ABRAHAM LINCOLN

A History, Vol. X
(in 10 volumes)

ABRAHAM LINCOLN

A History, Vol. X
(in 10 volumes)

JOHN M. HAY
JOHN G. NICOLAY

COSIMOCLASSICS

NEW YORK

Abraham Lincoln: A History, Vol. X (in 10 volumes)
Cover Copyright © 2009 by Cosimo, Inc.

Abraham Lincoln: A History, Vol. X (in 10 volumes)
was originally published in 1917.

For information, address:
P.O. Box 416, Old Chelsea Station
New York, NY 10011

or visit our website at:
www.cosimobooks.com

Ordering Information:
Cosimo publications are available at online bookstores. They may
also be purchased for educational, business or promotional use:
- *Bulk orders:* special discounts are available on bulk orders for reading
groups, organizations, businesses, and others. For details contact
Cosimo Special Sales at the address above or at info@cosimobooks.com.
- *Custom-label orders:* we can prepare selected books with your cover or
logo of choice. For more information, please contact Cosimo at
info@cosimobooks.com.

Cover Design by www.popshopstudio.com

ISBN: 978-1-60520-686-8

Booth had done his work efficiently. His principal subordinate, the young Floridian called Payne, had acted with equal audacity and cruelty, but not with equally fatal result. He had made a shambles of the residence of the Secretary of State, but among all his mangled victims there was not one killed. At eight o'clock that night he received his final orders from Booth, who placed in his hands a knife and revolver, and a little package like a prescription, and taught him his lesson. Payne was a young man, hardly of age, of herculean strength, of very limited mental capacity, blindly devoted to Booth, who had selected him as the fitting instrument of his mad hatred...

—from Chapter XV: "The Fate of the Assassins"

LIFE MASK OF ABRAHAM LINCOLN.

Drawn by Kenyon Cox from a copy of the mask made by Clark Mills in February, 1865.
The original mask is owned by Colonel John Hay.

ILLUSTRATIONS

VOL. X

LIFE MASK OF ABRAHAM LINCOLN....................*Frontispiece*
Drawn by Kenyon Cox from a copy of the mask made by Clark
Mills in February, 1865. The original mask is owned by
Colonel John Hay.

PAGE

GENERAL GEORGE H. THOMAS............................... 16
From a photograph.

GENERAL JOHN B. HOOD 24
From a photograph by Anderson-Cook.

GENERAL ALEXANDER P. STEWART 32
From a photograph.

COMMANDER WM. B. CUSHING 48
From a photograph by Brady.

ADMIRAL DAVID D. PORTER................................. 64
From a photograph by Brady.

GENERAL ALFRED H. TERRY 72
From a photograph by Brady.

WILLIAM LLOYD GARRISON 80
From a photograph by Rockwood.

GENERAL JOHN B. GORDON................................ 160
From a photograph.

GENERAL A. A. HUMPHREYS............................... 168
From a photograph by Anthony.

GENERAL CHARLES GRIFFIN............................... 176
From a photograph.

GENERAL A. P. HILL 184
From a photograph by Anderson-Cook.

GENERAL FRANCIS C. BARLOW 192
From a photograph by Brady.

GENERAL GEORGE A. CUSTER 200
From a photograph by Gardner.

GENERAL JOHN GIBBON...................................... 208
From a photograph by Brady.

GENERAL GODFREY WEITZEL 216
From a photograph by Anthony.

GENERAL W. T. SHERMAN................................... 224
From a photograph by Brady.

GENERAL OLIVER O. HOWARD............................... 224
From a photograph by Brady.

GENERAL JOHN A. LOGAN.......... 224
From a photograph by Brady.

GENERAL WILLIAM B. HAZEN 224
From a photograph by Brady.

GENERAL JEFF. C. DAVIS.................................. 224
From a photograph by Brady.

GENERAL HENRY W. SLOCUM.............................. 224
From a photograph by Brady.

GENERAL WADE HAMPTON. 232
From a photograph.

GENERAL J. A. MOWER 240
From a photograph by Brady.

GENERAL JAMES H. WILSON 256
From a photograph by Wm. Klauser.

GENERAL U. S. GRANT..................................... 272
From a photograph taken by Walker in 1875.

ABRAHAM LINCOLN 288
From a photograph taken March 6, 1865.

DIAGRAM OF THE BOX IN FORD'S THEATER.................. 294
From the drawing in the War Department.

STAGE AND PROSCENIUM BOXES OF FORD'S THEATER AS THEY
APPEARED ON THE NIGHT OF PRESIDENT LINCOLN'S AS-
SASSINATION... 296
From photographs.

DIAGRAM OF THE HOUSE IN WHICH PRESIDENT LINCOLN DIED 300
From the original prepared by Major A. F. Rockwell, April 15,
1865.

THE FUNERAL CAR...... 318
From a photograph by P. Relyea.

THE LINCOLN MONUMENT AT SPRINGFIELD 324
From a photograph by G. A. W. Pittman.

MAPS

VOL. X

	PAGE
HOOD'S TENNESSEE CAMPAIGN	2
BATTLE OF FRANKLIN	14
BATTLE OF NASHVILLE	26
COAST OF THE CAROLINAS	40
FORT FISHER	56
BATTLE OF FIVE FORKS.	170
FROM PETERSBURG TO APPOMATTOX COURT HOUSE	176
BATTLE OF BENTONVILLE	236

TABLE OF CONTENTS

Vol. X

CHAPTER I. FRANKLIN AND NASHVILLE

Hood's Plan of Invasion. His Dream of Conquest. His Movement toward Tennessee. The Responsibility of Thomas. His Force. Forrest's Raid on Johnsonville. Hood at Tuscumbia. He Crosses the Tennessee and Moves for Columbia. Schofield Arrives there First. Hood Attempts to Flank Schofield at Spring Hill. His Failure. Schofield Arrives at Franklin. Hood Attacks Him. The Battle of Franklin. Repulse of the Confederates. Their Heavy Losses. Schofield Retires to Nashville. Hood Follows. Thomas Prepares to Attack Him. Impatience of General Grant. He Resolves to Supersede Thomas. A Spell of Bad Weather. Thomas Attacks Hood on the 15th of December. The Battle of Nashville. Hood Driven Eight Miles. The Fight of the 16th. Rout of Hood's Army. The Pursuit. Hood Driven into Mississippi and His Army Dispersed 1

CHAPTER II. THE ALBEMARLE

The Building of the *Albemarle*. The Attack and Capture of Plymouth. The *Albemarle* Attacks the Union Fleet, and Retires to Plymouth. Plans for her Destruction. William B. Cushing. His Adventures. His Expedition Against the *Albemarle*. Incidents of

the Night. The *Albemarle* Destroyed. Escape of
Cushing. Received as One From the Dead. Plymouth
Captured by the United States Navy 38

CHAPTER III. FORT FISHER AND WILMINGTON

Blockade Running. Importance of the Port of Wil-
mington. Profits of the Blockade Runners. Activity
of the Navy. An Expedition Planned Against Fort
Fisher. The Powder Boat Scheme. The Relations of
Porter, Butler, and Weitzel. Mutual Recriminations.
Delays. The Powder Boat Exploded Without Results.
The Force under Butler Lands. The Fort Bombarded
by the Navy. Weitzel Decides Against Attacking.
The Troops Reëmbark and Return to Fort Monroe.
Grant Censures Butler and Relieves Him. A New
Expedition Starts under Terry. The Troops Land and
Assault the Fort. Capture of Fort Fisher. The Move-
ment on Wilmington. Schofield Enters Wilmington
on the 22d of February. The March to Goldsboro'.
Battle of Kinston. Occupation of Goldsboro' and
Junction with Sherman 52

CHAPTER IV. THE THIRTEENTH AMENDMENT

Colfax Elected Speaker. Lincoln's Annual Message
of 1863 on Emancipation. Constitutional Amendments
Proposed. Trumbull's Amendment. Thirteenth
Amendment Passed by the Senate, and Defeated by
the House. Lincoln and the Baltimore Platform.
Lincoln's Annual Message of 1864 on Amending the
Constitution. Ashley Moves to Reconsider the Vote
on the Thirteenth Amendment. Debate in the House.
Progressive Democratic and Border State Members.
Sumner and the Raritan Bill. House Passes the Thirteenth Amendment. Lincoln's Address. The Thirteenth Amendment Ratified. Amendments of 1861
and 1865 Contrasted 72

CHAPTER V. BLAIR'S MEXICAN PROJECT

Lincoln's Annual Message of 1864 on Peace. Francis
P. Blair, Sr., Permitted to go South. His Letters to
Jefferson Davis. His Visit to Richmond. His Inter-

view with Jefferson Davis. His Scheme Concerning
Mexico. Davis's Replies and Questions. His Letter to
Blair about Peace for "The Two Countries." Lin-
coln's Letter to Blair about Peace for "Our One
Common Country." Blair's Return Visit to Richmond.
Davis's Consultation with His Cabinet. Appoints
Stephens, Hunter, and Campbell Peace Commission-
ers. His Double-meaning Instruction 91

CHAPTER VI. THE HAMPTON ROADS CONFERENCE
Stephens, Hunter, and Campbell Ask Leave to Visit
Washington. Major Eckert's Mission. Lincoln Sends
Seward to Meet the Commissioners. His Instructions.
The Commissioners and Grant. Grant's Telegram to
Stanton. Lincoln Goes to Fort Monroe. Interview Be-
tween Lincoln, Seward, and the Commissioners. The
Points of Discussion. No Agreement Reached. Lin-
coln's Suggestion to Stephens. The Commissioners Re-
port to Jefferson Davis. Davis's Message and Speech . 113

CHAPTER VII. THE SECOND INAUGURAL
Lincoln's Proposed Message and Proclamation. His
Proposal Disapproved by the Cabinet. Statement of
Secretary Welles. Statement of Secretary Usher. Lin-
coln's Message About the Hampton Roads Conference.
Joint Resolution About Insurrectionary States. Lin-
coln's Message on Signing the Joint Resolution. The
Presidential Count. Lincoln's Reply to the Notifica-
tion Committee. His Second Inauguration. The Sec-
ond Inaugural. Lincoln's Letter to Weed 132

CHAPTER VIII. FIVE FORKS
The Agony of the Confederacy. Worthlessness of the
Currency. High Prices. Rigor of the Conscription.
Desertions. Mutual Recriminations. Disaffection.
Decline in Value of Slave Property. Despair of the
Confederate State Department. Lee in Supreme
Command. Overtures for Military Negotiations. Lin-
coln Forbids Them. Lee and Davis on the Evacuation
of Richmond. Gordon's Sortie at Fort Stedman. Its
Partial Success and Final Failure. Grant Resolves to

Move to the Left. His Plans. Sherman's Visit. The
Army of the Potomac. Sheridan's Views. Grant's
Purpose Fully Developed. Sheridan at Dinwiddie
Court House. The Battle of Five Forks. Warren
Relieved. Relations Between Him and Grant . . 148

CHAPTER IX. APPOMATTOX
Grant Orders Assault on the Confederate Lines at
Petersburg. Success of Wright and Parke. Death
of A. P. Hill. Capture of Forts Gregg and Whit-
worth. Lee Driven Back to His Inner Line. He
Evacuates Petersburg. Reception of the News in
Richmond. Lee's Flight and Grant's Pursuit. Lee
at Amelia Court House. The Battle of Sailor's Creek.
Humphreys and Wright Defeat the Confederates.
Read's Self-sacrifice. " Let the Thing be Pressed."
The Race to Appomattox. Lee's Optimism. Not
Shared by His Generals. Grant's Summons to Sur-
render. Exchange of Letters. Sheridan at Appo-
mattox. Ord and Griffin Come Up. The Way Barred.
Lee Surrenders. Grant's Liberal Terms. The Number
Surrendered. No Salutes Fired. Meeting of Lee
and Grant After the Surrender. 175

CHAPTER X. THE FALL OF THE REBEL CAPITAL
Prospects in Richmond. Davis's Last Message. Lee
Directs the Evacuation of Richmond. A Fateful
Sunday. Departure of the Rebel Government. Dis-
order and Pillage. The Confederates Burn Richmond.
General Ewell's Statement. The City Surrendered to
General Weitzel. Arrival of the Union Army. Rich-
mond Under the Stars and Stripes. Order, Relief,
and Peace 199

CHAPTER XI. LINCOLN IN RICHMOND
Captain Robert T. Lincoln. The President's Visit to
Grant. Interview of Lincoln, Grant, Sherman, and
Porter. Lincoln's Visit to Petersburg. His Visit to
Richmond. Presidential Entry into the Fallen Capital.
Interviews with Judge Campbell. Lincoln's Memoran-
dum. His Directions About the Virginia Legislature.

Notification to Grant. Campbell's Letter to the Legislative Committee. The Call to the Legislature. Campbell's Misconstruction. · Weitzel's Mistake. The Meeting Revoked by the President 213

CHAPTER XII. JOHNSTON'S SURRENDER

Sherman's March Northward. His Forces. The Country Traversed. Columbia Captured and Burned. The March to the Great Pedee. Fayetteville Taken. Johnston Supersedes Beauregard. The Confederate Forces. The Battles of Averysboro' and Bentonville. Sherman Enters Goldsboro'. Stoneman's Raid Towards Lynchburg. Wilson's Expedition. He Defeats Forrest and Captures Selma. Sherman Prepares for a Final Campaign. The News of Lee's Surrender. Sherman Marches to Raleigh. Johnston Proposes a Suspension of Hostilities. Negotiations. The Sherman-Johnston Memorandum. It is Disapproved by Grant and the Government. Grant Arrives at Sherman's Headquarters. Johnston Surrenders on the Appomattox Terms. Sherman's Controversy with Halleck and Stanton 229

CHAPTER XIII. THE CAPTURE OF JEFFERSON DAVIS

Flight of the Rebel Government. Davis's Danville Proclamation. The Halt at Greensboro'. Davis's Interviews with Johnston and Beauregard. Johnston's Statement. Mallory's Statement. Negotiations with Sherman. Davis's Stay at Charlotte. Davis's Orders and Johnston's Refusal. Wilson Sends Harnden and Pritchard in Pursuit. Capture of the Camp near Irwinville. Davis's Statement. Lawton's Statement. Reagan's Statement. Imprisonment and Indictment of Davis. President Johnson's Amnesty. The Death of Jefferson Davis 255

CHAPTER XIV. THE FOURTEENTH OF APRIL

Good Friday, a Day of Thanksgiving. Restoration of the Flag at Fort Sumter. Solemn Ceremonies. Oration by Henry Ward Beecher. Meeting of the Cabinet at Washington. The President's Dream. Discussion of Plans for Peace. " Enough Lives Have Been Sacrificed." The President's Last Words to His Cabinet. He Passes the Day with His Family. Threats of Assassination. The President's Treatment of Them. Confederate Propositions. The Final Plot. The Conspirators. Wilkes Booth and His Accomplices. Booth's Preparations at the Theater. The President in His Box. The Strange Fate of all His Party. The Shot Fired. The Flight of Booth. The Death of Abraham Lincoln 277

CHAPTER XV. THE FATE OF THE ASSASSINS

The Attempted Assassination of Seward. The Flight and Capture of Payne. Booth Gains the Navy Yard Bridge. His Escape into Maryland. Receives Aid and Comfort. Passages From His Diary. Shot on the 26th of April. Trial of the Surviving Conspirators. Their Execution. John H. Surratt 303

CHAPTER XVI. THE MOURNING PAGEANT

The General Sorrow. No Public Rejoicing Over the Downfall of the Rebellion. The Attitude of the Radicals in Congress. President Johnson Takes the Oath of Office. The Funeral Ceremonies in Washington. The Journey to Springfield Begun. Harrisburg. Philadelphia. New York. Through New York State. Ohio. Cleveland. Indiana and the West. Chicago. The Interment at Oak Ridge. Building of the Monument. Its Dedication. Speech of President Grant . 314

CHAPTER XVII. THE END OF REBELLION

" The Back of Rebellion Broken." Fears of an Indefinite Prolongation of the War. These Fears Unfounded. Surrender of Taylor to Canby and Farrand to Thatcher. Kirby Smith's Threats and Surrender. Wilson's Paroles. Recruiting Stopped. Reduction of the Army. Sale of Material. The Grand Review of the 23d and 24th of May. The Army of the Potomac. Sherman's Army. The Lesson of the War. The Mustering out of Army and Navy. The New Grand Divisions. The Insurrection Proclaimed at an End. The Losses and Expense of the War. The Growth of the Country in Four Years 326

Chapter XVIII. Lincoln's Fame

The Voice of Official Europe. France. England. Germany. The Common People of Europe. Lincoln Best Appreciated at Home. The Element of Legend. Emerson's Opinion. The Fame of Lincoln a Growing Force in This Country and Abroad. The Foundation of it. His Writings. His Public Work. His Military Capacity. His Moral Qualities. His Name the Possession of the Whole Country 341

ABRAHAM LINCOLN

CHAPTER I

FRANKLIN AND NASHVILLE

WHILE Sherman was planning his march to the sea General Hood was devising a counter scheme of invasion. In spite of the rebuffs he had suffered at every encounter of arms since he had attained the object of his ambition by replacing Johnston, his hope and his courage had suffered no diminution. He had come to the West thoroughly imbued, as he says, with the spirit of Lee and Jackson. He thought by persisting in a series of flank attacks he would sooner or later destroy the National army. His courage and energy were equal to any demands that could be made upon them. His mental capacity was so limited that he was unable to see the obstacles in his way. Even now, after all the wasteful defeats which his rashness had inflicted upon his army, he was dreaming of a succession of victories more brilliant than any which had illustrated the career of his great prototype in Virginia. Although he had retreated from the front of Sherman, on the unani-

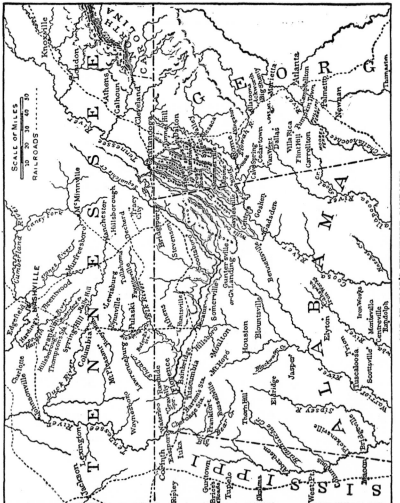

MAP OF HOOD'S TENNESSEE CAMPAIGN.

mous report of all the officers he consulted that
his army was in no condition to fight a pitched
battle with Sherman's force, yet even while he
halted at the Cross Roads he decided, he says, to
cross the Tennessee at Guntersville, to destroy
Sherman's communications, to move upon Thomas
and Schofield, and rout and capture their armies
before they could reach Nashville. He intended
then — we are quoting his own words — to march
upon that city, where he would supply his army
and reënforce it by accessions from Tennessee; he
would then march northeast, pass the Cumberland
River, move into Kentucky, take position with his
left at Richmond and his right at Hazel Green,
then, threatening Cincinnati, recruit his army from
Kentucky and Tennessee. The dream that had
beguiled Kirby Smith still had power with Hood;
"the former State," he said, "was reported, at
this juncture, to be more aroused and embittered
against the Federals than at any period of the
war." He was imbued, he said, with the belief
that he could accomplish this stupendous feat
while Sherman was debating the alternative of
following him, or marching through Georgia. But
this scheme was merely the prelude to greater
achievements; if Sherman should return to confront him or should follow him from Georgia into
Tennessee and Kentucky he hoped then to be in
condition to offer battle, and if blest with victory,
to send reënforcements to General Lee, or to march
through the gaps in the Cumberland Mountains
and take Grant in rear; even if Sherman should
beat him he considered that this enterprise was
still open to him. Thus, he says, he believed he

CHAP. I.

Hood,
"Advance
and
Retreat,"
p. 268.
could "defeat Grant, and allow General Lee, in command of our combined armies, to march upon Washington or turn upon and annihilate Sherman." This fantastic vision seemed as easy as " good morning" to the courageous heart and narrow mind of General Hood.

Eager as Sherman was to march southward, and little as he cared for what damage Hood might do in the rear, he was for a long time uncertain what Report Committee on Conduct of the War, 1865–66. Supplement, Vol. I., p. 232. course he should pursue in reference to him. On the 17th of October he had said to Thomas that Hood would not dare to go into Tennessee. If he wants to, " let him go; and then we can all turn on him and he cannot escape"; and on the 26th, after his reconnaissance to Gadsden had revealed the fact that the rebel army had gone, he again said to Thomas, " If it turns up at Guntersville I will be after it; but if it goes, as I believe, to Decatur and beyond, I must leave it to you at present, and push for the heart of Georgia." Even after he was satisfied that Hood had gone towards Decatur, he told Halleck that he would wait a few days to hear what headway Hood was making and that he might yet turn to Tennessee, though it would be a great Sherman to Halleck, Oct. 27. Report Committee on Conduct of the War. Supplement, Part I., p. 242. pity to take a step backward. " I think," he adds, with his humorous coolness, "it would be better even to let him ravage the State of Tennessee, provided he does not gobble up too many of our troops."

Hood,
"Advance
and
Retreat,"
p. 274.
Hood's intention, as we have seen, was really to cross at Guntersville, in which case he would have had Sherman upon his heels; but he postponed his ruin a few weeks by passing further west. The reason he gives for this course was his lack of cav-

alry and his desire to effect a junction with General Forrest before crossing. He did not even
attempt to cross at Decatur, or, at least, the movement he made in this direction, which was promptly
checked by General Granger, in garrison there,
with considerable loss to the Confederates, Hood
insists was intended merely as a slight demonstration.

Sherman, though he sometimes complains of
Hood's baffling eccentricities, seems to have read
his mind on many occasions like an open book.
He telegraphed on the 28th of October, not knowing of the result at Decatur, that Hood would not
assault that place and that Granger did not want
too many men. The next day he received information of Hood's feeble demonstration against it,
and of Granger's successful sortie, in which he
killed and wounded a considerable number of Confederates and captured over a hundred. Granger
added his belief that Hood would go to Tuscumbia before crossing; he was evidently out of supplies, as the first thing the prisoners asked for was
something to eat. Hood continued on his way
west and reached Tuscumbia, on the south bank
of the Tennessee, on the 31st of October.

General Grant's doubts of the wisdom of Sherman's movement southward, which were so strong
on the 1st of November that he recommended him
to beat Hood before he started, gave way before
Sherman's intense eagerness to be off, and on the
2d, as we have seen, he gave his full consent.
From that moment there was no question that one
of the gravest responsibilities of the war rested
upon the broad shoulders of General Thomas.

This weighty load was well placed. Sherman said, "General Thomas is well alive to the occasion, and better suited to the emergency than any man I have." He might have gone further and said that no man then alive on the continent was better suited to the work in hand. Grant, it is true, never rated Thomas at his real value; but he acquiesced in Sherman's opinion on this as on almost all other occasions. Sherman's confidence was full and unlimited. He issued an order that "in the event of military movements or the accidents of war separating the general in command from his military division, Major-General George H. Thomas, commanding the Department of the Cumberland, would exercise command over all the troops and garrisons not absolutely in the presence of the General-in-Chief." The Departments of the Ohio and Tennessee were thus placed completely under his command. Thomas had not sought these honors or responsibilities; he accepted them most reluctantly. "I do not wish," he said, "to be in command of the defense of Tennessee unless you and the authorities in Washington deem it absolutely necessary"; but having once accepted the charge he executed it with all that human courage and human wisdom could bring to the task.

During the whole month of November the situation was extremely grave. Hood's army had, by the utmost exertion, been recruited up to its full strength. He himself says that desertions had ceased, and he started, at least, with his organization perfect and his subordinate generals entirely in harmony with him, now that Hardee was gone; with three corps of infantry, commanded by Gen-

erals S. D. Lee, Cheatham, and Stewart, comprising
a force variously estimated at from 40,000 to 45,000;
and he was accompanied besides by a formidable
body of cavalry, under Forrest, of 10,000 to 12,000.
Thomas's force was, on the 1st of November, greatly
inferior to that of Hood. A large part of it was
dispersed along the garrisoned posts of the southern frontier of Tennessee, and this, of course, could
not be displaced. His movable force he estimated
at 22,000 infantry, and a little over 4000 cavalry.
He received about this time some 12,000 new recruits
from the North; but these did not make up his
losses by the expiration of terms of service and by
the furloughing of soldiers going North. The forces
upon which he most relied were the Fourth Corps,
under Stanley, and the Twenty-third Corps, under
Schofield; and he was promised in addition to these
an excellent corps under A. J. Smith, which had
been serving temporarily under Rosecrans. At the
time of the battle of Nashville, however, Thomas
had at hand of all arms, about 55,000.

1864.
Report of
Major-
General
Thomas,
Committee
on Conduct
of the War.
Supple-
ment,
Part I.,
p. 369.

As soon as Thomas learned that Hood had appeared in force on the Tennessee, Schofield and
Stanley were ordered to be concentrated at Pulaski;
but before this could be accomplished Forrest had
made an attack at Johnsonville, one of Thomas's
bases of supply on the Tennessee River, and,
after a feeble and discreditable resistance on the
part of the garrison of the place, had caused the
destruction of several transports and a large
amount of valuable Government property. Schofield arrived at Nashville on the 5th, when the Nov., 1864.
advance of his corps was immediately dispatched
to Johnsonville by rail; but on reaching there he

found that Forrest, having done all the damage possible, had retreated. Schofield left the place sufficiently garrisoned, and with the rest of his command marched to join the Fourth Corps at Pulaski, and to assume command of all the troops in that vicinity. Though Stanley's commission as major-general antedated his, Schofield had the higher rank as commander of a department. His orders from Thomas were to retard the advance of Hood into Tennessee as much as possible, without risking a general engagement, until Smith's command should arrive from Missouri, and General J. H. Wilson, who had been put in command of all the cavalry in the department,—and who came indorsed by Grant with the prediction that he would increase the efficiency of that arm fifty per cent.,—had time to remount the cavalry regiments whose horses had been taken for Kilpatrick.

A fortnight had been spent by Hood and Beauregard at Tuscumbia and the contemplated campaign discussed by them in all its bearings. On

the 6th of November Hood telegraphed to Jefferson Davis his intention to move into Tennessee, to which Mr. Davis answered, that if Sherman, as reported, had "sent a large part of his force southward,

you may first beat him in detail and subsequently, without serious obstruction or danger to the country in your rear, advance to the Ohio River." On the 12th, which was the day on which communication ceased between Sherman and Thomas, Hood telegraphed again to the Confederate President, giving his reasons for not having fought Sherman ; saying he did not then regard his army as in proper condition for a pitched battle, but that it was now

in excellent spirits and confidence. He also ac- CHAP. I.
counted for his delays of the last few weeks by
saying that Forrest had not been able to join him; Hood,
that as soon as he could come up, which would be "Advance and
in a few days, he should move forward. He moved Retreat," p. 274.
across to Florence on the north bank of the Tennessee on the 13th; Forrest reported the next day, and
Hood brought his entire army across the river.

Sherman's intentions were not long a secret to
the Confederates, and, his formidable movement to
the south being now fully developed, Beauregard
ordered Hood, on the 17th of November, to "take
the offensive at the earliest practicable moment
striking the enemy while thus dispersed, and by
these means distract Sherman's advance into
Georgia"; and on the same day, telegraphing to Ibid., p. 277.
General Howell Cobb, who was reporting in panic
and terror the advance of Sherman, Beauregard
said, "Victory in Tennessee will relieve Georgia."
Three days later Beauregard again charged Hood to Nov. 20, 1864.
"push on active offensive immediately," and on the Ibid., p. 281.
21st, Hood, with his usual alacrity, put his army in
motion, feeling sure that he was to gain the victory
so much needed and desired. The storms which in
Sherman's neighborhood had been no more than
refreshing showers, in Middle Tennessee had turned Dispatches of Nov. 19,
the roads to mire; neither Schofield nor Thomas from Thomas
believed that it was possible for the Confederates and Schofield
to move in such weather, but nevertheless Hood to each other.
pushed forward with his habitual vigor intent on
coming upon Schofield's rear and cutting him off
from Columbia; and in this daring plan he almost
succeeded. In spite of snow, sleet, and rain he
pushed northward, and it was only by an equally

CHAP. I.
1864.
vigorous and energetic march on the night from the 23d to the 24th of November that Schofield reached Columbia first. Forrest's cavalry was on the Mount Pleasant pike almost in sight of the town when Cox's division moved at double-quick, marched across from the Pulaski road, and held back
Cox,
"Franklin
and
Nashville,"
p. 65.
the Confederates until Stanley's head of column arrived and a strong position was taken up by the whole command, covering the town on the south.

Disappointed in his first effort to march around Schofield, Hood determined to proceed by the right flank, crossing the river some distance above Columbia, and move upon Schofield's line of communications at Spring Hill. He had not yet given up his hope of renewing in the West the exploits of Stonewall Jackson. "I had beheld," he said, "with admiration the noble deeds and grand results achieved by the immortal Jackson in similar manœuvres." He waited only one day to prepare this movement, and as he had always thought, since the 22d of July, that if he had been present in Hardee's flanking movement he could have destroyed McPherson's army, he determined this time to accomplish a closer imitation of Jackson at Chancellorsville, by riding at the head of his own flanking column. He bridged
Nov., 1864.
the river during the night of the 28th, three miles above Columbia, and crossing at daybreak he rode at the head of Granbury's brigade of Cleburne's division, giving instructions to remaining corps to follow, and to keep well closed up. He left General S. D. Lee at Columbia with two divisions and most of the artillery to make a heavy demonstration against Schofield and to follow him if he retired.

In anticipation of this movement Stanley had been sent with two divisions of the Fourth Corps to Spring Hill, Cox having been left at Columbia to prevent or delay Hood's crossing there. Colonel P. S. Post's brigade was at the same time sent up the river in observation and soon reported the movement of infantry north of the stream. Fearing that this force, the strength of which was not yet developed, might come in upon the flank near Rutherford's Creek, Nathan Kimball's division halted at that point, while Stanley passed on with G. D. Wagner's division to Spring Hill, where he arrived a little before noon. In the mean time Forrest had been encountered by Wilson near Hurt's Corners, and a brisk engagement took place between them, Forrest with his largely superior force gradually crowding Wilson to the north in such a way as to give the Confederates command of the direct road from Rally Hill to Spring Hill. When Stanley, with his one division, arrived at the latter point there was brisk skirmishing on every side of him for the possession of the road, which increased throughout the afternoon.

The disposition made of Wagner's division was admirably effective; Emerson Opdycke's and J. Q. Lane's brigades covering the village and protecting the trains, while L. P. Bradley occupied a wooded knoll some three-quarters of a mile east of the pike, which commanded the approaches from that direction. By great good fortune Wagner had not only his own battery of artillery, but Captain Lyman Bridges, the artillery chief of the corps, had come up with six more batteries, not with any idea of fighting a battle, but simply to get them as far as pos-

sible on the road to Franklin; but the moment he
arrived at Spring Hill, scenting the conflict, he
placed all his guns in battery on a commanding
point west of the road, where they did efficient
service.

The first demonstration upon the place came from
Cheatham's corps, which Hood accompanied in person, having left Stewart's corps at Rutherford's
Creek; Cleburne's division, one of the finest in the
Confederate army, under command of a general
whose fighting qualities were proverbial, was so
hotly received by Bradley's small brigade, and by
the utterly disproportionate fire from Bridges'
batteries, that it was impossible for the Confederates to believe that the force opposed to them was
so small. Bradley's brigade was, however, very
roughly handled. Its heroic commander being severely wounded it fell back under charge of Colonel
Joseph Conrad towards the road, and there, with
Lane's and Opdycke's brigades, made so stout a resistance that evening came on, to Hood's almost
frantic disappointment, before the Franklin pike
was reached. As he saw himself missing the
great stroke upon which he had built such hopes,
he assailed his generals with furious reproaches and
adjurations. Bringing up Stewart from Rutherford's Creek he threw him to the right of Cheatham,
with orders to take the pike at all hazards, although
night had already fallen. But it was too late.
Stewart's men went into bivouac within a few
hundred yards of the road which Wagner's division, by good fighting and admirable judgment
on the part of everybody concerned, still held, and
with it the salvation of Schofield's army.

General Lee had succeeded in retaining General Cox with the Twenty-third Corps all day at Columbia. In the afternoon, Schofield, becoming convinced that Hood with his main army was moving upon his rear, ordered Cox to withdraw as soon as it was dark. He himself took T. H. Ruger's division, and pushed for Spring Hill. The enemy was so close to the road that Schofield had repeatedly to brush his pickets away from the path as he advanced. He reached Spring Hill about seven o'clock, and there learned that Thompson's Station, a few miles further north, was occupied by the enemy. Posting a strong force to the east of the road, to protect his marching column, he hurried on with Ruger's division to Thompson's Station, the enemy retiring as he approached. He then returned to Spring Hill, meeting there the head of Cox's column, which had come up with the greatest celerity from Columbia. The whole force then started for Franklin, and marched all night with its heavy trains and invaluable artillery past the sleeping army of Hood. Several times during the night the trains were delayed by slight obstructions, and it seemed as if they must be abandoned, or a battle be fought to save them; but by mingled good fortune and good management they all got through, the head of the column arriving at Franklin a little before daylight on the 30th, and the rest coming up during the forenoon.

Schofield's orders were to cross the Harpeth River, to hold Hood in check there, and retire gradually upon Nashville, for Thomas now felt ready to fight at that place. Smith's detachment of the Army of the Tennessee had at last begun to

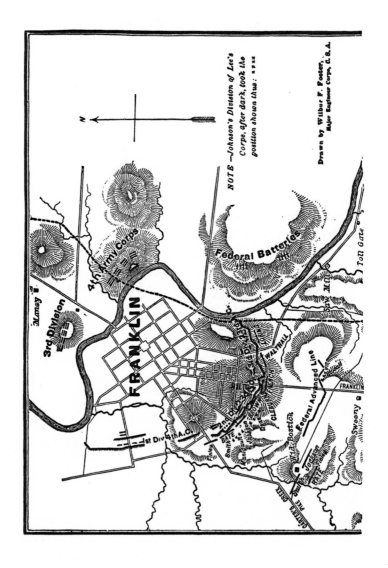

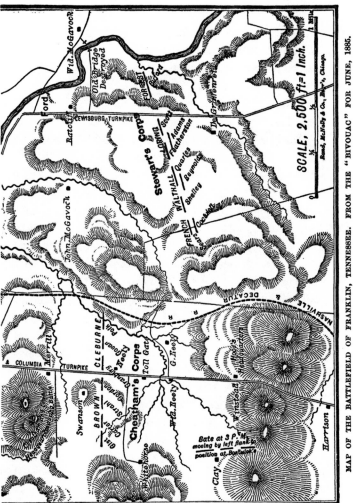

MAP OF THE BATTLEFIELD OF FRANKLIN, TENNESSEE. FROM THE "BIVOUAC" FOR JUNE, 1885.

Chap. I. arrive from Missouri, and Thomas was now equal
or superior in infantry to Hood. But, to Schofield's
surprise and annoyance, he found no means of
Nov.30,1864. crossing the river. He had destroyed his pontoons
at Columbia, they being too heavy and cumbrous
for the transportation at his disposition. Those he
had requested from Nashville had not been sent;
the light and movable train which had belonged to
Thomas's army had gone with Sherman to Georgia.
A staff and an army like that of Schofield's wastes
no time in regrets; they scarped the banks on both
sides of the river and made a sort of ford; they tore
several houses to pieces, and with the planking
floored the railroad bridge; they sawed the old
Cox,
"Franklin,
and
Nashville,"
p. 85. posts of the county bridge down to the level of the
water, and hastily covered the stumps with planks.
Thus in a few hours they had three practicable
bridges, and began at once crossing the artillery
and trains. T. J. Wood's division, with some guns,
took position in an abandoned work called Fort
Granger, on the north side, where they commanded
the bridges.

But while these operations were going on it became necessary to provide for receiving Hood's
attack on the other side of the village. The
Twenty-third Corps was posted on both sides of the
main road, upon which Hood's army was expected.
The village of Franklin stands in a bend of the
Harpeth River, so that Cox, who commanded the
lines, had his left on the stream, and extended
across the Columbia pike to the Carter's Creek
pike, but could not reach to the bend of the river
on the other side. Kimball's division was, therefore, given the duty of closing the line on that

GENERAL GEORGE H. THOMAS.

flank. The instant the men were assigned their positions they went to work with instinctive alacrity to build such slight breastworks as the means at hand afforded. The roadway was left open to enable a double line of wagons and artillery to pass, and this opening was protected by a retrenchment a few rods further back.

CHAP. I.

Cox,
"Franklin
and
Nashville,"
p. 84.

Wagner's division, which had held the lines at Spring Hill all the day before, and which had brought up the rear in a long night march, came in about noon. Colonel Opdycke's brigade, which had formed the rear guard, and upon which had fallen the double duty of beating back Hood's advance, and driving forward the weary and limping recruits of Schofield's army, now came inside the lines, and was posted as a reserve in rear of the center. Wagner's other two brigades were left outside the principal line, about half a mile forward on the Columbia pike, with instructions to observe the enemy, and to retire as soon as the Confederates showed a disposition to advance in force. The weary soldiers threw themselves down for a little repose behind their breastworks; neither Schofield nor his corps commanders imagined that a great battle was to burst upon them in a few moments. The artillery and trains were nearly all across the river by the middle of the afternoon, and Schofield had issued orders for the troops to pass over at six o'clock. But there was a state of things in the Confederate army which made any moderate or prudent measures impossible to Hood. His failure to destroy Schofield at Spring Hill had so embittered and exasperated him that he was ready for any enterprise, however desperate.

Ibid., p. 86.

Nov.30,1864.

The irritation had communicated itself to his principal officers; his reproaches had stung them beyond endurance; and, therefore, on arriving in sight of Schofield's army, in position on the south bank of the Harpeth, there was no thought of anything among the Confederate commanders but immediate and furious attack. All the Confederate accounts agree in describing this spirit in Hood's army on the morning of the 30th of November, though Hood and his generals entirely disagree as to the cause of it.[1] Generals Cheatham and John C. Brown, and, according to their account, General Cleburne also, ascribed it to Hood's unreasonable and angry censures of their conduct the day before, while Hood attributes the new spirit of the army to mortification for the great opportunity lost and a renewed access of admiration and confidence towards himself.

The assault was made at about four o'clock. The Confederates never rushed forward to battle with more furious impetus, and by a strange accident it seemed for a moment as if this desperate assault of Hood was to succeed, and he was to gain the glory he so ardently longed for of a success like Stonewall Jackson's best. Wagner's two brigades, that had been left outside the line with instructions to retire before becoming actually engaged with the enemy, stayed too long. The wide and heavy lines of Cheatham and Stewart had enveloped them on both flanks and the bayonets of Hood's center were almost touching them when they

---

[1] Hood's "Advance and Retreat," p. 294 et seq. General Cheatham's paper, read at a meeting of Confederate officers at Louisville — "Southern Historical Society Papers." Vol. IX.

turned and ran for the Union lines. They rushed
over the parapets on either side of the pike, the
Confederates following immediately after them,
overwhelming and carrying to the rear the troops
who were defending the breastworks. A gap of
about one thousand feet was instantly made in the
Union lines; Hood's battalions were rapidly con-
verging to this point. If the damage were not
immediately repaired, it would be irreparable;
with a superior force wedged into the Union center, short work would have been made of the two
wings, and nothing but annihilation would have
been left for Schofield's army.

General D. S. Stanley, the commander of the
Fourth Corps, seeing from the north side of the
river the Confederate advance, started at the instant for his line. He reached it just as the breach
was made and the confused mass of fugitives and
Confederates came pouring to the rear. The only
force available at the instant to meet them was
Opdycke's brigade, which had fought all the day
before at Spring Hill and afterwards had marched
all night; but even while Stanley was galloping to
order Opdycke to lead his men to the charge he
saw that gallant commander taking position himself on the right of his line; seeing that no orders
were necessary he gave none, but placed himself
at the left of this heroic brigade. A shout rose
among the veteran soldiers about him, "We can go
where the general can"; and the brigade, supported on the right and left by Cox's men, who instantly rallied to the rescue, rushed forward and
regained the lines. Opdycke's magnificent courage
met its adequate reward. He fought on horseback

till his revolver was empty, then dealt about him with the butt of his pistol, and descending from his horse seized the musket of a fallen soldier, and fought like a private until the intrenchments were regained. Although four regimental commanders fell in this furious charge, Opdycke was unhurt. Stanley did not fare so well; his horse was killed under him and he received a serious wound in the neck and was carried to the rear.

The battle did not cease with this fierce onset and repulse. All along the line the Confederates made attack after attack. Hood sitting on horseback, a little way behind his lines, sent them forward again and again with furious orders " to drive the Yankees into the river." To show with what desperate gallantry the Confederates were led, it need only be said that six generals were killed on or near the parapets, six were wounded, and one captured. Cleburne closed his brilliant career in front of the Union breastworks. John Adams charged his horse over the ditch, leaped it, and horse and rider were killed upon the parapet. General O. F. Strahl fought with his men in the ditch until evening came; he was struck down; he turned over the command to Colonel F. E. P. Stafford, but while his men were carrying him to the rear he was struck twice more and killed. Stafford took up his fallen sword and carried on the fight with a courage which will form the theme of fable and legend in time to come. An eye witness says that his men were piled about him in such numbers that when at last he was shot dead he could not fall, but was found the next morning, partially upright, as if still commanding the gallant dead who surrounded him.

Cox, "Franklin and Nashville," p. 95.

Along the whole line the attack and defense were
carried on, until nothing but the flashes of the
muskets could be seen in the darkness, with the
same furious gallantry on the one side and
the same immovable determination on the other.

Few battles so frightfully destructive are recorded
in the wars of modern times. In the terrible fight at
Ezra Church, a Union picket shouted across the
lines to a Confederate with that friendly chaff common to both armies, "I say, Johnny, how many of
you are there left?" To which the undaunted Confederate replied, "About enough for another killing." On this terrible afternoon at Franklin, Hood's
army suffered the last killing it was able to endure. Hood,
He admitted in his dispatch to Richmond a loss of "Advance and Retreat,"
"about 4500"; but Thomas in his careful report p. 330.
foots the Confederate loss at 6252, of which all but Thomas, Report.
700 were killed and wounded. Schofield's loss was Committee on Conduct
very much less, amounting to 2326 in all, of which of the War. Supplement, Part I., p. 372.
Wagner's unfortunate division lost 1200. Had it
not been for the mistake made in those two advanced brigades, Schofield's army would have
slaughtered Hood's at its leisure. Thomas, in his
grave and sober manner, thus sums up the result
of this signal victory: "It not only seriously
checked the enemy's advance and gave General
Schofield time to move his troops and all his property to Nashville, but it also caused deep depression
among the men of Hood's army, making them
doubly cautious in their subsequent movements." Ibid.

Schofield reported the day's work to Thomas and
by his advice and direction fell back during the
night to Nashville. His retreat was entirely unmolested; for Wilson, while the battle was going

on at Franklin, had met and checked Forrest, holding him at the river and driving some of his detachments back. Schofield's army, on arriving at Nashville, occupied a position selected for it in advance by General Thomas. General Schofield held the left extending to the Nolensville pike; the Fourth Corps, under the command of General Wood, held the center, and the Sixteenth Corps under General A. J. Smith, who had just arrived in time to assist in the defense of Tennessee, occupied the right, his flank resting on the Cumberland River below the city. Wilson, with his cavalry, was stationed first at Schofield's left, but Steedman's provisional command having arrived at
Nashville on the evening of the 1st of December Wilson was moved to the north side of the river and Steedman occupied the space from Schofield's left to the Cumberland.

Hood, as if driven by his evil genius, followed rapidly after Schofield and sat down before Nashville. He was aware, he said, of the reënforcements which had reached Thomas, and which had brought the strength of the National army above his own, but he was in the position of a desperate gamester who has so little to lose that he feels it better policy to stake all than to leave the game. He knew that Mr. Davis was urgent in his orders for the reënforcement of the Army of Tennessee from Texas; he hoped that with this expected accession he might still realize the roseate dreams with which he had started out on this ill-starred campaign. He trusted to the chapter of accidents to give him some dazzling successes which would draw the Tennesseeans and Kentuckians to his standard.

He formed his line of battle in front of Nashville
on the 2d of December. Lee's corps took the center,
astride the Franklin pike, Stewart occupied the
left, and Cheatham the right, their flanks widely
extending towards the Cumberland River, and
Forrest's cavalry filling the gap. But no sooner
had he established himself there than, as if determined to give himself no chance in the impending
battle, he detached Forrest on the 5th with W. B.
Bate's division of infantry to invest and capture, if
possible, the garrison of Murfreesboro', commanded
by General Rousseau. This expedition totally failed.
A sally was made on the 7th by some of Rousseau's
troops under General Milroy, who won that day a
merited consolation for his disaster at Winchester,
and inflicted a sharp defeat upon Bate's infantry,
which was thereupon recalled to Nashville; while
Forrest, in this useless adventure, remained away
from Hood too far to be recalled when he was
most needed.

While General Hood was strengthening his intrenchments and waiting in vain for good news
from Forrest, and the arrival of reënforcements
from across the Mississippi, which were never to
come, Thomas upon his side was completing in his
unhurried and patient manner his preparations for
a crushing blow. He would have been ready to
strike in about a week after Hood's arrival. Nothing exhibits more vividly the tension of spirit
which had come with four years of terrible war,
than the fact that the Administration at Washington, which had patiently allowed McClellan to
sit motionless in front of Johnston from July to
February, began to urge Thomas to move against

CHAP. I. Hood within twenty-four hours of the victory at Franklin. General Grant felt and exhibited this impatience in a much stronger degree. He not only sent out daily messages urging immediate action, but betrayed an irritation which reads strangely in the light of Thomas's career. He carried this feeling much further than the civil authorities at Washington, though it is true that Mr. Van Horne, "History of the Army of the Cumberland." Vol. II., p. 253. Stanton, in a strain of whimsical exaggeration, wrote to Grant on the 7th of December, "If he [Thomas] waits for Wilson to get ready, Gabriel will be blowing his last horn." Grant the next day telegraphed to Halleck, "If Thomas has not struck yet he ought to be ordered to hand over his command to Ibid. Schofield." Halleck replied, showing that the Government at Washington, impatient as they felt for immediate action, cherished a higher regard for Thomas than that felt by the General-in-Chief. "If you wish General Thomas relieved," he said, "give the order. No one here will, I think, interfere. The responsibility, however, will be yours, as no Halleck to Grant, Dec. 8, Ibid. one here, so far as I am informed, wishes General Thomas removed."

This dispatch saved General Thomas his command for a few days longer; but Grant refused to be placated. Thomas telegraphed him on the 8th in extenuation of his not having attacked Hood that he could not concentrate his troops and get their transportation in order in shorter time than it had been done. Halleck answered, expressing the deep dissatisfaction of Grant at Thomas's delay, and Grant, on the 9th, with growing indignation, requested Halleck to telegraph orders re- Ibid., p. 255. lieving Thomas at once and placing Schofield in

GENERAL JOHN B. HOOD.

command. These orders were immediately written out, but before they were transmitted to Nashville Thomas reported in his usual manly and reasonable style, "I regret that General Grant should feel dissatisfaction at my delay in attacking the enemy. I feel conscious that I have done everything in my power to prepare, and that the troops could not have been gotten ready before this. And if he should order me to be relieved I will submit without a murmur. A terrible storm of freezing rain has come on since daylight, which will render an attack impossible till it breaks." On the receipt of this dispatch the authorities took the responsibility of delaying the order for Thomas's relief until Grant could be consulted, and he, the same evening, suspended the order until, as he said, "it is seen whether he will do anything."

Van Horne, "History of the Army of the Cumberland." Vol. II., p. 255.

Ibid., p. 256.

The spell of bad weather announced by Thomas in this dispatch continued for six days. It made any movement of either army impracticable. The rain froze as it fell, covering road and field with a thick coating of ice, upon which it was impossible for men to march, and on which every effort to move cavalry resulted in serious casualties to men and horses. General Grant knew this;[1] but his fear that Hood might elude Thomas and lead him in a race to the Ohio River became so overpowering that it clouded his better judgment, and his dispatches of censure and vehement command came raining in day by day upon Thomas, causing that most subordinate and conscientious of soldiers

[1] He says in his "Memoirs," Vol. II., p. 380: "The rain was falling, and freezing as it fell, so that the ground was covered with a sheet of ice that made it very difficult to move."

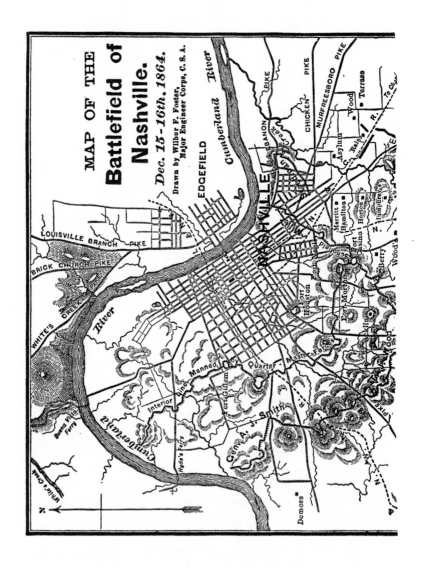

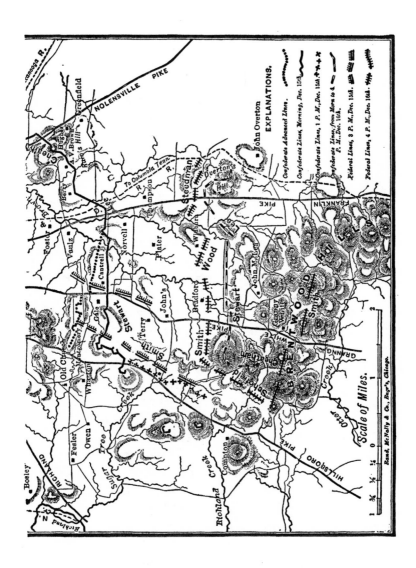

Chap. I. exquisite pain, but never for an instant disturbing the calm equipoise of his mind. He replied from day to day, acknowledging the receipt of orders, and promising to execute them at the earliest moment possible. "The whole country," he said, on Van Horne, "History of the Army of the Cumberland." Vol. II., p. 257. the 11th, "is covered with a perfect sheet of ice and sleet, and it is with difficulty that troops are able to move about on level ground." On the 12th it was no better. He again described in a dispatch the utter impossibility of moving men or horses, and his belief that an attack at this time would only Ibid. result in a useless sacrifice of life.

It is hard to believe, and painful to write, that after the receipt of this truthful and loyal statement, General Grant dispatched General John A. Logan, who was then visiting him at City Point, to relieve General Thomas at Nashville. He directed him, however, not to deliver the order or publish it until he reached his destination, and then, if Thomas had moved, not to deliver it at all. Even after Logan had started, Grant's uneasiness at the situation so gained upon him that he himself started for Nashville, and was met at Washington by news which electrified the country, saved General Thomas his command, and established him immutably in the respect and affection of his country. Thomas nowhere appears to greater advantage, not even on the hills of Chickamauga opposing his indomitable spirit to the surging tide of disaster and defeat, than he does during this week, opposing his sense of duty to the will of his omnipotent superior, and refusing to move one hour before he thought the interests of the country permitted it, even under the threat of

removal and disgrace. In answer to Halleck's last CHAP. I.
peremptory dispatch, he replied on the evening of
the 14th of December: "The ice having melted away 1864.
to-day, the enemy will be attacked to-morrow morning"; and the next night he sent this laconic dis- Van Horne,
"History of
the Army
of the Cum-
berland."
Vol. II.,
p. 258.
patch, "Attacked enemy's left this morning; drove
it from the river below city very nearly to Franklin
pike — distance about eight miles."

The frightful storms of rain and sleet which had
held Thomas as if spell-bound had interfered
equally with the mobility of Hood. Neither one
nor the other could stir. Still, without the slightest trepidation, the Confederate chief waited for
Thomas's attack, feeling sure, as he says in his
report, "that I could defeat him and thus gain
possession of Nashville with abundant supplies for Hood,
"Advance
and
Retreat,"
p. 331.
the army. This would give me possession of Tennessee." So late as the 11th of December he wrote
in a most encouraging strain to the Confederate
Secretary of War, making suggestions as to his
spring campaign, and saying with unconscious
humor, "I think the position of this army is
now such as to force the enemy to take the in- Ibid., p. 357.
itiative."

On the morning of the 15th of December, in the 1864.
midst of a heavy fog which masked the movements
of Thomas's army, he threw it forward to the long
desired attack. It was the sort of weather which
from time immemorial had been held as a justification for absolute inaction. The warm rains had
changed the sleety roads and fields to a sea of
mire, through which the troops floundered painfully. To divert Hood's attention from his real
purpose, Thomas had ordered Steedman to demon-

strate heavily with his command against the Confederate right, east of the Nolensville pike, orders which that energetic commander carried out with such tumultuous zeal as to draw Hood's attention almost entirely to that side of the field. Wilson's cavalry and Smith's infantry corps then moved out along the Hardin pike and commenced the grand movement of the day, by wheeling to the left, and advancing against the left flank of Hood's position. Wilson first struck the enemy along Richland Creek, which bounds the city on the west, and drove him rapidly, making numerous captures, until he came upon a detached redoubt, intended as a protection to Hood's left flank, which was carried in splendid style by a portion of Edward Hatch's dismounted troopers; another work and some hundreds of prisoners were immediately after captured by the combined assault of Smith's and Wilson's men.

But finding that Smith had not gone as far to the right as he had hoped, Thomas directed Schofield to move the Twenty-third Corps to the right of General Smith, by this means enabling the cavalry to act more freely upon Hood's left flank and rear. Schofield's two divisions, admirably commanded by Generals Couch and Cox, marched with great spirit and swiftness to the position assigned them and gained ground rapidly all the afternoon. The Fourth Corps, under General T. J. Wood, which held the center of the Union line, assaulted about one o'clock Hood's advanced position at Montgomery Hill, a gallant feat of arms executed by the brigade of Colonel P. Sidney Post. From this point a rapid advance was made, the whole line working steadily forward until Hood was driven everywhere from his position, and forced back to a new line having its right and left flank respectively on the Overton and the Brentwood Hills, his left occupying a commanding range of hills on the east of the Franklin pike; his center stretched across from that road to another a mile to the west called the Granny White turnpike; both flanks were refused and strongly intrenched to the east and west and to the south, while the main line fronted northward. The Union lines closed rapidly about him, and in this position both sides waited for the morning.

The events of the day had filled the Union army with confidence and enthusiasm, and at early dawn on the morning of the 16th Thomas sent his whole line forward. Wood pressed the Confederate skirmishers across the Franklin pike, and swinging a little to the right, advanced due south, driving the enemy before him, until he came upon his new main line of works, constructed during the night on Overton's Hill. Steedman marched out on the Nolensville pike and formed on the left of Wood, the latter general taking command of both corps. Smith connected with Wood's right, his corps facing southward, while Schofield began the morning's work in the position where night had overtaken him, his line running almost due southward and perpendicular to that of Wood. Thomas now rode along the entire line surveying every inch of the field, and at last gave orders that the movement should continue against the Confederate left. His entire line was closely crowding that of Hood, there being only a space of 600 yards between them.

Chap. I.   At about three o'clock, Post's brigade, which had on the day before so gallantly carried Montgomery Hill, was ordered by General Wood to assault the Dec. 16, 1864. works on the Overton Heights.   C. R. Thompson's brigade of colored troops of Steedman's command joined in this desperate enterprise.   "Our men," says Thomas, "moved steadily onward up the hill until near the crest, when the reserve of the enemy rose and poured into the assaulting column a most destructive fire, causing the men first to waver and then to fall back, leaving their dead and wounded, black and white indiscriminately mingled, lying amidst the abatis, the gallant Colonel Post Thomas, Report. among the wounded." [1] This was the only Confederate success of the day; but it was enough to excite the wildest hopes in the always sanguine breast of General Hood. Sitting on his horse and observing the repulse of Post's storming party, he says, "I had matured the movement for the next morning. The enemy's right flank, by this hour, Hood, "Advance and Retreat," p. 303. stood in air some six miles from Nashville, and I had determined to withdraw my entire force during the night and attack this exposed flank in rear"; still intent on his reverent imitation of Stonewall Jackson. But even at the moment he was maturing this strategic scheme, his line, he says, "broke at all points," and he "beheld for the first and only time Ibid. a Confederate army abandon the field in confusion."

Immediately after Post's assault had failed, the commands of Smith and Schofield advanced to the

---

[1] Colonel Post was reported among the killed; the reports were afterwards corrected to "mortally wounded"; but he survived to receive the promotion he had so gallantly won, was afterwards Consul-General of the United States at Vienna, and is now (1890) a Member of Congress.

GENERAL ALEXANDER P. STEWART.

work assigned them, and with marvelous celerity and success they burst over the enemy's works in every direction, "carrying all before them, irreparably breaking his lines in a dozen places and capturing all his artillery and thousands of prisoners." The result was so sudden and so overwhelming that neither side was quite prepared for it.

CHAP. I.

Thomas, Report Committee on Conduct of the War, 1865–66. Supplement, Vol. I., p. 377.

Wilson had been making rapid progress with his cavalry on the extreme right, and had come to report his success to Thomas, who stood with Schofield directing operations; he saw the rush for the Confederate position and galloped back to his command to share in the final struggle; but as Cox says, "Before he could get half way there the whole Confederate left was crushed in like an egg-shell; . . . the arch was broken, there were no reserves to restore it, and from right and left the Confederate troops peeled away from the works in wild confusion." With the exception of the casualties in the gallant rush made by Post's and Thompson's brigades Thomas's entire loss was but slight. The Confederates abandoned their artillery, rushed across the Granny White road to the Franklin pike, and poured in a disorganized mass down the only avenue to the South which was left open to them. No rout during the war was ever more complete. Thomas captured in the two days 4462 prisoners, including 287 officers of all grades from that of major-general, fifty-three pieces of artillery, and thousands of small arms.

Cox, "Franklin and Nashville," p. 123.

Dec. 15 and 16, 1864.

Thomas, Report.

One or two of the brigades that still retained their organization formed as a rear guard on the Franklin pike, under command of S. D. Lee, and during the first hours of the night efficiently maintained a certain show of resistance to the pursuing cavalry. Night quickly closed in, and a drenching rain came down which made pursuit extremely difficult. General Grant was never satisfied with the swiftness and efficiency of Thomas's pursuit of Hood's beaten army; yet with the exception of that historic chase which began at Petersburg and ended at Appomattox there was no other pursuit of a beaten army during the war so energetic, so prolonged, and so fruitful. The cavalry column came up with the enemy's rear guard four miles north of Franklin. They charged it in front and flank, capturing 413 prisoners and three colors. They drove the Confederates through Franklin, capturing 2000 wounded in the hospitals there, and liberated some hundreds of Union prisoners. The cavalry pressed on, followed by the infantry, who moved with such expedition as was possible over the frightful roads, incumbered by all the débris of two armies.

On the 18th, the enemy crossed Harpeth River, destroying the bridges behind them. The profuse rains of the month now began to show their effects in the swollen water-courses. At Rutherford's Creek they found the stream, which was usually a rivulet, a foaming torrent. It took two days to get the command across; material for a bridge over Duck River was hastily pushed forward to that point so that Wood crossed late on the 22d, and got into position on the Pulaski road. Hood's army, though still retreating at the top of their speed, had by this time gained the powerful assistance of Forrest, who had joined them at Columbia; and Hood had formed a strong rear guard of four

thousand infantry, under E. C. Walthall,— Lee CHAP. I.
having been wounded on the 17th,— and all his
available cavalry. "With the exception of his rear
guard," says Thomas, "his army had become a dis-
heartened and disorganized rabble of half-armed and
barefooted men, who sought every opportunity to
fall out by the wayside and desert their cause to put
an end to their sufferings." On Christmas morning Thomas, still continuing the pursuit, drove the
enemy out of Pulaski, and chased him towards
Lamb's Ferry over roads which had become almost
impassable "and through a country devoid of sus-
tenance for man and beast." The Confederates
were, however, more fleet than their pursuers; the
swollen rivers and other accidents everywhere
favored them, and during the 26th and 27th Hood
crossed the Tennessee River.

Thomas,
Report
Committee
on Conduct
of the War.
Supple-
ment.
Part I.,
p. 379.

Dec., 1864.

Even here he did not feel in safety, but continued his headlong retreat to Tupelo, Mississippi. From there, on the 13th of January, he
sent a dispatch to the Confederate War Department requesting to be relieved from the command
of the army. After consultation with General
Beauregard, he issued furloughs to most of his
Tennessee troops; his army, what there was of it,
rapidly melted away. Four thousand of them
went to join Maury at Mobile. It is hard to say
what became of the rest. After the pressure of
public opinion had forced the Richmond authorities to the bitter necessity of reappointing General
Johnston to the command of that spectral army
which was expected to oppose the triumphal march
of Sherman to the North, the three corps of Hood's
army which reported to him consisted of 2000 men

1865.

Hood,
"Advance
and
Retreat,"
p. 307.

CHAP. I. under C. L. Stevenson,— S. D. Lee's successor,—
2000 under Cheatham, and 1000 under Stewart; in
addition to these there were, he says, little parties
Johnston,
"Narrative
of Military
Opera-
tions,"
pp. 372, 373. who gradually made their way into North Carolina, as groups and individuals, and were brought
to him at last by General S. D. Lee.   The pursuit of Hood's retreating army was not continued
1864. longer by Thomas.   On the 29th of December, a
small force of cavalry of only 600 men, under
command of Col. W. J. Palmer, of the Fifteenth
Pennsylvania, went roving through North Alabama and Mississippi striking the enemy here and
there, destroying one day his pontoon trains, on
another day a large supply train, sabering and
shooting his mules, attacking the Confederate general W. W. Russell near Thorn Hill, routing him,
capturing some prisoners, burning some wagons,
and then proceeding at his leisure back to camp
at Decatur, after a march of over 250 miles, reporting a loss of one killed and two wounded.

Mr. Davis promptly complied with Hood's request for relief, and he bade farewell on the 23d of
January, 1865, to what was left of the army of
50,000 men which Johnston had led with such
unfailing prudence and wisdom from Tunnel Hill
to Atlanta, and which Hood had dashed to pieces
against the National breastworks on every field
from Atlanta to Nashville.   Hood then visited Virginia, was kindly received by Jefferson Davis, with
whom he always remained a favorite, even amid
the impending ruin of the Confederacy, and was
on his way to Texas with instructions to bring a
new army from that remote but gallant State to
the rescue of the falling cause, when he heard of

Lee's surrender. He tried for many days to cross the Mississippi, several times, as he says, "hotly chased by Federal cavalry through the wood and cane-brakes"; but, at last, making a virtue of necessity, he surrendered to General John W. Davidson, at Natchez, on the 31st of May.

Chap. I.

Hood, "Advance and Retreat," p. 311.

1865.

CHAPTER II

THE ALBEMARLE

THE successive captures and recaptures of the town of Plymouth, in North Carolina, were episodes of the war so unimportant that they would scarcely claim a place in history were it not for the memorable naval fights in the spring of 1864 in which the Confederate ironclad *Albemarle* gained great distinction, and the splendid heroism of a young sailor, by which, in the autumn of the same year, she was destroyed. This famous vessel was slowly and painfully constructed, far inland, in a cornfield on the banks of the Roanoke River, about thirty miles below Weldon. The same officer who had changed the *Merrimac* into the ironclad *Virginia* used the experience acquired in that service in the building of the *Albemarle*. Nearly everything requisite in shipbuilding was lacking; but, in spite of all difficulties, the vessel was built at last, and slid from the bluff into the river without springing a leak. She measured 152 feet in length, 45 in width, and, with her armor on, drew eight feet. In general construction she resembled all the other Confederate ironclads. Her casement, or shield, was sixty feet long, sloping to the deck at an angle of forty-five degrees; plated with two courses of two-

Gilbert
Elliott,
"Battles
and
Leaders."
Vol. IV.,
p. 626.

inch iron, rolled at the Tredegar Works. She was
armed with two rifled Brooke guns, mounted on
pivot carriages, so disposed that each gun commanded three portholes. Her beak was of oak,
plated with two-inch iron. She was a year under
construction; rumors of her progress occasionally
transpired, and the brave and vigilant commander,
C. W. Flusser, to whom her first sortie was to be
mortal, warned the department in the summer of
1863 that a formidable craft was in preparation in
the river.

It would have required no considerable expedition to destroy her in the yard, but General Grant's
attention was at that time fully occupied with other
matters. She was not completed until April, 1864,
and her first service under her captain, J. W. Cooke,
was to assist General Hoke in an attack upon the
town of Plymouth, which was held by a small Union
force under General H. W. Wessels. Hoke's division marched down and surrounded the place, his
two flanks resting on the river above and below the
town. It was the task of the *Albemarle* to clear
away the navy from the river front. The attack
began on the 18th of April, and lasted all day, with
no advantage to the Confederates, Wessels's troops,
and the two gunboats *Miami* and *Southfield*, under
the intelligent direction of Flusser, repulsing every
attempt to take the place; but on the next day the
intervention of the *Albemarle* put a different face
on the affair. She dropped down the river in front
of the town by night, the fire of the fort rattling
harmlessly against her shield. Flusser, warned of
her coming, made ready for action, and steamed up to
meet her with the *Miami* and the *Southfield* chained

MAPS OF THE COAST OF THE CAROLINAS.

together. The adversaries met in the first glimmer
of dawn. The ram struck the *Miami* a slight blow,
and, passing on, with one thrust of her beak tore
open the side of the *Southfield*, which filled and sank
almost immediately. The *Miami* opened upon the
ram with her batteries, with results fatal only to
her own brave commander. Flusser, who was personally firing the first shots, was struck by a fragment of a Dahlgren shell, rebounding from the iron
side of the ram, and instantly killed. His successor
in command seeing that if he remained he would
simply be sacrificing his vessel uselessly, retired
down the river to Albemarle Sound. The post of
Plymouth, surrounded on every side, fell into the
hands of the Confederates.

The destruction of the *Albemarle* was thencefor-
ward the principal object of the naval squadron
in the Sound. Captain Melancton Smith, an able
and experienced officer, was dispatched to the scene
of action for that especial service. He rapidly made
the necessary arrangements for attack. His main
reliance was upon his guns and torpedoes; ramming was to be resorted to in the discretion of commanders, though the peculiar construction of the
double enders, of which his fleet consisted, rendered this a doubtful expedient. The *Albemarle*
did not wait to be attacked, but sallied forth
at midday of the 5th of May, with the intention
of clearing both Albemarle and Pamlico Sounds of
the Union fleet, and, if possible, regaining control
of Hatteras Inlet. She was attended by the transport *Cotton Plant*, and the captured storeship *Bombshell*. Smith speedily got his vessels under way,
the flagship *Mattabesett* leading, the *Sassacus* and

CHAP. II.

1864.

Report of
Acting-
Master
Wells.

Lee,
Orders,
April 23,
1864.
Report
Secretary
of the
Navy,
Dec. 5, 1864.

Gilbert
Elliott,
"Century
Magazine,"
July, 1888.

Chap. II. the rest of the fleet following, eight vessels in all, carrying 32 guns, besides 23 howitzers. Against this heavy armament the undaunted ironclad came May 5, 1864. on with her two guns; and so enormous is the power of invulnerability that the fight was not altogether unequal. We feel in reading the epics and sagas of the past, that Achilles and Siegfried are safe no matter what the number of their adversaries, unless the exposed heel or the mark of the linden leaf is touched. Without the ironclads in Mobile Bay, all the valor of Farragut would have been of no avail against the tough sides of the *Tennessee.* The *Cotton Plant* was at once ordered back out of danger, and the *Bombshell,* at the first onset of the Union fleet, surrendered; but the *Albemarle* held her own sturdily; her two pivot guns, working in safety and at leisure, seemed to quadruple themselves by dint of efficiency.

The battle began at a quarter before five o'clock; the *Albemarle* fired two damaging shots into the *Mattabesett* and then tried to ram her, but the swifter ship evaded the blow and poured a broadside upon the ironclad. The *Sassacus* coming up did the same, and the other vessels in succession Gilbert Elliott, "Century Magazine," July, 1888. did what they could; their principal danger was firing into, or fouling, each other. Their fire was by no means ineffective; the boats of the *Albemarle* were shot away, her smoke-stack so injured that it almost ceased to draw, many of her plates were started and shattered, and her after gun was broken and disabled; but to the eyes of the officers in the Union fleet, this concentrated fire appeared to have no more effect on the iron sides of the monster than so much thistle-down. Lieutenant-Commander

F. A. Roe, of the *Sassacus*, therefore resolved to try the desperate expedient of ramming the iron-clad. He drew off to a distance of some 200 yards, and putting on a full head of steam rushed upon the *Albemarle* at a speed of ten knots an hour. He struck her just abaft the casemate on the starboard side with a shock which caused every timber to groan, though nothing gave way. There was a moment of consternation on board the ram, but seeing they did not sink the crew immediately rallied to their guns and continued the fight. The *Sassacus* steamed heavily, hoping to force the ram under water; and in this Roe might have met the success his bravery deserved, but for a shot from the *Albemarle* which passed through his boiler, and in an instant filled his vessel with scalding steam, disabling his engine and sixteen men. Crippled as he was, his engine room inaccessible, the vessel filled with smoke and steam and the shrieks of scalded sailors, Roe still fought his guns with imperturbable gallantry, hurling upon the *Albemarle* his hundred-pound shot, which rebounded in pieces on his own deck. He slowly dropped out of the fight, and a period of considerable confusion ensued, as the result of two mistakes; the flag of the *Albemarle* being shot away, it was thought she had surrendered, and the *Wyalusing* erroneously reported herself as sinking; this caused a temporary cessation of the battle, which was not renewed with much energy until night closed in.

The *Albemarle*, whose riddled smoke-stack refused to draw, was able, by burning the lard and bacon on board, to steam back to Plymouth.

Chap. II.

Roe, Report, May 6, 1864. Report Secretary of the Navy.

Ibid

She had gained great glory throughout the Confederacy by her two battles, and Captain Cooke was promoted to the command of the rebel navy on the coast of North Carolina. With a few knots more speed she could have destroyed the whole Union fleet; as it was, the capture of a fort with a brigade of prisoners, the destruction of a gunboat, and a drawn battle lasting a full afternoon with a squadron mounting 55 pieces, were no inconsiderable claims to renown. She came out of the Roanoke but once after this battle; on the 24th of May she was seen by a picket boat, apparently dragging for torpedoes. A single shot fired at her caused her to retire up the stream. She lay at her berth by the wharf at Plymouth until the 27th of October, when her name was associated forever with one still more glorious.

Of course the Navy Department could not count upon this long inaction, and so long as the *Albemarle* lay substantially unhurt at Plymouth she was a source of constant anxiety to the squadron in the Sound. They had no ironclads of sufficiently light draft to cross the bar at Hatteras Inlet; several were in course of construction, but it was not safe to wait for their completion. A party of volunteers from the *Wyalusing* was sent to destroy the ram with torpedoes, late in May; but an untoward accident, the fouling of their line by a schooner, prevented a success which was merited by their courage and good conduct. September had come before the plan and the man were found that were adapted to the work. The scheme was to fit out two small steam launches rigged with spar torpedoes, and armed with howitzers, which should try to reach the ram at night by surprise; the man was Lieutenant William B. Cushing, who had attracted the attention of his superiors by several noteworthy examples of coolness and daring. Once he had landed by night with two boat crews at the town of Smithville, being rowed under the very guns of Fort Caswell, walked with three men to General Louis Hébert's headquarters, captured an officer of engineers, the general himself being absent in Wilmington, and had come safely away with his prisoner, from a post garrisoned by a thousand men.

At another time, having volunteered to destroy the ironclad *Raleigh*, supposed to be lying in the Cape Fear River, he went in his cutter up the stream, eluding the sentries on either shore, landed within seven miles of Wilmington, thoroughly reconnoitered the place, found the *Raleigh* a total wreck, and after three days of adventures in which his luck and daring were equally amazing he was intercepted on his return down the river in the moonlight by a whole fleet of guard boats and his escape apparently cut off. Turning about, he found himself confronted by a schooner filled with troops. Instead of surrendering he dashed for New Inlet; and, seconded by his crew, who always seemed when with him as insensible to danger as himself, he escaped into the breakers, where the enemy dared not follow, and safely rejoined his ship. His perfect coolness in critical emergencies was a matter of temperament rather than calculation. He prepared everything in advance with a care and judgment remarkable in one so young; but when the time of action came, the immediate peril of death was nothing more than a gentle stimulant to him; he enjoyed it as he would a frolic. He was a handsome youth, 21 years of age; six feet high; with a beardless face and bright auburn hair.

After conferences with Admiral Lee and Mr. Fox, the Assistant Secretary of the Navy, Cushing went to New York and found two launches, at the Brooklyn Navy Yard, suited to his purpose. They were 46 feet in length, $9\frac{1}{2}$ feet wide, and drew about 40 inches. While they were being equipped for the work by Engineer-in-Chief W. W. Wood of the navy, Cushing visited his mother in Fredonia, N. Y., and confided to her his intention, saying he needed her prayers. Returning to New York he took his launches out and tested his torpedoes, and then started them southward, by way of Chesapeake Bay; one of them on the way was attacked by guerrillas and burned. At Hampton Roads Cushing refitted his only remaining boat, and passing through the Dismal Swamp came to Roanoke Island. There he gave out that he was bound for Beaufort and steamed away by night to join the fleet which was lying off the mouth of the Roanoke River, the senior officer being Commander W. H. Macomb, whose flagship was the *Shamrock.*

Here for the first time Cushing disclosed to his officers and men the purpose of his expedition, leaving them free to go or stay as they preferred; all wanted to go with him.[1] Several others volunteered, among them Paymaster Francis H. Swan, whose anxiety for a fight was paid by a severe

[1] In this chapter we have made free use of Cushing's admirable account of his expedition, printed in "Battles and Leaders of the Civil War," Vol. IV., p. 634. We have also used J. Russell Soley's "The Blockade and the Cruisers."

wound and four months in Libby prison; W. L.
Howarth, Cushing's tried and trusted companion in
former adventures, and two other master's mates,
Thos. S. Gay and John Woodman; two engineer
officers, Steever and Stotesbury, and eight men. A
cutter from the *Shamrock* was taken in tow with
eleven men; their duty was to board the wreck of
the *Southfield*, if the guard which was known to be
posted there should discover the party as they
passed. A false start was made on the night of the
26th; the boat ran aground, and so much time was
wasted in getting her off that the expedition was
postponed for twenty-four hours. At midnight, Cushing, Report, Oct. 30, 1864.
in rain and storm, the devoted little party set
forth. Fortune favored them at first; they passed Report Secretary of the Navy.
the wreck of the *Southfield* without a hail, and
came in view of the few lights of Plymouth.

The little noise made by the low-pressure engines
was muffled with tarpaulins, which also concealed
every ray of light from the launch. Cushing
stood near the bow, connected by lines with every
part of the boat as the brain is by nerves with
every limb. He held a line by which he was to de-
tach the torpedo from the spar which carried it,
when it should have been shoved under the over-
hang of the ram; another, by which he was to
explode it after it had floated up to a point of contact; and two more, one attached to the wrist and
one to the ankle of the engineer, by which he directed
the movements of the boat. He had two complete plans in his mind; one was — to use his own
nervous phrase — "to take the *Albemarle* alive," by
landing some distance below, stealing up, and dash-
ing on her from the wharf; but just as he was

sheering in close to the lower wharf he heard a dog
bark, a sentry hail, and a moment afterwards a shot
was fired. Instantly dismissing his first plan, Cushing ordered the cutter to cast loose and row to capture the *Southfield's* picket; and then, putting on all
steam, he rushed for the ram, whose black bulk
loomed in the darkness before him. By the light
of a fire on the wharf he discovered that she was surrounded by a boom of logs extending all around
her for the express purpose of protecting her against
torpedoes. A brisk fire opened on the launch from
the ship and the shore, but his keen intelligence
was only sharpened by the danger, and he saw at
a glance that on the course he was taking he could
not get over the boom. He therefore sheered off a
hundred yards, and then turning came at full speed
to strike the logs at right angles, hoping thus to
slide over them, and getting inside the sort of pen
they formed, to reach the ram.

The fire had by this time become severe; Swan
was wounded; Cushing's clothes were torn by three
bullets; the sole of his shoe was carried away, but
he was unhurt and very happy. Being hailed again,
as he dashed forward, he shouted, "Leave the ram.
We are going to blow you up," a response as considerate as it proved truthful. His crew, catching the
infection, also chaffed the Confederates, while Cushing, not wishing to let the enemy do all the firing,
sent a charge of canister among them at short
range, which, he said, "served to moderate their
zeal and disturb their aim." The launch touched
the logs and slid gently over them; the spar was
lowered; Cushing, as cool in that shower of deadly
missiles, and in face of a hundred-pound rifle,

Cushing,
"Narra-
tive,"
ut supra.

COMMANDER WILLIAM B. CUSHING.

whose muzzle he could now plainly see, as a skilled Chap. II.
artisan at his bench, watched for the proper instant,
detached the torpedo with a line held in his
right hand, waited a moment for it to rise under
the hull of the ram, and then pulled with the left Oct. 27, 1864.
hand, which had just been cut by a bullet. At the
same instant the 100-pounder was fired; the
grape shot, at ten feet range, came roaring over
Cushing and his crew, just missing them; but the
torpedo had done its work, and a suffocating mass
of water rose from the side of the *Albemarle* and
fell upon the launch, half filling it, and drenching
the crew. Cushing, who thought his boat had been Cushing, Report, Oct. 30, 1864. Report Secretary of the Navy.
pierced by the shot from the ram, saw there was
no hope of saving her; being summoned to surrender he refused, and ordered his crew to save
themselves; he threw off his sword, revolver, coat,
and shoes and jumped into the water.

The *Albemarle's* commander did not at first real- Captain A. F. Warley.
ize what had happened. He heard a dull report as
of an unshotted gun; a fragment of wood fell at
his feet. He sent a carpenter to examine the hull,
who reported " a hole big enough to drive a wagon
in." The *Albemarle* was resting in the mud; she
had sunk so little her own officers did not perceive
it, and the victors were unconscious of their success.
The men in the launch were captured, all but three,
who had followed Cushing in his desperate leap
into the icy river. Two of these were drowned;
the third got ashore and was saved.

Perhaps no event of his life gave such proof of
Cushing's extraordinary nerve and endurance as
his escape. He swam out in the darkness, knowing
there was no shelter for him but the fleet, twelve

miles away. He evaded the rebel boats which were rowing about the river until he was well out of sight. Nearing the shore, he found Woodman drowning, and kept him up ten minutes with his own fast-failing strength, but could not bring him to land. Cushing at last managed to reach the muddy shore, and fell, half in and half out of the water; there he lay until daybreak, unable to move.

When the dawn came, he found himself lying on the edge of a swamp, in full view of a sentry, not forty steps from a fort. When the sun had warmed his chilled limbs a little, he attempted to crawl away from his exposed position, and, being covered with mud, he succeeded, by sliding on his back, inch by inch, though soldiers were several times almost near enough to tread on him. After gaining the swamp he wandered for several hours among the cypresses, scratched and torn at every step by thorns and briers. At last he found an aged negro, and the disposition he made of him is noteworthy. Instead of employing him to assist in his escape, Cushing plied him with greenbacks and texts of Scripture until he induced him to go into Plymouth and get news of the last night's affair.

The tidings he brought back were such a cordial to the forlorn victor, that he plunged into the swamp with new heart and hope. In the afternoon he came upon a stream where there was a picket post of soldiers who had a small skiff fastened to a cypress root in the water. Watching them till they sat down to eat, he swam to the boat, noiselessly unfastened it, and drew it around a bend in the river, then got in and paddled for life and liberty. He floated on through twilight to darkness, out of

the Roanoke into the broad Sound; the night was
providentially still and calm; he steered by the
stars till he reached the picket vessel *Valley City;*
he had strength enough left to give a feeble hail,
then fell with a splash into the water in the bottom
of his boat. He had paddled, he says, "every minute for ten successive hours, and for four my body
had been 'asleep,' with the exception of my two
arms and brain." At first they took the skiff for a
torpedo boat, and were more inclined to give him a
volley of musketry than to pick him up; but he
soon established his identity, refreshed himself, and
went to report to the flagship, where he was received as one risen from the dead with salutes of
rejoicing; the night air became gay with rockets,
and all hands were called to cheer ship. Perhaps
the most remarkable words in the simple narrative
this heroic youth has left of his strange adventure
are these, with which it closes: "In the morning I
was again well in every way, with the exception of
hands and feet, and had the pleasure of exchanging
shots with the batteries that I had inspected on the
day previous."

On the 30th of October, Commander Macomb,
having ascertained that the direct channel was obstructed, passed into the Roanoke above Plymouth
by Middle River, and thus took the place in reverse.
A spirited engagement between the fleet and the
forts began about eleven in the morning of the
31st; a fortunate shot from the *Shamrock* exploded
the enemy's magazine, and the Confederates hastily
evacuated their works; the victorious sailors, rowing ashore, captured the rear guard with twenty-two
cannon and a large quantity of stores.

CHAPTER III

CHAP. III.

1864.

THE ports of Wilmington and Savannah, after the capture of New Orleans and the strict blockade of Charleston, and especially after the occupation of Mobile Bay, became the most important and valuable means of communication with the outside world which were left to the Confederacy. In spite of the utmost efforts of the National vessels, an extensive trade was carried on between these ports and those West Indian islands which had been taken as points of transshipment for the contraband goods exported from England to the Confederacy, and for the cotton which formed the only coin by which the South paid its debts to Europe. There was a peculiarity about the harbor of Wilmington which rendered it the favorite port of entry for blockade runners. The city stands on the Cape Fear River, about twenty-eight miles from the sea. There is a good entrance to the river at its mouth, and another by New Inlet, six miles in a straight line to the north; the space between them, merely sand and shallow water, is called Smith's Island, the southern extremity of which is the sharp headland of Cape Fear, beyond which stretch the Frying Pan Shoals for ten miles. The southern

entrance was protected by Fort Caswell; the north- CHAP. III.
ern by Fort Fisher; between the two, on the mainland, was the village of Smithville, where the
blockaders lay in wait, watching their chance to
dart out to sea by one or the other sally-port. Those
wishing to enter would wait outside till evening
fell, and then dash in through the blockading fleet
to the safe shelter of the guns of one or the other
fort.

Legitimate trade had ceased immediately on the
proclamation of the blockade by the President; but
the necessities of the Confederacy and the hope of
enormous profits by enterprising English adven-
turers formed together so powerful a stimulus to
blockade running that, as a matter of course, it at
once assumed a considerable development, and for
a time actually increased in proportion to the means
taken to suppress it. The Confederates had little
use for their cotton, except as a medium of exchange; it therefore fell to a lower price than usual
in the South; while the dearth of it in England
and in the North caused an enormous increase in
its value in those countries. The difference between eight cents a pound, at which it could be
purchased in Wilmington, and two shillings, at
which it could be sold in Liverpool, afforded a
profit which would compensate for almost any
possible risk. Three successful voyages would pay
for a vessel; and the odds against a blockade runner were nothing like so great as that. A single
ship, the *R. E. Lee*, ran the blockade twenty-one Soley,
"The
Blockade
and the
Cruisers,"
p. 156.
times between December, 1862, and November,
1863, carrying abroad six thousand bales of cotton.
This was a case of extraordinary success, but it was

CHAP. III.

Soley, "The
Blockade
and the
Cruisers,"
p. 94.

the opinion of our naval officers that two-thirds of
the vessels attempting to enter Wilmington during
the first half of 1864 were successful. It is true
that sixty steamers running the blockade were captured or destroyed by the squadron before Wilmington; but in many cases these had more than
paid for themselves before their fate overtook them.

And yet the blockade was one of the most effective ever seen in war. Captures to the amount
of many millions of dollars were made, and the
shore was strewn with the wrecks of ships which
were destroyed in the attempt to escape. In the
latter part of 1864 the blockade was greatly increased in stringency. Three cordons of ships were
drawn about the blockaded ports; the first as close
as it could lie to the shore, and the third one hundred and thirty miles from land. Even through all
these toils the long, narrow, and swift steel cruisers
sometimes made their way. But the proportion of
those which were captured grew so large that the industry languished. The most prudent had retired
with their gains, and the business was no longer what
it had been. The Government of the United States
might have been satisfied with the results of the
blockade but for its tremendous expense. To watch
the port of Wilmington required a vast armada;
and it was for this reason, fully as much as to put
a stop to contraband trade, that the Navy Department and the President constantly urged upon the
military authorities a joint expedition of the army
and navy against Fort Fisher.

Mr. Welles had from time to time during the war
tried to effect this purpose, but it was not until the
autumn of 1864 that he could get the promise of a

military force to assist the naval attack. He at CHAP. III.
once took measures to make ready as great a force
as possible and offered the command of it to Welles to
Admiral Farragut. His health, which had been Farragut, Sept. 5, 1864.
seriously impaired by his incessant exertions and
exposures in the Gulf, compelled that energetic officer to decline this appointment; it was then given
to Rear-Admiral D. D. Porter, who had greatly
distinguished himself by his zeal and ability in
command of the Mississippi squadron. "A fleet
of naval vessels," says Mr. Welles, "surpassing in
numbers and equipments any which had assem- Report
bled during the war, was collected with dispatch Secretary of the
at Hampton Roads." General Grant promised an Navy, 1865, p. iv.
expeditionary force of over six thousand men.

It was the wish of the President and the War
Department that General Gillmore should have
command of these troops; but that brave and
capable officer had fallen under General Grant's
displeasure, and he had substituted General Godfrey Weitzel. Being informed of the plan proposed Weitzel went down to New Inlet in the
last days of September, and with the assistance 1864.
of Rear-Admiral S. P. Lee made a thorough reconnaissance of the place. He found Fort Fisher
a most formidable work. The Confederates had
made the best use of the long leisure afforded them,
and had built an imposing fortress on the narrow
sandspit which runs northward from New Inlet between Cape Fear River and the sea. A small out-
work called Fort Buchanan was built on the shore
of the Inlet. A half mile to the north Fort Fisher
stretched all the way across the narrow peninsula,
at that point only about five hundred yards wide.

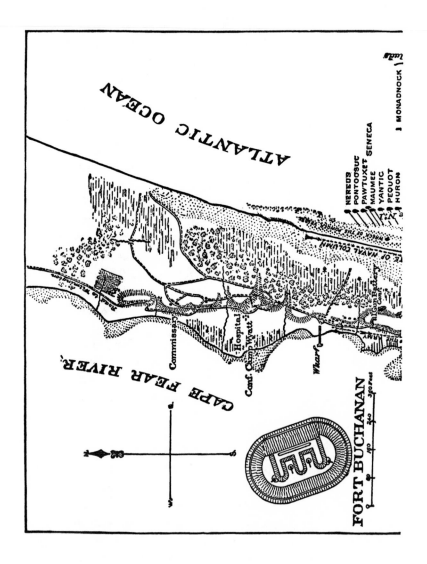

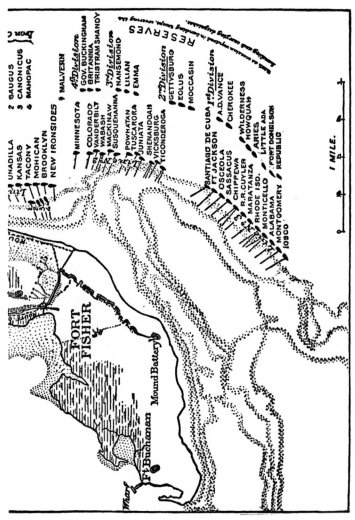

MAP OF THE NAVAL AND MILITARY ATTACKS ON FORT FISHER, JANUARY 15, 1865, SHOWING
DIRECTION OF FIRE OF UNION VESSELS.

NOTE: The flag-ship *Malvern* (placed on the map behind the *New Ironsides*) had no fixed position.

Chap. III. The land face looked north; the sea face east, running along the beach for thirteen hundred yards. The northern front mounted twenty-one guns and three mortars, the sea front twenty-four. The work was so extensive that if it had consisted of its vast parapet alone it would have protected only those immediately under the wall. They had therefore built an extraordinary series of traverses, made bomb-proof; so that Fort Fisher really consisted of something like a dozen small forts in one inclosure.

Report Committee on the Conduct of the War, 1864–65. Part II., p. 68.

Weitzel returned and reported the result of his observations to Grant, who told him he did not think he would start the expedition; that the navy had advertised it too widely by rendezvousing the fleet at Hampton Roads — a charge which seems hardly reasonable, as the fleet could not sail without a rendezvous. The plan lay in abeyance for several weeks. It was taken up with renewed spirit on account of an idea conceived by General Butler, suggested by reading of the great destruction consequent upon an explosion of gunpowder at Erith, England. He supposed that firing a large mass of powder some four hundred yards from Fort Fisher would for the moment paralyze the garrison, and so injure the work as to render its capture easy. This plan, after it had been tried and failed, seemed very ridiculous, and every one concerned in the affair, except Butler, made haste to disavow all responsibility for it. But no one thought it ridiculous when it was suggested. General Butler says: "It was readily embraced by the Secretary of the Ibid., p. 4. Navy, and with more caution by the President." After a thorough study of the subject by accom-

plished officers of the army and navy it was decided that the experiment was worth trying; the
Louisiana, a boat of little value, was selected and
fitted out, and loaded with two hundred and thirty-
five tons of powder.

It was then the first week in December; Sher- 1864.
man was approaching Savannah, and General
Grant, in view of the weakening of the garrison
of Wilmington by the detachment of troops to
meet the victors of Atlanta, was anxious for the
expedition to be off. He afterwards said that he
had never dreamed of General Butler's going   Report
with it; that he had given his orders to Weitzel Committee
on Conduct
through Butler, his department commander, as of the War,
1864–65.
required by military courtesy, without any thought Part II.,
p. 52.
of his going in person. Butler contradicted this
statement, insisting that his purpose was known Ibid.,
to Grant from the beginning. However this may pp. 10, 11.
be, the expedition started under the worst possible auspices. Weitzel, who had been selected
to command it, never read his orders, which had
been communicated by Grant to Butler, and not
shown to Weitzel. In these orders Grant had
said: "The object of the expedition will be gained
on effecting a landing on the mainland between
Cape Fear River and the Atlantic, north of the
north entrance to the river. Should such landing
be effected, whether the enemy hold Fort Fisher
or the batteries guarding the entrance to the river
there, the troops should intrench themselves, and
by coöperating with the navy effect the reduction Grant
to Butler,
and capture of those places." It was an oversight Dec. 6, 1864.
Ibid., p. 10.
almost incredible that General Butler did not say
a word to Weitzel of these clear and important in-

CHAP. III. structions. To make a bad matter worse neither
Butler nor Weitzel was on good terms with Admiral Porter, who was to command the fleet.

The history of this unfortunate expedition, as
written by the principal participators, is little more
than a series of mutual recriminations. The fleet
1864. sailed from Hampton Roads on the 13th of December, and the transports with six thousand five
hundred troops on the next day. From the lack
of a good understanding, so essential in such cases,
they did not arrive together at the rendezvous.
Butler went at once to New Inlet, but Admiral
D. D.
Porter,
"Naval
History
of the
Civil War,"
p. 693. Porter put in at Beaufort to " coal and receive ammunition," as he says, "for now that the expedition
had waited two months there was no particular
hurry." When the admiral was ready to go in and
explode the powder boat, on the 18th, Butler suggested delay until the sea, which had grown rough,
should subside. A gale came on which lasted several days, and which the fleet at anchor rode out
in the most creditable manner. When the storm
abated Porter again informed Butler, who in his
turn had gone to Beaufort for coal and water, that
the powder boat would be exploded on the night
of the 23d of December. Admiral Porter seems
up to this time to have expected a great effect
from the explosion. He suggested to Butler that
Report
Committee
on Conduct
of the War,
1864–65.
Part II.,
p. 18. even at a distance of 25 miles the explosion might
affect the boilers of his steamers ; and in another
letter he says, " The powder vessel is as complete
as human ingenuity can make her."

She was towed to her place near the beach, four
hundred yards from the fort, by the *Wilderness*,
under the charge of two of the bravest and most ac-

complished officers of the navy, Commander Alex.
C. Rhind and Lieutenant S. W. Preston, both of
them volunteers. Every contingency was provided
for; it was even arranged between those two devoted sailors that if she were boarded by the enemy and in danger of capture, Preston, at a signal
given by Rhind, was to stick a lighted candle into
a bag of powder. All this devotion, however, was
to go for nothing; there is even a touch of the
comic about this daring deed of two of the most
heroic men our navy has known. They lighted
their fuses, and kindled a fire of pine knots in the
cabin of the *Louisiana,* and then jumped into their
boats and pulled for the *Wilderness.* The fuses
were set for an hour and a half; the *Wilderness*
steamed out to sea. The whole fleet waited with
breathless apprehension for the result. The explosion took place at forty-five minutes past one;
there was a blaze on the horizon, a dull detonation,
and nothing more. There was little or no concus-
sion felt on ship or shore. It was General Butler's
opinion that the ignition was imperfect; in fact,
that not more than one-tenth of the powder was
burned.

At daylight, the admiral got his fleet under way
and stood in towards the fort in line of battle. He
attacked in fine style and soon silenced the guns
of the fortress, to all appearance; though, as it
turned out, little damage was done. At evening
General Butler arrived with some of the transports,
but as it was too late to land the fleet retired to a
safe anchorage. The next day was Christmas; the
transports were all on hand, and under cover of
the guns of the fleet, which kept up an annoying

CHAP. III. fire all the morning, the troops began to land about five miles north of the fort. Weitzel took the first five hundred as a reconnoitering party and pushed Dec. 25, 1864. rapidly towards the fort, capturing on the way the small garrison of an outlying earthwork. On questioning the prisoners, he found they belonged to Hoke's division, which he had left at Richmond; and that the rest of the brigade to which they belonged was a mile and a half to the rear. This convinced him that the garrison of Fort Fisher had been newly strengthened, and this impression was deepened by the fact that the next squad he captured said they were outside the fort because the bomb-proofs were full. This was not encouraging information, but he pushed on, advancing his skirmish line to within 150 yards of the fort, and from a knoll had a good view of the interior of the work. What he saw powerfully impressed him; the fort was practically uninjured, and seemed to him, with its thick parapets, its bastions in high relief, its bomb-proof traverses, the strongest work he had seen during the war. Weitzel was a brave and intelligent soldier, but he had been engaged in five assaults of intrenchments, three times attacking, twice defending the works. On all five occasions, the party attacking was repulsed; and Weitzel decided naturally enough that he would not advise an attack upon a work stronger than any he had ever attacked in vain or defended successfully.

Weitzel, Testimony. Report Committee on Conduct of the War, 1864-65. Part II., pp. 72, 73.

Weitzel reported to Butler the result of his reconnaissance, which was confirmed by General C. B. Comstock of Grant's staff, who had also reconnoitered the work. Upon this report, General Butler

made the capital mistake of the expedition. Grant's Chap. III.
orders were clear and explicit; the landing itself
was to be regarded as a success; if the work did
not fall at once, the troops were to stay there and
intrench themselves, and, with the help of the
navy, reduce and capture the place. General Butler chose to assume that he had not effected a
landing, because all of his troops had not yet got
ashore; the weather began to look unfavorable;
he therefore resolved to abandon the enterprise Report Committee on Conduct of the War, 1864–65. Part II., p. 80.
and return to Fort Monroe. Even then he did not
show his orders to Weitzel, who said afterwards
that if he had known of their existence he would
have advised differently.

While the generals afloat were coming to this
unfortunate conclusion, one of the officers ashore
had made up his mind in the opposite sense.
General N. M. Curtis, a man of unusual physical
strength, courage, and energy, had pushed his advance almost to the parapet of the fort. The fire
of the navy had been so severe as to confine the
garrison in great part to the bomb-proof, so that
Curtis's men were hardly molested in their approach. They came so near that they captured a
mounted courier; one man climbed the parapet
and brought away a flag which had been shot
away. Curtis was burning with eagerness to
assault; his men shared his enthusiasm. Of course
it cannot be said whether he would have succeeded
or not, though his spirit so infected General Comstock that he changed his mind, and now believed
the movement practicable. But the orders were
given to reëmbark, and slowly and reluctantly
Curtis drew away his men from the coveted prize

he believed was in his hands. The reëmbarkation of the 2500 who had landed took as much time as would have been required to put the whole force on shore. The weather grew worse the next day, and a portion of Curtis's brigade remained on shore until the 27th without molestation by the Confederates.

On the evening of that day General Butler arrived at Fort Monroe and sent a brief telegram to General Grant announcing his return and the failure of the expedition. On the 3d of January he made a more detailed report, throwing the blame of the failure upon Admiral Porter, saying that the first delay of three days of good weather, was due to the navy not being on hand when the army arrived; that the powder boat was prematurely exploded; that Porter should have run by the fort and thus blockaded Wilmington; that Hoke's division was in front of him, making the enemy's force greater than his own; that the experience of Port Hudson and Fort Wagner convinced him that so strong a work as Fisher could not be taken by assault. Upon this General Grant made a merciless indorsement to the effect that he had never intended that Butler should go with the expedition, and that he was in error in stating that he came back in " obedience to his instructions." Grant immediately relieved General Butler from command, which closed his military career. He was summoned before the Committee on the Conduct of the War a few days later, and defended himself with his usual vigor and adroitness, and the Committee in their report, after hearing Grant and Porter, fully justified the action of Butler.

ADMIRAL DAVID D. PORTER.

The President was deeply disappointed by the untoward result of the expedition. Finding that Admiral Porter and the Navy Department were still confident that an attack, if properly made, would succeed, without losing a moment of time in regrets and without even waiting for the official reports of the affair, he directed that Admiral Porter should hold his position off Fort Fisher and that the Secretary of the Navy should send in his name a telegram to General Grant inviting him to a renewed coöperation in attacking the fort. To this Grant instantly acceded. He sent back the same force which had gone before, Adelbert Ames's and Charles J. Paine's divisions, adding Joseph C. Abbott's brigade of the Twenty-fourth Corps, and assigned to command the expedition General Alfred H. Terry.

A landing was effected on the 13th of January. In this case there was no room for doubt or vacillation. The failure of Butler was a sufficient education for Terry. He knew he was sent there to take the fort. He proceeded with the greatest energy and singleness of purpose to do this. His first work was to draw a strong line of contravallation across the narrow sandspit about two miles north of the fort to protect his rear against any attack from Wilmington; this was completed by a hard night's work; at eight in the morning Terry's foothold on the peninsula was secured; Paine and Abbott were placed in this line. Under cover of the fire of the fleet, which now worked with splendid zeal and activity under the stimulus of the hope and gratification occasioned by the return of the army, Ames's division, with Curtis in the lead, moved

CHAP. III.

Welles to Grant, Dec. 29, 1864. Report of Secretary of the Navy, 1865, p. 71.

1865.

Terry, Report, Jan. 25, 1865.

CHAP. III. down the river to within six hundred yards of the fort, where Terry, Curtis, and Comstock made a careful reconnaissance. Curtis felt himself at home on this ground; he was as ready as ever to assault, and an attack was arranged for the afternoon of Jan., 1865. the 15th. Ames was to move on the land face with his division, and the navy, inspired by a noble emulation, undertook to attack the bastion at the sea-angle at the same time. In the morning Col. William Lamb, in "Southern Historical Society Papers." Vol. X., p. 356. Porter began and carried on perhaps the most tremendous fire to which a fort has ever been subjected from a fleet. Nothing could withstand the rain of projectiles which he poured upon Fort Fisher. At first the Confederate cannoneers stood stoutly enough to their guns, while the infantry huddled in their bomb-proofs; but the fire was too hot for human endurance; one by one the guns of the fort were dismounted or destroyed, until hardly a response came from the parapets to the thunder of the ships.

Jan. 15, 1865. At two o'clock Curtis began to move forward against the land face of the fort; Galusha Pennypacker and Louis Bell following in close support. They went forward rapidly, availing themselves of every inequality of the ground, under a severe fire of musketry, until being near enough for the final rush the fleet was signaled to change the direction of its fire, and Curtis led his brigade directly at the bastion by the river. At the same instant the naval force gallantly led by Commander K. R. Breese attempted to storm the bastion on the sea beach. This attempt failed, with the loss of many brave men; notably of Lieutenants S. W. Preston and B. H. Porter, two of the most brilliant and

promising officers in the service; but the diver- CHAP. III.
sion thus made was of great advantage to Curtis
in distracting the attention of the garrison at a
critical moment. The irresistible rush of his brigade carried them over the parapet and Penny- Jan. 15, 1865.
packer gained the palisade from the earthwork
to the river. They were both now inside the
works and ready to take them in reverse; but
here they found that their labor was only be-
gun. The system of traverses was so complete Terry, Report. "Rebellion Record." Vol. XI., p. 429.
that it required nearly a dozen separate actions to
carry the fort. The garrison under Colonel William Lamb, an officer of high bravery and intelligence, fought with desperate courage; but the
progress of the National soldiers, though slow and
hotly disputed, was never once checked. The routed
sailors and marines took charge of the line in the
rear and Abbott was set free to reënforce the
storming party in the traverses. It was growing
dark when the last rush was made which cleared
the fort. It was a well-won victory, not lightly
gained. Curtis was terribly wounded in the head;
Pennypacker had a severe wound, the gallant
Bell was killed at the head of his brigade. The
garrison fled to Fort Buchanan at the southern
extremity of Federal Point, where late in the evening they surrendered. Colonel Lamb and General
W. H. C. Whiting, the latter having taken part in Ibid.
the action, though not in command, both severely
wounded, were taken prisoners.

The forts at the mouth of the river were immediately abandoned, rendering the victory complete
and extremely valuable. One hundred and sixty-
nine cannon in all were captured, and more than

CHAP. III. two thousand prisoners. But, better than all this, the fleet could now enter the harbor, and the days of blockade running were at an end. A comical afterpiece—here, as at Savannah—followed the great drama. Two English vessels after the fort had been taken made their way by night through the fleet and gave the customary signals, which were answered satisfactorily by General Terry, under the dictation of an intelligent negro; the vessels came in, their officers reported, and were informed that their ships were prizes.

On the day that Terry was preparing to storm

Jan. 14, 1865. Fort Fisher General Schofield received his orders from Grant to move the Twenty-third Corps to the east. He came as rapidly as possible by river and by rail to Washington, and reporting in person to Grant at Fort Monroe went with him to Fort Fisher, where, with Terry and Porter, the plan of the coming campaign was arranged. Schofield

Schofield, was placed in command of the new department of
Report,
Apr. 3, 1865. North Carolina, and the first task assigned to him was the capture of Wilmington, to serve as a base for Sherman if anything should interrupt his march to Goldsboro'; and next, to open the route from New Berne to Goldsboro', and concentrate his army there to meet Sherman and be ready for any duty which the exigencies of the campaign might require.

The first division of the Western troops that ar-

Feb. 9, 1865. rived was that of General J. D. Cox, followed a few days later by part of D. N. Couch's; and with these

Ibid. and Terry's force Schofield moved on Wilmington. The Confederate general Hoke had intrenched himself with his own and what was left of Whiting's troops across Federal Point, on a line from Myrtle Sound to Cape Fear River, and beyond the river a heavy earthwork called Fort Anderson guarded the right bank. Cox and Ames marched against this position on the 17th, by the right bank of the stream; Terry moved up the left bank, a strong force of gunboats between them; Schofield kept his headquarters on a steamboat. The fort was attacked by the fleet at long range; and two of Cox's brigades demonstrated against it, while the rest of his force made a detour to the west to come in upon its rear. Thus threatened from every side the Confederate garrison evacuated the place, abandoning ten pieces of heavy ordnance and retreating to Town Creek, half way to Wilmington, halted in a strong position well covered by swamps.

Ames, with his division, went back to the left bank, where Hoke's principal force was opposing Terry. Cox cleverly turned the Confederate position at Town Creek, and, coming in upon their rear, dislodged and routed them, capturing two guns and nearly four hundred prisoners; the rest of them made their escape to Wilmington. Cox pushed on with great energy the next day and came opposite to the city, which was shrouded in smoke, and gave other signs of evacuation. Terry had been stoutly resisted by Hoke — who was covering his purpose of retreat by this judicious action — and Schofield had ordered Cox to cross the river and join the army on the left bank; but Cox, seeing that Wilmington was in extremity, took the responsibility of disobeying his orders and explaining the situation to Schofield. His conduct was approved, and at daybreak on the 22d of February Schofield cele-

CHAP. III.

Schofield,
Report.
"Rebellion
Record."
Vol. XI.,
p. 383.

brated the birthday of Washington by an unopposed entry into Wilmington.

The next thing to be done was to gain possession of Goldsboro', the point designated for the junction with Sherman. It was decided that New Berne afforded a better base for that movement, as well as for Sherman's subsequent operations, than Wilmington. Cox was therefore sent to New Berne to prepare it for that purpose, and to set on foot the necessary repairs to the railway between New Berne and Goldsboro'. In the prosecution of this work he advanced to the neighborhood of Kinston, on the Neuse River, about half way to Goldsboro', where, on the morning of the 8th of March, he was attacked with great spirit by the Confederate forces, under General Bragg, consisting of Hoke's command and some of the débris of Hood's army. One of Cox's regiments, in advance of his main line, was routed and captured. The ease with which this success was achieved was most encouraging to Bragg, who came up energetically against Cox's force in position, but was easily repulsed. The attack was renewed the next day with unabated courage, and although the Confederates were again repulsed, General Schofield, who had arrived on the field, sent urgent orders to Couch to hasten his march across country from Wilmington. Before he arrived, Bragg had retired through Goldsboro' to concentrate with the rest of Johnston's force, who were preparing to resist Sherman's northward march. Schofield occupied Kinston on the 14th, bridged the Neuse, and opened up communication with New Berne by river. Terry, marching directly upon Goldsboro' from Wilming-

Cox,
"The
March
to the Sea,"
p. 159.

March, 1865.

ton, secured the crossing of the Neuse south of that
city, which Schofield occupied on the 21st of March,
and made ready for the reception of Sherman; who,
on the 23d, here completed his march through the
Carolinas.

CHAPTER IV

THE THIRTEENTH AMENDMENT

WE have enumerated with some detail the series of radical antislavery measures enacted at the second session of the Thirty-seventh Congress, which ended July 17, 1862 — the abolition of slavery in the District of Columbia; the prohibition of slavery in the National Territories; the practical repeal of the fugitive-slave law; and the sweeping measures of confiscation which in different forms decreed forfeiture of slave property for the crimes of treason and rebellion. When this wholesale legislation was supplemented by the President's preliminary Emancipation Proclamation of September 22, 1862, and his final Edict of Freedom of January 1, 1863, the institution had clearly received its *coup de grâce* in all except the loyal border States. Consequently the third session of the Thirty-seventh Congress, ending March 4, 1863, occupied itself with this phase of the slavery question only to the extent of an effort to put into operation the President's plan of compensated abolishment. That effort took practical shape in a bill to give the State of Missouri fifteen millions on condition that she would emancipate her slaves; but the proposition failed, largely through the op-

GENERAL ALFRED H. TERRY.

position of a few conservative Members from Missouri, and the session adjourned without having by
its legislation advanced the destruction of slavery.

When Congress met again in December, 1863,
and organized by the election of Schuyler Colfax
of Indiana as Speaker, the whole situation had
undergone further change. The Union arms had
been triumphant — Gettysburg had been won and
Vicksburg had capitulated; Lincoln's Edict of Freedom had become an accepted fact; fifty regiments
of negro soldiers carried bayonets in the Union
armies; Vallandigham had been beaten for governor in Ohio by a hundred thousand majority; the
draft had been successfully enforced in every district of every loyal State in the Union. Under
these brightening prospects, military and political,
the more progressive spirits in Congress took up
anew the suspended battle with slavery which the
institution had itself invited by its unprovoked
assault on the life of the Government.

The President's reference to the subject in his
annual message was very brief: "The movements
by State action for emancipation in several of the
States not included in the Emancipation Proclamation are matters of profound gratulation. And
while I do not repeat in detail what I have heretofore so earnestly urged upon this subject, my general views and feelings remain unchanged; and I
trust that Congress will omit no fair opportunity
of aiding these important steps to a great consum- Annual
Message,
mation." His language had reference to Maryland, Dec. 8, 1863.
where during the autumn of 1863 the question of
emancipation had been actively discussed by political parties, and where at the election of November

CHAP. IV. 4, 1863, a legislature had been chosen containing a considerable majority pledged to emancipation.

More especially did it refer to Missouri, where, notwithstanding the failure of the fifteen-million compensation bill at the previous session, a State Convention had actually passed an ordinance of emancipation, though with such limitations as rendered it unacceptable to the more advanced public opinion of the State. Prudence was the very essence of Mr. Lincoln's statesmanship, and he doubtless felt it was not safe for the Executive to venture farther at that time. "We are like whalers," he said to Governor Morgan one day, "who have been long on a chase: we have at last got the harpoon into the monster, but we must now look how we steer, or with one 'flop' of his tail he will send us all into eternity."

Carpenter, in Raymond, "Life of Abraham Lincoln," p. 752.

Senators and Members of the House, especially those representing antislavery States or districts, did not need to be so circumspect. It was doubtless with this consciousness that J. M. Ashley, a Republican Representative from Ohio, and James F. Wilson, a Republican Representative from Iowa, on the 14th of December, 1863,—that being the earliest opportunity after the House was organized,—introduced the former a bill and the latter a joint resolution to propose to the several States an amendment of the Constitution prohibiting slavery throughout the United States. Both the propositions were referred to the committee on the judiciary, of which Mr. Wilson was chairman; but before he made any report on the subject it had been brought before the Senate, where its discussion attracted marked public attention.

"Globe," Dec. 14, 1863, pp. 19, 21.

Senator John B. Henderson, who with rare cour- CHAP. IV.
age and skill had, as a progressive Conservative,
made himself one of the leading champions of Mis- Henry
Wilson,
"History
of the Anti-
slavery
Measures
in
Congress,"
p. 251.
souri emancipation, on the 11th of January, 1864,
introduced into the Senate a Joint Resolution proposing an amendment to the Constitution that
slavery shall not exist in the United States. It is
not probable that either he or the Senate saw any
near hope of success in such a measure. The resolution went to the committee on the judiciary, apparently without being treated as a matter of pressing
importance. Nearly a month had elapsed when
Mr. Sumner also introduced a Joint Resolution,
proposing an amendment that " everywhere within
the limits of the United States, and of each State
or Territory thereof, all persons are equal before the law, so that no person can hold another
as a slave." He asked its reference to the select "Globe,"
Feb. 8, 1864,
p. 521.
committee on slavery, of which he was chairman;
but several Senators argued that such an amendment properly belonged to the committee on the
judiciary, and in this reference Mr. Sumner finally
acquiesced. It is possible that this slight and
courteously worded rivalry between the two committees induced earlier action than would otherwise have happened, for two days later Lyman
Trumbull, chairman of the judiciary commit- Feb. 10.
tee, reported back a substitute in the following
language, differing from the phraseology of both
Mr. Sumner and Mr. Henderson:

ARTICLE XIII.

SECTION 1. Neither slavery nor involuntary servitude,
except as a punishment for crime, whereof the party shall

Chap. IV.

"Globe,"
Mar. 28,
1864, p. 1313.
have been duly convicted, shall exist within the United States, or any place subject to their jurisdiction.

Section 2. Congress shall have power to enforce this article by appropriate legislation.

Even after the committee on the judiciary by this report had adopted the measure, it was evidently thought to be merely in an experimental stage, for more than six weeks elapsed before the Senate again took it up for action. On the 28th of March, however, Mr. Trumbull formally opened debate upon it in an elaborate speech. The discussion was continued from time to time until the 8th of April. As the Republicans had almost unanimous control of the Senate, their speeches, though able and eloquent, seemed perfunctory and devoted to a foregone conclusion. Those which attracted most attention were the arguments of Reverdy Johnson of Maryland and Mr. Henderson of Missouri,— Senators representing slave States,— advocating the amendment. Senator Sumner, whose pride of erudition amounted almost to vanity, pleaded earnestly for his phrase, "All persons are equal before the law," copied from the Constitution of revolutionary France. But Jacob M. Howard of Michigan, one of the soundest lawyers and clearest thinkers of the Senate, pointed out the inapplicability of the words, and declared it safer to follow the Ordinance of 1787, with its historical associations and its well adjudicated meaning.

There was, of course, from the first no doubt whatever that the Senate would pass the constitutional amendment, the political classification of that body being thirty-six Republicans, five Conditional Unionists, and nine Democrats. Not only was the whole Republican strength, thirty-six votes, CHAP. IV. cast in its favor, but two Democrats,— Reverdy Johnson of Maryland and James W. Nesmith of Oregon,— with a political wisdom far in advance of their party, also voted for it, giving more than the two-thirds required by the Constitution.

When, however, the Joint Resolution went to the House of Representatives there was such a formidable party strength arrayed against it as to foreshadow its failure. The party classification of the House stood one hundred and two Republicans, seventy-five Democrats, and nine from the border States, leaving but little chance of obtaining the required two-thirds vote in favor of the measure. Nevertheless there was sufficient Republican strength to secure its discussion; and when it came up on the 31st of May the first vote showed "Globe," May 31, 1864, p. 2612. seventy-six to fifty-five against rejecting the Joint Resolution.

We may infer that the conviction of the present hopelessness of the measure greatly shortened the debate upon it. The question occupied the House only on three different days — the 31st of May, when it was taken up, and the 14th and 15th of June. The speeches in opposition all came from 1864. Democrats; the speeches in its favor all came from Republicans, except one. From its adoption the former predicted the direst evils to the Constitution and the Republic; the latter the most beneficial results in the restoration of the country to peace and the fulfillment of the high destiny intended for it by its founders. Upon the final question of its passage the vote stood: yeas, ninety-three; nays, sixty-five; absent or not voting, twenty-three. Of those voting in favor of the Resolution eighty-seven were Republicans and four were Democrats.[1] Those voting against it were all Democrats. The resolution, not having secured a two-thirds vote, was thus lost; seeing which Mr. Ashley, Republican, who had the measure in charge, "Globe,"
June 15,
1864, p. 2995. changed his vote so that he might, if occasion arose, move its reconsideration.

The ever-vigilant public opinion of the loyal States, intensified by the burdens and anxieties of the war, took up this far-reaching question of abolishing slavery by constitutional amendment with an interest fully as deep as that manifested by Congress. Before the Joint Resolution had failed in the House of Representatives the issue was already transferred to discussion and prospective decision in a new forum.

When on the 7th of June, 1864, the National Republican Convention met in Baltimore, the two most vital thoughts which animated its members were the renomination of Mr. Lincoln and the success of the constitutional amendment. The first was recognized as a popular decision needing only the formality of an announcement by the Convention; and the full emphasis of speech and resolution was therefore centered on the latter, as the dominant and aggressive reform upon which the party would stake its political fortunes in the coming campaign.

It is not among the least of the evidences of President Lincoln's political sagacity and political courage

[1] The Democrats voting for the Joint Resolution were Moses F. Odell and John A. Griswold of New York, Joseph Baily of Pennsylvania, and Ezra Wheeler of Wisconsin, the latter having made the only speech in its favor from the Democratic side.

that it was he himself who supplied the spark that fired this train of popular action. The editor of the "New York Independent," who attended the Convention, and who with others visited Mr. Lincoln immediately after the nomination, printed the following in his paper of June 16, 1864: "When one of us mentioned the great enthusiasm at the Convention, after Senator E. D. Morgan's proposition to amend the Constitution, abolishing slavery, Mr. Lincoln instantly said, 'It was I who suggested to Mr. Morgan that he should put that idea into his opening speech.'"[1]

The declaration of Morgan, who was chairman of the National Republican Committee, and as such called the Convention to order, immediately found an echo in the speech of the temporary chairman, the Rev. Dr. Robert J. Breckinridge. The indorsement of the principle by the eminent Kentucky divine, not on the ground of party but on the high philosophy of true universal government and of genuine Christian religion, gave the announcement an interest and significance accorded to few planks in party platforms. The permanent chairman,

---

[1] William Lloyd Garrison, in a speech at a meeting in the Boston Music Hall on February 4, 1865, called to rejoice over the passage of the XIIIth Amendment, bore the following testimony to the President's initiative: "And to whom is the country more immediately indebted for this vital and saving amendment of the Constitution than, perhaps, to any other man? I believe I may confidently answer — to the humble railsplitter of Illinois — to the Presidential chain-breaker for millions of the oppressed — to Abraham Lincoln! (Immense and long continued applause, ending with three cheers for the President.) I understand that it was by his wish and influence that that plank was made a part of the Baltimore platform; and taking his position unflinchingly upon that platform, the people have overwhelmingly sustained both him and it, in ushering in the year of jubilee." — "The Liberator," February 10, 1865.

William Dennison, reaffirmed the doctrine of Morgan and Breckinridge, and the thunderous applause of the whole Convention greeted the formal proclamation of the new dogma of political faith in the third resolution of the platform :

Resolved, That as slavery was the cause and now con· stitutes the strength of this rebellion, and as it must be always and everywhere hostile to the principles of republican government, justice and the National safety demand its utter and complete extirpation from the soil of the Republic; and that while we uphold and maintain the acts and proclamations by which the Government in its own defense has aimed a death blow at this gigantic evil, we are in favor, furthermore, of such an amendment to the Constitution, to be made by the people, in conformity with its provisions, as shall terminate and forever prohibit the existence of slavery within the limits or the jurisdiction of the United States.

We have related elsewhere how upon this and the other declarations of the platform the Republican party went to battle and gained an overwhelming victory — a popular majority of 411,281, an electoral majority of 191, and a House of Representatives of 138 Unionists to 35 Democrats. In view of this result the President was able to take up the question with confidence among his official recommendations; and in the annual message which he transmitted to Congress on the 6th of December, 1864, he urged upon the Members whose terms were about to expire the propriety of at once carrying into effect the clearly expressed popular will. Said he :

" Tribune
Almanac,"
1865.
p. 20.

At the last session of Congress a proposed amendment of the Constitution, abolishing slavery throughout the United States, passed the Senate, but failed, for lack of the requisite two-thirds vote, in the House of Representa-

WILLIAM LLOYD GARRISON.

tives. Although the present is the same Congress, and CHAP. IV.
nearly the same members, and without questioning the wisdom or patriotism of those who stood in opposition, I venture to recommend the reconsideration and passage of the measure at the present session. Of course the abstract question is not changed, but an intervening election shows, almost certainly, that the next Congress will pass the measure if this does not. Hence there is only a question of *time* as to when the proposed amendment will go to the States for their action. And as it is to so go at all events, may we not agree that the sooner the better? It is not claimed that the election has imposed a duty on Members to change their views or their votes any further than, as an additional element to be considered, their judgment may be affected by it. It is the voice of the people, now for the first time heard upon the question. In a great National crisis like ours unanimity of action among those seeking a common end is very desirable — almost indispensable. And yet no approach to such unanimity is attainable unless some deference shall be paid to the will of the majority, simply because it is the will of the majority. In this case the common end is the maintenance of the Union; and among the means to secure that end, such will, through the election, is most clearly declared in favor of such constitutional amendment.

Lincoln,
Annual
Message,
Dec. 6, 1864.

On the 15th of December Mr. Ashley gave notice that he would, on the 6th of January, 1865, call up the constitutional amendment for reconsideration; and accordingly, on the day appointed, he opened the new debate upon it in an earnest speech. General discussion followed from time to time, occupying perhaps half the days of the month of January. As at the previous session, the Republicans all favored, while the Democrats mainly opposed it; but the important exceptions among the latter showed what immense gains the proposition had made in popular opinion and in Congressional willingness to recognize and embody it. The logic of

"Globe,"
Dec. 15,
1864, p. 53.

CHAP. IV. events had become more powerful than party creed or strategy. For fifteen years the Democratic party had stood as sentinel and bulwark to slavery; and yet, despite its alliance and championship, the peculiar institution was being consumed like dry leaves in the fire of war. For a whole decade it had been defeated in every great contest of Congressional debate and legislation. It had withered in popular elections, been paralyzed by confiscation laws, crushed by executive decrees, trampled upon by marching Union armies. More notable than all, the agony of dissolution had come upon it in its final stronghold — the constitutions of the slave States. Local public opinion had throttled it in West Virginia, in Missouri, in Arkansas, in Louisiana, in Maryland; and the same spirit of change was upon Tennessee, and even showing itself in Kentucky.

Here was a great revolution of ideas, a mighty sweep of sentiment, which could not be explained away by the stale charge of sectional fanaticism, or by alleging technical irregularities of political procedure. Here was a mighty flood of public opinion, overleaping old barriers and rushing into new channels. The Democratic party did not and could not shut its eyes to the accomplished facts. "In my judgment," said William S. Holman of Indiana, "the fate of slavery is sealed. It dies by the rebellious hand of its votaries, untouched by the law. Its fate is determined by the war; by the measures of the war; by the results of the war. These, sir, must determine it, even if the Constitution were amended." He opposed the amendment, he declared, simply because it was unnecessary.

"Globe,"
Jan. 11,
1865, p. 219.

Though few other Democrats were so frank, all their speeches were weighed down by the same consciousness of a losing fight, a hopeless cause. The Democratic leader of the House, and lately defeated Democratic candidate for Vice-President, George H. Pendleton, opposed the amendment, as he had done at the previous session, by asserting that three-fourths of the States did not possess constitutional power to pass it, this being — if the paradox be excused — at the same time the weakest and the strongest argument: weakest, because the Constitution in terms contradicted the assertion; strongest, because under the circumstances nothing less than unconstitutionality could justify opposition.

But while the Democrats as a party thus persisted in a false attitude, more progressive Members had the courage to take independent and wiser action. Not only did the four Democrats — Moses F. Odell and John A. Griswold of New York, Joseph Baily of Pennsylvania, and Ezra Wheeler of Wisconsin — who supported the amendment at the first session again record their votes in its favor, but they were now joined by thirteen others of their party associates, namely: Augustus C. Baldwin of Michigan; Alexander H. Coffroth and Archibald McAllister of Pennsylvania; James E. English of Connecticut; John Ganson, Anson Herrick, Homer A. Nelson, William Radford, and John B. Steele of New York; Wells A. Hutchins of Ohio; Austin A. King and James S. Rollins of Missouri; and George H. Yeaman of Kentucky; and by their help the favorable two-thirds vote was secured. But special credit for the result must not be accorded to these alone. Even more than of

"Globe," Jan. 31, 1865, p. 531.

Northern Democrats must be recognized the courage and progressive liberality of Members from the border slave States — one from Delaware, four from Maryland, three from West Virginia, four from Kentucky, and seven from Missouri, whose speeches and votes aided the consummation of the great act; and finally, something is due to those Democrats, eight in number, who were absent without pairs, and thus, perhaps not altogether by accident, reduced somewhat the two-thirds vote necessary to the passage of the Joint Resolution.

Mingled with these influences of a public and moral nature it is not unlikely that others of more selfish interest, operating both for and against the amendment, were not entirely wanting. One, who was a member of the House, writes: "The success of the measure had been considered very doubtful, and depended upon certain negotiations the result of which was not fully assured, and the particulars of which never reached the public." So also one of the President's secretaries wrote on the 18th of January:

George W. Julian, " Political Recollections," p. 250.

I went to the President this afternoon at the request of Mr. Ashley, on a matter connecting itself with the pending amendment of the Constitution. The Camden and Amboy Railroad interest promised Mr. Ashley that if he would help postpone the Raritan railroad bill over this session they would in return make the New Jersey Democrats help about the amendment, either by their votes or absence. Sumner being the Senate champion of the Raritan bill, Ashley went to him to ask him to drop it for this session. Sumner, however, showed reluctance to adopt Mr. Ashley's suggestion, saying that he hoped the amendment would pass anyhow, etc. Ashley thought he discerned in Sumner's manner two reasons: (1) That if the present Senate resolution were not adopted by the

House, the Senate would send them another in which CHAP. IV. they would most likely adopt Sumner's own phraseology and thereby gratify his ambition; and (2) that Sumner thinks the defeat of the Camden and Amboy monopoly would establish a principle by legislative enactment which would effectually crush out the last lingering relics of the States rights dogma. Ashley therefore desired the President to send for Sumner, and urge him to be practical and secure the passage of the amendment in the manner suggested by Mr. Ashley. I stated these points to the President, who replied at once: "I can do nothing with Mr. Sumner in these matters. While Mr. Sumner is very cordial with me, he is making his history in an issue with me on this very point. He hopes to succeed in beating the President so as to change this Government from its original form and make it a strong centralized power." Then calling Mr. Ashley into the room, the President said to him, "I think I understand Mr. Sumner; and I think he would be all the more resolute in his persistence on J. G. N., "Personal Memoranda." MS. the points which Mr. Nicolay has mentioned to me if he supposed I were at all watching his course on this matter."

The issue was decided in the afternoon of the 31st of January, 1865. The scene was one of unusual interest. The galleries were filled to overflowing; the Members watched the proceedings with unconcealed solicitude. "Up to noon," said a contemporaneous formal report, "the pro-slavery Report of Special Committee of the Union League Club of New York. Pamphlet. party are said to have been confident of defeating the amendment, and, after that time had passed, one of the most earnest advocates of the measure said, ''T is the toss of a copper.'" There were the usual pleas for postponement and for permission to offer amendments or substitutes, but at four o'clock the House came to a final vote, and the roll-call showed, yeas, 119; nays, 56; not voting, 8. Scattering murmurs of applause had followed the announcement of affirmative votes from several of the

Democratic Members. This was renewed when by direction of the Speaker the clerk called his name and he voted aye. But when the Speaker finally announced, " The constitutional majority of two-thirds having voted in the affirmative, the Joint Resolution is passed," "the announcement" — so continues the official report printed in the "Globe" — "was received by the House and by the spectators with an outburst of enthusiasm. The Members on the Republican side of the House instantly sprung to their feet, and, regardless of parliamentary rules, applauded with cheers and clapping of hands. The example was followed by the male spectators in the galleries, which were crowded to excess, who waved their hats and cheered loud and long, while the ladies, hundreds of whom were present, rose in their seats and waved their handkerchiefs, participating in and adding to the general excitement and intense interest of the scene. This lasted for several minutes."

"Globe,"
Jan. 31,
1865, p. 531.

"In honor of this immortal and sublime event," cried Ebon C. Ingersoll of Illinois, "I move that the House do now adjourn," and against the objection of a Maryland Democrat the motion was carried by a yea and nay vote.

A salute of one hundred guns soon made the occasion the subject of comment and congratulation throughout the city.[1] On the following night

---

[1] By inadvertence the Joint Resolution proposing the Thirteenth Amendment was sent to the President, who formally signed it on February 1, the day after its passage by the House. Subsequently (February 7) the Senate adopted a resolution declaring that "such approval was unnecessary to give effect to the action of Congress"; Senator Trumbull stating in his explanatory remarks that the Supreme Court of the United States in a case arising in 1798 had decided that "the negative of the President applies

a considerable procession marched with music to CHAP. IV.
the Executive Mansion to carry popular greetings
to the President. In response to their calls, Mr.
Lincoln appeared at a window and made a brief
speech, of which only an abstract report was preserved, but which is nevertheless important as
showing the searching analysis of cause and effect
which this question had undergone in his mind,
the deep interest he felt in, and the far-reaching
consequences he attached to the measure and its
success.

He supposed the passage through Congress of the constitutional amendment for the abolishment of slavery
throughout the United States was the occasion to which
he was indebted for the honor of this call. The occasion
was one of congratulation to the country and to the whole
world. But there is a task yet before us — to go forward
and have consummated by the votes of the States that
which Congress had so nobly begun yesterday. He had
the honor to inform those present that Illinois had already
to-day done the work. Maryland was about half through,
but he felt proud that Illinois was a little ahead. He
thought this measure was a very fitting if not an indispensable adjunct to the winding up of the great difficulty.
He wished the reunion of all the States perfected, and so
effected as to remove all causes of disturbance in the future; and to attain this end it was necessary that the
original disturbing cause should, if possible, be rooted
out. He thought all would bear him witness that he had
never shrunk from doing all that he could to eradicate
slavery, by issuing an Emancipation Proclamation. But
that proclamation falls far short of what the amendment
will be when fully consummated. A question might be
raised whether the proclamation was legally valid. It

only to the ordinary cases of legislation. He has nothing to do
with the proposition or adoption
of amendments to the Constitution."— "Globe," February 7,
1865, pp. 629, 630. A similar
inadvertence occurred when the
amendment of 1861 was passed;
it was signed by President
Buchanan.

might be urged that it only aided those that came into our lines, and that it was inoperative as to those who did not give themselves up; or that it would have no effect upon the children of slaves born hereafter; in fact, it would be urged that it did not meet the evil. But this amendment is a king's cure-all for all the evils. It winds the whole thing up. He would repeat that it was the fitting, if not the indispensable, adjunct to the consummation of the great game we are playing. He could not but congratulate all present — himself, the country, and the whole world — upon this great moral victory.

Widely divergent views were expressed by able constitutional lawyers in both branches of Congress as to what, in the anomalous condition of the country, would constitute a valid ratification of the Thirteenth Amendment; some contending that ratification by three-fourths of the loyal States would be sufficient, others that three-fourths of all the States, whether loyal or insurrectionary, would be necessary. We have seen that Mr. Lincoln, in his speech on Louisiana reconstruction, while expressing no opinion against the first proposition, nevertheless declared, with great argumentative force, that the latter " would be unquestioned and unquestionable "; and this view appears to have governed the action of his successor.

As Mr. Lincoln mentioned with just pride in his address, Illinois was the first State to ratify 1865. the amendment, taking her action on February 1, the day after the Joint Resolution was passed by the House of Representatives; and ratification by other States continued in the following order: Rhode Island, February 2, 1865; Michigan, February 2, 1865; Maryland, February 3, 1865; New York, February 3, 1865; West Virginia, February

3, 1865; Maine, February 7, 1865; Kansas, February 7, 1865; Massachusetts, February 8, 1865;
Pennsylvania, February 8, 1865; Virginia,. February 9, 1865; Ohio, February 10, 1865; Missouri,
February 10, 1865; Indiana, February 16, 1865;
Nevada, February 16, 1865; Louisiana, February
17, 1865; Minnesota, February 23, 1865; Wisconsin,
March 1, 1865; Vermont, March 9, 1865; Tennessee, April 7, 1865; Arkansas, April 20, 1865; Connecticut, May 5, 1865; New Hampshire, July 1,
1865; South Carolina, November 13, 1865; Alabama,
December 2, 1865; North Carolina, December 4,
1865; Georgia, December 9, 1865; Oregon, December 11, 1865; California, December 20, 1865; Florida,
December 28, 1865; New Jersey, January 23, 1866;
Iowa, January 24, 1866; Texas, February 18, 1870.

Without waiting for the ratification by the last
six of these States, Mr. Seward, who remained as
Secretary of State in the Cabinet of President
Johnson, made official proclamation on December
18, 1865, that the Legislatures of twenty-seven
States, constituting three-fourths of the thirty-six
States of the Union, had ratified the amendment,
and that it had become valid as a part of the Constitution of the United States. It needs to be
noted that four of the States constituting this number of twenty-seven were Virginia, Louisiana, Tennessee, and Arkansas, whose reconstruction had
been effected under the direction and by the
authority of President Lincoln.

The profound political transformation which the
American Republic had undergone can perhaps best
be measured by contrasting for an instant the two
constitutional amendments which Congress made

it the duty of the Lincoln Administration to submit officially to the several States. The first was
that offered by Thomas Corwin, chairman of the
Committee of Thirty-three, in February, 1861, and
passed by the House of Representatives, yeas, 133;
nays, 65; and by the Senate, yeas, 24; nays, 12.
It was signed by President Buchanan as one of his
last official acts, and accepted and indorsed by
Lincoln in his inaugural address. The language of
that amendment was:

"No amendment shall be made to the Constitution
which will authorize or give to Congress the power
to abolish or interfere within any State with the domestic institutions thereof, including that of persons
held to labor or service by the laws of said State."

Between Lincoln's inauguration and the outbreak
of war, the Department of State, under Seward,
transmitted this amendment of 1861 to the several
States for their action; and had the South shown
a willingness to desist from secession and accept it
as a peace offering, there is little doubt that the
required three-fourths of the States would have
made it a part of the Constitution. But the South
refused to halt in her rebellion, and the thunder of
Beauregard's guns against Fort Sumter drove away
all further thought or possibility of such a ratification; and within four years Congress framed and
the same Lincoln Administration sent forth the
amendment of 1865, sweeping out of existence by
one sentence the institution to which it had in its
first proposal offered a virtual claim to perpetual
recognition and tolerance. The "new birth of
freedom," which Lincoln invoked for the nation
in his Gettysburg address, was accomplished.

Appendix,
"Globe,"
Mar. 2, 1861,
p. 350.

CHAPTER V

THE triumphant reëlection of Mr. Lincoln in November, 1864, greatly simplified the political conditions as well as the military prospects of the country. Decisive popular majorities had pointedly rebuked the individuals who proclaimed, and the party which had resolved, that the war was a failure. The verdict of the ballot-box not only decided the continuance of a war administration and a war policy, but renewed the assurance of a public sentiment to sustain its prosecution. When Congress convened on the 6th of December, and the President transmitted to that body his annual message, he included in his comprehensive review of public affairs a temperate but strong and terse statement of this fact and its potent significance. Inspired by this majestic manifestation of the popular will to preserve the Union and maintain the Constitution, he was able to speak of the future with hope and confidence. But with characteristic prudence and good taste, he uttered no word of boasting and indulged in no syllable of acrimony; on the contrary, in terms of fatherly kindness, he again offered the rebellious States the generous conditions he had previously tendered them by various acts and declarations, and specifi-

CHAP. V. cally in his amnesty proclamation of December 8, 1863. The statement of the whole situation with its alternative issues was so admirably compressed into the closing paragraphs of his message as to leave no room for ignorance or misunderstanding:

Dec. 6, 1864.
The National resources, then, are unexhausted, and, as we believe, inexhaustible. The public purpose to reëstablish and maintain the National authority is unchanged, and, as we believe, unchangeable. The manner of continuing the effort remains to choose. On careful consideration of all the evidence accessible, it seems to me that no attempt at negotiation with the insurgent leader could result in any good. He would accept nothing short of severance of the Union — precisely what we will not and cannot give. His declarations to this effect are explicit and oft-repeated. He does not attempt to deceive us. He affords us no excuse to deceive ourselves. He cannot voluntarily re-accept the Union; we cannot voluntarily yield it. Between him and us the issue is distinct, simple, and inflexible. It is an issue which can only be tried by war, and decided by victory. If we yield, we are beaten; if the Southern people fail him, he is beaten. Either way, it would be the victory and defeat following war.

What is true, however, of him who heads the insurgent cause is not necessarily true of those who follow. Although he cannot re-accept the Union, they can. Some of them, we know, already desire peace and reunion. The number of such may increase. They can, at any moment, have peace simply by laying down their arms, and submitting to the National authority under the Constitution. After so much, the Government could not, if it would, maintain war against them. The loyal people would not sustain or allow it. If questions should remain, we would adjust them by the peaceful means of legislation, conference, courts, and votes, operating only in constitutional and lawful channels. Some certain, and other possible, questions are, and would be, beyond the Executive power to adjust; as, for instance, the admission of members into Congress, and whatever might require the appropriation of money. The Executive power itself would be greatly diminished by the cessation of actual war. Pardons and remissions of forfeitures, however, would still be within Executive control.

In what spirit and temper this control would be exercised can be fairly judged of by the past. A year ago general pardon and amnesty, upon specified terms, were offered to all, except certain designated classes; and it was, at the same time, made known that the excepted classes were still within contemplation of special clemency. . . . In presenting the abandonment of armed resistance to the national authority, on the part of the insurgents, as the only indispensable condition to ending the war on the part of the Government, I retract nothing heretofore said as to slavery. I repeat the declaration made a year ago, that "While I remain in my present position I shall not attempt to retract or modify the Emancipation Proclamation, nor shall I return to slavery any person who is free by the terms of that proclamation, or by any of the acts of Congress." If the people should, by whatever mode or means, make it an Executive duty to reënslave such persons, another, and not I, must be their instrument to perform it. In stating a single condition of peace, I mean simply to say that the war will cease on the part of the Government whenever it shall have ceased on the part of those who began it.

Annual Message, Dec. 6, 1864.

The country was about to enter upon the fifth year of actual war; but all the indications were pointing unmistakably to a speedy collapse of the rebellion. This foreshadowed disaster to the Confederate armies gave rise to another volunteer peace project and negotiation, which, from the boldness of its animating thought and the official prominence of its actors, assumes a special importance.

The veteran politician, Francis P. Blair, Sr., who, as a young journalist, thirty-five years before, had helped President Jackson throttle the South Carolina nullification; who, from his long political and personal experience at Washington, perhaps

knew better than almost any one else the individual
characters and tempers of Southern leaders; and
who, moreover, was ambitious to crown his remarkable career with another dazzling chapter of political intrigue, conceived that the time had arrived
when he might perhaps take up the rôle of a successful mediator between the North and the South.
He gave various hints of his desire to President
Lincoln, but received neither encouragement nor
opportunity to unfold his plans. " Come to me
after Savannah falls," was Lincoln's evasive reply;
and when, on the 22d of December, Sherman announced the surrender of that city as a National
Christmas gift Mr. Blair hastened to put his design into execution. Three days after Christmas the
President gave him a simple card bearing the words:

Allow the bearer, F. P. Blair, Sr., to pass our lines, go
South, and return.

MS.   December 28, 1864.   A. LINCOLN.

With this single credential he went to the camp
of General Grant, from which he forwarded, by the
usual flags of truce, the following letters to Jefferson Davis at Richmond:

HEADQUARTERS ARMIES OF THE UNITED STATES,
December 30, 1864.
JEFFERSON DAVIS, President, etc., etc.
MY DEAR SIR: The loss of some papers of importance
(title papers), which I suppose may have been taken by
some persons who had access to my house when General
Early's army were in possession of my place, induces me
to ask the privilege of visiting Richmond and beg the
favor of you to facilitate my inquiries in regard to them.
MS.   Your most obedient servant,
F. P. BLAIR.

HEADQUARTERS ARMIES OF THE UNITED STATES,
December 30, 1864.

JEFFERSON DAVIS, President, etc., etc.

MY DEAR SIR: The fact stated in the inclosed note may serve to answer inquiries as to the object of my visit, which, if allowed by you, I would not communicate fully to any one but yourself. The main purpose I have in seeing you is to explain the views I entertain in reference to the state of the affairs of our country, and to submit to your consideration ideas which in my opinion you may turn to good and possibly bring to practical results— that may not only repair all the ruin the war has brought upon the nation, but contribute to promote the welfare of other nations that have suffered from it. In candor I must say to you in advance that I come to you wholly unaccredited except in so far as I may be by having permission to pass our lines and to offer to you my own suggestions — suggestions which I have submitted to no one in authority on this side the lines, and will not, without my conversation with you may lead me to suppose they may lead to something practicable. With the hope of such result, if allowed, I will confidentially unbosom my heart frankly and without reserve. You will of course hold in reserve all that is not proper to be said to one coming, as I do, merely as a private citizen and addressing one clothed with the highest responsibilities. Unless the great interests now at stake induce you to attribute more importance to my application than it would otherwise command I could not expect that you would invite the intrusion. I venture however to submit the matter to your judgment.

Your most obedient servant,

F. P. BLAIR.

MS.

Mr. Davis returned a reply with permission to make the visit; but by some mischance it did not reach Mr. Blair till after his patience had become exhausted by waiting and he had returned to Washington. Proceeding then to Richmond he was received by Jefferson Davis in a confidential

Davis, "Rise and Fall of the Confederate Government," Vol. II., p. 612.

interview on the 12th of January, 1865, which he
thoroughly described in a written report of which
we quote the essential portions:

"I introduced the subject to Mr. Davis by giving
him an account of the mode in which I obtained
leave to go through the lines, telling him that the
President stopped me when I told him 'I had kindly
relations with Mr. Davis, and at the proper time I
might do something towards peace,' and said, 'Come
to me when Savannah falls'— how after that event
he shunned an interview with me, until I perceived
he did not wish to hear me, but desired I should go
without explanation of my object. I then told Mr.
Davis that I wanted to know if he thought fit to
communicate it, whether he had any commitments
with European powers which would control his
conduct in making arrangements with the Government of the United States. He said in the most
decisive manner that there were none, that he had
no commitments; and expressed himself with some
vehemence that he was absolutely free and would
die a freeman in all respects. This is pretty much
his language; it was his sentiment and manner
certainly. I told him that that was an all-important
point, for if it were otherwise I would not have
another word to say. I then prefaced the reading
of the paper — which I had intended to embody in
a letter to him, or present in some form if I could
not reach him, or if I were prevented from seeing
him personally — by saying that it was somewhat
after the manner of an editorial and was not of a
diplomatic character. . . He replied that he gave
me his full confidence, knew that I was an earnest man, and believed I was an honest man, and

Blair,
Report.
MS.
Jan., 1865.

said he reciprocated the attachment which I had
expressed for him and his family; that he was
under great obligations to my family for kindnesses
rendered to his, that he would never forget them,
and that even when dying they would be remem-
.bered in his prayers. I then read the paper to him.

CHAP. V.

Blair,
Report.
MS.
Jan., 1865.

" ' *Suggestions submitted to Jefferson Davis,
President, etc. etc.*

" ' The Amnesty Proclamation of President Lincoln in connection with his last message to Congress, referring to the termination of the rebellion,
presents a basis on which I think permanent
peace and union between the warring sections
of our country may be reëstablished. The amnesty offered would doubtless be enlarged to secure these objects and made to embrace all who
sincerely desired to renew and confirm their allegiance to the Government of the United States by
the extinction of the institution which originated
the war against the National Republic. . . Slavery
no longer remains an insurmountable obstruction to
pacification. You propose to use the slaves in some
mode to conquer a peace for the South. If this
race be employed to secure the independence of the
Southern States by risking their lives in the service, the achievement is certainly to be crowned
with their deliverance from bondage. . . Slavery,
" the cause of all our woes," is admitted now on all
sides to be doomed. As an institution all the world
condemns it.

" ' This expiation made, what remains to distract
our country ? It now seems a free-will offering on
the part of the South as essential to its own safety.

VOL. X.—7

CHAP. V.

Blair,
Report.
MS.
Jan., 1865.

Being made, nothing but military force can keep
the North and South asunder. . . We see them
coming together again, after momentary rupture,
along the Ohio, the Mississippi, upon the Gulf, the
Potomac, and gradually in the interior wherever
defense is assured from the military power that
at first overthrew the Government.   It is now
plain to every sense that nothing but the inter-
position of the soldiery of foreign tyrannies can
prevent all the States from resuming their places
in the Union, casting from them the demon of dis-
cord.   The few States remaining in arms that made
the war for slavery as the *sine qua non* now propose to surrender it, and even the independence
which was coveted to support it, as a price for
foreign aid.

" ' Slavery abandoned, the issue is changed and
war against the Union becomes a war for monarchy;
and the cry for independence of a government that
assured the independence of the Southern States of
all foreign powers and their equality in the Union,
is converted into an appeal for succor to European
potentates, to whom they offer, in return, homage
as dependencies!   And this is the price they propose to pay for success in breaking up the National
Government!   But will the people who have consented to wage this war for an institution once
considered a property, now that they have abandoned it, continue the war to enslave themselves?
Would they abandon slavery to commend themselves to the protection of European monarchies,
and thus escape the embrace of that national
Republic as a part of which they have enjoyed
almost a century of prosperity and renown?   The

whole aspect of the controversy upon this view CHAP. V.
is changed. The patriarchal domestic institution
given up, and the idea of independence and " being
let alone " in happy isolation surrendered to obtain Blair, Report. MS. Jan., 1865.
the boon of foreign protection under the rule of
monarchy.

" ' The most modern exemplification of this programme for discontented Republican States defeating their popular institution by intestine hostilities
is found in the French emperor's Austrian deputy,
Maximilian, sent to prescribe for their disorders. . .
The design of Louis Napoleon in reference to
conquest on this continent is not left to conjecture. With extraordinary frankness he made a
public declaration that his object was to make the
Latin race supreme in the Southern section of the
North American continent. This is a Napoleonic
idea. The great Napoleon, in a letter or one of his
dictations at St. Helena, states that it had been his
purpose to embody an army of negroes in San
Domingo, to be landed in the slave States with
French support to instigate the blacks there to insurrection, and through revolution effect conquest.
Louis Napoleon saw revolution involving the
struggle of races and sections on the question of
slavery made to his hand, when he instantly re-
curred to his uncle's ideas of establishing colonies
to create commerce and a navy for France and
to breed the material for armies to maintain his
European empire. . .

" ' Jefferson Davis is the fortunate man who now
holds the commanding position to encounter this
formidable scheme of conquest, and whose fiat can
at the same time deliver his country from the

CHAP. V.

Blair,
Report.
MS.
Jan., 1865.

bloody agony now covering it in mourning. He can drive Maximilian from his American throne, and baffle the designs of Napoleon to subject our Southern people to the "Latin race." With a breath he can blow away all pretense for proscription, conscription, or confiscation in the Southern States, restore their fields to luxuriant cultivation, their ports to the commerce of the world, their constitutions and their rights under them as essentially a part of the Constitution of the United States to that strong guaranty under which they flourished for nearly a century not only as equals, but down to the hour of conflict the prevalent power on the continent. . .

"'To accomplish this great good for our common country President Lincoln has opened the way in his amnesty proclamation and the message which looks to armistice. Suppose the first enlarged to embrace all engaged in the war; suppose secret preliminaries to armistice enable President Davis to transfer such portions of his army as he may deem proper for his purpose to Texas, held out to it as the land of promise; suppose this force on the banks of the Rio Grande, armed, equipped, and provided, and Juarez propitiated and rallying the Liberals of Mexico to give it welcome and support — could it not enter Mexico in full confidence of expelling the invaders, who, taking advantage of the distractions of our own Republic, have overthrown that of Mexico and established a foreign despotism to rule that land and spread its power over ours? I know Romero, the able, patriotic minister who represents the Republic of Mexico near our Government. He is intimate with my son

Montgomery, who is persuaded that he could in- Chap. v.
duce Juarez to devolve all the power he can command on President Davis — a dictatorship, if
necessary — to restore the rights of Mexico and Blair, Report. MS. Jan., 1865.
her people and provide for the stability of its Gov-
ernment. With such hopes inspiring and a veteran
army of invincibles to rally on, such a force of
Mexicans might be embodied as would make the
conquest of the country the work of its own people
under able leading.

" ' But if more force were wanted than these Mexican recruits and the army of the South would supply, would not multitudes of the army of the North,
officers and men, be found ready to embark in an
enterprise vital to the interests of our whole Republic ? The Republican party has staked itself on
the assertion of the Monroe Doctrine proposed by
Canning and sanctioned by a British cabinet. The
Democrats of the North have proclaimed their
adhesion to it, and I doubt not from the spirit exhibited by the Congress now in session, however
unwilling to declare war, it would countenance all
legitimate efforts short of such result to restore
the Mexican Republic. . .

" ' He who expels the Bonaparte-Hapsburg dy-
nasty from our Southern flank, which General
Jackson in one of his letters warned me was the
vulnerable point through which foreign invasion
would come, will ally his name with those of
Washington and Jackson as a defender of the
liberty of the country. If in delivering Mexico he
should model its States in form and principle to
adapt them to our Union and add a new Southern
constellation to its benignant sky while rounding

off our possession on the continent at the Isthmus, and opening the way to blending the waters of the Atlantic and Pacific, thus embracing our Republic in the arms of the ocean, he would complete the work of Jefferson, who first set one foot of our colossal Government on the Pacific by a stride from the Gulf of Mexico. Such achievement would be more highly appreciated in the South, inasmuch as it would restore the equipoise between the Northern and Southern States—if indeed such sectional distinctions could be recognized after the peculiar institution which created them had ceased to exist.'"

It is of course possible that the hard mental processes in political metaphysics through which Jefferson Davis had forced his intellect in pursuing the ambitious hallucinations which led him from loyalty to treason, had blighted all generous sentiment and healthy imagination. But if his heart was yet capable of a single patriotic memory and impulse, strange emotions must have troubled him as he sat listening to the reading of this paper by the man who had been the familiar friend, the trusted adviser, it might almost be said the confidential voice, of Andrew Jackson. It was as though the ghost of the great President had come from his grave in Tennessee to draw him a sad and solemn picture of the ruin and shame to which he was bringing, and had almost brought, the American Republic, especially "his people" of the Southern States—nationality squandered, slavery doomed, and his Confederacy a supplicant for life at the hands of European despotisms. If he did not correctly realize the scene and hour in all its impressiveness, he seems at least to have tacitly

acknowledged that his sanguinary adventure in
statesmanship was moribund, and that it was high
time to listen earnestly to any scheme which might
give hope of averting from himself and his ad-
herents the catastrophe to whose near approach he
could no longer shut his eyes. Mr. Blair's report
thus narrates the remainder of the interview:

"I then said to him, 'There is my problem, Mr.
Davis; do you think it possible to be solved?'
After consideration he said, 'I think so.' I then
said, 'You see that I make the great point of this
matter that the war is no longer made for slavery,
but monarchy. You know that if the war is kept
up and the Union kept divided, armies must be
kept afoot on both sides, and this state of things has
never continued long without resulting in monarchy
on one side or the other, and on both generally.'
He assented to this, and with great emphasis remarked that he was like Lucius Junius Brutus, and
uttered the sentiment ascribed to him in Shakspere,
without exactly quoting it:

> There was a Brutus once that would have brooked
> The eternal devil to keep his state in Rome
> As easily as a king.

Then he said, that he was thoroughly for popular
government, that this feeling had been born and
bred in him. Touching the project, he said, of
bringing the sections together again, the great difficulty was the excessive vindictiveness produced by
outrages perpetrated in the invaded States during
the war. He said reconcilement must depend, he
thought, upon time and events, which he hoped
would restore better feelings, but that he was cer-

tain that no circumstance would have a greater effect than to see the arms of our countrymen from the North and the South united in a war upon a foreign power assailing principles of government common to both sections and threatening their de-

struction. And he said he was convinced that all the powers of Europe felt it their interest that our people in this quarrel should exhaust all their energies in destroying each other, and thus make them a prey to the potentates of Europe, who felt that the destruction of our Government was necessary to the maintenance of the monarchical principles on which their own were founded.

"I told him that I was encouraged by finding him holding these views, and believed that our country, if impressed with them, as I thought it might be universally, would soon resume its happy unity. He said I ought to know with what reluctance he had been drawn out of the Union; that he labored to the last moment to avoid it; that he had followed the old flag longer and with more devotion than anything else on earth; that at Bull Run, when he saw the flag he supposed it was his own hanging on the staff,— they were more alike then than now,— and when the flag of the United States unfurled itself in the breeze he saw it with a sigh, but he had to choose between it and his own, and he had to look to it as that of an enemy. He felt now that it was laid up, but the circumstances to which he had adverted might restore it and reconcilement be easier. With regard to Mexico, if the foreign power was driven out, it would have to depend on the events there to make it possible to connect that country with this and restore the equipoise to which I looked; nobody could foresee how things would shape themselves. . .

CHAP. V.

"Touching the matter of arrangement for reconcilement proposed by me, he remarked that all depended upon well-founded confidence, and, looking at me with very significant expression, he said, 'What, Mr. Blair, do you think of Mr. Seward?' I replied: 'Mr. Seward is a very pleasant companion; he has good social qualities, but I have no doubt that where his ambition is concerned his selfish feelings prevail over all principle. I have no doubt he would betray any man, no matter what his obligations to him, if he stood in the way of his selfish and ambitious schemes. But,' I said, 'this matter, if entered upon at all, must be with Mr. Lincoln himself. The transaction is a military transaction, and depends entirely upon the Commander-in-Chief of our armies. If he goes into it he will certainly consider it as the affair of the military head of the Government. Now I know that Mr. Lincoln is capable of great personal sacrifices — of sacrificing the strongest feelings of his heart, of sacrificing a friend when he thinks it necessary for the good of the country; and you may rely upon it, if he plights his faith to any man in a transaction for which he is responsible as an officer or a man, he will maintain his word inviolably.' Mr. Davis said he was glad to hear me say so. He did not know Mr. Lincoln; but he was sure I did, and therefore my declaration gave him the highest satisfaction. As to Mr. Seward, he had no confidence in him himself, and he did not know any man or party in the South that had any.

Blair,
Report.
MS.
Jan., 1865.

CHAP. V.
"In relation to the mode of effecting the object about which we had been talking, he said 'we ought soon to have some understanding, because things to be done or omitted will depend upon it'; that he Blair Report. MS. Jan., 1865. was willing to appoint persons to have conferences, without regard to forms; that there must be some medium of communication; that he would appoint a person or persons who could be implicitly relied on by Mr. Lincoln; that he had on a former occasion indicated Judge Campbell, of the Supreme Court, as a person who could be relied on. I told him he was a person in whom I had unbounded confidence, both as regarded talents and fidelity.

"In reply to some remarks that I made as to the fame he would acquire in relieving the country from all its disasters, restoring its harmony, and extending its dominion to the Isthmus, he said what his name might be in history he cared not. If he could restore the prosperity and happiness of his country, that was the end and aim of his being. For himself, death would end his cares, and that was very easy to be accomplished.

"The next day after my first interview he sent Blair, Report, MS. Printed in full in Serial Chapter. "Century," Oct., 1889. me a note, saying he thought I might desire to have something in writing in regard to his conclusion, and therefore he made a brief statement which I brought away."

Davis, "Rise and Fall of the Confederate Government." Vol. II., pp. 612 et seq. The substantial accuracy of Mr. Blair's report is confirmed by the memorandum of the same interview which Jefferson Davis wrote at the time and has since printed. In this conversation the rebel leader took little pains to disguise his entire willingness to enter upon the wild scheme of military conquest and annexation which could easily be read between the lines of a political crusade to rescue the Monroe Doctrine from its present peril. If Mr. Blair felt elated at having so quickly made a convert of the Confederate President, he was still further gratified at discovering yet more favorable symptoms in his official surrounding at Richmond. In the three or four days he spent at the rebel capital he found nearly every prominent personage convinced of the hopeless condition of the rebellion, and even eager to seize upon any contrivance to help them out of their direful prospects. The letter which he bore from Jefferson Davis to be shown to President Lincoln was in the following language:

RICHMOND, VIRGINIA, 12 Jany., '65.
F. P. BLAIR, Esq.

SIR: I have deemed it proper, and probably desirable to you, to give you, in this form, the substance of remarks made by me, to be repeated by you to President Lincoln, etc., etc. I have no disposition to find obstacles in forms, and am willing now, as heretofore, to enter into negotiations for the restoration of peace; and am ready to send a commission whenever I have reason to suppose it will be received, or to receive a commission, if the United States Government shall choose to send one. That, notwithstanding the rejection of our former offers, I would, if you could promise that a commissioner, minister, or other agent would be received, appoint one immediately, and renew the effort to enter into conference, with a view to secure peace to the two countries.

Yours, etc.,
JEFFERSON DAVIS.

But the Government councils at Washington were not ruled by the spirit of political adventure. Abraham Lincoln had a loftier conception of patriotic duty and a higher ideal of national ethics. The proposal to divert his nation, "conceived in Liberty," from its grand task of preserving for humanity "government of the people, by the people, for the people," and degrade its heroic struggle and sacrifice to the low level of a joint filibustering foray, which, instead of crowning his work of emancipation, might perhaps eventuate in a renewal, extension, and perpetuation of slavery, did not receive from him an instant's consideration. His whole interest in Mr. Blair's mission was in the despondency of the rebel leaders which it disclosed, and the possibility of bringing them to an acknowledgment of their despair and the abandonment of their resistance. His only response to the overture thus half officially brought to his notice was to open the door of negotiation a little wider than he had done before, but for the specific and exclusive objects of union and peace. As an answer to Jefferson Davis's note he therefore wrote Mr. Blair the following:

WASHINGTON, January 18, 1865.
F. P. BLAIR, Esq.

SIR: You having shown me Mr. Davis's letter to you of the 12th instant, you may say to him that I have constantly been, am now, and shall continue ready to receive any agent whom he, or any other influential person now resisting the National authority, may informally send to me, with the view of securing peace to the people of our one common country.

Yours, etc.,

A. LINCOLN.

With this note Mr. Blair returned to Richmond, giving Mr. Davis such feeble excuses as he could hastily frame why the President had rejected his overture for a joint invasion of Mexico,[1] alleging that Mr. Lincoln was embarrassed by radical politicians and could not use "political agencies." Mr. Blair then, but again without authority, proposed a new project, namely, that Grant and Lee should enter into negotiations, the scope and object of which, however, he seems to have left altogether vague. The simple truth is evident that Mr. Blair was, as best he might, covering his retreat from an abortive intrigue. He soon reported to Davis that military negotiation was out of the question.

Jefferson Davis therefore had only two alternatives before him—either to repeat his stubborn ultimatum of separation and independence, or frankly to accept Lincoln's ultimatum of reunion. The principal Richmond authorities knew, and some of them had tacitly admitted, that their Confederacy was nearly in collapse. Vice-President Stephens, in a secret session of the rebel Senate, had pointed out that "we could not match our opponents in numbers, and should not attempt to cope with them in direct physical power," and advocated a Fabian policy which involved the abandonment of Richmond. Judge Campbell, rebel Assistant Secretary of War, had collected facts

Stephens, "War Between the States." Vol. II., pp. 587–589.

[1] "He [Blair] then unfolded to me," writes Jefferson Davis in his book, "the embarrassment of Mr. Lincoln on account of the extreme men, in Congress and elsewhere, who wished to drive him into harsher measures than he was inclined to adopt; whence it would not be feasible for him to enter into any arrangement with us by the use of political agencies; that if anything beneficial could be effected it must be done without the intervention of the politicians. He therefore suggested that Generals Lee and Grant might enter into an arrangement by which hostilities would be suspended, and a way paved for the restoration of peace. I responded that I would willingly intrust to General Lee such negotiation as was indicated."—Davis, "Rise and Fall of the Confederate Government." Vol. II., pp. 616, 617.

CHAP. V.

Jones, "A Rebel War Clerk's Diary." Vol. II., p. 384.

Jan. 11, 1865.
and figures, which a few weeks later he embodied in a formal report, showing the South to be in practical exhaustion. Lee sent a dispatch saying he had not two days' rations for his army. Richmond was already in a panic at rumors of evacuation. Flour was selling at a thousand dollars a barrel in Confederate currency. The recent fall of Fort Fisher had closed the last avenue through which blockade runners could bring them foreign supplies. Governor Brown of Georgia was refusing to obey orders from Richmond and character- Ibid., p. 395. izing them as "usurping" and "despotic." Under such circumstances a defiant cry of independence would not reassure anybody; nor, on the other hand, was it longer possible to remain silent. Mr. Blair's first visit to Richmond had created general interest. Old friends plied him with eager questions and laid his truthful answers concerning their gloomy prospects solemnly to heart. The fact of his secret consultation with Davis transpired. When Mr. Blair came a second time and held a second secret consultation with the rebel President wonder and rumor rose to fever heat.

Impelled to take action, Mr. Davis had not the courage to be frank. He called, first, Vice-President Stephens, and afterwards his Cabinet, to a discussion of the project. A peace commission of three was appointed, consisting of Alexander H. Stephens, Vice-President; R. M. T. Hunter, Senator and ex-Secretary of State, and John A. Campbell, Assistant Secretary of War — all of them convinced that the rebellion was hopeless, and yet unwilling to admit the logical consequences and necessities. The drafting of instructions for the

guidance of the commissioners was a difficult prob- CHAP. V.
lem, since the explicit condition prescribed by Mr.
Lincoln's note was that he would only receive an
agent sent him "with the view of securing peace to
the people of our one common country." The astute Benjamin
Mr. Benjamin, rebel Secretary of State, in order to to Davis,
May 17,
make the instructions "as vague and general as   1877.
"Southern
possible," proposed the simple direction to confer Historical
Society
"upon the subject to which it relates." His action Papers."
Vol. IV.,
and language were broad enough to carry the infer- pp., 212-214.
ence that in his secret heart he, too, was sick of
rebellion and ready to make terms. Whether it
was so meant or not, his chief refused to receive
the delicate suggestion.

With the ruin and defeat of the Confederate
cause staring him full in the face Davis could
bring himself neither to a dignified refusal nor to
a resigned acceptance of the form of negotiation as
Mr. Lincoln had tendered it. Even in the gulf of
war and destitution into which he had led his
people he could not forego the vanity of mas-
querading as a champion. He was unwilling,
says Mr. Benjamin, to appear to betray his trust
as Confederate President. "You thought, from regard to your personal honor, that your language
ought to be such as to render impossible any malignant comment on your actions." But if so, why Ibid., p. 213.
not adopt the heroic alternative and refuse to negotiate? Why resort to the yet more humiliating
absurdity of sending a commission on terms which
he knew Mr. Lincoln had pointedly rejected?[1]

[1] [INDORSEMENT BY MR. LINCOLN.]   the original, of which the within
"To-day [January 28] Mr.   is a copy, and left it with him;   1865.
Blair tells me that on the 21st   that at the time of delivering it
instant he delivered to Mr. Davis   Mr. Davis read it over twice in

CHAP. V Instead of Mr. Benjamin's phraseology, Jefferson Davis wrote the following instruction to the commissioners, which carried a palpable contradiction on its face.

RICHMOND, January 28, 1865.

In conformity with the letter of Mr. Lincoln, of which the foregoing is a copy, you are requested to proceed to "Southern Historical Society Papers." Vol. IV., p. 214. Washington City for informal conference with him upon the issues involved in the existing war, and for the purpose of securing peace to the two countries.

Your obedient servant,

JEFFERSON DAVIS.

Autograph MS. Mr. Blair's presence, at the close of which he (Mr. Blair) remarked that the part about ' our one common country' related to the part of Mr. Davis's letter about 'the two countries,' to which Mr. Davis replied that he so understood it.   A. LINCOLN."

CHAPTER VI

THE HAMPTON ROADS CONFERENCE

WITH this double-meaning credential the commissioners presented themselves at the Union lines near Richmond on the evening of January 29, 1865, and, instead of frankly showing their authority, asked admission " in accordance with an understanding claimed to exist with Lieutenant-General Grant, on their way to Washington as peace commissioners." The application being telegraphed to Washington, Mr. Stanton answered that no one should be admitted under such character or profession until the President's instructions were received. Mr. Lincoln, being apprised of the application, promptly dispatched Major Thomas T. Eckert an officer of the War Department, with written directions to admit the commissioners under safe conduct if they would say in writing that they came for the purpose of an informal conference on the basis of his note of January 18 to Mr. Blair, "with the view of securing peace to the people of our one common country." Before this officer arrived, however, the commissioners reconsidered the form of their application and addressed a new one to General Grant, asking permission " to proceed to Washington to hold a conference with President Lincoln upon the sub-

Wilcox to Parke, 1865. MS.

Stanton to Ord, Jan. 29, 1865, 10 P. M. MS.

Lincoln to Eckert, Jan. 30, 1865. MS.

ject of the existing war, and with a view of
Stephens,
Campbell,
and Hunter
to Grant,
Jan. 30,
1865. MS. ascertaining upon what terms it may be terminated, in pursuance of the course indicated by him
in his letter to Mr. Blair of January 18, 1865."

Pursuant to this request, they were provisionally
conveyed to Grant's headquarters. One of them
records with evident surprise the unostentatious
surroundings of the General-in-Chief. "I was instantly struck with the great simplicity and perfect naturalness of his manners, and the entire
absence of everything like affectation, show, or
even the usual military air or *mien* of men in his
position. He was plainly attired, sitting in a log
cabin, busily writing on a small table, by a
kerosene lamp. It was night when we arrived.
There was nothing in his appearance or surroundings which indicated his official rank. There were
neither guards nor aids about him. . . He furnished us with comfortable quarters on board one
of his dispatch boats. The more I became acquainted with him, the more I became thoroughly
impressed with the very extraordinary combination
of rare elements of character which he exhibited.
During the time, he met us frequently and conversed
freely upon various subjects, not much upon our
Stephens,
"War
between
the States."
Vol. II.,
p. 597. mission. I saw, however, very clearly that he was
very anxious for the proposed conference to take
place."

The commissioners' note to Grant had been a
substantial compliance with the requirement of
President Lincoln; and so accepting it, the latter,
on the 31st of January, sent Secretary Seward
to meet them, giving him for this purpose the
following written instructions.

EXECUTIVE MANSION,
WASHINGTON, January 31, 1865.

Hon. WILLIAM H. SEWARD, Secretary of State:

You will proceed to Fortress Monroe, Virginia, there to meet and informally confer with Messrs. Stephens, Hunter, and Campbell, on the basis of my letter to F. P. Blair, Esq., of January 18, 1865, a copy of which you have. You will make known to them that three things are indispensable, to wit: *First.* The restoration of the national authority throughout all the States. *Second.* No receding by the Executive of the United States on the slavery question from the position assumed thereon in the late annual message to Congress, and in preceding documents. *Third.* No cessation of hostilities short of an end of the war, and the disbanding of all forces hostile to the Government. You will inform them that all propositions of theirs, not inconsistent with the above, will be considered and passed upon in a spirit of sincere liberality. You will hear all they may choose to say, and report it to me. You will not assume to definitely consummate anything.   Yours, etc.,

ABRAHAM LINCOLN.   MS.

Mr. Seward started on the morning of February 1, and simultaneously with his departure the President repeated to General Grant the monition which the Secretary of War had already sent him two days before through Major Eckert. " Let nothing which is transpiring change, hinder, or delay your military movements or plans." Grant responded to the order, promising that no armistice should ensue, adding, " The troops are kept in readiness to move at the shortest notice, if occasion should justify it." Major Eckert[1] arrived while Mr. Seward was yet on his way. On informing the commissioners of the

Lincoln to
Grant,
Feb. 1, 1865.
MS.

Grant
to Lincoln,
Feb. 1, 1865.
MS.

---

[1] Major Eckert was personally acquainted with Mr. Stephens, and the meeting between them was one of peculiar interest, as Stephens had been the means of saving Eckert's life from a secession mob in Georgia at the outbreak of the war.

CHAP. VI. President's exact requirement they replied by presenting Jefferson Davis's instruction. This was receding from the terms contained in their note to Grant, and Major Eckert promptly notified them that they could not proceed further unless they complied strictly with President Lincoln's terms. Thus at half-past nine on the night of February 1 the mission of Stephens, Hunter, and Campbell was practically at an end. It was never explained why they took this course, for the next day they again changed their minds. The only conjecture which seems plausible is that they hoped to persuade General Grant to take some extraordinary and dictatorial step. One of them hints as much in a newspaper article written long after the war.
"We had tried," he wrote, "to intimate to General Grant, before we reached Old Point, that a settlement generally satisfactory to both sides could be more easily effected through him and General Lee by an armistice than in any other way. The attempt was in vain." The general had indeed listened to them with great interest and in their eagerness to convert him they had probably indulged in stronger phrases of repentance than they felt. About an hour after the commissioners refused Major Eckert's ultimatum General Grant telegraphed the following to Secretary Stanton, from which it will be seen that at least two of the commissioners had declared to him their personal willingness "to restore peace and union."

Hunter, in "Southern Historical Society Papers." Vol. III., p. 175 (April, 1877).

February 1, 10:30 P. M., 1865.
Hon. EDWIN M. STANTON, Secretary of War:
Now that the interview between Major Eckert, under his written instructions, and Mr. Stephens and party has

ended, I will state confidentially, but not officially, to become a matter of record, that I am convinced, upon conversation with Messrs. Stephens and Hunter, that their intentions are good and their desire sincere to restore peace and union. I have not felt myself at liberty to express even views of my own, or to account for my reticency. This has placed me in an awkward position, which I could have avoided by not seeing them in the first instance. I fear now their going back without any expression from any one in authority will have a bad influence. At the same time I recognize the difficulties in the way of receiving these informal commissioners at this time, and do not know what to recommend. I am sorry, however, that Mr. Lincoln cannot have an interview with the two named in this dispatch, if not all three now within our lines. Their letter to me was all that the President's instructions contemplated to secure their safe conduct, if they had used the same language to Major Eckert.

U. S. GRANT, Lieut.-General. MS.

On the morning of February 2, President Lincoln went to the War Department, and, reading Major Eckert's report, was about to recall Mr. Seward by telegraph, when Grant's dispatch was placed in his hands. The communication served to change his purpose. Resolving not to neglect the indications of sincerity here described, he immediately telegraphed in reply, " Say to the gentlemen I will meet them personally at Fortress Monroe as soon as I can get there." The commissioners by this time had decided to accept Mr. Lincoln's terms, which they did in writing to both Major Eckert and General Grant, and thereupon were at once conveyed from General Grant's headquarters at City Point to Fort Monroe, where Mr. Lincoln joined Secretary Seward on the same night.

1865.

MS.

On the morning of February 3, 1865, the rebel commissioners were conducted on board the *River Queen*, lying at anchor near Fort Monroe, where President Lincoln and Secretary Seward awaited them; and in the saloon of that steamer an informal conference of four hours' duration ensued. It was agreed beforehand that no writing or memorandum should be made at the time, so that the record of the interview remains only in the separate accounts which each of the rebel commissioners afterwards wrote out from memory, neither Mr. Seward nor President Lincoln ever having made any report in detail. Former personal acquaintance made the beginning easy and cordial, through pleasant reminiscences of the past and mutual inquiries after friends. In a careful analysis of these reports, thus furnished by the Confederates themselves, the first striking feature is the difference of intention between the parties. It is apparent that Mr. Lincoln went, honestly and frankly in all friendliness, to offer them the best terms he could to secure peace and reunion, but to abate no jot of official duty and personal dignity; while the main thought of the commissioners was to evade the express condition on which they had been admitted to conference; to seek to postpone the vital issue; and to propose an armistice, by debating a mere juggling expedient, against which they had in a private agreement with one another already committed themselves.

Mr. Stephens began the discussion by asking whether there was no way of restoring the harmony and happiness of former days; to which Mr. Lincoln replied, "There was but one way that he

knew of, and that was, for those who were resisting the laws of the Union to cease that resistance."
Mr. Stephens rejoined that they had been induced
to believe that both parties might for a while leave
their present strife in abeyance and occupy themselves with some continental question till their anger
should cool and accommodation become possible.

Here Mr. Lincoln interposed promptly and
frankly : " I suppose you refer to something that
Mr. Blair has said. Now it is proper to state at
the beginning that whatever he said was of his
own accord, and without the least authority from
me. When he applied for a passport to go to Richmond, with certain ideas which he wished to make
known to me, I told him flatly that I did not want
to hear them. If he desired to go to Richmond of
his own accord, I would give him a passport; but
he had no authority to speak for me in any way
whatever. When he returned and brought me Mr.
Davis's letter, I gave him the one to which you
alluded in your application for leave to cross the
lines. I was always willing to hear propositions
for peace on the conditions of this letter, and on no
other. The restoration of the Union is a *sine qua
non* with me, and hence my instructions that no
conference was to be held except upon that basis."

Despite this express disavowal, Mr. Stephens
persisted in believing that Mr. Lincoln had come
with ulterior designs, and went on at considerable
length to elaborate his idea of a joint Mexican expedition, to be undertaken during an armistice and
without a prior pledge of ultimate reunion. Such
an expedition, he argued, would establish the
" right of self-government to all peoples on this

CHAP. VI. continent against the dominion or control of any
European power." Establishing this principle of the
right of peoples to self-government would neces-
Feb. 3, 1865. sarily also establish, by logical sequence, the right
of States to self-government; and, present passions
being cooled, there would ensue "an Ocean-bound
Federal Republic, under the operation of this *Continental Regulator*—the ultimate absolute sov-
ereignty of each State." His idea was that "all
the States might reasonably be expected, very
soon, to return, of their own accord, to their
former relations to the Union, just as they came
together at first by their own consent, and for their
mutual interests. Others, too, would continue to
join it in the future, as they had in the past. This
Stephens,
"War
between
the States."
Vol. II.,
pp. 600-604. great law of the system would effect the same
certain results in its organization as the law of
gravitation in the material world."

Mr. Stephens does not seem to have realized how
comically absurd was his effort to convert President
Lincoln to the doctrine of secession by this very
transparent bit of cunning, and the others listened
with considerate and patient gravity. Mr. Seward
at length punctured the bubble with a few well-
directed sentences, when Mr. Hunter also inter-
vened to express his entire dissent from Mr.
Stephens's proposal. "In this view," reports Mr.
Stephens naïvely, "he expressed the joint opinion
of the commissioners; indeed, we had determined
not to enter into any agreement that would require
the Confederate arms to join in any invasion of
Ibid., p. 608. Mexico." But the rebel Vice-President fails to
record why, under these circumstances, he had
opened this useless branch of the discussion.

At this stage President Lincoln brought back the conversation pointedly to the original object of the conference: "He repeated that he could not entertain a proposition for an armistice on any terms while the great and vital question of reunion was undisposed of. That was the first question to be settled. He could enter into no treaty, convention, or stipulation, or agreement with the Confederate States, jointly or separately, upon that or any other subject, but upon the basis first settled, that the Union was to be restored. Any such agreement, or stipulation, would be a *quasi* recognition of the States then in arms against the National Government, as a separate power. That he never could do."

"This branch of the discussion," also reports Judge Campbell, "was closed by Mr. Lincoln, who answered that it could not be entertained; that there could be no war without the consent of Congress, and no treaty without the consent of the Senate of the United States; that he could make no treaty with the Confederate States, because that would be a recognition of those States, and that this could not be done under any circumstances; that unless a settlement were made there would be danger that the quarrel would break out in the midst of the joint operations; that one party might unite with the common enemy to destroy the other; that he was determined to do nothing to suspend the operations for bringing the existing struggle to a close to attain any collateral end. Mr. Lincoln in this part of the conversation admitted that he had power to make a military convention, and that his arrangements under that

Stephens, "War between the States." Vol. II., p. 608.

CHAP. VI.
Campbell,
in
" Southern
Magazine,"
Dec., 1874,
p. 191.

might extend to settle several of the points mentioned, but others it could not."

The theory of secession as a conservative principle, and the bait of a joint expedition to steal
Mexico under guise of enforcing the Monroe Doctrine, being thus cleared away, the discussion turned
to the only reasonable inquiry which remained.
Judge Campbell asked how restoration could be
effected if the Confederate States would consent,
mentioning important questions, such as the disbandment of the army, confiscation acts on both
sides, the effect of the Emancipation Proclamation,
representation in Congress, the division of Virginia, and so on, which would inevitably arise and
require immediate adjustment. On these various
topics much conversation ensued, which, even as
briefly reported, is too long to be quoted entire.
It will be more useful to condense, under specific
Feb. 3, 1865. headings, the substantial declarations and offers
which the commissioners report Mr. Lincoln to
have made.

I. RECONSTRUCTION.— The shortest way the insurgents could effect this, he said, was " by disbanding their armies and permitting the National
authorities to resume their functions." Mr. Seward
called attention to that phrase of his annual message where he had declared, " In stating a single
condition of peace, I mean simply to say that the
war will cease on the part of the Government
whenever it shall have ceased on the part of those
who began it." As to the rebel States being admitted to representation in Congress, " Mr. Lincoln
very promptly replied that his own individual

opinion was they ought to be. He also thought
they would be; but he could not enter into any
stipulation upon the subject. His own opinion
was that when the resistance ceased and the National authority was recognized the States would
be immediately restored to their practical relations
to the Union."

II. CONFISCATION ACTS.—"Mr. Lincoln said that
so far as the confiscation acts and other penal acts
were concerned, their enforcement was left entirely
with him, and on that point he was perfectly
willing to be full and explicit, and on his assurance   Stephens,
perfect reliance might be placed. He should exer-   "War
                                                        between
cise the power of the Executive with the utmost   the States."
                                                        Vol. II.,
liberality." "As to all questions," says Judge   pp. 609, 612,
Campbell's report, "involving rights of property,   and 617.
the courts could determine them, and that Congress
would no doubt be liberal in making restitution of   Campbell,
                                                        in
confiscated property, or by indemnity, after the   "Southern
                                                        Magazine,"
passions that had been excited by the war had   Dec., 1874,
been composed."   p. 192.

III. THE EMANCIPATION PROCLAMATION.—"Mr.
Lincoln said that was a judicial question. How the
courts would decide it he did not know, and could
give no answer. His own opinion was that as the
proclamation was a war measure, and would have
effect only from its being an exercise of the war
power, as soon as the war ceased it would be inoperative for the future. It would be held to apply
only to such slaves as had come under its operation while it was in active exercise. This was his
individual opinion, but the courts might decide the
other way, and hold that it effectually emancipated
all the slaves in the States to which it applied at

CHAP. VI.

Stephens,
"War
between
the States."
Vol. II.,
pp. 610, 611.
the time. So far as he was concerned, he should leave it to the courts to decide. He never would change or modify the terms of the proclamation in the slightest particular."

At another point in the conversation " he said it was not his intention in the beginning to interfere with slavery in the States; that he never would have done it if he had not been compelled by necessity to do it to maintain the Union; that the subject presented many difficult and perplexing questions to him; that he had hesitated for some time, and had resorted to this measure only when driven to it by public necessity; that he had been in favor of the General Government prohibiting the extension of slavery into the Territories, but did not think that that Government possessed power over the subject in the States, except as a war measure; and that he had always himself been in favor of emancipation, but not immediate emancipation, even by the States. Many evils attending this Ibid.,
pp. 613, 614. appeared to him."

Recurring once more to the subject of emancipation, " he went on to say that he would be willing to be taxed to remunerate the Southern people for their slaves. He believed the people of the North were as responsible for slavery as the people of the South; and if the war should then cease, with the voluntary abolition of slavery by the States, he should be in favor, individually, of the Government paying a fair indemnity for the loss to the owners. He said he believed this feeling had an extensive existence at the North. He knew some who were in favor of an appropriation as high as four hundred millions of dollars for this purpose.

'I could mention persons,' said he, 'whose names would astonish you, who are willing to do this if the war shall now cease without further expense, and with the abolition of slavery as stated.' But on this subject, he said, he could give no assur- ance — enter into no stipulation. He barely ex- pressed his own feelings and views, and what he believed to be the views of others upon the subject."

Stephens, "War between the States." Vol. II., p. 617.

IV. THE DIVISION OF VIRGINIA.—"Mr. Lincoln said he could only give an individual opinion, which was, that Western Virginia would continue to be recognized as a separate State in the Union."

V. THE THIRTEENTH AMENDMENT.— Mr. Seward brought to the notice of the commissioners one topic which to them was new; namely, that only a few days before, on the 31st of January, Congress had passed the Thirteenth Amendment to the Con- stitution, which, when ratified by three-fourths of the States, would effect an immediate abolition of slavery throughout the entire Union. The reports of the commissioners represent Mr. Seward as say- ing that if the South would submit and agree to immediate restoration, the restored States might yet defeat the ratification of this amendment, inti- mating that Congress had passed it "under the predominance of revolutionary passion," which would abate on the termination of the war. It may well be doubted whether Mr. Seward stated the case as strongly as the commissioners intimate, since he himself, like Mr. Lincoln and his entire cabinet, had favored the measure. It is probable that the commissioners allowed their own feelings and wishes to color too strongly the hypothesis he stated, and to interpret as a probability what

1865.

he mentioned as only among the possible events of the future.

It will be seen that in what he said upon these various propositions Mr. Lincoln was always ex- tremely careful to discriminate between what he was authorized under the Constitution to do as Executive, and what would devolve upon coördinate branches of the Government under their own powers and limitations. With the utmost circumspection he pointed out the distinctions between his personal opinions and wishes and his official authority. More especially, however, did he repeat and emphasize the declaration that he would do none of the things mentioned or promised without a previous pledge of reunion and cessation of resistance. "Even in case the Confederate States should entertain the proposition of a return to the Union," says Mr. Stephens's narrative, "he persisted in asserting that he could not enter into any agreement upon this subject [reconstruction], or upon any other matters of that sort, with parties in arms against the Government. Mr. Hunter interposed, and in illustration of the propriety of the Executive entering into agreements with persons in arms against the acknowledged rightful public authority referred to repeated instances of this character between Charles I. of England and the people in arms against him. Mr. Lincoln in reply to this said: 'I do not profess to be posted in history. On all such matters I will turn you over to Seward. All I distinctly recollect about the case of Charles I. is that he lost his head.'"

The pertinent retort reduced Mr. Hunter to his last rhetorical resource — a complaint that the

Confederate States and their people were by
these terms forced to unconditional surrender
and submission. To this Mr. Seward replied with
patience and dignity, " That no words like unconditional submission had been used, or any
importing or justly implying degradation, or humiliation even, to the people of the Confederate
States. . . Nor did he think that in yielding to
the execution of the laws under the Constitution
of the United States, with all its guarantees and
securities for personal and political rights, as they
might be declared to be by the courts, could be
properly considered as unconditional submission
to conquerors, or as having anything humiliating
in it. The Southern people and the Southern
States would be under the Constitution of the
United States, with all their rights secured thereby, Stephens,
in the same way, and through the same instrumen- "War
between
talities, as the similar rights of the people of the the States."
Vol. II.,
other States were." pp. 616, 617.

The reader will recall that in his last annual
message President Lincoln declared his belief,
based " on careful consideration of all the evidence
accessible," that it was useless to attempt to negotiate with Jefferson Davis, but that the prospect
would be better with his followers. Mr. Lincoln
had evidently gone to Fort Monroe in hope of
making some direct impression upon Stephens and
Hunter, whom Grant represented as having such
good intentions " to restore peace and union."
Seizing the proper opportunity, he pressed upon
Stephens the suggestion of separate State action
to bring about a discontinuance of hostilities.
Addressing him, he said:

"If I resided in Georgia, with my present sentiments, I 'll tell you what I would do if I were in
your place. I would go home and get the Governor
of the State to call the Legislature together, and get
them to recall all the State troops from the war;
elect Senators and Members to Congress, and ratify
this constitutional amendment prospectively, so as
to take effect — say in five years. Such a ratification would be valid, in my opinion. I have looked
into the subject, and think such a prospective ratification would be valid. Whatever may have been
the views of your people before the war, they must
be convinced now that slavery is doomed. It cannot last long in any event, and the best course, it
seems to me, for your public men to pursue would
Stephens,
" War
between
the States."
Vol. II.,
p. 614. be to adopt such a policy as will avoid, as far as
possible, the evils of immediate emancipation.
This would be my course, if I were in your place."

The salutary advice was wasted. Mr. Stephens
was a very incarnation of political paradoxes. Perhaps in all the South there was not another man
whose personal desires were so moderate and correct, and whose political theories were so radical
and wrong. At the beginning he had opposed
secession as premature and foolish, war as desperate and ruinous; yet, against his better judgment,
he had followed his " corner-stone" theory of slavery and his "supremacy" theory of States rights
to the war and the ruin he foretold. Now, at the
end of four years' experiment, he still clung obstinately to his new theory of secession as a " continental regulator," and the vain hope that Mr. Lincoln would yet adopt it. When at last the parties
were separating, with friendly handshakings, he

asked Mr. Lincoln to reconsider the plan of an CHAP. VI.
armistice on the basis of a Mexican expedition.
"Well, Stephens," replied Mr. Lincoln, "I will re- Stephens, "War between the States." Vol. II., pp. 610-618.
consider it; but I do not think my mind will
change." And so ended the Hampton Roads conference.

The commissioners returned to Richmond in great
disappointment, and communicated the failure of
their efforts to Jefferson Davis, whose chagrin was
as great as their own. They had all caught eagerly
at the hope that this negotiation would somehow
extricate them from the dilemmas and dangers
whose crushing portent they realized, but had no
power to avert except by surrender; and now,
when this last hope failed them, they were doubly
cast down. Campbell says he "favored negotia- Campbell, "Recollections," etc. Pamphlet.
tions for peace"—doubtless meaning by this
language that he advocated the acceptance of the
proffered terms. Stephens yet believed that Mr.
Lincoln would be tempted by the Mexican scheme
and would reconsider his decision. He therefore
advised that the results of the meeting should be
kept secret; and when the other commissioners
and Davis refused to follow this advice, he gave up
the Confederate cause as hopeless, withdrew from Stephens, "War between the States." Vol. II., pp. 624-626.
Richmond, abandoned the rebellion, and went into
retirement. His signature to the brief public report
of the commissioners stating the result of the Hampton Roads Conference was his last participation in
the ill-starred enterprise.

Davis took the only course open to him after refusing the honorable peace which Mr. Lincoln had
tendered. He transmitted the commissioners' report to the rebel Congress with a brief and dry

CHAP. VI. message, stating that the enemy refused any terms except those the conqueror may grant; and then arranged as vigorous an effort as the circumstances permitted, once more to " fire the Southern heart." A public meeting was called, and on the evening 1865. of February 6, Jefferson Davis and others made speeches at the African Church,[1] which, judging from the meager reports that were printed, were as denunciatory and bellicose as the bitterest Confederate could have wished. Davis, particularly, is represented to have excelled himself in defiant heroics. " Sooner than we should ever be united again," he said, " he would be willing to yield up everything he had on earth — if it were possible he would sacrifice a thousand lives"; and further announced his confidence that they would yet "compel the Yankees, in less than twelve "Richmond months, to petition us for peace on our own Dispatch," Feb. 7, 1865. terms." He denounced President Lincoln as " His

---

[1] This meeting at the African Church was supplemented, a few days later, by a grand concerted effort at public speech-making at different places in Richmond, intended to electrify the South. Pollard, the Southern historian, thus describes it: " All business was suspended in Richmond; at high noon processions were formed to the different places of meeting; and no less than twenty different orators, composed of the most effective speakers in Congress and the cabinet, and the most eloquent divines of Richmond, took their stands in the halls of legislation, in the churches and the theaters, and swelled the eloquence of this last grand appeal to the people and armies of the South. . . It was an extraordinary day in Richmond; vast crowds huddled around the stands of the speakers or lined the streets; and the air was vocal with the efforts of the orator and the responses of his audience. It appeared indeed that the blood of the people had again been kindled. But it was only the sickly glare of an expiring flame; there was no steadiness in the excitement; there was no virtue in huzzas; the inspiration ended with the voices and ceremonies that invoked it; and it was found that the spirit of the people of the Confederacy was too weak, too much broken, to react with effect or assume the position of erect and desperate defiance."—Pollard, " The Lost Cause," pp. 684, 685.

Majesty Abraham the First," and said "before the
campaign was over he and Seward might find
'they had been speaking to their masters.'"

This extravagant rhetoric would seem merely
grotesque were it not embittered by the reflec-
tion that it was the signal which carried many
additional thousands of brave soldiers to bloody
graves in continuing a palpably hopeless miiitary
struggle.

CHAP. VI.

Jones,
"A Rebel
War Clerk's
Diary."
Vol. II.,
p. 411.

CHAPTER VII

THE SECOND INAUGURAL

WE have seen what effect the Hampton Roads Conference produced upon Jefferson Davis, and to what intemperate and wrathful utterance it provoked him. Its effect upon President Lincoln was almost directly the reverse. His interview with the rebel commissioners doubtless strengthened his former convictions that the rebellion was waning in enthusiasm and resources, and that the Union cause must triumph at no distant day. Secure in his renewal of four years' personal leadership, and hopefully inspirited by every sign of early victory in the war, his only thought was to shorten, by generous conciliation, the period of the dreadful conflict. His temper was not one of exultation, but of broad, patriotic charity, and of keen, sensitive personal sympathy for the whole country and all its people, South as well as North. His conversation with Stephens, Hunter, and Campbell had probably revealed to him glimpses of the undercurrent of their anxiety that fraternal bloodshed and the destructive ravages of war might somehow come to an end.

To every word or tone freighted with this feeling, the magnanimous and tender heart of Presi-

dent Lincoln sincerely responded. As a ruler and CHAP. VII.
a statesman, he was clear in his judgment and
inflexible in his will to reëstablish union and maintain freedom for all who had gained it by the
chances of war; but also as a statesman and a
ruler, he was ready to lend his individual influence and his official discretion to any measure of mitigation and manifestation of good-will
that, without imperiling the union of the States,
or the liberty of the citizen, might promote acquiescence in impending political changes, and
abatement and reconcilement of hostile sectional
feelings. Filled with such thoughts and purposes,
he spent the day after his return from Hampton
Roads in considering and perfecting a new proposal,
designed as a peace-offering to the States in rebellion. On the evening of February 5, 1865, he called
his Cabinet together and read to them the following
draft of a message and proclamation, which he had
written during the day, and upon which he invited
their opinion and advice :

Fellow-citizens of the Senate and House of Representatives : I respectfully recommend that a joint resolution,
substantially as follows, be adopted, so soon as practi- Feb. 5, 1865
cable, by your honorable bodies : "Resolved by the Senate
and House of Representatives of the United States of
America in Congress assembled, That the President of
the United States is hereby empowered, in his discretion,
to pay four hundred millions of dollars to the States of
Alabama, Arkansas, Delaware, Florida, Georgia, Kentucky, Louisiana, Maryland, Mississippi, Missouri, North
Carolina, South Carolina, Tennessee, Texas, Virginia, and
West Virginia, in the manner and on the conditions fol-
lowing, to wit : The payment to be made in six per cent.
Government bonds, and to be distributed among said
States *pro rata* on their respective slave populations as

shown by the census of 1860, and no part of said sum to be paid unless all resistance to the National authority shall be abandoned and cease, on or before the first day of April next; and upon such abandonment and ceasing of resistance one-half of said sum to be paid, in manner aforesaid, and the remaining half to be paid only upon the amendment of the National Constitution recently proposed by Congress becoming valid law, on or before the first day of July next, by the action thereon of the requisite number of States."

The adoption of such resolution is sought with a view to embody it, with other propositions, in a proclamation looking to peace and reunion.

Whereas, a joint resolution has been adopted by Congress, in the words following, to wit:

Now therefore I, Abraham Lincoln, President of the United States, do proclaim, declare, and make known, that on the conditions therein stated, the power conferred on the Executive in and by said joint resolution will be fully exercised; that war will cease and armies be reduced to a basis of peace; that all political offenses will be pardoned; that all property, except slaves, liable to confiscation or forfeiture, will be released therefrom, except in cases of intervening interests of third parties; and that liberality will be recommended to Congress upon MS. all points not lying within Executive control.

It may be said with truth that this was going to Feb., 1864. the extreme of magnanimity toward a foe already in the throes and helplessness of overwhelming defeat — a foe that had rebelled without adequate cause and was maintaining the contest without reasonable hope. But Mr. Lincoln remembered that the rebels, notwithstanding all their offenses and errors, were yet American citizens, members of the same nation, brothers of the same blood. He remembered, too, that the object of the war, equally with peace and freedom, was the maintenance of one government and the perpetuation of one

Union. Not only must hostilities cease, but dissension, suspicion, and estrangement be eradicated.
As it had been in the past, so it must again become
in the future — not merely a nation with the same
Constitution and laws, but a people united in feeling, in hope, in aspiration. In his judgment, the
liberality that would work reconciliation would be
well employed. Whether their complaints for the
past were well or ill founded, he would remove
even the temptation to complain in the future.
He would give them peace, reunion, political pardon, remission of confiscation wherever it was in
his power, and securing unquestioned and universal
freedom through the constitutional amendment, he
would at the same time compensate their loss of
slavery by a direct money equivalent.

It turned out that he was more humane and
liberal than his constitutional advisers. The indorsement of his own handwriting on the manuscript draft of his proposed message records the
result of his appeal and suggestion :

" FEBRUARY 5, 1865. To-day these papers, which
explain themselves, were drawn up and submitted
to the Cabinet and unanimously disapproved by
them.   A. LINCOLN."

It would appear that there was but little discussion of the proposition. The President's evident
earnestness on the one side, and the unanimous dissent of the Cabinet on the other, probably created
an awkward situation which could be best relieved
by silence on each hand. The diary of Secretary
Welles gives only a brief mention of the important
incident, but it reflects the feeling which pervaded
the Cabinet chamber :

MONDAY, February 6, 1865.

There was a Cabinet meeting last evening. The President had matured a scheme which he hoped would be successful in promoting peace. It was a proposition for paying the expense of the war for two hundred days, or four hundred millions, to the rebel States, to be for the extinguishment of slavery or for such purpose as the States were disposed. This, in few words, was the scheme. It did not meet with favor, but was dropped. The earnest desire of the President to conciliate and effect peace was manifest, but there may be such a thing as so overdoing as to cause a distrust or adverse feeling. In the present temper of Congress the proposed measure, if a wise one, could not be carried through successfully; I do not think the scheme could accomplish any good results. The rebels would misconstrue it if the offer were

MS.   made. If attempted and defeated it would do harm.

The statement of Secretary Usher, written many years afterward from memory, also records the deep feeling with which the President received the non-concurrence of his Executive Council: "The members of the Cabinet were all opposed. He seemed somewhat surprised at that and asked, 'How long will the war last?' No one answered, but he soon said: 'A hundred days. We are spending now in carrying on the war three millions a day, which will amount to all this money, besides all the lives.' With a deep sigh he added,

"New York Tribune," Sept. 13, 1885.   'But you are all opposed to me, and I will not send the message.'"

The entry made by Secretary Welles in his diary on the morning after the Cabinet meeting, as to the amount and time, is undoubtedly the correct one, coinciding as it does with the President's manuscript. But the discrepancy in the figures of the two witnesses is of little moment. Both ac-

counts show us that the proposal was not based
on sentiment alone, but upon a practical arith-
metical calculation. An expenditure of three or
four hundred millions was inevitable; but his plan
would save many precious lives, would shield
homes and hearths from further sorrow and desolation, would dissolve sectional hatred, and plant fraternal good-will. Though overborne in opinion,
clearly he was not convinced. With the words, "You
are all opposed to me," sadly uttered, Mr. Lincoln
folded up the paper and ceased the discussion of
what was doubtless the project then nearest his
heart. We may surmise, however, that, as he wrote
upon it the indorsement we have quoted and laid it
away, he looked forward to a not distant day when,
in the new term of the Presidency to which he was
already elected, the Cabinet would respond more
charitably to his own generous impulses.

Few Cabinet secrets were better kept than this
proposal of the President and its discussion. Since
the subject was indefinitely postponed, it was, of
course, desirable that it should not come to the
knowledge of the public. Silence was rendered
easier by the fact that popular attention in the
North busied itself with rumors concerning the
Hampton Roads Conference. To satisfy this curi-
osity a resolution of the House of Representatives,
passed on February 8, requested the President to
communicate such information respecting it as he
might deem not incompatible with the public interest. With this request Mr. Lincoln complied on
the 10th, by a message containing all the correspondence, followed by a brief report touching the
points of conference:

Chap. VII.

1865.

"Globe,"
Feb. 8, 1865,
p. 665.

CHAP. VII. On the morning of the 3d the three gentlemen, Messrs. Stephens, Hunter, and Campbell, came aboard of our steamer, and had an interview with the Secretary of State and myself of several hours' duration. No question of preliminaries to the meeting was then and there made or mentioned. No other person was present; no papers were exchanged or produced; and it was, in advance, agreed that the conversation was to be informal and verbal merely. On our part, the whole substance of the instructions to the Secretary of State, hereinbefore recited, was stated and insisted upon, and nothing was said inconsistent therewith; while, by the other party, it was not said that in any event or on any condition they ever would consent to reunion; and yet they equally omitted to declare that they never would so consent. They seemed to desire a postponement of that question, and the adoption of some other course first, which, as some of them seemed to argue, might or might not lead to reunion; but which course, we thought, would amount to an indefinite postponement. MS. The conference ended without result.

"Globe,"
Feb. 10, 1865,
pp. 730–735. A short discussion occurred in the House on the motion to print this message, but it did not rise above the level of an ordinary party wrangle. The few Democrats who took part in it complained of the President for refusing an armistice, while the Republicans retorted with Jefferson Davis's condition about the "two countries" and the more recent declarations of his Richmond harangue, announcing his readiness to perish for independence. On the whole, both Congress and the country were gratified that the incident had called out Mr. Lincoln's renewed declaration of an unalterable resolve to maintain the Union. Patriotic hope was quickened and public confidence strengthened by noting once more his singleness of purpose and steadfastness of faith. No act of his could have formed a more fitting prelude to his second inauguration, which

was now rapidly approaching, and the preliminary
steps of which were at this time being consummated.

A new phase of the reconstruction question was
developed in the usual Congressional routine of
counting the electoral votes of the late Presidential election. Former chapters have set forth
the President's general views on reconstruction,
and shown that though the executive and legislative branches of the Government differed as to the
theory and policy of restoring insurrectionary
States to their normal Federal functions, such difference had not reached the point of troublesome
or dangerous antagonism. Over the new question
also dissension and conflict were happily avoided.
By instruction to his military commanders and in
private letters to prominent citizens Mr. Lincoln
had strongly advised and actively promoted the
formation of loyal State governments in Louisiana,
Tennessee, and Arkansas, and had maintained the
restored Government of Virginia after the division
of that State and the admission of West Virginia
into the Union, and had officially given them the
recognition of the Executive Department of the
Government. The Legislative Department, however, had latterly withheld its recognition, and
refused them representation in Congress. The
query now arose whether the popular and electoral
votes of some of those States for President should
be allowed and counted.

The subject was taken up by the House, which,
on January 30, passed a joint resolution naming the
insurrectionary States, declaring them to have been
" in armed rebellion " on the 8th of November,

CHAP. VII.
"Globe,"
Jan. 30,
1865, p. 505.
1864, and not entitled to representation in the electoral college. A searching debate on this resolution arose in the Senate, which called out the best legal talent of that body. It could not very consistently be affirmed that Louisiana, Tennessee, and Arkansas, held by Federal troops and controlled by Federal commanders in part at least, were "in armed rebellion" on election day, under whatever constitutional theory of reconstruction. The phraseology was finally amended to read that the rebel States "were in such condition on the 8th day of November, 1864, that no valid election for electors of President and Vice-President of the United States, according to the Constitution and laws thereof, was held therein on said day," and in this "Globe,"
Feb. 4, 1865,
pp. 595, 602. form the joint resolution was passed by both Houses. Joint resolutions of Congress have all the force and effect of laws, and custom requires the President to approve them in the same manner as regular acts. His signature in this case might therefore be alleged to imply that he consented to or adopted a theory of reconstruction at variance with his former recommendation and action. To avoid the possibility of such misconstruction, Mr. Lincoln sent Congress a short message, in which he said:

> The joint resolution, entitled "Joint resolution declaring certain States not entitled to representation in the electoral college," has been signed by the Executive, in deference to the view of Congress implied in its passage and presentation to him. In his own view, however, the two Houses of Congress, convened under the twelfth article of the Constitution, have complete power to exclude from counting all electoral votes deemed by them to be illegal; and it is not competent for the Executive to

defeat or obstruct that power by a veto, as would be
the case if his action were at all essential in the matter.
He disclaims all right of the Executive to interfere in any
way in the matter of canvassing or counting electoral   Lincoln,
                                                          Message,
votes; and he also disclaims that, by signing said resolu-   Feb. 8, 1865.
tion, he has expressed any opinion on the recitals of the   "Globe,"
                                                            Feb. 10, 1865,
preamble, or any judgment of his own upon the subject   p. 711.
of the resolution.

In anticipation of possible debate and contention
on the subject of counting the electoral votes of
reconstructed States, Congress had, on February 6,
adopted what afterwards became famous as the
Twenty-second Joint Rule, which directed in substance that all such questions should be decided,
not by the joint convention of the two Houses, but
by each House for itself without debate, the two
Houses having temporarily separated for that pur-   "Globe,"
                                                      Feb. 6, 1865,
pose; and requiring the concurrence of both for   pp. 608, 628.
any affirmative action, or to count a vote objected
to.   When the two Houses met in joint convention
on the eighth day of February, mention was made
by the Vice-President, presiding, that "The Chair
has in his possession returns from the States of
Louisiana and Tennessee; but in obedience to the
law of the land, the Chair holds it to be his duty   "Globe,"
                                                      Feb. 8, 1865,
not to present them to the Convention." No   p. 668.
member insisted on having these returns opened,
since they could not possibly change the result.
Only the returns therefore from the loyal States,
including West Virginia, were counted, showing
212 electoral votes for Lincoln, and 21 for Mc-
Clellan.[1] The Vice-President thereupon announced

---

[1] Since the Presidential elec-   uary, 29, 1861, casting three
tion of 1860 three additional   electoral votes; West Virginia,
States had been admitted into   June 19, 1863, casting five elec-
the Union, namely, Kansas, Jan- toral votes; and Nevada, October

CHAP. VII.

"Globe,"
Feb. 8, 1865,
p. 669.

"that Abraham Lincoln of the State of Illinois, having received a majority of the whole number of electoral votes, is duly elected President of the United States for four years, commencing on the fourth day of March, 1865."

The usual committee was appointed to wait upon Mr. Lincoln and notify him of his second election; and in response to their announcement he read the following brief address:

"With deep gratitude to my countrymen for this mark of their confidence; with a distrust of my own ability to perform the duty required, under the most favorable circumstances, and now rendered doubly difficult by existing National perils; yet with a firm reliance on the strength of our free Government and the eventual loyalty of the people to the just principles upon which it is founded, and, above all, with an unshaken faith in the Supreme Ruler of Nations, I accept this trust. Be pleased to signify this to the respective Houses of Congress."[1]

In the informal friendly conversation which followed, the President said to the committee, in substance: "Having served four years in the depths of a great and yet unended National peril, I can view this call to a second term in nowise more

31, 1864, entitled to three electoral votes, but casting only two because of a vacancy.

The States which voted for Lincoln were: California, Connecticut, Illinois, Indiana, Iowa, Kansas, Maine, Maryland, Massachusetts, Michigan, Minnesota, Missouri, Nevada, New Hampshire, New York, Ohio, Oregon, Pennsylvania, Rhode Island, Vermont, West Virginia, and Wisconsin.

The States which voted for McClellan, were: Delaware, Kentucky, and New Jersey.

[1] MS. The reply reported by the notification committee, and printed in the "Congressional Globe," is incorrect, having apparently been written out from memory, intermingling an abstract of the formal paper which the President read, with the informal conversation that succeeded.

flattering to myself than as an expression of the CHAP. VII.
public judgment that I may better finish a difficult
work in which I have labored from the first than "Globe,"
March 1,
1865, p. 1263.
could any one less severely schooled to the task."

The formal inauguration of Mr. Lincoln for his
second Presidential term took place at the appointed
time, March 4, 1865. There is little variation in
the simple but impressive pageantry with which
this official ceremony is celebrated. The principal
novelty commented upon by the newspapers was
the share which the hitherto enslaved race had for
the first time in this public and political drama.
Civic associations of negro citizens joined in the
procession, and a battalion of negro soldiers formed
part of the military escort. The weather was sufficiently favorable to allow the ceremonies to take
place on the eastern portico, in view of a vast
throng of spectators. Imaginative beholders, who
were prone to draw augury and comfort from
symbols, could rejoice that the great bronze Statue
of Freedom now crowned the dome of the Capitol,
and that her guardianship was justified by the fact
that the Thirteenth Amendment virtually blotted
slavery from the Constitution. The central act of
the occasion was President Lincoln's second
inaugural address, which enriched the political
literature of the Union with another master-
piece, and which deserves to be quoted in full.
He said:

FELLOW-COUNTRYMEN: At this second appearing to Mar. 4, 1865
take the oath of the Presidential office, there is less
occasion for an extended address than there was at the
first. Then, a statement, somewhat in detail, of a course
to be pursued, seemed fitting and proper. Now, at the
expiration of four years, during which public declara-

tions have been constantly called forth on every point and phase of the great contest which still absorbs the attention and engrosses the energies of the nation, little that is new could be presented. The progress of our arms, upon which all else chiefly depends, is as well known to the public as to myself; and it is, I trust, reasonably satisfactory and encouraging to all. With high hope for the future, no prediction in regard to it is ventured.

On the occasion corresponding to this four years ago, all thoughts were anxiously directed to an impending civil war. All dreaded it — all sought to avert it. While the inaugural address was being delivered from this place, devoted altogether to saving the Union without war, insurgent agents were in the city seeking to destroy it without war — seeking to dissolve the Union, and divide effects, by negotiation. Both parties deprecated war; but one of them would make war rather than let the nation survive; and the other would accept war rather than let it perish. And the war came.

One-eighth of the whole population were colored slaves, not distributed generally over the Union, but localized in the Southern part of it. These slaves constituted a peculiar and powerful interest. All knew that this interest was, somehow, the cause of the war. To strengthen, perpetuate, and extend this interest was the object for which the insurgents would rend the Union, even by war; while the Government claimed no right to do more than to restrict the territorial enlargement of it. Neither party expected for the war the magnitude or the duration which it has already attained. Neither anticipated that the cause of the conflict might cease with, or even before, the conflict itself should cease. Each looked for an easier triumph, and a result less fundamental and astounding. Both read the same Bible, and pray to the same God; and each invokes his aid against the other. It may seem strange that any men should dare to ask a just God's assistance in wringing their bread from the sweat of other men's faces; but let us judge not, that we be not judged. The prayers of both could not be answered — that of neither has been answered fully. The Almighty has his own purposes. "Woe unto the world because of offenses! for it must needs be that offenses come; but woe to that man by whom the offense cometh." If we shall suppose that American slavery is one of those offenses which, in the providence of God, must needs come, but which, having continued through his appointed time, he now wills to remove, and that he gives to both North and South this terrible war, as the woe due to those by whom the offense came, shall we discern therein any departure from those divine attributes which the believers in a living God always ascribe to him? Fondly do we hope — fervently do we pray — that this mighty scourge of war may speedily pass away. Yet, if God wills that it continue until all the wealth piled by the bondman's two hundred and fifty years of unrequited toil shall be sunk, and until every drop of blood drawn with the lash shall be paid by another drawn with the sword, as was said three thousand years ago, so still it must be said, "The judgments of the Lord are true and righteous altogether."

With malice toward none; with charity for all; with firmness in the right, as God gives us to see the right, let us strive on to finish the work we are in; to bind up the nation's wounds; to care for him who shall have borne the battle, and for his widow, and his orphan — to do all which may achieve and cherish a just and lasting peace among ourselves, and with all nations.

The address being concluded, Chief-Justice Chase administered the oath of office; and listeners who heard Abraham Lincoln for the second time repeat, "I do solemnly swear that I will faithfully execute the office of President of the United States, and will, to the best of my ability, preserve, protect, and defend the Constitution of the United States," went from the impressive scene to their several homes with thankfulness and with confidence that the destiny of the country and the liberty of the citizen were in safe keeping. "The fiery trial" through which he had hitherto walked showed him possessed of the capacity, the courage, and the will to keep the promise of his oath.

CHAP. VII. Among the many criticisms passed by writers and thinkers upon the language of the second inaugural, none will so interest the reader as that of Mr. Lincoln himself, written about ten days after its delivery, in the following letter to a friend:

DEAR MR. WEED: Every one likes a compliment. Thank you for yours on my little notification speech and on the recent inaugural address. I expect the latter to wear as well as, perhaps better than, anything I have produced; but I believe it is not immediately popular. Men are not flattered by being shown that there has been a difference of purpose between the Almighty and them. To deny it, however, in this case, is to deny that there is a God governing the world. It is a truth which I thought needed to be told, and, as whatever of humiliation there is in it falls most directly on myself, I thought others might afford for me to tell it.

Lincoln to Weed, Mar. 15, 1865. Weed, "Memoirs." Vol. II., pp. 449, 450.

A careful student of Mr. Lincoln's character will also find this inaugural address instinct with another meaning, which, very naturally, the President's own comment did not touch. The eternal law of compensation, which it declares and applies to the sin and fall of American slavery, in a diction rivaling the fire and the dignity of the old Hebrew prophecies,[1] may, without violent inference, be interpreted

[1] Mgr. Dupanloup, Bishop of Orleans, in a letter, dated 2d April, 1865, to M. Auguste Cochin, acknowledging the receipt of Lincoln's second inaugural, said: " J'ai lu ce document avec la plus religieuse émotion, avec l'admiration la plus sympathique. ... M. Lincoln exprime, avec une solennelle et touchante gravité, les sentiments qui, j'en suis sûr, envahissent les âmes d'élite, au Nord comme au Sud. Quel beau jour lorsque l'union des âmes se fera là, dans la vraie et parfaite lumière de l'Évangile. Mais quel beau jour déjà lorsque le chef deux fois élu d'un grand peuple tient un langage chrétien, trop absent, dans notre Europe, du langage officiel des grandes affaires, annonce la fin de l'esclavage, et prépare les embrassements de la justice et de la miséricorde dont l'Écriture Sainte a parlé. Je vous remercie de m'avoir fait lire cette belle page de l'histoire des grands hommes."

to foreshadow an intention to renew at a fitting CHAP. VII.
moment the brotherly good-will gift to the South
which has been treated of in the first part of
this chapter. Such an inference finds strong cor-
roboration in the phrases which closed the last
public address he ever made, and which we have Ante,
elsewhere quoted in full. On Tuesday evening, Vol. IX., pp. 457-463.
April 11, a considerable assemblage of citizens of 1865.
Washington gathered at the Executive Mansion to
celebrate the victory of Grant over Lee. The rather
long and careful speech which Mr. Lincoln made on
that occasion was, however, less about the past than
the future. It discussed the subject of reconstruction, as illustrated in the case of Louisiana, showing
also how that issue was related to the questions of
emancipation, the condition of the freedmen, the
welfare of the South, and the ratification of the
constitutional amendment. "So new and unprecedented is the whole case," he concluded, "that no
exclusive and inflexible plan can safely be prescribed as to details and collaterals. Such exclusive and inflexible plan would surely become a new
entanglement. Important principles may and must
be inflexible. In the present situation, as the
phrase goes, it may be my duty to make some new
announcement to the people of the South. I am
considering, and shall not fail to act when satisfied
that action will be proper." Can any one doubt
that this "new announcement" which was taking
shape in his mind would again have embraced and
combined justice to the blacks and generosity to
the whites of the South, with union and liberty
for the whole country?

CHAPTER VIII

CHAP. VIII.
1864

FROM the hour of Mr. Lincoln's reëlection the Confederate cause was doomed. The cheering of the troops which greeted the news from the North was heard within the lines at Richmond and at Petersburg, and although the leaders maintained to the end their attitude of defiance, the impression rapidly gained ground among the people that the end was not far off. The stimulus of hope being gone, they began to feel the pinch of increasing want. Their currency had become almost worthless. In October a dollar in gold was worth thirty-five dollars in Confederate money; a month later it brought fifty dollars; with the opening of the new year the price rose to sixty dollars, and soon after to seventy; and despite the efforts of the Confederate treasury, which would occasionally rush into the market and beat down the price of gold ten or twenty per cent. in a day, the currency gradually depreciated until a hundred for one was offered and not taken.

As a result of this vanishing value of their money a portentous rise took place in the prices of all the necessaries of life. It is hard for a people to recognize that their money is good for nothing; to do this is to confess that their Government has failed: it was natural, therefore, for the unhappy citizens of Richmond to think that monstrous prices were being extorted for food, clothing, and fuel, when, in fact, they were paying no more than was reasonable. The journals and diaries of the time are filled with bitter execrations against the extortioners and forestallers; but when we translate their prices into the gold standard, we wonder how the grocers and clothiers lived. To pay a thousand dollars for a barrel of flour was enough to strike a householder with horror; but ten dollars is not a famine price. A suit of clothes cost from one thousand to fifteen hundred dollars; but if you divide this sum by seventy-five, there is very little profit left for the tailor. High prices, however, even if paid in dry leaves, are a hardship when dry leaves are not plentiful; and there was scarcity, even of Confederate money, in the South. In Richmond, which lived upon the war, the dearth was especially evident. The clerks in the departments received say four thousand dollars a year, hardly enough for a month's provisions. Skilled mechanics fared somewhat better. They could earn, so long as they kept out of the army, something like six thousand dollars a year. Statesmanship was cheap. A congressman's pay was five thousand five hundred dollars; but most of the civil officers of the Government managed to get their supplies at cost prices from the military stores. It was illegal; but they could not have lived otherwise, and they doubtless considered their lives necessary to their country.

The depreciation of the Confederate currency was an unmistakable symptom of a lack of confidence in the course of affairs, since it did not arise from inflation. On the contrary, George A. Trenholm, the Secretary of the Treasury, did all he could to check this dangerous tendency, going so far as to incur the reproaches of many who imagined his action enhanced prices. All dealers instinctively felt the money was worthless, and their only object was to get it out of their hands as soon as possible, at whatever prices, in exchange for objects of real value. One Confederate diarist records with indignation that he saw a Jew buy at auction an old set of tablespoons for $575, and makes this a cause of complaint against the Government, which permits men to acquire in this way the means of running away. Anybody who was able to leave the country became the object of the envy and hatred of those who remained behind. They began to treat their own financial system with contempt. When the officer in charge of the Treasury Note Bureau at Columbia, alarmed at the approach of Sherman, asked where he was to go, he could get no attention to his inquiries; one high functionary advising that he go to the devil.

Jones, "A Rebel War Clerk's Diary." Vol. II., p. 361.

Jan., 1865. Jones, "A Rebel War Clerk's Diary." Vol. II., p. 384.

At every advance of General Grant's lines a new disturbance and alarm was manifested in Richmond, the first proof of which was always a fresh rigor in the enforcement, not only of existing conscription laws, but of the arbitrary orders of the frightened authorities. After the capture of Fort Harrison, on the north side of the James, squads of guards were sent into the streets with directions to arrest every able-bodied man they met. They paid

no regard to passes or to certificates of exemption
or detail, but hurried the unhappy civilians off to
the field, or herded them, pending their assignment
to companies, within the railings of the public
square. Two members of the Cabinet, John H.
Reagan and George Davis, were thus arrested on
the streets by the zealous guards in spite of their
protestations, though they were, of course, soon
recognized and released. The pavements were
swept of every class of loiterers; the clerks in the
departments with their exemptions in their pockets
were carried off, whether able to do duty or not.
It is said by one Confederate writer that the
medical boards were ordered to exempt no one
who seemed capable of bearing arms for ten days,
and he mentions an instance where a man died, Jones,
"A Rebel
War Clerk's
on the eleventh day of his service, of consump- Diary."
Vol. II.,
tion. Human nature will not endure such a p. 305.
strain as this: a week after this sweeping of
Richmond for recruits, General William M. Gardner reported that more than half the men thus
dragged to the trenches had deserted. Of those
who remained, the members of influential families
came, one by one, back to the town on various
pretexts, increasing the bitterness of feeling among
those too poor or too obscure to rescue their sons
and brothers.

Desertion grew too common to punish. Almost
every man in the Confederacy was, by statute or
decree, liable to military service, and yet hundreds
of thousands of them were not in the army. If
men were to be shot for deserting it would have
been a question whether there were soldiers enough
to shoot them. Mr. Davis acted prudently in remit-

CHAP. VIII. ting the death sentences laid before him, although this occasioned great dissatisfaction in the army. Near the end of the year 1864 Longstreet reported one hundred men of Pickett's division as in the guard-house for desertion, attributing the blame for it to the numerous reprieves which had been granted, no one having been executed for two months. General Lee sent this report to Richmond Nov.29,1864. with his approval, which gave great offense to the Confederate President. He returned the paper with an indorsement to the effect that the remis- Jones, "A Rebel War Clerk's Diary," pp. 343, 344. sion of sentences was not a proper subject for the criticism of a military commander.

As disaster increased, as each day brought its catastrophe, the Confederate Government steadily lost ground in the confidence and respect of the Southern people. It is characteristic of every fail- ing revolt that in the hour of ruin the participators turn upon one another with reproaches, often as causeless and unjust as those they cast upon their legitimate government. Mr. Davis and his coun- cilors now underwent this natural retribution. They were doing their best, but they no longer got any credit for it. From every part of the Confed- eracy came complaints of what was done, demands for what it was impossible to do. Some of the States were in a condition near to counter-revolution. Governor Brown of Georgia made no pretense of concealing his contumacy. The march of Sherman across his State seemed to have emancipated him from any feeling of obligation to the Confederacy. His letters to Richmond from that moment lost all color of allegiance. The feeling in North Carolina was little better. A slow paralysis was benumbing the limbs of the insurrection, and even at the heart its vitality was plainly declining.

The Confederate Congress, which had hitherto been the mere register of the President's will, now turned upon him and gave him wormwood to drink. On the 19th of January they passed a reso- lution making Lee general-in-chief of the army. This Mr. Davis might have borne with patience, although it was intended as a notification to him that his meddling with military affairs must come to an end. But far worse was the necessity put upon him, as a sequel to this act,— and in con- formity with a resolution of Congress and of the Vir- ginia Legislature,— of reappointing General Joseph E. Johnston to the command of the army which was to resist Sherman's victorious march to the North. After this he might say that the bitterness of death was past. The Virginia delegation in Con- gress passed a vote of want of confidence in the Government's conduct of the war. Mr. Seddon, considering his honor impugned, and being not un- willing to lay down a thankless task, resigned his Pollard, "The Lost Cause," p. 653. post of Secretary of War. Mr. Davis at first wished him to reconsider his action, claiming that such a declaration from Congressmen was beyond their functions and subversive of the President's consti- tutional jurisdiction; but Mr. Seddon insisted, and General John C. Breckinridge was appointed in his place in February, for the few weeks that remained before the final crash. Warnings of serious de- moralization came daily from the army; even that firm support to the revolt seemed crumbling. Dis- affection was so rife in official circles in Richmond that it was not thought politic to call public atten-

CHAP. VIII.

Jones,
"A Rebel
War Clerk's
Diary."
Vol. II.,
p. 390.

1865.

1864.

tion to it by repression. A detective reported a Member of Congress as uttering treasonable language, and for his pains was told at the War Department that matters of that sort were none of his business.

It is a curious and instructive thing to note how the act of emancipation had by this time virtually enforced itself in Richmond. The value of slave property was gone. It is true that a slave was still occasionally sold, at a price less than one-tenth of what he would have brought before the war. But servants could be hired of their nominal owners at a barley-corn rate; six dollars in gold would pay the hire of a good cook for a year — merely enough to keep up the show of vassalage. In effect any one could hire a negro for his keeping, which was all that anybody in Richmond got for his work. Even Mr. Davis had at last become docile to the stern teachings of events. In his message of November he had recommended the employment of 40,000 slaves in the army,— not as soldiers it is true, save in the last extremity,— with emancipation to come later.

The determined buoyancy and fanfaronade of the rebel department of State had finally given way. On the 27th of December Mr. Benjamin wrote his last important instruction to John Slidell. It is nothing less than a cry of despair. He recounts the courage and fortitude with which the South has withstood for four years the attack of " an arrogant and domineering race, vengeful, grasping, and ambitious "; the very adjectives show a vast change from the Southern tone of former years. He complains bitterly of the attitude of foreign nations while the South is fighting the battles of England and France against the North; he asks with agonized earnestness what it is they want. "Are they determined never to recognize the Southern Confederacy until the United States assent to such action on their part? Do they propose under any circumstances to give other and more direct aid to the Northern people in attempting to enforce our submission to a hateful Union? If so, it is but just that we be apprized of their purposes, to the end that we may then deliberately consider the terms, if any, upon which we can secure peace from the foes to whom the question is thus surrendered, and who have the countenance and encouragement of all mankind in the invasion of our country, the destruction of our homes, the extermination of our people."

If, on the other hand, he continues, there be any conditions under which England and France will be willing to grant recognition, a frank exposition of such conditions "is due to humanity. It is due now, for it may enable us to save many lives most precious to our country, by consenting to such terms in advance of another year's campaign." With this alternative,—with the frantic offer to submit to any terms which Europe may impose as the price of recognition, and with the scarcely veiled threat of making peace with the North unless Europe should speedily act—the Confederate Department of State closed its four years of fruitless activity.

Lee assumed command of all the Confederate forces on the 9th day of February. His situation was one of unprecedented gloom. The day before,

Benjamin
to Slidell,
Dec. 27, 1864
MS., Con-
federate
Archives.

Ibid.

Long,
"Memoirs
of R. E.
Lee," p. 679.

CHAP. VIII.
Feb. 8, 1865.
he had reported to Richmond that his troops, who
had been in line of battle for two days at Hatcher's
Run, exposed to the bitter winter weather, had
been without meat for three days. " If some change
is not made," he said, " and the commissary department reorganized, I apprehend dire results; . . . you
must not be surprised if calamity befalls us." Mr.
Davis indorsed this discouraging dispatch with
words of anger and command easy to write : " This
is too sad to be patiently considered; . . . criminal
neglect or gross incapacity. . . Let supplies be had
by purchase or borrowing." A prodigious effort
was made, and the danger of starvation for the
moment averted, but no permanent improvement
resulted in the situation of affairs. The armies of
the Union were closing in from every point of the
compass. Grant was every day pushing his formidable left wing nearer the only roads by which Lee
could escape; Thomas was threatening the Confederate communications from Tennessee; Sheridan
was moving for the last time up the Valley of the
Shenandoah to abolish Early ; while from the South
the redoubtable columns of Sherman — the men
who had taken Vicksburg, who had scaled the
heights of Chattanooga, and, having marched
through Georgia, had left Savannah loyal and
Charleston evacuated — were moving northward
with the steady pace and irresistible progress of
a tragic fate. It was the approach of this portent which affected the nerves of the Confederate
leaders more than the familiar proximity of Grant.
Beauregard, and afterwards Johnston, were ordered
to " destroy Sherman." Beauregard, after his kind,
showed his Government its duty in loud and valiant

Long,
" Memoirs
of R. E.
Lee,"
pp. 678, 679.

Breckin-
ridge to
Lee, Feb. 21,
1865.

words.   He advised Mr. Davis to send him at once
heavy reënforcements "to give the enemy battle
and crush him"; "then to concentrate all forces
against Grant, march to Washington and dictate
a peace"— a plan of limpid simplicity, which was
not adopted. Johnston superseded the brilliant
Louisianian the next day, and thereafter did what
he could — with the scraps and remnants of an
army allowed him — to resist the irresistible.

A singular and significant attempt at negotiations
was made at this time by General Lee. He was now
so strong in the confidence of the people of the
South, and the Government at Richmond was so
rapidly becoming discredited, that he could doubtless have obtained the popular support, and compelled the assent of the Executive to any measures
he thought proper for the attainment of peace.
From this it was easy for him and for others to
come to the wholly erroneous conclusion that General Grant held a similar relation to the Government and people of the United States. General Lee
seized upon the pretext of a conversation reported
to him by General Longstreet, as having been held
with General E. O. C. Ord under an ordinary flag
of truce for exchange of prisoners, to address a letter
to Grant, sanctioned by Mr. Davis, saying he had
been informed that General Ord had said that General Grant would not decline an interview with a
view to "a satisfactory adjustment of the present
unhappy difficulties by means of a military convention," providing Lee had authority to act. He therefore proposed to meet General Grant, "with the
hope that upon an interchange of views it may
be found practicable to submit the subjects of con-

CHAP. VIII.

Badeau,
"Military
History of
U. S.
Grant."
Vol. III.,
pp. 400, 401. troversy between the belligerents to a convention of the kind mentioned." In such event he said he was "authorized to do whatever the result of the proposed interview may render necessary or advisable."

Grant at once telegraphed these overtures to Washington. Stanton received his dispatch at the Capitol, where the President was, according to his custom, passing the last night of the session for the convenience of signing bills. The Secretary handed the telegram to Mr. Lincoln, who read it in silence. He asked no advice or suggestion from any one about him, but taking a pen, wrote with his usual slowness and precision a dispatch in Stanton's name, which he showed to Seward and then handed to Stanton to be signed, dated, and sent. The language is that of an experienced ruler, perfectly sure of himself and of his duty:

Mar. 3, 1865.

Badeau,
"Military
History of
U. S.
Grant."
Vol. III.,
pp. 401, 402. The President directs me to say that he wishes you to have no conference with General Lee unless it be for capitulation of General Lee's army, or on some minor or purely military matter. He instructs me to say that you are not to decide, discuss, or confer upon any political questions. Such questions the President holds in his own hands, and will submit them to no military conferences or conventions. Meanwhile you are to press to the utmost your military advantages.

General Grant, on the receipt of this instruction, wrote, in answer to General Lee, that he had no authority to accede to his proposition — such authority being vested in the President of the United States alone; he further explained that General Ord's language must have been misunderstood. Grant reported to Washington what he had done, adding that he would in no case exceed his authority, or omit to press all advantages to the utmost of his ability. This closed the last avenue of hope to the Confederate authorities of any compromise by which the dread alternative of utter defeat or unconditional surrender might be avoided.[1]

Early in March General Lee came to Richmond and had a conference with Mr. Davis on the measures to be adopted in the crisis which he saw was imminent. The General-in-Chief had not taken his advancement seriously. He had not sympathized in the slight which it involved towards the civil government; he had positively refused to assume the dictatorial powers with which the Richmond Congress had clearly intended to invest him; he had ostentatiously thanked " the President alone" for a promotion which in reality came from the President's enemies and critics. He continued to the end, in accordance with the constitution of the Confederate States, to treat Mr. Davis as the Commander-in-Chief of the forces. He now laid before him the terrible facts by which the army was environed: Richmond and Petersburg must be evacuated before many days; a new seat for the Confederate Government, a new base of defense for the armies must be taken up farther south and west.

There is a direct contradiction between Mr. Davis and the friends of General Lee as to the

[1] Jefferson Davis refers to this incident in his message of March 13 to the Confederate Congress, and says: "It thus appears, that neither with the Confederate authorities, nor the authorities of any State, nor through the commanding generals, will the Government of the United States treat or make any terms or agreement whatever for the cessation of hostilities. There remains then for us no choice but to continue this contest to a final issue"; etc.— "Annual Cyclopædia, 1865," p. 719.

CHAP. VIII.

Davis,
" Rise and
Fall of the
Confed-
erate Gov-
ernment."
Vol. II.,
p. 648.
manner in which the former received this communication. Mr. Davis says he suggested an immediate withdrawal, but that General Lee said his
horses were too weak for the roads in their present
state, and that he must wait till the ground became
firmer. But General Long, who gives General Lee as
his authority, says that the President overruled the
general; that Lee wanted then to withdraw his
forces and take up a line behind the Staunton
Long,
"Memoirs
of R. E.
Lee," p. 403. River, from which point he might have indefinitely protracted the war. However this may be,
they were both agreed that sooner or later the
Richmond lines must be abandoned; that the next
move should be to Danville; that a junction was
to be formed with Johnston; Sherman was to be
destroyed; a swarm of recruits would come in after
this victory; and Grant, being caught away from
" Rise
and Fall
of the
Confed-
erate Gov-
ernment."
Vol. II.,
pp. 648, 649. his base, was to be defeated and Virginia delivered
from the invader. Mr. Davis gravely set forth this
programme as his own, in his book written sixteen
years after the war.

But before he turned his back forever upon those
lines he had so stoutly defended, before he gave up
to the nation the capital of the State for whose
sake he had deserted his flag, Lee resolved to dash
once more at the toils by which he was surrounded.
He placed half his army under the command of
General John B. Gordon, with orders to break
through the Union lines at Fort Stedman, and to
take possession of the high ground behind them.
The reticence in which General Lee enveloped
himself in his last years has left his closest friends
in doubt as to his real object in this apparently
desperate enterprise. General Gordon, who takes

GENERAL JOHN B. GORDON.

to himself the greater share of responsibility for Chap. VIII.
the plan, says: "I decided that Fort Stedman
could be taken by a night assault, and that it
might be possible to throw into the breach thus Gordon to Davis, "Rise and Fall of the Confederate Government," pp. 650, 651.
made in Grant's lines a sufficient force to disorgan-
ize and destroy the left wing of his army before he
could recover and concentrate his forces."

It is certainly true that any fort can be taken,
by day or night, if the assaulting party has men
enough and is willing to pay the price; but to
take a place which cannot be held is not what we
expect from a wise and experienced general. Grant
had, with singular prescience, looked for some such
movement from Lee a month before. He had
ordered Parke, then in command of the Ninth Feb. 22, 1865.
Corps, to be ready to meet an assault on his center
and to let his commanders understand they were
to lose no time in bringing all their resources to
bear on the point of danger. "With proper alacrity
in this respect," he adds, "I would have no objection to seeing the enemy get through." This is one
of the most characteristic phrases we have met with
in Grant's orders. It throws the strongest light both
on his temperament and on the mastery of his
business at which he had arrived. A month beforehand he foresaw Gordon's attack, prepared for it,
and welcomed the momentary success which attended it. Under such generalship an army's lines
are a trap into which entrance is suicide.

The assault was made with great spirit at half-
past four on the morning of the 25th of March. Its
initial success was due to a singular cause. The
opposing lines at the point chosen were only 150
yards apart; the pickets were only fifty yards from

CHAP. VIII. each other; it was therefore a favorite point of departure for those Confederates who were tired of the war. Desertions had of late become very numerous and had naturally been encouraged in every way; orders had been issued allowing deserters to bring their arms with them. When Mar.25,1865. Gordon's skirmishers came stealing through the darkness they were at first mistaken for an unusually large batch of deserters, and they overpowered several picket posts without a shot being fired. The storming party at once followed, took the trenches with a rush, and in a few minutes had possession of the main line on the right of Stedman. Turning on the fort, they soon drove out the garrison or made them prisoners. It was the dark hour before dawn, and the defense could not distinguish friends from foes; for a little while General Parke, who acted with his usual vigor and intelligence, was unable to make headway against the invisible enemy who swarmed on both sides of the breach in the lines. General N. B. McLaughlen, who was posted to the left of Fort Stedman, at once got to work and recaptured an outlying battery with the bayonet, and then hurrying into the fort in ignorance of its capture was made prisoner.

As soon as it was light, Parke's troops advanced from every direction to mend the breach; R. B. Potter on the left, Willcox on the right, and John F. Hartranft, who had been held in reserve, attacking directly from the high ground in the rear. The last two, between them, first made short work of the Confederate detachments that were moving on the City Point road and telegraph and searching in vain for three forts in the rear of Stedman which they

had been ordered to take; there were no such forts, Cᴀᴘ. VIII.
Humphreys says, where Gordon thought they were; Hum-phreys,
the forts commanding Stedman were part of the "The Virginia
main line. By half-past seven Parke had his task Campaign of '64 and
well in hand. He had repulsed the Confederate '65," p. 317.
attack to the right and left of Fort Stedman, recaptured two of the detached batteries, forced the Mar.25,1865.
enemy with heavy loss back into the fort, and concentrated upon them a heavy artillery fire from
three sides. The artillery under the direction of
General J. C. Tidball worked with splendid energy
and precision. Hartranft's division carried Fort
Stedman by assault, and Gordon withdrew to the
Confederate lines what he was able to save of his
attacking force. The cross fire of artillery was
now so withering that few of the Confederates
could get back, and none could come to their assistance. General Parke captured 1949 prisoners,
including seventy-one officers and nine stands of
colors; his own total loss was about 1000.

But this heavy loss was not the only damage the
Confederates suffered. Humphreys and Wright, in
command of the troops on the Union left, who were
to be routed and dispersed according to General
Lee's plan, on being informed of the racket in the
center, correctly assuming that Parke could take
care of himself, instantly searched the lines in their
front to see if they had been essentially weakened to support Gordon's attack. They found
they had not; but in the process of gaining this
information they captured the enemy's intrenched
picket lines in front of them, which, in spite of repeated attempts to regain them, were firmly held,
and gave inestimable advantage to the Union army

CHAP VIII. in the struggle of the next week. The net results
therefore to General Lee of the day's work were a
bitter disappointment, a squandering of four thousand of his best troops against half that number
on the other side, and the loss of his intrenched
picket line, which brought such dangerous neighbors as Wright and Humphreys within arm's-
length of him.

For several weeks General Grant's chief anxiety
had been lest Lee should abandon his lines. At
first he feared a concentration of Lee and Johnston against Sherman; but when the victorious
Army of the West had arrived at Goldsboro' and
formed connection with Schofield his anxiety on
that score was at rest, and there only remained a
keen eagerness to make an end of the Army of
Northern Virginia. "I was afraid," he says, "every
morning that I would awake from my sleep to hear
that Lee had gone, and that nothing was left but a
picket line." Still — just as Lee, though feeling
every hour of waiting was fraught with danger,
was prevented from moving by the bad roads and
the Richmond complications — Grant, although
burning to attack, was delayed by the same cause
of bad roads, and by another. He did not wish to
move until Sheridan had completed the work assigned him in the Valley and joined either Sherman or the army at Petersburg.

But at last, satisfied with Sheridan's progress
and with Sherman's condition, he resolved to wait
no longer, and on the 24th of March, at the very
moment when Gordon was making his arrangements for the next day's sortie, Grant issued his
order for the great movement to the left which was

Grant,
"Personal
Memoirs."
Vol. II.,
p. 424.

1865.

to finish the war. He intended to begin on the
29th, but Lee's desperate dash of the 25th appeared
to the Union commander to indicate an intention
to secure a wider opening to the Danville road to
facilitate an immediate move of the Confederates
westward, and he felt more than ever that not a
moment was to be lost. Sheridan reached City
Point on the 26th, and Sherman came up from
North Carolina for a brief visit the next day. He
said he would be ready to move on the 10th of
April, and laid before Grant a plan for a coöpera-
tive campaign, which was of course satisfactory, as
was usually everything that Sherman proposed, but
which the swift rush of events soon rendered superfluous. The President was also there, and an interesting conversation took place between these
famous brothers-in-arms and Mr. Lincoln, after
which Sherman went back to Goldsboro' and Grant
began pushing his army to the left with even more
than his usual iron energy.

It was a great army; it was the result of all the
power and wisdom of the Government, all the devotion of the people, all the intelligence and teach-
ableness of the soldiers themselves, and all the
ability and character which the experience of a
mighty war had developed in the officers. Few
nations have produced better corps commanders
than Sheridan, Warren, Humphreys, Ord, Wright,
and Parke, taking their names as they come in the
vast sweep of the Union lines from Dinwiddie
Court House to the James in the last days of March;
north of the James was Weitzel, vigilant and
capable. Between Grant and the Army of the
Potomac was Meade, the incarnation of industry,

Chap. VIII. zeal, and talent; and in command of all was Grant, then in his best days, the most extraordinary military temperament this country has ever seen. When unfriendly criticism has exhausted itself, the fact remains, not to be explained away by any reasoning, subtle or gross, that in this tremendous war he accomplished more with the means given him than any other two on either side. The means given him were enormous, the support of the Government was intelligent and untiring; but others had received the same means and the same support — and he alone captured three armies. The popular instinct which hails him as our greatest general is correct; and the dilettante critics who write ingenious arguments to prove that one or another of his subordinates or his adversaries was his superior will please for a time their diminishing coteries, and then pass into silence without damaging his robust fame.

The numbers of the respective armies in this last grapple have been the occasion of endless controversy. We take the figures given by General Humphreys — not merely on account of his profound study of the subject and personal acquaintance with it, but because we consider him the most thoroughly candid and impartial man who has written the history of this army. The effective force of infantry of the Army of the Potomac was 69,000; of field artillery, 6000, with 243 guns. The effective force of infantry of the Army of the James was 32,000; of field artillery, 3000, with 126 guns, and 1700 cavalry, though General Ord took with him only about one-half his infantry; Sheridan's cavalrymen, present for duty, 13,000; the grand total

of all arms was 124,700. Lee's infantry numbered
46,000; his field artillery, 5000; his cavalry, 6000;
in all, 57,000.

Grant's plan, as announced in his instructions
of March 24, was at first to dispatch Sheridan to
reach and destroy the South Side and Danville
railroads, at the same time moving a heavy force   Grant,
   Report.
to the left, primarily to insure the success of Sheri-   " Personal
  Memoirs."
dan's raid,[1] and then to turn Lee's position. But   Vol. II.,
   p. 616.
his purpose grew and developed every hour, and
before he had been a day away from his winter
headquarters he had given up the comparatively
narrow scheme with which he started and had
adopted the far bolder and more comprehensive
plan, which he carried out to his immortal honor.

It is probable that to General Sheridan belongs
a part of the credit of this change of plan. He
often said, in conversation with his friends, that
he was delighted after his victory over Early at
Waynesboro' to find such difficulties in crossing
the James as prevented his going south to Sherman, and justified him—neglecting his alternative
orders to return to Winchester—in turning east
and uniting with the Army of the Potomac. He   Sheridan,
  "Memoirs."
felt that the war was nearing its end and desired   Vol. II.,
   p. 119.
his cavalry to be in at the death. He thought it
best that the Eastern army, which had thus far won
scanty laurels when compared with the Western,
should have the glory of this final victory; and
when he arrived at City Point and found General
Grant's plans once more contemplated the possi-

[1] Grant wrote to Sherman on lowing Sheridan. But I shall be   Sherman,
March 22: "I shall start with along myself, and will take ad-   "Memoirs."
no distinct view further than vantage of anything that turns   Vol. II.,
holding Lee's forces from fol- up."   p. 323.

Sheridan,
"Memoirs."
Vol. II.,
p. 128.
Grant,
"Personal
Memoirs."
Vol. II.,
p. 437.

CHAP. VIII. bility of sending his cavalry to Sherman and bringing that commander, after disposing of Johnston,
to share in the destruction of Lee, Sheridan urged
the General-in-Chief to finish the work immediately
with the Army of the Potomac, that had so richly
merited the glory which would come of the fruition
of their long years of blood and toil.   Grant seems
to have assured Sheridan that his orders would
not require him to go to Sherman except in a
remote contingency, and that they had been prepared as a "blind" in case of failure. Both commanders were full of the spirit of victory.   On the
evening of the 29th of March, Sheridan's cavalry
was at Dinwiddie Court House, and the left of the
moving force of infantry extended to the Quaker
road—almost to Lee's right flank on the White
Oak Ridge. Grant's purpose had now taken complete shape in his mind. From his tent on Gravelly
Creek he wrote to Sheridan, telling him the position of all his corps, and adding in simple words,
which will stir the blood of every reader for ages
to come, "I now feel like ending the matter . . .
before going back." He ordered Sheridan not to
cut loose and go after the railroads, but to push for

Grant,
Report,
"Personal
Memoirs."
Vol. II.,
p. 621.

the enemy's right rear. "We will act all together
as one army here, until it is seen what can be done
with the enemy."

The next day Sheridan advanced to Five Forks,
where he found a heavy force of the enemy. Lee,
justly alarmed by Grant's movements, had drawn
all his available troops out of the trenches, dispatched a sufficient force under Fitzhugh Lee to
Five Forks to hold that important cross-roads, and
had taken personal command of the rest on the

GENERAL A. A. HUMPHREYS.

White Oak Ridge. A heavy storm of rain began
the night of the 29th, continuing more than twenty-
four hours, and greatly impeded the march of the
troops. Warren, on the morning of the 31st, worked
his way towards the White Oak road; but before
he reached it Lee came out of his lines and attacked
Warren's advanced division (Ayres's) with such impetus that it was driven back on the main line
at Gravelly Run. There, gallantly supported by
General Miles of Humphreys's corps, who made a
spirited attack on Lee's left flank, Warren held his
own, and in the afternoon moved forward and
drove the enemy into his works.

Lee, not satisfied with opposing Sheridan at Five
Forks with cavalry, had, on the 30th, sent Pickett
there with some 7000 infantry, which, with nearly
an equal force of cavalry, was too much for the
Union horse to handle. Sheridan was, therefore,
on the 31st, forced back to Dinwiddie Court House. Grant, Report, "Personal Memoirs." Vol. II., p. 621.
"Here," says Grant, "Sheridan displayed great
generalship." He fought with obstinate tenacity,
disputing every inch of ground, deploying his cavalry on foot, leaving only men enough with his
horses to guard them. He gave Pickett and Lee a
hard day's work on the way to Dinwiddie, and at
night reported his situation to Grant in his usual
tone of valorous confidence. Grant, indeed, was far
more disturbed than Sheridan. He rained orders
and suggestions all night upon Meade, Warren, and
Sheridan, the purpose of which was to effect a concentration at daylight on that portion of the enemy
in front of Sheridan. Warren, giving his troops,
who had been marching and fighting for three days,
a few hours' needed rest, came in on Sheridan's

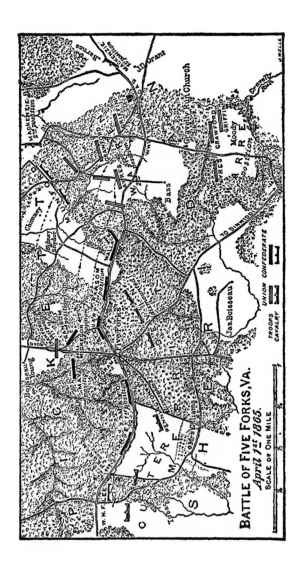

BATTLE OF FIVE FORKS, VA.
April 1st 1865.
SCALE OF ONE MILE

right about dawn. But Pickett, seeing that he was
out of position, did not wait to be caught between
the two Union columns; he withdrew noiselessly
during the night[1] and resumed his strongly intrenched post at Five Forks. Grant, in ignorance
of this timely flight of Pickett, was greatly incensed
at Warren for not having done what is now seen
to have been impossible to do, since Pickett was
gone before the hour when Grant wished Warren
to attack him. The long-smoldering dislike of
Warren, which had been for months increasing in
Grant's mind, now blazed out into active hostility,
and he sent an aide-de-camp to Sheridan, suggesting that Warren be relieved from his command.[2]

Sheridan hurried up to Five Forks with his cavalry, leaving Warren to bring up the Fifth Corps.
Filled, as Sheridan was all this day, with the most
intense martial ardor, his judgment and control of
his troops were never more powerful and comprehensive. He pressed with his cavalry the retreating Confederates until they came to Five Forks,
and then assigned to Merritt the duty of demon-

[1] The testimony of the Confederate generals in the Warren
court of inquiry shows that Pickett and Fitzhugh Lee, anticipating Warren's arrival at daybreak,
resolved to retire at ten o'clock
on the night of the 31st of March,
and that the movement began at
once. "Nearly everything on
wheels," Fitzhugh Lee said,
"was away by midnight." At
daylight the cavalry moved, covering the rear of the infantry.—
Warren Court of Inquiry, p.
469. General W. H. F. Lee's
testimony is to the same effect,
p. 536.

[2] Thorough inquiry among the
friends of both generals seems to
establish the fact that Grant's
animosity towards Warren arose
from the habit Warren had of discussing his orders, suggesting
changes in plans of battle, and
movements in support of his own.
Grant regarded this habit as lacking in respect to himself, and
although Warren was looked upon
as one of the ablest and most
devoted officers in the army, it
was evident that sooner or later
Grant's irritation would come to
a point which would prove ruinous to Warren.

CHAP. VIII. strating strongly on Pickett's right, while with the
infantry of the Fifth Corps he was to strike the left
flank, which ran along the White Oak road about
three-quarters of a mile east from Five Forks and
then made a return of a hundred yards to the
north, perpendicular to the road. It was the old
tactics of the Valley repeated, with the additional
advantage in this case that, if successful, he would
drive Pickett westward and cut him off from Lee.
To guard against any interruption from the east
R. S. Mackenzie had been sent to take possession
of the White Oak road, some three miles east of the
Forks, a task which he promptly performed, and
then came back to take his position on the right of
the Fifth Corps.

April 1, 1865. The battle was fought almost as it was planned:
the only difference between conception and execution arose from the fact that it had not been practicable to ascertain the precise position of the
enemy's left flank, lest the attempt might put them
on their guard. Ayres's division was on the left,
Crawford on the right, Griffin behind Crawford,
and in this way they moved to the attack about four
o'clock. Warren, understanding that the enemy's
lines reached farther down the road than was the
case, sent Ayres, his smallest division, in a direction which brought it against the angle, and Crawford and Griffin were moving across the road and
altogether past the left of the enemy into the
woods, when the heavy firing in front of Ayres
warned Warren of his error, and he immediately
bestirred himself to rectify it, sending his aides in
every direction, and finally riding off into the woods
to bring back Crawford and Griffin to the point

where they were so greatly needed. All this occupied considerable time, and in the mean while the
brunt of the battle fell upon Ayres's division. They
were hardly strong enough for the work thus acci-
dentally assigned them, and there might have been
a serious check at that moment but for the providential presence of Sheridan himself, who, with a
fury and vehemence founded on the soundest judgment, personally led the troops in their attack on
the intrenchments. Those who saw him that day
will tell the story to their latest breath, how, holding the colors in his hand, with a face darkened
with smoke and anger, and with sharp exhortations
that rang like pistol-shots, he gathered up the fal-
tering battalions of Ayres and swept like a spring
gust over Pickett's breastworks.

Meanwhile Warren was doing similar work on
the right. He had at last succeeded in giving his
other two divisions the right direction, and came in
on the reverse of the enemy's lines. At one moment, finding some hesitation in a part of Crawford's force, "Warren, riding forward," says
Humphreys, "with the corps flag in his hand, led
his troops across the field." His horse was shot
dead in the final charge. The dusk of evening
came down on one of the most complete and momentous victories of the war. Pickett was absolutely routed; every man was driven from the field
except the killed and wounded, and the prisoners,
who were gathered in to the number of some five
thousand, with a great quantity of guns and colors.
As the battle was ending, Sheridan sent an order
to Warren relieving him of his command and directing him to report to General Grant for orders.

CHAP. VIII. It does not come within the compass of this work to review all the circumstances which led General Grant to entertain so rooted a dislike to Warren, and General Sheridan, who had but a slight acquaintance with him,[1] to adopt his chief's opinions. In removing him from command they were perfectly justified. Honestly holding the opinion they held of him, it was their duty to prevent the evils they thought might result from his retention in so important a trust. But it is not improper here to say that a court of inquiry, which General Warren succeeded in obtaining after General Grant had for twelve years denied it to him, decided that the impressions under which Grant and Sheridan acted were erroneous, and that Warren did his whole duty at Five Forks. Grant never changed his opinion of him. It is true he offered him another command the next day, and soon afterwards he was given an important department to administer; but the General-in-Chief was always implacable towards him. Even in his "Memoirs," in the midst of the compliments he pays to the memory of Warren, he shows his increasing prejudice in one phrase. In his report of 1865 he said Warren was relieved "about the close of this battle"; in p. 444. his "Memoirs" he says "the troops were then brought up and the assault successfully made" — *after* Warren was relieved.

---

[1] " As we had never been thrown much together, I knew but little of him."—Sheridan, "Memoirs." Vol. II., p. 168.

CHAPTER IX

APPOMATTOX

the war: Lee's right had been shattered and
routed; his line, as he had long predicted, had been
stretched westward until it broke; there was no
longer any hope of saving Richmond, or even of
materially delaying its fall. But General Lee apparently thought that even the gain of a day was of
value to the Richmond Government, and what was
left of the Army of Northern Virginia was still so
perfect in discipline and obedience that it answered
with unabated spirit and courage every demand
made upon it. It is painful to record or to read
the story of the hard fighting of the 2d of April; 1865.
every drop of blood spent on the lines of Petersburg that day seems to have been shed in vain.

Parke and Wright had been ordered on the 30th
of March to examine the enemy's works in their
respective fronts with a view to determine whether
it was practicable to carry them by assault; they
had both reported favorably. After the great
victory of Five Forks, Grant, whose anxiety for
Sheridan seems excessive, thought that Lee would
reënforce against him heavily,[1] when, in fact Lee

Badeau,
"Military
History of
U. S.
Grant."
Vol. III.,
p. 503.

[1] Grant to Ord: "I have just heard from Sheridan. . . Everything
the enemy has will probably be pushed against him."

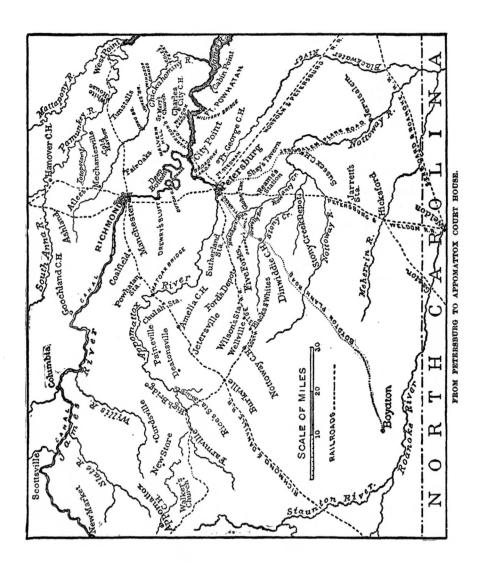

FROM PETERSBURG TO APPOMATTOX COURT HOUSE.

GENERAL CHARLES GRIFFIN.

had already sent to his right all the troops that
could be spared, and Sheridan had routed them.
To relieve Sheridan and to take advantage of any
weakness in Lee's extended front, Grant now
ordered an assault all along the lines. The answers
came in with electric swiftness and confidence:
Wright said he would "make the fur fly"; Ord
promised to go into the Confederate lines "like a
hot knife into butter." The ground, however, in
front of Ord was so difficult that Grant gave him
no positive orders to assault, but, on the contrary,
enjoined upon him great vigilance and caution.
Similar instructions were given to Humphreys;
Miles, of his corps, was ordered westward on the
White Oak road to help Sheridan, and Wright and
Parke were directed to attack at four o'clock on the
morning of the 2d. Grant's principal anxiety was
lest Lee should get away from Petersburg and
overwhelm Sheridan on the White Oak road. Lee
was thinking of nothing of the kind. The terrible
blow his right had received seemed to have stunned
him. He waited, with a fortitude not far from
despair, for the attack which the morning was sure
to bring, making what hasty preparations were in
his power for the coming storm.

It came with the first glimmer of dawn. Wright,
who had carefully studied the ground in his front,
from the safe point of vantage he had gained the
day of Gordon's ill-fated sortie, had selected the
open space in front of Forts Fisher and Walsh as
the weak point in the Confederate harness. Not
that it was really weak, except in comparison with
the almost impregnable works to right and left: the
enemy's front was intersected by marshy rivulets;

a heavy abatis had to be cut away under musketry fire from the parapets and a rain of artillery from the batteries. It was a quarter to five before there was light enough to guide the storming columns; but at that instant they swarmed forward, rushing over the Confederate pickets with too much momentum to be delayed a minute, and, gaining the main works, made them their own after a brief but murderous conflict. In fifteen minutes Wright lost eleven hundred men. They wasted not an instant after this immense success. Some pushed on in the ardor of the assault across the Boydton road as far the South Side Railroad; the gallant Confederate general A. P. Hill rode unawares upon a squad of these skirmishers, and, refusing to surrender, lost his life at their hands. But the main body of the troops wisely improved their victory. A portion of them worked resolutely to the right, meeting strong resistance from the Confederates under Wilcox; the larger part re-formed with the celerity that comes from discipline and experience, and moved down the reverse of the captured lines to Hatcher's Run, where, about seven o'clock, having swept everything before them and made large captures of men and guns, they met their comrades of the Twenty-fourth Corps, whom they joined, facing about and marching over ground cleared of the enemy till the left closed in on the Appomattox River.

Parke also assaulted at the earliest light, meeting with a success on the outer line equally brilliant and important, capturing four hundred yards of intrenchments with many guns, colors, and prisoners. But there was in front of him an interior line,

heavily fortified, and here the enemy, under General Gordon, not only made a stand, but resumed
the offensive and assaulted several times during
the day, without success, the lines which Parke had
seized in the morning and hastily reversed. On the
left Humphreys displayed his usual intelligent
energy; as soon as he heard of the success of
Wright and Parke, on his right, he attacked with
Hays's division the Confederate redoubt at Crow's
house, capturing the works, the guns, and most of
the garrison, while upon his left Mott's division
drove the enemy out of their works at Burgess's
Mill. Humphreys wanted to concentrate his whole
corps against the scattered enemy by the Claiborne road; but General Meade countermanded
the movement. Mott and Hays were ordered towards Petersburg, and Miles, who had been holding
the White Oak road for Sheridan, was therefore left
alone to deal with Heth's division, which had hastily
intrenched itself near Sutherland's Station, and here
a sharp fight took place. Miles, twice repulsed,
stuck obstinately to his task, and about three o'clock
whipped and dislodged the enemy, making large
captures, and driving him off towards the Appomattox and Amelia Court House.

Two forts—Gregg and Whitworth—on the main
line of the Confederate intrenchments west of
Petersburg made a stout resistance to the National
troops. The former was a very strong work, surrounded by a deep and wide wet ditch, flanked by
fire to the right and left. It was an ugly thing to
handle, but Robert S. Foster's and J. W. Turner's
divisions of Gibbon's corps assaulted with unflinch-
ing valor, meeting a desperate resistance. Every

advantage, except that of numbers, was on the side of its brave defenders, and they put twice their own numbers *hors du combat* before they surrendered. Gibbon reports a loss of 714 killed and

Apl. 2, 1865. wounded ; 55 Confederate dead were found in the work. After Gregg had fallen, Turner's men made short work of Fort Whitworth, and the Confederates, from the Appomattox to the Weldon road, fell slowly back to their inner line of works near Petersburg, now garrisoned by Longstreet's troops, who had come in from the north side of the James.

The attack of Wright, though it must have been anticipated, came upon General Lee with the stunning effect of lightning. Before the advance of the National army had been reported to Lee or A. P.

W. H.
Taylor,
" Four
Years with
General
Lee,"
p. 149.

Hill, they saw squads of men in blue scattered about the Boydton road, and it was in riding forward to ascertain what the strange apparition meant that General Hill lost his life. General Lee, in full uniform, with his dress sword, which he seldom wore, but which he had put on that morning in honor of the momentous day he saw coming, — being determined with that chivalrous spirit of his to receive adversity splendidly, — watched from the lawn in front of his headquarters the formidable advance of the National troops before whom his weakened lines were breaking into spray, and then, mounting

J. E.
Cooke,
" Life of
R. E. Lee,"
p. 447.

his iron-gray charger, slowly rode back to his inner line. There his ragged troops received him with shouts and cheers, which showed there was plenty of fight left in them ; and there he spent the day in making preparations for the evacuation which was now the only resort left him. He sent a dispatch to Richmond, carrying in brief and simple words

the message of despair to the Confederate authori- Chap. IX.
ties : " I see no prospect of doing more than holding Long,
"Memoirs
of
R. E. Lee,"
p. 691.
our position here till night.   I am not certain I can
do that." He succinctly stated the disaster that
had befallen him, announced his purpose of concentrating on the Danville road, and advised that all
preparations be made for leaving Richmond that Apl. 2, 1865
night.

Some Confederate writers express surprise that
General Grant did not attack and destroy Lee's
army on the afternoon of the 2d of April; but this
is a view, after the fact, easy to express. Wright's
and Humphreys's troops on the Union left had been
on foot for eighteen hours; they had fought an important battle, marched and countermarched many
miles, and were now confronted by Longstreet's
fresh corps, behind formidable works, led by the
best of Lee's generals ; while the attitude of the
force under Gordon, on the south side of the town,
was such as to require the close attention of Parke.
Grant, anticipating an early retirement of Lee from
his citadel, wisely resolved to avoid the waste and
bloodshed of an immediate assault on the inner
lines at Petersburg. He ordered Sheridan to get
upon Lee's line of retreat, sent Humphreys to
strengthen him; then, directing a general bombardment for five o'clock the next morning, and an
assault at six, he gave himself and his soldiers
a little of the rest they had so richly earned, and
which they so seriously needed, as a restorative
after the labors past and a preparation for the
labors to come.

He had telegraphed during the day to President
Lincoln, who was at City Point, the great day's

news as it developed hour by hour. He was particularly happy at the large captures. " How many prisoners ? " was always the first question as an aide-de-camp came galloping in with news of success. Prisoners he regarded as so much net gain : he was weary of slaughter ; he wanted the war ended with the least bloodshed possible. It was with the greatest delight that he was able to telegraph on this Sunday afternoon, " The whole captures since the army started out gunning will not amount to less than twelve thousand men and probably fifty pieces of artillery."

Badeau, "Military History of U. S. Grant." Vol. III., p. 526.

General Lee, after the first shock of the breaking of his lines, soon recovered his usual *sang froid*, and bent all his energies to saving his army and leading it out of its untenable position on the James to a point from which he could effect a junction with Johnston in North Carolina. The place selected for this purpose was Burkeville, at the crossing of the South Side and Danville roads, fifty miles from Richmond, whence a short distance would bring him to Danville, where the desired junction might be made. Even in this ruin of the Confederacy, when the organized revolt which he had sustained so long with the bayonets of his soldiers was crashing about his ears, he was able still to cradle himself in the illusion that it was only a campaign that had failed ; that he might withdraw his troops, form a junction with Johnston, and continue the war indefinitely in another field. Whatever we may think of his judgment, it is impossible not to admire the coolness of a general who, in the midst of irremediable disaster such as encompassed Lee on the afternoon of the 2d of April, could write

1865.

such a letter as he wrote to Jefferson Davis under
date of three o'clock. He began it by a quiet and
calm discussion of the question of negro recruit-
ment; promised to give his attention to the business
of finding suitable officers for the black regiments;
hoped the appeal Mr. Davis had made to the governors would have a good effect; and, altogether,
wrote as if years of struggle and effort were before
him and his chief. He then went on to narrate the
story of the day's catastrophe and to give his plans
for the future. He closed by apologizing for writ- Davis,
ing "such a hurried letter to your Excellency," on "Rise and
the ground that he was "in the presence of the erate Gov-
enemy, endeavoring to resist his advance." pp. 660, 661.

At nightfall all his preparations were completed.
He mounted his horse, and riding out of the town
dismounted at the mouth of the road leading to
Amelia Court House, the first point of rendezvous,
where he had directed supplies to be sent, and
standing beside his horse, the bridle reins in his
hand, he watched his troops file noiselessly by in
the darkness. At three o'clock the town, which Apl. 3, 1865.
had been so long and so stoutly defended, was
abandoned; only a thin line of skirmishers was left
in front of Parke, and before daybreak he pierced
the line in several places, gathering in the few
pickets that were left. The town was formally surrendered to Colonel Ralph Ely at half-past four,
anticipating the capitulation which some one else
offered to General Wright a few minutes later.
Meade reported the news to Grant, and received the order to march his army immediately
up the Appomattox by the river road; Grant,
divining the intentions of Lee, dispatched an of-

ficer to Sheridan, directing him to push with all speed to the Danville road with Humphreys and Griffin and all the cavalry.

Thus the flight and the pursuit began almost at the same moment. The swift-footed Army of Northern Virginia was now racing for its life; and Grant, inspired with more than his habitual tenacity and energy, and thoroughly aroused to the tremendous task of ending the war at once, not only pressed his enemy in the rear, but hung upon his flank, and strained every nerve to get in his front. It is characteristic of him that he did not even allow himself the pleasure of entering Richmond, which, deserted by those who had so often promised to protect it, and wrapped in flames lighted by the reckless hands of Confederate officials, surrendered April, 1865. to Weitzel early on the morning of the 3d.

All that day Lee pushed forward towards Amelia Court House. He seemed in higher spirits than usual. As one who has long been dreading bankruptcy feels a great load taken from his mind when his assignment is made, so the Virginian chief, when he drew out from the ruin and conflagration in which the Confederate dream of independent power was passing away, and marched with his men into the vernal fields and woods of his native State, was filled with a new sense of encouragement and cheer. "I have got my army safe out of its breastworks," he said, "and in order to follow me the enemy must abandon his lines, and can J. E. Cooke, "Life of derive no further benefit from his railroads or R. E. Lee," p. 451. James River." But he was now dealing with the man who, in Mississippi, had boldly swung loose from his base of supplies in an enemy's country, in

GENERAL A. P. HILL.

face of an army equal to his own, and had won a CHAP. IX.
victory a day without a wagon train.

There was little fighting the first day except
among the cavalry. Custer attacked the Confederates at Namozine Church, and later in the day
Merritt's cavalry had a sharp contest with Fitzhugh Lee at Deep Creek. On the 4th, Sheridan,
who was aware of Lee's intention to concentrate
at Amelia Court House, brought his cavalry with
great speed to Jetersville, about eight miles southwest of the Court House, where Lee's army was
resting. Sheridan intrenched, and sent tidings of
his own and the enemy's position to Grant, and on
the afternoon of the next day the Second and Apl. 5, 1865.
Sixth Corps came up. A terrible disappointment
awaited General Lee on his arrival at Amelia Court
House. He had ordered, he says, supplies to be
forwarded there; but when his half-starved troops
arrived on the 4th of April they found that no food
had been sent to meet them, and nearly twenty-
four hours were lost in collecting subsistence for
men and horses. "This delay was fatal and could
not be retrieved."[1] The whole pursuing force was
south and stretching out to the west of him, when
he started on the night of the 5th of April to make 1865.
one more effort to reach a place of temporary
safety. Burkeville, the junction of the Lynchburg

---

[1] Lee's report of the surrender (Long, "Memoirs of R. E. Lee," p. 693). Other Confederate writers insist that the train which should have borne these supplies to Lee was directed to Richmond to assist the flight of the Confederate authorities (Pollard, "Lost Cause," p. 703). Jefferson Davis ("Rise and Fall." Vol. II., p. 668) denounces the whole story as a malignant calumny, and gives voluminous statements from Confederate officers to confute it. But there seems no reason to doubt General Lee's statement, made to Mr. Davis in his report at the time.

and Danville roads, was in Grant's possession; the way to Danville was barred, and the supply of provisions from the south cut off. Lee was compelled to change his route to the west; and he now started for Lynchburg, which he was destined never to reach.

It had been Meade's intention to attack Lee at Amelia Court House on the morning of the 6th of April, but before he reached that place he discovered that Lee's westward march had already begun, and that the Confederates were well beyond the Union left. Meade quickly faced his army about and started in pursuit. A running fight ensued for fourteen miles; the enemy, with remarkable quickness and dexterity, halting and partly intrenching themselves from time to time, and the National forces driving them out of every position, moving so swiftly that lines of battle followed closely on the skirmish line. At several points the cavalry, on this and the preceding day, harassed the moving left flank of the Confederates and worked havoc on the trains, on one occasion causing a grievous loss to history by burning Lee's headquarters baggage with all its wealth of returns and reports. Sheridan and Meade pressed so closely at last that Ewell's corps was brought to bay at Sailor's Creek, a rivulet running northward into the Appomattox. Here an important battle, or rather series of battles, took place, with fatal results to Lee's fast-vanishing army. The Fifth Corps held the extreme right and was not engaged. Humphreys, coming to where the roads divided, took the right fork and drove Gordon down towards the mouth of the creek. A sharp battle was fought about

dark, which resulted in the total defeat of the Chap. IX.
Confederates, Humphreys capturing 1700 prisoners, Humphreys,
"The
Virginia
Campaign
of '64
and '65,"
p. 381.
13 flags, 4 guns, and a large part of the main trains;
Gordon making his escape in the night to High
Bridge with what was left of his command. Wright,
on the left-hand road, had also a keen fight, and
won a most valuable victory. With Wheaton's and
Seymour's divisions he attacked Ewell's corps, in
position on the banks of the creek, enveloping him
with the utmost swiftness and vehemence; Sheridan, whose cavalry had intercepted the Confederates, ordered Crook and Merritt to attack on the
left, which was done with such vigor — Davies's
horsemen riding over the enemy's breastworks at a
single rush — that, smitten in front and flank, unable
either to stand or to get away, Ewell's whole force
was captured on the field. The day's loss was
deadly to Lee, not less than eight thousand in all;
among them such famous generals as Ewell, Kershaw, G. W. Custis Lee, M. D. Corse, and others
were prisoners.

In the mean time Ord, under Sheridan's orders, Apl. 6, 1865.
had moved rapidly along the Lynchburg road to
Rice's Station, where he found Longstreet's corps
intrenched, and night came on before he could get
into position to attack. General Theodore Read,
Ord's chief-of-staff, had gone still farther forward
with eighty horsemen and five hundred infantry
to burn High Bridge, if possible. In the attempt
to execute this intention he fell in, in the neighborhood of Farmville, with two divisions of Confederate cavalry under Rosser and T. T. Munford. One
of the most gallant and pathetic battles of the
war took place. General Read, Colonel Francis

Chap. ix. Washburn, and all the cavalry officers with Read
were killed and the rest captured; the Confederate loss was also heavy. Read's generous self-
sacrifice halted the Confederate army for several
hours. Longstreet lost the day at Rice's Station
waiting for Anderson, Ewell, and Gordon to unite
with him. They were engaged in a fruitless attempt to save their trains, which resulted, as we
have seen, in the almost total loss of the trains,
in the capture of Ewell's entire force, and in the
routing and shattering of the other commands.
The day's work was of incalculable value to the
National arms. Sheridan's unerring eye appreciated the full importance of it; his hasty report
ended with the words, "If the thing is pressed,
I think that Lee will surrender." Grant sent the
dispatch to President Lincoln, who instantly replied, "Let the thing be pressed."

Hum-
phreys,
" The
Virginia
Campaign
of '64 and
'65," p. 385.

Badeau,
"Military
History of
U. S.
Grant."
Vol. III.,
p. 581.

April, 1865.

In fact, after nightfall of the 6th Lee's army
could only flutter like a wounded bird with one wing
shattered; there was no longer any possibility of
escape. Yet General Lee found it hard to relin-
quish the illusions of years, and his valiant heart
still dreamed of evading the gathering toils and
forming somewhere a junction with Johnston and
indefinitely prolonging the war. As soon as night
had come down on the disastrous field of Sailor's
Creek, he again took up his weary march westward.
Longstreet marched for Farmville, crossed to the
north bank of the Appomattox, and on the 7th
moved out on the road which ran through Appomattox Court House to Lynchburg. His famishing
troops had found provisions at Farmville, and
with this refreshment marched with such celerity

that Grant and Sheridan, with all the energy they
could breathe into their subordinates, could not
head them off, or bring them to decisive battle that
day. Nevertheless the advance of the Union army
hung close upon the heels of the Confederates.
The rear corps under Gordon had burned the railroad bridge near Farmville behind them; but
General Barlow, sending his men forward at Apl. 7, 1865.
double-quick, saved the wagon bridge, and the
Second Corps crossed over without delay and continued the chase, Humphreys taking the northern
road, and sending Barlow by the railroad bed along
the river. Barlow overtook Gordon's rear, working
great destruction among his trains. Humphreys
came up with the main body shortly after noon,
and pressing them closely held them till evening,
expecting Barlow to join him, and Wright and
Crook to cross the river and attack from the south,
a movement which the swollen water and the destruction of the bridge prevented. General Irvin
Gregg's brigade had indeed succeeded in getting
over, but was attacked by an overwhelming force
of Confederate cavalry,— three divisions,— Gregg
being captured, and his brigade driven back. This
trivial success in the midst of unspeakable disaster
delighted General Lee. He said to his son, W. H.
F. Lee, "Keep your command together and in
good spirits, General; do not let it think of sur- J. E. Cooke,
"Life of
R. E. Lee,"
p. 455.
render. I will get you out of this."

But his inveterate optimism was not shared by
his subordinates. A number of his principal officers,
selecting General William N. Pendleton as their
spokesman, made known to him on the 7th their
belief that further resistance was useless, and

CHAP. IX.
Apl. 7, 1865. advised surrender. General Lee replied: "I trust it has not come to that. . . We have yet too many bold men to think of laying down our arms." Besides, he feared that if he made the first overtures for capitulation Grant would regard it as a confession of weakness, and demand unconditional surrender. But General Grant did not wish to drive a gallant antagonist to such extremes. On this same day, seeing how desperate was Lee's condition, and anxious to have an end of the now useless strife, he sent him this courteous and generous
Long, "Memoirs of R. E. Lee," p. 417.

Apl. 7, 1865. summons:

The results of the last week must convince you of the hopelessness of further resistance, on the part of the Army of Northern Virginia, in this struggle. I feel that it is so, and regard it as my duty to shift from myself the responsibility of any further effusion of blood, by asking of you the surrender of that portion of the Confederate States army known as the Army of Northern Virginia.
Grant, "Personal Memoirs." Vol. II., pp. 478, 479.

This letter was sent at night through Humphreys's lines to Lee, who at once answered: "Though not entertaining the opinion you express on the hopelessness of further resistance on the part of the Army of Northern Virginia, I reciprocate your desire to avoid useless effusion of blood, and therefore, before considering your proposition, ask the terms you will offer on condition of its surrender."
Ibid., p. 479.

The forlorn remnant of the Confederate army stole away in the night, on the desperate chance of finding food at Appomattox and a way of escape to Lynchburg, and at daybreak the hot pursuit was resumed by the Second and Sixth Corps. All this day the flight and chase continued, through a portion of Virginia never as yet wasted by the passage

of hostile armies. The air was sweet and pure, CHAP. IX.
scented by opening buds and the breath of spring;
the early peach trees were in flower; the sylvan by-
paths were slightly shaded by the pale-green foliage
of leafing trees. Through these quiet solitudes the
diminishing army of Lee plodded on, in the apa-
thetic obedience which is all there is left to brave
men when hope is gone, and behind them came the
victorious legions of Grant, inspired to the forget-
fulness of pain and fatigue by the stimulus of a
prodigious success. Sheridan, on the extreme left,
by unheard-of exertions, at last accomplished the
important task of placing himself squarely on Lee's
line of retreat. His advance, under George A.
Custer, captured, about sunset on the evening of
the 8th, Appomattox Station with four trains of April, 1865.
provisions, then attacked the rebel force advancing
from Farmville, and drove it towards the Court
House, taking twenty-five guns and many prisoners. A reconnaissance revealed the startling
fact that Lee's whole army was coming up the
road. Though he had nothing but cavalry, Sheridan, with undaunted courage, resolved to hold
the inestimable advantage he had gained, sending a request to Grant to hurry up the required
infantry support, saying that if Gibbon and Griffin
could get to him that night, they might "perhaps
finish the job in the morning." He added, with Badeau,
"Military
History of
U. S.
Grant."
Vol. III.,
p. 594.
singular prescience, referring to the negotiations
which had been opened, "I do not think Lee
means to surrender until compelled to do so."
This was strictly true. When Grant received
Lee's first letter he replied on the morning of the
8th, saying: "Peace being my great desire, there is

CHAP. IX. but one condition I would insist upon, namely, that the men and officers surrendered shall be disqualified from taking up arms again against the Government of the United States until properly exchanged. I will meet you, or will designate officers to meet any officers you may name for the same purpose, at any point agreeable to you, for the purpose of arranging definitely the terms upon which the surrender of the Army of Northern Virginia will be received."

Humphreys, "The Virginia Campaign of '64 and '65," p. 439.

But in the course of the day a last hope seemed to have come to Lee that he might yet reach Appomattox in safety and thence make his way to Lynchburg — a hope utterly fallacious, for Stoneman was now on the railroad near Lynchburg. He therefore, while giving orders to his subordinates to press with the utmost energy westward, answered General Grant's letter in a tone more ingenious than candid, reserving, while negotiations were

Apl. 8, 1865. going on, the chance of breaking away. He said:

I received at a late hour your note of to-day. In mine of yesterday I did not intend to propose the surrender of the Army of Northern Virginia, but to ask the terms of your proposition. To be frank, I do not think the emergency has arisen to call for the surrender of this army; but as the restoration of peace should be the sole object of all, I desired to know whether your proposals would lead to that end. I cannot, therefore, meet you with a view to surrender the Army of Northern Virginia; but as far as your proposal may affect the Confederate States forces under my command, and tend to the restoration of peace, I should be pleased to meet you at 10 A. M. to-morrow, on the old stage road to Richmond between the picket lines of the two armies.

Grant, "Personal Memoirs." Vol. II., p. 627.

Grant was not to be entrapped into a futile negotiation for the restoration of peace. He doubtless had in view the President's peremptory instructions

GENERAL FRANCIS C. BARLOW.

of the 3d of March, forbidding him to engage in any
political discussion or conference, or to entertain
any proposition except for the surrender of armies.
He therefore answered General Lee on the morning of the 9th of April with perfect courtesy, but
with unmistakable frankness, saying: "I have no
authority to treat on the subject of peace. The
meeting proposed for 10 A. M. to-day could lead to
no good. I will state, however, General, that I am
equally anxious for peace with yourself, and the
whole North entertains the same feeling. The terms
upon which peace can be had are well understood.
By the South laying down their arms they will hasten
that most desirable event, save thousands of human
lives and hundreds of millions of property not
yet destroyed. Seriously hoping that all our diffi-   Grant,
culties may be settled without the loss of another   "Personal Memoirs."
life, I subscribe myself, etc." He dispatched this   Vol. II., p. 627.
letter to Lee and then set off to the left, where
Sheridan was barring Lee's last avenue of escape.

It appears from General Lee's report, made three
days after the surrender, that he had no intention
on the night of the 8th of giving up the fight. He
ordered Fitz Lee, supported by Gordon, in the
morning " to drive the enemy from his front, wheel
to the left and cover the passage of the trains, while   Long,
Longstreet . . . should close up and hold the posi-   "Memoirs of
tion." He expected to find only cavalry on the   R. E. Lee," p. 694.
ground, and thought even his remnant of infantry
could break through Sheridan's horse while he
himself was amusing Grant with platonic discussions in the rear. But he received, on arriving at
the rendezvous he had suggested, not only Grant's
stern refusal to enter into a political negotiation,

but other intelligence which was to him the trump of doom. Ord and Griffin had made an almost incredible march of about thirty miles during the preceding day and night, and had come up at daylight to the post assigned them in support of Sheridan; and when Fitzhugh Lee and Gordon made their advance in the morning and the National cavalry fell slowly back, in obedience to their orders, there suddenly appeared before the amazed Confederates a formidable force of infantry filling the road, covering the adjacent hills and valley, and barring as with an adamantine wall the further progress of the army of the revolt. The marching of the Confederate army was over forever.

The appalling tidings were instantly carried to. Lee. He at once sent orders to cease hostilities, and, suddenly brought to a sense of his real situation, sent a note to Grant, asking an interview in accordance with the offer contained in Grant's letter of the 8th for the surrender of his army. Grant had created the emergency calling for such action. As Sheridan was about to charge on the huddled mass of astonished horse and foot in front of him a flag of truce was displayed, and the war was at an end. The Army of Northern Virginia was already captured. "I've got 'em, like that!" cried Sheridan, doubling up his fist, fearful of some ruse or evasion in the white flag. The Army of the Potomac on the north and east, Sheridan and Ord on the south and west, completely encircled the demoralized and crumbled army of Lee. There was not another day's fighting in them. That morning at three o'clock Gordon had sent word to Lee that he had fought his corps "to a frazzle," and could

Badeau,
"Military
History of
U. S.
Grant."
Vol. III.,
p. 601.

do nothing more unless heavily supported by Chap. IX. Longstreet. Lee and his army were prisoners of Long, "Memoirs of R. E. Lee," p. 421. war before he and Grant met at Appomattox.

The meeting took place at the house of Wilmer McLean, in the edge of the village. Lee met Grant at the threshold, and ushered him into a small and barely furnished parlor, where were soon assembled the leading officers of the National army. General Lee was accompanied only by his secretary, Colonel Charles Marshall. A short conversation led up to a request from Lee for the terms on which the surrender of his army would be received. Grant briefly stated the terms which would be accorded. Lee acceded to them, and Grant wrote the following Apl. 9, 1865. letter:

In accordance with the substance of my letter to you of the 8th inst., I propose to receive the surrender of the Army of Northern Virginia on the following terms, to wit: Rolls of all the officers and men to be made in duplicate; one copy to be given to an officer designated by me, the other to be retained by such officer or officers as you may designate. The officers to give their individual paroles not to take up arms against the Government of the United States until properly exchanged; and each company or regimental commander sign a like parole for the men of their commands. The arms, artillery, and public property to be parked and stacked, and turned over to the officer appointed by me to receive them. This will not embrace the side-arms of the officers, nor their private horses or baggage. This done, each officer and man will be allowed Facsimile of original MS. Grant, "Memoirs." Vol. II., p. 496. to return to their homes, not to be disturbed by United States authority so long as they observe their parole and the laws in force where they may reside.

General Grant says in his "Memoirs" that up to the moment when he put pen to paper he had not thought of a word that he should write. The terms he had verbally proposed, and which Lee had accepted, were soon put in writing, and there he might have stopped. But as he wrote, a feeling of sympathy for his gallant antagonist gradually came over him, and he added the extremely liberal terms with which his letter closed. The sight of Lee's sword, an especially fine one, suggested the paragraph allowing officers to retain their side-arms; and he ended with a phrase which he had evidently not thought of, and for which he had no authority, which practically pardoned and amnestied every man in Lee's army — a thing he had refused to consider the day before, and which had been expressly forbidden him in President Lincoln's order of the 3d of March.[1] Yet so great was the joy over the crowning victory, so deep was the gratitude of the Government and the people to Grant and his heroic army, that his terms were accepted as he wrote them, and his exercise of the Executive prerogative of pardon entirely overlooked. It must be noticed here, however, as a few days later it led the greatest of Grant's generals into a serious error.

Lee must have read the memorandum of terms with as much surprise as gratification. He said the permission for officers to retain their side-arms would have a happy effect. He then suggested and gained another important concession — that those of the cavalry and artillery who owned their own horses should be allowed to take them home to put in their crops. Lee wrote a brief reply accepting the

---

[1] The President, in his Amnesty Proclamation of December 8, 1863, expressly excepted officers above the rank of colonel, all who left seats in Congress to aid the rebellion, and all who resigned commissions in the army or navy of the United States and afterwards participated in the rebellion. The terms granted to General Lee's army at Appomattox practically extended amnesty to many persons in these classes.

terms. He then remarked that his army was in a CHAP. IX.
starving condition, and asked Grant to provide
them with subsistence and forage, to which he at Apl. 9, 1865.
once assented, and asked for how many men the
rations would be wanted. Lee answered, "About Grant, "Personal Memoirs." Vol. II., p. 495.
twenty-five thousand," and orders were at once
given to issue them. The number surrendered
turned out to be even larger than this. The paroles
signed amounted to 28,231. If we add to this the
captures at Five Forks, Petersburg, and Sailor's
Creek, the thousands who deserted the failing cause
at every by-road leading to their homes, and filled
every wood and thicket between Richmond and
Lynchburg, we can see how considerable an army
Lee commanded when Grant "started out gunning."
Yet every Confederate writer, speaker, and singer
who refers to the surrender says, and will say forever, that Lee surrendered only seven thousand
muskets.

With these brief and simple formalities one of
the most momentous transactions of modern times
was concluded. The news soon transpired, and the
Union gunners prepared to fire a National salute;
but Grant would not permit it. He forbade any
rejoicing over a fallen enemy, who he hoped would
hereafter be an enemy no longer. The next day he
rode to the Confederate lines to make a visit of
farewell to General Lee. Sitting on horseback be- Ibid., p. 497.
tween the lines, the two heroes of the war held a
friendly conversation. Lee considered the war at
an end, slavery dead, the National authority restored; Johnston must now surrender — the sooner
the better. Grant urged him to make a public appeal to hasten the return of peace; but Lee, true to

his ideas of subordination to a government which had ceased to exist, said he could not do this without consulting the Confederate President.   They parted with courteous good wishes, and Grant, without pausing to look at the city he had taken or the enormous system of works which had so long held him at bay, intent only upon reaping the peaceful results of his colossal victory, and putting an end to the waste and the burden of war, hurried away to Washington to do what he could for this practical and beneficent purpose.   He had done an inestimable service to the Republic : he had won immortal honor for himself ; but neither then nor at any subsequent period of his life was there any sign in his words or his bearing of the least touch of vainglory.   The day after Appomattox he was as simple, modest, and unassuming a citizen as he was the day before Sumter.

CHAPTER X

THE FALL OF THE REBEL CAPITAL

SINCE the visit of Blair and the return of the rebel commissioners from the Hampton Roads Conference, no event of special significance had excited the authorities or people of Richmond. February and March passed away in the routine of war and politics, which at the end of four years had become familiar and dull. To shrewd observers in that city things were going from bad to worse. Stephens, the Confederate Vice-President, had abandoned the capital and the cause and retired to Georgia to await the end. Judge John A. Campbell, though performing the duties of Assistant Secretary of War, made, among his intimate friends, no concealment of his opinion that the last days of the Confederacy had come. The members of the rebel Congress, adjourning after their long and fruitless winter session, gave many indications that they never expected to reassemble. A large part of their winter's work had been to demonstrate without direct accusation that it was the Confederate maladministration which was wrecking the Southern cause. On his part Jefferson Davis prolonged their session a week to send them his last message — a dry lecture to prove that the blame rested en-

CHAP. X.

1865.

Jones, "A Rebel War Clerk's Diary." Vol. II., p. 450.

tirely on their own shoulders. The last desperate measure of rebel statesmanship, the law to permit masters to put their slaves into the Southern armies to fight for the rebellion, was so palpably illogical and impracticable that both the rebel Congress and the rebel President appear to have treated it as the merest legislative rubbish; or else the latter would scarcely have written in the same message, after stating that "much benefit is anticipated from this measure," that "The people of the Confederacy can be but little known to him who supposes it possible they would ever consent to purchase, at the cost of degradation and slavery, permission to live in a country garrisoned by their own negroes, and governed by officers sent by the conqueror to rule over them."

Davis, Message, Mar. 13, 1865. "Annual Cyclopædia," 1865, pp. 718, 719.

Jefferson Davis was strongly addicted to political contradictions, but we must suppose even his cross-eyed philosophy capable of detecting that a negro willing to fight in slavery in preference to fighting in freedom was not a very safe reliance for Southern independence. The language as he employs it here fitly closes the continuous official Confederate wail about Northern subjugation, Northern despotism, Northern barbarity, Northern atrocity, and Northern inhumanity which rings through his letters, speeches, orders, messages, and proclamations with monotonous dissonance during his whole four years of authority.

Of all the Southern people none were quite so blinded as those of Richmond. Their little bubble of pride at being the Confederate capital was ever iridescent with the brightest hopes. They had no dream that the visible symbols of Confederate

GENERAL GEORGE A. CUSTER.

Government upon which their eyes had nourished
their faith would disappear almost as suddenly as
if an earthquake had swallowed them. Poverty,
distress, and desolation had indeed crept into their
homes, but the approach had been slow, and miti-
gated by the exaltations of a heroic self-sacrifice.

All accounts agree that when on Sunday morning, April 2, 1865, the people of Richmond went
forth to their places of worship, they had no
thought of imminent calamity. The ominous signs
of such a possibility had escaped their attention. A
few days before, Mrs. Jefferson Davis with her children had left Richmond for the South and sent a
part of her furniture to auction. So also several
weeks before, the horses remaining in the city had
been impressed to collect the tobacco into conve- Jones,
" A Rebel
War Clerk's
nient warehouses where it could be readily burned Diary."
Vol. II.,
to prevent its falling into Yankee hands. p. 438.

But the significance of these and perhaps other
indications could not be measured by the general
populace. In fact for some days a rather unusual
quiet had prevailed. That morning Jefferson Davis
was in his pew in St. Paul's Church when, before
the sermon was ended, an officer walked up the
aisle and handed him a telegram from General Lee
at Petersburg, dated at half-past ten that morning,
in which he read, "My lines are broken in three
places; Richmond must be evacuated this evening." He rose and left the church; whereupon
the officer handed the telegram to the rector, who
as speedily as possible brought the services to
a close, making the announcement that General
Ewell, the commander at Richmond, desired the
military forces to assemble at three o'clock in the

afternoon. The news seems also to have reached in some form one or two of the other churches, so that though no announcement of the fact was made, the city little by little became aware of the impending change.

The fact of its being Sunday, with no business going on and rest pervading every household, doubtless served to moderate the shock to the public. Yet very soon the scene was greatly transformed. From the Sabbath stillness of the morning the streets became alive with bustle and activity. Jefferson Davis had called his Cabinet and officials together, and the hurried packing of the Confederate archives for shipment was soon in progress. Citizens who had the means made hasty preparations for flight; the far greater number who were compelled to stay were in a flutter to devise measures of protection or concealment. The banks were opened and depositors flocked thither to withdraw their money and valuables. A remnant of the Virginia Legislature gathered in the Representatives' Hall at the Capitol to debate a question of greater urgency than had ever before taxed their wisdom or eloquence. In another room sat the municipal council, for once impressed with the full weight of its responsibility. Meanwhile the streets were full of hurrying people, of loaded wagons, of galloping military officers conveying orders.

One striking sketch of that wild hurry-skurry deserves to be recorded. "Lumkin, who for many years had kept a slave-trader's jail, also had a work of necessity on hand—fifty men, women, and children, who must be saved to the missionary institution for the future enlightenment of Africa.

Although it was the Lord's day (perhaps he was CHAP. X. comforted by the thought that 'the better the day the better the deed') the coffle-gang was made Apl. 2, 1865. up in the jail-yard, within pistol shot of Davis's parlor window, within a stone's throw of the Monumental Church, and a sad and weeping throng, chained two and two, the last slave-coffle that shall ever tread the streets of Richmond, were hurried "Atlantic to the Danville depot." But the "institution," like Monthly," June, 1865. the Confederacy, was already *in extremis*. The account adds that the departing trains could afford no transportation for this last slave cargo, and the gang went to pieces, like every other Richmond organization, military and political.

Evening had come, and the confusion of the streets found its culmination at the railroad depots. Military authority made room for the fleeing President and his Cabinet, and department officials and their boxes of more important papers. The cars were overcrowded and overloaded long before the clamoring multitude and piles of miscellaneous baggage could be got aboard, and by the occasional light of lanterns flitting hither and thither the wheezing and coughing trains moved out into the darkness. The Legislature of Virginia and the Governor of the State departed in a canal boat towards Lynchburg. All available vehicles carrying fugitives were leaving the city by various country roads, but the great mass of the population, unable to get away, had to confront the dread certainty that only one night remained before the appearance of a hostile army with the power of death and destruction over them and their homes.

How this power might be exercised, present
signs were none too reassuring. Since noon, when
the fact of evacuation had become certain, the
whole fabric of society seemed to be crumbling to
pieces. Military authority was concentrating its
energy on only two objects, destruction and departure. The civil authority was lending a hand,
for the single hasty precaution which the city
council could ordain was that all the liquors in the
city should be emptied out. To order this was one
thing, to have it rigorously executed would be asking quite too much of the lower human appetites,
and while some of the street gutters ran with alcohol,
enough was surreptitiously consumed to produce a
frightful state of excitement and drunkenness. No
picture need be drawn of the possibilities of violence
and crime which must have haunted the timid
watchers in Richmond who listened all night to the
shouts, the blasphemy, the disorder that rose and
fell in the streets, or who furtively noted the signs
of pillage already begun. And how shall we follow
their imagination, passing from these acts of the
friends of yesterday to what they might look for
from the enemies expected to-morrow? And
there was that final horror of horrors, the negro
soldiers, held up to their dread by the presidential message of Jefferson Davis only two weeks
before! What now of the fear of servile insurrection, the terrible specter they had secretly
nursed from their very childhood? It is scarcely
possible they can have escaped such meditations
even though already weary and exhausted with the
surprises and labors of the day, with the startling
anxieties of the evening, with the absorbing care of

burying their household silver and secreting their
yet more precious personal ornaments and tokens of
affection.   In Europe, a thousand wars have rendered such experiences historically commonplace;
in America, let us hope that a thousand years of
peace may render their repetition impossible.

Full of dangerous portent as had been the night,
the morning became yet more ominous.   Long before day sleepers and watchers alike were startled
by a succession of explosions which shook every
building.   The military authorities were blowing
up the vessels in construction at the river.   These
were nine in number, three of them ironclads of
four guns each, the others small wooden ships.[1]
Next, the arsenal was fired; and, as many thousands of loaded shells were stored here, there succeeded for a period the sounds of a continuous
cannonade.   Already fire had been set to the warehouses containing the collected tobacco and cotton,
among which loaded shells had also been scattered
to insure more complete destruction.

There is a conflict of testimony as to who is responsible for the deplorable public calamity which
ensued.   The rebel Congress had passed a law
ordering the Government tobacco and other public
property to be burned, and Jefferson Davis states
that the general commanding had advised with the
mayor and city authorities about precautions
against a conflagration.   On the other hand, Lieu-

---

[1] "The following is a list of the vessels destroyed: *Virginia*, flagship, ironclad, four guns; *Richmond*, ironclad, four guns; *Fredericksburg*, ironclad, four guns; *Nansemond*, wooden, two guns; *Hampton*, wooden, two guns; *Roanoke*, wooden, one gun; *Torpedo*, tender; *Shrapnel*; *Patrick Henry*, school-ship." — Porter, Report, April 5, 1865. Report, Secretary of the Navy, 1865-66.

tenant-General Ewell, the military commander, has authorized the statement that he not only earnestly warned the city authorities of the certain consequences of the measure, but that he took the responsibility of disobeying the law and military orders. " I left the city about seven o'clock in the morning," he writes; " as yet nothing had been fired by my orders; yet the buildings and depot near the railway bridge were on fire, and the flames were so close as to be disagreeable as I rode by them." [1] By this time the spirit of lawlessness and hunger for pillage had gained full headway. The rear guard of the retreating Confederates set the three great bridges in flames, and while the fire started at the four immense warehouses and various points, and soon uniting in an uncontrollable conflagration was beginning to eat out the heart of the city, a miscellaneous mob went from store to store, and with a beam for a battering ram smashed in the

[1] The full report of these occurrences, written by General Ewell, seems never to have been printed.

Lossing, writing from both the written statement and verbal explanations of General Ewell, says: " General Ewell earnestly warned the city authorities of the danger of acting according to the letter of that resolution; for a brisk wind was blowing from the south which would send the flames of the burning warehouses into the town and imperil the whole city. Early in the evening a deputation of citizens called upon President Davis and remonstrated against carrying out that order of Congress, because the safety of the city would be jeopardized. He was then in an unamiable state of mind, and curtly replied, ' Your statement that the burning of the warehouses will endanger the city is only a cowardly pretext to save your property for the Yankees!' After Davis's departure a committee of the city council, at the suggestion of General Ewell, went to the War Office to remonstrate with whomsoever might represent the department, against the execution of the perilous order. Major Melton rudely replied in language which was almost an echo of that of his superior, and General Ewell, in spite of his earnest remonstrances, was ordered to cause the four warehouses near the river to be set on fire at three o'clock in the morning."— Lossing, in "The Independent " (New York), March 11, 1886.

doors so that the crowd might freely enter and plunder the contents. This rapacity, first directed towards bread and provision stores, gradually extended itself to all other objects until mere greed of booty rather than need or usefulness became the ruling instinct, and promoted the waste and destruction of that which had been stolen.

Into this pandemonium of fire and license there came one additional terror to fill up its dramatic completeness. "About ten o'clock," writes an eyewitness, "just before the entrance of the Federal army, a cry of dismay rang all along the streets which were out of the track of the fire, and I saw a crowd of leaping, shouting demons, in party-colored clothes, and with heads half shaven. It was the convicts from the penitentiary, who had overcome the guard, set fire to the prison, and were now at liberty. Many a heart which had kept its courage to this point quailed at the sight. Fortunately, they were too intent upon securing their freedom to do much damage."

It is quite probable that the magnitude and rapidity of the disaster served in a measure to mitigate its evil results. The burning of seven hundred buildings, comprising the entire business portion of Richmond, warehouses, manufactories, mills, depots, and stores, all within the brief space of a day, was a visitation so sudden, so unexpected, so stupefying as to overawe and terrorize even wrong-doers, and made the harvest of plunder so abundant as to serve to scatter the mob and satisfy its rapacity to quick repletion.

Before a new hunger could arise, assistance, protection, and relief were at hand. The Mayor and

CHAP. X.

Apl. 3, 1865.

Mary Tucker Magill, in "The Independent" (New York), Jan. 7, 1886.

citizens' committee who went forth met General Weitzel a little before seven o'clock in the morning, near Gilliss Creek, outside the limits of Richmond, where a detachment of Union pickets, numbering sixty or seventy men, under command of Lieutenant Royal B. Prescott had also arrived. Here an informal surrender took place, a ceremony which was repeated with more formality in the capital at a later hour. This incident over, the general and his staff proceeded into the city, followed by Lieutenant Prescott and his force, and preceded by a squad of the general's orderlies [1] from the Fourth Massachusetts Cavalry, commanded by Major A. H. Stevens, and established headquarters in the house lately occupied by Jefferson Davis. Lieutenant Prescott reached Capitol Square soon after seven o'clock; at that hour there was no flag flying, but Major Stevens soon arrived and hoisted two cavalry guidons over the State House. [2] Mean-

S. M. Thompson, "Thirteenth Regiment New Hampshire Volunteer Infantry," p. 559.

[1] We here use General Weitzel's phrase in a letter to Horace Greeley, dated March 9, 1869; but T. Thatcher Graves, M. D., of Providence, R. I., has written a long and interesting narrative of the event, in which he says: "As soon as it was light General Weitzel ordered Colonel E. E. Graves, senior aide-de-camp, and Major Atherton H. Stevens, Jr., Provost Marshal, to take a detachment of forty men from the two companies of the Fourth Massachusetts Cavalry (white) attached to our headquarters, and . . . press forward towards Richmond on a reconnaissance."

It may have been this force, or a part of it, which General Weitzel's letter designates as "a squad of my orderlies."

[2] Dr. Graves's MS. narrative says "Colonel Graves and Major Stevens each took a guidon and ascended to the roof of the Capitol, and, hauling down the Confederate flag," they proceeded to hoist theirs upon the Capitol.

Lieutenant Prescott relates that no flag was flying over the Capitol when he entered the grounds, but that one suddenly appeared on the roof, raised by a colored boy of seventeen, named Richard G. Forrester, who stated he had been a page or errand boy employed in the Capitol; also that it was a flag used before the ordinance of secession, but which the secessionists then took down and threw among rubbish under the roof of the building. He further stated that he had carried it

GENERAL JOHN GIBBON.

while, from the meeting at Gilliss Creek, and probably on information gathered from the Mayor,
General Weitzel had sent an aide back ·" with
orders to get the first brigade he could find, and
bring it in to act as provost guard." This proved
to be General E. H. Ripley's brigade of General
Charles Devens's division of the Twenty-fourth
Army Corps. The brigade was headed by General
Devens, with the Thirteenth New Hampshire Volunteers as its leading regiment, and marched into
the city with colors flying and bands playing,
reaching the Capitol grounds a little after eight
o'clock; from where the force was sent in various
directions on the urgent duties of the hour.

Soon afterward there occurred what was to the
inhabitants the central incident of the day — the
event which engrossed their solicitude even more

Chap. X.

Weitzel,
Testimony.
Report
Committee
on Conduct
of the War,
1864-65.
Part I.,
pp. 522, 523.

Col. G. A.
Bruce
to the
Authors,
Dec. 14,
1889. MS.

Apl. 3, 1865.

home, concealed it, and that —
"when I saw you 'uns comin'"
— he drew the old flag from its
hiding place, and ran to the Capitol and raised it. Whether this
was an old Union flag, a Virginia
State flag, or some early form
of Confederate flag, is left in
doubt.

As a continuation of the incidents of the flag raising, we also
quote from a letter written us by
Loomis L. Langdon, Colonel First
Artillery U. S. A., who, after
mentioning the two cavalry guidons hoisted by Major Stevens,
continues:

"Some hours after that, without my personally knowing then
of Major Stevens's movements,
my artillery began the march to
Richmond, then almost in sight.
As chief of artillery of the
Twenty-fifth Corps, I rode with

General Weitzel. On the way to
the city young Johnston Livingston De Peyster rode alongside
of me, and during a conversation
showed me a flag he had attached
to his saddle, and as we neared
the city he invited me to go to the
roof of the State House and hoist
the flag with him. Together we
passed through the Senate Chamber and up some dark passages, in
which the gas jets were still burning, and got on the roof. . . The
wind blew a hurricane. After a
good deal of trouble we 'bent' on
our flag, but found our progress
impeded by something bulky at
the top of the flagstaff. This we
pulled down, and the bulky object
proved to be two cavalry guidons
(U. S. flags) belonging to the
Fourth Massachusetts Cavalry,
which Major Stevens had
hoisted."

Letter
dated
Feb. 24,
1890.

than the vanished rebel government, the destroyed city, or the lost cause. General Weitzel's direction calling in the provost guard had been accompanied by another that all the rest of his troops should remain outside the city to take possession of the inner line of redoubts. This second order, however, failed to reach the Fifth Massachussets Cavalry, a colored regiment under command of Colonel Charles Francis Adams, posted on the extreme right of the Union line, who instead obeyed an earlier request from General Devens to advance into the city; and this colored regiment therefore, led by a grandson of President John Quincy Adams, shared with the six white regiments of General Ripley's brigade the honor of a march into the rebel capital on the day of its surrender. The arrival of these colored soldiers was to the people of Richmond the visible realization of the new order to which four years of rebellion and war had brought them. The prejudices of a lifetime cannot be instantly overcome, and the rebels of Richmond doubtless felt that this was the final drop in their cup of misery and that their "subjugation" was complete.

It is related that about this time, as by a common impulse, the white people of Richmond disappeared from the streets, and the black population streamed forth with an apparently instinctive recognition that their day of jubilee had at last arrived. To see this compact, organized body of men of their own color, on horseback, in neat uniforms, with flashing sabers, with the gleam of confidence and triumph in their eyes, was a palpable living reality to which their hope and pride, long repressed, gave instant response. They greeted them with expressions of welcome in every form — cheers, shouts, laughter, and a rattle of exclamations—as they rushed along the sides of the streets to keep pace with the advancing column and feast their eyes on the incredible sight; while the black Union soldiers rose high in their stirrups and with waving swords and deafening huzzas acknowledged the fraternal reception.

But there was little time for holiday enjoyment. The conflagration was roaring, destruction was advancing; fury of fire, blackness of smoke, crash of falling walls, obstruction of débris, confusion, helplessness, danger, seemed everywhere. The great Capitol Square on the hill had become the refuge of women and children and the temporary storing-place of the few household effects they had saved from the burning. From this center, where the Stars and Stripes again floated, there now flowed back upon the stricken city, not the doom and devastation for which its people looked, but the friendly help and protection of a generous army bringing them peace, and the spirit of a benevolent Government tendering them forgiveness and reconciliation. Up to this time it would seem that not an organization had been proposed and but feeble efforts made to stay the ravages of the flames. The public spirit of Richmond was crushed by the awful catastrophe.

The advent of the Union army breathed a new life into this social paralysis. The first care of the officers was to organize resistance to fire, to reëstablish order and personal security, and convert the unrestrained mob of whites and blacks into a regulated energy, to save what remained of the city from the needless burning and pillage to which its own friends had devoted it, against remonstrance and against humanity. And this was not all. Begin-

ning that afternoon and continuing many days, these "Yankee invaders" fed the poor of Richmond, and saved them from the starvation to which the law of the Confederate Congress, relentlessly executed by the Confederate President and some of his subordinates, exposed them.

CHAPTER XI

A LITTLE more than two months before these events, President Lincoln had written to General Grant: "Please read and answer this letter as though I was not President, but only a friend. My son, now in his twenty-second year, having graduated at Harvard, wishes to see something of the war before it ends. I do not wish to put him in the ranks, nor yet to give him a commission, to which those who have already served long are better entitled, and better qualified to hold. Could he, without embarrassment to you, or detriment to the service, go into your military family with some nominal rank, I, and not the public, furnishing his necessary means? If no, say so without the least hesitation, because I am as anxious and as deeply interested that you shall not be encumbered as you can be yourself."

Grant replied as follows: "Your favor of this date in relation to your son serving in some military capacity is received. I will be most happy to have him in my military family in the manner you propose. The nominal rank given him is immaterial, but I would suggest that of captain, as I have three staff-officers now, of considerable service, in

CHAP. XI.

Lincoln to Grant, Jan. 19, 1865. MS.

CHAP. XI. no higher grade. Indeed, I have one officer with only the rank of lieutenant who has been in the service from the beginning of the war. This, however will make no difference, and I would still say give the rank of captain.— Please excuse my writ-Grant to Lincoln, Jan. 21, 1865. MS. ing on a half sheet. I have no resource but to take the blank half of your letter." The President's son therefore became a member of Grant's staff with the rank of captain, and acquitted himself of the duties of that station with fidelity and honor.

We may assume that it was the anticipated important military events rather than the presence of Captain Robert T. Lincoln at Grant's headquarters which induced the General on the 20th of March, 1865, to invite the President and Mrs. Lincoln to make a visit to his camp near Richmond; and on the 22d they and their younger son Thomas, nicknamed "Tad," proceeded in the steamer *River Queen* from Washington to City Point, where General Grant with his family and staff were "occupying a pretty group of huts on the bank of the James River, overlooking the harbor, which was full of vessels of all classes, both war and merchant, Sherman, "Memoirs." Vol. II., p. 324. with wharves and warehouses on an extensive scale." Here, making his home on the steamer which brought him, the President remained about ten days, enjoying what was probably the most satisfactory relaxation in which he had been able to indulge during his whole Presidential service. It was springtime and the weather was moderately steady; his days were occupied visiting the various camps of the great army in company with the General.

"He was a good horseman," records a member of CHAP. XI.
the General's staff, "and made his way through
swamps and over corduroy roads as well as the
best trooper in the command. The soldiers invari-
ably recognized him and greeted him, wherever he Gen.
Horace
Porter,
in "The
Century
Magazine,"
Oct., 1885.
appeared amongst them, with cheers that were no
lip service, but came from the depth of their
hearts." Many evening hours were passed with
groups of officers before roaring camp-fires, where
Mr. Lincoln was always the magnetic center of
genial conversation and lively anecdote. The interest of the visit was further enhanced by the
arrival at City Point, on the evening of March 27, 1865.
of General Sherman, who, having left General
Schofield to command in his absence, made a hasty
trip to confer with Grant. He was able to gratify
the President with a narrative of the leading incidents of his great march from Atlanta to Savannah
and from Savannah to Goldsboro', North Carolina.
In one or two informal interviews in the after cabin
of the *River Queen*, Lincoln, Grant, Sherman, and
Rear-Admiral Porter enjoyed a frank interchange
of opinion about the favorable prospects of early
and final victory, and of the speedy realization of
the long hoped for peace. Sherman and Porter
affirm that the President confided to them certain
liberal views on the subject of reconstructing State
governments in the conquered States which do not
seem compatible with the very guarded language
of Mr. Lincoln elsewhere used or recorded by him.
It is fair to presume that their own enthusiasm
colored their recollection of the President's expressions, though it is no doubt true that he spoke of
his willingness to be liberal to the verge of prudence,

and that he even gave them to understand that he would not be displeased at the escape from the country of Jefferson Davis and other principal rebel leaders.

On the 29th of March the party separated, Sherman returning to North Carolina, and Grant starting on his final campaign to Appomattox. Five days later Grant informed Mr. Lincoln of the fall of Petersburg, and on his request the President made a flying visit to that town for another brief conference with the General. Here, also, amid the wildest enthusiasm, the President again reviewed the victorious regiments of Grant, marching through Petersburg in pursuit of Lee. The capture of Richmond was hourly expected, and that welcome information reached Lincoln after his return to City Point.

Between the receipt of this news and the following forenoon, but before any information of the great fire had been received, a visit to Richmond was arranged for the President and Admiral Porter.[1] Ample precautions were taken at the start; the President went in the *River Queen* with her escort the *Bat;* Admiral Porter went in his flagship, the *Malvern;* the transport *Columbus* carried a small cavalry escort and ambulances for the party. A tug used at City Point to convey the President to and from the landing to the *River*

---

[1] Since this chapter appeared in serial form, Major C. B. Penrose, U. S. A., who was detailed by Secretary Stanton to accompany President Lincoln on his visit, has permitted the editor of "The Century Magazine," to print in the June number, 1890, a copy of the skeleton diary he kept at the time, from which we have been able to fill up the historical narrative with much greater accuracy. The authors are also indebted to Major Penrose for much additional information.

GENERAL GODFREY WEITZEL.

Queen at her anchorage in the harbor, also went along. The little flotilla steamed cautiously up the James River beyond Drewry's Bluff, distant twenty-eight to thirty miles from City Point by the very tortuous windings of the river. Some distance above Drewry's Bluff the rebels had obstructed the stream by formidable rows of piling, leaving only a small passage which they could easily close if necessary.

Arriving at these obstructions, the further progress of the larger vessels was for the moment found impossible. Admiral Farragut visited Richmond immediately after its fall; and on this morning of April 4 came down from that city to meet the President, on the rebel flag-of-truce boat *Allison*, which had escaped destruction. By an accident to her machinery the *Allison* had swung across the opening in the piles, and was held in place by the current. Instead of patiently waiting until she could be moved, it was resolved to proceed without the vessels. The Presidential party was transferred to the twelve-oared barge of Admiral Porter; a guard of twenty or thirty marines was put aboard the tug, and the tug, taking the barge in tow, managed to pass through the opening in the piles partly obstructed by the *Allison*. But when the obstructions had been passed, the President insisted that the tug should return and help the *Allison* out of her difficulty. In doing this, the tug got aground, and the mishap left the party no alternative but to proceed in the barge, rowed by the Admiral's twelve sailors, without other escort of any kind; and in this manner the President traversed the remaining distance to Richmond. No

accident befell them; they passed the suburb of
Rockett's and proceeded to the neighborhood of the
Manchester Bridge, effecting a landing one square
above Libby Prison, where there was neither officer,
nor wagon, nor escort to meet and receive them.

Never in the history of the world did the head
of a mighty nation and the conqueror of a great
rebellion enter the captured chief city of the insurgents in such humbleness and simplicity. As
the party stepped from the barge, they found a
guide among the contrabands who quickly crowded
the streets; for the probable coming of the President had been circulated through the city. Ten of
the sailors, armed with carbines, were formed as a
guard, six in front and four in rear, and between
these the party, consisting of the President, Admiral Porter, Captain C. B. Penrose of the Army,
Captain A. H. Adams of the Navy, and Lieutenant
W. W. Clemens of the Signal Corps, placed themselves, all being on foot; and in this order the improvised street procession walked a distance of
perhaps a mile and a half to the center of Richmond. It was a long and fatiguing march, the
probability of which had not been foreseen at
starting. We quote from a private letter of Captain Penrose, written on April 10, 1865, a vivid
description of its attendant scenes:

"On Tuesday we started for Richmond, and
arrived there just thirty-six hours after Jefferson
Davis had left. Here again was a perfect ovation
of blacks and poor whites. The boat with our escort ran aground, so we pulled up to the city in
Admiral Porter's barge. When we arrived, there
was a rush for the President, and as we had but

ten sailors as a guard, and had to walk over a mile
and a half to headquarters, it seemed foolhardy in
the President to go. However we went through
without accident; but I never passed a more anxious time than in this walk. In going up (and we
were amongst the very first boats) we ran the risk of
torpedoes and the obstructions; but I think the risk
the President ran in going through the streets of
Richmond was even greater, and shows him to have
great courage. The streets of the city were filled
with drunken rebels, both officers and men, and all
was confusion. . . A large portion of the city was
still on fire."

The imagination may easily fill up the picture of
a gradually increasing crowd, principally of negroes,
following the little group of marines and officers
with the tall form of the President in its center;
and, having learned that it was indeed Mr. Lincoln,
giving expression to wonder, joy, and gratitude in
a variety of picturesque emotional ejaculations
peculiar to the colored race, and for which there
was ample time while the little procession made its
tiresome march, whose route cannot now be traced.

At length the party reached the headquarters of
General Weitzel, established in the very house
occupied by Jefferson Davis as the Presidential
mansion of the Confederacy, and from which he
had fled less than two days before. Here Mr. Lincoln was glad of a chance to sit down and rest,
and a little later to partake of refreshments which
the general provided. An informal reception,
chiefly of Union officers, naturally followed, and
later in the afternoon General Weitzel went with
the President and Admiral Porter in a carriage,

CHAP. XI. guarded by an escort of cavalry, to visit the Capitol, the burnt district, Libby Prison, Castle Thunder, and other points of interest about the city; and of Apl. 4, 1865. this afternoon drive also no narrative in detail by an eye-witness appears to have been written at the time.

It was probably before the President went on this drive that there occurred an interview on political topics which forms one of the chief points of interest connected with his visit. Judge John A. Campbell, rebel Assistant Secretary of War, remained in Richmond when on Sunday night the other members of the Confederate Government fled, and on Tuesday morning he reported to the Union military governor, General G. F. Shepley, and informed him of his "submission to the military Campbell, authorities." Learning from General Shepley that Pamphlet. Mr. Lincoln was at City Point, he asked permission to see him. This application was evidently communicated to Mr. Lincoln, for shortly after his arrival a staff-officer informed Campbell that the requested interview would be granted, and conducted him to the President at the general's headquarters, where it took place. The rebel general J. R. Anderson and others were present as friends of the judge, and General Weitzel as the witness of Mr. Lincoln. Campbell, as spokesman, "told the President that the war was over," and made inquiries about the measures and conditions necessary to secure peace. Speaking for Virginia, he "urged him to consult and counsel with her public men, and her citizens, as to the restoration of peace, civil order, and the renewal of her relations as a member of the Ibid. Union."

In his pamphlet, written from memory long afterwards, Campbell states that Mr. Lincoln replied "that my general principles were right, the trouble was how to apply them"; and no conclusion was reached except to appoint another interview for the following day on board the *Malvern*. This second interview was accordingly held on Wednesday, April 5, Campbell taking with him only a single citizen of Richmond, as the others to whom he sent invitations were either absent from the city or declined to accompany him. General Weitzel was again present as a witness. The conversation apparently took a wide range on the general topic of restoring local governments in the South, in the course of which the President gave Judge Campbell a written memorandum,[1] embracing an outline of

CHAP. XI.

1865.

[1] "As to peace, I have said before, and now repeat, that three things are indispensable:

"1. The restoration of the national authority throughout the United States.

"2. No receding by the Executive of the United States on the slavery question from the position assumed thereon in the late annual message, and in preceding documents.

"3. No cessation of hostilities short of an end of the war, and the disbanding of all forces hostile to the Government. That all propositions coming from those now in hostility to the Government, not inconsistent with the foregoing, will be respectfully considered and passed upon in a spirit of sincere liberality.

"I now add that it seems useless for me to be more specific with those who will not say that they are ready for the indispensable terms, even on conditions to be named by themselves. If there be any who are ready for these indispensable terms, on any conditions whatever, let them say so, and state their conditions, so that the conditions can be known and considered. It is further added, that the remission of confiscation being within the executive power, if the war be now further persisted in by those opposing the Government, the making of confiscated property at the least to bear the additional cost will be insisted on, but that confiscations (except in case of third party intervening interests) will be remitted to the people of any State which shall now promptly and in good faith withdraw its troops from further resistance to the Government. What is now said as to the remission of confiscation has no reference to supposed property in slaves."

President Lincoln, Memorandum printed in Campbell Pamphlet, pp. 9, 10.

conditions of peace which repeated in substance
the terms he had proffered the rebel commissioners
(of whom Campbell was one) at the Hampton
Roads Conference on the 3d of February, 1865.
The only practical suggestion which was made has
been summarized as follows by General Weitzel in
a statement written from memory, as the result of
the two interviews : " Mr. Campbell and the other
gentlemen assured Mr. Lincoln that if he would
allow the Virginia Legislature to meet, it would at
once repeal the ordinance of secession, and that
then General Robert E. Lee and every other Virginian would submit ; that this would amount to
the virtual destruction of the Army of Northern
Virginia, and eventually to the surrender of all
Weitzel,
in " Phila-
delphia
Times." the other rebel armies, and would insure perfect
peace in the shortest possible time."

Out of this second conference, which also ended
without result, President Lincoln thought he saw
an opportunity to draw an immediate and substan-
1865. tial military benefit. On the next day (April 6) he
wrote from City Point, where he had returned, the
following letter to General Weitzel, which he immediately transmitted to the general by the hand
of Senator Morton S. Wilkinson, in whose presence
he wrote it, and who was on his way from City
Point to Richmond :

It has been intimated to me that the gentlemen who
have acted as the Legislature of Virginia in support of
the rebellion may now desire to assemble at Richmond,
and take measures to withdraw the Virginia troops and
other support from resistance to the General Government.
If they attempt it, give them permission and protection,
until, if at all, they attempt some action hostile to the
United States, in which case you will notify them, give

them reasonable time to leave, and at the end of which time arrest any who remain. Allow Judge Campbell to see this, but do not make it public.

CHAP. XI.

Lincoln to Weitzel, April 6, 1865. Weitzel, Testimony, Report of Committee on Conduct of the War, 1864-65. Part I., p. 521.

This document bears upon its face the distinct military object which the President had in view in permitting the rebel Legislature to assemble, namely, to withdraw immediately the Virginia troops from the army of Lee, then on its retreat towards Lynchburg. It could not be foreseen that Lee would surrender the whole of that army within the next three days, though it was evident that the withdrawal of the Virginia forces from it, under whatever pretended State authority, would contribute to the ending of the war quite as effectually as the reduction to an equal extent of that army by battle or capture. The ground upon which Lincoln believed the rebel Legislature might take this action is set forth in his dispatch to Grant of the same date, in which he wrote:

Secretary Seward was thrown from his carriage yesterday and seriously injured. This with other matters will take me to Washington soon. I was at Richmond yesterday and the day before, when and where Judge Campbell, who was with Messrs. Hunter and Stephens in February, called on me, and made such representations as induced me to put in his hands an informal paper repeating the propositions in my letter of instructions to Mr. Seward, which you remember, and adding "that if the war be now further persisted in by the rebels, confiscated property shall at the least bear the additional cost, and that confiscation shall be remitted to the people of any State which will now promptly and in good faith withdraw its troops and other support from the resistance to the Government." Judge Campbell thought it not impossible that the rebel legislature of Virginia would do the latter, if permitted, and accordingly I ad-

CHAP. XI. dressed a private letter to General Weitzel, with permission for Judge Campbell to see it, telling him (General W.) that if they attempt this to permit and protect them, unless they attempt something hostile to the United States, in which case to give them notice and time to leave, and to arrest any remaining after such time. I do not think it very probable that anything will come of this, but I have thought best to notify you, so that if you should see signs you may understand them. From your recent dispatches, it seems that you are pretty effectually withdrawing the Virginia troops from opposition to the Government. Nothing that I have done, or probably shall do, is to delay, hinder, or interfere with your work.

Lincoln to
Grant,
April 6, 1865.

That Mr. Lincoln well understood the temper of leading Virginians when he wrote that he had little hope of any result from the permission he had given is shown by what followed. When, on the morning of April 7, General Weitzel received the President's letter of the 6th, he showed it confidentially to Judge Campbell, who thereupon called together a committee, apparently five in number, of the Virginia rebel Legislature, and instead of informing them precisely what Lincoln had authorized, namely, a meeting to "take measures to withdraw the Virginia troops and other support from resistance to the General Government," the judge in a letter to the committee (dated April 7) formulated quite a different line of action.

1865.

I have had, since the evacuation of Richmond, two conversations with Mr. Lincoln, President of the United States. . . The conversations had relation to the establishment of a government for Virginia, the requirement of oaths of allegiance from the citizens, and the terms of settlement with the United States. With the concurrence and sanction of General Weitzel he assented to the application not to require oaths of allegiance from the citizens.

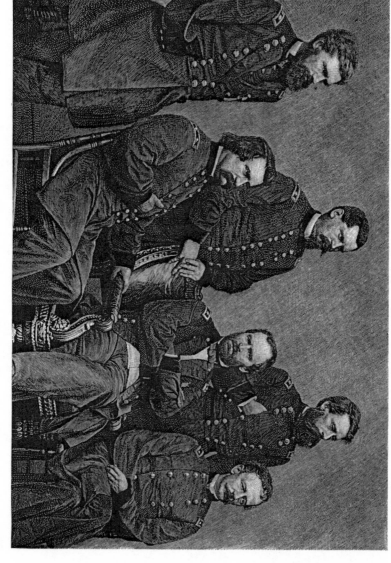

GENERAL O. O. HOWARD.   GENERAL W. B. HAZEN.   GENERAL W. T. SHERMAN.   GENERAL H. W. SLOCUM.
GENERAL JOHN A. LOGAN.   GENERAL JEFF C. DAVIS.

He stated that he would send to General Weitzel his de- CHAP. XI.
cision upon the question of a government for Virginia.
This letter was received on Thursday, and was read by
me. . . The object of the invitation is for the government
of Virginia to determine whether they will administer the Apl. 7, 1865.
laws in connection with the authorities of the United
States. I understand from Mr. Lincoln, if this condition
be fulfilled, that no attempt would be made to establish Campbell,
Pamphlet.
or sustain any other authority.

The rest of Campbell's long letter related to safe-
conducts, to transportation, and to the contents
of the written memorandum handed by Lincoln to
him at the interview on the *Malvern* about general
conditions of peace. But this memorandum contained no syllable of reference to the "government
of Virginia," and bore no relation of any kind to
the President's permission to "take measures to
withdraw the Virginia troops," except its promise
"that confiscations (except in case of third party
intervening interests) will be remitted to the people
of any State which shall now promptly and in good
faith withdraw its troops from further resistance to
the Government." Going a step further, the committee next prepared a call inviting a meeting of
the General Assembly, announcing the consent of
"the military authorities of the United States to
the session of the legislature in Richmond," and
stating that "The matters to be submitted to the
legislature are the restoration of peace to the State
of Virginia, and the adjustment of questions involving life, liberty, and property that have arisen
in the States as a consequence of the war." When Ibid.
General Weitzel indorsed his approval on the call
"for publication in the 'Whig' and in hand-bill
form," he does not seem to have read, or if he

read, to have realized, how completely President Lincoln's permission had been changed and his authority perverted. Instead of permitting them to recall Virginia soldiers, Weitzel was about to allow them authoritatively to sit in judgment on all the political consequences of the war "in the States."

General Weitzel's approval was signed to the call on April 11, and it was published in the "Richmond Whig" on the morning of the 12th. On that day the President, having returned to Washington, was at the War Department writing an answer to a dispatch from General Weitzel, in which the general defended himself against the Secretary's censure for having neglected to require from the churches in Richmond prayers for the President of the United States similar to those which prior to the fall of the city had been offered up in their religious services in behalf of "the rebel chief, Jefferson Davis, before he was driven from the capital." Weitzel contended that the tone of President Lincoln's conversations with him justified the omission. Mr. Lincoln was never punctilious about social or official etiquette towards himself, and he doubtless felt in this instance that neither his moral nor political well-being was seriously dependent upon the prayers of the Richmond rebel churches. To this part of the general's dispatch he therefore answered: "I have seen your dispatches to Colonel Hardie about the matter of prayers. I do not remember hearing prayer spoken of while I was in Richmond, but I have no doubt you acted in what appeared to you to be the spirit and temper manifested by me while there."

Having thus generously assumed responsibility for Weitzel's alleged neglect, the President's next thought was about what the Virginia rebel Legislature was doing, of which he had heard nothing since his return from City Point. He therefore included in this same telegram of April 12 the following inquiry and direction: " Is there any sign of the rebel Legislature coming together on the understanding of my letter to you ? If there is any such sign, inform me what it is. If there is no such sign, you may withdraw the offer."

To this question General Weitzel answered briefly, " The passports have gone out for the legislature, and it is common talk that they will come together." It is probable that Mr. Lincoln thought that if after the lapse of five days the proposed meeting had progressed no farther than "common talk," nothing could be expected from it. It would also seem that at this time he must have received, either by telegraph or by mail, copies of the correspondence and call which Weitzel had authorized, and which had been published that morning. The President therefore immediately wrote and sent to General Weitzel a long telegram, in which he explained his course with such clearness that its mere perusal sets at rest all controversy respecting either his original intention of policy or the legal effect of his action and orders, and by a final revocation of the permission he had given brought the incident to its natural and appropriate termination:

I have just seen Judge Campbell's letter to you of the 7th. He assumes, it appears to me, that I have called the insurgent legislature of Virginia together, as the rightful

CHAP. XI.

Apl. 12, 1865.
legislature of the State, to settle all differences with the United States. I have done no such thing.[1] I spoke of them not as a legislature, but as " the gentlemen who have acted as the legislature of Virginia in support of the rebellion." I did this on purpose to exclude the assumption that I was recognizing them as a rightful body. I dealt with them as men having power *de facto* to do a specific thing, to wit: " to withdraw the Virginia troops and other support from resistance to the General Government," for which, in the paper handed to Judge Campbell, I promised a special equivalent, to wit: a remission to the people of the State, except in certain cases, of the confiscation of their property. I meant this and no more. Inasmuch, however, as Judge Campbell misconstrues this, and is still pressing for an armistice, contrary to the explicit statement of the paper I gave him, and particularly as General Grant has since captured the Virginia troops, so that giving a consideration for their withdrawal is no longer applicable, let my letter to you and the paper to Judge Campbell both be withdrawn or

Lincoln to Weitzel, Apl. 12, 1865. Campbell, Pamphlet.
countermanded, and he be notified of it. Do not now allow them to assemble, but if any have come allow them safe return to their homes.

[1] The account given by Admiral Porter of this transaction, in his "Naval History," p. 799, is evidently written from memory, without consultation of dates or documents, and is wholly inaccurate as well in substance as in detail.

CHAPTER XII

JOHNSTON'S SURRENDER

SHERMAN soon wearied of the civil administration of Savannah and of the adjacent region of Georgia which had suddenly grown loyal. He received in January a visit from the Secretary of War, in which many matters pertaining to the care of captured property and the treatment of reclaimed territory were discussed and settled. But the business which lay nearest to Sherman's heart, and occupied most of his time, was the preparation for his march northward of five hundred miles which was to bring him in upon Grant's left wing to finish the war, either on the banks of the Roanoke or the James. He pushed forward, with his accustomed untiring zeal, the work required to put his magnificent army in position to traverse the wide pine barrens, the spreading swamps, and the deep rivers that lay between him and his goal; and so rapid was his progress that he would have found himself ready to start by the middle of January had it not been for the torrents of rain which fell during that month, swelling the Savannah River out of its bed and flooding the rice fields on its shore for miles around. He made a lodgment meanwhile at Pocotaligo, where the railroad to Charleston

Sherman, "Memoirs." Vol. II., p. 255.

CHAP. XII. crosses the Combahee, meeting so little resistance as to convince him that there was a sensible diminution of the energy of the Confederates. The weather cleared away bright and cold at the end of 1865. January, and with the opening days of February the great march to the North was begun. Howard commanded the right wing, consisting of the Fifteenth and Seventeenth Army Corps, under Logan and Blair; Slocum the left wing, the Fourteenth Sherman, "Memoirs." Vol. II., p. 268. Corps, under Jeff. C. Davis, and the Twentieth under A. S. Williams; the cavalry was led by Kilpatrick; a grand total of 60,000 men; added to this Grant had promised him important reënforcements on the way. He had abundant stores, with what he could collect on the march, of food and forage, and ammunition enough for a great battle. Fortunately, this last was never to be used.

The whole campaign in fact is mainly interesting to the military student as one of the most remarkable marches which history records. It amazed the Confederate commanders that Sherman should have thought of advancing before the waters subsided. There is no account of another such march. From Savannah to Goldsboro' is a distance of 425 miles. The country is for the most part low and at that season wet, intersected by innumerable rivers and streams, bordered by swamps, traversed by roads hardly deserving the name, mere quaking causeways in a sea of mud. The advance guard frequently waded through water waist deep. The country was almost as destitute of maps as the region of the Congo; every step forward was made gropingly. At the crossing of the Salkehatchie by Logan's corps, it was found the stream had fifteen channels, all of which had to be bridged. The roads were CHAP. XII. impassable to artillery or train wagons until corduroyed; under the heavy weight the logs gradually sank till another layer was necessary, and this toilsome process had to be repeated indefinitely, Cox, "The March to the Sea," pp. 171, 172. "bridging chaos for hundreds of miles," as General Cox calls it. There are few instances of equal energy and success in the conquest of physical conditions. General Sherman himself, when it was all over, compared the march northward with the march to the sea, in relative importance as ten to one.

He had little except the forces of nature to fight with on the way. By skillfully feigning to right and left he produced the impression that both Charleston and Augusta were threatened, while he marched almost unopposed to Columbia. Charleston being thus turned fell like a ripe fruit into the hands of Dahlgren and Gillmore on the 18th of February; General Hardee hurrying northward to 1865. Cheraw, on the Great Peedee. There was nothing like organized resistance at the beginning of the march, even at points where it was expected. When Howard drew near the railroad between Charleston and Augusta, he paused to deploy his leading division to be ready for battle. While thus engaged, a man came galloping down the road, whom he recognized as one of his own foragers, on a white horse, with a rope bridle, shouting, "Hurry up, General, we've got the railroads." A vital line of communication had been captured by a squad of Sherman, "Memoirs." Vol. II., p. 274. "bummers," while the generals were preparing for a serious battle. Beauregard and Wade Hampton, who were both in Columbia, had neither the means nor the disposition to make any effectual resistance. General Sherman entered the place on the 17th of February. That night a great part of the town was destroyed by fire, ignited, Sherman says, by the burning cotton bales which had been set on fire by the retreating Confederates. In spite of all that could be done to check the conflagration it raged all night, and left the capital of South Carolina a heap of ashes.[1]

Sherman did everything in his power to relieve the houseless and destitute people; he provided shelter for many, gave five hundred beef cattle to the mayor, and took measures to maintain public order after the army should be gone. He destroyed the railroad for many miles, and, after a halt of two days, resumed his march to the North.

After leaving Columbia the country was less difficult and the rate of progress more rapid. With no more delay than was necessary to destroy the railroads of the State, the army pushed on towards the Great Peedee. This was a most important stage in the journey. Sherman felt if he crossed that river prosperously there lay no serious obstacle before him south of the Cape Fear, and that river he expected to find in the possession of the National forces. Hardee, after evacuating Charleston, had established himself in formidable works at Cheraw, but Sherman flanked him out of them with his left

[1] General Wade Hampton and other Confederate writers charge General Sherman with the malicious burning of Columbia. We consider General Sherman's assertion to be a sufficient disproof of this charge. He had, it is true, ordered the public buildings to be destroyed, but he had expressly directed General Howard to "spare libraries, asylums, and private dwellings." Any one acquainted with Sherman's character would believe that if he had ordered the town to be destroyed he would have admitted and defended the act.

GENERAL WADE HAMPTON.

wing, and the right wing, under Howard, crossed
the Peedee and took the town on the 3d of March,
with 28 pieces of artillery, 3000 small arms, and a
great quantity of stores. Hardee and Hampton retreated rapidly to Fayetteville, on the Cape Fear;
Sherman following with equal celerity entered that
place on the 11th, and established communications
with the splendid force which Schofield had brought
from Tennessee to the North Carolina coast. At
Fayetteville Sherman destroyed the arsenal with
all its valuable machinery. If he could have foreseen the speedy close of the war this would not
have been done. There was now apparently no
obstruction to the concentration of all his forces at
Goldsboro', a place of the utmost value and importance; being the point where the railroads running
from the coast to the Tennessee mountains, and
from Wilmington to Richmond, crossed each other
— to hold which was sooner or later to strangle the
Confederate army in Virginia.

But Sherman was not to accomplish this final
stage of his last great march without meeting a
more determined resistance than he had as yet encountered. Beauregard, who was enfeebled by
long illness, in body and mind, had been superseded on the 23d of February by General Joseph
E. Johnston, who had received from Lee the comprehensive order to "concentrate all available
forces and drive back Sherman." He immediately
assumed command, not flattering himself that he
could defeat his formidable adversary, but determined to do everything in his power to keep his
army together in such condition that when the end
came he might obtain fair terms of peace.

His army, though wholly inadequate to the task of driving back Sherman, was by no means contemptible. It is almost impossible to determine with any accuracy the numbers of the Confederates at this stage of the war; Jefferson Davis, General Johnston, and General Beauregard differ widely; but a careful examination of all their statements and reports indicates that Johnston could command, with Hardee's troops and the remnants of what Thomas had left on foot of Hood's army, something like 30,000 men. He had to give Bragg a portion of this force to oppose the march of Schofield from the coast, and with the rest he did what he could to delay Sherman's inevitable progress.

With the exception of occasional cavalry skirmishes of little importance, in one of which— 1865. on the 10th of March—Hampton surprised and came near capturing Kilpatrick, the two armies came into collision only twice. At Averysboro' on the 16th of March, Slocum, with the left wing, found Hardee intrenched between the Cape Fear and a neighboring swamp. Sherman, riding with that wing, personally directed the brief engagement which ensued; Hardee was driven from his position and retired in the night, and Sherman pursued his march, going to the right to join Howard. General Johnston having by this time come to the conclusion that Sherman was moving upon Goldsboro' concentrated nearly all his force, about 20,000 men, at Bentonville, where on the 19th a severe fight took place between him and Slocum, commanding the left wing of Sherman's army. Slocum, finding the enemy too strong in numbers and position to be swept aside, reported the condition of things to Sherman, who instantly started for the CHAP. XII. scene of action, bringing up his right wing to Slocum's support. He found Johnston established on the south side of Mill Creek very much as Hood had found Schofield at Franklin; Johnston's position was even stronger, his whole left being covered by a brook running through a swamp which seemed at first sight impassable. Sherman found among his prisoners representatives of so many brigades and divisions, the phantom relics of Hood's army, that he over-estimated the numbers opposed to him; and therefore instead of at once overpowering Johnston's force he proceeded with unusual caution.

On the afternoon of the 21st, General Joseph A. March, 1865. Mower, who held the extreme right of the National line, made his way with great boldness and skill through the difficult swamp in his front, and with two brigades pushed close to the bridges in Johnston's rear. If he had been supported he could have cut off Johnston's retreat. But Sherman did not think it wise to risk a general engagement at that moment, and ordered Mower to withdraw, which he did under the fire of the forces which Johnston hurriedly threw against him. The day's work was the last fight of the two great armies; it elated the Confederates beyond what it was worth; they cannot be made to believe, to this day, that Mower withdrew under orders. Sherman in his "Memoirs" blames himself for not having Vol. II., p. 304. followed up Mower's success; but the result justified his wise forbearance. The war ended just as soon as it would have done if he had plunged among the swampy thickets at Bentonville, and

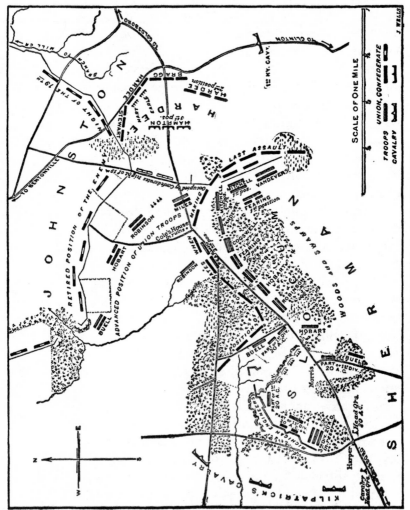

BATTLE OF BENTONVILLE, N. C., MARCH 19, 1865.

sacrificed thousands of lives in a murderous grapple with Johnston's veterans.

Johnston made good his retreat in the night, and Sherman hurried on to Goldsboro'; he rode into the place at the head of his troops on the 23d, find- ing that Schofield had arrived there the day before. The grand junction was accomplished, the great Army of the West was once more united; the heroes of Franklin and Nashville shook hands with those who had marched to the sea. Sherman, with his 90,000 veterans, trained to marching and fighting under conditions before unknown to the world, was henceforth not only invincible, but irresistible. The days of the Confederacy were numbered when he rode into Goldsboro'; there was nothing left to do but to gather up the fragments of the revolt.

From every quarter the triumphant legions of the Union were moving to consummate victory. At the same moment that the armies of Sherman and Schofield came together at Goldsboro', two splendidly equipped cavalry expeditions were moving east and south from Thomas's department, the one under J. H. Wilson to the pacification of Alabama, the other, under Stoneman, to destroy Lee's last avenue of supply or escape in the mountainous region where the boundaries of Virginia, North Carolina, and Tennessee come together. Thomas had already, in the month of December, sent Stoneman with two brigades to sweep East Tennessee clear of the enemy. He then crossed over into Virginia, and ascending the Valley of the Holston to Saltville destroyed the extensive and valuable salt works at that place, the iron manufactories at Marion, and the leadworks of Wythe County. He drove Breckinridge out of the country, and into the Secretaryship of War at Richmond, burnt bridges, twisted rails, and captured some guns and prisoners. On the 22d of March he started out again, this time moving towards Lynchburg, to head off the expected retreat of Lee. He did not pursue his old track up the Holston, as there was a small Confederate force along that river which might have delayed him; but crossed the Blue Ridge by way of the Watauga, to the Yadkin, and thence turning sharply to the north reached Wytheville without opposition. Here he destroyed a large depot of Confederate supplies, and rendered useless by the 7th of April some ninety miles of railroad to the west of Lynchburg, so that if Lee had broken through Sheridan's lines at Appomattox, he would have met capture or famine immediately beyond. On the 9th, not knowing what weighty transactions were making the day forever memorable, Stoneman pushed southward, and on the 12th defeated Pemberton and Gardner and captured Salisbury, N. C., with its enormous wealth of stores, accumulated with the utmost toil and pain, in the last throes of the Confederacy, as a reserve stock for Lee's army. He destroyed everything, in accordance with his orders, not aware of the situation which made this havoc unnecessary, and went back to Tennessee.

The ride of Wilson's troopers into Alabama was one of the most important and fruitful expeditions of the war, and justified by its celerity, its boldness, and good judgment the high encomium with which Grant sent Wilson to Thomas. After the battle of Nashville and the dispersion of Hood's army, Wil-

son had passed the rest of the winter in drilling
and equipping his force; and he swung loose from
the Tennessee River on the 23d of March, with
three fine divisions commanded by Generals Eli
Long, Emory Upton, and Edward McCook, a
train of 250 wagons especially adapted for
rapid traveling, and packed with small rations
and ammunition; he relied on the country for
bread and meat. Arriving at Jasper he received
information of the movements of Forrest, who
commanded the Confederate forces in his front,
which determined him to sacrifice everything to
swift marching. He left his trains behind, well
guarded, made his men fill their haversacks with
food, and pushed on with such relentless energy
that the scattered detachments of Forrest could
make no stand, nor accomplish any effective concentration against him. He sent flying columns
to the right and left to destroy public property and
stores, but led his main column so impetuously
that even the energetic and rough-riding Forrest
could nowhere turn long enough to fight.

At Hillsboro' Wilson reached a bridge so hot on
the heels of the enemy that they could not destroy
it. Coming to Montevallo on the 31st, he wrought
great destruction of iron furnaces and collieries
in the few hours he could spare; but still pushed
forward, driving the enemy, who, though constantly increased by additional detachments, could
not gain time enough to make an effectual resistance. At last Forrest, having collected all his
available force in a strong position at Plantersville,
six miles north of Selma, gave battle for that important railroad and manufacturing center, and

met with a total defeat, his lines being broken and his forces driven helter-skelter into Selma. Wilson wasted not an instant after his victory, although it was won on a day in which he marched twenty-four miles; at dawn on April 2 he closed in upon Selma and spent the day establishing his lines and searching the works. Richard Taylor had fled in the morning to Demopolis, intending to bring back a relieving force; but it was not Wilson's habit to allow time for this. He assaulted the works late in the evening and carried them at every point after a hot but brief conflict. Forrest escaped in the confusion and joined a portion of his command which had been cut off at Marion by Wilson's swift marching. If the Confederacy had not been already wounded to death, the loss of Selma would have been almost irreparable; their greatest manufacturing arsenal was there, and enormous stores of every kind. Wilson, after destroying everything which could be of advantage to the enemy, moved east on Macon, Georgia, and it was reserved for a detachment of his troops to capture the fugitive Confederate President on his flight towards the Florida coast.

Sherman returned to Goldsboro' from his journey to City Point on the 30th of March; he was able to come by rail from New Berne, so rapidly had the skill of his engineers repaired the ruined road. He set himself at once to the reorganization of his army and the replenishment of his stores, so as to be able to move by the 10th of April, the day agreed upon with Grant — the day after the deluge, as it turned out. He still thought there was a hard campaign with desperate fighting before him; he

GENERAL J. A. MOWER.

superseded Williams by Mower in command of CHAP. XII.
the Twentieth Corps, because he considered the
latter superior in tactical fighting qualities. With
that vast army, greater than Grant's, under him,
supplied now by rail from Morehead and Wilmington with all that the nation's imperial wealth could
afford, with the broken rebellion tottering to its
fall in every Southern State, he was still as careful
and as laborious in every particular of his preparation for his next march as if he were beginning a
great war with an equal adversary. He had not
comprehended the full measure of his own success.
So late as the 24th of March he wrote to Grant, "I
feel certain, from the character of the fighting, Sherman, "Memoirs." Vol. II., p. 316.
that we have got Johnston's army afraid of us" —
as if that were not natural under the circumstances.
Grant, himself, up to the last, remained singularly
modest and reserved in his expectations. His
mind was full of care on Sherman's account, dur- Grant to Sherman, Mar. 16, 1865, Ibid., p. 312.
ing all his triumphal march northward. "When
I hear that you and Schofield are together," he
wrote, "with your back upon the coast, I shall feel
that you are entirely safe against anything the
enemy can do." Safe — with those armies, the
phrase does not sin by exaggeration.

Even on the 6th of April, when the news of the 1865.
fall of Richmond and the flight of Lee and the
Confederate Government towards Danville reached
Goldsboro', Sherman was still unable to understand
the full extent of the National triumph. "Of
course," he says, "I inferred that General Lee
would succeed in making junction with General
Johnston, with at least a fraction of his army, some- Sherman, "Memoirs." Vol. II., p. 343.
where to my front." He admired and respected

CHAP. XII. Grant, so far as a man might short of idolatry, yet
the long habit of respect for Lee led him to think
the Confederates would somehow get away. He
had, on the day before, drawn up elaborate and
detailed orders for the march which was to begin
April, 1865. in earnest on the 12th, and be directed to Warren-
ton, near the Roanoke River. He now changed his
plan and prepared to move straight upon Johnston's army, which was at Smithfield, half way to
Raleigh.

He started promptly on the morning of the
10th; the next day he reached Smithfield, finding it abandoned, Johnston having retired to
Raleigh, burning his bridges. While these were
repairing, Sherman received the great news from
Appomattox. He issued a brief and sententious
order in his happiest vein: " Glory to God and our
country," he said, " and all honor to our comrades
in arms toward whom we are marching! A little
more labor, a little more toil on our part, the great
Sherman,
"Memoirs."
Vol. II.,
p. 344. race is won, and our Government stands regenerated
after four long years of war." A young staff officer
galloped along the lines of the Army of the Ohio
shouting the glorious news to the troops who were
lying at ease in the warm spring sunshine on either
side of the road. His words were received with
wild rejoicing; they meant peace, an end of march-
Captain
A. J. Ricks,
"How I
Carried the
News of
Lee's
Surrender
to the Army
of the
Ohio." ing and battle, an end of hatred and strife, a return
to home and its loves and duties. The troops broke
into strange antics, eminent officers of the highest
rank and dignity turned somersaults on the grass.
One soldier, as he caught the shouted tidings, yelled
Cox,
"March to
the Sea,"
p. 213. back at the galloping Mercury, " You are the man
we have been looking for these three years." Even

the inhabitants of the country shared in the general CHAP. XII.
joy; the worn and weary women caught up their
ragged children and cried, "Now father will come
home."

Sherman, definitely relieved from the apprehension of a junction of the Confederate armies, had
now no fear except of a flight and dispersal of
Johnston's force into guerrilla bands. If they ran
away he felt he could not catch them; the country
was too open for that; they could scatter and meet
again at appointed rendezvous and continue a par- Sherman,
"Memoirs."
tisan warfare indefinitely. He could not be ex- Vol. II.,
p. 344.
pected to know that this resolute enemy, who had
met him on a hundred fields with such undaunted
valor, was sick to the heart of war and longing for
peace. The desire for more fighting survived only
in a group of fugitive politicians, flying from a
danger which did not exist, through the pine
forests and woodlands of the Carolinas.

Entering Raleigh on the morning of the 13th, April, 1865.
Sherman turned his heads of column in the direction of Salisbury and Charlotte, hoping to cut off
the southward march of Johnston. He made no
great haste, for thinking Johnston superior to him
in cavalry he wanted Sheridan to arrive before pushing the Confederates to extremities. He tried to
persuade the civil authorities at Raleigh to remain
at their posts; but the governor, Zebulon B. Vance,
had fled, fearing arrest and imprisonment. The
next day Kilpatrick, who was far in front with the
cavalry, reported that a flag of truce had arrived
with a communication from General Johnston. It
reached Sherman in Raleigh; it was dated the 13th
of April, and was in these words: "The results of

CHAP. XII. the recent campaign in Virginia have changed the relative military condition of the belligerents. I am therefore induced to address you, in this form, the inquiry whether, in order to stop the further effusion of blood and devastation of property, you are willing to make a temporary suspension of active operations, and to communicate to Lieutenant-General Grant, commanding the armies of the United States, the request that he will take like action in regard to other armies — the object being to permit the civil authorities to enter into the needful arrangements to terminate the existing war."

Johnston, "Narrative of Military Operations," p. 400.

This proposition, which was simply for an armistice to enable the National and the Confederate Governments to negotiate on equal terms, had been dictated by Jefferson Davis, who had then reached Greensboro' on his flight southward, written down by S. R. Mallory, and merely signed and sent by General Johnston. It was inadmissible, even offensive in its terms; but General Sherman, anxious for peace and incapable of discourtesy to a brave enemy, took no notice of its language, and answered at once in terms so unreserved and so cordial that they probably encouraged the Confederates to ask for better conditions of surrender than they had expected to receive. " I am fully empowered," he said, "to arrange with you any terms for the suspension of further hostilities between the armies commanded by you and those commanded by myself, and will be willing to confer with you to that end." He gave notice that he would limit his advance to certain points, and asked Johnston to stay in his present position pending negotiations. He suggested the Appomattox conditions as a basis of

Ibid.

Sherman, "Memoirs." Vol. II., p. 347.

action; and promised to obtain from Grant and
Stoneman a suspension of hostilities. Johnston,
who after sending his letter had marched with his
army towards Greensboro', received Sherman's
reply on the 16th, when he was within a few
miles of that place. He hurried to Greensboro' to
submit the letter to Jefferson Davis, who was the
real principal so far in the negotiation, but found
that he had started for Charlotte; and Johnston,
therefore, arranged a meeting for noon the next
day, the 17th, at the house of a Mr. Bennett on the
Raleigh road.

The two great antagonists, who had dealt each
other so many sturdy blows during two years, at
last met, not without emotion, which was height-
ened by Sherman's communicating to Johnston
the news he had that morning received of the
murder of Mr. Lincoln. The Confederate general
expressed his unfeigned sorrow at this calamity,
which smote the South, he said, as deeply as the
North, and in this mood of sympathy the discussion began.[1] Sherman said frankly that he could
not recognize the Confederate civil authority as
having any existence, and could neither receive nor
transmit to Washington any proposition coming
from them. He expressed his ardent desire for an
end to devastation, and offered Johnston the same
terms offered by Grant to Lee. Johnston replied
that he would not be justified in such a capitulation, but suggested that they might arrange the terms
of a permanent peace. The suggestion pleased

[1] In our account of this discussion we have relied mainly
on General Johnston's "Narrative" which General Sherman
indorses as "quite accurate and
correct."

Sheridan,
"Memoirs."
Vol. II.,
p. 350.

CHAP. XII. General Sherman; the prospect of ending the war without the shedding of another drop of blood was so tempting to him that he did not sufficiently consider the limits of his authority in the matter; and besides, his heart was melted at the sight of his gallant adversary so completely at his mercy. He afterwards said in his report of the transaction: "To push an army whose commander had so frankly and honestly confessed his inability to cope with me were cowardly and unworthy of the brave men I led." Questions arising as to a general amnesty and as to the power of Johnston to bring about the surrender of the Confederate forces in Texas consumed the afternoon and the generals parted to meet the next day.

May 9,
Sherman,
Report
Committee
on Conduct
of the War,
1865.
Vol. III.,
p. 8.

General Sherman, going back to Raleigh, found all his general officers eagerly in favor of the negotiations he had begun, and thus confirmed in his own prepossessions, he renewed the discussion at noon on the 18th. Here he committed a grave error in assenting to Johnston's proposition to introduce John C. Breckinridge into the discussion—not as Secretary of War, they agreed, but as an officer of the general's staff. Reagan, the Confederate Postmaster-General, who was somewhere in the background, sent in a written scheme of capitulation, which Johnston read as a basis of agreement. Sherman at last—after listening to a speech by Breckinridge, seized a pen and wrote with an ease and rapidity which surprised Johnston the following memorandum of agreement: —

Johnston,
"Narrative of
Military
Operations,"
p. 405.

Apl. 18, 1865. "1. The contending armies now in the field to maintain the *status quo* until notice is given by the commanding general of any one to its opponent, and reasonable time, — say, forty-eight hours — allowed.

" 2. The Confederate armies now in existence to be disbanded and conducted to their several State capitals, there to deposit their arms and public property in the State arsenal; and each officer and man to execute and file an agreement to cease from acts of war, and to abide the action of the State and Federal authority. The number of arms and munitions of war to be reported to the Chief of Ordnance at Washington City, subject to the future action of the Congress of the United States, and, in the mean time, to be used solely to maintain peace and order within the borders of the States respectively.

" 3. The recognition by the Executive of the United States of the several State governments, on their officers and Legislatures taking the oaths prescribed by the Constitution of the United States, and, where conflicting State governments have resulted from the war, the legitimacy of all shall be submitted to the Supreme Court of the United States.

" 4. The reëstablishment of all the Federal Courts in the several States, with powers as defined by the Constitution of the United States and of the States respectively.

" 5. The people and inhabitants of all the States to be guaranteed, so far as the Executive can, their political rights and franchises, as well as their rights of person and property, as defined by the Constitution of the United States and of the States respectively.

CHAP. XII. "6. The Executive authority of the Government of the United States not to disturb any of the people by reason of the late war, so long as they live Apl. 18, 1865. in peace and quiet, abstain from acts of armed hostility and obey the laws in existence at the place of their residence.

"7. In general terms—the war to cease; a general amnesty, so far as the Executive of the United States can command, on condition of the disbandment of the Confederate armies, the distribution of the arms, and the resumption of peaceful pursuits by the officers and men hitherto composing said armies.

"Not being fully empowered by our respective principals to fulfill these terms, we individually and officially pledge ourselves to promptly obtain Sherman, "Memoirs." Vol. II., pp. 356, 357. the necessary authority, and to carry out the above programme."

This agreement was signed by the two generals.

Thus the wisdom of Lincoln's peremptory order to Grant of the 3d of March was completely vindicated; no general in the field could be trusted to make terms of peace involving the future relations of the States with the National Government. On the Confederate side in this affair the military commander had completely effaced himself, while General Sherman, who had begun most properly with the offer of Grant's terms at Appomattox, had in the two days' negotiations set on foot by Jefferson Davis and carried on by Reagan and Breckinridge, ended by making a treaty of peace with the Confederate States. But two things must always be said in his defense. Neither the Government nor General Grant had ever communicated to him the

President's instructions of the 3d of March for- CHAP. XII.
bidding Grant to "decide, discuss, or to confer
upon any political question"; a neglect for which
both were to blame. Secondly, Grant, in over-
stepping his powers by granting pardon and
amnesty to all the officers of Lee's army, had
naturally created in Sherman's mind the impression
that he might with equal propriety venture upon
the exercise of similar powers. He says also in
justification of his action, that Mr. Stanton, when
at Savannah, had spoken of the terrible financial
strain of the war, and had made him believe that
the termination of this waste was an object so desirable that great sacrifices should be made to
obtain it.

But when all possible explanations have been
made, the fact remains that General Sherman,
though perfectly loyal and subordinate to the civil
authorities, so far as obedience to orders was concerned, ready to lay down his life at any moment
at their command, had the low opinion of civilians
which is so common to soldiers, and thought the
generals in the field more competent to make peace
or war than the politicians in Washington. A year
before he had said to Grant, "Even in the seceded
States, your word *now* would go further than a   Sherman
to Grant,
President's proclamation or an act of Congress";   Mar. 10,
1864.
and now, three days after this agreement had been   Apl. 21, 1865.
dispatched to Washington for approval, he returned
to the political aspect of the matter in a letter to
Johnston, referring to the question of slavery, and
saying, "Although, strictly speaking, this is no
subject of a military convention, yet I am honestly
convinced that our simple declaration of a result

CHAP. XII. will be accepted as good law everywhere. Of
Report
Committee
on Conduct
of the War,
1865.
Vol. III.,
p. 16. course I have not a single word from Washington
on this or any other point of our agreement, but I
know the effect of such a step by us will be universally accepted."

On the same day these confident words were
written the text of the agreement arrived in Wash-
ington. The moment Grant read it he saw that
it was entirely inadmissible; he submitted it to
President Johnson, the Cabinet was hastily called
Grant to
Sherman,
April 21,
1865.
Sherman,
"Memoirs."
Vol. II.,
p. 360. together and the whole negotiation disapproved.
General Grant was ordered to give Sherman notice
of the disapproval, and to direct him to resume hos-
tilities at once. Lincoln's instructions of the 3d of
March were repeated — somewhat tardily, it must
be confessed — to Sherman as his rule of action.
All this was a matter of course, and even General
Sherman could not properly, and perhaps would
not, have objected to it. But the calm spirit of
Lincoln was now absent from the councils of the
Government; and it was not in Andrew Johnson and
Mr. Stanton to pass over a mistake like this, even
in the case of one of the most illustrious captains
of the age. They ordered Grant to proceed at once
to Sherman's headquarters, and to direct operations against the enemy, and what was worse than
all, Mr. Stanton printed in the newspapers of the
country the reasons of the Government for dis-
approving the agreement expressed in terms of the
sharpest censure of General Sherman. This publication did not for some weeks come under General
Sherman's eye.

General Grant arrived at Sherman's headquarters
April, 1865. on the 24th, and made known to him the Govern-

ment's disapproval of his proceedings. Sherman, with prompt obedience, announced the fact to Johnston, demanded the surrender of his immediate command on the Appomattox terms, pure and simple; and gave forty-eight hours' notice of the termination of the truce. General Johnston had already received, on the same day, from Mr. Davis, at Charlotte, the approval of the Confederate Government for the convention of the 18th. Mr. Davis, April, 1865. before giving his consent to the agreement, required from General Breckinridge, his Secretary of War, a report as to the desirability of ratifying the convention. This report set forth the desperate condition of affairs, the favorable terms proposed, the impossibility of negotiations ‑on equal terms. He therefore advised Mr. Davis to execute the convention so far as it was in his power, and to recommend its acceptance by the States, and finally to "return "Southern Historical to the States and the people the trust which you Society Papers." are no longer able to defend." Thinking the war Vol. XII., pp. 100–102. at an end, Johnston had drawn from the Treasury Agent, in his camp, the sum of $39,000 in silver, which he distributed among his troops, each man and officer getting a dollar. So far as he was concerned, the war was certainly over; for he could no longer hold his troops together. Eight thousand Johnston, "Narra- of them left their camps and went home in the tive of Military week of the truce, many of them riding away on Opera- tions," the artillery horses and train mules. When John- p. 410. ston communicated to Mr. Davis the failure of his negotiations and asked instructions, the Confederate President suggested that he disband the infantry with instructions to come together at some rendezvous, and try to escape with the cavalry and

Chap. XII. light guns. This futile and selfish direction General Johnston deliberately and wisely refused to obey. He told General Breckinridge plainly that this plan contemplated merely the safety of the "high civil functionaries," and made no provision for the protection of the people and the prevention of bloodshed among the soldiers. He counseled the immediate flight of President Davis, and added, "Commanders believe the troops will not fight again." Thinking "it would be a great crime to prolong the war," he therefore assumed the responsibility of making an end of strife, and answered Sherman's summons by inviting another conference at Bennett's house, where the two commanders met on the 26th of April, and Johnston surrendered all the Confederate forces in his command, which in territory happened to be coextensive with that of Sherman, on the same terms granted Lee at Appomattox.

"Southern Historical Society Papers." Vol. XII., p. 98.

1865.

By a supplemental agreement, Schofield allowed the Confederates the use of their field transportation to get to their homes, and for use on their farms; each brigade to retain one-seventh of their arms till they arrived at the capital of their State; officers and men to retain their own horses and property; General Canby was requested to give water transportation to those living beyond the Mississippi; besides this, Sherman, when he was informed by the Confederate commander that his supplies were exhausted, gave him 250,000 rations. Never was a beaten enemy treated so like a friend.

Johnston, "Narrative of Military Operations," p. 418.

Sherman instantly made the orders necessary for closing up the work in his department and for starting the troops on their march homeward. The paroling of the Confederate force occupied about a CHAP. XII. week. Thirty-seven thousand, officers and men, were paroled in North Carolina — and these were exclusive of the thousands who deserted their camps during the suspension of hostilities; some sixty thousand surrendered as reported by Wilson in Georgia and Florida. General Johnston closes his account of this transaction with these generous words, as creditable to him as to those of whom he writes: "The United States troops that remained in the Southern States on *military* duty conducted themselves as if they thought that the object of the war had been the restoration of the Union. They treated the people around them as they would have done those of Ohio or New York, if stationed among them, as their fellow-citizens."[1]

Sherman did not pretend to relish or approve the decision of the Government in regard to his diplomacy. He submitted like a soldier, carried out his orders punctually; but he said to Stanton plainly that the Government had made a mis- Sherman, "Memoirs." Vol. II., p. 362. take. He wrote on the 25th to Grant, then present with him at headquarters, "I now apprehend that the rebel armies will disperse; and instead of deal- April, 1865. ing with six or seven States, we will have to deal with numberless bands of desperados, headed by such men as Mosby, Forrest, Red Jackson, and others, who know not, and care not for danger and its consequences." He did not know that Forrest Ibid. had at last got all the fighting he wanted at Wilson's hands, and that Mosby was soon to be a Federal office-holder. Sherman was preparing to

---

[1] He adds in a footnote: "This language excludes those of the Freedmen's Bureau."

CHAP. XII.
April, 1865.
go to Savannah to direct the further operations of Wilson's cavalry, when on the 28th he received a New York paper containing Stanton's bulletin in regard to his convention with Johnston. This naturally roused him to great wrath; he wrote an eloquent and fiery defense of his conduct to Grant, but hastened on his journey to Savannah nevertheless, made all needful provision for Wilson, and then returned to find still further cause of indignation. General Grant had transferred his headquarters to Washington, and Halleck had been made commander of the Armies of the Potomac and the James. In this capacity, filled with new zeal on the occasion of the Johnston convention, Halleck had ordered Meade's army, disregarding the truce, to push forward against Johnston and to attack him, regardless of Sherman's orders. These orders, though they were nullified by the surrender,

Bowers to
Sherman,
and
Sherman to
Bowers,
May 25 and
26, 1865.
Report
Committee
on Conduct
of the War,
1865.
Vol. III.,
p. 20.
had injudiciously been published. This new insult completed the measure of Sherman's anger. He broke out into open defiance of the authorities who he thought were persecuting him with deliberate malice, and declared in a report to Grant that he would have maintained his truce at any cost of life. When Grant suggested that this was uncalled for, and offered him an opportunity to correct the report, Sherman refused to do so, avowing his readiness to obey all future orders of the President and the General, but insisting that his record should stand as written. He declined to meet Halleck in Richmond and warned him to keep out of his way, and on arriving in Washington publicly refused the proffered hand of Stanton at the grand review of the armies.

CHAPTER XIII

THE CAPTURE OF JEFFERSON DAVIS

WHEN Jefferson Davis and the remnant of the Confederate Cabinet, with the more important of their department archives, left Richmond on the night of April 2, in consequence of Lee's retreat, they proceeded to Danville, southwest of Richmond, arriving there the following morning. In a conference between Davis and Lee, in which the probability of abandoning Richmond was discussed, they had agreed upon this point at which to endeavor to unite the armies of Lee and Johnston, first to attack and beat Sherman and then return and defeat Grant. But Grant, so far from permitting Lee to execute the proposed junction, did not even allow him to reach Danville. Lee had been pressed so hard that he had not found opportunity to inform Davis where he was going, and this absence of news probably served to give Davis an intimation that their preconcerted plans were not likely to reach fulfillment. Nevertheless, the rebel President made a show of confidence; rooms were obtained, and, he says, the " different departments resumed their routine labors," though it may be doubted whether in these labors they earned the compensation which the Confederate States promised them.

Ch. XIII.

April, 1865.

Two days after his arrival at Danville, Jefferson Davis added one more to his many rhetorical efforts to "fire the Southern heart." On the 5th he issued a proclamation, in which, after reciting the late disasters in as hopeful a strain as possible, he broke again into his never-failing grandiloquence:

We have now entered upon a new phase of the struggle. Relieved from the necessity of guarding particular points, our army will be free to move from point to point, to strike the enemy in detail far from his base. Let us but will it and we are free.

Animated by that confidence in your spirit and fortitude which never yet failed me, I announce to you, fellow-countrymen, that it is my purpose to maintain your cause with my whole heart and soul; that I will never consent to abandon to the enemy one foot of the soil of any of the States of the Confederacy; that Virginia — noble State, whose ancient renown has been eclipsed by her still more glorious recent history; whose bosom has been bared to receive the main shock of this war; whose sons and daughters have exhibited heroism so sublime as to render her illustrious in all time to come — that Virginia, with the help of the people and by the blessing of Providence, shall be held and defended, and no peace ever be made with the infamous invaders of her territory.

Davis, "Rise and Fall of the Confederate Government." Vol. II., p. 677.

If, by the stress of numbers, we should be compelled to a temporary withdrawal from her limits or those of any other border State, we will return until the baffled and exhausted enemy shall abandon in despair his endless and impossible task of making slaves of a people resolved to be free.

In his book, Davis is frank enough to admit that this language, in the light of subsequent events, may fairly be said to have been oversanguine. He probably very soon reached this conviction, for almost before the ink was dry on the document a son of General Henry A. Wise, escaping through the Federal lines on a swift horse, brought him infor-

GENERAL JAMES H. WILSON.

mation of the surrender of Lee's army to Grant. CH. XIII.
Rumor also reaching him that the Federal cavalry
was pushing southward west of Danville, the Confederate Government again hastily packed its
archives into a railroad train and moved to Greensboro', North Carolina. Its reception at this place
was cold and foreboding. The headquarters of the
government remained on the train at the depot.
Only Jefferson Davis, and Secretary Trenholm who
was ill, were provided with lodgings. From this
point Davis sent a dispatch to General Johnston,
soliciting a conference, either at Greensboro' or at
the general's headquarters; and in response to this
request Johnston went without delay to Greensboro', arriving there on the morning of April 12. 1865.
Within an hour or two both Generals Johnston
and Beauregard were summoned to meet the Confederate President in a council of war, there being
also present the members of the rebel Cabinet,
namely: Benjamin, Secretary of State; Mallory,
Secretary of the Navy, and Reagan, Postmaster-
General. The meeting was held in a room some
twelve by sixteen feet in size, on the second floor Frank H. Alfriend, "Life of Jefferson Davis," p. 623.
of a small dwelling, and contained a bed, a few
chairs, and a table with writing-materials.

The infatuation under which Davis had plunged
his section into rebellion against the Government,
pitting the South, with its disparity of numbers[1] and
resources against the North, still beset him in the
hour of her collapse and the agony of her surrender. He had figured out how the united armies of Lee

---

[1] "Dividing their free population between the two sections,
and the odds were six and a half
millions against twenty and a half
millions."— Alfriend, "Life of
Jefferson Davis," p. 573.

CH. XIII. and Johnston could successively demolish Sherman and Grant, but he could not grasp the logic of common sense that by the same rule the united armies of Grant and Sherman would make short work of Johnston alone whenever they could reach him. The spirit of obstinate confidence with which he

Apl. 12, 1865. entered upon the interview may be best inferred from the description of it, written by the two principal actors themselves. Davis says: "I did not think we should despair. We still had effective armies in the field, and a vast extent of rich and productive territory both east and west of the Mississippi, whose citizens had evinced no disposition to surrender. Ample supplies had been collected in the railroad depots, and much still remained to be placed at our disposal when needed by the army in North Carolina. . . My motive, therefore, in holding an interview with the senior generals of the army in North Carolina was not to learn their opinion as to what might be done by negotiation

Davis, with the United States Government, but to derive
"Rise and
Fall of the from them information in regard to the army under
Confed- their command, and what it was feasible and
erate Gov-
ernment." advisable to do as a military problem."
Vol. II.,
pp. 679, 680.

Johnston's statement shows still more distinctly how impossible it was for Davis to lay aside the airs of dictator : " We had supposed that we were to be questioned concerning the military resources of our department, in connection with the question of continuing or terminating the war. But the President's object seemed to be to give, not to obtain, information ; for, addressing the party, he said that in two or three weeks he would have a large army in the field by bringing back into the ranks those

who had abandoned them in less desperate circum- CH. XIII.
stances, and by calling out the enrolled men whom Johnston,
the conscript bureau with its forces had been un- "Narra-
tive of
able to bring into the army. . . Neither opinions Military
Opera-
nor information was asked, and the conference tions,"
pp. 396, 397.
terminated."

Pollard, the Southern historian, is probably not
far wrong in saying that this "was an interview of
inevitable embarrassment and pain. The two generals [Johnston and Beauregard] were those who
had experienced most of the prejudice and injustice
of the President; he had always felt aversion for
them, and it would have been an almost impossible
excess of Christian magnanimity if they had not Pollard,
"Life of
returned something of resentment and coldness to Jefferson
Davis,
the man who, they believed, had arrogantly domi- with a
Secret
neered over them and more than once sought their History of
the Confed-
ruin." Now when Davis, without even the preface eracy,"
p. 514.
of asking their opinions, bade these two men resus-
citate his military and political power and trans-
form him from a fugitive to a commander-in-chief,
it is not to be wondered at that the interview
terminated without result.

Matters were thus left in an awkward situation
for all parties: the rebel chief had no promise of
confidence or support; the generals no authority
to negotiate or surrender; the Cabinet no excuse
to intervene by advice or protest to either party.
This condition was, however, opportunely relieved
by the arrival during the afternoon of the Secre- Apl. 12, 1865.
tary of War, Breckinridge, who was the first to
bring them the official and undoubted intelligence
of the surrender of Lee with his whole army, of
which they had hitherto been informed only by

CH. XIII. rumor, and which they had of course hoped to the last moment might prove unfounded. The fresh news naturally opened up another discussion and review of the emergency between the various individuals, and seems at length to have brought them to a frank avowal of their real feelings to each other in private.

Johnston, "Narrative of Military Operations," p. 397. Johnston and Beauregard, holding military counsel together, "agreed in the opinion that the Southern Confederacy was overthrown." This opinion Johnston also repeated to Breckinridge and Mallory, both of whom, it would seem, entertained the same view. The absence of anything like full confidence and cordial intimacy between Davis and his advisers is shown by the fact that these two members of his Cabinet were unwilling to tell their chief the truth which both recognized, and urged upon General Johnston the duty of making the unwelcome suggestion "that negotiations to end the war should be commenced." Breckinridge promised to bring about an opportunity; and it was evidently upon his suggestion that Davis called together a second conference of his Cabinet Ibid., p. 398. and his generals.

There is a conflict of statement as to when it took place. Both Davis and Mallory in their accounts group together all the incidents as if they occurred at a single meeting, which Mallory places April, 1865. on the evening of the 12th, while Johnston's account mentions the two separate meetings, the first on the morning of the 12th, and the second on the morning of the 13th; there being, however, substantial agreement between all as to the points discussed. Of this occasion, so full of historical interest, we fortunately have the records of two of the participants. General Johnston writes:

Being desired by the President to do it, we compared the military forces of the two parties to the war : ours, an army of about 20,000 infantry and artillery, and 5000 mounted troops; those of the United States, three armies that could be combined against ours, which was insignificant compared with either Grant's of 180,000 men, Sherman's of 110,000 at least, and Canby's of 60,000— odds of seventeen or eighteen to one, which in a few weeks could be more than doubled. I represented that under such circumstances it would be the greatest of human crimes for us to attempt to continue the war; for, having neither money nor credit, nor arms but those in the hands of our soldiers, nor ammunition but that in their cartridge-boxes, nor shops for repairing arms or fixing ammunition, the effect of our keeping the field would be, not to harm the enemy, but to complete the devastation of our country and ruin of its people. I therefore urged that the President should exercise at once the only function of government still in his possession, and open negotiations for peace. The members of the Cabinet present were then desired by the President to express their opinions on the important question. General Breckinridge, Mr. Mallory, and Mr. Reagan thought that the war was decided against Johnston, "Narrative of Military Operations," us, and that it was absolutely necessary to make peace. Mr. Benjamin expressed the contrary opinion. The latter made a speech for war much like that of Sempronius in pp. 398, 399. Addison's play.

Secretary Mallory's account is even more full of realistic vividness. He represents Davis, after introducing the dreaded topic by several irrelevant subjects of conversation and coming finally to " the situation of the country," as saying:

"Of course we all feel the magnitude of the moment. Our late disasters are terrible, but I do not think we should regard them as fatal. I think we can whip the

enemy yet, if our people will turn out. We must look at
matters calmly, however, and see what is left for us to do.
Whatever can be done must be done at once. We have
not a day to lose." A pause ensued, General Johnston
not seeming to deem himself expected to speak, when the
President said, "We should like to hear your views,
General Johnston." Upon this the general, without preface or introduction,— his words translating the expression which his face had worn since he entered the room,—
said, in his terse, concise, demonstrative way, as if seeking
to condense thoughts that were crowding for utterance:
"My views are, sir, that our people are tired of the war,
feel themselves whipped, and will not fight. Our country
is overrun, its military resources greatly diminished,
while the enemy's military power and resources were never
greater, and may be increased to any desired extent. We
cannot place another large army in the field ; and, cut off
as we are from foreign intercourse, I do not see how we
could maintain it in fighting condition if we had it. My
men are daily deserting in large numbers, and are taking my
artillery teams to aid their escape to their homes. Since
Lee's defeat they regard the war as at an end. If I march
out of North Carolina, her people will all leave my ranks.
It will be the same as I proceed south through South
Carolina and Georgia, and I shall expect to retain no
man beyond the by-road or cow-path that leads to his
house. My small force is melting away like snow before
the sun, and I am hopeless of recruiting it. We may perhaps obtain terms which we ought to accept." The tone
and manner, almost spiteful, in which the general jerked
out these brief, decisive sentences, pausing at every paragraph, left no doubt as to his own convictions. When he
ceased speaking, whatever was thought of his statements,
— and their importance was fully understood,— they
elicited neither comment nor inquiry. The President,
who during their delivery had sat with his eyes fixed upon
a scrap of paper, which he was folding and refolding ab-
stractedly, and who had listened without a change of position or expression, broke the silence by saying in a low, even
tone, "What do you say, General Beauregard ?" "I concur
in all General Johnston has said," he replied. Another
silence, more eloquent of the full appreciation of the condi-

tion of the country than words could have been, succeeded, during which the President's manner was unchanged.

CH. XIII.

Alfriend,
" Life of
Jefferson
Davis,"
pp. 623–625.

Davis's optimism had taken an obstinate form, and even after these irrefutable arguments and stern decisions he remained unconvinced. He writes that he " never expected a Confederate army to surrender while it was able either to fight or to retreat"; but, sustained only by the sophomoric eloquence of Mr. Benjamin, he had no alternative. He inquired of Johnston how terms were to be obtained; to which the latter answered, by negotiation between military commanders, proposing that he should be allowed to open such negotiations with Sherman. To this Davis consented, and, upon Johnston's suggestion, Secretary Mallory took up a pen and, at Davis's dictation, wrote down the letter to Sherman which we have quoted elsewhere, and the results of which have been related. The council of war over, General Johnston returned to his army to begin negotiations with Sherman. On the following day, April 14, Davis and his party, without waiting to hear the result, left Greensboro' to continue their journey southward.

Davis,
" Rise and
Fall of the
Confed-
erate Gov-
ernment."
Vol. II.,
p. 682.

April, 1865.

Alfriend,
" Life of
Jefferson
Davis,"
p. 625.

Burton N.
Harrison,
in " The
Century,"
Nov., 1883,
pp. 134, 137

The dignity and resources of the Confederate Government were rapidly shrinking; railroad travel had ceased on account of burned bridges, and it could no longer even maintain the state enjoyed in its car at Greensboro'. We are not informed what became of the archives; its personnel — President, Cabinet, and sundry staff officers — scraped together a lot of miscellaneous transportation, composed of riding horses, ambulances, and other vehicles, which, over roads rendered almost impassable by mud, made their progress to the last degree vexa-

Burton N.
Harrison,
in "The
Century,"
Nov., 1883.
p. 133.

CH. XIII.   tious and toilsome. The country was so full of
fugitives that horse-stealing seems to have become
for the time an admitted custom and privilege. We
have the statement of Davis's private secretary that
eight or ten young Mississippians, one of them an
officer, who volunteered to become the rebel President's body-guard, equipped themselves by "pressing" the horses of neighboring farmers, rendering
necessary a premature and somewhat sudden departure in advance of the official party. Obtaining
shelter by night when they could, and camping at
other times, the distinguished fugitives made their
way to Charlotte, North Carolina, where they arrived on the 18th of April.

1865.

Since the Confederate Government had considerable establishments at Charlotte, orders were
dispatched to the quartermaster to prepare ac-
commodations; and this request was reasonably
satisfied for all the members of the party except
its chief. The quartermaster met them near the
town and "explained that, though quarters could
be furnished for the rest of us, he had as yet been
able to find only one person willing to receive Mr.
Davis, saying the people generally were afraid that
whoever entertained him would have his house
burned by the enemy; that, indeed, it was understood threats to that effect had been made everywhere by Stoneman's cavalry. There seemed to be
nothing to do but to go to the one domicile offered.
It was on the main street of the town, and was
occupied by Mr. Bates, a man said to be of Northern birth, a bachelor of convivial habits, the local
agent of the Southern Express Company, apparently living alone with his negro servants, and

keeping a sort of 'open house,' where a broad, well-equipped sideboard was the most conspicuous feature of the situation—not at all a seemly place for Mr. Davis."

CH. XIII.
Burton N. Harrison, in "The Century," Nov., 1883, p. 136.

Mr. Davis was perforce obliged to accept this entertainment; and whether he failed to realize the significance of such treatment or whether he was moved by his suppressed indignation to a defiant self-assertion, when a detachment of rebel cavalry passing along the street saluted him with cheers and called him out for a speech, after the usual compliments to soldiers, he " expressed his own determination not to despair of the Confederacy, but to remain with the last organized band upholding the flag." And this feeling he again emphasized during his stay in Charlotte by a remark to his private secretary, " I *cannot* feel like a beaten man."

Ibid.

The stay at Charlotte was prolonged, evidently to wait for news from Johnston's army. No information came till April 23, when Breckinridge, Secretary of War, arrived, bringing the memorandum agreement made by Sherman and Johnston on the 18th. The memorandum seems to have been discussed at a Cabinet meeting held on the morning of the 24th, and Mr. Davis yielded to the advice they all gave him to accept and ratify the agreement. He wrote a letter to that effect, but almost immediately received further information, which Sherman communicated to Johnston, that the Washington authorities had rejected the terms and agreement, and directed Sherman to continue his military operations, and that Sherman had given notice to terminate the armistice. This

1865.
"Southern Historical Society Papers." Vol. XII., pp. 100, 102.
Davis, " Rise and Fall of the Confederate Government." Vol. II., p. 688.

change, coupled with the news of the assassination of President Lincoln, which the party had received on their arrival in Charlotte, stimulated the hopes of the rebel President, and he sent back instructions to Johnston to disband his infantry and retreat southward with so much of his cavalry and light artillery as he could bring away. Against the daily evidence of his own observation and the steady current of advice from his followers, he was still dreaming of some romantic or miraculous renewal of his chances and fortunes. And in his book, written fifteen years afterward, he makes no attempt to conceal his displeasure that General Johnston refused to obey his desperate and futile orders.

April, 1865. The armistice expired on the 26th, and the fugitive Confederate Government once more took up its southward flight. At starting, the party still made show of holding together. There were the President, most of the members of the Cabinet, several staff officers, and fragments of six cavalry brigades, counting about two thousand, which had escaped in small parties from Johnston's surrender. This was enough to form a respectable escort. There was still talk of the expedition turning westward and making its way across the Mississippi to join Kirby Smith and Magruder. But the meager accounts plainly indicate that Davis's advisers fed his hope for politeness' sake, or to furnish the only pastime with which it was possible to relieve the tedium of their journey; for as they proceeded the expedition melted away as if by enchantment. Davis directed his course toward Abbeville, South Carolina. Mr. Mallory records that though they had met no enemy, "At Abbeville the fragments of disorganized cavalry commands, which had thus far performed, in some respects, an escort's duty, were found to be reduced to a handful of men, anxious only to reach their homes as early as practicable, and whose services could not further be relied on. . . Almost every cross-road witnessed the separation of comrades in arms, who had long shared the perils and privations of a terrific struggle, now seeking their several homes to resume their duties as peaceful citizens."

Alfriend, "Life of Jefferson Davis," p. 630.

The members of the Cabinet, except Reagan, also soon dropped off on various pretexts. Benjamin decided to pursue another route, Breckinridge remained behind with the cavalry at the crossing of the Savannah River and never caught up. At Washington, Georgia, a little further on, Mallory halted "to attend to the needs of his family." Davis waited a whole day at Washington, and finding that neither troops nor leaders appeared, the actual situation seems at last to have dawned upon him. "I spoke to Captain Campbell of Kentucky, commanding my escort," he writes, "explained to him the condition of affairs, and telling him that his company was not strong enough to fight, and too large to pass without observation, asked him to inquire if there were ten men who would volunteer to go with me without question wherever I should choose." With these, two officers, three members of his personal staff, and Postmaster-General Reagan, he pushed ahead, still nursing his project of crossing the Mississippi River.

Davis, "Rise and Fall of the Confederate Government." Vol. II., p. 695.

Davis's private secretary had been sent ahead to join Mrs. Davis and her family party at Abbeville, South Carolina, and they continued their journey, in advance, with a comfortable wagon train. After passing Washington, in Georgia, reports of pursuit by Federal cavalry increased, and a more ominous rumor gained circulation that a gang of disbanded Confederates was preparing to plunder the train under the idea that it carried a portion of the official treasure. Apprehension of this latter danger induced the Confederate President to hurry forward and overtake his family, and during three days he traveled in their company. It seems to have been a dismal journey; the roads were bad, heavy storms were prevailing; signs of danger and prospects of capture were continually increasing, and they were sometimes compelled to start at midnight and push on through driving rain to make good their concealed flight.

1865. They halted about five o'clock in the afternoon of May 9, to camp and rest in the pine woods by a small stream in the neighborhood of Irwinville, Irwin County, near the middle of Southern Georgia. Here the situation was discussed, and it became clear that any hope of reaching the trans-Mississippi country was visionary. The determination was finally arrived at to proceed to the east coast of Florida, and by means of a small sailing vessel, stated to be in readiness, endeavor to gain the Texas coast by sea. It was also agreed that Davis should at once leave his family and push ahead with a few companions. Davis explains that he and his special party did not start ahead at nightfall, as had been arranged, because a rumor reached him that the expected rebel marauders would probably attack the camp that night, and that he delayed his departure for the protection of the women and children, still intending, however, to start during the night. With this view, his own and other horses remained saddled and ready. But the camp was undisturbed, and fatigue seems to have held its inmates in deep slumber until dawn of May 10, when, by a complete surprise, a troop of Federal cavalry suddenly captured the whole party and camp. There is naturally some variance in the accounts of the incident, but the differences are in the shades of coloring rather than in the essential facts.

Two expeditions had been sent from Macon by General James H. Wilson in pursuit of Jefferson Davis and his party — the one to scour the left, the other the right bank of the Ocmulgee River; one, under Lieutenant-Colonel Henry Harnden, commanding the 1st Wisconsin Cavalry, starting on the 6th, and the other, under Lieutenant-Colonel B. D. Pritchard, commanding the 4th Michigan Cavalry, starting on the 7th of May. Following different routes, these two officers met at the village of Abbeville, Georgia, in the afternoon of May 9, where they compared notes and decided to continue the pursuit by different roads. As the chase grew hot, smaller detachments from each party spurred on, learned the location of the slumbering camp, and posted themselves in readiness to attack it at daylight, but remained unconscious of each other's proximity.

The fugitives' camp was in the dense pine woods a mile and a half north of Irwinville. Pritchard had reached this village after midnight, obtained

CH. XIII. information about the camp, and procured a negro boy to guide them to it. Approaching to within half a mile, he halted, both to wait for daylight and to send his lieutenant, Purinton, with twenty-five dismounted men to gain the rear of the camp, but cautioning him that a part of Harnden's command would in all probability approach from that direction, and that he must avoid a conflict with them.

May 10, 1865. "At daybreak," writes Captain G. W. Lawton of Pritchard's force, "the order was passed in a whisper to make ready to enter the camp. The men were alive to the work. Mounting their horses, the column moved at a walk until the tents came in sight, and then, at the word, dashed in. The camp was found pitched on both sides of the road. On the left hand, as we entered, were wagons, horses, tents, and men; on the right were two wall-tents, G. W. Lawton, in "The Atlantic," Sept., 1865, p. 344. fronting from the road. All was quiet in the camp. We encountered no guards; if there were any out, they must have been asleep."

Just at this instant, however, firing was heard back of the camp, where Purinton had been sent. This created instant confusion, and Pritchard with most of his force rushed forward through the camp to resist a supposed Confederate attack. It turned out that, despite the precautions taken, the detachment of Pritchard's men under Purinton (the 4th Michigan) had met a detachment of Harnden's men (the 1st Wisconsin), and in the darkness they had mistaken and fired on each other, causing two deaths and wounding a number.

The rush of the cavalry and the firing of course aroused the sleepers, and as they emerged from their tents there was a moment of confusion, during which only one or two Federal soldiers remained in the camp. One of these had secured Davis's horse, which had stood saddled since the previous evening, and which a colored servant had just brought to his tent. Of what ensued, we give Mr. Davis's own account:

CH. XIII.

Lawton, in "The Atlantic," Sept., 1865, p. 344.

I stepped out of my wife's tent and saw some horsemen, whom I immediately recognized as cavalry, deploying around the encampment. I turned back and told my wife these were not the expected marauders, but regular troopers. She implored me to leave her at once. I hesitated, from unwillingness to do so, and lost a few precious moments before yielding to her importunity. My horse and arms were near the road on which I expected to leave, and down which the cavalry approached; it was, therefore impracticable to reach them. I was compelled to start in the opposite direction. As it was quite dark in the tent, I picked up what was supposed to be my "raglan," a waterproof light overcoat, without sleeves; it was subsequently found to be my wife's, so very like my own as to be mistaken for it; as I started, my wife thoughtfully threw over my head and shoulders a shawl. I had gone perhaps fifteen or twenty yards when a trooper galloped up and ordered me to halt and surrender, to which I gave a defiant answer, and dropping the shawl and raglan from my shoulders advanced toward him; he leveled his carbine at me, but I expected, if he fired, he would miss me, and my intention was in that event to put my hand under his foot, tumble him off on the other side, spring into his saddle and attempt to escape. My wife, who had been watching, when she saw the soldier aim his carbine at me, ran forward and threw her arms around me. Success depended on instantaneous action, and recognizing that the opportunity had been lost I turned back, and, the morning being damp and chilly, passed on to a fire beyond the tent.[1]

May 10, 1865.

Davis, " Rise and Fall of the Confederate Government," pp. 701, 702.

[1] It is but just to give the following narrative of Captain G. W. Lawton of the 4th Michigan Cavalry. It was printed in "The Atlantic Monthly" for September, 1865, and the reader may

272 ABRAHAM LINCOLN

CH. XIII.
May 10, 1864.

Colonel Pritchard relates in his official report:
"Upon returning to camp I was accosted by Davis
from among the prisoners, who asked if I was the
officer in command, and upon my answering him
that I was, and asking him whom I was to call him,

profitably compare it with Jefferson Davis's own narrative which is quoted in the text.

"Andrew Bee, a private of Company L went to the entrance of Davis's tent, and was met by Mrs. Davis, 'bareheaded and barefoot,' as he describes her, who, putting her hand on his arm, said:

"'Please don't go in there till my daughter gets herself dressed.'

"Andrew thereupon drew back, and in a few minutes a young lady (Miss Howell) and another person, bent over as with age, wearing a lady's 'waterproof,' gathered at the waist, with a shawl drawn over the head, and carrying a tin pail, appear, and ask to go to 'the run' for water. Mrs. Davis also appears, and says:

"'For God's sake, let my old mother go to get some water!'

"No objections being made, they passed out. But sharp eyes were upon the singular looking 'old mother.' Suddenly, Corporal Munyer of Company C, and others, at the same instant, discovered that the 'old mother' was wearing very heavy boots for an aged female, and the corporal exclaimed:

"'That is not a woman! Don't you see the boots?' and spurring his horse forward and cocking his carbine, compelled the withdrawal of the shawl, and disclosed Jeff. Davis.

"As if stung by this discovery

of his unmanliness, Jeff. struck an attitude, and cried out:

"'Is there a man among you? If there is, let me see him!'

"'Yes,' said the corporal, 'I am one; and if you stir, I will blow your brains out!'

"'I know my fate,' said Davis, 'and might as well die here.'

"But his wife threw her arms around his neck, and kept herself between him and the threatening corporal.

"No harm, however, was done him, and he was generally kindly spoken to; he was only stripped of his female attire.

"As a man he was dressed in a complete suit of gray, a light felt hat, and high cavalry boots, with a gray beard of about six weeks' growth covering his face.

"He said he thought that our Government was too magnanimous to hunt women and children that way.

"When Colonel Pritchard told him that he would do the best he could for his comfort, he answered:

"'I ask no favors of you.'

"To which surly reply the colonel courteously responded by assuring him of kind treatment.

"Arrangements were forthwith made to return to Macon. . .

"The members of Davis's staff submitted with better grace than he to the capture and march, and were generally quite communicative."

GENERAL ULYSSES S. GRANT.

From a photograph taken in 1875.

he replied that I might call him what or whomsoever I pleased. When I replied to him that I would call him Davis, and after a moment's hesitation he said that was his name, he suddenly drew himself up in true royal dignity and exclaimed, ' I suppose that you consider it bravery to charge a train of defenseless women and children, but it is theft, it is vandalism ! ' "

Ch. XIII.

Pritchard to Stanton, May 25, 1865.

That the correctness of the report may not be questioned, we add the corroborating statement of Postmaster-General Reagan, the sole member of the rebel Cabinet remaining with the party : " Colonel Pritchard did not come up for some time after Mr. Davis was made a prisoner. When he rode up there was a crowd, chiefly of Federal soldiers, around Mr. Davis. He was standing, and dressed in the suit he habitually wore. He turned toward Colonel Pritchard and asked, ' Who commands these troops ?' Colonel Pritchard replied, without hesitation, that he did. Mr. Davis said to him, ' You command a set of thieves and robbers. They rob women and children.' Colonel Pritchard then said, ' Mr. Davis, you should remember that you are a prisoner.' And Mr. Davis replied: 'I am fully conscious of that. It would be bad enough to be the prisoner of soldiers and gentlemen. I am still lawful game, and would rather be dead than be your prisoner.' "

J. H. Reagan, in "Annals of the War," p. 155.

Colonel Pritchard's official report gives the following list of the persons who fell into his hands : " I ascertained that we had captured Jefferson Davis and family (a wife and four children); John H. Reagan, his Postmaster-General; Colonels Harrison and Lubbock, A. D. C. to Davis; Burton N.

CH. XIII. Harrison, his private secretary; Major Maurin and Captain Moody, Lieutenant Hathaway; Jeff. D. Howell, midshipman in the rebel navy, and twelve private soldiers; Miss Maggie Howell, sister of Mrs. Davis; two waiting maids, one white and one black, and several other servants. We also captured five wagons, three ambulances, about fifteen horses, and from twenty-five to thirty mules. The train was mostly loaded with commissary stores and private baggage of the party."

The details of the return march are unnecessary; there is no allegation that the prisoners were ill 1865. treated. They arrived at Macon on May 13, both captors and prisoners having on the way first learned of the offer of a reward of one hundred thousand dollars for Davis's apprehension on the charge of having been an accomplice in the assassination of President Lincoln.

The assumption of Davis's guilt, and the proclamation offering the reward, were not based upon mere public excitement, but upon testimony given by witnesses who appeared before the Bureau of Military Justice, and which seemed conclusively to prove that the rebel President had taken part in that dreadful conspiracy. But this evidence was found to be untrustworthy; upon an investigation held by a Committee of Congress about a year later, several of these witnesses retracted their statements and declared that their testimony as given originally was false in every particular. No prosecution on this charge was therefore begun against Davis; but after an imprisonment of about two years in Fort Monroe, he was indicted and arraigned at Richmond before the United States Circuit Court for the District of Virginia for the crime of treason, and liberated on bail, Horace Greeley, Gerritt Smith, and Cornelius Vanderbilt having volunteered to become his principal bondsmen.

On the 3d of December, 1868, a motion was made to quash the indictment on the ground that the penalties and disabilities denounced against and inflicted on him for his alleged offense, by the third section of the Fourteenth Amendment of the Constitution of the United States, were a bar to any proceedings upon such indictment. The court, consisting of Chief-Justice Chase and Judge John C. Underwood, considered the motion, and two days later announced that they disagreed in opinion, and certified the question to the Supreme Court of the United States. Though not announced, it was understood that the Chief-Justice held the affirmative and Judge Underwood the negative.

Three weeks from that day President Johnson bestowed upon Mr. Davis and those who had been his followers a liberal and fraternal Christmas gift. On the 25th of December, 1868, he issued a proclamation supplementing the various prior proclamations of amnesty, which declared "unconditionally and without reservation, to all and to every person who directly or indirectly participated in the late insurrection or rebellion, a full pardon and amnesty for the offense of treason against the United States, or of adhering to their enemies during the late civil war, with restoration of all rights, privileges, and immunities, under the Constitution and the laws which have been made in pursuance thereof." The Government of course took no further action in the suit; and at a subsequent term of the Circuit Court the indictment was dismissed on motion of Mr. Davis's counsel. The ex-President of the Confederate States was thus relieved from all penalties for his rebellion except the disability to hold office imposed by the third section of the Fourteenth Amendment, which Congress refused to remove.

This ended the public career of Jefferson Davis. He returned to his home in Mississippi, where he lived unmolested nearly a quarter of a century after the downfall of his rebellion; emerging from his retirement only by an occasional letter or address. In some of these, as well as in his elaborate work entitled " The Rise and Fall of the Confederate Government," very guarded undertones revealed an undying animosity to the Government of the United States, whose destiny he had sought to pervert, whose trusts he had betrayed, whose honors he had repaid by attempting its destruction, and whose clemency he appeared incapable of appreciating even in his defeat. He died at New Orleans on December 6, 1889, while visiting that city.

CHAPTER XIV

THE 14th of April was a day of deep and tran- CHAP. XIV.
quil happiness throughout the United States. 1865.
It was Good Friday, observed by a portion of the
people as an occasion of fasting and religious
meditation; but even among the most devout
the great tidings of the preceding week exerted
their joyous influence, and changed this period of
traditional mourning into an occasion of general
and profound thanksgiving. Peace, so strenuously
fought for, so long sought and prayed for, with
prayers uttered and unutterable, was at last near at
hand, its dawn visible on the reddening hills. The
sermons all day were full of gladness; the Misereres
turned of themselves to Te Deums. The country
from morning till evening was filled with a solemn
joy; but the date was not to lose its awful significance in the calendar: at night it was claimed once
more, and forever, by a world-wide sorrow.

The thanksgiving of the nation found its principal expression at Charleston Harbor. A month
before, after Sherman had "conquered Charleston
by turning his back upon it," the Government resolved that the flag of the Union should receive a
conspicuous reparation on the spot where it had

first been outraged. It was ordered by the President that General Robert Anderson should, at the hour of noon on the 14th day of April, raise above the ruins of Fort Sumter the identical flag lowered and saluted by him four years before. In the absence of General Sherman the ceremonies were in charge of General Gillmore. Henry Ward Beecher, the most famous of the antislavery preachers of the North, was selected to deliver an oration. The surrender of Lee, the news of which arrived at Charleston on the eve of the ceremonies, gave a more transcendent importance to the celebration, which became at once the occasion of a national thanksgiving over the downfall of the rebellion. On the day fixed Charleston was filled with a great concourse of distinguished officers and citizens. Its long-deserted streets were crowded with an eager multitude, and gay with innumerable flags, while the air was thrilled from an early hour with patriotic strains from the many bands, and shaken with the thunder of Dahlgren's fleet, which opened the day by firing from every vessel a national salute of twenty-one guns. By eleven o'clock a brilliant gathering of boats, ships, and steamers of every sort had assembled around the battered ruin of the fort; the whole bay seemed covered with the vast flotilla, planted with a forest of masts, whose foliage was the triumphant banners of the nation. The Rev. Matthias Harris, the same chaplain who had officiated at the raising of the flag over Sumter, at the first scene of the war, offered a prayer; Dr. Richard S. Storrs and the people read, in alternate verses, a selection of psalms of thanksgiving and victory, beginning with these marvelous

words which have preserved for so many ages the CHAP. XIV.
very pulse and throb of the joy of redemption:

When the Lord turned again the captivity of Zion, we
were like them that dream.

Then was our mouth filled with laughter, and our
tongue with singing; then said they among the heathen,
The Lord hath done great things for them.

The Lord hath done great things for us; whereof we
are glad.

Turn again our captivity, O Lord, as the streams in the
south.

They that sow in tears shall reap in joy.

He that goeth forth and weepeth, bearing precious seed,
shall doubtless come again with rejoicing, bringing his
sheaves with him.

And at the close, before the Gloria, the people
and the minister read all together, in a voice that
seemed to catch the inspiration of the hour:

Some trust in chariots and some in horses: but we will
remember the name of the Lord our God.

We will rejoice in thy salvation, and in the name of our
God we will set up our banners.

General Townsend then read the original dispatch announcing the fall of Sumter, and precisely
as the bells of the ships struck the hour of noon,
General Anderson, with his own hands seizing the
halyards, hoisted to its place the flag which he had
seen lowered before the opening guns of rebellion.
As the starry banner floated out upon the breeze,
which freshened at the moment as if to embrace it,
a storm of joyful acclamation burst forth from the
vast assembly, mingled with the music of hundreds
of instruments, the shouts of the people, and the
full-throated roar of great guns from the Union and
the captured rebel forts alike, on every side of the

General
E. D.
Townsend,
afterwards
Adjutant-
General
U. S. A.

Apl. 14, 1865.

harbor, thundering their harmonious salute to the restored banner. General Anderson made a brief and touching speech, the people sang "The Star-Spangled Banner," Mr. Beecher delivered an address in his best and gravest manner, filled with an earnest, sincere, and unboastful spirit of nationality; with a feeling of brotherhood to the South, prophesying for that section the advantages which her defeat has in fact brought her; a speech as brave, as gentle, and as magnanimous as the occasion demanded. In concluding, he said, and we quote his words, as they embodied the opinion of all men of good will on this last day of Abraham Lincoln's life: "We offer to the President of these United States our solemn congratulations that God has sustained his life and health under the unparalleled burdens and sufferings of four bloody years, and permitted him to behold this auspicious consummation of that national unity for which he has waited with so much patience and fortitude, and for which he has labored with such disinterested wisdom."

At sunset another national salute was fired; the evening was given up to social festivities; the most distinguished of the visitors were entertained at supper by General Gillmore; a brilliant show of fireworks by Admiral Dahlgren illuminated the bay and the circle of now friendly forts, at the very moment when at the capital of the nation a little group of conspirators were preparing the blackest crime which sullies the record of the century.

In Washington also it was a day, not of exultation, but of deep peace and thankfulness. It was the fifth day after the surrender of Lee; the first

effervescence of the intoxicating success had passed
away. The President had, with that ever-present
sense of responsibility which distinguished him,
given his thoughts instantly to the momentous
question of the restoration of the Union and of
harmony between the lately warring sections. He
had, in defiance of precedent and even of his own
habit, delivered to the people on the 11th, from the
windows of the White House, his well-considered
views as to the measures demanded by the times.
His whole heart was now enlisted in the work of
"binding up the nation's wounds," of doing all
which might "achieve and cherish a just and
lasting peace."

Grant had arrived that morning in Washington
and immediately proceeded to the Executive Mansion, where he met the Cabinet, Friday being their
regular day of meeting. He expressed some anxiety
as to the news from Sherman, which he was expecting hourly. The President answered him in that
singular vein of poetic mysticism which, though
constantly held in check by his strong common-
sense, formed a remarkable element in his character.
He assured Grant that the news would come soon
and come favorably, for he had last night had his
usual dream which preceded great events. He
seemed to be, he said, in a singular and indescrib-
able vessel, but always the same, moving with
great rapidity towards a dark and indefinite shore;
he had had this dream before Antietam, Murfreesboro', Gettysburg, and Vicksburg. The Cabinet
were greatly impressed by this story; but Grant,
the most matter-of-fact of created beings, made the
characteristic response that "Murfreesboro' was no

CHAP. XIV. victory, and had no important results." The President did not argue this point with him, but repeated that Sherman would beat or had beaten Johnston; that his dream must relate to that, as he knew of no other important event which was likely at present to occur.[1]

Apl. 14, 1865. The subject of the discussion which took place in the Cabinet on that last day of Lincoln's firm and tolerant rule has been preserved for us in the notes of Mr. Welles. They were written out, it is true, seven years afterwards, at a time when Grant was President, seeking reëlection, and when Mr. Welles had followed Andrew Johnson into full fellowship with the Democratic party. Making whatever allowance is due for the changed environment of the writer, we still find his account of the day's conversation candid and trustworthy. The subject of trade between the States was the first that engaged the attention of the Cabinet. Mr. Stanton wished it to be carried on under somewhat strict military supervision; Mr. Welles was in favor of a more liberal system; Mr. McCulloch, new to the Treasury, and embarrassed by his grave responsibilities, favored the abolition of the Treasury agencies, and above all desired a definite understanding of the purpose of the Government. The President, seeing that in this divergence of views among men equally able and honest there lay the best chance of a judicious arrangement, appointed the three Secretaries as a commission with plenary power to examine the whole subject, announcing

"The Galaxy," April, 1872.

[1] This incident is told by the Hon. Gideon Welles in an article printed in "The Galaxy" for April, 1872. It was frequently related by Charles Dickens with characteristic amplifications. See also "George Eliot's Life." Vol. III., p. 82.

himself as content in advance with their conclu-
sións.

The great subject of the reëstablishment of civil
government in the Southern States was then taken
up. Mr. Stanton had, a few days before, drawn
up a project for an executive ordinance for the
preservation of order and the rehabilitation of
legal processes in the States lately in rebellion.
The President, using this sketch as his text, not
adopting it as a whole, but saying that it was substantially the result of frequent discussions in the
Cabinet, spoke at some length on the question of
reconstruction, than which none more important
could ever engage the attention of the Government. It was providential, he thought, that this
matter should have arisen at a time when it could
be considered, so far as the Executive was concerned, without interference by Congress. If they
were wise and discreet, they should reanimate the
States and get their governments in successful
operation, with order prevailing and the Union
reëstablished, before Congress came together in
December. The President felt so kindly towards
the South, he was so sure of the Cabinet under
his guidance, that he was anxious to close the period of strife without overmuch discussion.

He was particularly desirous to avoid the shedding of blood, or any vindictiveness of punishment.
He gave plain notice that morning that he would
have none of it. "No one need expect he would
take any part in hanging or killing these men, even
the worst of them. Frighten them out of the
country, open the gates, let down the bars, scare
them off," said he, throwing up his hands as if

scaring sheep. "Enough lives have been sacrificed; we must extinguish our resentments if we expect harmony and union."[1] He deprecated the disposition he had seen in some quarters to hector and dictate to the people of the South, who were trying to right themselves. He regretted that suffrage, under proper arrangement, had not been given to negroes in Louisiana, but he held that their constitution was in the main a good one. He was averse to the exercise of arbitrary powers by the Executive or by Congress. Congress had the undoubted right to receive or reject members; the Executive had no control in this; but the Executive could do very much to restore order in the States, and their practical relations with the Government, before Congress came together.

Mr. Stanton then read his plan for the temporary military government of the States of Virginia and North Carolina, which for this purpose were combined in one department. This gave rise at once to extended discussion, Mr. Welles and Mr. Dennison opposing the scheme of uniting two States under one government. The President closed the session by saying the same objection had occurred to him, and by directing Mr. Stanton to revise the document and report separate plans for the government of the two States. He did not wish the autonomy nor the individuality of the States de-

---

[1] Near the close of the war his old friend, Joseph Gillespie, asked him what was to be done with the rebels. He answered, after referring to the vehement demand prevalent in certain quarters for exemplary punishment, by quoting the words of David to his nephews, who were asking for vengeance on Shimei because "he cursed the Lord's anointed": "What have I to do with you, ye sons of Zeruiah, that ye should this day be adversaries unto me? Shall there any man be put to death this day in Israel?"

stroyed. He commended the whole subject to the most earnest and careful consideration of the Cabinet; it was to be resumed on the following Tuesday; it was, he said, the great question pending — they must now begin to act in the interest of peace.

These were the last words that Lincoln spoke to his Cabinet. They dispersed with these words of clemency and good-will in their ears, never again to meet under his wise and benignant chairmanship. He had told them that morning a strange story, which made some demand upon their faith, but the circumstances under which they were next to come together were beyond the scope of the wildest fancy. The day was one of unusual enjoyment to Mr. Lincoln. His son Robert had returned from the field with General Grant, and the President spent an hour with the young captain in delighted conversation over the campaign. He denied himself generally to the throng of visitors, admitting only a few friends.

Schuyler Colfax, who was contemplating a visit overland to the Pacific, came to ask whether the President would probably call an extra session of Congress during the summer. Mr. Lincoln assured him that he had no such intention, and gave him a verbal message to the mining population of Colorado and the Western slope of the mountains concerning the part they were to take in the great conquests of peace which were coming. In the afternoon he went for a long drive with Mrs. Lincoln. His mood, as it had been all day, was singularly happy and tender. He talked much of the past and the future; after four years of trouble and tumult he looked

CHAP. XIV. forward to four years of comparative quiet and normal work; after that he expected to go back to Illinois and practice law again. He was never Apl. 14, 1865. simpler or gentler than on this day of unprecedented triumph; his heart overflowed with sentiments of gratitude to Heaven, which took the shape usual to generous natures, of love and kindness to all men.

From the very beginning of his Presidency Mr. Lincoln had been constantly subject to the threats of his enemies and the warnings of his friends. The threats came in every form; his mail was infested with brutal and vulgar menace, mostly anonymous, the proper expression of vile and cowardly minds. The warnings were not less numerous; the vaporings of village bullies, the extravagances of excited secessionist politicians, even the drolling of practical jokers, were faithfully reported to him by zealous or nervous friends. Most of these communications received no notice. In cases where there seemed a ground for inquiry it was made, as carefully as possible, by the President's private secretary and by the War Department, but always without substantial result. Warnings that appeared to be most definite, when they came to be examined proved too vague and confused for further attention. The President was too intelligent not to know he was in some danger. Madmen frequently made their way to the very door of the Executive offices and sometimes into Mr. Lincoln's presence.[1] He had himself so sane

---

[1] All Presidents receive visits from persons more or less demented. Mr. Hayes, when about to retire one day from his working-room, asked his messenger if there was any one waiting to see

a mind, and a heart so kindly even to his enemies, that it was hard for him to believe in a political hatred so deadly as to lead to murder. He would sometimes laughingly say, "Our friends on the other side would make nothing by exchanging me for Hamlin," the Vice-President having the reputation of more radical views than his chief.

He knew indeed that incitements to murder him were not uncommon in the South. An advertisement had appeared in a paper of Selma, Alabama, in December, 1864, opening a subscription for funds to effect the assassination of Lincoln, Seward, and Johnson before the inauguration. There was more of this murderous spirit abroad than was suspected. A letter was found in the Confederate Archives from one Lieutenant Alston, who wrote to Jefferson Davis immediately after Lincoln's re-election, offering to "rid his country of some of her deadliest enemies by striking at the very heart's blood of those who seek to enchain her in slavery." This shameless proposal was referred, by Mr. Davis's direction, to the Secretary of War; and by Judge Campbell, Assistant Secretary of War, was sent to the Confederate Adjutant-General indorsed "for attention." We can readily imagine what reception an officer would have met with who should have laid before Mr. Lincoln a scheme to assassinate Jefferson Davis. It was the uprightness and the kindliness of his own heart that made him slow to believe that any such ignoble fury

Pitman, Conspiracy Trial, p. 51. W. Alston to Jefferson Davis. On file in the office of the Judge Advocate-General at Washington. Ibid., p. 52.

him. "Only two, and one of them is crazy." "Send in the sane one," said the President. A grave-looking man was introduced, who announced himself as the emperor of the world. The President rang the bell, and told the messenger if that was his idea of sanity to send in the maniac.

CHAP. XIV. could find a place in the hearts of men in their right minds.

Although he freely discussed with the officials about him the possibilities of danger, he always considered them remote, as is the habit of men constitutionally brave, and positively refused to torment himself with precautions for his own safety. He would sum the matter up by saying that both friends and strangers must have daily access to him in all manner of ways and places; his life was therefore in reach of any one, sane or mad, who was ready to murder and be hanged for it; that he could not possibly guard against all danger unless he were to shut himself up in an iron box, in which condition he could scarcely perform the duties of a President; by the hand of a murderer he could die only once; to go continually in fear would be to die over and over. He therefore went in and out before the people, always unarmed, generally unattended. He would receive hundreds of visitors in a day, his breast bare to pistol or knife. He would walk at midnight, with a single secretary or alone, from the Executive Mansion to the War Department and back. He would ride through the lonely roads of an uninhabited suburb from the White House to the Soldiers' Home in the dusk of evening, and return to his work in the morning before the town was astir. He was greatly annoyed when it was decided that there must be a guard stationed at the Executive Mansion, and that a squad of cavalry must accompany him on his daily ride; but he was always reasonable and yielded to the best judgment of others.

Four years of threats and boastings, of alarms

ABRAHAM LINCOLN.

From a photograph taken March 6, 1865.

that were unfounded, and of plots that came to
nothing thus passed away; but precisely at the
time when the triumph of the nation over the long
insurrection seemed assured, and a feeling of peace
and security was diffused over the country, one of
the conspiracies, not seemingly more important
than the many abortive ones, ripened in the sudden
heat of hatred and despair. A little band of malignant secessionists, consisting of John Wilkes Booth,
an actor, of a family of famous players, Lewis
Powell, alias Payne, a disbanded rebel soldier from
Florida, George Atzerodt, formerly a coachmaker,
but more recently a spy and blockade runner of the
Potomac, David E. Herold, a young druggist's
clerk, Samuel Arnold and Michael O'Laughlin,
Maryland secessionists and Confederate soldiers, Pitman,
pp. 350, 222.
and John H. Surratt, had their ordinary rendezvous
at the house of Mrs. Mary E. Surratt, the widowed 541 H St.
mother of the last named, formerly a woman of
some property in Maryland, but reduced by reverses
to keeping a small boarding-house in Washington.

Booth was the leader of the little coterie. He
was a young man of twenty-six, strikingly handsome, with a pale olive face, dark eyes, and that
ease and grace of manner which came to him of
right from his theatrical ancestors. He had played
for several seasons with only indifferent success;
his value as an actor lay rather in his romantic
beauty of person than in any talent or industry he
possessed. He was a fanatical secessionist; had
assisted at the capture and execution of John Brown,
and had imbibed at Richmond and other Southern
cities where he had played, a furious spirit of par-
tisanship against Lincoln and the Union party.

CHAP. XIV. After the reëlection of Mr. Lincoln, which rang the knell of the insurrection, Booth, like many of the secessionists North and South, was stung to the quick by disappointment. He visited Canada, consorted with the rebel emissaries there, and at last — whether or not at their instigation cannot certainly be said — conceived a scheme to capture the President and take him to Richmond. He spent a great part of the autumn and winter inducing a small number of loose fish of secession sympathies to join him in this fantastic enterprise. He seemed always well supplied with money, and talked largely of his speculations in oil as a source of income; but his agent afterwards testified that he never realized a dollar from that source; that his investments, which were inconsiderable, were a total loss. The winter passed away and nothing was accomplished. On the 4th of March, Booth was at the Capitol and created a disturbance by trying to force his way through the line of policemen who guarded the passage through which the President walked to the east front of the building. His intentions at this time are not known; he afterwards said he lost an excellent chance of killing the President that day.

Pitman,
p. 45.

He was
seized and
held back
by John W.
Westfall,
of the
Capitol
Police.

Pitman,
p. 45.

There are indications in the evidence given on the trial of the conspirators that they suffered some great disappointment in their schemes in the latter part of March, and a letter from Arnold to Booth, dated March 27, showed that some of them had grown timid of the consequences of their contemplated enterprise and were ready to give it up. He advised Booth, before going further, " to go and see how it will be taken in R—d." But timid

1865.

Ibid., p. 236.

as they might be by nature, the whole group was
so completely under the ascendency of Booth that
they did not dare disobey him when in his presence; and after the surrender of Lee, in an access
of malice and rage which was akin to madness, he
called them together and assigned each his part in
the new crime, the purpose of which had arisen
suddenly in his mind out of the ruins of the
abandoned abduction scheme. This plan was as
brief and simple as it was horrible. Powell, alias
Payne, the stalwart, brutal, simple-minded boy
from Florida, was to murder Seward; Atzerodt,
the comic villain of the drama, was assigned to
remove Andrew Johnson; Booth reserved for himself the most difficult and most conspicuous rôle of
the tragedy; it was Herold's duty to attend him as
a page and aid in his escape. Minor parts were
assigned to stage carpenters and other hangers-on,
who probably did not understand what it all meant.
Herold, Atzerodt, and Surratt had previously de-
posited at a tavern at Surrattsville, Maryland, owned
by Mrs. Surratt, but kept by a man named Lloyd,
a quantity of ropes, carbines, ammunition, and
whisky, which were to be used in the abduction
scheme. On the 11th of April Mrs. Surratt, being   1865.
at the tavern, told Lloyd to have the shooting irons
in readiness, and on Friday, the 14th, again visited
the place and told him they would probably be
called for that night.

The preparations for the final blow were made
with feverish haste; it was only about noon of the
14th that Booth learned the President was to go to
Ford's Theater that night. It has always been a
matter of surprise in Europe that he should have

been at a place of amusement on Good Friday; but the day was not kept sacred in America, except by the members of certain churches. It was not, throughout the country, a day of religious observance. The President was fond of the theater; it was one of his few means of recreation. It was natural enough that, on this day of profound national thanksgiving, he should take advantage of a few hours' relaxation to see a comedy. Besides, the town was thronged with soldiers and officers, all eager to see him; it was represented to him that appearing occasionally in public would gratify many people whom he could not otherwise meet. Mrs. Lincoln had asked General and Mrs. Grant to accompany her; they had accepted, and the announcement that they would be present was made as an advertisement in the evening papers; but they changed their minds and went North by an afternoon train. Mrs. Lincoln then invited in their stead Miss Harris and Major Henry R. Rathbone, the daughter and the stepson of Senator Ira Harris. The President's carriage called for these young people, and the four went together to the theater. The President had been detained by visitors, and the play had made some progress when he arrived. When he appeared in his box the band struck up "Hail to the Chief," the actors ceased playing, and the audience rose, cheering tumultuously; the President bowed in acknowledgment of this greeting and the play went on.

From the moment Booth ascertained the President's intention to attend the theater in the evening his every action was alert and energetic. He and his confederates, Herold, Surratt, and Atzerodt, were

seen on horseback in every part of the city. He
had a hurried conference with Mrs. Surratt before
she started for Lloyd's tavern. He intrusted to an
actor named Matthews a carefully prepared statement of his reasons for committing the murder,
which he charged him to give to the publisher of
the "National Intelligencer," but which Matthews,
in the terror and dismay of the night, burned without showing to any one. Booth was perfectly at
home in Ford's Theater, where he was greatly liked
by all the employees, without other reason than
the sufficient one of his youth and good looks.
Either by himself or with the aid of his friends he
arranged his whole plan of attack and escape during the afternoon. He counted upon address and
audacity to gain access to the small passage behind the President's box; once there, he guarded
against interference by an arrangement of a
wooden bar to be fastened by a simple mortice in
the angle of the wall and the door by which he
entered, so that the door could not be opened from
without. He even provided for the contingency
of not gaining entrance to the box by boring a
hole in its door, through which he might either
observe the occupants or take aim and shoot. He
hired at a livery stable a small, fleet horse, which
he showed with pride during the day to barkeepers
and loafers among his friends.

The moon rose that night at ten o'clock. A few
minutes before that hour he called one of the
underlings of the theater to the back door and left
him there holding his horse. He then went to a
saloon near by, took a drink of brandy, and, entering the theater, passed rapidly through the crowd in

CHAP. XIV.

Apl. 14, 1865.

John F.
Coyle, MS.
Statement.

CHAP. XIV.   rear of the dress circle and made his way to the passage leading to the President's box. He showed a

Apl. 14, 1865.   card to a servant in attendance and was allowed to pass in. He entered noiselessly, and, turning, fastened the door with the bar he had previously made ready, without disturbing any of the occupants of the box, between whom and himself there yet remained the slight partition and the door

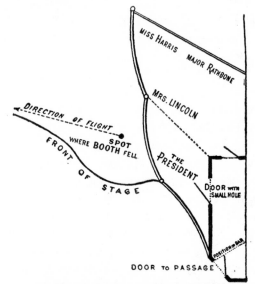

DIAGRAM OF THE BOX IN FORD'S THEATER.
(COPIED FROM THE DRAWING IN THE WAR DEPARTMENT.)

through which he had bored the hole. Their eyes were fixed upon the stage; the play was "Our American Cousin," the original version by Tom Taylor, before Sothern had made a new work of it by his elaboration of the part of *Dundreary*.

No one, not even the comedian on the stage, could ever remember the last words of the piece that were uttered that night — the last Abraham

Lincoln heard upon earth. The whole performance
remains in the memory of those who heard it a
vague phantasmagoria, the actors the thinnest of
specters. The awful tragedy in the box makes
everything else seem pale and unreal. Here were
five human beings in a narrow space — the greatest
man of his time, in the glory of the most stupendous success in our history, the idolized chief of a
nation already mighty, with illimitable vistas of
grandeur to come; his beloved wife, proud and
happy; a pair of betrothed lovers, with all the
promise of felicity that youth, social position, and
wealth could give them; and this young actor,
handsome as Endymion upon Latmos, the pet of
his little world. The glitter of fame, happiness,
and ease was upon the entire group, but in an
instant everything was to be changed with the
blinding swiftness of enchantment. Quick death
was to come on the central figure of that company
— the central figure, we believe, of the great and
good men of the century. Over all the rest the
blackest fates hovered menacingly — fates from
which a mother might pray that kindly death would
save her children in their infancy. One was to
wander with the stain of murder on his soul, with
the curses of a world upon his name, with a price
set upon his head, in frightful physical pain, till he
died a dog's death in a burning barn; the stricken
wife was to pass the rest of her days in melancholy
and madness; of those two young lovers, one was
to slay the other, and then end his life a raving
maniac.

The murderer seemed to himself to be taking part
in a play. Partisan hate and the fumes of brandy

STAGE AND PROSCENIUM BOXES OF FORD'S THEATER AS THEY

This drawing was made from two photographs by Brady, lent by W. R. Speare of Washington. One of the photographs (of the President's box, on the opposite page), supposed to be the earlier of the two, differs from the other photograph (showing the stage and all the boxes) as regards the three silk flags, apparently regimental flags, fixed at the sides and middle column of the box. Joseph S.

APPEARED ON THE NIGHT OF PRESIDENT LINCOLN'S ASSASSINATION.

Sessford, at the time assistant treasurer of the theater, is authority for the statement that the second photograph (presented to Mr. Speare by L. Moxley, who had it from Mr. Sessford) was taken three or four days after the assassination, when none of the decorations, except the regimental flags, had been removed. The portrait between the flags is an engraving of Washington.

CHAP. XIV.   had for weeks kept his brain in a morbid state.
Apl. 14, 1865.   He felt as if he were playing Brutus off the boards;
he posed, expecting applause. Holding a pistol in
one hand and a knife in the other, he opened the
box door, put the pistol to the President's head,
and fired; dropping the weapon, he took the knife
in his right hand, and when Major Rathbone sprang
to seize him he struck savagely at him. Major
Rathbone received the blow on his left arm, suffer-
ing a wide and deep wound. Booth, rushing forward, then placed his left hand on the railing of
the box and vaulted lightly over to the stage. It
was a high leap, but nothing to such a trained
athlete. He was in the habit of introducing what
actors call sensational leaps in his plays. In
"Macbeth," where he met the weird sisters, he
leaped from a rock twelve feet high. He would
have got safely away but for his spur catching in
the folds of the Union flag with which the front of the
box was draped. He fell on the stage, the torn flag
trailing on his spur, but instantly rose as if he had
received no hurt, though in fact the fall had broken
his leg; he turned to the audience, brandishing his
dripping knife, and shouting the State motto of
Virginia, " Sic Semper Tyrannis," [1] and fled rapidly
across the stage and out of sight. Major Rathbone had shouted, " Stop him ! " The cry went

[1] Mr. Leopold de Gaillard, writing on the 29th of April, 1865,
refers to these words of Booth,
which he calls a "stupid phrase,"
and not American in character.
"I remember," he adds, "but
one assassination adorned with a
Latin quotation, but it took place
in Florence, and in the sixteenth
century. Lorenzino treacher-
ously killed his cousin, Alexander
de Medici, who was in reality a
tyrant, and left in writing near
the body the line of Virgil on
Brutus: *Vincet amor patriæ lau-
dumque immensa cupido.* It was
the thirst of fame which was the
real incentive to these savage
deeds." — " Gazette de France,"
April 30, 1865.

out, "He has shot the President." From the
audience, at first stupid with surprise, and afterwards wild with excitement and horror, two or
three men jumped upon the stage in pursuit of the
flying assassin; but he ran through the familiar
passages, leaped upon his horse, which was in
waiting in the alley behind, rewarded with a kick
and a curse the call-boy who had held him, and
rode rapidly away in the light of the just risen
moon.

The President scarcely moved; his head drooped
forward slightly, his eyes closed. Colonel Rathbone, at first not regarding his own grievous hurt,
rushed to the door of the box to summon aid. He
found it barred, and on the outside some one was
beating and clamoring for entrance. He opened
the door; a young officer named Crawford entered;
one or two army surgeons soon followed, who
hastily examined the wound. It was at once seen
to be mortal. It was afterwards ascertained that
a large derringer bullet had entered the back of
the head on the left side, and, passing through the
brain, had lodged just behind the left eye. By
direction of Rathbone and Crawford, the President
was carried to a house across the street and laid
upon a bed in a small room at the rear of the
hall, on the ground floor. Mrs. Lincoln followed,
half distracted, tenderly cared for by Miss Harris.
Rathbone, exhausted by loss of blood, fainted, and
was carried home. Messengers were sent for the
members of the Cabinet, for the Surgeon-General, for
Dr. Robert K. Stone, the President's family physician; a crowd of people rushed instinctively to
the White House and, bursting through the doors,

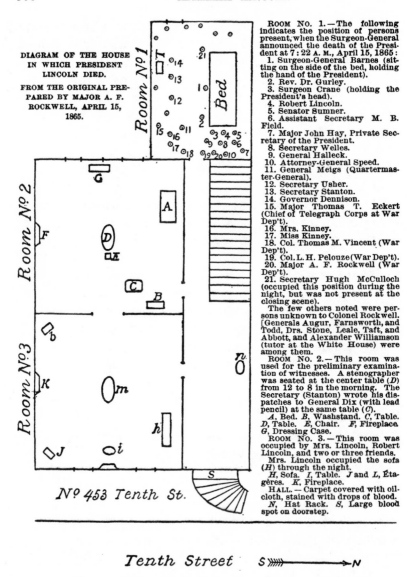

DIAGRAM OF THE HOUSE
IN WHICH PRESIDENT
LINCOLN DIED.

FROM THE ORIGINAL PRE-
PARED BY MAJOR A. F.
ROCKWELL, APRIL 15,
1865.

N? 453 Tenth St.

ROOM NO. 1.—The following indicates the position of persons present, when the Surgeon-General announced the death of the President at 7:22 A. M., April 15, 1865:

1. Surgeon-General Barnes (sitting on the side of the bed, holding the hand of the President).
2. Rev. Dr. Gurley.
3. Surgeon Crane (holding the President's head).
4. Robert Lincoln.
5. Senator Sumner.
6. Assistant Secretary M. B. Field.
7. Major John Hay, Private Secretary of the President.
8. Secretary Welles.
9. General Halleck.
10. Attorney-General Speed.
11. General Meigs (Quartermaster-General).
12. Secretary Usher.
13. Secretary Stanton.
14. Governor Dennison.
15. Major Thomas T. Eckert (Chief of Telegraph Corps at War Dep't).
16. Mrs. Kinney.
17. Miss Kinney.
18. Col. Thomas M. Vincent (War Dep't).
19. Col. L. H. Pelouze (War Dep't).
20. Major A. F. Rockwell (War Dep't).
21. Secretary Hugh McCulloch (occupied this position during the night, but was not present at the closing scene).

The few others noted were persons unknown to Colonel Rockwell. [Generals Augur, Farnsworth, and Todd, Drs. Stone, Leale, Taft, and Abbott, and Alexander Williamson (tutor at the White House) were among them.

ROOM NO. 2.—This room was used for the preliminary examination of witnesses. A stenographer was seated at the center table (*D*) from 12 to 8 in the morning. The Secretary (Stanton) wrote his dispatches to General Dix (with lead pencil) at the same table (*C*).

A, Bed. *B*, Washstand. *C*, Table. *D*, Table. *E*, Chair. *F*, Fireplace. *G*, Dressing Case.

ROOM NO. 3.—This room was occupied by Mrs. Lincoln, Robert Lincoln, and two or three friends.

Mrs. Lincoln occupied the sofa (*H*) through the night.

H, Sofa. *I*, Table. *J* and *L*, Étagères. *K*, Fireplace.

HALL.—Carpet covered with oilcloth, stained with drops of blood. *N*, Hat Rack. *S*, Large blood spot on doorstep.

Tenth Street   S »»»»————→ N

Fords Theatre

shouted the dreadful news to Robert Lincoln and
Major Hay, who sat gossiping in an upper room,
Mr. Nicolay being absent at Charleston, at the
flag-raising over Sumter. They ran downstairs.
Finding a carriage at the door, they entered it to
go to Tenth street. As they were driving away,
a friend came up and told them that Mr. Seward
and most of the Cabinet had been murdered. The
news was all so improbable that they could not
help hoping it was all untrue. But when they
got to Tenth street and found every thoroughfare blocked by the swiftly gathering thousands,
agitated by tumultuous excitement, they were
prepared for the worst. In a few minutes those
who had been sent for, and many others, were
gathered in the little chamber where the chief of
the state lay in his agony. His son was met at
the door by Dr. Stone, who with grave tenderness
informed him that there was no hope. After a
natural outburst of grief young Lincoln devoted
himself the rest of the night to soothing and com-
forting his mother.

The President had been shot a few minutes past
ten. The wound would have brought instant death
to most men, but his vital tenacity was extraordinary. He was, of course, unconscious from the
first moment; but he breathed with slow and
regular respiration throughout the night. As the
dawn came, and the lamplight grew pale in the
fresher beams, his pulse began to fail; but his face
even then was scarcely more haggard than those
of the sorrowing group of statesmen and generals
around him. His automatic moaning, which had
continued through the night, ceased; a look of

unspeakable peace came upon his worn features.
At twenty-two minutes after seven he died.
Stanton broke the silence by saying, "Now he
belongs to the ages." Dr. Gurley kneeled by the
bedside and prayed fervently. The widow came
in from the adjoining room supported by her son
and cast herself with loud outcry on the dead
body.

CHAPTER XV

THE FATE OF THE ASSASSINS

CHAP. XV.

Apl. 14, 1865.

BOOTH had done his work efficiently. His principal subordinate, the young Floridian called Payne, had acted with equal audacity and cruelty, but not with equally fatal result. He had made a shambles of the residence of the Secretary of State, but among all his mangled victims there was not one killed. At eight o'clock that night he received his final orders from Booth, who placed in his hands a knife and revolver, and a little package like a prescription, and taught him his lesson. Payne was a young man, hardly of age, of herculean strength, of very limited mental capacity, blindly devoted to Booth, who had selected him as the fitting instrument of his mad hatred. He obeyed the orders of his fascinating senior as exactly and remorselessly as a steel machine. At precisely the moment when Booth entered the theater, Payne came on horseback to the door of Mr. Seward's residence on Lafayette Square. Dismounting he pretended to be a messenger from the attending physician, with a package of medicine, and demanded immediate access to the sick-room of the Secretary. Mr. Seward had been thrown from his carriage a few days before and his right arm and jaw were fractured. The servant at the

Doster's Speech, Pitman, p. 314.

His true name was Lewis Thornton Powell.

In 1890 the residence of James G. Blaine, Secretary of State.

door tried to prevent Payne from going up the
stairs, but he persisted, and the noise the two men
made in mounting brought his son Frederick W.
Seward out into the hall.

The Secretary had been very restless and had
with difficulty at last been composed to sleep. Fearing that this restorative slumber might be broken,
Frederick Seward came out to check the intruders.
He met Payne at the head of the stairs, and after
hearing his story bade him go back, offering himself
to take charge of the medicine. Payne seemed for
an instant to give up his purpose in the face of this
unexpected obstacle, but suddenly turned and
rushed furiously upon Frederick Seward, putting
a pistol to his head. It missed fire, and he then
began beating him on the head with it, tearing his
scalp and fracturing his skull. Still struggling, the
two came to the Secretary's room and fell together
through the door. Frederick Seward soon became
unconscious and remained so for several weeks,
being perhaps the last man in the civilized world
who learned the strange story of the night. The
Secretary lay on the farther side of the bed from
the door; in the room was his daughter and a
soldier-nurse, Sergeant G. F. Robinson. They both
sprang up at the noise of the disturbance; Payne
struck them right and left out of his way, wounding Robinson with his knife; then rushed to the
bed and began striking at the throat of the crippled statesman, inflicting three terrible wounds
in his cheek and neck; the Secretary rolled off
between the bed and the wall.

Robinson had by this time recovered himself and
seized the assassin from behind, trying to pull him

away from the bed. He fought with the quickness
of a cat, stabbing Robinson twice severely over his
shoulder, in spite of which the sergeant still held on
to him bravely. Colonel Augustus Seward, roused
by his sister's screams, came in his nightdress into
the room, and seeing the two forms in this deadly
grapple thought at first his father was delirious
and was struggling with the nurse, but noting in
a moment the size and strength of the man, he
changed his mind and thought that the sergeant
had gone mad and was murdering the Secretary.
Nothing but madness was at first thought of anywhere to account for the night's work. He seized
Payne, and after a struggle forced him out of the
door — the assassin stabbing him repeatedly about
the head and face. Payne broke away at last and
ran rapidly downstairs, seriously wounding an attendant named Hansell on the way. He reached
the door unhurt, leaped upon his horse, and rode
leisurely away out Vermont Avenue to the eastern
suburb. When surgical aid arrived, the quiet
house, ordinarily so decorous and well ordered, the
scene of an affectionate home life and an unobtru-
sive hospitality, looked like a field hospital; five of
its inmates were bleeding from ghastly wounds,
and two of them — among the highest officials of
the nation — it was thought might never see the
light of another day; though all providentially
recovered.

The assassin left behind him in his flight his
bloodstained knife, his revolver, — or rather the
fragments of it, for he had beaten it to pieces over
the head of Frederick Seward, — and his hat. This
last apparently trivial loss cost him and one of his

fellow-conspirators their lives; for as soon as he had left the immediate scene of his crime, his perceptions being quickened by a murderer's avenging fears, it occurred to him that the lack of a hat would expose him to suspicion wherever he was seen; so, instead of making good his escape, he abandoned his horse and hid himself for two days in the woods east of Washington. Driven by hunger he at last resolved to return to the city, to the house on H street which had been the headquarters of the conspiracy. He made himself a cap from the sleeve of his woolen shirt, threw over his shoulder a pickax he had found in a trench, and coming into town under cover of the darkness knocked about midnight at Mrs. Surratt's door. As his fate would have it, the house was full of officers who had that moment arrested all the inmates and were about to take them to the office of the provost-marshal. Payne thus fell into the hands of justice, and the utterance of half a dozen words by him and the unhappy woman whose shelter he had sought was the death warrant of both. Being asked by Major Smith to give an account of himself, he said he had been hired by Mrs. Surratt to dig a drain for her. She was called out and asked if she knew him. Not being aware of what he had said, she raised her right hand, with uncalled-for solemnity, and said, "Before God, I do not know him, never saw him, and never hired him." These words, the evidence of a guilty secret shared between them, started a train of evidence which led them both to the scaffold.

Booth was recognized by dozens of people as he stood before the footlights and brandished his drip-

ping dagger in a Brutus attitude. His swift horse
quickly carried him beyond the reach of any hap-
hazard pursuit. He gained the navy-yard bridge
in a few minutes, was hailed by a sentry, but persuaded the sergeant of the guard that he was
returning to his home in Charles County, and that
he had waited in Washington till the moon should
rise. He was allowed to pass, and shortly afterwards Herold came to the bridge and passed over
with similar explanations. A moment later the
owner of the horse which Herold rode came up in
pursuit of his animal. He, the only honest man of
the three, was turned back by the guard—the
sergeant felt he must draw the line somewhere.
The assassin and his wretched acolyte came at
midnight to Mrs. Surratt's tavern. Booth, whose
broken leg was by this time giving him excruciat-
ing torture, remained outside on his horse, and
Herold went in, shouting to the inn-keeper to give
him "those things." Lloyd, knowing what was
meant, without a word brought the whisky, carbines, and field-glass which the Surratts had de-
posited there. Booth refused a gun, being unable
in his crippled condition to carry it. Herold told
Lloyd they had killed the President, and they rode
away, leaving Lloyd, who was a sodden drunkard
and contrabandist, unnerved by the news and by
his muddy perception of his own complicity in
the crime. He held his tongue for a day or two;
but at last, overcome by fear, told all that he knew
to the authorities. Booth and Herold pushed on
through the moonlight to the house of an acquaintance of Booth, a rebel sympathizer, a surgeon
named Samuel Mudd. The pain of his broken

bone had become intolerable and day was approaching; aid and shelter had become pressingly necessary. Mudd received them kindly, set Booth's leg, and gave him a room where he rested until the middle of the afternoon; Mudd had a crutch made for him, and in the evening sent them on their desolate way to the South.

If Booth had been in health there is no reason why he should not have remained at large a good while; he might even have made his escape to some foreign country, though, sooner or later, a crime so prodigious will generally find its perpetrator out. But it is easy to hide among a sympathizing people. Many a Union soldier, escaping from prison, walked hundreds of miles through the enemy's country, relying implicitly upon the friendship of the negroes. Booth, from the hour he crossed the navy-yard bridge, though he met with a considerable number of men, was given shelter and assistance by every one whose sympathies were with the South. After parting with Dr. Mudd, he and Herold went to the residence of Samuel Cox,[1] near Port Tobacco, and were by him given into the charge of Thomas Jones, a contraband trader between Maryland and Richmond, a man so devoted to the interests of the Confederacy that treason and murder seemed every-day incidents to be accepted as natural and necessary. He kept Booth and Herold in hiding, at the peril of his own life,

[1] What Booth and Herold were about during the week between the 15th and the 22d of April was not brought out upon the trial of the conspirators, but George Alfred Townsend, while making the extensive and careful studies for his historical novel, "Katy of Catoctin," reconstructed the entire itinerary of the assassin, and published an admirably clear account of it in "The Century Magazine" for April, 1884.

for a week, feeding and caring for them in the CHAP. XV. woods near his house, watching for an opportunity to ferry them across the Potomac. He did this while every woodpath was haunted by Govern- April, 1865. ment detectives, while his own neighborhood was under strong suspicion, knowing that death would promptly follow his detection, and that a reward was offered for the capture of his helpless charge which would make a rich man of any one who gave him up. So close was the search that Herold killed the horses on which they had ridden out of Washington for fear a neigh might betray their hiding-place.

With such devoted aid Booth might have wandered a long way; but there is no final escape but suicide for an assassin with a broken leg. At each painful move the chances of discovery increased. Jones was indeed able, after repeated failures, to row his fated guests across the Potomac. Arriving on the Virginia side, they lived the lives of hunted animals for two or three days longer, finding to their horror that they were received by the strongest Confederates with more of annoyance than enthusiasm — though none, indeed, offered to be- "Trial of J. H. Surratt," p. 402. tray them. At one house, while food was given him, hospitality was not offered. Booth wrote the proprietor a note, pathetic in its attempted dignity, inclosing five dollars — "though hard to spare" — for his entertainment.

He had by this time seen the comments of the newspapers on his work, and bitterer than death or wounds was the blow to his vanity. He con- Ibid., p. 310. fided his feelings of wrong to his diary: "I struck boldly, and not as the papers say; I walked with a firm step through thousands of his friends; was stopped, but pushed on. A colonel was at his side. I shouted *Sic Semper* before I fired. In jumping broke my leg. I passed all his pickets. Rode sixty miles that night, with the bone of my leg tearing the flesh at every jump." On Friday, the 21st, he writes: "After being hunted like a dog through swamps, woods, and last night chased by gunboats till I was forced to return, wet, cold, and starving, with every man's hand against me, I am here in despair. And why? For doing what Brutus was honored for — what made Tell a hero." He goes on comparing himself favorably with these stage heroes, and adds: "I struck for my country and that alone — a country that groaned beneath his tyranny and prayed for this end; and yet now behold the cold hand they extend to me." He was especially grieved that the grandiloquent letter he had intrusted to his fellow-actor Matthews — and which he in his terror had destroyed — had not been published.[1] He thought the Government had wickedly suppressed it; he was tortured with doubts whether God would forgive him, whether it would not be better to go back to Washington and "clear his name." "I am abandoned, with the curse of Cain upon me, when, if the world knew my heart, that one blow would have made me great." With blessings on his mother, upon his wretched

---

[1] He had written another letter in November, 1864, avowing his intention to abduct the President, and to enlist in the Southern army, signing it "A Confederate doing duty upon his own responsibility." He left this letter, sealed, in the hands of his brother-in-law, J. S. Clarke, the comedian. It was given by Mr. Clarke, after the assassination, to the United States authorities in Philadelphia and published in the "Press." It may be found in Raymond's "Life of Lincoln," pp. 793-796.

companion in crime and flight, upon the world which he thought was not worthy of him, he closed these strange outpourings, saying, " I do not wish to shed a drop of blood, but I must fight the course."

The course was soon ended. At Port Conway on the Rappahannock, Booth and Herold met three young men in Confederate uniforms. They were disbanded soldiers; but Herold, imagining that they were recruiting for the Southern army, told them his story with perfect frankness and even pride, saying, " We are the assassinators of the President," and asked their company into the Confederate lines. He was disappointed at learning they were not going South, but his confidence was not misplaced. The soldiers took the fugitives to Port Royal, and tried to get shelter for them, representing Booth as a wounded Confederate soldier. After one or two failures they found refuge on the farm of a man named Garrett on the road to Bowling Green.

On the night of the 25th of April a party under Lieutenant E. P. Doherty arrested, in his bed at Bowling Green, William Jett, one of the Confederate soldiers mentioned above, and forced him to guide them to Garrett's farm. Booth and Herold were sleeping in the barn. When called upon to surrender, Booth refused, and threatened to shoot young Garrett, who had gone in to get his arms. A parley took place, lasting some minutes. Booth offered to fight the party at a hundred yards, and when this was refused cried out in a theatrical tone, " Well, my brave boys, prepare a stretcher for me." Doherty then told him he would fire the barn; upon

CHAP. XV. this Herold came out and surrendered. The barn was fired, and while it was burning, Booth, who was clearly visible by the flames through the cracks in the building, was shot by Boston Corbett, a sergeant of cavalry, a soldier of a gloomy and fanatical disposition, which afterwards developed into insanity.[1] Booth was hit in the back of the neck, not far from the place where he had shot the President. He lingered about three hours in great pain, conscious but nearly inarticulate, and died at seven in the morning.

The surviving conspirators, with the exception of John H. Surratt, were tried by a military commission[2] sitting in Washington in the months of
1865. May and June. The charges against them specified that they were "incited and encouraged" to treason and murder by Jefferson Davis and the Confederate emissaries in Canada. This was not proved on the trial: the evidence bearing on the case showed frequent communication between Canada and Richmond and the Booth coterie in Wash-
Lewis F. Bates, Testimony. Pitman, p. 46. ington, and some transactions in drafts at the Montreal Bank, where Jacob Thompson and Booth both kept their accounts. It was shown by the sworn testimony of a reputable witness that Jefferson Davis at Greensboro', on hearing of the assassination, expressed his gratification at the news; but this, so far from proving any direct complicity in

[1] In 1890 he was still living in an insane asylum in Kansas.

[2] This commission was composed of officers not only of high rank and distinction, but of unusual weight of character. They were Generals David Hunter, Lew Wallace, August V. Kautz, Albion P. Howe, Robert S. Foster, James A. Ekin, Thomas M. Harris, Colonels C. H. Tompkins and D. R. Clendenin. The Judge Advocate and Recorder was Joseph Holt, assisted by the Hon. John A. Bingham and Colonel H. L. Burnett.

the crime, would rather prove the opposite, as a CHAP. XV
conscious murderer usually conceals his malice.[1]
Against all the rest the facts we have briefly stated
were abundantly proved, though in the case of
Mrs. Surratt the repugnance which all men feel at
the execution of a woman induced the commission
to unite in a recommendation to mercy, which
President Johnson, then in the first flush of his zeal
against traitors, disregarded.[2] Habeas corpus proceedings were then resorted to, and failed in virtue
of the President's orders to the military in charge
of the prisoners. The sentences were accordingly
executed: Mrs. Surratt, Payne, Herold, and Atzerodt were hanged on the 7th of July; Mudd, Arnold, 1865.
and O'Laughlin were imprisoned for life at the
Tortugas, though the term was afterwards shortened; and Spangler, the scene shifter at the theater,
was sentenced to six years in jail. John H. Surratt
escaped to Canada, where he lay in hiding some
months in a monastery, and in the autumn sailed
for England under an assumed name. He wandered
over Europe, enlisted in the Papal Zouaves, deserted
and fled to Egypt, where he was detected and brought
back to Washington in 1867. His trial lasted two
months and ended in a disagreement of the jury.

[1] Mr. Davis, in his "Rise and
Fall of the Confederate Government," contradicts this evidence
of Lewis F. Bates. He admits,
however, that the dispatch, being
read in his presence to the
troops with him, elicited cheers,
"as was natural at news of
the fall of one they considered
their most powerful foe"; and he
adds, "For an enemy so relentless, in the war for our subjugation, we could not be expected to
mourn." When captured by
Wilson he affected to think he
cleared himself of all suspicion
in this regard by saying that
Johnson was more objectionable
to him than Lincoln — not notic-
ing that the conspiracy contemplated the murder of both of
them.

[2] See argument of Edwards
Pierrepont, p. 77.

Vol. II.,
p. 683.

CHAPTER XVI

THE MOURNING PAGEANT

RECOUNTING the fate of these wretched male-factors has led us far afield. We will now return to the morning of the 15th of April and sketch, in brief and wholly inadequate words, the honors which the nation paid to its dead. The appalling news spread quickly over the country; millions of citizens learned at their breakfast tables that the President had been shot and was dying; and two hours after his death, when a squad of soldiers were escorting his mortal remains to the Executive Mansion, the dreadful fact was known at all the great centers of population. This was the first time the telegraph had been called upon to spread over the world tidings of such deep and mournful significance; it was therefore the first time the entire people of the United States had been called to deplore the passing away of an idol-ized leader even before his body was cold in death. The news fell with peculiar severity upon the hearts which were glowing with the joy of a great victory. For the last four days, in every city and hamlet of the land, the people were breaking forth into unusual and fantastic expressions of gaiety and content; bonfires flamed through the nights;

the days were uproarious with the firing of guns; CHAP. XVI.
the streets were hung with flags and wreaths, and
whatever decorations could be on the instant
improvised by a people not especially gifted with
the scenic sense; and committees were everywhere
forming to arrange for elaborate and official functions of joy.

Upon this mirth and expansion the awful in- April, 1865.
telligence from Washington fell with the crushing
and stunning effect of an unspeakable calamity.
In the sudden rigor of this unexpected misfortune
the country lost sight of the vast national success
of the past week; and it thus came to pass that
there was never any organized expression of the
general exultation or rejoicing in the North over
the downfall of the rebellion. It was unquestion-
ably best that it should be so; and Lincoln himself would not have had it otherwise. He hated
the arrogance of triumph; and even in his cruel
death he would have been glad to know that
his passage to eternity would prevent too loud
an exultation over the vanquished. As it was, the
South could take no umbrage at a grief so genuine
and so legitimate; the people of that section even
shared, to a certain degree, in the lamentations
over the bier of one whom in their inmost hearts
they knew to have wished them well.

There was one exception to the general grief too
remarkable to be passed over in silence. Among
the extreme radicals in Congress Mr. Lincoln's
determined clemency and liberality towards the
Southern people had made an impression so unfavorable that, though they were naturally shocked at
his murder, they did not among themselves con-

CHAP. XVI. ceal their gratification that he was no longer in their way. In a political caucus, held a few hours after the President's death, they resolved on an entire change of the Cabinet, and a "line of policy less conciliatory than that of Mr. Lincoln ; . . . the feeling was nearly universal "— we are using the language of one of their most prominent representatives —" that the accession of Johnson to the Presidency would prove a godsend to the country." The next day the Committee on the Conduct of the War called on the new President, and Senator Wade bluntly expressed to him the feeling of his associates : " Johnson, we have faith in you. By the gods, there will be no trouble now in running the Government." Before many months passed away they had opportunity to learn that violence of speech was no guarantee of political consistency.

George W. Julian, " Political Recollections," p. 255.

Ibid., p. 257.

In Washington, with this singular exception, the manifestation of the public grief was immediate and demonstrative. The insignia of rejoicing at once disappeared, and within an hour after the body of the President was taken to the White House the town was shrouded in black. Not only the public buildings, the stores and shops, and the better class of residences were draped in funeral decorations, but a still more touching proof of the affection with which the dead man was regarded was seen in the poorest class of houses, where the laboring men of both colors found means in their penury to afford some scanty show of mourning. The interest and the veneration of the people still centered in the White House, where, under a tall catafalque in the east room, the late chief of the state lay in the majesty of death, and not at the

modest tavern on Pennsylvania Avenue, where
the new President had his lodging. At eleven
o'clock Chief-Justice Chase administered the oath
of office to Andrew Johnson in the presence of a
few witnesses. He immediately summoned the
Cabinet for a brief meeting. William Hunter
was appointed Acting Secretary of State during
the interim of the disability of Mr. Seward and his
son, and directed to communicate to the country
and the world the change in the head of the Government brought about by the last night's crime.
It was determined that the funeral ceremonies in
Washington should be celebrated on Wednesday,
the 19th of April, and all the churches throughout
the country were invited to join at the same time
"in solemnizing the occasion" by appropriate
observances. All of the pomp and circumstance
which the Government could command was employed to give a fitting escort from the White
House to the Capitol, where the body of the President was to lie in state. A splendidly appointed
force of cavalry, artillery, and infantry formed the
greater part of the procession, which was completed by delegations from Illinois and Kentucky
as mourners, the new President, the Cabinet, the
ministers of foreign powers, and all the high officers
of the nation, legislative, judicial, and executive.
The pall-bearers comprised the leading members of
both Houses of Congress and the officers of the
highest rank in the army and navy.

The ceremonies in the east room were brief and
simple. The Rev. Dr. Hall of the Church of the
Epiphany read the burial service. Bishop Simpson of the Methodist Church, distinguished equally

CHAP. XVI. for his eloquence and his patriotism, offered a prayer, and the Rev. Dr. P. D. Gurley, at whose church the President and his family habitually attended worship, delivered a short address, commemorating, in language notably free from courtly flattery, the qualities of courage, purity, and sublime faith which had made the dead man great and

THE FUNERAL CAR.

useful. The coffin was carried to the funeral car, and the vast procession moved to the Capitol amid the tolling of all the bells in Washington, Georgetown, and Alexandria, and the booming of minute-guns at Lafayette Square, at the City Hall, and on Capitol hill. To associate the pomp of the day with the greatest work of Lincoln's life, a detachment of colored troops marched at the head of the line. In the rotunda, under the soaring dome of the Capitol, the coffin rested during the April, 1865. day and night of the 19th and until the evening of the next day. The people passed by in thousands to gaze on the face of the liberator — which had taken on in death an expression of profound happiness and repose, like that so often seen on the features of soldiers shot dead in battle.

It had been decided from the first that Lin- coln was to be buried at Springfield. Whenever a President dies, whose personality, more than his office, has endeared him to the people, it is proposed that his body shall rest at Washington; but the better instinct of the country, no less than the natural feelings of the family, insist that his dust shall lie among his own neighbors and kin. It is fitting that Washington shall sleep at Mount Vernon, the Adamses at Quincy, that even Harrison and Taylor and Garfield, though they died in office, should be conveyed to the bosom of the States which had cherished them and sent them to the service of the nation. So Illinois claimed her greatest citizen for final sepulture amid the scenes which witnessed the growth and development of his unique character. The town of Springfield set apart a lovely spot in its northern suburb for his grave and appropriated $20,000 — a large sum considering the size and wealth of the town — to defray the expenses of his funeral. As soon as it was announced that he was to be buried in Illinois every town and city on the route begged that the train might halt within its limits and give its people the opportunity of testifying their grief and their reverence. It was finally arranged that the funeral cortége should follow substantially the same route over which Lincoln had come in 1861 to take possession of the office to which he had given a new dignity and value for all time.

Governor John Brough of Ohio and John W. Garrett of Baltimore were placed in general charge of the solemn journey. A guard of honor consisting of a dozen officers of high rank in the army and

CHAP. XVI. navy[1] was detailed by their respective departments, which received the remains of the President
at the station in Washington at eight o'clock on
1865.   the morning of Friday, the 21st of April, and
the train, decked in somber trappings, moved out
towards Baltimore. In this city, through which,
four years before, it was a question whether the
President-elect could pass with safety to his life,
the train made a halt; the coffin was taken with
sacred care to the great dome of the Exchange, and
there, surrounded by evergreens and lilies, it lay for
several hours, the people passing by in mournful
throngs. Night was closing in, with rain and
wind, when the train reached Harrisburg, and the
coffin was carried through the muddy streets to the
State Capitol, where the next morning the same
scenes of grief and affection were seen. We need
not enumerate the many stopping places of this
dolorous pageant. The same demonstration was
repeated, gaining continually in intensity of feeling and solemn splendor of display, in every city
through which the procession passed. At Philadelphia a vast concourse accompanied the dead
President to Independence Hall; he had shown
himself worthy of the lofty fate he courted when,
on that hallowed spot, on the birthday of Washington, 1861, he had said he would rather be assas-
sinated than give up the principles embodied in the
Declaration of Independence. Here, as at many
other places, the most touching manifestations of
loving remembrance came from the poor, who
brought flowers twined by themselves to lay upon

[1] General E. D. Townsend represented the Secretary of War, Rear-
Admiral C. H. Davis the Secretary of the Navy.

the coffin. The reception at New York was worthy alike of the great city and of the memory of the man they honored. The body lay in state in the City Hall and a half million of people passed in deep silence before it. Here General Scott came, pale and feeble, but resolute, to pay his tribute of respect to his departed friend and commander.

The train went up the Hudson River by night, and at every town and village on the way vast crowds were revealed in waiting by the fitful glare of torches; dirges and hymns were sung as the train moved by. Midnight had passed when the coffin was borne to the Capitol at Albany, yet the multitude rushed in as if it were day, and for twelve hours the long line of people from northern New York and the neighboring States poured through the room.

Over the broad spaces of New York the cortége made its way, through one continuous crowd of mourners. At Syracuse thirty thousand people came out in a storm at midnight to greet the passing train with fires and bells and cannons; at Rochester the same solemn observances made the night memorable; at Buffalo—it was now the morning of the 27th—the body lay in state at St. James's Hall, visited by a multitude from the western counties. As the train passed into Ohio the crowds increased in density, and the public grief seemed intensified at every step westward; the people of the great central basin seemed to be claiming their own. The day spent at Cleveland was unexampled in the depth of emotion it brought to life, the warm devotion to the memory of the great man gone which was exhibited; some of the

CHAP. XVI. guard of honor have said that it was at that point
they began to appreciate the place which Lincoln
was to hold in history.   The authorities, seeing
April, 1865. that no building could accommodate the crowd
which was sure to come from all over the State,
wisely erected in the public square an imposing
mortuary tabernacle for the lying in state, brilliant
with evergreens and flowers by day, and innumerable gas jets by night, and surmounted by the
inscription, *Extinctus amabitur idem.* Impressive
religious ceremonies were conducted in the square
by Bishop McIlvaine, and an immense procession
moved to the station at night between two lines of
torchlights.   Columbus and Indianapolis, the State
capitals of Ohio and Indiana, were next visited.
The whole State, in each case, seemed gathered to
meet their dead hero; an intense personal regard
was everywhere evident; it was the man, not the
ruler, they appeared to be celebrating; the banners
and scrolls bore principally his own words: "With
malice toward none, with charity for all"; "The
purposes of the Lord are perfect and must prevail";
"Here highly resolve that these dead shall not
have died in vain"; and other brief passages from
his writings. On arriving in Chicago, on the 1st of
May, amid a scene of magnificent mourning, the
body was borne to the court-house, where it lay for
two days under a canopy of somber richness,
inscribed with that noble Hebrew lament, "The
beauty of Israel is slain upon thy high places."
From all the States of the Northwest an innumerable throng poured for these two days into Chicago,
and flowed, a mighty stream of humanity, past the
coffin of the dead President, in the midst of

evidences of deep and universal grief which was all the more genuine for being quiet and reserved.

The last stage of this extraordinary progress was the journey to Springfield, which began on the night of the 2d of May and ended at nine o'clock the next morning—the schedule made in Washington twelve days before having been accurately carried out. On all the railroads centering in Springfield the trains for several days had been crowded to their utmost capacity with people who desired to see the last of Abraham Lincoln upon earth. Nothing had been done or thought of for two weeks in Springfield but the preparations for this day; they were made with a thoroughness which surprised the visitors from the East. The body lay in state in the Capitol, which was richly draped from roof to basement in black velvet and silver fringe; within it was a bower of bloom and fragrance. For twenty-four hours an unbroken stream of people passed through, bidding their friend and neighbor welcome home and farewell, and at ten o'clock on the 4th of May the coffin lid was closed at last and a vast procession moved out to Oak Ridge, where the dead President was committed to the soil of the State which had so loved and honored him. The ceremonies at the grave were simple and touching. Bishop Simpson delivered a pathetic oration; prayers were offered and hymns were sung; but the weightiest and most eloquent words uttered anywhere that day were those of the Second Inaugural, which the committee had wisely ordained to be read over his grave, as the friends of Raphael chose the incom-

THE LINCOLN MONUMENT AT SPRINGFIELD.

parable canvas of the Transfiguration as the chief ornament of his funeral.

An association was immediately formed to build a monument over the grave of Lincoln. The work was in the hands of his best and oldest friends in Illinois, and was pushed with vigor. Few large subscriptions were received, with the exception of $50,000 voted by the State of Illinois and $10,000 by New York; but innumerable small contributions afforded all that was needed. The soldiers and sailors of the nation gave $28,000, of which the disproportionately large amount of $8,000 was the gift of the negro troops, whose manhood Lincoln had recognized by putting arms in their

hands.[1] In all $180,000 was raised, and the monu-
ment, built after a design by Larkin G. Mead, was
dedicated on the 15th of October, 1874. The day
was fine, the concourse of people was enormous;
there were music and eloquence and a brilliant deco-
rative display. The orator of the day was General
Richard J. Oglesby, who praised his friend with
warm but sober eulogy; General Sherman added his
honest and hearty tribute; and General Grant, twice
elected President, uttered these carefully chosen
words, which had all the weight that belongs to the
rare discourses of that candid and reticent soldier:

From March, 1864, to the day when the hand of the
assassin opened a grave for Mr. Lincoln, then President
of the United States, my personal relations with him
were as close and intimate as the nature of our respective
duties would permit. To know him personally was to
love and respect him for his great qualities of heart and
head, and for his patience and patriotism. With all his
disappointments from failures on the part of those to
whom he had intrusted commands, and treachery on
the part of those who had gained his confidence but
to betray it, I never heard him utter a complaint, nor cast
a censure, for bad conduct or bad faith. It was his
nature to find excuses for his adversaries. In his death
the nation lost its greatest hero; in his death the South
lost its most just friend.

[1] Besides contributing thus generously to the Springfield monument, the freed people gave
another touching instance of
their gratitude by erecting in a
public square on Capitol Hill in
Washington a noble group in
bronze, including Lincoln, and
entitled "Emancipation." The
subscription for this purpose was
started by a negro washerwoman.
The statue is by Thomas Ball.

CHAPTER XVII

THE END OF REBELLION

CH. XVII. IN the early years of the war, after every considerable success of the national arms, the newspapers were in the habit of announcing that "the back of the rebellion was broken." But at last the time came when the phrase was true; after April, 1865. Appomattox, the rebellion fell to pieces all at once, Lee surrendered less than one-sixth of the Confederates in arms on the 9th of April; the armies that still remained to them, though inconsiderable when compared with the mighty host under the national colors, were yet infinitely larger than any Washington had commanded, and were capable of strenuous resistance and of incalculable mischief. Leading minds on both sides thought the war might be indefinitely prolonged. We have seen that Jefferson Davis, after Richmond fell, issued his swelling manifesto, saying the Confederates had "now entered upon a new phase of the struggle," and that he would "never consent to abandon to the enemy one foot of the soil of any of the States of the Confederacy." Sherman to Grant, Report Committee on Conduct of the War, 1864–65. Part III., p. 18. General Sherman, so late as the 25th of April, said, "I now apprehend that the rebel armies will disperse; and instead of dealing with six or seven States, we will have to deal with numberless bands of desperadoes." Neither side comprehended fully the intense weariness of war that had taken possession of the South; and peace came more swiftly and completely than any one had ever dared to hope.

The march of Sherman from Atlanta to the sea and his northward progress through the Carolinas had predisposed the great interior region to make an end of strife, a tendency which was greatly promoted by Wilson's energetic and masterly raid. The rough usage received by Taylor and by Forrest at his hands, and the blow their dignity suffered in the chase of their fugitive President, made their surrender more practicable. An officer of Taylor's staff came to Canby's headquarters on the 19th of April to make arrangements for the sur render of all the Confederate forces east of the Mississippi not already paroled by Sherman and by Wilson — embracing some 42,000 men. On the 4th of May the terms were agreed upon and signed at the village of Citronelle in Alabama. General Taylor gives a picturesque incident of his meeting with General Canby. The Union officers invited the Confederates to a luncheon, and while the latter were enjoying a menu to which they had long been unaccustomed, the military band in attendance began playing "Hail, Columbia." Canby — with a courtesy, Taylor says, equal to anything recorded by Froissart — excused himself, and walked to the door; the music ceased for a moment, and then the air of " Dixie " was heard. The Confederates, not to be left in arrears of good-breeding, then demanded the national air, and the flag of the reunited country was toasted by both sides.

CH. XVII. The terms agreed upon were those accorded by Grant to Lee, with slight changes of detail, the United States Government furnishing transportation and subsistence on the way home to the men lately engaged in the effort to destroy it. The Confederates willingly testify to the cordial generosity with which they were treated. "Public property," says General Taylor, "was turned over and receipted for, and this as orderly and quickly as in time of peace between officers of the same service." At the same time and place the Confederate commodore Ebenezer Farrand surrendered to Rear-Admiral Henry K. Thatcher all the naval forces of the Confederacy in the neighborhood of Mobile — a dozen vessels and some hundreds of officers.

General E. Kirby Smith commanded all the insurgent forces west of the Mississippi. On him the desperate hopes of Mr. Davis and his flying Cabinet were fixed, after the successive surrenders of Lee and Johnston had left them no prospect in the East. They imagined they could move westward, gathering up stragglers as they fled, and, crossing the river, could join Smith's forces, and "form an army, which in that portion of the country, abounding in supplies and deficient in rivers and railroads, could have continued the war. . ." "To this hope," adds Mr. Davis, " I persistently clung."

1865   Smith, on the 21st of April, called upon his soldiers to continue the fight. " You possess the means of long resisting invasion. You have hopes of succor from abroad. . . The great resources of this department, its vast extent, the numbers, the discipline, and the efficiency of the army, will

secure to our country terms that a proud people
can with honor accept, and may, under the providence of God, be the means of checking the triumph
of our enemy and securing the final success of our
cause."

The attitude of Smith seemed so threatening
that Sheridan was sent from Washington to bring
him to reason. But he did not long hold his
position of solitary defiance. One more needless
·skirmish took place near Brazos, and then Smith
followed the example of Taylor, and surrendered
his entire force, some eighteen thousand, to General
Canby, on the 26th of May. The same generous   1865.
terms were accorded him that had been given to
Taylor — the Government fed his troops and carried them to their homes.

Meanwhile, General Wilson had been paroling
many thousands of prisoners, who wandered in
straggling parties within the limits of his command. One hundred and seventy-five thousand
men in all were surrendered by the different
Confederate commanders, and there were, in addition to these, about 99,000 prisoners in national
custody during the year ; one-third of these were
exchanged and two-thirds released. This was done
as rapidly as possible, by successive orders of the
War Department, beginning on the 9th of May and   1865.
continuing through the summer.

The first object of the Government was to stop
the waste of war. Recruiting ceased immediately
after Lee's surrender; the purchase of arms and
supplies was curtailed, and measures were taken
to reduce as promptly as possible the vast military
establishment. It had grown during the last few

CH. XVII. months to portentous dimensions. The impression that a great and final victory was near at hand, the stimulus of the national hope, the prospect of a brief and prosperous campaign, had brought the army up to the magnificent complement of a million men.[1] The reduction of this vast armament, the retrenchment of the enormous expenses incident to it, were immediately undertaken with a method and despatch which were the result of four years' thorough and practical training, and which would have been impossible under any other circumstances. Every chief of bureau was ordered, on 1865. the 28th of April, to proceed at once to the reduction of expenses in his department to a peace footing, and this before Taylor or Smith had surrendered, and while Jefferson Davis was still at large. The transportation department gave up the railroads of the South to their owners, mainly in better condition than that in which they had been received. They began without delay to sell the immense accumulation of draught animals; eight million dollars were realized from that source within the year. The other departments also disposed of their surplus stores. The stupendous difference which the close of the war at once caused in the finances of the country may be seen in the fact that the appropriations for the army in the fiscal year succeeding the war were $33,814,461 as against $516,240,131 for the preceding year. The army of a million men was brought down, with incredible ease and celerity, to one of twenty-five thousand.

Before the great army melted away into the

[1] May 1, 1865, the aggregate was 1,000,516.—Johnson, Message, December 4, 1865. Appendix, "Globe," p. 4.

greater body of citizens the soldiers enjoyed CH. XVII.
one final triumph, a march through the capital,
undisturbed by death or danger, under the eyes of
their highest commanders, military and civilian,
and the representatives of the people whose nationality they had saved. The Army of the Potomac and
the army of Sherman — such corps of them as were
stationed within reach, waiting their discharge —
were ordered to pass in review before General
Grant and President Johnson, in front of the
Executive Mansion, on the 23d and 24th of May. 1865.
Those who witnessed this solemn yet joyous
pageant will never forget it, and will pray that
their children may never witness anything like it.
For two whole days this formidable host, eight
times the number of the entire peace establishment,
marched the long stretch of Pennsylvania Aver.ue,
starting from the shadow of the dome of the Capitol,
and filling that wide thoroughfare to Georgetown
with their serried mass, moving with the easy, yet
rapid pace of veterans in cadence step. On a platform in front of the White House stood the President and all the first officers of the state, the judges
of the highest court, the most eminent generals and
admirals of the army and the navy. The weather,
on both days, was the finest a Washington May
could afford; the trees of Lafayette Square were
leafing out in their strong and delicate verdure.

The Army of the Potomac, which for four years
had been the living bulwark of the capital, was
rightly given the precedence. Meade himself rode
at the head of his column, then came the cavalry
headed by Merritt — Sheridan having already
started for his new command in the Southwest.

Custer, commanding the Third Division, had an opportunity of displaying his splendid horsemanship, as his charger, excited beyond control by the pomp and martial music, bolted near the Treasury, and dashed with the speed of the wind past the reviewing stand, but was soon mastered by the young general, who was greeted with stormy applause as he rode gravely by the second time, covered with garlands of flowers, the gifts of friends on the pavement. The same graceful guerdon was given all the leading commanders; even subalterns and hundreds of private soldiers marched decked with these fragrant offerings. The three infantry corps, the Ninth, under Parke, the Fifth, under Griffin,— though Warren was on the stand, hailed with tumultuous cheers by his soldiers,— and the Second, under Humphreys, moved swiftly forward. Wright, with the Sixth, was too far away to join in the day's parade.[1] The memory of hundreds of hard-fought battles, of saddening defeats and glorious victories, of the dead and maimed comrades who had fallen forever out of the thinned ranks, was present to every one who saw the veteran divisions marching by under the charge of generals who had served with them in every vicissitude of battle and siege — trained officers like Crook and Ayres, and young and brilliant soldiers who had risen like rockets from among the volunteers, such as Barlow and Miles. Every brigade had its days of immortal prowess to boast, every tattered guidon had its history.

May, 1865.   On the 24th Sherman's army marched in review. The general rode in person at the head of his

[1] His corps was reviewed on the 7th of June.

troops, and was received by the dense multitude
that thronged the avenue with a tumult of raptur-
ous plaudits which might have assured him of the
peculiar place he was to hold thereafter in the
hearts of his fellow-citizens. He and his horse
were loaded with flowers; and his principal commanders were not neglected. Howard had just
been appointed chief of the Freedmen's Bureau,
and therefore Logan commanded the right wing of
the Army of the Tennessee, the place he had hoped
for, and, his friends insist, deserved, when McPherson fell; Hazen had succeeded to the Fifteenth
Corps, and Frank Blair, a chivalrous and martial
figure, rode at the head of the Seventeenth. Slocum
led the left wing,— the Army of Georgia,— consisting of the Twentieth Corps under Mower, and the
Fourteenth under J. C. Davis. The armies of
Meade and Sherman were not exclusively from the
East and West respectively; for Sherman had the
contingent which Hooker and Howard had brought
to Chattanooga from the East; and there were
regiments from as far West as Wisconsin and
Minnesota in the Army of the Potomac. But
Sherman's troops were to all intents and purposes
Western men, and they were scanned with keen
and hospitable interest by the vast crowd of spectators, who were mainly from the East. There was
little to choose between the two armies: a trifle
more of neatness and discipline, perhaps, among
the veterans of Meade; a slight preponderance in
physique and in swinging vigor of march among
the Westerners; but the trivial differences were
lost in the immense and evident likeness, as of
brothers in one family. There was a touch of the

grotesque in the march of Sherman's legions which
was absent from the well-ordered corps of Meade.
A small squad of bummers followed each brigade,
in their characteristic garb and accessories; small
donkeys loaded with queer spoils; goats and game
cocks, regimental pets, sitting gravely on the backs
of mules; and pickaninnies, the adopted children
of companies, showed their black faces between
the ranks, their eyes and teeth gleaming with
delight.

As a mere spectacle, this march of the mightiest
host the continent has ever seen gathered together
was grand and imposing, but it was not as a spectacle alone that it affected the beholder most deeply.
It was not a mere holiday parade; it was an army
of citizens on their way home after a long and
terrible war. Their clothes were worn with toilsome marches and pierced with bullets; their
banners had been torn with shot and shell and lashed
in the winds of a thousand battles; the very drums
and fifes that played the ruffles as each battalion
passed the President had called out the troops to
numberless night alarms, had sounded the onset
at Vicksburg and Antietam, had inspired the
wasted valor of Kenesaw and Fredericksburg,
had throbbed with the electric pulse of victory at
Chattanooga and Five Forks. The whole country
claimed these heroes as a part of themselves, an
infinite gratification forever to the national self-
love; and the thoughtful diplomatists who looked
on the scene from the reviewing stand could not
help seeing that there was a conservative force in
an intelligent democracy which the world had
never before known.

With all the shouting and the laughter and the
joy of this unprecedented ceremony there was one
sad and dominant thought which could not be
driven from the minds of those who saw it — that
of the men who were absent, and who had, nevertheless, richly earned the right to be there. The
soldiers, in their shrunken companies, were conscious of the ever-present memories of the brave
comrades who had fallen by the way; and in the
whole army there was the passionate and unavail-
ing regret that their wise, gentle, and powerful
friend, Abraham Lincoln, was gone forever from
the house by the avenue, where their loyal votes,
supporting their loyal bayonets, had contributed
so much to place him.

The world has had many lessons to learn from
this great war: the naval fight in Hampton Roads
opened a new era in maritime warfare; the marches
of Sherman disturbed all previous axioms of
logistics; the system of instantaneous intrenchments, adopted by the soldiers of both sides in the
latter part of the war, changed the whole character
of modern field tactics. But the greatest of all
the lessons afforded to humanity by the Titanic
struggle in which the American Republic saved its
life is the manner in which its armies were levied,
and, when the occasion for their employment was
over, were dismissed. Though there were periods
when recruiting was slow and expensive, yet there
were others, when some crying necessity for troops
was apparent, that showed almost incredible speed
and efficiency in the supply of men. Mr. Stanton,
in his report for 1865, says: "After the disasters
on the Peninsula, in 1862, over 80,000 troops were

CH. XVII.

Appendix,
"Globe,"
1865-66,
pp. 10, 11.

enlisted, organized, armed, equipped, and sent into the field in less than a month. Sixty thousand troops have repeatedly gone to the field within four weeks; and 90,000 infantry were sent to the armies from the five States of Ohio, Indiana, Illinois, Iowa, and Wisconsin within twenty days."

This certainly shows a wealth of resources nothing less than imperial, and a power of commanding the physical and moral forces of the nation which has rarely been paralleled. Even more important, by way of instruction and example, was the lesson given the nations by the quick and noiseless dispersion of the enormous host when the war was done. The best friends of the Republic in Europe feared for it in this crisis, and those who disbelieved in the conservative power of democracy were loud in their prophecies of the trouble which would arise on the attempt to disband the army. A million men, with arms in their hands, flushed with intoxicating victory, led by officers schooled in battle, loved and trusted — were they not ready for any adventure? Was it reasonable to believe that they would consent to disband and go to work again at the bidding of a few men in black coats at Washington? Especially after Lincoln was dead, could the tailor from Tennessee direct these myriads of warriors to lay down their arms and melt away into the everyday life of citizens? In America there was no anxiety on this score among the friends of the Union. Without giving the subject a thought they knew there was no danger. The war had been made to execute the laws and to save the national existence, and when those objects were attained there was no thought among the soldiers,

from the general to the humblest file-closer, but to
wait for the expected orders from the civil authorities for their disbandment.

The orders came as a mere matter of course, and
were executed with a thoroughness and rapidity
which then seemed also a matter of course, but
which will appear more and more wonderful to
succeeding generations. The muster-out began on
the 29th of April, before Lincoln was borne to his
grave, before Davis was caught, before the rebels
of the trans-Mississippi had ceased uttering their
boasts of eternal defiance. First the new recruits,
next the veterans whose terms were nearly expired,
next those expensive corps the cavalry and artillery,
and so on in regular order. Sherman's laurel-
crowned army was the first to complete its muster-
out, and the heroic Army of the Potomac was not
far behind it. These veterans of hundreds of bat-
tlefields were soon found mingled in all the pursuits
of civic activity. By the 7th of August 641,000
troops had become citizens; by the middle of
November over 800,000 had been mustered out —
without a fancy in any mind that there was anything else to do.

The Navy Department had not waited for the
return of peace to begin the reduction of expenses.
As soon as Fort Fisher fell the retrenchment began,
and before Grant started on his last campaign considerable progress had been made in that direction.
By the 1st of May the squadrons were reduced one-
half, and in July but thirty steamers comprised the
entire blockading squadron on the Atlantic and the
Gulf. The Potomac and Mississippi flotillas were
wholly discontinued in another month. When Mr.

Welles made his annual report, in December, he could say: "There were in the several blockading squadrons in January last, exclusive of other duty,
Report
of the
Secretary
of the Navy
for 1865,
p. x.
471 vessels and 2455 guns. There are now but 29 vessels remaining on the coast, carrying 210 guns, exclusive of howitzers." Superfluous vessels were sold by hundreds and the money covered into the Treasury; thousands of the officers and sailors who had patriotically left the merchant service to fight under the national flag went back to the pursuits of peace.

For the purposes of pacification and the reëstablishment of the national authority the country was divided into five grand divisions — that of the Atlantic, commanded by Meade; the Mississippi, by Sherman; the Gulf, by Sheridan; the Tennessee, by Thomas; and the Pacific, by Halleck. These again were subdivided into nineteen departments, and we print here the names of the generals commanding them for the last time, as a roll of the men who survived the war, most favored by fortune and their own merits: Hooker, Hancock, Augur, Ord, Stoneman, Palmer (J. M.), Pope, Terry, Schofield, Sickles, Steedman, Foster (J. G.), Wood (T. J.), Wood (R. C.), Canby, Wright, Reynolds (J. J.), Steele, McDowell. The success or failure of these soldiers in administering the trust confided to them, their relations to the people among whom they were stationed, and to the President who succeeded to the vacant chair of Lincoln, form no part of the story we have attempted to tell.

1865.   On the 13th of June the President proclaimed the insurrection at an end in the State of Tennessee; it was not until the second day of April, 1866,

that he proclaimed a state of peace as existing in
the rest of the United States, and then he excepted
the State of Texas; on the 20th of August, in the
same year, he made his final proclamation, announcing the reëstablishment of the national
authority in Texas, and thereupon he concluded,
"I do further proclaim that the said insurrection is
at an end, and that peace, order, tranquillity, and
civil authority now exist in and throughout the
whole of the United States of America."

Thus the war ended. The carnage and the waste
of it had surpassed the darkest forebodings, the
most reckless prophecies. On the Union side
2,200,000 men had enlisted; [1] on the Confederate,
about 1,000,000. Of these 110,000 Union soldiers
were killed or mortally wounded in battle; [2] a quarter of a million died of other causes. The total of
deaths by the war on the Northern side amounted
to 360,282. The number of the Confederate dead
cannot be accurately ascertained; it ranges between 250,000 and 300,000. The expense of the
war to the Union, over and above the ordinary expenses of the government, was about $3,250,000,000;
to the Confederacy less than half that amount,
about $1,500,000,000.

It seems a disheartening paradox to the lovers of
peace that all this homicide and spoil gave only a
new impulse to the growth and the wealth of the
nation. We have seen how the quick eye of Lincoln recognized the fact, on the very night of election, that the voting strength of the country was

---

[1] There were 2,690,401 names
on the rolls, but these included
reënlistments.

[2] Sixty-seven thousand and fif-
ty-eight killed · 43,012 died of
wounds.

greater in 1864 than it had been in 1860, and the census of 1870 showed a prodigious advance in prosperity and population. The 31,443,321 of 1860 had in the ten troubled years of war and reconstruction increased to 38,558,371; and the wealth of the country had waxed in an astonishing proportion, from $16,159,616,068 to $30,068,518,507. Even the reconquered States shared in this enormous progress.

CHAPTER XVIII

LINCOLN'S FAME

THE death of Lincoln awoke all over the world a quick and deep emotion of grief and admi- ration. If he had died in the days of doubt and gloom which preceded his reëlection, he would have been sincerely mourned and praised by the friends of the Union, but its enemies would have curtly dismissed him as one of the necessary and misguided victims of sectional hate. They would have used his death to justify their malevolent forebodings, to point the moral of new lectures on the instability of democracies. But as he had fallen in the moment of a stupendous victory, the halo of a radiant success enveloped his memory and dazzled the eyes even of his most hostile critics. That portion of the press of England and the Continent which had persistently vilified him now joined in the universal chorus of elegiac praise.[1] Cabinets and courts which had been cold

[1] One of the finest poems on the occasion of his death was that in which the London "Punch" made its manly recantation of the slanders with which it had pursued him for four years:

> Beside this corpse that bears for winding-sheet
> The Stars and Stripes he lived to rear anew,
> Between the mourners at his head and feet,
>   Say, scurrile jester, is there room for you?

> Yes, he had lived to shame me from my sneer,
>   To lame my pencil, and confute my pen;
> To make me own this hind of princes peer,
>   This rail-splitter a true-born king of men.

or unfriendly sent their messages of condolence. The French Government, spurred on by their Liberal opponents, took prompt measures to express their admiration for his character and their horror at his taking-off. In the Senate and the Chamber of Deputies the imperialists and the republicans vied with each other in utterances of grief and of praise; the Emperor and the Empress sent their personal condolences to Mrs. Lincoln.

In England there was perhaps a trifle of self-consciousness at the bottom of the official expressions of sympathy. The Foreign Office searched the records for precedents, finding nothing which suited the occasion since the assassination of Henry IV. The sterling English character could not, so gracefully as the courtiers of Napoleon III., bend to praise one who had been treated almost as an enemy for so long. When Sir George Grey opened his dignified and pathetic speech in the House of Commons, by saying that a majority of the people of England sympathized with the North, he was greeted with loud protestations and denials on the part of those who favored the Confederacy. But his references to Lincoln's virtues were cordially received, and when he said that the Queen had written to Mrs. Lincoln with her own hand, "as a widow to a widow," the House broke out in loud cheering. Mr. Disraeli spoke on behalf of the Conservatives with his usual dexterity and with a touch of factitious feeling. "There is," he said, "in the character of the victim, and even in the accessories of his last moments, something so homely and innocent, that it takes the question, as it were, out of all the pomp of history and the

ceremonial of diplomacy; it touches the heart of CH. XVIII.
nations and appeals to the domestic sentiment
of mankind."

In the House of Lords the matter was treated
with characteristic reticence. The speech of Lord
Russell was full of that rugged truthfulness, that
unbending integrity of spirit, which appeared at
the time to disguise his real friendliness to America,
and which was only the natural expression of a
mind extraordinarily upright, and English to the
verge of caricature. Lord Derby followed him in
a speech of curious elegance, the object of which
was rather to launch a polished shaft against
his opponents than to show honor to the dead
President; and the address proposed by the
Government was voted. While these reserved and
careful public proceedings were going on, the heart
of England was expressing its sympathy with the
kindred beyond sea by its thousand organs of
utterance in the press, the resolutions of municipal
bodies, the pulpit, and the platform.

In Germany the same manifestations were seen of
official expressions of sympathy from royalty and
its ministers, and of heartfelt affection and grief
from the people and their representatives. Otto von
Bismarck, then at the beginning of the events which
have made his career so illustrious, gave utterance
to the courteous regrets of the King of Prussia;
the eloquent deputy, William Loewe, from his place
in the House, made a brief and touching speech.
"The man," he said, "who accomplished such great
deeds from the simple desire conscientiously to perform his duty, the man who never wished to be more
nor less than the most faithful servant of his people,

CH. XVIII. will find his own glorious place in the pages of history. In the deepest reverence I bow my head before this modest greatness, and I think it is especially agreeable to the spirit of our own nation, with its deep inner life and admiration of self-sacrificing devotion and effort after the ideal, to pay the tribute of veneration to such greatness, exalted as it is by simplicity and modesty."

Two hundred and fifty members of the Chamber signed an address to the American minister in Berlin, full of the cordial sympathy and admiration felt, not only for the dead President, but for the national cause, by the people of Germany. "You are aware," they said, "that Germany has looked with pride and joy on the thousands of her sons who in this struggle have placed themselves so resolutely on the side of law and right. You have seen with what pleasure the victories of the Union have been hailed, and how confident the faith in the final triumph of the great cause and the restoration of the Union in all its greatness has ever been, even in the midst of calamity." Workingmen's clubs, artisans' unions, sent numberless addresses, not merely expressive of sympathy, but conveying singularly just appreciations of the character and career of Lincoln. His death seemed to have marked a step in the education of the people everywhere.

In fact it was among the common people of the entire civilized world that the most genuine and spontaneous manifestations of sorrow and appreciation were produced, and to this fact we attribute the sudden and solid foundation of Lincoln's fame. It requires years, perhaps centuries, to build the structure of a reputation which rests upon the CH. XVIII. opinion of those distinguished for learning or intelligence; the progress of opinion from the few to the many is slow and painful. But in the case of Lincoln the many imposed their opinion all at once; he was canonized, as he lay on his bier, by the irresistible decree of countless millions. The greater part of the aristocracy of England thought little of him, but the burst of grief from the English people silenced in an instant every discordant voice. It would have been as imprudent to speak slightingly of him in London as it was in New York. Especially among the Dissenters was honor and reverence shown to his name. The humbler people instinctively felt that their order had lost its wisest champion.

Not only among those of Saxon blood was this outburst of emotion seen. In France a national manifestation took place which the Government disliked, but did not think it wise to suppress. The students of Paris marched in a body to the American Legation to express their sympathy. A two-cent subscription was started to strike a massive gold medal; the money was soon raised, but the committee was forced to have the work done in Switzerland. A committee of French Liberals brought the medal to the American minister, to be sent to Mrs. Lincoln. "Tell her," said Eugène Pelletan, "the heart of France is in that little box." The inscription had a double sense; while honoring the dead Republican, it struck at the Empire. "Lincoln — the Honest Man; abolished slavery, reëstablished the Union; Saved the Republic, without veiling the Statue of Liberty."

CH. XVIII. Everywhere on the Continent the same swift apotheosis of the people's hero was seen. An Austrian deputy said to the writer, "Among my people his memory has already assumed superhuman proportions; he has become a myth, a type of ideal democracy." Almost before the earth closed over him he began to be the subject of fable. The Freemasons of Europe generally regard him as one of them — his portrait in Masonic garb is often displayed; yet he was not one of that brotherhood. The Spiritualists claim him as their most illustrious adept, but he was not a Spiritualist; and there is hardly a sect in the Western world, from the Calvinist to the atheist, but affects to believe he was of their opinion.

A collection of the expressions of sympathy and condolence which came to Washington from foreign governments, associations, and public bodies of all sorts was made by the State Department, and afterwards published by order of Congress. It forms a large quarto of a thousand pages, and embraces the utterances of grief and regret from every country under the sun, in almost every language spoken by man.

But admired and venerated as he was in Europe, he was best understood and appreciated at home. It is not to be denied that in his case, as in that of all heroic personages who occupy a great place in history, a certain element of legend mingles with his righteous fame. He was a man, in fact, especially liable to legend. We have been told by farmers in Central Illinois that the brown thrush did not sing for a year after he died. He was gentle and merciful, and therefore he seems in a certain class of annals to have passed all his time in soothing misfortune and pardoning crime. He had more than his share of the shrewd native humor, and therefore the loose jest-books of two centuries have been ransacked for anecdotes to be attributed to him. He was a great and powerful lover of mankind, especially of those not favored by fortune. One night he had a dream, which he repeated the next morning to the writer of these lines, which quaintly illustrates his unpretending and kindly democracy. He was in some great assembly; the people made a lane to let him pass. "He is a common-looking fellow," some one said. Lincoln in his dream turned to his critic and replied, in his Quaker phrase, "Friend, the Lord prefers common-looking people: that is why he made so many of them." He that abases himself shall be exalted. Because Lincoln kept himself in such constant sympathy with the common people, whom he respected too highly to flatter or mislead, he was rewarded by a reverence and a love hardly ever given to a human being. Among the humble working people of the South whom he had made free, this veneration and affection easily passed into the supernatural. At a religious meeting among the negroes of the Sea Islands a young man expressed the wish that he might see Lincoln. A gray-headed negro rebuked the rash aspiration: "No man see Linkum. Linkum walk as Jesus walk—no man see Linkum."[1]

But leaving aside these fables, which are a natural enough expression of a popular awe and love,

[1] Mr. Hay had this story from Captain E. W. Hooper immediately after it happened. It has been told with many variations.

CH. XVIII. it seems to us no more just estimate of Lincoln's relation to his time has ever been made — nor perhaps ever will be — than that uttered by one of the wisest and most American of thinkers, Ralph Waldo Emerson, a few days after the assassination. We cannot forbear quoting a few words of this remarkable discourse, which shows how Lincoln seemed to the greatest of his contemporaries: "A plain man of the people, an extraordinary fortune attended him. Lord Bacon says, 'Manifest virtues procure reputation; occult ones fortune.' . . His occupying the chair of state was a triumph of the good sense of mankind and of the public conscience. . . . He grew according to the need; his mind mastered the problem of the day; and as the problem grew, so did his comprehension of it. Rarely was a man so fitted to the event. . . It cannot be said that there is any exaggeration of his worth. If ever a man was fairly tested, he was. There was no lack of resistance, nor of slander, nor of ridicule. . . . Then what an occasion was the whirlwind of the war! Here was no place for holiday magistrate, nor fair-weather sailor; the new pilot was hurried to the helm in a tornado. In four years — four years of battle-days — his endurance, his fertility of resources, his magnanimity, were sorely tried and never found wanting. There by his courage, his justice, his even temper, his fertile counsel, his humanity, he stood a heroic figure in the center of a heroic epoch. He is the true history of the American people in his time; the true representative of this continent — father of his country, the pulse of twenty millions throbbing in his heart, the thought of their minds articulated by his tongue."

The quick instinct by which the world recognized CH. XVIII. him, even at the moment of his death, as one of its greatest men, was not deceived. It has been confirmed by the sober thought of a quarter of a century. The writers of each nation compare him with their first popular hero. The French find points of resemblance in him to Henry IV.; the Dutch liken him to William of Orange; the cruel stroke of murder and treason by which all three perished in the height of their power naturally suggests the comparison, which is strangely justified in both cases, though the two princes were so widely different in character. Lincoln had the wit, the bonhomie, the keen, practical insight into affairs of the Béarnais; and the tyrannous moral sense, the wide comprehension, the heroic patience of the Dutch patriot, whose motto might have served equally well for the American President — *Sævis tranquillus in undis.* European historians speak of him in words reserved for the most illustrious names. Merle d'Aubigné says, "The name of Lincoln will remain one of the greatest that history has to inscribe on its annals." Henri Martin predicts nothing less than a universal apotheosis: " This man will stand out in the traditions of his country and the world as an incarnation of the people, and of modern democracy itself." Emilio Castelar, in an oration against slavery in the Spanish Cortes, called him "humblest of the humble before his conscience, greatest of the great before history."

In this country, where millions still live who were his contemporaries, and thousands who knew him personally, where the envies and jealousies

CH. XVIII. which dog the footsteps of success still linger in the hearts of a few, where journals still exist that loaded his name for four years with daily calumny, and writers of memoirs vainly try to make themselves important by belittling him, his fame has become as universal as the air, as deeply rooted as the hills. The faint discords are not heard in the wide chorus that hails him second to none and equaled by Washington alone. The eulogies of him form a special literature. Preachers, poets, soldiers, and statesmen employ the same phrases of unconditional love and reverence. Men speaking with the authority of fame use unqualified superlatives. Lowell, in an immortal ode, calls him "New birth of our new soil, the first American." General Sherman says, "Of all the men I ever met, he seemed to possess more of the elements of greatness, combined with goodness, than any other." General Grant, after having met the rulers of almost every civilized country on earth, said Lincoln impressed him as the greatest intellectual force with which he had ever come in contact.

Sherman, "Memoirs." Vol. II., p. 328.

He is spoken of, with scarcely less of enthusiasm, by the more generous and liberal spirits among those who revolted against his election and were vanquished by his power. General Longstreet calls him "the greatest man of rebellion times, the one matchless among forty millions for the peculiar difficulties of the period." An eminent Southern orator, referring to our mixed Northern and Southern ancestry, says: "From the union of those colonists, from the straightening of their purposes and the crossing of their blood, slowly

"Battles and Leaders." Vol. II., p. 405.

perfecting through a century, came he who stands
as the first typical American, the first who comprehended within himself all the strength and
gentleness, all the majesty and grace of this
republic — Abraham Lincoln."

It is not difficult to perceive the basis of this
sudden and world-wide fame, nor rash to predict
its indefinite duration. There are two classes of
men whose names are more enduring than any
monument — the great writers; and the men of
great achievement, the founders of states, the
conquerors. Lincoln has the singular fortune to
belong to both these categories; upon these broad
and stable foundations his renown is securely
built. Nothing would have more amazed him
while he lived than to hear himself called a man
of letters; but this age has produced few greater
writers. We are only recording here the judgment
of his peers. Emerson ranks him with Æsop and
Pilpay in his lighter moods, and says: "The
weight and penetration of many passages in his
letters, messages, and speeches, hidden now by the
very closeness of their application to the moment,
are destined to a wide fame. What pregnant defi-
nitions, what unerring common-sense, what foresight, and on great occasions what lofty, and more
than national, what human tone! His brief speech
at Gettysburg will not easily be surpassed by words
on any recorded occasion."

His style extorted the high praise of French
Academicians; Montalembert commended it as a
model for the imitation of princes. Many of his
phrases form part of the common speech of mankind. It is true that in his writings the range of

CH. XVIII. subjects is not great; he is concerned chiefly with
the political problems of the time, and the moral
considerations involved in them. But the range
of treatment is remarkably wide; it runs from the
wit, the gay humor, the florid eloquence of his
stump speeches to the marvelous sententiousness
and brevity of the letter to Greeley and the address
at Gettysburg, and the sustained and lofty grandeur
of the Second Inaugural.

The more his writings are studied in connection
with the important transactions of his age the
higher will his reputation stand in the opinion of
the lettered class. But the men of study and
research are never numerous; and it is principally
as a man of action that the world at large will
regard him. It is the story of his objective life
that will forever touch and hold the heart of mankind. His birthright was privation and ignorance
— not peculiar to his family, but the universal environment of his place and time; he burst through
those enchaining conditions by the force of native
genius and will; vice had no temptation for him;
his course was as naturally upward as the skylark's;
he won, against all conceivable obstacles, a high
place in an exacting profession and an honorable
position in public and private life; he became the
foremost representative of a party founded on an
uprising of the national conscience against a secular
wrong, and thus came to the awful responsibilities
of power in a time of terror and gloom. He met
them with incomparable strength and virtue. Caring for nothing but the public good, free from envy
or jealous fears, he surrounded himself with the
leading men of his party, his most formidable

rivals in public esteem, and through four years of CH. XVIII.
stupendous difficulties he was head and shoulders
above them all in the vital qualities of wisdom,
foresight, knowledge of men, and thorough comprehension of measures. Personally opposed, as the
radicals claim, by more than half of his own party
in Congress, and bitterly denounced and maligned
by his open adversaries, he yet bore himself with
such extraordinary discretion and skill, that he
obtained for the Government all the legislation it
required, and so impressed himself upon the national mind that without personal effort or solicita-
tion he became the only possible candidate of his
party for reëlection, and was chosen by an almost
unanimous vote of the Electoral Colleges.

His qualities would have rendered his administration illustrious even in time of peace; but when
we consider that in addition to the ordinary work
of the executive office he was forced to assume
the duties of Commander-in-Chief of the National
forces engaged in the most complex and difficult
war of modern times, the greatness of spirit as
well as the intellectual strength he evinced in that
capacity is nothing short of prodigious. After
times will wonder, not at the few and unimportant
mistakes he may have committed, but at the intui-
tive knowledge of his business that he displayed.
We would not presume to express a personal opinion in this matter. We use the testimony only of
the most authoritative names. General W. T. Sherman has repeatedly expressed the admiration and
surprise with which he has read Mr. Lincoln's
correspondence with his generals, and his opinion
of the remarkable correctness of his military views.

CH. XVIII. General W. F. Smith says: "I have long held to the opinion that at the close of the war Mr. Lincoln was the superior of his generals in his comprehension of the effect of strategic movements and the "Lincoln Memorial Album," p. 555. proper method of following up victories to their legitimate conclusions." General J. H. Wilson holds the same opinion; and Colonel Robert N. Scott, in whose lamented death the army lost one of its most vigorous and best-trained intellects, frequently called Mr. Lincoln "the ablest strategist of the war."

To these qualifications of high literary excellence, and easy practical mastery of affairs of transcendent importance, we must add, as an explanation of his immediate and world-wide fame, his possession of certain moral qualities rarely combined, in such high degree, in one individual. His heart was so tender that he would dismount from his horse in a forest to replace in their nest young birds which had fallen by the roadside; he could not sleep at night if he knew that a soldier-boy was under sentence of death; he could not, even at the bidding of duty or policy, refuse the prayer of age or helplessness in distress. Children instinctively loved him; they never found his rugged features ugly; his sympathies were quick and seemingly unlimited. He was absolutely without prejudice of class or condition. Frederick Douglass says he was the only man of distinction he ever met who never reminded him by word or manner of his color; he was as just and generous to the rich and well born as to the poor and humble — a thing rare among politicians. He was tolerant even of evil: though no man can ever have lived with a loftier scorn of meanness and selfishness, he yet recognized their existence CH. XVIII. and counted with them. He said one day, with a flash of cynical wisdom worthy of La Rochefoucauld, that honest statesmanship was the employment of individual meannesses for the public good. He never asked perfection of any one; he did not even insist, for others, upon the high standards he set up for himself. At a time before the word was invented he was the first of opportunists. With the fire of a reformer and a martyr in his heart he yet proceeded by the ways of cautious and practical statecraft. He always worked with things as they were, while never relinquishing the desire and effort to make them better. To a hope which saw the Delectable Mountains of absolute justice and peace in the future, to a faith that God in his own time would give to all men the things convenient to them, he added a charity which embraced in its deep bosom all the good and the bad, all the virtues and the infirmities of men, and a patience like that of nature, which in its vast and fruitful activity knows neither haste nor rest.

A character like this is among the precious heirlooms of the Republic; and by a special good fortune every part of the country has an equal claim and pride in it. Lincoln's blood came from the veins of New England emigrants, of Middle State Quakers, of Virginia planters, of Kentucky pioneers; he himself was one of the men who grew up with the earliest growth of the Great West. Every jewel of his mind or his conduct sheds radiance on each portion of the nation. The marvelous symmetry and balance of his intellect and character may have owed something to this varied envi-

CH. XVIII. ronment of his race, and they may fitly typify the variety and solidity of the Republic. It may not be unreasonable to hope that his name and his renown may be forever a bond of union to the country which he loved with an affection so impartial, and served, in life and in death, with such entire devotion.

INDEX

INDEX

Abbot, Dr. E. W., present at Lincoln's deathbed, X, 300.

Abbott, Joseph C., Bvt. Brig. Gen. U. S. Vols.: in second Fort Fisher expedition, X, 65.

Abercrombie, John J., Bvt. Brig. Gen. U. S. A.: persuades Patterson not to attack, IV, 346.

Adams, A. H., Capt. U. S. N. : in Lincoln's visit to Richmond, X, 218.

Adams, Charles Francis, M. C., U. S. Min. to England: Freesoil nominee for Vice-President, I, 277; member of House Committee of Thirty-three, II, 417; resolution in that committee, III, 216; sails for Europe, IV, 268; first interview with Lord John Russell, 276; warns Lord Russell against receiving Southern commissioners, 277; answers about the blockade, V, 1; complains of governor of Nassau for refusing coal to U. S. vessels, VI, 50; notifies British government of the building of the *Oreto*, 51, 52; interview with Lord Russell about the *Oreto*, 52; notifies Lord Russell of the building of the *290* or *Alabama*, 53; directs Craven to intercept the *Alabama*, 53; sends Lord Russell legal opinion about the *Alabama*, 54; notifies Lord Russell of further Confederate naval enterprises in Great Britain, 57; dispatch to Seward on disposition of British government, 57; correspondence with Lord Russell on proposed changes in the Foreign Enlistment Act, 58; presents evidence to Lord Russell of proposed violation of British neutrality, 58; interview with Lord Russell, March 26, 1863, 59; correspondence with Lord Russell about Confederate rams, VIII, 258, 259.

Adams, Charles Francis, Jr., Bvt. Brig. Gen. U. S. Vols.: regiment of, enters Richmond, X, 210.

Adams, Henry A., Capt. U. S. N.: ordered not to land Vogdes's company, III, 168; refuses to land Vogdes's company, IV, 7; dispatch to Secretary of Navy, 7, 8; lands reënforcements, 12, 13.

Adams, J. H., Comr. of S. C.: arrives in Washington, III, 62; interview with Pres. Buchanan, 70.

Adams, John, Conf. Brig. Gen.: killed at Franklin, X, 20.

Adams, John Quincy, sixth Pres. U. S. : address against Texas annexation, I, 230; dispatch embodying the Monroe doctrine, VII, 405; message about Monroe doctrine, 406.

Adrain, Garnett B., M. C.: plan of compromise, II, 422.

Agnew, Daniel, Chief Justice Sup. Ct. of Pa.: defeats and succeeds Chief Justice Lowrie, VII, 13, 376.

Aiken, William, M. C.: votes for, for Speaker of House of Representatives, I, 364.

Alabama, State of, secession movement in, III, 185; joint resolutions authorizing convention, 185; military appropriation in, 185; proclamation of Gov. Moore, 185; election of delegates, 185; meeting and resolutions of convention, 186; seizure of Mount Vernon arsenal, and of Forts Morgan and Gaines, 186; ordinance of secession passed Jan. 11, 1861, 188; Provisional Congress of seceding States, 196–212; battle of Mobile Bay, Aug. 5, 1864, IX, 230–239; siege of Mobile, 239–242; surrender of Mobile, April 11, 1865, 242; ratifies Thirteenth Amendment, X, 89; capture of Selma, April 2, 1865, 240.

Alabama, The (or 290), Conf. cruiser: built in Liverpool under builder's number 290, VI, 53; sails from Liverpool, 54; receives armament and crew at Western Islands, 55; commanded by Capt. Raphael Semmes, 55; declared in commission as a Confederate cruiser, 55; procedure of, 55; sinks the *Hatteras*, 56; correspondence about, VIII, 254, 255; enters harbor of Cherbourg, France, IX, 142; blockaded by the *Kearsarge*, 144; sunk by the *Kearsarge*, 146-149.

Albemarle, The, Conf. ironclad: building of, X, 38, 39; sinks the *Southfield*, 39-41; battle with the Union fleet, 41-43; sunk by Cushing, 49.

Albert, Prince Consort: draft of note to Lord Russell, V, 28.

Alden, James, Rear Adm. U. S. N.: mission to Gosport navy yard, IV, 145, 146; commands the *Richmond* in Farragut's fleet, V, 261; commands the *Brooklyn* in battle of Mobile Bay, IX, 232, 233.

Alexander, E. P., Conf. Col.: in battle of Gettysburg, VII, 262; opinion about Gettysburg, 271.

Alexandra, The, case of, VIII, 256, 257.

Allen, William F., member of commission on New York enrollment, VII, 41.

Allison, William B., M. C., U. S. Sen.: votes for re-passage of National Bank Act, VI, 245.

Almonte, Juan Nepomuceno, Mex. Gen. and diplomatist: notification to the United States concerning Texas, I, 241; expulsion demanded by Juarez, VI, 45; representations to the French, 46; member of Mexican Provisional Government, VII, 398.

Alston, W., Conf. Lieut.: proposition to Jefferson Davis, X, 287.

Altoona, Pa., meeting of governors at, Sept. 24, 1862, VI, 164-166.

Alvarez, Juan, Mex. Gen.: commands Mexican reserves in Guerrero, VII, 396.

American Baptist Missionary Union, resolutions supporting emancipation, VI, 316.

American Board of Foreign Missions, resolutions supporting the war and emancipation, VI, 317.

American Knights, Order of, VIII, 2-27.

American, or Know-Nothing, Party, influence on elections in 1854, I, 358; nominates Fillmore for President in 1856, II, 24; action in Illinois in 1856, 24, 25.

Ames, Adelbert, Bvt. Maj. Gen. U. S. A.: at battle of Bermuda Hundred, VIII, 398; in siege of Richmond, IX, 431; in second Fort Fisher expedition, X, 65; in assault on Fort Fisher, 66; in advance on Wilmington, 69.

Ames, Edward R., D.D., Bish. M. E. Church: appointed commissioner to visit Union prisoners of war, VII, 449.

Ammen, Daniel, Rear Adm. U. S. N.: commands U. S. monitor *Patapsco* in attack on Charleston, VII, 67.

Ammen, Jacob, Brig. Gen. U. S. Vols.: brigade deployed under fire at Pittsburg Landing, V, 333.

Ampudia, Pedro de, Mex. Gen.: opposed to Gen. Taylor, I, 249.

Anderson, C. D., Conf. Brig. Gen.: surrenders Fort Gaines, IX, 238.

Anderson, Hiram, Jr., Col. U. S. Vols.: killed at Cold Harbor, VIII, 405.

Anderson, J. R., Conf. Brig. Gen.: present at interview of Lincoln and Campbell, X, 220-222.

Anderson, Larz, recommends McClellan for command at Cincinnati, IV, 282.

Anderson, Mrs. Robert, valuable manuscripts from, II, 347; loyalty of, 347.

Anderson, Richard H., Conf. Lieut. Gen.: in battle of Chancellorsville, VII, 101; in march on Spotsylvania, VIII, 368; in battle of Spotsylvania, 375, 381; in battle of Cold Harbor, 391; in Shenandoah campaign, IX, 293-295, 297; starts for Lee's army, 298; in siege of Richmond, 432; in retreat to Appomattox, X, 188.

Anderson, Robert, Bvt. Maj. Gen. U. S. A.: signs Lincoln's discharge in Black Hawk war, I, 96; ordered to command Charleston forts, II, 346, 348; antecedents of, 346, 347; interview with Gen. Scott, 347; interview with Floyd, 348; assumes command of Charleston Harbor, 349; asks reenforcements, 351-354; visit to the mayor of Charleston, 356, 357; Floyd's instructions to, by Buell, 387, 388; suggests to Foster to arm his workmen, 442; instructions from Secretary of War, III, 36, 40; description of Fort Moultrie, 37; letter reporting guardboat, 44; asks for instructions, 45; resolves to abandon Fort Moultrie, 46; letter to his wife, 46; preparations to occupy Fort Sumter, 47; transfers his command to Sumter, 52; reports his movement to Washington, 54; refuses Gov. Pickens's demand that he return to Moultrie, 57; reply to Floyd's inquiry, 65; calls council of war to consider the firing on the *Star of the West*, 105; letter demanding explanations and threatening to close the harbor, 106; letter deciding to refer the question to Washington, 108; letter refusing to surrender Fort Sumter to Gov. Pickens, and proposing to report the matter to Washington, 112, 113; reports beginning of Morris Island battery, 123; opinion on reënforcing Fort Sumter, 377; comment on Fox's suggestion, 390; reported declarations of, IV, 20; reply to Beauregard's conditions, 21, 22; letters about evacuation, 24, 25; letter about his instructions, 26, 27; reply to instructions, 40, 41; refuses to evacuate Fort Sumter, 46; proposition about evacuation, 47; agreement with Wigfall, 60; capitulation of, 60; evacuates Fort Sumter, 61; sails for New York, 61; commissioned to organize Kentucky troops, 235; letter to Lincoln, 236, 237; invited by Kentucky legislature to command, V, 46; moves headquarters to Louisville, 49; relieved from command in Kentucky, 52; raises U. S. flag over Fort Sumter, April 14, 1865, X, 278–280.

Anderson, Thomas L., M. C. : plan of compromise, II, 424.

Anderson, W. G., letter to Lincoln demanding explanations, I, 211.

Andersonville prison, situation of, VII, 465, 466; Col. Chandler's report on, 465, 466.

Andrew, John A., Gov. of Mass. : request to Baltimore authorities, IV, 119; dispatch to Cameron, 120; appoints B. F. Butler brigadier general, 133; correspondence with Butler about slave insurrection, 385, 386; obtains authority to raise colored troops, VI, 462; regiments organized by, 463.

Andrews, George L., Bvt. Maj. Gen. U. S. Vols. : interrogates Col. J. L. Logan about negro prisoners of war, VII, 454, 455.

Antietam, Md., battle of, Sept. 17, 1862, VI, 139–141; losses at, 141.

Appomattox, Va., Lee's surrender at, April 9, 1865, X, 195–197.

Archer, James J., Conf. Brig. Gen. : in battle of Gettysburg, VII, 240.

Arguelles, José Augustin, Lieut. Gov. of Colon, Cuba: business of, in New York, IX, 45; charged with selling recaptured Africans in Cuba, 45; extradition of, asked by Spain, 46; arrest and delivery of 46; Senate resolution demanding information concerning, 46; Seward's answer concerning, 46, 47.

Argyll, Duke of, alleged views on the *Alabama*, VI, 54.

Arista, Mariano, Mex. Gen. : attacks Gen. Taylor, I, 242; defeated by Taylor at Palo Alto, 261.

Arkansas, State of, admitted as a State, I, 324; response to Lincoln's proclamation, IV, 90, 249; course of secession movement in, 248, 249; convention called, 248; arsenal at Little Rock seized, 249; conditional secession ordinance voted down by the convention, 249; the governor's revolutionary acts, 249; secession ordinance passed, May 6, 1861, 249; Battle of Pea Ridge, March 6–8, 1862, V, 291, 292; John S. Phelps appointed military governor, VI, 346; Lincoln's letter to Steele and Phelps, Nov. 18, 1862, about reconstruction, 350; condition of, described by Hindman, 372; Hindman sent to command rebel troops in, 373; Maj. Gen. T. H. Holmes assigned to command rebel troops in, 380; battle of Prairie Grove, Dec. 7, 1862, 383; capture of Arkansas Post, Jan. 11, 1863, VII, 140; Gen. Steele occupies Little Rock, VIII, 411; Union regiments formed in, 412; Union organization in, 412; State convention at Little Rock, Jan. 8, 1864, 414; Constitution amended, to abolish slavery, 415; provisional State government inaugurated, 415; Isaac Murphy appointed governor, 415; election ordered by Gen. Steele, 415, 417; vote on the Constitution, 416, 417; Murphy elected governor, 417; State government inaugurated, 417; legislature organized, 417; Fishback and Baxter elected to U. S. Senate, 418; election for Congress, 418; ratifies Thirteenth Amendment, X, 89.

Arkansas, The, Conf. ram : set on fire, VII, 122.

Arkansas Post, Ark., capture of, Jan. 11, 1863, VII, 140.

Arman, Jean L., French shipbuilder: receives assurances from Napoleon the Third, VIII, 271; agreement with Bullock about Confederate ships, 279; sells Confederate ships, 279; interview with Napoleon, 279.

Armies of the United States, strength of, reported, April 5, 1861, IV, 65; numbers of, spring of 1862, VII, 2; call for 300,000 volunteers, July 2, 1862, 3; call for 300,000 nine-months militia, Aug. 4, 1862, 3; statement of successive calls for, 8; muster out and reduction of, X, 329, 330, 337; grand review of, at Washington, 331, 335; number of, during the war, 339.

Armistead, Lewis A., Conf. Brig. Gen.: strength of brigade after Antietam, VI, 143; killed at Gettysburg, VII, 267.

Armstrong, Frank C., Conf. Brig. Gen.: in battles of Atlanta, IX, 286.

Armstrong, Jack, wrestles with Lincoln, I, 80, 81.

Armstrong, James, Capt. U. S. N.: assists Lieut. Slemmer, III, 163; surrenders Pensacola navy yard, 164.

Arnold, Isaac N., M. C.: complaint about Scripps, IX, 361.

Arnold, L. G., Bvt. Maj. U. S. A.: sent to occupy Fort Jefferson, III, 134.

Arnold, Samuel, in conspiracy to assassinate Lincoln, X, 289; tried and imprisoned, 312, 313.

Arthur, Chester A., twenty-first Pres. U. S.: action on case of Gen. Fitz-John Porter, VI, 13.

Asboth, Alexander, Bvt. Maj. Gen. U. S. Vols.: commands a division under Frémont, IV, 429.

Ashley, James M., M. C.: favors Lincoln's renomination, IX, 62; House bills on reconstruction, 449–453; House bill to abolish slavery by Constitutional amendment, X, 74; changes vote on Thirteenth Amendment, 78; calls up Thirteenth Amendment for reconsideration, 81; interview with Lincoln, 84, 85; interview with Nicolay, 84, 85.

Ashmore, John D., M. C.: signs secession address, II, 436.

Ashmun, George, M. C.: amendment on the Mexican war, I, 259; chairman of Chicago Convention, 1860, II, 266.

Aspinwall, W. H., recommends McClellan for command at Cincinnati, IV, 282; advises McClellan it is his duty to submit to Lincoln's proclamation, VI, 180.

Atchison, David R., U. S. Sen., acting Vice-Pres. under Pierce: remarks on Missouri Compromise, I, 340, 341; interview with Douglas, and proposition to him; 346; organizes political conspiracy in Missouri, 397; speech advising Missourians to vote slavery into Kansas, 399; town named in his honor, 402; resigns office of President pro tem. of Senate, 408; leads Platte County riflemen against Lawrence in Wakarusa war, 443; sustains Lawrence agreement, 447; takes part in destroying Free State Hotel, 455; joins third raid against Lawrence, II, 16; yields to Gov. Geary's commands, 16.

Atherton, Sir William, opinion on the Alabama, VI, 54.

Atkins, Smith D., Bvt. Maj. Gen. U. S. Vols.: in March to the Sea, IX, 481.

Atkinson, Henry, Brig. Gen. U. S. A.: summons Black Hawk to return, I, 89; commands regulars in Black Hawk war, 91.

Atlanta, Ga., siege of, July 22 to Sept. 1, 1864, IX, 270–289; occupied by Sherman, 289.

Atlanta, The, rebel ram: captured by the Weehawken, XII, 79–81.

Atzerodt, George A., in conspiracy to assassinate Lincoln, X, 289; receives Booth's directions to remove Andrew Johnson, 291, 292; tried and hanged, 312, 313.

Augur, C. C., Bvt. Maj. Gen. U. S. A.: instructions about political arrests, VIII, 40; present at Lincoln's deathbed, X, 300; made Department commander, 338.

Averill, William W., Bvt. Maj. Gen. U. S. A.: defeats Ramseur's division, IX, 175; drives McCausland from Hancock, Md., 178; defeats McCausland at Moorefield, 178; in Sheridan's army, 182; in Shenandoah campaign, 295, 296; in battle of Winchester, 303.

Avery, W. L., Capt. U. S. Vols.: in battle of Chattanooga, VIII, 149.

Avery, William W., presents majority report in Charleston Convention, II, 233, 234.

Ayres, Romeyn B., Bvt. Maj. Gen. U. S. A.: in march to Five Forks, X, 169; in battle of Five Forks, 172; at grand review in Washington, 332.

Bad Axe, battle of, I, 94, 95.

Bailey, Joseph, Bvt. Maj. Gen. U. S. Vols.: builds dams on Red River, VIII, 298–301.

Bailey, Joshua F., special Treasury agent: action of, IX, 86, 87.

Bailey, Maj., commands battalion in Black Hawk war, I, 91.

Bailey, Theodorus, Rear Adm. U. S. N.: commands "Column of the Red" in passage of Forts Jackson and St. Philip, V, 261; destruction of rebel gunboats, 262, 263; sent by Farragut to confer with mayor of New Orleans, 267.

Baily, Joseph, M. C.: first vote for Thirteenth Amendment, X, 78; second vote for Thirteenth Amendment, 83.

Baird, Absalom, Bvt. Maj. Gen. U. S. A.: command of, in Army of Kentucky, VIII, 44; withdraws from Bragg's attack, 79; in battle of Chickamauga, 85, 88, 89, 92–94,

98, 104; in battle of Chattanooga, 135, 146, 151, 152, 155; in March to the Sea, IX, 481.
Baird, Mrs., Lincoln's letter concerning, V, 143.
Baker, Edward D., M. C.: U. S. Sen., Bvt. Maj. Gen. U. S. Vols.: protest against the Judicial Reform scheme, I, 164, 165; nominated for Illinois State Senate, 182; oratorical powers, 220; elected to Congress from Springfield district, 223; commands regiment in Mexican war, 250; speech in House of Representatives, 252-255; resumes his seat in Congress, 255; succeeds to command of Shields's brigade at Cerro Gordo, 255; elected to Congress from Galena district, 290; introduces Lincoln at his first inauguration, III, 327; killed at Ball's Bluff, IV, 456, 457.
Baldwin, Augustus C., M. C.: vote for Thirteenth Amendment, X, 83.
Baldwin, John B., interview with Lincoln, III, 423-426.
Baldwin, P. P., Col. U. S. Vols.: in battle of Murfreesboro, VI, 286.
Ball's Bluff, Va., battle of, Oct. 21, 1861, IV, 455-457.
Baltimore, Md., condition of, in January and February, 1861, III, 304-307; secession feeling in, IV, 110; arrival of the 6th Massachusetts, 111; soldiers attacked by the mob, 113; march across the city, 116; mass-meeting in Monument Square, 119; railroad bridges burned, 121; railroads refuse to transport troops, 124; transit of troops through, reëstablished, 172, 173; occupied by Butler, 173, 174.
Baltimore Convention, 1852, Democratic National: meets in June, I, 332; votes: for Lewis Cass, 332 — for William L. Marcy, 332 — for James Buchanan, 332 — for Stephen A. Douglas, 332; nominates Franklin Pierce, 332.
Baltimore Convention, 1864, Republican National: adopts resolution affirming Monroe doctrine, VII, 421; meeting of, June 7, 1864, IX, 65; address of E. D. Morgan, 65; Rev. R. J. Breckinridge made temporary chairman, 65; Breckinridge's speech, 65-67; William Dennison made permanent chairman, 67, 68; action of committee on credentials, 68, 69; Henry J. Raymond reports platform, 69-71; Lincoln renominated for President, 71, 72; Andrew Johnson nominated for Vice-President, 72-74; resolution advocating Thirteenth Amendment, X, 80.

Bancroft, George, Sec. of Navy under Polk, historian, Min. to Prussia: remarks at a New York meeting, V, 202; letter to Lincoln suggesting "an increase of free States," 203; letter to Lincoln about suspension of habeas corpus, VIII, 36, 37.
Banks, Nathaniel P., Speaker H. R., Maj. Gen. U. S. Vols.: chosen Speaker of House of Representatives under plurality rule, I, 364; receives votes for Vice-President in Philadelphia Convention, II, 35; appointed major general of U. S. volunteers, IV, 309; succeeds Gen. Butler at Baltimore, 309; supersedes Patterson at Harper's Ferry, 356; assumes command at Ball's Bluff, 457; assigned to command Fifth Army Corps, V, 169; pursues Jackson up the Valley, 401; retreat to the Potomac, 402; commands corps in Army of Virginia, VI, 1; ordered to Culpeper Court House, 5; attacks Jackson at Cedar Mountain and is repulsed, Aug. 9, 1862, 6; report of negro troops organized, 455; expedition to Department of the Gulf, VII, 311; sends Gen. Grover to occupy Baton Rouge, 313; sends expedition to Galveston, 313; makes demonstration against Port Hudson, 314; expedition to Alexandria, La., 314, 315; correspondence with Grant about coöperation, 315-317; expedition against Port Hudson, 317; effects junction with C. C. Augur, 317; first assault on Port Hudson, May 25, 1863, 317; second assault on Port Hudson, June 14, 1863, 317; siege of Port Hudson, May 25 to July 9, 1863, 317-322; ordered to occupy some portion of Texas, VIII, 286; sends expedition to Sabine Pass, 286; defeat of Franklin at Sabine Pass, Sept. 8, 1863, 287; expedition to the Rio Grande, 287, 288; occupies Brownsville and Point Isabel, 287; captures works at Aransas Pass, 287; occupies Fort Esperanza, Nov. 30, 1863, 287, 288; accepts Halleck's plan for Red River campaign, 288; march towards Shreveport, 291, 292; battle of Sabine Cross Roads, April 8, 1864, 292-294; battle of Pleasant Hill, April 9, 1864, 295; retreats down Red River, 296-301; plan for obtaining cotton, 305; replies to the President, 427; plan of reconstruction in Louisiana, 428-430; orders election for State officers in Louisiana, 431-433; orders election for State convention in Louisiana, 435.

Baptist Convention of New York, resolutions supporting emancipation, VI, 315.

Baptist State Convention of Alabama, resolution supporting secession, VI, 331.

Barbour, James, M. C.: suggested for the Cabinet, III, 365.

Barclay, Clement, information to Lincoln about Hooker, VII, 200.

Barksdale, William, M. C., Conf. Brig. Gen.: signs secession address, II, 436 ; in battle of Ball's Bluff, IV, 458.

Barlow, Francis C., Maj. Gen. U. S. Vols.: wounded at Gettysburg, VII, 242 ; in Army of Potomac, VIII, 353; in battle of the Wilderness, 362, 364; in battle of Spotsylvania, 376, 379, 380, 386; in battle of Cold Harbor, 401; in attack on Petersburg, IX, 411; in march to Appomattox, X, 189; at grand review in Washington, 332.

Barnard, J. G., Bvt. Maj. Gen. U. S. A.: attends council of war, V, 167; says Yorktown should have been assaulted, 367; says batteries should have been opened on Yorktown as fast as completed, 372; comment on battle of Seven Pines, 391 ; criticism on battle of Gaines's Mill, 429, 430; advises McClellan's withdrawal from the James, 457.

Barnes, Albert, resolutions offered at meeting of American Board of Foreign Missions, VI, 317.

Barnes, James, Bvt. Maj. Gen. U. S. Vols.: in battle of Gettysburg, VII, 254.

Barnes, Joseph K., Bvt. Maj. Gen. U. S. A.: present at Lincoln's deathbed, X, 300.

Barney, Hiram, Collector of New York: present at Lincoln's Cooper Institute speech, II, 217.

Barnwell, R. W., Comr. of S. C.: arrives in Washington, III, 62 ; interview with Pres. Buchanan, 70.

Barry, William F., Bvt. Maj. Gen. U. S. A.: chief of artillery at Washington, IV, 441; opinion about siege operations at Yorktown, V, 372.

Barton, Seth M., Conf. Brig. Gen.: in battle of Champion's Hill, VII, 191.

Bate, Wm. B., Conf. Maj. Gen. U. S. Sen.: in battle of Chattanooga, VIII, 152; defeated by Milroy, X, 23.

Bates, Edward, M. C.: Atty. Gen. under Lincoln : candidate before Chicago Convention, 1860, II, 256, 263, 271 ; vote for, on first ballot, 273 ; vote for, on second ballot, 274 ; vote for, on third ballot, 275 ; visits Lincoln at Springfield, III, 351 ; accepts office

of Attorney General, 352; appointed Attorney General, 372 ; extract from diary, 380, 381; first opinion on Sumter, 388; second opinion on Sumter, 432 ; opinion on Maryland matters, IV, 166 ; diary of, on the Trent affair, V, 35, 36; signs remonstrance against McClellan's continuance in command, VI, 21; favors immediate announcement of first emancipation proclamation, 128; opinion on the admission of West Virginia, 308, 309; suggestions for final emancipation proclamation, 419, 420; opinion on the Fort Pillow massacre, 482; review of the Merryman case, VIII, 28 ; resignation of, IX, 343-346 ; declines a district judgeship, 344, 345; controversy with Butler, 441, 442.

Bates, Lewis F., entertains Jefferson Davis, X, 264, 265.

Bates, Richard, son of Edward Bates : thanks to, for use of manuscripts, V, 36.

Baton Rouge, La., barracks and arsenal seized, III, 192.

Battle, C. A., Conf. Brig. Gen. : in battle of Winchester, IX, 301.

Baxter, Elisha, elected U. S. Senator from Arkansas, VIII, 418.

Bayard, James A., U. S. Sen. : deprecates making paper money legal tender, VI, 235.

Bazaine, François Achille, Marshal of France: defeats Comonfort, VII, 397.

Beall, John Yates, takes possession of the Philo Parsons, VIII, 19; scuttles the Island Queen, 19; attempts to wreck a railroad train, 19, 20; sentenced to death by court martial, 20; petition for commutation of sentence of, 20 ; respited by Pres. Lincoln, 20; execution of, 20, 21.

Beatty, John, Brig. Gen. U. S. Vols. : in battle of Chickamauga, VIII, 92 ; in battle of Chattanooga, 148.

Beauregard, G. T., Conf. Gen.: interview with Fox, III, 389; report on Sumter, 397; telegram to commissioners, IV, 3 ; proposes conditions to Anderson, 21 ; apologizes to Anderson, 22 ; letter to Walker, 23; reports batteries ready, 29; letter to Anderson about mails, 30 ; permits Gov. Pickens to open Anderson's mail, 39 ; demands evacuation of Sumter, 46; second proposition about evacuation, 46 ; notice of attack, 47; ratifies Wigfall's negotiations, 60, 61; sent to command Manassas Junction, 322 ; in command at Bull Run, 342; first plan of battle, 347; changes his plan, 347; battle of Bull

Run, July 21, 1861, 348-351; endeavors to check Confederate defeat, 348; congratulatory order about Ball's Bluff, 458; council of war at Fairfax Court House, V, 153, 154; attends council of war at Bowling Green, 185; evacuates Columbus, 303; joins Johnston near Corinth, 321; second in command of Confederate army at Pittsburg Landing, 321; council of Confederate commanders; advises change of plan, 322; attack on Union troops, April 6, 1862, 325; advances his headquarters to Shiloh Church, 325, 326; orders rebel attack to cease, 333; force of, at Corinth, 338; evacuates Corinth, 341; plans to fortify Vicksburg, 346; preparations for defending Charleston, VII, 66, 67; plan for a boarding assault on the Union fleet, 82, 83; letter about Vallandigham, 340; opposes Terry's demonstration against James Island, 427; correspondence with Gillmore about Gen. Hunter, 437-439; correspondence with Gillmore about bombardment of Charleston, 439-441; comments on defense of Charleston, 442, 443; commands defense of Richmond and Petersburg, VIII, 393; dispatches to Seddon, 396; plan of campaign, 396, 397; battle of Bermuda Hundred, May 16, 1864, 397-399; defense of Petersburg, IX, 410, 411; in siege of Petersburg, 428; given command over Hood and Taylor, 473; approves Hood's Tennessee campaign, 476; directs Hood to take the offensive, X, 9; suggests plan to Davis, 156,157; superseded by Johnston, 233; interviews with Davis and Johnston, 257-263.

Beaver Dam Creek, Va., rebels repulsed at, June 26, 1862, V, 425; losses at, 425.

Bee, H. P., Conf. Brig. Gen.: defeated at Cane River, VIII, 297.

Beecher, Rev. Henry Ward, oration at Fort Sumter flag-raising, X, 278, 280.

Bell, John, M. C., Sec. of War under W. H. Harrison, U. S. Sen.: opposes first Nebraska Bill, I, 340; nominated for President by Constitutional Union Party, II, 253; subsequent course on secession, 254; letter of acceptance, 281; electoral votes for, 294.

Bell, Louis, Col. U. S. Vols.: killed in assault on Fort Fisher, X, 66, 67.

Bellows, W. H., D. D., Pres. Sanitary Commission: consults with Mr. Lincoln, VI, 330.

Belmont, August, Min. to The Hague: calls Democratic National Convention to order, IX, 254, 255.

Belmont, Mo., battle of, Nov. 7, 1861, V, 113, 114.

Benedict, Lewis, Col. U. S. Vols.: killed at Pleasant Hill, VIII, 295.

Benham, Henry W., Bvt. Maj. Gen. U. S. A.: leads pursuit against Garnett, IV, 337.

Benjamin, Judah P., U. S. Sen., Conf. Sec. of State: comments on Douglas's recusancy, II, 163,164; signs address commending the Charleston disruption, 245, 246; signs secession address, 436; signs the Senatorial secession caucus resolutions, III, 181; appointed Confederate Attorney General, 212; telegram about East Tennessee bridge-burners, V, 77; instructions about bridge-burners, 78; sends Brownlow within the Union lines, 80; authorizes Slidell to submit propositions to Napoleon III., VI, 77-79; accepts arrangement about rebel privateers, VII, 450; interview with Jaquess and Gillmore, IX, 208-211; report of Jaquess-Gilmore interview with Jefferson Davis, 211, 212; suggests instructions to Peace Commissioners, X, 111, 112; dispatch to Slidell, 154, 155; present at interview of Davis and Johnston, 257-263; leaves Davis's party, 267.

Bennett, James Gordon, editor of N. Y. "Herald:" interview with F. P. Blair, Sr., IX, 248.

Benton, Thomas H., U. S. Sen.: votes against Nebraska bill, I, 270.

Bermuda Hundred, Va., battle of, May 16, 1864, VIII, 397-399; losses at, 399.

Berry, Hiram G., Maj. Gen. U. S. Vols.: killed at Chancellorsville, VII, 104.

Berry, Richard, signs Thomas Lincoln's marriage bond, I, 23, 24.

Berry, William F., partner of Lincoln in a store, I, 110.

Berry, Wm. W., Col. U. S. Vols.: in battle of Chattanooga, VIII, 151.

Berthier, Gen., defeated by Mexicans, VI, 47.

Biddle, Charles J., M. C.: opposes bill for draft, VII, 5.

Bidwell, Daniel D., Brig. Gen. U. S. Vols.: skirmish near Washington, IX, 172; killed at Cedar Creek, 321.

Big Black, Miss., battle of, May 17, 1863, VII, 192.

Bigler, William, Gov. of Penn., U. S. Sen.: explains caucus action on the Toombs bill, II, 94; speech in Charleston Convention,

239; member of Senate Committee of Thirteen, 414; propositions in that committee, III, 222.

Bingham, John A., M. C., Min. to Japan: plan of compromise, II, 422; bill to aid emancipation in Maryland, VIII, 457; assistant judge advocate in trial of Lincoln's assassins, X, 312.

Binney, Horace, M. C.: comment on opinion in Merryman case, IV, 175, 176; pamphlet, "Writ of Habeas Corpus," VIII, 29–31.

Birney, David B., Maj. Gen. U. S. Vols.: in battle of Chancellorsville, VII, 99, 101; in battle of Gettysburg, 250, 251; testimony about Gettysburg, 269; in Army of the Potomac, VIII, 353; in battle of the Wilderness, 362, 366; in battle of Spotsylvania, 376, 379, 380; in attack on Petersburg, IX, 411; in siege of Petersburg, 432; in siege of Richmond, 427, 431.

Birney, James G., votes for, for President, I, 231.

Birney, William, Bvt. Maj. Gen. U. S. Vols.: in siege of Richmond, IX, 431.

Bismarck, Prince, Chancellor of German Empire: speech on Lincoln's death, X, 344.

Bissell, George B.: marshals first Wide Awakes, II, 285.

Bissell, J. W., Col. U. S. Vols.: canal of, at Island No. 10, V, 297.

Bissell, William H., M. C., Gov. of Ill.: commands regiment in Mexican war, I, 250; his political antecedents, II, 25–27; in battle of Buena Vista, 26; challenged by Jefferson Davis, 27; nominated for governor of Illinois, 29; elected governor, 43.

Blackburn's Ford, Va., engagement at, July 18, 1861, IV, 343.

Black, Jeremiah S., Atty. Gen. and Sec. of State under Buchanan: controversy with Douglas, II, 184, 185; opinions on disunion, 360–362; appointed Secretary of State, III, 66; sustains Anderson's movement, 67; announces his intention to resign, 80; memorandum criticizing Buchanan's reply to South Carolina commissioners, 80–82; letter to Gen. Scott, 157, 158; answer to Tyler about the *Brooklyn*, 166; circular to foreign governments, IV, 267; criticisms of Stanton, V, 131.

Black Hawk, Chief of Sac Indians: treaty with, I, 87, 88; crosses the Mississippi River with his warriors into Illinois, 89; Gov. Reynolds calls for volunteers to expel them, 89; defeats Stillman, 91; defeated at battle of Bad Axe, 95; capture of, 95; speech to Pres. Jackson at Washington, 95; death of, 96.

Blaine, James G., U. S. Sen., Sec. of State under Garfield and Benjamin Harrison: votes for re-passage of National Bank Act, VI, 245.

Blair, Francis P., Jr., M. C., Maj. Gen. U. S. Vols.: lecture in New York, II, 217; elected to Congress, IV, 206; reëlected in 1860, 207; member of Union Safety Committee at St. Louis, 212; delivers the President's order to Harney, 222; takes his seat in Congress, 404; quarrel with Frémont, 413, 414; member of Select Committee on Emancipation, VI, 395; in assault on Chickasaw Bluffs, VII, 133; march to Edwards's Station, 188; candidate for Speaker of House of Representatives, 381; returns to the army, 393; in march to Chattanooga, VIII, 132; in Sherman's march to Knoxville, 182; joins Sherman's army, IX, 27; Congressional investigation of, 80; speech attacking Chase, 80; in battle of Atlanta, 272, 273, 286; comment on his brother's resignation, 341, 342; in March to the Sea, 481; in march to Columbia, X, 230; at grand review in Washington, 333.

Blair, Francis P., Sr., interview with R. E. Lee, IV, 98; interview with Bryant, IX, 248; interview with Greeley, 248; interview with Bennett, 248; interview with McClellan, 248, 249; letters to Jefferson Davis, X, 94, 95; visit to Richmond, 95, 96; interview with Jefferson Davis, 96–106; second interview with Davis, 109, 110.

Blair, H. P., suggests Wide Awake uniform, II, 285.

Blair, Jacob B., M. C.: second interview with Lincoln about compensated emancipation, VI, 112.

Blair, Montgomery, P. M. Gen. under Lincoln: argument in Dred Scott case, II, 64; recommended for the Cabinet, III, 368; selected for the Cabinet, 369; appointed Postmaster General, 372; first opinion on Sumter, 386; second opinion on Sumter, 432; statement about Lee, IV, 98; testimony concerning Frémont, 402, 403; visits Frémont, 313; deprecates policy of military emancipation, VI, 129; comment on preliminary emancipation proclamation, 161–163; opinion on admission of West Virginia, 306–308; suggestions for final emancipation proclamation, 419; opinion on the Fort Pillow massacre, 482; conversation with Lincoln about Frank Blair, VII, 392; political antecedents of, IX, 333–335; opposes Henry Winter Davis, 335, 336; opposes Colfax for Speaker, 337; relations to the Cabinet, 337; controversy with Halleck, 338; Lincoln asks his resignation, 340, 341; declines Spanish or Austrian mission, 342.

Blake, George S., commodore U. S. N.: commandant U. S. Naval Academy, IV, 136.

Blatchford, Richard M., authorized to make government purchases, IV, 137; authorized to organize troops, 138; proposed for Assistant Treasurer at New York, IX, 93.

Bledsoe, Albert T., Conf. Asst. Sec. of War: prominent lawyer of Illinois, I, 213.

Blenker, Louis, Brig. Gen. U. S. Vols.: attends council of war, V, 167.

Bliss, Z. R., Lieut. Col. U. S. A.: censured for Petersburg mine affair, IX, 425.

Blow, Henry T., Min. to Venezuela, M. C.: approves Lincoln's message, IX, 110.

Blunt, James G., Maj. Gen. U. S. Vols.: called to aid Missouri campaign, VI, 379; battle of Prairie Grove, Dec. 7, 1862, 383.

Boggs, C. S., Rear Adm. U. S. N.: commands the *Varuna* in Farragut's fleet, V, 261; sinking of the *Varuna*, 263.

Boggs, W. R., Conf. Capt.: sent to Pensacola, IV, 11.

Bogue, Vincent, navigates Sangamon River with steamboat *Talisman*, I, 85, 86.

Bogus Laws of Kansas, provisions about slavery, etc., I, 419–421; ignored by Kansas Free State party, 428, 429, 432.

Bogus Legislature of Kansas, vote electing, I, 411; convened by the governor at Pawnee, 414; J. H. Stringfellow elected Speaker of House, 415; Thomas Johnson elected Speaker of Council, 415; passes Act to remove seat of government to Shawnee Mission, 415; reassembles at Shawnee Mission, 415; petitions the President to remove Gov. Reeder, 417; copies and adopts Revised Statutes of Missouri, 419; concurrent resolution " to know but one issue, slavery," 425; analysis of vote for, 438, 439.

Bond,——, favorably mentioned by Lincoln, I, 292.

Bonds of United States, $10,000,000 negotiated by Sec. Cobb, III, 239; authorized by act of Feb. 8, 1861, 242; authorized by Morrill Tariff Act, 243; issue of " Five-twenty " bonds, VI, 240, 241.

Bonham, Milledge L., M. C., Conf. Brig. Gen.: signs secession address, II, 436; advises with Trescott about withdrawing Gov. Pickens's letter, III, 6.

Bonzano, M. F., elected to Congress in Louisiana, VIII, 437.

Boone, Anna, first cousin of Daniel Boone : marries Abraham Lincoln of Pennsylvania, I, 4.

Boone, Anna, sister of Daniel Boone, I, 5.

Boone, Daniel, explorer and pioneer; explores Kentucky, I, 6; captured by the Indians, 6; meets his brother Squire Boone in Kentucky, 6; spends three months alone in the wilderness, 7; disaster near Cumberland Gap, 7; escorts a party of surveyors through Kentucky, 8; commands three garrisons, 8; personal characteristics, 8, 9; report of battle of the Blue Licks, 9; member of Henderson's legislature, 9; deprived of his Kentucky homestead, 13.

Boone, George, trustee of Mordecai Lincoln, I, 5.

Boone, Squire, father of Daniel Boone: appraiser of Mordecai Lincoln's estate, I, 6.

Boone, Squire, younger brother of Daniel Boone : meets Daniel Boone in Kentucky, I, 6; returns to the eastern settlements, 7.

Boonville, Mo., battle of, June 17, 1861, IV, 224.

Booth, John Wilkes, personal description, X, 289, 290; conspiracy to abduct Lincoln, 290; creates disturbance at Lincoln's second inauguration, 290; conspiracy to assassinate Lincoln, 291, 292; gives a letter to Matthews, 293; shoots Pres. Lincoln, 296; wounds Maj. Rathbone, 296; flight of, 297; escape from Washington, 307; assisted by Samuel Mudd, 307, 308; assisted by Samuel Cox, 308; rowed across the Potomac by Thomas Jones, 308, 309; diary of, 309–311; assisted by William Jett, 311; goes to Garrett's farm, 311; shot by Boston Corbett, 312.

Booth, L. W., Maj. U. S. Vols.: refuses to surrender Fort Pillow, VI, 479; killed at Fort Pillow, April 12, 1864, 479.

Boteler, A. R., M. C.: motion to appoint House Committee of Thirty-three, II, 415.

Botts, John Minor, M. C.: interview with Lincoln, III, 423; describes the Baldwin interview, 424, 425.

Bouligny, John E., M. C.: loyalty of, III, 193; retains his seat in House of Representatives, 195; mission to New Orleans, VI, 349.

Boutwell, George S., M. C., Sec. of Treas. under Grant, U. S. Sen.: member of Peace Convention, III, 230; reports Lincoln's statement about Altoona meeting, VI, 164, 165; votes for re-passage of National Bank Act, 245; approves Lincoln's message, IX, 109.

Bowen, John S., Conf. Brig. Gen.: brigade of, at Grand Gulf, VII, 165; defense of Port Gibson, 170, 171; evacuates Grand Gulf, 172; in battle of Champion's Hill, 189-192; advises capitulation of Vicksburg, 302; sent with flag of truce to Grant, 302; present at Pemberton's interview with Grant, 303.

Bowie, James, Col. Tex. army : defense of the Alamo, I, 233.

Boyce, William W., M. C.: member of House Committee of Thirty-three, II, 417; refuses to attend its meetings, III, 214.

Boynton, H. V., Bvt. Brig. Gen. U. S. Vols.: in battle of Chattanooga, VIII, 151.

Bradford, A. W., Gov. of Md.: complaints about negro recruiting in Maryland, VI, 464; election of, VIII, 450; complaint about negro enlistments, 459; complaints about Maryland elections, 462; proclamation about Schenck's election order, 464; proclamation declaring Constitution adopted, 468.

Bradley, L. P., Bvt. Brig. Gen. U. S. A.: in march to Franklin, X, 11, 12.

Bragg, Braxton, Conf. Gen.: dispatches about Fort Pickens, IV, 9-11, 13; commands Confederate right wing at Pittsburg Landing, V, 321; invades Kentucky, VI, 274; march toward Louisville, 276; move toward Lexington, 276; attempts to inaugurate a Confederate government at Frankfort, 277; attacked by Union forces at Perryville, 278; withdraws his army to Harrodsburg, 279; retreats from Kentucky, 279; pursued by Buell, 279; takes position at Murfreesboro, Tenn., 282; plan of battle at Murfreesboro, 284, 285; begins the battle, Dec. 31, 1862, 285; dispatch announcing victory, 290; attacks Rosecrans, Jan. 2, 1863, 292; retreats to Tullahoma, 294; raids in Kentucky, VIII, 49, 50; organizes cavalry raid into northern States, 52; retreats to Chattanooga, 62; reënforced, 63; retreat from Chattanooga, 73; prepares to take the offensive, 76; gives orders to attack Thomas, 78; orders movement against Crittenden, 79; blames Polk, 80; battle of Chickamauga, Sept. 18-

20, 1863, 83-107; blockades the Tennessee River, 113; comment on Longstreet's advice, 113, 114; opposes Union advance on Lookout Valley, 126; interview with Jefferson Davis, 127; battle of Chattanooga, Nov. 23-25, 1863, 134-157; made chief of staff to Jefferson Davis, 326; comment on Beauregard's plan, 396, 397; proposes plan to Johnston, IX, 5-8; in defense of Goldsboro, X, 70.

Brainard, Cephas, present at Lincoln's Cooper Institute speech, II, 217.

Braine, J. C., Conf. mutineer : in capture of the Chesapeake, VIII, 14.

Bramlette, Thomas E., Brig. Gen. U. S. Vols., Gov. of Ky.: occupies Lexington, V, 51; objects to arming negroes, VI, 463.

Branch, Lawrence O'B., M. C., Conf. Brig. Gen.: resolutions in House of Representatives about quartering troops at the Capital, III, 147; defeated by Porter, V, 385; joins J. R. Anderson, 386.

Brandy Station, Va., cavalry battle at, June 9, 1863, VII, 205, 206.

Brannan, J. M., Bvt. Maj. Gen. U. S. A.: in battle of Chickamauga, VIII, 85, 88, 92, 94, 95, 98-101, 104; reports against attack on Missionary Ridge, 130.

Branson, Jacob, arrest and rescue of, I, 441.

Braxton, Carter M., Conf. Lieut. Col.: in battle of Winchester, IX, 301.

Breckinridge, Judge, introduces bill in Missouri Convention to accept compensated abolishment, VI, 391.

Breckinridge, J. C., Vice-Pres. with Buchanan, Conf. Maj. Gen. and Sec. of War: nominated for Vice-President, II, 39; circulates Dred Scott decision, 73, 74; nominated for President at Baltimore, 251; letter of acceptance, 281; electoral votes for, 294; popular vote for and against, 358; presides at the Presidential count, III, 145; announces election of Lincoln, 146; call of ceremony on Lincoln, 317; leaves Kentucky, to join the South, IV, 244; complains of usurpation, 383; flight from Lexington, V, 51; commands Confederate reserve at Pittsburg Landing, 321; in battle of Murfreesboro, VI, 283, 292; defeat of, 292; threat of retaliation, 477; sent to attack Baton Rouge, VII, 122; defeated at Baton Rouge, 122; fortifies Port Hudson, 122; joins Johnston's army in Mississippi, 294; in battle of Chickamauga, VIII, 92, 106; in battle of Chattanooga, 145; in battle of Cold Harbor,

401; witnesses skirmish near Washington, IX, 172; in battle of Winchester, 303; in campaign of Cedar Creek, 312; appointed Confederate Secretary of War, X, 153; interview with Sherman and Johnston, 246-248; report on the Sherman-Johnston agreement, 251; arrives at Greensboro, 259; present at interview of Davis and Johnston, 260-263; interview with Davis at Charlotte, 265; leaves Davis's party, 267.

Breckinridge, R. J., D.D., LL.D.: report to Presbyterian General Assembly, VI, 219, 220; temporary chairman of Baltimore Convention, IX, 65; speech of, 65-67.

Breese, K. Randolph, Capt. U. S. N.: in assault on Fort Fisher, X, 66.

Breese, Sidney, Judge Ill. Sup. Ct., U. S. Sen.: discussion at Illinois State Fair, I, 375.

Bridges, Lyman, Capt. U. S. Vols.: in march to Franklin, X, 11, 12.

Briggs, James A.: present at Lincoln's Cooper Institute speech, II, 217.

Bright, John, M. P.: remarks on the American war, VIII, 261.

Brinckerhoff, Jacob, M. C.: agrees to Wilmot Proviso, I, 268.

Bristow, Francis M., M. C.: member of House Committee of Thirty-three, II, 417.

Broadhead, James O.: member of Union Safety Committee at St. Louis, IV, 212.

Broderick, David C., U. S. Sen.: votes against Lecompton Constitution, II, 130; opposes a Congressional slave code, 175.

Brooke, John R., Bvt. Maj. Gen. U. S. Vols.: wounded at Cold Harbor, VIII, 404.

Brooklyn, The, U. S. sloop of war: ordered to reënforce Fort Pickens, III, 164; Tyler's inquiries and Buchanan's answers concerning, 166; ordered not to land Capt. Vogdes's company, 168.

Brooks, Preston S., M. C.: assaults Sen. Sumner, II, 49-51; House Committee recommends his expulsion, 53; censured by the House, 53; resigns his seat, is reëlected, and resumes his seat, 53; challenges Sen. Wilson, 54; challenges Burlingame, 55; death, 56.

Brooks, T. B., Maj. U. S. Vols.: engineering work against Fort Wagner, VII, 433, 434.

Brooks, W. T. H., Maj. Gen. U. S. Vols.: brigade of, attacks Dam No. 1, V, 368.

Brough, John, Gov. of Ohio: nominated governor of Ohio, VII, 355; in charge of funeral cortège of Lincoln, X, 319.

VOL. X.—24

Brown, ——, nominated for Congress, I, 255.

Brown, Albert G., M. C., U. S. Sen.: demands a Congressional slave code, II, 174; remarks of, 174, 175; Senate discussion, 400, 407, 410; signs secession address, 436; signs Senatorial secession caucus resolutions, III, 281.

Brown, B. Gratz, U. S. Sen.: telegram to Lincoln about Missouri Senatorial election, VI, 397; elected U. S. Senator, VIII, 470; statement about Schofield, 471; signs call for Cleveland Convention, IX, 32; absent from Cleveland Convention, 34; amendment to Reconstruction Act, 119.

Brown, George W., mayor of Baltimore, starts for the scene of rioting, IV, 114; heads the Massachusetts companies, 116; speech in Monument Square, 119; order to burn railroad bridges, 120; telegram to Secretary of War, 123; requests that transit of troops be stopped, 125; interview with Lincoln, 130.

Brown, Harvey, Bvt. Maj. Gen. U. S. A.: commands troops to protect Washington, III, 145; sails for Fort Pickens, IV, 6, 7; takes command of Fort Pickens, 16.

Brown, John, revolt against Lawrence agreement, I, 447; followers of, dispersed by Col. Sumner, II, 2; biographical notice, 190, 191; Kansas guerrilla acts, 191; the Pottawatomie massacre, 191; personal characteristics, 192, 193; collects funds and arms, 194; contract for pikes, 194; gathers and drills recruits, 195; the Peterboro council, 196-199; scheme of slave liberation, 197, 198; the Chatham meeting, 200, 201; postponement and preparation, 202, 203; change of plan, 203; Harper's Ferry, 203, 204; the Kennedy farm, 204; his campaign, 204-208; captured by Col. Lee, 208; trial and execution, 208, 209; Senate investigation, 209, 210.

Brown, Joseph E., Gov. of Ga., U. S. Sen.: reply to Gov. Gist about proposed secession, II, 310, 311; recommendations of, III, 189; orders seizure of Fort Pulaski, 190; orders seizure of Augusta arsenal, 191; withdraws Georgia militia from Hood's command, IX, 470.

Brown, Owen, son of John Brown: concerned in the Harper's Ferry invasion, II, 195.

Brown, Salmon, son of John Brown: statement about Pottawatomie massacre, II, 191.

Brown, William G., M. C.: second interview with Lincoln about compensated emancipation, VI, 112.

Browne, J. H., correspondent of New York "Tribune": cruelly treated as prisoner of war, VII, 458.

Brownell, Francis E., Lieut. U. S. A.; kills the assassin of Ellsworth, IV, 314.

Brownell, H. H., acting ensign U. S. N. : in battle of Mobile Bay, IX, 233.

Browning, Orville H., U. S. Sen., Sec. of Int. under Johnson: opinion of Lincoln's malady, I, 187; member of Bloomington Convention, II, 28; suggestions for Lincoln's inaugural address, III, 319, 322, 333, 334.

Brownlow, William G., Gov. of Tenn., U. S. Sen.: arrested, V, 80; sent into Union lines, 80; signs call for Union Convention at Nashville, VIII, 440; elected governor of Tennessee, 449.

Brumfield, ——; marries aunt of the Pres. Lincoln, I, 23.

Brumfield, Nancy Lincoln, youngest child of Abraham Lincoln, the President's grandfather, I, 5.

Brune, John C., elected to Maryland legislature, IV, 165.

Bruner, J. B., member of committee to distribute Union arms, IV, 237.

Bryant, William Cullen, editor of "New York Evening Post": leaves Democratic party, I, 277; presides over Cooper Institute meeting, II, 217; letter to Lincoln, III, 257; signs memorial about Frémont and colored troops, VI, 456; effort to postpone Republican National Convention, IX, 57, 58; interview with F. P. Blair, Sr., 248.

Buchanan, Franklin, Capt. U. S. N., Adm. Conf. navy: resigns from Washington navy yard, IV, 141; on board the *Tennessee*, IX, 227; battle of Mobile Bay, Aug. 5, 1864, 230-239; wounded at Mobile Bay, 237.

Buchanan, James, fifteenth Pres. of U. S.: votes for, in Baltimore Convention, 1852, I, 332; nominated for President, II, 39; elected President, 40; popular and electoral vote for, 40, 41; vote of Illinois for, 43; inserts a new clause in his inaugural address, 72; appoints R. J. Walker governor of Kansas Territory, 93; approves Walker's inaugural address, 95; letter to Gov. Walker about submitting Lecompton Constitution to popular vote, 102, 103; letter to Gov. Walker about the Washington "Union," 110-112; quarrel with

Douglas, 120; letter to Silliman and others, 121; message indorsing Lecompton Constitution, 122; transmits Lecompton Constitution to Congress, 125-127; favors acquisition of Cuba, 129; sends detachment of marines to capture John Brown, 207; schism between himself and Douglas, 228; speech at Washington, 282; interview with Jefferson Davis, 326; comments on Gen. Scott's "Views," 341; his opportunity, 358, 359; Cabinet conference on disunion, 360-363; annual message, Dec. 4, 1860, 365-371; message unsatisfactory, 372; declares Federal government has no power to coerce a State, 375; acquiescence in Gist's suggestion, 379; truce with South Carolina Representatives, 383-386; memorandum on Cass's resignation, 392, 393; Cabinet discussion with Floyd, 394, 395; answer to Cass, 396, 397; letter to Cass, 397, 398; proclamation of fasting and prayer, 435; letter to Gov. Pickens refusing to give up Fort Sumter, III, 4; sends Caleb Cushing to Gov. Pickens, 11; informed of Floyd's secret orders to Anderson, 39; issues a modifying order, 40; appoints interview with South Carolina commissioners, 63; informed by commissioners of Anderson's movement, 64; requests Floyd's resignation, 65; postpones interview with commissioners, 67; determines to await official information from Anderson, 69; interview with commissioners, 70; draft of reply to commissioners, 74; special message of Jan. 8, 1861, 78, 140; authorizes Black to amend his reply to South Carolina commissioners, 80; amended reply to commissioners, 82; declines to receive the commissioners' rejoinder, 86; authorizes Holt to act as Secretary of War, 89; appoints Holt Secretary of War *ad interim*, 89; nominates Holt Secretary of War, 89; postpones orders for expedition to relieve Sumter, 91; promises Secretary Thompson not to renew the orders without Cabinet discussion, 92; says "reënforcements must be sent," 93; note to Slidell, 131; nominates Collector for Charleston, 133; authorizes measures to protect Washington, 137; recommends restoration of Missouri Compromise line, 140; refuses to publish Holt's report, 149; revokes orders for military parade, Feb. 22, 1861, 150; renews the order, 151; letter to Tyler about parade, 152; interview with Hayne, 153; reply to Sen.

C. C. Clay, 159, 160; instructs Holt to reply to secession Senators, 160; interview with Tyler, 165; reply to Tyler about the *Brooklyn*, 166; reply to Hayne, 171; special message transmitting Virginia peace resolutions, 228; signs joint resolution for Constitutional Amendment, 236; signs Morrill Tariff Act, 243; receives visit of ceremony from Lincoln, 317; accompanies Lincoln at inauguration, 325; takes leave of Lincoln at the White House, 344; dismisses Gen. Twiggs from army, IV, 191; foreign opinion of his non-coercion doctrine, 266, 267.

Buckingham, C. P., Brig. Gen. U. S. Vols.: delivers to McClellan the order for his removal, VI, 189; delivers to Burnside order to take command of Army of the Potomac, 196.

Buckley, Harrison, obtains peace warrant against Branson, I, 441.

Buckmaster, Nathaniel, Brigade Maj. Ill. Vols.: musters out volunteers for Black Hawk war, I, 96.

Buckner, Simon B., Conf. Lieut. Gen.: interviews with McClellan, IV, 202; organizes Kentucky State Guard, 230; conference with Davis, V, 43; made Conf. Brig. Gen., 43; occupies Bowling Green, 45; sent to reënforce Fort Donelson, 185; attacks McClernand's division, 196; repulsed by McClernand, 196; attends council of war in Donelson, 198; advises capitulation, 198; proposes armistice to Grant, 199; surrenders unconditionally, 199; plan to capture Louisville, VIII, 52, 53; retreat to Loudon, 72; called from the Hiawassee, 76; sent to execute orders issued to Hill, 78; in battle of Chickamauga, 84, 88; in battle of Chattanooga, 145; expects Burnside at Cumberland Gap, 162.

Buell, Don Carlos, Maj. Gen. U. S. Vols.: memorandum of instructions to Anderson, II, 387, 388; assigned to command in Kentucky, V, 65; answer to Johnson and Maynard, 68; reply to McClellan, 68; suggests plan, 69; asks for more troops for Kentucky, 70; reply to Lincoln's inquiry, 70; promises to obey instructions, 73; abandons East Tennessee movement, 73; reply to Lincoln about coöperation, 100; answer to Lincoln about Bowling Green, 101; advises Tennessee and Cumberland expedition, 101, 102; orders Thomas to dislodge Zollicoffer, 116; reply to McClellan about Tennessee movement, 188; re-

calls Nelson's division, 304; informs Halleck of his intended advance on Nashville, 304; advances opposite Nashville, 311; offers Halleck aid against Columbus, 313; ordered to march to the Tennessee, 317; delay at Duck River, 318; arrival with his army on battlefield of Pittsburg Landing, 333; directs placing of his army, 333; interview with Grant, 334; attacks the enemy, April 7, 1862, 334; defeat and retreat of Confederates, 335; ordered to advance toward Chattanooga, 351; assigned to command center of Halleck's army, 337; concentrates forces at Murfreesboro, VI, 276; march to Louisville, 276; relieved from command, 276; order relieving him withdrawn, 277; appoints Thomas second in command, 277; prepares to attack Bragg, 277; battle of Perryville, Oct. 8, 1862, 278; pursuit of Bragg, 279; moves toward western Tennessee, 279; ordered to East Tennessee, 280; reply to Halleck's order, 280; superseded by Rosecrans, 281.

Buell, George P., Bvt. Brig. Gen. U. S. A.: in battle of Chickamauga, VIII, 98.

Buford, A., Conf. Brig. Gen.: threat at Columbus, Ky, VI, 480.

Buford, Jefferson, arrives in Kansas, I, 448; denounces sack of Lawrence, 456.

Buford, John, Maj. Gen. U. S. Vols.: cavalry successes under, VII, 215; occupies Gettysburg, 239.

Bullen, J. D., Col. U. S. Vols.: repulses rebel attack on Donaldsonville, VII, 321.

Bullitt, Capt., survey of lands at the falls of Ohio, I, 15.

Bullock, James D., Commander Confederate navy: makes provisional contracts for building Confederate ships in France, VIII, 272; letter to Mallory, 277, 278; agreement with Arman about Confederate ships, 279; reports action of French Minister of Marine, 279; fits out Confederate ram *Stonewall*, IX, 136; fits out Confederate cruiser *Shenandoah*, 155.

Bull Run, Va.: battle of, July 21, 1861, IV, 348–351; summary of forces engaged, 351; losses in, 357; second battle of, Aug. 30, 1862, VI, 10.

Bunch, Robert, Brit. consul at Charleston: dispatch to Lord Lyons, IV, 279; exequatur revoked, 280; carried home, 280.

Burbridge, S. G., Brig. Gen. U. S. Vols.: defeats Morgan, VIII, 58.

Burch, John C., M. C.: member of House
Committee of Thirty-three, II, 417.

Burgess, J. M., member of Lincoln's suite,
III, 290.

Burlingame, Anson, M. C., Min. to China:
denounces Brooks's assault, II, 54; challenged by Brooks, 55; accepts the challenge, 55; favors reëlection of Douglas,
139.

Burnett, Henry C., M. C : resolution of inquiry, III, 147.

Burnett, H. L., Bvt. Brig. Gen. U. S. Vols. :
assistant judge advocate in trial of Lincoln's assassins, X, 312.

Burnham, Hiram, Brig. Gen. U. S. Vols. :
killed at Richmond, IX, 431.

Burnside, Ambrose E., Maj. Gen. U. S. Vols.:
commands provisional brigades at Wash-
ington, IV, 441; organizes coast division,
V, 241; commands expedition against
Roanoke Island, 242; instructions from
McClellan, 242; assigned to command
Department of North Carolina, 242; expedition sails, Jan. 11, 1862, 242; attacks
Roanoke Island, 244; captures Roanoke
Island, Feb. 8, 1862, 245; captures Elizabeth City, Feb. 10, 1862, 246; captures
New Berne, March 14, 1862, 246; captures
Fort Macon, April 26, 1862, 247; recalled
to the James River in Virginia, 248;
crosses Antietam Bridge, VI, 140; attacks
Lee's right wing, 140; recommends renewal of the fight, 144; assigned to command Army of Potomac, Nov. 5, 1862,
189; receives order to command Army
of Potomac, 196; his feeling at the promotion, 196, 197; proposes a new plan of
campaign, 198; refuses Sumner and
Hooker permission to cross the Rappahannock, 199; arrives at Fredericksburg,
199; interview with the President, Nov. 27,
1862, 200; crosses his army at Fredericksburg, 202; visit to his generals, 202; orders
sent to Franklin, 203; battle of Fredericksburg, Dec. 13, 1862, 203-208; controversy
with Franklin about his action, 204;
orders Sumner to assault Marye's Heights,
205; orders Hooker to assault Marye's
Heights, 206; assault on Marye's Heights
repulsed, 206-208; orders Ninth Corps to
assault Marye's Heights, Dec. 14, 1862, 208;
advised by Sumner against assaulting,
209; consults his officers, 209; withdraws
his army to Falmouth, Dec. 15, 1862, 209;
his report and magnanimity, 210, 211; the
army discouraged, 212; prepares for another movement, 213; restrained by dispatch from the President, 213; interview
with Lincoln, 214; alleged letter to Lincoln, Jan. 1, 1863, 216; asks permission to
advance, 217; the "Mud March" of Jan.
21, 1863, 217; prepares order dismissing
certain general officers, 219, 220; tenders
resignation to the President, 220; takes
command of Department of the Ohio,
VII, 328; issues Order No. Thirty-eight,
332; arrests and imprisons Vallandigham,
332; tries Vallandigham by military commission, 333, 334; approves finding and
sentence, 334, 335; written address against
habeas corpus for Vallandigham, 335, 336;
starts for East Tennessee, VIII, 162; occupies Knoxville, 163; tenders his resignation, 165; places his army on half
rations, 170; resigns a second time, 170; report from East Tennessee, 172; correspondence with Grant about Longstreet, 173;
withdraws to Knoxville, 174; forces of,
175; advises Sherman to return with part
of his force to Grant, 184; succeeded
in East Tennessee by Foster, 185; joins
Meade's army, 353; march to the Wilderness, 358; in battle of the Wilderness, 363,
364; in battle of Spotsylvania, 375, 377, 378,
381, 383; in battle of North Anna, 389; in
battle of Cold Harbor, 391, 404; in siege of
Petersburg, IX, 412, 420; explosion of
Petersburg mine, 421, 422; assault at Petersburg mine, 422-425; relieved from command, 425; censured for Petersburg mine
affair, 425; exonerated by Committee on
Conduct of the War, 426.

Bushnell, Orsamus, signs memorial about
Frémont and colored troops, VI, 456.

Butler, A. P., U. S. Sen. : Sumner's personal
criticism of, II, 48, 49; death of, 56.

Butler, Benjamin F., Maj. Gen. U. S. Vols.,
M. C.: report in Charleston Convention,
II, 235; appointed brigadier general of
Massachusetts militia, IV, 133; dispatch
from Philadelphia, 134; correspondence
with Gov. Hicks and mayor of Annapolis,
136; occupies railroad buildings at Annapolis, 154; signifies his willingness to arrest Maryland legislature, 166; assigned
to command Department of Annapolis,
169; occupies Relay House, 170; occupies
Baltimore, 173; seizes rebel arms, 173, 174;
appointed major general of U. S. volunteers, 308; assigned to command Fort
Monroe, 308; offers Gov. Hicks aid against
slave insurrection, 385; correspondence

with Gov. Andrew about slave insurrection, 385, 386; reply to Col. Mallory, 387; employs and feeds fugitive slaves, 389; asks instructions about fugitive slaves, 393; commands troops in Hatteras expedition, V, 12; reports victory at Hatteras, 13; commands troops sent to Ship Island, 253; commands land forces in Farragut's expedition against New Orleans, 271; effects a landing at quarantine, 272; occupies Forts Jackson and St. Philip, 275; occupies New Orleans, May 1, 1862, 275; supplies New Orleans with provisions, 276; proclaims martial law, 276; proclaimed an outlaw by Jefferson Davis, 277; orders arrest, trial, and execution of Mumford, 278; description of disloyalty in New Orleans, 281; publishes his "Woman Order," 281; letter to mayor about Order No. Twenty-eight, 281, 282; criticized by Lord Palmerston, 282; reply to Lord Palmerston in his farewell address, 282, 283; efficiency of military government, 284; assessments and charities, 284, 285; public health maintained, 285; quarantine and yellow fever, 285, 286; punishes rebel contumacy and intrigue, 286, 287; arrests a Norfolk clergyman, VI, 334; letter about recruits in New Orleans, 446, 447; refuses to sanction Phelps's organization of negro troops, 448, 449; his regiment of free negroes, 450, 451; organizes three additional regiments, 451, 452; placed in charge of exchange of prisoners at Fort Monroe, VII, 460; letter to Ould demanding withdrawal of Confederate menace to negro troops and their officers, 462; insists on his claim to command, VIII, 392; lands at Bermuda Hundred, 393; battle of Bermuda Hundred, May 16, 1864, 397, 399; receives votes for Vice-President at Baltimore Convention, IX, 72; sent to New York to preserve order at Presidential election, 373-375; attack on Petersburg, June 15-19, 1864, 407, 412; command at Bermuda Hundred, 412; in siege of Richmond, 433, 434; controversy with Peirpoint, 439-442; controversy with Edward Bates, 441, 442; plan of powder boat, X, 58, 59; accompanies Fort Fisher expedition, 59, 60; returns from Fort Fisher expedition, 63, 64; relieved by Grant, 64; justified by Committee on Conduct of the War, 64.

Butler, William, relates incident about Lincoln, I, 101, 102; friendship for Lincoln, 153; challenged by Shields, 209;

recommended by Lincoln for pension agent, 291.

Butterfield, Daniel, Bvt. Maj. Gen. U. S. A.: in battle of Fredericksburg, VI, 206; order to Sedgwick at Chancellorsville, VII, 105; controversy about Meade's intention at Gettysburg, 248.

Butterfield, Justin, appointed commissioner of the General Land Office, I, 293; his wit, 293, 294.

Butz, Caspar, attends Cleveland Convention, IX, 34.

Byrnes, Richard, Col. U. S. A.: killed at Cold Harbor, VIII, 404.

Cabell, W. L., Conf. Brig. Gen.: captured by Pleasonton, VIII, 479.

Cadwalader, George, Maj. Gen. U. S. Vols.: refuses obedience to habeas corpus, IV, 174, 175; refuses obedience to writ of attachment, 175.

Cadwalader, John, Judge U. S. Circ. Ct.: decides draft law is constitutional, VII, 13.

Calderon Collantes, Saturnino, Spanish statesman: reply to Great Britain about joint intervention in Mexico, VI, 37; comment on U. S. treaty with Great Britain to suppress African slave trade, 61.

Caldwell, C. H. B., Commodore U. S. N.: commands the *Itasca* in Farragut's fleet, V, 261.

Calhoun, John, appoints Lincoln deputy surveyor, I, 115; speech in canvass of 1836, 130; defeated for Congress, 223; appointed surveyor general of Kansas, 374; discussion at Illinois State fair, 375; speech at Leavenworth meeting, 440; arrested on account of "candlebox" election fraud, II, 106; presides over Lecompton Constitutional Convention, 107; signs Lecompton Constitution, 108; proposal to Gov. Walker, 109; proclaims votes cast for Lecompton Constitution, 114, 115; authority of, under Lecompton Constitution, 121; declares it adopted, 125; carries it to Washington, 125.

Calhoun, John C., Sec. of War under Monroe, Vice-Pres. with J. Q. Adams: diplomatic dispatch of, I, 227; attacks Pres. Polk's policy, 262.

California, State of, territory of, acquired, I, 325; forms Free State Constitution, 327; proposition to divide into two States, 327; admitted as a free State, 328; ratifies Thirteenth Amendment, X, 89.

Calvert, Charles B., M. C.: second interview with Lincoln about compensated emancipation, VI, 111.

Cameron, R. A., Bvt. Maj. Gen. U. S. Vols.: in battle of Sabine Cross Roads, VIII, 294; in battle of Pleasant Hill, 295.

Cameron, Simon, U. S. Sen., Sec. of War under Lincoln: candidate before Chicago Convention, 1860, II, 256, 263, 271; votes for: on first ballot, 273 — on second ballot, 274; letter to Lincoln, III, 250; invited by Lincoln to Springfield, 355; tendered Cabinet appointment, 355; tender recalled, 355; epistolary contest about, 360; appointed Secretary of War, 372; first opinion on Sumter, 387; signs instructions to Anderson drafted by Lincoln, IV, 28; statement about Lee, 98; warning to Gov. Hicks, 105; orders Annapolis route kept open, 170; telegram to Gov. Yates, 194; orders provisions stopped at Cairo, Ill., 200; letters to governors, 254, 255; reports Washington safe, 357; instructions to Butler about fugitive slaves, 389, 390; rules about fugitive slaves, 394; visit to Frémont, 429; reports Frémont's situation, 430; military consultation with Sherman, V, 53, 54; views on arming slaves, 125, 126; appointed Minister to Russia, 128; censured by the House of Representatives, 129, 130; defended by Lincoln in a special message, 130; note to Lincoln about renomination, IX, 53; in Baltimore Convention, 71; advises against the draft, 364.

Campbell, James H., M. C., Min. to Sweden: member of House Committee of Thirty-three, II, 417.

Campbell, John A., Assoc. Justice U. S. Sup. Ct., Conf. Comr.: statement regarding Dred Scott case, II, 67, 68, 71; opinion in Dred Scott case, 72; letter against disunion, III, 186; becomes Confederate commissioners' intermediary, 404, 405; first visit to Seward, 406, 407; interviews with Seward, 409, 410; report to Jefferson Davis, 411, 412; note to Seward, IV, 36; letter to the commissioners, 37; letter to Jefferson Davis, 148, 149; resignation of, 261; warning to Jefferson Davis, 261, 262; appointed Peace Commissioner, X, 110; asks permission to go to Washington, 113; interview with Grant, 114–116; interview with Lincoln, 118–129; report to Davis, 129; interviews with Lincoln, 220–222; interview with Weitzel, 224–226;

letter about interview with Lincoln, 224, 225; indorsement on Alston's proposition, 287.

Camp Jackson, formed at St. Louis, IV, 209; captured by Lyon, 213, 214.

Canada, Parliament suspends Judge Coursol from office, VIII, 26; authorities rearrest St. Albans raiders, 26; refunds money stolen by raiders, 26.

Canby, E. R. S., Bvt. Maj. Gen. U. S. A.: report on exchange of prisoners, VII, 445; assigned to command Military Division of the West Mississippi, VIII, 301; siege of Mobile, IX, 239–242; receives Taylor's surrender, X, 327, 328; receives E. Kirby Smith's surrender, 328, 329; made Department Commander, 338.

Cantey, James, Conf. Brig. Gen.: arrives at Resaca, IX, 12; in battles of Resaca, 13.

Carey, ——, receives votes for Vice-President in the Philadelphia Convention, II, 35.

Carlile, John S., M. C., U. S. Sen.: second interview with Lincoln about compensated emancipation, VI, 111.

Carlin, Thomas, Gov. of Ill.: action on internal improvement system, I, 160.

Carlin, Wm. P., Bvt. Maj. Gen. U. S. A.: reënforces Sheridan at Perryville, VI, 278; in battle of Murfreesboro, 286; in battle of Chattanooga, VIII, 143, 148; in March to the Sea, IX, 481.

Carpenter, ——, elected to Illinois legislature in 1834, I, 122.

Carr, ——, remarks in Cleveland Convention, IX, 36.

Carr, E. A., Bvt. Maj. Gen. U. S. A.: in battle of Port Gibson, VII, 171; march to Edwards's Station, 187; in battle of Champion's Hill, 191; in battle of the Big Black, 192.

Carrick's Ford, Va., battle of, July 13, 1861, IV, 337.

Carrington, H. B., Bvt. Brig. Gen. U. S. A.: estimate of number of arms brought into Indiana by American Knights, VIII, 2.

Carroll, Samuel S., Bvt. Maj. Gen. U. S. A.: in battle of Fredericksburg, VI, 206; in battle of Gettysburg, VII, 258; wounded in battle of the Wilderness, VIII, 363; in battle of Spotsylvania, 377; wounded at Spotsylvania, 382.

Carroll, W. H., Conf. Brig. Gen.: moves his command to East Tennessee, V, 77.

Carter, Samuel P., Lieut. U. S. N., Bvt. Maj. Gen. U. S. Vols.: organizes Union regiments of Tennesseeans, V, 59; in march to East Tennessee, 162; welcomed to Knoxville, 163.

Cartter, David K., Chief Justice Sup. Ct. D. C.: delegate to Chicago Convention, 1860, II, 275; announces change of vote to Lincoln, 275.

Cartwright, Mrs., death of, I, 248.

Cartwright, Peter, elected to Illinois legislature, I, 109; Democratic candidate against Lincoln for Congress, 245; career as a Methodist preacher, 246–248.

Casey, Samuel L., M. C.: second interview with Lincoln about compensated emancipation, VI, 112; member of Select Committee on Emancipation, 395.

Casey, Silas, Bvt. Maj. Gen. U. S. A.: commands provisional brigades at Washington, IV, 441: division attacked by D. H. Hill, V, 388.

Cass, Lewis, U. S. Sen., Min. to France, Sec. of State under Buchanan: nominated for President, I, 277; popular and electoral votes for, 282; votes for, in Baltimore Convention, 1852, 332; presents Topeka Constitution to the Senate, 430; instructions to Gov. Walker, II, 95; admonishes Acting Gov. Stanton to conform to the views of the President, 116; opinion on disunion, 361, 362; resignation of, 392; letter to Buchanan, 397; explanations to Holt, 398, 399.

Castelar, Emilio, President of the Spanish Republic: eulogy of Lincoln, X, 349.

Castle Pinckney, S. C., condition of, II, 343; inspected by Maj. Porter, 345; Anderson sent to command, 346; thirty workmen sent to, 442; occupied by the rebels, III, 60, 61.

Catholic Church, supports the government and the war, VI, 325.

Cato, Sterling G., Assoc. Justice Kas. Ter.: found in the Missouri camp, II, 19; issues writ of mandamus, 105; issues writ of habeas corpus in behalf of John Calhoun, 106.

Catron, John, Assoc. Justice U. S. Sup. Ct.: opinion in Dred Scott case, II, 72.

Cedar Creek, Va., battle of, Oct. 19, 1864, IX, 316–326.

Cedar Mountain, Va., engagement at, Aug. 9, 1862, VI, 6.

Chaffee, C. C., M. C.: inherits ownership of Dred Scott, II, 81; emancipates Dred Scott and his family, 81.

Chalmers, J. R., Conf. Brig. Gen., M. C.: assists in capture of Fort Pillow, VI, 479.

Chamberlain, Joshua L., Bvt. Maj. Gen. U. S. Vols.: in attack on Petersburg, IX, 411.

Chambersburg, Pa., burned by McCausland, July 30, 1864, IX, 176, 177.

Champion's Hill, Miss., battle of, May 16, 1863, VII, 189–192; losses at, 192.

Chancellorsville, Va., battle of, May 1–3, 1863, VII, 96–107; losses at, 111.

Chandler, D. T., Conf. Lieut. Col.: report on Andersonville prison, VII, 465–468.

Chandler, Zachariah, U. S. Sen., Sec. of Int. under Grant: interview with Lincoln, IV, 467; interview with McClellan, 467; offers resolution to investigate battle of Ball's Bluff, V, 150; member of Committee on Conduct of the War, 150; urges active army operations, 151; votes for National Bank Act, VI, 244; criticism on Weed and Morgan, VII, 388, 389; approves Lincoln's message, IX, 109; interview with Lincoln about Reconstruction Act, 120, 121; opposes recognition of Louisiana, 455.

Chantilly, Va., engagement at, Sept. 1, 1862, VI, 11.

Chapman, G. H., Bvt. Maj. Gen. U. S. Vols.: wounded at Winchester, IX, 304.

Charleston Convention, 1860, Democratic National: meets April 23, 1860, II, 227; sentiments of delegates, 228–231; Caleb Cushing made chairman, 232; Committee on Platform, 232; majority report by Avery, 233, 234; minority report by Payne, 234, 235; Butler's report, 235; speech of Yancey, 237; speech of Pugh, 238; speech of Bigler, 239; second majority and minority reports, 239, 240; minority report adopted, 240; Cotton State delegates secede, 240–242; balloting for candidates, 243, 244; adjourned to meet in Baltimore, 244; Seceders' Convention in Charleston, 244, 245; adjourns to meet in Richmond, 245; address of Southern Senators, 245, 246; reassembles at Baltimore, 250; second disruption 251; original Convention nominates Douglas, 251; seceders' Convention nominates Breckinridge, 251.

Charleston, S. C., public buildings seized by Gov. Pickens, III, 59; attack on defenses of, April 7, 1863, VII, 65–71; bombardment of, Aug. 23, 1863, 439–441; capture of, Feb. 18, 1865, X, 231; flag-raising over Fort Sumter, 277–280.

Chase, Salmon P., U. S. Sen., Sec. of Treas. under Lincoln, Chief Justice U. S. Sup. Ct.: leaves the Democratic party, I, 277; address against Nebraska bill, 360;

speeches in Illinois, 369; candidate before Chicago Convention, 1860, II, 255, 263, 271; votes for: on first ballot, 273 — on second ballot, 274 — on third ballot, 275; member of Peace Convention, III, 230; letter to Lincoln, 245; invited by Lincoln to Springfield, 359; visits Springfield, 359; conference with Lincoln, 359; appointed Secretary of Treasury, 372; first opinion on Sumter, 385; second opinion on Sumter, 430; letter to Lincoln about loan, IV, 78; complaining note to Lincoln, 166, 167; loans negotiated by, 377; diary of, on *Trent* affair, V, 36, 37; memorandum of McClellan's intention to attack, 164; visits Fort Monroe, 234; reconnoiters landings opposite Fort Monroe, 235, 236; accompanies advance on Norfolk, 236, 237; favors removal of McClellan from command of Army of Potomac, VI, 3; signs remonstrance against McClellan's continuance in command, 21; supervises freedmen in the Department of the South, 93; favors employment of negro soldiers, 124; prefers emancipation through local military commanders, 129; describes Lincoln's reading of preliminary emancipation proclamation, 158-160; comment on emancipation proclamation, 163; early loans negotiated by, 226; estimates for fiscal year ending June 30, 1862, 227; conference with New York bankers, 228, 229; report of December, 1861, 229; asks increased appropriations, 229; suspends specie payments, 230; recommends making paper money legal tender, 231-233; legal-tender decision of, as Chief Justice, 235, 236; sales of cash gold by, 239; system of temporary loans, 240; issues Five-twenty bonds, 240, 241; urges system of national banks, 242; report of December, 1862, 242, 243; comment on national-bank system, 245, 246; personal attitude towards the President and Cabinet, 254; letters and diary criticizing the Administration, 255-257; attitude towards McClellan, 257, 258; attitude towards Shields, 259; remarks to Hooker, 259; advice to Gen. Butler, 259, 260; conversation with Thurlow Weed, 262; present at interview between Lincoln, Cabinet, and Republican Senators, 266; tenders his resignation, 267; Lincoln declines to accept his resignation, 268; letter to Seward about Cabinet crisis, 268; letter to Lincoln about Cabinet crisis, 269; resumes

duty as Secretary of Treasury, 270; opinion on admission of West Virginia, 301-303; suggestions for final emancipation proclamation, 416-418; opinion on the Fort Pillow massacre, 481; announces fear of financial embarrassment, VIII, 111; at council of war, 112; at military conference, 236; letters: to Sprague, 311 — to Spencer, 311 — to Leavitt, 312 — to Dixon, 312, 313 — to Gilbert, 313 — to Ball, 313 — to Hall, 314 — to Lincoln about Pomeroy's circular, 321 — to Hall about Lincoln's nomination, 324, 325 — criticizing Lincoln, IX, 81-83; action of, on appointments, 83-85; defends Special Agent Bailey, 86, 87; asks renomination of Howard, 87; writes his resignation, 88; letter to Lincoln about Howard, Dixon, and Loomis, 88; tenders his resignation, 90; urges M. B. Field for Assistant Treasurer at New York, 92; resignation of, 94; comments on his official life, 101-103; comment on Lincoln's reconstruction veto, 123, 124; recommends suspension of draft, 364; opposed to Lincoln, 367; desire to become Chief Justice, 386, 387; relations to the President, 387-391; recommended and opposed for Chief Justiceship, 391-393; appointed Chief Justice, 394, 395; advice on reconstruction, 396-398; course of, on politics, 398-401; judicial action of, 401; certificate of division in the Jefferson Davis case, X, 275; administers oath to Andrew Johnson, 317.

Chase, W. H., Conf. Col.: threatens Fort Pickens, III, 164.

Chatfield, John L., Col. U. S. Vols.: killed in second assault on Fort Wagner, VII, 431.

Chattanooga, Tenn., occupied by Rosecrans, Sept. 9, 1863, VIII, 73; battle of, Nov. 23-25, 1863, 134-157.

Cheatham, B. F., Conf. Brig. Gen.: in battle of Murfreesboro, VI, 293; in battle of Chickamauga, VIII, 88, 91, 92, 101; in battle of Chattanooga, 145; in battle of Atlanta, IX, 273; in army of Hood, X, 7; in march to Franklin, 12, 18; in battle of Franklin, 18; in campaign against Nashville, 23; joins Johnston, 36.

Cheever, Rev. George B., signs calls for Cleveland Convention, IX, 31; fails to attend Convention, 34.

Chesapeake, The, U. S. merch. str.: captured by Confederate mutineers, VIII, 14-16.

Chetlain, Augustus L., Capt. U. S. Vols.: captain of Galena company, IV, 287.

Chew, R. S., sent as messenger to Charleston, IV, 35; report of, 35.

Chicago Convention, 1860, Republican National: meeting of, May 16, 1860, II, 255, 259, 265; leading candidates in, 255, 256, 263; the Wigwam, 265; organization of, 265, 266; platform reported, 266, 267; Giddings's amendment, 268; Curtis's speech, 269; platform adopted, 269; ballotings, 272-275; Lincoln nominated for President, 275-277; Hamlin nominated for Vice-President, 277.

Chicago Convention, 1864, Democratic National: convened, Aug. 29, 1864, IX, 252, 253; called to order by August Belmont, 254, 255; Horatio Seymour made chairman, 256; James Guthrie chairman of Platform Committee, 256, 257; adopts Vallandigham's resolution declaring the war a failure, 257; McClellan nominated for President, 258; G. H. Pendleton nominated for Vice-President, 258, 259; adjourns subject to call of Executive National Committee, 259.

Chickamauga, Tenn., battle of, Sept. 18-20, 1863, VIII, 84-107.

Chickasaw, The, Union monitor: in battle of Mobile Bay, IX, 236-238.

Chickasaw Bluffs, Miss., assault on, Dec. 28, 29, 1862, VII, 133, 134.

Chicora, The, Conf. ram: attempts to break blockade at Charleston, VII, 59-61.

Chipman, Norton P., Bvt. Brig. Gen. U. S. Vols.: carries Grant's dispatch to Sheridan, IX, 293.

Chiriqui, District of, project for colonization in, VI, 357, 358; Prof. Henry's report on coal of, 358, 359.

Choctaw, The, Union gunboat, assists defense of Milliken's Bend, VII, 293.

Christian Commission, work of, VI, 329.

Churchill, T. J., Conf. Brig. Gen.: surrenders Fort Hindman, VII, 140; in battle of Pleasant Hill, VIII, 295.

Cincinnati, The, Union gunboat: sunk at Vicksburg, VII, 293.

Cisco, John J., Asst. Treas. in New York: suggests system of temporary loans, VI, 240; resigns, IX, 91; withdraws his resignation, 94.

Clanton, James H., Conf. Brig. Gen.: defeated by Steele, IX, 240.

Clark, Daniel, U. S. Sen.: substitute for Crittenden compromise plan, III, 226; his substitute adopted by the Senate, 227; letter to Lincoln, VII, 375.

Clark, Edward, Gov. of Texas: succeeds Houston as governor of Texas, IV, 187.

Clark, George Rogers, capture of Kaskaskia and Vincennes, I, 15.

Clay, Cassius M., Maj. Gen. U. S. Vols., Min. to Russia: captured in Mexico, I, 260; letter advocating fusion, 368; speeches in Illinois, 369; receives votes for Vice-President in Philadelphia Convention, II, 35; lecture in New York, 217; votes for, in Chicago Convention, 1860: on second ballot, 274 — on third ballot, 275; escorted by first Wide-Awakes, 285; organizes Clay Battalion, IV, 106.

Clay, Clement C., Jr., U. S. Sen., Conf. agent in Canada: supports demand for Congressional Slave Code, II, 175; interview with Buchanan, III, 159; signs the Senatorial Secession Caucus resolutions, 181; offered safe-conduct to Washington, IX, 190; replies he is not accredited from Richmond, 191.

Clay, Henry, Speaker H. R., Sec. of State under J. Q. Adams, U. S. Sen.: Whig nominee for President in 1844, I, 223-235; political and official career, 223, 224; devotion of his followers, 224; views on Texas annexation, 228-230; defeated for President, 231, 235; leader of compromise of 1850, 328; comment on provision of fugitive slave law, III, 25; dispatch about Monroe doctrine, VII, 406.

Clayton, William, testimony about American Knights, VIII, 6, 7.

Cleburne, Patrick R., Conf. Maj. Gen.: in battle of Chickamauga, VIII, 92, 101; in battle of Chattanooga, 145, 154; in march to Franklin, X, 10, 12, 18; killed at Franklin, 20.

Clemens, Jere, U. S. Sen.: letter of, III, 188.

Clemens, Sherrard, M. C.: remarks on value of slaves, I, 321.

Clemens, W. W., Bvt. Maj. U. S. A.: in Lincoln's visit to Richmond, X, 218.

Clements, Andrew J., M. C.: elected to Congress, V, 57; second interview with Lincoln about compensated emancipation, VI, 112; member Select Committee on Emancipation, 395.

Clendenin, D. R., Bvt. Brig. Gen. U. S. Vols.: member of military commission for trial of Lincoln's assassins, X, 312.

Cleveland Convention, 1864, of "Radical Democracy": called to meet, May 31, 1864, IX, 29; meets in Chapin's Hall, 33; presided over by John Cochrane, 34, 35;

platform of, 37; nominates Frémont for President, 39; nominates John Cochrane for Vice-President, 39; criticism of Arguelles case, 47.

Clingman, Thomas L., M. C., U. S. Sen.: interviews with Thompson, II, 325, 326; Senate discussion, 400, 410; attacks Lincoln's inaugural as an announcement of war, III, 399.

Clopton, David, M. C.: House discussion, II, 416; signs secession address, 436.

Cobb, Howell, Sec. of Treas. under Buchanan, Conf. Maj. Gen.: instructions to Martin, II, 109; prevents publication of certain letters, 111; interviews with Floyd, 317; opinion on disunion, 361-363; resignation of, 391; letter to Buchanan, 391-392; secession address, 392; elected chairman of Provisional Congress of seceding States, III, 197; services to the rebellion, 204; financial management of, 238; reports on public debt, 239; negotiates $10,000,000, 239; buys up six per cents of 1868 at sixteen per cent. premium, 241; says there will be no war, IV, 261; financial acts recapitulated, VI, 224, 225; meeting with Wool to arrange exchange of prisoners, VII, 449, 450; letter to Seddon suggesting that Union prisoners opposed to Lincoln be paroled, 462.

Cobb, Thomas R. R., insidious suggestion of, III, 190.

Cobb, W. R. W., M. C.: House discussion, II, 421.

Coburn, John, Bvt. Brig. Gen. U. S. Vols.: defeated by Van Dorn and Wheeler, VIII, 50.

Cochrane, John, M. C., Brig. Gen. U. S. Vols.: plan of compromise, II, 422; interview with Lincoln, VI, 213; presides over Cleveland Convention, IX, 34, 35; nominated for Vice-President by Cleveland Convention, 39; accepts nomination, 42, 43; withdraws from Presidential campaign, 44.

Cocke, P. St. George, Conf. Brig. Gen.: number of his command, IV, 162; suggestions to Lee, 322.

Codding, Ichabod, member of Bloomington Convention, II, 28.

Coffee, A. M., Maj. Gen. Kas. militia: driven out of Kansas, II, 2.

Coffroth, Alexander H., M. C.: vote for Thirteenth Amendment, X, 83.

Cogswell, Milton, Col. U. S. Vols.: in battle of Ball's Bluff, IV, 456, 457.

Cold Harbor, Va., battle of, June 1-12, 1864, VIII, 391, 400-405; losses at, 404.

Cole, Charles H., plot to capture the Michigan, VIII, 18, 19; capture of, 19.

Coles, Edward, Gov. of Ill.: elected through division of proslavery party, I, 143; indicted and fined, 145.

Colfax, Mrs., valuable manuscripts from, II, 180.

Colfax, Schuyler, M. C., Vice-Pres. with Grant: interviews with Douglas, II, 139; correspondence with Lincoln, 178-180; recommended for Postmaster-General, III, 353; candidate for Speaker of House of Representatives, VII, 391; elected Speaker of the Thirty-eighth Congress, 394; denies being in the Chase movement, VIII, 315; interview with Lincoln, X, 285.

Collamer, Jacob, M. C., P. M. Gen. under Taylor, U. S. Sen.: receives votes for Vice-President in Philadelphia Convention, II, 35; member of committee to investigate the John Brown raid, 210; votes before Chicago Convention, 1860, 271; votes for, on first ballot, 273; Senate discussion, 406; member of Senate Committee of Thirteen, 414; remarks on legal tender, VI, 234, 235; votes against National Bank Act, 244; votes for re-passage of the Act, 244; present at interview between Lincoln, Cabinet, and Republican Senators, 266; defends bill for draft, VII, 4; discourages opposition to Lincoln, IX, 367.

Collier, Robert, Lord Monkswell: legal opinion on the building of the Alabama, VI, 54.

Collins, Napoleon, Rear Adm. U. S. N.: commands U. S. steamer Wachusett, IX, 129; challenges the Florida, 130; captures the Florida at Bahia, 131-133; ordered before a court martial, 133.

Colonization, appropriation for, V, 216; discussed in Cabinet, VI, 124; Lincoln's belief in, 354; his views as expressed in the Lincoln-Douglas debates, 355; recommendations concerning, in Lincoln's first annual message, 355; Congressional appropriations for, 356, 357; Seward's circular respecting, 357; offers from foreign governments, 357; the district of Chiriqui, 357, 358; Prof. Henry's report on Chiriqui coal, 358, 359; contract for a colony on Ile A'Vache, Hayti, 360; Lincoln cancels his contract, 362; new contract signed, 362; emigrants sail for Ile A'Vache, 363;

Bernard Kock as governor of the colony, 363; Kock driven from the island, 364; arrival of Special Agent Donnohue at Ile A'Vache, 364; Donnohue's report, 365, 366; relief to the colonists, 365; colonists brought back to the United States, 366; recommended in Lincoln's annual message of Dec. 1, 1862, 400.

Colorado, Territory of, organized as a Territory, III, 237; instructs delegates in favor of Lincoln's renomination, IX, 56.

Colquitt, Alfred H., Conf. Brig. Gen., U. S. Sen.: in battle of Bermuda Hundred, VIII, 398.

Colston, R. E., Conf. Brig. Gen.: in battle of Chancellorsville, VII, 103.

Columbia, S. C., occupied by Sherman, Feb. 17, 1865, X, 232.

Colvin, Andrew J., reads letter from Robinson to Cleveland Convention, IX, 38.

Committee on the Conduct of the War, appointed, V, 150; report on Fort Pillow massacre, VI, 479; exonerates Burnside, IX, 426; justifies Butler's action at Fort Fisher, X, 64; calls on President Johnson, 316.

Comonfort, Ignacio, Mex. Gen.: defeated by Bazaine, VII, 397; captured and killed, 400.

Comstock, C. B., Bvt. Maj. Gen. U. S. Vols.: reconnoiters Fort Fisher, X, 62, 66.

Confederate Commissioners, arrive at Washington, III, 397, 398; theory of Seward's intentions, 398, 399; plan of action, 399, 400; ask an unofficial interview of Seward, 401; demand an official interview, 402; report to Toombs, March 12, 1861, 402, 403 — March 15, 1861, 408; ask further instructions, 413; telegrams about expeditions, IV, 2, 3; ask an official answer, 37; report failure of their mission, 37.

Confederate Congress, authorizes organization of provisional government, III, 212, 213; authorizes provisional army and navy, 212, 213; appoints commissioners to Washington, 213; Davis transmits correspondence with Campbell, 405; session of April 29 to May 21, 1861, IV, 263; Acts of, 263, 264; removes seat of Confederate government to Richmond, 264; law to punish Union officers of negro troops, VI, 472; law authorizing negro soldiers for rebel service, 487; peace resolutions in, VII, 364, 365; resolutions on Mexican affairs, 422, 423; suspends writ of habeas corpus, VIII, 42.

Confederate States of America, government formed by seceding States, III, 198; Provisional Constitution adopted Feb. 8, 1861, 198; name of, adopted by Provisional Congress, 198; permanent Constitution adopted March 11, 1861, 198; summary of laws by the Provisional Congress, 212; league with Virginia, IV, 159.

Confiscation Acts, amendment to, First Session Thirty-seventh Congress, freeing slaves, IV, 380–382; amendment to, Second Session Thirty-seventh Congress, VI, 98; new Act, Second Session Thirty-seventh Congress, 100–102; discussed at Hampton Roads Conference, X, 123.

Congregational Conference of Massachusetts, resolutions supporting the war, VI, 317, 318.

Congregational General Association of New York, New Jersey, and Pennsylvania, resolutions supporting the war and emancipation, VI, 318.

Congress, The, Union sailing frigate: at Newport News, V, 223; prepares for action, 223; shelled and burned by the *Merrimac*, 225; surrender of, 225.

Congress of the United States, authorizes 50,000 volunteers for Mexican war, I, 250; Robert C. Winthrop chosen Speaker, 259; slavery question in, 263–266; Wilmot Proviso, 279, 280; rejects Jefferson's draft of Ordinance of 1784, 316; adopts Ordinance of 1877, 316; Nebraska Bill passed by the House, 338; Nebraska Bill introduced in Senate, 339; Senate caucus agreement on slavery, 344; Dixon's amendment, 346; Douglas's amendments, 349, 350; Kansas-Nebraska Act passed, 351; party division in Thirty-fourth, 362, 364; Republicans support Topeka Constitution, 430; Douglas's report in Senate against Topeka Constitution, 431; sends investigating committee to Kansas, 431, 432, 451; attack on Sumner by Preston S. Brooks, II, 50, 51; Wilson's announcement, 52; Seward moves for a committee of investigation, 52; Mason proposes to elect the committee by ballot, 52; report of committee, 52; House committee report, 53; House censures Brooks, 53; rejects Lecompton Constitution, 130, 131; Crittenden-Montgomery substitute for Lecompton Constitution, 131; English bill passed, 133; Senate committee appointed to investigate John Brown raid, 209; Wm. Pennington elected Speaker,

Congress of the United States — *continued.*
215; Senate Committee of Thirteen appointed, 414; House Committee of Thirty-
three appointed, 417; propositions submitted to that committee, 422-426; passes
Fugitive Slave law of 1850, III, 26; Holt
confirmed as Secretary of War, 89; select
Committee of Five appointed by House of
Representatives, 141; reports of that committee, 143, 144; proceedings of Presidential count, 145; Branch's House resolution
about quartering troops at the Capital, 147;
Burnett's resolution of inquiry in House
of Representatives, 147; Sickles's House
resolution to celebrate Feb. 22, 148;
action of House Committee of Thirty-
three, 214-217; action of Senate Committee of Thirteen, 219-222; Senate action on
Crittenden Compromise, 225; Senate action on Clark substitute, 226, 227; Senate
action on resolutions of Peace Convention, 233; Constitutional Amendment
(Thirteenth) proposed by, 235; admits
Kansas as a State, 237; organizes Territories of Dakota, Colorado, and Nevada,
237; financial measures, 240, 242-244; convened in extra session, July 4, 1861, by
Lincoln's proclamation, IV, 77; convenes
July 4, 1861, under the President's proclamation, 370; Galusha A. Grow elected
Speaker, 370; Lincoln's message to, 371-
375; war measures of, 375, 378; financial
legislation, 377, 378; the Crittenden resolution, 379; first Confiscation Act, 380-382;
the President's acts legalized, 382-384; adjourned, Aug. 6, 1861, 384; House of Representatives censures Cameron, V, 129, 130;
Joint Committee on the Conduct of the
War appointed, 150; passes Lincoln's
joint resolution for compensated abolishment, 214; passes Act of immediate emancipation in District of Columbia, 216; appropriation for colonization, 216; Act of,
restoring and retiring Gen. Porter, VI, 13;
Senate ratifies and House approves treaty
with Great Britain to suppress African
slave trade, 61; resolutions declaring
foreign intervention useless, mischievous,
and unfriendly, 88, 89; antislavery enactments, 97; army forbidden to return fugitive slaves, 98; virtual amendment of
Fugitive Slave law, 98; Act for recognition
of Hayti and Liberia, 99; prohibition of
slavery in the Territories, 99; Act abolishing slavery in District of Columbia, 100;
provisions of Confiscation Act emanci

pating slaves, 100, 101; provisions for
emancipation through military service,
101, 102; Lincoln's draft of veto message
on the Confiscation Act, 102; 103; attitude
of Border State representatives, 105, 106;
Yeaman offers resolution censuring emancipation proclamation, 171; Fessenden
offers resolution indorsing emancipation
proclamation, 171; loan of $250,000,000,
227; direct tax of $20,000,000, 227; demand
notes authorized, 228; Act to make paper
money legal tender, 235, 236; demand
notes made legal tender, 236; Act to prevent speculations in gold, 239; repeal of
the Act, 239; system of temporary loans,
240; authorizes certificates of indebtedness, 240; authorizes Five-twenty bonds,
241; bill for National Bank Act introduced, 241; National Bank Act passed,
243, revised and re-passed, 244; application of West Virginia for admission to the
Union, 298, 299; report of Senate Committee on Territories thereon, 299; conditions
of bill to admit the new State, 299; Senate
bill passed, 299; passage of bill by the
House, 299; action touching reconstruction, 348; Flanders and Hahn admitted to
seats in, 353; appropriations for colonization, 356, 357; repeal of appropriations
for colonization, 367; White's select committee on emancipation, 395; committee
reports bill to aid emancipation in Delaware, Maryland, Virginia, Kentucky, Tennessee, and Missouri, 395; Henderson introduces bill in Senate to aid Missouri
emancipation, 396; Noell introduces bill
in House to aid Missouri emancipation,
396; House bill passed, Jan. 6, 1863, 396;
Senate amendment to House bill passed
Feb. 12, 1863, 396; failure of amended bill in
the House, 397; laws authorizing colored
soldiers, 441, 442; Hunter's answer to the
Wickliffe resolution, 443; Act including
colored men in enrollment for draft, 467;
bill introduced for enrolling and calling
out national forces, VII, 4; Senate bill for
draft introduced in House, 4; Colfax
elected Speaker, 394; G. C. Smith's resolutions in House of Representatives supporting the war, 395; Henry Winter
Davis's resolution on Mexico passed by
the House, 408; Senate action on Trumbull's resolution about political prisoners,
VIII, 31; Act to indemnify the President
for suspending writ of habeas corpus,
33-36; passes Act authorizing the Presi-

dent to suspend writ of habeas corpus, 33-36; Powell's Senate resolution about political prisoners, 39, 40; passes bill to revive grade of lieutenant general, 334, 335; refuses to admit Senators and Representatives from Arkansas, 418; Senate resolution demanding information concerning Arguelles case, IX, 46; passes Reconstruction Act, 120; admits Joseph Segar to seat in House of Representatives, 437; House of Representatives defeats Ashley's reconstruction bills, 449-453; resolution of thanks to Sherman, 494; Trumbull reports Thirteenth Amendment, X, 75; Senate adopts Thirteenth Amendment, 77; House rejects Thirteenth Amendment, 77, 78; House reconsideration of Thirteenth Amendment, 81; House adopts Thirteenth Amendment, 85, 86; joint resolution about electoral votes, 139, 140; Presidential count, Feb. 8, 1865, 141, 142.

Conkling, James C., invites Lincoln to Republican mass meeting at Springfield, VII, 379.

Conkling, Roscoe, M. C., U. S. Sen.: offers resolution to investigate battle of Ball's Bluff, V, 150; introduces Lincoln's joint resolution recommending compensated abolishment, 214; deprecates making paper money legal tender, VI, 235; declines to join opposition to Lincoln, IX, 367.

Connecticut, State of, instructs delegates in favor of Lincoln's renomination, IX, 55; ratifies Thirteenth Amendment, X, 89.

Conrad, C. M., U. S. Sen., Sec. of War under Fillmore, Conf. Brig. Gen.: appointed Confederate commissioner to negotiate exchange of prisoners, VII, 449.

Conrad, Joseph, Bvt. Brig. Gen. U. S. Vols.: in march to Franklin, X, 12.

Constitution of the United States, origin of compromises of, I, 318; allowed each State two Senators, 318; relative representation of North and South in Congress when Constitution was formed, 318; provisions concerning slave trade, 318; alleged violation by Fugitive Slave law of 1850, III, 28.

Constitutional Amendments offered in House of Representatives by Mr. Corwin, III, 235; adopted by House of Representatives, Feb. 28, 1861, 235; adopted in Senate, March 2, 1861, 235; approved by Buchanan, 236; commended in Lincoln's inaugural, 236; not acted on by the States, 236;

Thirteenth Amendment adopted, X, 75, 77, 78, 80, 81, 85-89, 125, 126.

Constitutional Union Party, National convention of, meets at Baltimore, May 9, 1860, II, 252, 253; nominates John Bell for President and Edward Everett for Vice-President, 253, 254; candidates and platform, 280; electors chosen by, 294.

Contrabands, origin of the term, IV, 388, 389; Lincoln modifies War Department instruction about employing, V, 124.

Cook, B. C., M. C.: speech in Illinois legislature against Nebraska bill, I, 366, 367; nominates Lincoln in Baltimore Convention, IX, 71, 72.

Cook, Daniel Pope, M. C.: defeated for Congress, I, 64; relates frontier incident, 145.

Cooke, J. W., Commander Conf. navy: commands the Albemarle, X, 39.

Cooke, P. St. George, Bvt. Maj. Gen. U. S. A.: military measures of, II, 7; "cannon" argument to the Border Ruffians, 17.

Cooper, Peter, signs memorial about Frémont and colored troops, VI, 456.

Cooper, Samuel, Conf. Adj. Gen.: issues general order that Generals Hunter and Phelps be treated as outlaws, VI, 471.

Corbett, Sergt. Boston, shoots Booth, X, 312.

Corinth, Miss., captured by Halleck, May 30, 1862, V, 340, 341; battle of, Oct. 3, 4, 1862, VII, 116-118.

Corse, J. M., Bvt. Maj. Gen. U. S. Vols.: in battle of Chattanooga, VIII, 146; sent to Rome, Ga., IX, 281; wounded at Allatoona, 474; in March to the Sea, 481.

Corwin, Thomas, M. C., U. S. Sen., Sec. of Treas. under Fillmore, Min. to Mexico: chairman of House Committee of Thirty-three, II, 417; character of, III, 215; submits report from House Committee of Thirty-three, 216; letters to Lincoln, 218, 255; offers Constitutional amendment in House of Representatives, 235; heads protest against insult to French legation, VI, 32; proposes guarantee by the United States of interest on the Mexican debt, 38.

Cosby, George B., Conf. Brig. Gen.: sent to reënforce Early, IX, 327; sent to Breckinridge, 328.

Cotton, cultivation in Southern States, I, 319; increased production of, 321; embarrassments to international relations from want of, VI, 62; Lincoln's letter about, IX, 447, 448.

Couch, Darius N., Maj. Gen. U. S. Vols.: repulses Huger's brigade at Malvern Hill, V, 438; in battle of Chancellorsville, VII, 104; second in command during Hooker's accident, 104; present at council of war, 109; militia force under, in Pennsylvania, 221; in battle of Nashville, X, 30; in advance on Wilmington, 68, 69; in advance on Goldsboro', 70.

Course, M. D., Conf. Brig. Gen.: captured in retreat to Appomattox, X, 187.

Coursol, Michel J. C., Canadian judge: discharges St. Albans raiders from custody, VIII, 24; suspended from office by Canadian Parliament, 26.

Covode, John, M. C.: member of Committee on Conduct of the War, V, 150.

Cowan, Edgar, U. S. Sen.: votes against National Bank Act, VI, 244.

Cowley, Earl, Brit. Ambass. in Paris: communicates reports concerning intentions of France and Spain in Mexico, VI, 42.

Cox, J. D., Maj. Gen. U. S. Vols.: commands under Burnside at Antietam, VI, 140; advance north of Dalton, IX, 11; in battle of Kenesaw Mountain, 25; in march to Franklin, X, 10, 11, 13, 16; in battle of Franklin, 19; in battle of Nashville, 30, 33; in advance on Wilmington, 68, 69; in advance on Goldsboro', 70.

Cox, Samuel, assists Booth and Herold, X, 308.

Cox, Samuel S., M. C., Min. to Turkey: plan of compromise, II, 422; opposes bill for draft, VII, 5; candidate for Speaker of House of Representatives, 391; seconds motion to nominate McClellan for President, IX, 258.

Craige, Burton, M. C.: signs secession address, II, 436.

Crane, Charles, Brig. Gen. U. S. A.: present at Lincoln's deathbed, X, 300.

Craven, Tunis A. M., Commander U. S. N.: death of, in Mobile Bay, IX, 232.

Craven, T. T., Rear Adm. U. S. N.: ordered to collect boats on the Potomac, IV, 451; requests sea-service, 452; commands the Brooklyn in Farragut's fleet, V, 261; report of, 264.

Crawford, A. M. L., Bvt. Maj. U. S. Vols.: directs Lincoln's removal from Ford's Theater, X, 296.

Crawford, Andrew, teacher of Pres. Lincoln, I, 34.

Crawford, Martin J., M. C., Conf. Comr.: signs secession address, II, 436; arrives in Washington, III, 397; interview with Campbell, 405, 406; dispatch to Beauregard, IV, 26-29.

Crawford, Samuel W., Bvt. Maj. Gen. U. S. A.: remains with rearguard in Moultrie, III, 50, 51; in battle of Gettysburg, VII, 255, 268; captures prisoners from Hood, 269; in Army of Potomac, VIII, 353; in battle of the Wilderness, 361; in battle of Five Forks, X, 172, 173.

Crisfield, John W., M. C.: report of Lincoln's interview with Border Slave State Representatives, V, 212-214; second interview with Lincoln about compensated emancipation, VI, 111; remarks on Maryland emancipation, VIII, 452, 457.

Crittenden, Geo. B., Conf. Maj. Gen.: commands under Zollicoffer, V, 116.

Crittenden, John J., Atty. Gen. under W. H. Harrison and Fillmore, U. S. Sen., M. C.: originates Crittenden-Montgomery substitute, II, 131; correspondence with Lincoln, 142; calls Baltimore Convention to order, 253; loyalty of, 254; Senate discussion, 404; member of Senate Committee of Thirteen, 414; propositions in House Committee of Thirty-three, III, 221; services of, 223, 224; renews propositions of compromise in Senate, 224; plan voted on by Senate, 225; telegram of, 227; moves to substitute resolutions of Peace Convention for his own, 233; position on secession, IV, 228; letter to Gen. Scott, 233; his conspicuous example of loyalty, 371; offers the Crittenden resolution, 379; speech on Confiscation Act, 381; position as leader of Border State Representatives, VI, 106; second interview with Lincoln about compensated emancipation, 111.

Crittenden, Thomas L., Maj. Gen. U. S. Vols.: commands division of Buell's army in battle of Pittsburg Landing, V, 333; appointed by Rosecrans to command left wing of Army of the Cumberland, VI, 281; in battle of Murfreesboro, 292; march on Chattanooga, VIII, 71; in battle of Chickamauga, 84, 85, 96, 103; in battle of Chattanooga, 135.

Crocker, M. M., Brig. Gen. U. S. Vols.: division of, added to McPherson's corps, VII, 172; in engagement at Raymond, 178; in battle of Champion's Hill, 189-192.

Crockett, David, M. C.: defense of the Alamo, I, 233.

Crook, George, Bvt. Maj. Gen. U. S. A.: command of, in Army of Kentucky, VIII, 44; defeated by Early, IX, 175; in Sheridan's army, 182; in Shenandoah campaign, 295, 297; in battle of Winchester, 301; in battle of Fisher's Hill, 307, 309; in battle of Cedar Creek, 316, 317, 320, 324; sent to Grant, 329; in march to Appomattox, X, 187, 188; at grand review in Washington, 332.

Crosby, Pierce, Commodore U. S. N.: commands the *Pinola* in Farragut's fleet, V, 261; in siege of Mobile, IX, 242.

Cross, Edward E., Col. U. S. Vols.: killed at Gettysburg, VII, 255.

Croxton, J. T., Bvt. Maj. Gen. U. S. Vols.: in battle of Chickamauga, VIII, 88.

Cruft, Charles, Bvt. Maj. Gen. U. S. Vols.: in battle of Chattanooga, VIII, 140, 141, 152.

Crume, Ralph, marries aunt of the President, I, 23.

Cullom, Shelby M., Gov. of Ill., U. S. Sen.: prominent lawyer of Illinois, I, 214.

Cumberland, The, Union razeed frigate: at Newport News, V, 223; prepares for action, 223; rammed and sunk by the *Merrimac*, 223, 224; heroism of officers and crew, 224.

Curry, J. L. M., M. C.: signs secession address, II, 436.

Curtin, A. G., Gov. of Penn., Min. to Russia, M. C.: appoints Patterson major general of Pennsylvania militia, IV, 315; conference with Seward about recruiting, VI, 117; originates Altoona meeting of governors, 165; reports organization in Pennsylvania for resisting the draft, VII, 3; reëlected governor of Pennsylvania, 13, 375, 376; information to Lincoln about Hooker, 200; care of Gettysburg dead and wounded, VIII, 189.

Curtis, Benjamin R., Assoc. Justice U. S. Sup. Ct.: dissenting opinion in Dred Scott case, II, 77-79; pamphlet against Lincoln's administration, VII, 370.

Curtis, George Ticknor, argument in Dred Scott case, II, 64.

Curtis, George William, speech in Chicago Convention, 1860, II, 269; letter to Lincoln announcing his renomination, IX, 77.

Curtis, N. M., Bvt. Maj. Gen. U. S. Vols.: action at Fort Fisher, X, 63; in second Fort Fisher expedition, 65; in assault on Fort Fisher, 66; wounded, 67.

Curtis, Samuel R., M. C., Maj. Gen. U. S. Vols.: member of House Committee of Thirty-three, II, 417; opinion on Frémont, IV, 431; sends order of removal to Frémont, 435; commands in southwest Missouri, V, 92; midwinter campaign of, 288; reports that he is capturing prisoners and materials, 289; congratulatory order of Feb. 18, 1862, 289; advances to Cross Hollow, 289; retires to Sugar Creek, 291; battle of Pea Ridge, March 6-8, 1862, 291, 292; defeats Van Dorn's army, 292; march down the White River, VI, 381; assigned to command of Department of Missouri, 381; assumes command, Sept. 24, 1862, 382; battle of Prairie Grove, Dec. 7, 1862, 383; interview with Gov. Gamble, 388, 389; explains system of provost marshals in Missouri, 389, 390.

Cushing, Alonzo H., Lieut. U. S. A.: killed at Gettysburg, VII, 267.

Cushing, Caleb, Atty. Gen. under Pierce, Min. to Spain: comment on Reeder's action, I, 413; address before U. S. Supreme Court, II, 70; presides over Charleston Convention, 232; construction of the "two-thirds rule," 243; resigns chairmanship of Charleston Convention, 251; messenger from Buchanan to Gov. Pickens, III, 11; interview with Gov. Pickens, 12; invited by South Carolina legislature to attend signing of ordinance of secession, 13.

Cushing, William B., Commander U. S. N.: daring of, X, 45, 46; prepares expedition against the *Albemarle*, 46-48; destroys the *Albemarle*, 49; escape of, 49-51.

Custer, George A., Bvt. Maj. Gen. U. S. A.: made brigadier general of U. S. volunteers, VII, 232; in battle of Gettysburg, 268; in Sheridan's expedition to join Butler, VIII, 370; in battle of Yellow Tavern, 371; in Shenandoah campaign, IX, 295; in battle of Cedar Creek, 317, 323-325; in battle of Waynesboro, 330; in march to Appomattox, X, 185, 191; at grand review in Washington, 332.

Cutler, Lysander, Bvt. Maj. Gen. U. S. Vols.: in battle of Gettysburg, VII, 240.

Cutler, R. King, elected U. S. Senator from Louisiana, VIII, 437.

Cutts, J. M., Jr., Bvt. Lieut. Col. U. S. A.: comment on Burnside's Order No. 38, VII, 329.

Dabney, R. L., D. D., Conf. Major: adjutant and biographer to Stonewall Jackson, V, 399.

Dahlgren, John A., Rear Adm. U. S. N.:
in charge of Washington navy yard, IV,
141, 142; ordered to make preparations to
obstruct the Potomac, V, 227; relieves Du
Pont in command of Charleston fleet,
VII, 85; assumes command of naval
forces at Charleston, 424, 425; bombardment of Fort Sumter, August to October,
1863, 435, 441, 442; council of war, 442; interview with Sherman, IX, 489; captures
Charleston, X, 231; festivities at Sumter
flag-raising, 278, 280.

Dahlgren, Ulric, Col. U. S. Vols.: death
of, VIII, 252.

Dakota, Territory of, organized as a Territory, II, 237.

Dallas, Ga., battles of, May 25 to June 4,
1864, IX, 17-19.

Dallas, George M., Vice-Pres. with Polk,
Min. to England: receives Lord Russell's
answer, IV, 268.

Daly, Judge Charles P., letter about prisoners of war, VII, 448.

Dana, Charles A., Asst. Sec. of War under
Lincoln: dispatches about Rosecrans,
VIII, 117-120.

Dana, N. J. T., Maj. Gen. U. S. Vols.:
wounded at Antietam, VI, 139; commands expedition to the Rio Grande,
VIII, 287.

Daniel, Junius, Conf. Brig. Gen.: killed at
Spotsylvania, VIII, 382.

Daniel, Peter V., Assoc. Justice U. S. Sup.
Ct.: opinion in Dred Scott case, II, 72.

D'Aubigné, Jean Henri Merle, Swiss historian: eulogy of Lincoln, X, 349.

Davidson, John W., Bvt. Maj. Gen. U. S. A.:
receives Hood's surrender, X, 37.

Davies, H. E., Maj. Gen. U. S. Vols.: in
march to Appomattox, X, 187.

Davis, Charles H., Rear Adm. U. S. N.: succeeds Foote in command of Union gunboat flotilla, V, 302; advances gunboats
upon Memphis, 342; river battle at Memphis, June 6, 1862, 344; joins Farragut
above Vicksburg, 348; represents Secretary of Navy at Lincoln's funeral, X, 320.

**Davis, David, Justice U. S. Sup. Ct., U. S.
Sen.:** opinion of Lincoln as a lawyer, I,
301-303; member of Bloomington Convention, II, 28; member of Mr. Lincoln's
suite, III, 290; attends meeting of Lincoln's suite, 314.

Davis, Garrett, M. C., U. S. Sen.: Union declarations, IV, 236; advice about organizing Kentucky troops, 236, 237; member of
committee to distribute Union arms, 237;
describes rebel proceedings in Kentucky,
243, 244; second interview with Lincoln
about compensated emancipation, VI,
111; Senate resolution for National Convention, VII, 365.

Davis, George, Conf. Atty. Gen.: arrest
of, X, 151.

Davis, G. T. M., declares in favor of Clay,
I, 260.

Davis, Henry Winter, M. C.: member of
House Committee of Thirty-three, II, 417;
suggested for the Cabinet, III, 364, 369;
announces himself a Union candidate for
Congress, IV, 94; resolutions about Mexico, VII, 408; report on diplomatic correspondence about Mexico, 410; relations
to Lincoln, IX, 112-115; reconstruction
bill of, 115-117; speech on reconstruction
bill, 117-119; signs Wade-Davis manifesto,
124-127; opposed to Lincoln, 367; advocates Ashley's reconstruction bills, 452.

**Davis, Jefferson, Sec. of War under Pres.
Pierce, U. S. Sen., Conf. Pres.:** relates
interview of Democratic Senators with
Pres. Pierce, I, 349; instructions of, on
rebellion, II, 5; indorsement on Gen.
Smith's report, 9; challenges Wm. H.
Bissell, 27; supports demand for Congressional slave code, 175; member of
committee to investigate John Brown
raid, 210; Senate resolutions of, 229, 230;
voted for in Charleston Convention,
244; signs address commending Charleston disruption, 245, 246; Senate debate
with Douglas, 247-250; inconsistency of,
249; interview with Buchanan, 326; advice
on Buchanan's message, 365; statement
about orders to Anderson, 389; claims
the suggestion to leave an ordnance sergeant in charge of Charleston forts, 395;
called by Floyd to influence Buchanan,
395; Senate discussion, 402, 407, 410, 411;
member of Senate Committee of Thirteen,
414; signs secession address, 436; refuses
to serve on Senate Committee of Thirteen, 437; reconsiders his refusal, 437;
prints South Carolina Commissioners' rejoinder to Buchanan in Senate speech, III,
86, 141; member of caucus committee of
secession Senators, 180, 181; signs Senatorial secession caucus resolutions, 181;
speech at Vicksburg, 183, 184; elected
President of the Confederate States, Feb.
9, 1861, 198; inaugurated, Feb. 18, 1861, 198;
theory of, on State equality, considered,

200; biographical summary, 204; States-rights fanaticism of, 205-207; compared and contrasted with Lincoln, 207-210; opposing declarations on disunion, 210-212; Cabinet of, 212; assumes control of military operations in seceded States, 212; sundry executive acts of, 212; sends commissioners to Washington, 213, 396; asks to be excused from serving on Senate Committee of Thirteen, 219; is persuaded to serve, 219; proposition in that committee, 220; transmits Campbell's statement to Confederate Congress, 405; answer to Campbell, 412, 413; letter to Campbell, IV, 32; proclamation offering letters of marque to privateers, 88; telegram to Gov. Letcher to sustain Baltimore, 160; attitude and confidence of, 262, 263; convenes rebel Congress, 263; recommendations for Southern armies, 264; negotiations with Mr. Bunch, 279; sends Johnston to command Harper's Ferry, 317; arrives on Bull Run battlefield, 350; letter to Lincoln about *Savannah* privateersmen, V, 10; approves Confederate invasion of Kentucky, 44; direction to prevent persecution in East Tennessee, 60; approves Benjamin's orders about bridge-burners, 78; council of war at Fairfax Court House, 153, 154; directs Johnston to draw back to a less exposed position, 163; uncertain about McClellan's destination, 176; message of approval to mayor of New Orleans, 269; proclamation of outlawry against Butler and his officers, 277, 278; comment on, 279; criticism of Butler's "Woman Order," 283; comment on, 283, 284; sends his family to a place of safety, 379; baptized and confirmed, 379; friendship for Lee, 422; criticism on Lee's plan for attacking McClellan, 424; present on battlefield of Gaines's Mill, 428; present with Lee at Malvern Hill, 438; censure of Hindman, VI, 373; proclaims Butler and his officers outlaws, 471; language of his message, 472; on employing rebel negro troops, 485, 486; letter to Gov. Smith, March 30, 1865, about colored recruits for the rebel army, 486, 487; appoints Johnston to command Confederate armies in the West, VII, 129; visits Chattanooga, Jackson, and Vicksburg, 130; orders reënforcements from Bragg to Pemberton, 130; holds conference with Johnston and Pemberton at Grenada, Miss., 131; controversy with Johnston, 183; correspondence with Johnston about Vicksburg, 296; conference with his Cabinet and Stephens about peace mission to Washington, 371, 372; authorizes Stephens to proceed to Washington, 372; refers suggestions about prisoners to his Secretary of War, 447; declares rebel soldiers paroled at Vicksburg exchanged, 457; proclamations establishing martial law, VIII, 41; proclamation of banishment, 41; requests Confederate Congress to suspend habeas corpus, 41, 42; visit to Bragg, 127; speeches after visiting Bragg, 128; advises Bragg to send expedition against Burnside, 167; directs Longstreet to join Bragg, 180; comments on action of England, 262-264; suggestions to Johnston, 327; directions to Johnston, 333; instructions to Johnston, IX, 5; comment on case of the *Rappahannock*, 142; interview with Jaquess and Gilmore, 208-211; comment on Northern politics, 245; accepts Hood's plan, 281; interview with Hood, 471-473; gives Hardee command of South Carolina and Florida, 472; gives Beauregard command over Hood and Taylor, 473; interview with F. P. Blair, Sr., X, 96-106; letter to Blair about peace negotiations, 107; second interview with Blair, 109, 110; appoints peace commissioners, 110; instructions to peace commissioners, 111, 112; speech in Richmond, 130, 131; appoints Johnston to command rebel Western armies, 153, 157; comment on Lee's report, 156; conference with Lee, 159, 160; last message of, 199, 200; receives news at St. Paul's Church, 201; departure from Richmond, 202, 203; dictates proposal of armistice to Sherman, 244, 263; approves the Sherman-Johnston agreement, 251, 265; instructions to Johnston, 251, 252, 266; arrives at Danville, 255; proclamation of, 256; goes to Greensboro, 257; interviews with Johnston and Beauregard, 257-263; goes to Charlotte, N. C., 263, 264; interview with Breckinridge at Charlotte, 265; goes to Abbeville, S. C., 266, 267; camps near Irwinville, Ga., 268; captured with his family, May 10, 1865, 270-274; statement about his capture, 271; indictment of, 274, 275; indictment dismissed, 276; death of, 276; comment on Lincoln's assassination, 312, 313.

Davis, Mrs. Jefferson, captured with her husband, X, 274.

Davis, Jefferson C., Bvt. Maj. Gen. U. S. A.:

assists Capt. Foster in destroying material in Fort Moultrie, III, 55; in engagement near Milford, V, 91; in battle of Murfreesboro, VI, 285; in battle of Chickamauga, VIII, 89, 95, 96; in battle of Chattanooga, 135; in battle of Kenesaw Mountain, IX, 22, 23; in March to the Sea, 481; in march to Columbia, X, 230; at grand review in Washington, 333.

Davis, Reuben, M. C.: member of House Committee of Thirty-three, II, 417; House discussion, 421; signs secession address, 436.

Dawes, E. C., Maj. U. S. Vols.: statement about Chickamauga, VIII, 106.

Dawes, Henry L., M. C., U. S. Sen.: statement about Stanton, II, 365; member of Select Committee of Five, III, 142; votes for re-passage of National Bank Act, VI, 245; opposes Ashley's reconstruction bills, IX, 450.

Dawson, John, elected to Illinois legislature in 1834, I, 122; one of the "Long Nine," 128; recommended for marshal by Lincoln, 183.

Dayton, William L., U. S. Sen., Min. to France: nominated for Vice-President, II, 35; candidate before Chicago Convention, 1860, 255, 263, 271; votes for: on first ballot, 273 — on second ballot, 274 — on third ballot, 275; sails for France, IV, 268; interview with Drouyn de l'Huys about mediation, VI, 63; interviews with Drouyn de l'Huys, VII, 403, 409, 410; presents letters to Drouyn de l'Huys about Confederate shipbuilding in France, VIII, 277; correspondence about the *Rappahannock*, IX, 138; correspondence about the *Alabama*, 143.

De Camp, John, Rear Adm. U. S. N.: commands the *Iroquois* in Farragut's fleet, V, 261.

De Courcy, John F., Col. U. S. Vols.: brigade of, assaults Chickasaw Bluffs, VII, 134.

De Jarnette, Daniel C., M. C.: remarks in House of Representatives, III, 147; resolutions in Confederate Congress about Mexico, VII, 422, 423.

Delafield, Richard, Bvt. Maj. Gen. U. S. A.: expected in Washington, IV, 96.

Delahay, Mark W., U. S. Dist. Judge: receives votes for delegate, I, 430.

Delano, Columbus, M. C., Sec. of Int. under Grant: in Baltimore Convention, IX, 71.

Delaware, State of, attitude on Lincoln's proclamation, IV, 92, 93; Lincoln's plan for compensated emancipation in, V, 206, 207; action of legislature on Lincoln's plan, 208.

De Leon, E., sent to Europe by Confederate government to subsidize the press, VI, 79.

Demers, George W., effort to nominate Grant in Cleveland Convention, IX, 39.

Democratic Party, the Cincinnati Convention, II, 38; the Cincinnati platform, 39, 40; defeats and victories, 227; convention of, at Charleston, 227-244; differences, North and South, 228, 230; adjourned meetings of Charleston Convention at Baltimore, 250; candidates and platforms in 1860, 279, 280; electors chosen by, 294; nominates Vallandigham for governor of Ohio, VII, 350, 351; National Convention at Chicago, Aug. 29, 1864, IX, 252-259; McClellan nominated for President, 258; Pendleton nominated for Vice-President, 258, 259.

Dennison, William, Gov. of Ohio, P. M. Gen. under Lincoln: dispatch to Cameron, IV, 283; appoints McClellan major general of Ohio militia, 285; permanent chairman of Baltimore Convention, IX, 67, 68; notifies Lincoln of his renomination, 75; appointed Postmaster General, 342, 343; at Cabinet meeting, April 14, 1865, X, 284; present at Lincoln's deathbed, 300.

Denver, J. W., appointed Secretary of Kansas Territory, II, 116.

De Peyster, Livingston, hoists flag over Richmond State House, X, 209.

Derby, Earl of, Prime Min. of Eng.: speech on Lincoln's death, X, 343.

De Saussure, W. G., Conf. Lieut. Col.: reports Fort Moultrie untenable, III, 118, 119.

Devens, Charles, Bvt. Maj. Gen. U. S. Vols., Atty. Gen. under Hayes: in battle of Ball's Bluff, IV, 455, 456; brigade from division of, occupies Richmond, X, 209.

Devin, Thomas C., Bvt. Maj. Gen. U. S. Vols.: in battle of Cedar Creek, IX, 325.

Dickey, W. H., Bvt. Brig. Gen. U. S. Vols.: in Red River expedition, VIII, 292; in battle of Pleasant Hill, 295.

Dickinson, Daniel S., U. S. Sen.: voted for, in Charleston Convention, II, 244; signs memorial about Frémont and colored troops, VI, 456; receives votes for Vice-President at Baltimore Convention, IX, 72-74; opposed to Lincoln, 367.

Disraeli, Benjamin, Lord Beaconsfield, English Prime Minister, speech on Lincoln's death, X, 342, 343.

District of Columbia, militia called out, IV, 67; slave trade prohibited in 1850, V, 215; Act to emancipate slaves in, 216; Lincoln's special message, April 16, 1861, 216, 217; Washington threatened by Early, IX, 169–173.

Diven, A. S., M. C.: appointed provost marshal general for New York, VII, 15.

Dix, Miss Dorothea, Supt. of hospitals: report about Confederate prisoners, VII, 465.

Dix, John A., U. S. Sen., Sec. of Treas. under Buchanan, Maj. Gen. U. S. Vols., Min. to France: appointed Secretary of Treasury, III, 132; telegram of "Shoot him on the spot," 133; letter to Mrs. Blodgett, 133; awards $3,230,000 Treasury notes, 242; authorized to make government purchases, IV, 137; appointed major general of U. S. volunteers, 309; assigned to command at Baltimore, 356; intention to resign, 363; transferred to Fort Monroe, V, 413; sends ten regiments to McClellan, 413; loans negotiated by, VI, 225; answer to Lincoln about colored troops, 453; letters to Seymour about the draft, VII, 36, 37; creates a panic in Richmond, 221; arranges cartel with D. H. Hill for exchange of prisoners, 451; instructions about pursuing Confederate raiders from Canada, VIII, 24, 25; appointed by Lincoln to examine cases of State prisoners, 33.

Dixon, Archibald, U. S. Sen.: offers amendment repealing Missouri Compromise, I, 344; Douglas proposes to adopt his amendment, 347; opinion on slavery, 357.

Dixon, James, M. C., U. S. Sen.: votes against National Bank Act, VI, 244; criticism on Sumner, VII, 388; favors rejection of Howard, IX, 87; recommends Goodman for Collector, 87; interview with Chase, 88; approves Lincoln's message, 109.

Doblado, Manuel, Mex. statesman: executes Convention of Soledad with Prim, VI, 44.

Dodge, Grenville M., Maj. Gen. U. S. Vols.: raid through northern Alabama, VIII, 51; in march to Chattanooga, 132; in battles of Atlanta, IX, 270, 272.

Doherty, E. P., Lieut. U. S. A.: arrests William Jett, X, 311; arrests Herold, 311, 312.

Doles, George, Conf. Brig. Gen.: killed at Cold Harbor, VIII, 400.

Donaldson, Edward, Rear Adm. U. S. N.: commands the Sciota in Farragut's fleet, V, 261.

Donaldson, J. B., Marshal Kas. Ter.: issues proclamation calling for help to execute the law, I, 453; refuses to protect Lawrence, 454.

Donelson, Andrew J., Min. to Russia and Germany: letter about Texas, I, 241; nominated for Vice-President, II, 24.

Doniphan, Col. Alexander W., speech condemning Polk administration, I, 260.

Donnohue, D. C., special agent to examine colony at Ile A'Vache, VI, 364; report to the government, 365, 366; relief to the colonists, 365; brings colonists back to the United States, 366.

Doolittle, James R., U. S. Sen.: member of committee to investigate the John Brown raid, II, 210; member of Senate Committee of Thirteen, 414; votes for re-passage of National Bank Act, VI, 245; advocates recognition of Louisiana, IX, 455.

Dorsey, Hazel, teacher of Pres. Lincoln, I, 34.

Doubleday, Abner, Bvt. Maj. Gen. U. S. A.: ordered to take his company to Fort Sumter, III, 50; takes possession of the fort, 53; statement about notice of relief expedition, 103; letters of, from Fort Moultrie, forwarded to Lincoln, 248; fires first gun from Sumter, IV, 51; in battle of Gettysburg, VII, 239, 240, 242; wounded at Gettysburg, 269; testimony about Gettysburg, 269.

Douglas, Stephen A., M. C., U. S. Sen.: legal fee of, I, 62; present at Vandalia, 1834, 124; made Circuit Attorney, 126; defeated for Congress in 1838, 157; appointed Judge of Illinois Supreme Court, 163; first meeting with Lincoln, 163; bill of, to reform the judiciary, 164; rencontre with Francis, 181; rencontre with Stuart, 182; elected U. S. Senator, 251, 252; votes against Wilmot Proviso, 269; political career, 330, 331; personal characteristics, 330, 331; choice of "Young America" for Presidential candidate, 331–333; chairman of Senate Committee on Territories, 331, 335; votes for, in Baltimore Convention, 332; declarations against renewing slavery agitation, 333, 334; defends Missouri Compromise, 334, 335; reports second Nebraska bill, 343; reply to Atchison's proposition.

346; interview with Dixon; proposes to adopt his amendment, 347; introduces Kansas-Nebraska Act, 349; conversation with Hamlin, 350; retort to petition of New England clergymen, 361; speech at Chicago, September, 1854, 371; speech in Springfield, Ill., at State fair, Oct. 3, 1854, 375, 379; speech at Peoria, Ill., Oct. 16, 1854, 380; Senate report against Topeka Constitution, 431; defeated in Cincinnati Convention, II, 38; speech at Springfield, Ill., defending the Dred Scott decision, 82–84; introduces enabling bill for Kansas, 93; indorses Walker's Kansas policy, 95; quarrel with Buchanan, 120; denounces Lecompton Constitution, 123–125; votes against Lecompton Constitution, 130; opposes English bill, 133; candidate for Senator, 135; begins the Senatorial campaign, 144; agrees to joint discussion, 145; skill in debate, 147; criticism of Lincoln's "House divided against itself" speech, 148; questions to Lincoln at Ottawa, 156, 157; answers to Lincoln, 160, 161; the Freeport doctrine, 160, 161; reëlected Senator, 165; deposed from chairmanship of Senate Committee on Territories, 170; speech at Memphis, 172, 173; speech at New Orleans, 173; speech at Baltimore, 174; answers Sen. Brown's questions, 175; letter to Dorr, 176; allusions to Lincoln's views, 183; "Harper's Magazine" article, 184; controversy with Black, 184, 185; advocates a law to punish conspiracies, 210, 211; schism between himself and Buchanan, 228; attitude as a Presidential candidate, 229; position at Charleston, 231; voted for in Charleston Convention, 243, 244; fails to receive nomination at Charleston, 244; Senate debate with Jefferson Davis, 247–250; nominated for President at Baltimore, 251; letter of acceptance, 281; campaign tour, 282, 283; repudiates fusion, 290; electoral votes for, 294; Senate discussion, 404, 405; member of Senate Committee of Thirteen, 414; motion at Presidential count, III, 145; propositions in Senate Committee of Thirteen, 221; call of ceremony on Lincoln, 317; calls Lincoln's inaugural a manifesto of peace, 399; interview with Lincoln, IV, 80; Senate speech, 81; speech at Bellair, O., 82; announces his support of the war, 85; speech before legislature of Illinois, 84; death of, June 3, 1861, 84; statement about Gen. Scott, 103.

Douglass, Frederick, Min. to Hayti: present at John Brown's council, II, 196; assists in raising colored troops in Massachusetts, VI, 463; statement about Lincoln's reply about retaliation, 474; eulogy of Lincoln, X, 354.

Downes, John, Commander U. S. N.: commands monitor Nahant in attack on Charleston, VII, 69; sent to attack the Atlanta, 79.

Draft Act, approved March 3, 1863, VII, 5; provisions of, 5, 6; National forces subject to, 7; quotas and deficiencies, 8; decided constitutional by Judge Cadwalader, 13; decided unconstitutional by Supreme Court of Pennsylvania, 13; Supreme Court of Pennsylvania reverses its decision, 13; opposition to commutation clause, 26.

Draft in insurrectionary States, Confederate law for, VII, 29, 30.

Draft riots, in New York, VII, 17–26; remarks of Gov. Seymour, July 4, 1863, 17; comments of newspapers, 17, 18; riot of July 13, 1863, 18–23; attack on colored orphan asylum, 21; attack on "Tribune" office, 21; murder of Col. H. T. O'Brien, 21, 22; remarks of Gov. Seymour, July 13, 1863, 22, 23; Gov. Seymour's proclamation of July 14, 1863, 23; riot of July 16, 1863, 24; address of Archbishop Hughes, July 17, 1863, 24, 25; riot in Boston, 26.

Drake, C. D., U. S. Sen., Chief Justice U. S. Ct. of Claims: reads address of radical committee to Lincoln, VIII, 215; letter to Lincoln about Missouri politics, 477.

Draper, Lyman C., Sec. of Wis. Hist. Soc.: information about lands owned by Abraham Lincoln, grandfather of the President, I, 11.

Drayton, Percival, Capt. U. S. N.: commands Union monitor Passaic in attack on Charleston, VII, 67; commands the Hartford in Mobile Bay, IX, 231.

Drayton, Thomas F., letters to Gov. Gist: Nov. 3, 1860, II, 319, 320 — Nov. 6, 1860, 320 — Nov. 8, 1860, 320 — Nov. 16, 1860, 321 — Nov. 19, 1860, 321, 322, 323 — Nov. 23, 1860, 323, 324.

Dred Scott decision, its origin, II, 59; the St. Louis local court declares Dred Scott free, 61; decision reversed by Supreme Court of Missouri, 61; suit renewed in the U. S. Circuit Court, 63; Scott and his family declared slaves, 63; appeal to the U. S. Supreme Court, 63; counsel in the case, 64; argument and re-argument, 64; opinion of Justice Nelson, 66; Mr. Buchanan's announcement, 72; decision announced, 72; opinions by all the justices, 72, 73; points of the decision, 73–76; dissenting opinions, 77–80; effect of, on politics, 81. See also SCOTT, DRED.

Dresser, Rev. Charles, marries Abraham Lincoln and Mary Todd, I, 200.

Drouyn de l'Huys, French Min. of Foreign Affairs: interview with Dayton about mediation, VI, 63; dispatch to Mercier proposing a conference between North and South, 68–70; interviews with Dayton about Mexico, VII, 403, 409, 410; relations with Slidell, VIII, 269, 270; interview with Slidell, 276, 277; interview about the *Alabama*, IX, 143; protests against combat of *Kearsarge* and *Alabama*, 145; interview with Slidell, 153–155.

Drum, R. C., Adjt. Gen. U. S. A.: statement concerning mustering out of Lincoln's regiment, I, 96, 97.

Drummond, Thomas, U. S. Circ. Judge: opinion of Lincoln as a lawyer, I, 303, 304.

Dubois, Jesse K., relates Lincoln's influence in the legislature, I, 138.

Duer, Denning, offered appointment of Assistant Treasurer at New York, IX, 91, 92.

Duffié, Alfred N., Brig. Gen. U. S. Vols.: in Sheridan's army, IX, 182.

Duke, Basil W., Conf. Brig. Gen.: statements about Morgan's raid, VIII, 53–56.

Duncan, J. K., Conf. Brig. Gen.; statement about ironclad *Louisiana*, V, 274.

Duncan, Joseph, M. C., Gov. of Ill.: elected to Congress, I, 64; refers slavery resolutions to legislature, 149, 150.

Duncan, William, Capt. U. S. Vols.: in March to the Sea, IX, 488.

Dunlap, George W., M. C.: second interview with Lincoln about compensated emancipation, VI, 111.

Dunn, William McKee, M. C.: member of House Committee of Thirty-three, II, 417; resolution in that committee, 433.

Dupanloup, Mgr., Bishop of Orleans: comment on Lincoln's second inaugural, X, 146.

Du Pont, Samuel F., Rear Adm. U. S. N.: ordered to gather a fleet, V, 14; commands fleet in Port Royal expedition, 16; commands expedition to occupy coast of Florida, 250, 251; directs Fort McAllister to

be attacked, VII, 61, 64; assaults defenses of Charleston, April 7, 1863, 65–71; report on the attack on Charleston, 71, 72; asks to be relieved, 75, 76; relieved by Dahlgren, 85.

Durant, Thomas J., president of Free State General Committee in New Orleans, 419; appointed attorney general for Louisiana, VIII, 419.

Durrett, Col. Reuben T., information from, concerning the settlement of the Lincolns in Kentucky, I, 11.

Duval, Hiram F., Bvt. Brig. Gen. U. S. Vols.: in the battle of Winchester, IX, 303.

Duval, Isaac H., Bvt. Maj. Gen. U. S. Vols.: wounded at Winchester, IX, 304.

Eads, James B., civil engineer: authorized to build Western gunboats, V, 118.

Early, Jubal A., Conf. Lieut. Gen.: lays York, Pa., under contribution, VII, 220; marches to join Ewell, 233; in battle of Gettysburg, 242; losses at Rappahannock Station, VIII, 245; in battle of the Wilderness, 361, 367; in battle of Spotsylvania, 375, 376, 381, 385; in battle of Cold Harbor, 391, 400; begins campaign against Washington, IX, 160; advance to Winchester, 161; moves through passes of South Mountain, 161; advance into Maryland, 164, 165; battle of Monocacy, July 9, 1864, 165; orders attack on Washington, 169, 170; council of war, 171; retreat from Washington, 173, 174; defeats Crook at Kernstown, 175; Shenandoah campaign, Aug. 10 to Sept. 19, 1864, 291–299; battle of Winchester, Sept. 19, 1864, 299–305; battle of Fisher's Hill, Sept. 22, 1864, 306–310; retires to Brown's Gap, 310; comment on his defeat, 311, 312; campaign of Cedar Creek, Oct. 6–18, 1864, 312–315; battle of Cedar Creek, Oct. 19, 1864, 316–326; return to Cedar Creek, 327, 328; winter quarters at Staunton, 329; battle of Waynesboro, March 2, 1865, 329–331; superseded by Echols, 331.

Eastport, The, Union gunboat: blown up in Red River, VIII, 297.

Echols, John, Conf. Brig. Gen.: supersedes Early, IX, 331.

Eckert, Thomas T., Bvt. Brig. Gen. U. S. Vols.: sent to meet peace commissioners, X, 113; ultimatum to peace commissioners, 116; present at Lincoln's deathbed, 300.

Ector, M. D., Conf. Brig. Gen.: joins Johnston's army in Mississippi, VII, 294.

Edmundson, Henry A., M. C.: acquainted with Brooks's design, II, 49; course disapproved by the House, 53.

Edwards, B. F., recommended for marshal by Lincoln, I, 183.

Edwards, Cyrus, candidate for governor of Illinois, I, 160; favorably mentioned by Lincoln for appointment, 293.

Edwards, Ninian, Gov. of Ill.: assists E. D. Baker, I, 221.

Edwards, Ninian W., one of the "Long Nine," I, 128; speech in canvass of 1836, 130.

Egan, T. W., Bvt. Maj. Gen. U. S. Vols.: in battle of Hatcher's Run, IX, 434.

Eighth Massachusetts Militia, arrival in Philadelphia, IV, 133; arrives before Annapolis, 135; landed at Annapolis, 154; march to Annapolis Junction, 155.

Ekin, James A., Brig. Gen. U. S. A.: member of military commission for trial of Lincoln's assassins, X, 312.

Elkin, David, preacher in Indiana, I, 31.

Elkin, Col. William F., one of the "Long Nine," I, 128; nominated for sheriff, 183.

Ella and Annie, The, Union gunboat: starts to take the *Chesapeake* to the United States, VIII, 15; returns to Halifax under orders, 15.

Ellet, Alfred W., Brig. Gen. U. S. Vols.: succeeds Charles Ellet, Jr., in command of ram fleet, V, 348; joins Farragut above Vicksburg, 348; assists defense of Milliken's Bend, VII, 293.

Ellet, Charles, Jr., Col. U. S. Vols.: employed by Stanton to extemporize a ram fleet, V, 343; description of his rams, 343; joins Davis in advance against Memphis, 343; river battle at Memphis, 344; wounded at Memphis, 344; death, 345.

Ellis, John W., Gov. of N. C.: reply to Gov. Gist about proposed secession, II, 307, 308; answer to Lincoln's call for troops, IV, 90.

Ellsworth, E. E., Col. U. S. Vols.: member of Lincoln's suite, III, 290; commands expedition to occupy Alexandria, IV, 312; assassination of, 313; funeral honors to, 314.

Ely, Alfred, M. C.: captured at Bull Run, IV, 354.

Ely, Ralph, Bvt. Brig. Gen. U. S. Vols.: receives surrender of Petersburg, X, 183.

Emancipation, Frémont's proclamation of, in Missouri, IV, 416, 417; Lincoln revokes Frémont's proclamation, 420; discussed in President's message of Dec. 3, 1861, V, 204, 205; Lincoln's plan for compensated emancipation in Delaware, 206, 207; action of Delaware legislature, 208; Lincoln's message of March 6, 1862, recommending compensated abolishment, 209, 210; Lincoln's interview with Border Slave State Representatives, 212-214; Congress passes Lincoln's joint resolution for compensated abolishment, 214; emancipation in District of Columbia, 215-217; Hunter's order of, in Georgia, Florida, and South Carolina, VI, 90; President revokes Hunter's order, 94-96; Act abolishing slavery in District of Columbia, 100; provisions of Confiscation Act emancipating slaves, 100, 101; provisions for, through military service, 101, 102; Lincoln's draft of veto message on Confiscation Act, 102, 103; Lincoln's second interview with Border State Representatives, 108-111; Lincoln decides to adopt military emancipation, 121; Lincoln reads draft of his first proclamation to the Cabinet, 125; Lincoln postpones first proclamation, 130; Lincoln's preliminary proclamation issued, 164; provisions of West Virginia Constitution respecting, 299; conditions of Senate bill to admit West Virginia, 299; gradual emancipation in the new State, 312; legislative acts concerning, 312, 313; slavery abolished in West Virginia, 313; indorsed: by American Baptist Missionary Union, 316 — by American Board of Foreign Missions, 317 — by Congregational General Association of New York, New Jersey, and Pennsylvania, 318 — by Lutheran General Synod, 318, 319 — by Moravian Synod, 319 — by Presbyterian General Assembly, 319-321 — by United Presbyterian Church General Assembly, 321 — by Reformed Presbyterian Church, 322 — by New School Presbyterians, 322, 323 — by Protestant Episcopal Church, Diocese of Pennsylvania, 323, 324; action on, of Society of Friends, 326-329; Breckinridge's bill in Missouri Convention of 1862 for compensated abolishment, 391; bill laid on the table, 391; mass convention of emancipationists at Jefferson City, Mo., 392, 393; victory in November election, 1862, in Missouri, 394; bill in Congress to aid, in Delaware,

Maryland, Virginia, Kentucky, Tennessee, and Missouri, 395; Henderson's Senate bill to aid, in Missouri, 396; Noell's House bill to aid, in Missouri, 396, 397; discussed in Lincoln's annual message of Dec. 1, 1862, 399–401; emancipation proclamation of Jan. 1, 1863, 429; ordinance of prospective emancipation in Missouri, VIII, 209; adopted by Arkansas, 415; adopted by Louisiana, 435, 436; adopted by Tennessee, 447, 448; Tennessee legislature ratifies Thirteenth Amendment, 449; adopted: by Maryland, 466 — by Missouri, 484 — in Virginia, IX, 438, 439; Lincoln's message of Dec. 8, 1863, about, X, 73, 74; Trumbull reports Thirteenth Amendment, 75; Senate adopts Thirteenth Amendment, 77; House rejects Thirteenth Amendment, 77, 78; House adopts Thirteenth Amendment, 85, 86; Thirteenth Amendment ratified, 88, 89; discussed at Hampton Roads Conference, 123–125; Lincoln's draft of message, Feb. 5, 1865, 133–135.

Emerson, Dr., owner of Dred Scott, II, 58.

Emerson, Ralph Waldo, remarks on John Brown's execution, II, 211; criticism of Lincoln's style, X, 351.

Emory, W. H., Bvt. Maj. Gen. U. S. A.: left in command at New Orleans, VII, 320, 321; in Red River expedition, VIII, 292; in battle of Sabine Cross Roads, 294; in battle of Pleasant Hill, 295; arrives in Washington, IX, 171; in battle of Winchester, 303; in battle of Fisher's Hill, 307, 309; in battle of Cedar Creek, 317, 320, 321, 324.

England, public opinion favorable to the South, IV, 266; reply to Black's circular, 267; proclamation of neutrality, 268; indirect negotiations with Jefferson Davis, 279; alleged causes of intervention in Mexico, VI, 33; signs tripartite convention, 38; withdraws from Mexican expedition, 45; interpretation of the Queen's proclamation of neutrality, 50; permits building of Confederate cruisers, 51; treaty with the United States to suppress African slave trade, 60, 61; invited by France to mediate in American affairs, 63; refuses to join France in effort to obtain armistice in the United States, 65; instructions to the governor-general of Canada about Confederate raiders, VIII, 25.

English, James E., M. C., Gov. of Conn.,

U. S. Sen.: vote for Thirteenth Amendment, X, 83.

English, Dr. R. W., mediator in the Lincoln-Shields duel, I, 207.

English, William H., M. C.: plan of compromise, II, 423.

Ericsson, John, civil engineer: plan of the Monitor, V, 219, 220.

Erwin, W. R., G. R. Sec. of Union League: transmits resolution of Union League to Lincoln, IX, 75.

Estrada, Gutierrez de, Mex. diplomatist: sent to offer the crown of Mexico to Maximilian, VII, 398, 399; notifies Maximilian of the action of the Mexican notables, 411.

Etheridge, Emerson, M. C., Clerk of H. R.: alleged plot of, VII, 389–391.

Eustis, George, Sec. to Confederate Commissioners, V, 23; removed from the Trent, 23, 24.

Evans, Nathan G., Conf. Brig. Gen.: report about Ball's Bluff, IV, 458; strength of command after Antietam, VI, 143; joins Johnston's army in Mississippi, VII, 294.

Evarts, William M., Sec. of State under Hayes, U. S. Sen.: chairman of New York delegation in Chicago Convention, II, 262; nominates Seward, 271; moves to make Lincoln's nomination unanimous, 277; authorized to organize troops, IV, 138; eulogy of Chase, VI, 223, 225, 226.

Everett, Edward, M. C., Min. to England, Sec. of State under Fillmore, U. S. Sen.: nominated for Vice-President by Constitutional Union party, II, 254; biographical notice, VIII, 192, 193; oration at Gettysburg, 194–199; letter to Lincoln, 203.

Ewell, Richard S., Conf. Lieut. Gen.: commands under Lee on the Peninsula, V, 428; in battle of Cedar Mountain, VI, 6; with Lee at Sharpsburg, 139; commands corps of Lee's army, VII, 201; corps of, moves northward, 205; invests Winchester, 208; crosses the Potomac, 217, 218; occupies Carlisle, Pa., 220; marches towards Gettysburg, 233; in battle of Gettysburg, 242, 244, 246, 249, 258; commands Confederate left at Gettysburg, 249; commands right wing of Army of Northern Virginia, VIII, 352; marches to attack Grant, 358; in battle of the Wilderness, 360, 361, 363; in battle of Spotsylvania,

375, 380, 385; in siege of Richmond, IX, 431; captured in retreat to Appomattox, X, 186–188; evacuates Richmond, 201, 206.

Ewing, Hugh, Bvt. Maj. Gen. U. S. Vols.: in battle of Chattanooga, VIII, 134, 139.

Ewing, Gen. William L. D., elected U. S. Senator, I, 126.

Fairfax, D. M., Rear Adm. U. S. N.: sent on board the *Trent*, V, 22; commands gunboat *Nantucket* in attack on Charleston, VII, 69.

Fannin, James W., killed at Goliad, I, 233.

Farnsworth, E. J., Brig. Gen. U. S. Vols.: made brigadier general, VII, 232; killed at Gettysburg, 268.

Farnsworth, John F., Brig. Gen. U. S. Vols.: present at Lincoln's deathbed, X, 300.

Farragut, David G., Adm. U. S. N.: selected to command expedition against New Orleans, V, 255; service and loyalty, 255, 256; his confidence and enthusiasm, 257; instructed to capture New Orleans, 258; leads "Column of the Blue" in the passage of Forts Jackson and St. Philip, 261; passage of the forts, April 24, 1862, 262; Confederate gunboats destroyed, 262, 263; the *Hartford* on fire, 264, 265; the fleet at New Orleans, 266; sends Bailey to confer with the mayor, 267; correspondence with the mayor, 267, 268; orders Morris to raise the flag over the Mint, April 27, 1862, 268; threatens to bombard the city, 269; raises Union flag over New Orleans, April 29, 1862, 269; places Butler in command of New Orleans, 275; ascends Mississippi River to Vicksburg, 346; demand for surrender of Vicksburg refused, 347; returns to New Orleans, 348; reascends Mississippi River to Vicksburg, 348; passes Vicksburg batteries, 348; applies to Halleck for land forces, 349; descends river to New Orleans, 350; passes batteries at Port Hudson, VII, 314; joins Banks's expedition at Alexandria, La., 314, 315; on board the *Hartford* in Mobile Bay, IX, 231; battle of Mobile Bay, Aug. 5, 1864, 231–239; lashes himself to the mast, 233; offered command of Fort Fisher expedition, X, 55.

Farrand, Ebenezer, Capt. Conf. navy: surrenders Confederate steamers, IX, 242; surrenders Confederate naval forces to Thatcher, X, 328.

Fellows, J. Q. A., receives votes for governor of Louisiana, VIII, 432.

Felton, S. M., Pres. P., W., and B. R. R.: precautions to protect Philadelphia, Wilmington, and Baltimore railroad, III, 304, 306; employs Detective Pinkerton, 304; railroad services, IV, 128, 129.

Ferrandini, C., conspiracy and testimony, III, 306.

Ferrero, Edward, Bvt. Maj. Gen. U. S. Vols.: censured for Petersburg mine affair, IX, 421, 425.

Ferry, Orris S., M. C., Bvt. Maj. Gen. U. S. Vols., U. S. Sen.: member of House Committee of Thirty-three, II, 417.

Fessenden, S. C., M. C.: resolution in House of Representatives indorsing emancipation proclamation, VI, 171.

Fessenden, William P., U. S. Sen., Sec. of Treas. under Lincoln: attends meeting at Seward's house, III, 263; remarks on legal tender, VI, 234; votes for National Bank Act, 244; present at interview between Lincoln, Cabinet, and Republican Senators, 266; appointed Secretary of Treasury, IX, 99–101; resignation of, X, 348; recommends Chase for Chief Justice, 391.

Field, A. P., elected to Congress in Louisiana, VIII, 437.

Field, Charles W., Conf. Maj. Gen.: in siege of Richmond, IX, 427, 433.

Field, David D., M. C.: present at Lincoln's Cooper Institute speech, II, 217; member of Peace Convention, III, 230.

Field, M. B., Asst. Sec. of Treas.: appointment as Assistant Treasurer at New York asked by Chase, IX, 92; present at Lincoln's deathbed, X, 300.

Filley, O. D., member of Union Safety Committee at St. Louis, IV, 212.

Fillmore, Millard, thirteenth Pres. U. S.: nominated for Vice-President, I, 276; elected Vice-President, 282; nominated for President by Know-Nothing party, II, 24; popular and electoral vote for, 40, 41; signs Fugitive Slave law of 1850, III, 26.

Finances of the U. S., financial measures, III, 238–244; suspension of specie payments, VI, 230; Act to make paper money legal tender, 235, 236; demand-notes made legal tender, 236; speculation in gold, 238, 239; system of temporary loans, 240; Five-twenty bonds, 240, 241; National Bank Act, 241–243; review of Confederate finances, 247–252.

Fish, Hamilton, Gov. of N. Y., U. S. Sen., Sec. of State under Grant: appointed commissioner to visit Union prisoners of war, VII, 449.

Fishback, Wm. M., elected U. S. Senator from Arkansas, VIII, 418.

Fisher, George P., M. C., Judge Sup. Ct. D. C.: elected to Congress, V, 206; urges Delaware to accept Lincoln's plan of compensated emancipation, 206, 207; second interview with Lincoln about compensated emancipation, VI, 112; member of Select Committee on Emancipation, 395.

Fisher's Hill, Va., battle of, Sept. 22, 1864, IX, 306-310.

Fitch, Graham N., M. C., U. S. Sen.: member of committee to investigate John Brown raid, II, 210.

Five Forks, Va., battle of, April 1, 1865, X, 172-174.

Flagg, W. J., recommends McClellan for command at Cincinnati, IV, 282.

Flanders, B. F., M. C., Gov. of La.: elected to Congress, VI, 353; admitted to a seat, 353; receives votes for governor of Louisiana, VIII, 437.

Fletcher, Job, one of the "Long Nine," I, 128.

Fletcher, Thomas C., Gov. of Mo.: proclamation about law and order, VIII, 486; declines to commit himself for Lincoln, IX, 368.

Florida, State of, admitted as a State, I, 324; secession ordinance passed, Jan. 10, 1861, III, 163, 183; forts and navy yard at Pensacola surrendered, Jan. 12, 1861, 163, 164, 183; secession movement in, 182; population in 1860, 182; seizure of arsenal at Appalachicola, 183; seizure of Fort Marion, 183; Fort Pickens reënforced, IV, 12, 13, 16; secession intrigues at Key West, 15; eastern coast occupied by Union troops, V, 251; Gillmore's expedition to, VIII, 281-285; Lincoln's letter about reconstruction in, 282, 283; Major Hay's mission to, 282, 283; failure of reconstruction in, 283; battle of Olustee, Feb. 20, 1864, 285; ratifies Thirteenth Amendment, X, 89.

Florida, The, Conf. cruiser: burns American trading-vessels, IX, 128, 129; captured by the Wachusett, 131-133; sinks at Hampton Roads, 133.

Floyd, John B., Sec. of War under Buchanan, Conf. Brig. Gen.: extracts from diary of, II, 316, 317, 360, 363; interviews with Trescott, Thompson, Cobb, and others, 317;

interviews with Drayton, 319, 321; suggestions about sale of arms, 323, 324; approves Foster's requisition, 344; ignores Gen. Scott, 347; interview with Anderson, 348; reply to Anderson, 355, 356; opinion on disunion, 362, 363; sends Buell to Anderson, 387; approves the Buell memorandum, 388; Cabinet discussion with Buchanan, 394, 395; approves requisition for forty muskets, 441; refuses requisition for one hundred muskets, 442; orders Foster to return the muskets, 446; requested by Buchanan to resign, III, 65; telegram of inquiry to Anderson, 65; demands withdrawal of Anderson and his garrison from Charleston, 67; Stanton's statement about, 73, 74; resignation of, 74; favors of, to secessionists, 128; orders heavy guns from Pittsburg to the South, 128; sends Hardee to drill and inspect a camp of instruction in Virginia, 418; sent to reënforce Fort Donelson, V, 185; attends council of war in Fort Donelson, 198; relinquishes command to Pillow, 198; leaves Fort Donelson, 198.

Flusser, Charles W., Lieut. Comm. U. S. N.: commands Union gunboat Miami, X, 39; killed at Plymouth, 41.

Fogg, George G., Min. to Switzerland, U. S. Sen.: letter to Lincoln, III, 256.

Follansbee, Albert S., Capt. 6th Mass. Militia: in Baltimore riot, IV, 115.

Foot, Solomon, M. C., U. S. Sen.: votes against National Bank Act, VI, 244; votes for re-passage of the Act, 244.

Foote, Andrew H., Rear Adm. U. S. N.: gunboat reconnaissance to Fort Henry, V, 106; asks permission to attack Fort Henry, 119; capture of Fort Henry, 120-122; arrives at Fort Donelson, 195; attacks with gunboats, 195; wounded, 195; conference with Grant, 196; declines to attack Island No. 10 at close range, 296; sends gunboats past Island No. 10, 298; receives surrender of Island No. 10, April 7, 1862, 299; directed to bombard Fort Pillow, 301; relinquishes command of gunboat flotilla, 302; helps Grant to occupy Clarksville, 310; designated to relieve Du Pont, VII, 85; death, 85.

Foote, Henry S., U. S. Sen., Gov. of Miss.: defeats Davis for governor in Mississippi, III, 206; peace resolution in Confederate Congress, VII, 364, 365.

Foote, John A., presents resolutions of New School Presbyterians to the President, VI, 323.

Forbes, B., member of Lincoln's suite, III, 290.

Forbes, Hugh, adventurer employed by John Brown, II, 195; discloses John Brown's projects, 201.

Force, M. F., Bvt. Maj. Gen. U. S. Vols.: comment on battle of Pittsburg Landing, V, 324; estimate of troops engaged at Pittsburg Landing, 326.

Ford, Thomas, Gov. of Ill.: statement about the effect of slavery in Illinois, I, 51; historian of Illinois, 133.

Ford, Thomas H., receives votes for Vice-President in Philadelphia Convention, II, 35.

Forey, Elie Frédéric, Marshal of France: sent to Mexico with 35,000 men, VI, 46; defeated before Puebla, 47; siege of Puebla, VII, 396, 397; occupies City of Mexico, 397; organizes provisional government, 397, 398.

Forman, Colonel, in Mexican war, I, 250.

Forney, John H., Conf. Maj. Gen.: advises capitulation of Vicksburg, VII, 302.

Forney, John W., editor of Philadelphia "Press:" favors Lincoln's renomination, IX, 63.

Forquer, George, prominent lawyer of Illinois, I, 213.

Forrest, Nathan B., Conf. Lieut. Gen.: captures Fort Pillow, April 12, 1864, VI, 479; first report about capture of Fort Pillow, 479; threat at Paducah, 480; letter to Washburn, 480; raid against Grant's line of communications, VII, 127; captures prisoners at Brentwood, VIII, 50; captures Col. Streight, 52; defeats W. S. Smith, 331; in army of Hood, X, 7; in march to Franklin, 10, 11; expedition against Murfreesboro, 23; in retreat of Hood, 34; defeated by Wilson, 239, 240.

Forsyth, John, Conf. Comr.: arrives in Washington, III, 398; letter to Walker, 404.

Fort Delaware, Del., reënforced, III, 135.

Fort Donelson, Tenn., garrison of, Feb. 8, 1862, V, 192; reënforced by Buckner, Floyd, and Pillow, 192; invested by Grant, Feb. 12, 1862, 193; description of, 193; attacked by Foote's gunboats, 195; council of Confederate commanders, 197; flight of Floyd and Pillow, 198; surrender, Feb. 16, 1862, 199, 200.

Fort Fisher, N. C., situation and strength of, X, 53, 55-58; first expedition against,

organized, 54, 55; failure of first expedition against, 60, 61; capture of, Jan. 15, 1865, 67.

Fort Henry, Tenn., capture of, Feb. 6, 1862, V, 121, 122.

Fort Jackson, La., seized by governor of Louisiana, III, 192; situation on the Mississippi, V, 254; armament and defenses, 259; bombardment by mortar flotilla begun, April 18, 1862, 260; Union fleet passes the fort, April 24, 1862, 261-266; mutiny in, 273; surrender of, April 28, 1862, 273; occupied by Butler, 275.

Fort Macon, N. C., captured by Union forces April 26, 1862, V, 247.

Fort McAllister, Ga., attacked by Union monitor Montauk, Jan. 27 and Feb. 1, 1863, VII, 61-63.

Fort McHenry, Md., reënforced, III, 135.

Fort Monroe, Va., importance and condition, III, 94; defensive preparations of, 135.

Fort Moultrie, S. C., condition of, II, 343, 440; inspected by Maj. Porter, 345; Anderson sent to command, 346; intrigue to possess, 379, 380; temporary defenses, 440; dismantled and abandoned by Anderson, III, 55; occupied by the rebels, 61.

Fort Pickens, Fla., occupied by Lieut. Slemmer, III, 163; truce at, 168; joint instructions concerning, 168; situation of, 437: plan to reënforce, 437, 438; reënforced by Vogdes's company and marines, IV, 12, 13; reënforced by the Meigs expedition, 16.

Fort Pillow, Tenn., Lincoln's address concerning, VI, 478; report of Committee on Conduct of the War, 479; capture of, by Forrest, April 12, 1864, 479; massacre of negro troops, 479; Forrest's first report, 479.

Fort Pulaski, Ga., seized by governor of Georgia, III, 190; description of, V, 248; operations against, by Gen. Gillmore, 249, 250; surrender, April 11, 1862, 250.

Fort St. Philip, La., seized by governor of Louisiana, III, 192; situation on the Mississippi, V, 254; armament and defenses, 259; bombardment by mortar flotilla begun, April 18, 1862, 260; Union fleet passes the fort, April 24, 1862, 261-266; surrender of, April 28, 1862, 273; occupied by Butler, 275.

Fort Sumter, S. C., condition of, II, 343; inspected by Maj. Porter, 345; Anderson sent to command, 346; workmen prove untrustworthy, 442; occupied by Anderson, III, 53; plans and orders to relieve, 90; expedition postponed, 91; expedition in the *Star of the West*, 96; possession of, demanded by commissioners from Gov. Pickens, 111; surrender refused to Pickens by council of war, 111; siege of, begun, 126; plan to relieve, under Capt. Ward, 172; preparations for bombardment, IV, 47, 48; condition of, 49; bombardment begun, 50; returns fire, 51; barracks catch fire, 53; course of the fleet, 54–56; fire on second day, 57, 58; negotiations for surrender, 59–61; evacuated by Anderson, April 14, 1861, 61; news of attack upon, 69, 70, 76; attacked by Du Pont's ironclads, April 7, 1863, VII, 65, 66, 67–71; Anderson raises flag over, April 14, 1865, X, 278.

Fort Wagner, S. C., siege operations against, July, 1863, VII, 425–437; first assault, July 11, 1863, 427; second assault, July 18, 1863, 429–431; evacuated, Sept. 7, 1863, 437.

Foster, John G., Bvt. Maj. Gen. U. S. A.: sent to repair Charleston forts, II, 343, 439; requisition for forty muskets, 344, 441; inspects Charleston forts with Anderson, 349; report about Fort Sumter, 351; constructs temporary defenses in Fort Moultrie, 440; letter to War Department, 442, 443; receives forty muskets, 443; correspondence about them, 444, 445; interview with Charlestonians, 445, 446; reply to the Secretary of War, 446, 447; reports movement of guard-steamer, III, 44; remains with a rearguard in Fort Moultrie, 50, 51; destroys material in Moultrie, 55; final visit to Charleston, 55; withdraws with rearguard from Moultrie, 56; comment on Maj. Anderson's delay, 109; reports military operations against Fort Sumter, 126; defensive preparations in Sumter, IV, 19; plants mines at Sumter, 20; prepares for the expected relief ship, 41; reports observations on Sumter bombardment, 52, 53; report of Wigfall's interview with Anderson, 60; commands division under Burnside, V, 242; commands center in attack on Roanoke Island, 244; report of victory of Feb. 8, 1862, 245; report of victory at New Berne, 246, 247; sent to relieve Burnside, VIII, 175; succeeds Burnside in East Tennessee, 185; interview with Grant, 332; in March to the Sea, IX, 487; made Department commander, X, 338.

Foster, Lafayette S., U. S. Sen.: Senate discussion, II, 406.

Foster, Robert S., Bvt. Maj. Gen. U. S. Vols.: in assault on Petersburg, X, 179; member of military commission for trial of Lincoln's assassins, 312.

Fox, Gustavus V., Asst. Sec. of Navy under Lincoln: plan to reënforce Fort Sumter, III, 383–385; visits Sumter, 389; report to the President, 389; memorandum for Sumter expedition, 433; sails for Sumter, IV, 28, 29; disappointed at non-arrival of the *Powhatan* and tugs, 55; qualifications, V, 4; called to council at the White House, 221; opinion on Potomac rebel batteries, 221, 222; sent to Fort Monroe, 222; witnesses fight of *Monitor* and *Merrimac*, 222; present at council about expedition against New Orleans, 254; testimony about operations against Yorktown, 361; precaution for Lincoln's safety, IX, 169.

France, public opinion favorable to the South, IV, 266; reply to Black's circular, 267; follows England's proclamation of neutrality, 268; indirect negotiations with Jefferson Davis, 279; insult to legation of, in Mexico, VI, 32: alleged causes of intervention in Mexico, 33; signs tripartite convention, 38; apprehensions of disturbed relations with the United States on account of French expedition to Mexico, 63; invites England and Russia to mediate between the United States and the rebels, 63; proposes to England and Russia joint effort to obtain armistice in the United States for six months, 64.

Francis, D. G., suggests Wide Awake uniform, II, 285.

Francis, Simeon, editor of "Sangamo Journal": assaulted by Douglas, I, 181.

Franciscus, G. C., conference with Judd, Pinkerton, and Sanford, III, 310.

Franklin, Tenn., battle of, Nov. 30, 1864, X, 18–21; losses at, 21.

Franklin, W. B., Bvt. Maj. Gen. U. S. A.: invited to a conference with Lincoln, V, 156; recommends movement against the rebels, 157; attends council of war, 167; division of, sent to the Peninsula, 365; assigned by McClellan to command provisional army corps, 382; established north of the Chickahominy, 385; moves towards the James River, 433; interview with Lincoln at Harrison's Landing, 453; advises McClellan's withdrawal from the James, 457; storms the crest of South

Mountain, VI, 136; corps engaged at Antietam, 140; recommends renewal of the attack, 144; commands Union left at Fredericksburg, 202; in battle of Fredericksburg, 203, 204; controversy with Burnside, 204; advice against the "Mud March," 217, 218; letter to Halleck, criticizing Burnside, 218; relieved from command, 221; commands expedition to Sabine Pass, VIII, 286; defeat at Sabine Pass, 287; organizes Red River expedition, 289; in battle of Sabine Cross Roads, 293, 294; suggested for command of Middle Military Division, IX, 179.

Frazer, J. W., Conf. Brig. Gen.: surrenders to Burnside, VIII, 165.

Fredericksburg, Va., campaign of, begun, VI, 199; the Rappahannock crossed, 202; battle of, Dec. 13, 1862, 203–208; army withdraws to Falmouth, 209; Union and Confederate loss, 210.

Free-soil Party, influence in politics, I, 352–356; address of Free-soilers in Congress, 360.

Free State Party of Kansas, beginnings of, in Lawrence, I, 427; non-conformity to bogus laws, 427–429; ex-Gov. Reeder nominated for Territorial delegate, 428; elects delegates to Constitutional Convention, 429; elects State officers under Topeka Constitution, 429, 430; mass Convention at Topeka, II, 97; refuses to vote for delegates, 100; resolves to vote at October election, 1857, 104; elects majority of legislature, 104.

Frelinghuysen, Frederick T., U. S. Sen., Sec. of State under Garfield: member of Peace Convention, III, 230.

Frelinghuysen, Theodore, U. S. Sen.: Whig nominee for Vice-President in 1844, I, 225.

Frémont, John C., U. S. Sen., Maj. Gen. U. S. A.: nominated for President, II, 32; his career, 33, 34; popular and electoral vote for, 40, 41; vote for, in Chicago Convention, 1860, on first ballot, 273; suggested for Secretary of War, III, 362; orders Grant's regiment to Missouri, IV, 294; his national prominence, 401, 402; appointed major general of U. S. army, 402; assigned to command the Western Department, 402; steamboat expedition to Cairo, 406; declares martial law and fortifies St. Louis, 411, 412; defective administration, 412; quarrel with F. P. Blair, Jr., 413, 414; proclaims military emancipation in Missouri, 416, 417; issues deeds of manumission, 417;

letter to Lincoln explaining his proclamation, 418, 419; takes the field in Missouri, 428; organizes his army in five divisions, 429; removed from command, 435; design to occupy Columbus, V, 48; reports Jackson's advance to attack him, 404; ordered to Harrisonburg, 404; promises to be at Strasburg May 31, 1862, 408; chooses wrong route, 408; explains his delay, 408, 409; pursues Jackson up the Valley, 410; battle of Cross Keys, June 8, 1862, 411; refuses to serve under Pope, 412; relieved from command, 412; commands corps in Army of Virginia, VI, 1; succeeded by Sigel, 1; reply to Sumner about colored troops, 457–459; nominated for President by Cleveland Convention, IX, 39; accepts nomination of Cleveland Convention, 41, 42; withdraws from Presidential campaign, 43, 44.

Frémont, Mrs., visit to President Lincoln, IV, 413–415; letter to Lamon, 434, 435.

French, S. G., Conf. Maj. Gen.: attack on Allatoona, IX, 473, 474.

French, William H., Bvt. Maj. Gen. U. S. A.: in battle at Fredericksburg, VI, 205; losses in his division, 206; assigned to command Third Corps, VIII, 231; crosses the Rappahannock at Kelly's Ford, 243; in movement at Mine Run, 248, 249.

Friend, Jesse, married great-aunt of the President, I, 24.

Frost, D. M., Conf. Brig. Gen.: commands Camp Jackson, IV, 209; surrenders Camp Jackson, 214.

Fry, James B., Bvt. Maj. Gen. U. S. A., Prov. Mar. Gen.: relates interview between Lincoln and Stanton, V, 145, 147; criticism of Lord Wolseley's article and Gen. McClellan, 384; report of, VII, 1; appointed provost marshal general, 6; criticisms on Enrollment Act, 41–48.

Fry, Speed S., Brig. Gen. U. S. Vols.: kills Zollicoffer in battle, V, 116, 117.

Fugitive Slave Law, origin of Act of 1793, III, 20, 21; decision of U. S. Supreme Court in 1842 concerning, 23; Webster's proposed amendment to Act of 1850, 25; Clay's proposed amendment to Act of 1850, 25; Winthrop's comment on provision of, 25, 26; bill prepared by Mason, 26; passed by Congress, 26; signed by Fillmore, 26; provisions of, 26, 27; incidents attending enforcement of, 29; declared constitutional by U. S. Supreme Court, 31; Lincoln's opinion on, 33; virtual amendment of, VI, 98.

Fugitive slaves, Constitutional provisions respecting, I, 318; active pursuit of, III, 29; Cameron's instructions to Butler about, IV, 389, 390; Lincoln's instructions to Gen. Scott about, 391; Cameron's rules about, 394; Wool's regulations about, 396; law forbidding army to return, VI, 98.

Fuller, W. P., describes origin of Wide Awakes, II, 284, 285.

Gaines, The, Conf. gunboat: burned in Mobile Bay, IX, 234.

Gaines's Mill, Va., battle of, June 27, 1862, V, 428–430.

Galena, The, Union ironclad: in battle of Mobile Bay, IX, 234.

Gamble, Hamilton R., appointed provisional governor of Missouri, IV, 225; organizes Missouri State Militia, V, 96; order creating Enrolled Missouri Militia, VI, 375; registration of rebel sympathizers, 376; general order correcting errors in enrolled militia, 376; provisional regiments organized, 377; interview with Gen. Curtis, 388; message to Convention about compensated abolishment, 392; message to legislature about emancipation, 394; conditions about colored recruiting in Missouri, 464; calls Missouri Convention together, VIII, 207; offers his resignation, 207; letter to Lincoln demanding protection for provisional State government, 226; proclamation to people of Missouri, 226, 227; death, 470.

Ganson, John, M. C.: vote for Thirteenth Amendment, X, 83.

Gantt, E. W., M. C.: made prisoner of war, VIII, 410; withdraws from secession, 410.

Gardiner, Henry C.: signs memorial about Frémont and colored troops, VI, 456.

Gardner, Franklin, Conf. Maj. Gen.: forces of, under Pemberton, VII, 164; directed to evacuate Port Hudson, 295; besieged in Port Hudson, May 25, 1863, 317; surrenders Port Hudson, July 4, 1863, 323.

Gardner, John L., Bvt. Brig. Gen. U. S. A.: commands Charleston forts, II, 343; asks reënforcements, 344; complaints concerning, 345; removed from command, 346; satisfied with Foster's temporary defenses, 441.

Gardner, Wm. M., Conf. Brig. Gen.: report on desertions, X, 151; defeated by Stoneman, 238.

Garesché, Julius P., Lieut. Col. U. S. A.: killed at Murfreesboro, VI, 289.

Garfield, James A., M. C., Maj. Gen. U. S. Vols., twentieth Pres. U. S.: votes for re-passage of National Bank Act, VI, 245; dissents from opinions of Rosecrans's council of war, VIII, 59; letter to Chase, 63, 64; in battle of Chickamauga, 102; approves Lincoln's message, IX, 109.

Garnett, Richard B., Conf. Brig. Gen.: strength of brigade after Antietam, VI, 143.

Garnett, Robert S., Conf. Brig. Gen.: sent to western Virginia, IV, 332, 333; fortifies Laurel Hill and Rich Mountain, 333; commands pass at Laurel Hill, 333; retreat, 336; killed at Carrick's Ford, 337.

Garrard, James, Gov. of Ky.: patent of lands to Abraham Lincoln, the President's grandfather, I, 11.

Garrard, J. H., member of committee to distribute Union arms, IV, 237.

Garrett, J. W., Pres. of B. & O. R. R.: telegram from, II, 131; in charge of funeral cortège of Lincoln, X, 319.

Garrison, William Lloyd, editor of "The Liberator": anti-slavery editorials of, I, 148.

Gartrell, L. J., M. C.: signs secession address, II, 436.

Gasset, Manuel, Span. Gen.: commands troops of Spanish expedition to Mexico, VI, 41.

Gaulden, W. B., speech in Charleston Convention, II, 268.

Gay, Thomas S., U. S. N.: in expedition against the *Albemarle*, X, 47.

Geary, John W., Gov. of Kas. Ter., Bvt. Maj. Gen. U. S. Vols., Gov. Penn.: appointed governor of Kansas, II, 9; arrival at Leavenworth, 11; letter to Secretary Marcy, 11, 12; inaugural address, 13; proclamations disbanding Missourians, 13; military measures of, 14–20; speech to Border Ruffians, 16; vetoes the Convention Act, 91; resignation of, 91; flight in disguise, 91; in march on Lookout Valley, VIII, 125; engagement in Lookout Valley, 126; in battle of Chattanooga, 140–143, 152; in battles of Dallas, IX, 18; in March to the Sea, 481.

Gentry, James, employs Lincoln to go to New Orleans, I, 44.

Gentry, Meredith P., M. C.: suggested for the Cabinet, III, 364.

Georgia, State of, popular vote at Presidential election, 1860, III, 189; electors chosen by legislature, 189; military appropriation, 190 ; Convention bill passed, 190; election for delegates, 190 ; seizure of Fort Pulaski ordered, 190; meeting of Convention, 190; secession ordinance passed, Jan. 19, 1861, 191; seizure of Augusta arsenal by Gov. Brown, 191 ; contest in, over secession, III, 266 ; speeches of Toombs and others at Milledgeville, 266 ; Stephens's Union speech in reply, 266; platform of 1850, 269; Fort Pulaski captured by Union army, April 11, 1862, V, 250 ; Brunswick occupied by Union troops, 251; battles of Resaca, May 13–16, 1864, IX, 13, 14; battles of Dallas, May 25 to June 4, 1864, 17–19; battles of Kenesaw Mountain, June 9–30, 1864, 19–25; battle of Peach Tree Creek, July 20, 1864, 269; siege of Atlanta, July 22 to Sept. 1, 1864, 270–289; Sherman occupies Atlanta, 289; siege of Savannah, Dec. 10–20, 1864, 487–492; Sherman occupies Savannah, Dec. 21, 1864, 492; ratifies Thirteenth Amendment, X, 89; capture of Jefferson Davis, May 10, 1865, 270–274.

Georgia, The, Conf. cruiser: commanded by Wm. L. Maury, IX, 137, 138 ; captured by the *Niagara*, 138.

German Reformed Synod, resolutions supporting the war, VI, 318.

Getty, George W., Bvt. Maj. Gen. U. S. A. : member of advisory board to reëxamine Porter court-martial case, VI, 13 ; in Army of Potomac, VIII, 353 ; wounded in battle of the Wilderness, 362, 363 ; sent to Washington, IX, 164; skirmish near Washington, 172 ; in battle of Cedar Creek, 320, 321, 323, 324.

Gettysburg, Penn., situation of, VII, 236–238 ; battle of, July 1–3, 1863, 239–268 ; dedication of cemetery, Nov. 19, 1863, VIII, 191–202.

Geyer, Henry S., U. S. Sen.: argument in Dred Scott case, II, 64.

Gibbon, John, Bvt. Maj. Gen. U. S. A.: in battle of Chancellorsville, VII, 106; wounded at Gettysburg, 269; in Army of Potomac, VIII, 353; in battle of the Wilderness, 362; in battle of Spotsylvania, 376; in battle of Cold Harbor, 401 ; in assault on Petersburg, X, 179, 180.

Giddings, Joshua R., M. C., Consul Gen. to Canada: approves Lincoln's bill abolishing slavery in District of Columbia, I, 286; remarks on Missouri Compromise, 339; address against Nebraska bill, 360; speeches in Illinois, 369; receives votes

for Vice-President in Philadelphia Convention, II, 35; amendment to Chicago platform, 268.

Gilbert, Charles C., Brig. Gen. U. S. Vols. : command of, in Army of Kentucky, VIII, 44.

Gillespie, Joseph, anecdote of Lincoln, I, 162.

Gillmore, Quincy A., Bvt. Maj. Gen. U. S. A.: operations against Fort Pulaski, V, 249, 250; capture of Fort Pulaski, April 11, 1862, 250; appointed to relieve Gen. Hunter, VII, 85; commands Department of the South, 424, 425; correspondence with Beauregard about Gen. Hunter, 437–439 ; correspondence with Beauregard about bombardment of Charleston, 439–441; bombardment of Fort Sumter, August to October, 1863, 435, 441, 442; comments on Fort Wagner, 442, 443; resolves on expedition to Florida, VIII, 281, 282; interview with Seymour at Baldwin, 283; telegram to Seymour, 283, 284 ; directs Seymour not to advance, 284 ; ordered to Virginia, 285; commands Tenth Corps under Butler, 392, 393; in battle of Bermuda Hundred, 398; captures Charleston, X, 231; in charge of Fort Sumter flag-raising, 278, 280.

Gilmer, John A., M. C.: correspondence with Lincoln, III, 283; suggested by Seward for the Cabinet, 362; tendered Cabinet appointment through Seward, 363; promises Seward an answer, 363 ; letter to Lincoln, 364.

Gilmor, Harry, Conf. Maj.: burns Gunpowder Bridge, IX, 165.

Gilmore, J. R., obtains permission for himself and Jaquess to go South, IX, 206, 207 ; visit to Richmond, 208; interview with Davis and Benjamin, 208–211.

Gist, S. R., Conf. Brig. Gen.: sent east of Jackson, Miss., VII, 185 ; joins Johnston's army, 294.

Gist, William H., Gov. of S. C.: letter to Southern governors proposing secession, II, 306, 307 ; convenes South Carolina legislature, 328 ; message to legislature, 329 ; letter to Trescott, 379.

Gittings, ——, Pres. N. C. R. R.: tenders a dinner to Mr. Lincoln and family, III, 308.

Gladstone, William Ewart, Prime Min. of England: remarks about American war, VIII, 260, 261.

Glendale, Va., battle of, June 30, 1862, V, 435.

Glover, Samuel T., member of Union Safety Committee at St. Louis, IV, 212.

Godwin, A. C., Conf. Brig. Gen.: defeated at Rappahannock Station, VIII, 243; killed at Winchester, IX, 304.

Godwin, Parke, editor of N. Y. "Evening Post": signs memorial about Frémont and colored troops, VI, 456.

Goldsboro', N. C., occupied by Schofield, March 21, 1865, X, 70, 71; occupied by Sherman, March 23, 1865, 237.

Goldsborough, L. M., Rear Adm. U. S. N.: visited by Lincoln, Stanton, and Chase, V, 234: commands fleet in Roanoke Island expedition, 242; attacks shore batteries on Roanoke Island, Feb. 7, 1862, 243; destruction of rebel fleet, Feb. 10, 1862, 246; testimony about operations against Yorktown, 361.

Gollaher, Austin, saves Abraham Lincoln from drowning, I, 27.

Gooch, Daniel W., M. C.: member of Committee on Conduct of the War, V, 150.

Goodloe, J. K., member of committee to distribute Union arms, IV, 237.

Goodman, Edward, recommended for Collector, IX, 87.

Gordon, James B., Conf. Brig. Gen.: killed in battle of Yellow Tavern, VIII, 371.

Gordon, John B., Conf. Lieut. Gen., U. S. Sen.: in Army of Northern Virginia, VIII, 354; in battle of the Wilderness, 367; in battle of Cold Harbor, 404; in battle of Winchester, IX, 300, 301; in battle of Fisher's Hill, 306; in battle of Cedar Creek, 316, 317, 320, 322, 325; assault of Fort Stedman, X, 161–164; in defense of Petersburg, 179; in retreat to Appomattox, 186–189, 194.

Gordon, Nathaniel P., trial and execution for crime of slave-trading, VI, 99.

Gorman, Willis A., Brig. Gen. U. S. Vols.: demonstration at Edwards's Ferry, IV, 455; repulses Confederate attack, 458.

Gortschakoff, Prince Alexander Michaelowitsch, Vice-Chancellor of Russia: comment on French proposal to obtain armistice in the United States, VI, 65, 66; remarks to Bayard Taylor, 66.

Gosport Navy Yard, Va.: measures for protection of, IV, 145; burning of, 147.

Gott, Daniel, M. C.: resolution about slave trade in the District of Columbia, I, 286.

Gourdin, Robert N., circular of The 1860 Association, II, 305.

Grady, Henry W., editor of Atlanta "Constitution": eulogy of Lincoln, X, 350.

Graham, Charles K., Bvt. Maj. Gen. U. S. Vols.: wounded and captured at Gettysburg, VII, 255.

Graham, Menton, assists Lincoln to study surveying, I, 115.

Graham, William M., Bvt. Brig. Gen. U. S. A.: testimony about Gettysburg, VII, 269.

Grammar, John, member of Illinois legislature, I, 65.

Granbury, H. B., Conf. Brig. Gen.: in march to Franklin, X, 10.

Grand Gulf, Miss., bombardment of, April 29, 1863, VII, 167.

Granger, Gordon, Bvt. Maj. Gen. U. S. A.: commands Army of Kentucky, VIII, 44; drives Bragg's rearguard out of Shelbyville, 62; in battle of Chickamauga, 101; in battle of Chattanooga, 135; ordered to Knoxville, 154; in Sherman's march to Knoxville, 182; enters Knoxville under Sherman, 183; lands troops at Mobile Bay, IX, 230; in siege of Mobile Bay, 240.

Granger, R. S., Bvt. Maj. Gen. U. S. A.: checks Hood at Decatur, X, 5.

Grant, Lewis A., Bvt. Maj. Gen. U. S. Vols.: in battle of Cedar Creek, IX, 321.

Grant, Mrs., invited by Mrs. Lincoln to Ford's Theater, X, 292.

Grant, U. S., Gen. and Gen. in Chief U. S. A., eighteenth Pres. of U. S.: arrives in Springfield, IV, 286; declines captaincy of Galena company, 287; employed at special duties, 287, 288; letter offering his services, 289; biographical notice of, 290–292; goes to visit McClellan, 292; appointed colonel of the 21st Illinois Volunteers, 293; his march from Springfield, 295, 296; occupies Paducah, V, 49; ordered to make a demonstration in Tennessee, 104; reconnoitres Fort Henry, 106; personal characteristics, 111; early military duties in Missouri, 112; commands at Cairo, 112; ordered to clear southeast Missouri of rebels, 112; battle of Belmont, Nov. 7, 1861, 113, 114; plan to attack Fort Henry, 119, 120; capture of Fort Henry, Feb. 6, 1862, 120–122; intention to capture and destroy Fort Donelson, 187; delayed by high water, 192; invests Fort Donelson, Feb. 12, 1862, 193; conference with Foote, 196; asks Foote to renew gunboat attack, 197; orders charge by Smith's division, 197; demands "unconditional surrender," 199; receives surrender

Grant, U. S. — *continued.*

of Fort Donelson, Feb. 16, 1862, 200; report of capture, 200; appointed major general of U. S. volunteers, 200; occupies Clarksville, 310; sends Nelson to occupy Nashville, 311; ordered to command expedition up the Tennessee, 311; ordered to remain at Fort Henry, 312; ordered to resume his command, 312; assumes command, 320; neglects proper precautions, 320; ignorance of rebel advance; reports main Confederate army at Corinth, 322; position of his divisions, 323; learns of arrival of Nelson's division of Buell's army, 328; goes to Pittsburg Landing on morning of April 6, 1862, 329; directions about the battle, 329; requests Buell's advance to come to the battlefield, 329; orders Lew Wallace to the battlefield, 329; controversy about intentions of, 331; interview with Buell, 334; attacks the enemy, April 7, 1862, 334; defeat and retreat of Confederates, 334; assigned to command right wing of Halleck's army, 337; assigned to duty as second in command under Halleck, 337; asks to be relieved from duty, 337; action on Porter court-martial case, VI, 12, 13; order expelling Jews from his Department, 339; letter to Lincoln about negro troops, 466; assigned to command in West Tennessee, VII, 112; sends Rosecrans and Ord to attack Iuka, 113; suggests to Halleck movement in rear of Vicksburg, 119; correspondence with Halleck about campaigns, 122, 123; arranges plan of operations with Sherman, 123; marches to Grenada, Miss., 124; proposes river expedition against Vicksburg, 124; appoints Sherman to command Vicksburg expedition, 125; returns to Holly Springs and Memphis, 127, 128; orders McClernand to return to Mississippi, 140, 141; controversy with McClernand, 141-143; divides his army into army corps, 144; prepares for the Vicksburg campaign, 146; supersedes McClernand in command of Vicksburg expedition, 146; failure of the Vicksburg canal, 146, 147; failure of the Lake Providence route, 147, 148; failure of the Yazoo Pass route, 148, 149; failure of the Steele's Bayou route, 150-152; resolves to join Banks, 153; marches to De Schroon's, 167, 168; orders for his march, 169; crosses the Mississippi to Bruinsburg, 169; orders McPherson to Willow Springs, 172; rides to Grand Gulf, 173; announces his campaign against Vicksburg, 174; engagement at Raymond, May 12, 1863, 177, 178; battle of Jackson, May 14, 1863, 182, 183; censure of McClernand, 183; march to Edwards's Station, 187; battle of Champion's Hill, May 16, 1863, 189-192; battle of the Big Black, May 17, 1863, 192; arrives before Vicksburg, 195, 196; first assault on Vicksburg, May 19, 1863, 282, 283; second assault on Vicksburg, May 22, 1863, 283-288; relieves McClernand from command, 288; assigns Ord to succeed McClernand, 288; siege of Vicksburg, May 22 to July 4, 1863, 288-305; interview with Pemberton, 303; letter to Pemberton proposing terms of surrender, 304, 305; occupies Vicksburg, 305-307; prisoners captured at Vicksburg, 306-310; correspondence with Banks about coöperation, 315-317; made major general in U. S. army, 325; instructions to Butler about exchange of prisoners, 461; suggestions to Rosecrans, VIII, 45; meets Stanton at Indianapolis, 119; assigned to command Military Division of the Mississippi, 119; telegraphs Thomas to hold Chattanooga, 120; statement about Rosecrans, 121; interview with Rosecrans, 122; orders Smith's plan carried out, 123; orders Thomas to attack Missionary Ridge, 129; revokes the order, 130; plans of battle, 133; battle of Chattanooga, Nov. 23-25, 1863, 134-157; correspondence with Burnside about Longstreet, 173; directions to Banks, 290; plans in Tennessee, 329, 330; orders to Thomas, 332; interview with Foster, 332; appointed lieutenant general, 335; goes to Washington, 336; letter of thanks to Sherman and McPherson, 336, 337; interview with Lincoln, 340, 341; reply on receiving his commission as lieutenant general, 342; conversation with Lincoln about his duties, 343; visits Gen. Meade, 344; returns to the West, 344, 345; establishes headquarters at Culpeper Court House, 347; visits Washington, 347; erroneous statement about Lincoln, 347, 348; plan of, 348-351; strength of Army of Potomac, 352; reply to Lincoln's letter, 355; begins Virginia campaign, May 4, 1864, 357; crosses the Rappahannock, 357, 358; battle of the Wilderness, May 5, 6, 1864, 360-367; begins march to Spotsylvania, 368; position at Spotsylvania, 369, 370; battle of Spotsylvania, May 8-19, 1864, 372-385; dispatch to Halleck, "I propose to fight it out on this line," 378, 379; telegrams to Halleck, 382, 383; battle of North Anna, May 23-27, 1864, 387-390; telegram to Halleck, 389, 390; battle of Cold Harbor, June 1-12, 1864, 391, 400-405; orders to Butler, 392; comment on battle of Cold Harbor, 405, 406; dispatch to Halleck about campaign, 406, 407; instructions to Sherman, IX, 1, 2; sends Sixth Corps to Washington, 164; recalls troops to Petersburg, 174; asks a call for 300,000 men, 176; suggests Franklin and Meade for command of Middle Military Division, 179; sends Sheridan north on temporary duty, 179; instructs Sheridan to put himself "south of the enemy," 179; interview with Hunter and Sheridan at Monocacy, 180-182; notifies Sheridan that Early is reënforced, 293, 294; visits Sheridan, 299; comment on Sheridan, 326; movement across James River, 406, 407; begins siege of Petersburg, June 19, 1864, 412; comment on assault at Petersburg mine, 425; siege of Richmond, 427; correspondence with Sherman, 468, 469, 478, 479; advises Sherman to move north by water, 490; orders removal of Thomas, X, 24; sends Logan to relieve Thomas, 28; starts for Nashville, 28; orders for first Fort Fisher expedition, 59, 60; relieves Butler from command, 64; sends second expedition to Fort Fisher, 65; interview with Peace Commissioners, 114-116; telegram to Stanton, 117; telegraphs Lee's proposition to Stanton, 158; reply to Lee's proposition, 158, 159; orders for march to Five Forks, 164, 167; officers and forces of, 165-167; march to Five Forks, 169-172; battle of Five Forks, April 1, 1865, 172-174; assault at Petersburg, April 2, 1865, 175-181; orders to Sheridan and Humphreys, 181; telegrams to Lincoln, 181, 182; march to Appomattox, 183-195; asks Lee to surrender, 190; proposes to receive Lee's surrender, 192; informs Lee, "I have no authority to treat on the subject of peace," 193; interview with Lee at Appomattox, 195; receives Lee's surrender, April 9, 1865, 195-197; farewell visit to Lee, 197, 198; return to Washington, 198; reply to Lincoln about his son, 214; interview with Lincoln, Sherman, and Porter, 215; interview with Lincoln at Petersburg, 216; at Cabinet meeting about Sherman's agreement, 250; sent to Sherman's headquarters, 250; at Cabinet meeting, April 14, 1865, 281;

invited by Mrs. Lincoln to Ford's Theater, 292; eulogy of Lincoln at Springfield, 325; at grand review in Washington, 331; eulogy of Lincoln, 353.

Granville, Earl, protests against an offer of mediation to the United States, VI, 67.

Greeley, Horace, editor of N. Y. "Tribune," M. C.: explains opposition to Clay, I, 229; attacked in the street at Washington, II, 52; favors reëlection of Douglas, 139; letter about the Illinois campaign, 140, 141; present at Lincoln's Cooper Institute speech, 217; delegate for Oregon in Charleston Convention, 1860, 264; editorials on secession, III, 253, 254; letter to Lincoln, 258; letter to Lincoln about Bull Run, IV, 366; suggests French mediation to Mercier, VI, 83, 84; criticism of Lincoln in N. Y. "Tribune," 151, 152; signs memorial about Frémont and colored troops, 456; opposes Lincoln's renomination, IX, 64; approves Lincoln's message, 110; letter to Lincoln about peace, 186, 187; suggests that Clay and Thompson desire to confer about peace, 188, 189; goes to Niagara Falls, 190; proposes to accompany commissioners to Lincoln, 190, 191; interview with Confederate emissaries, 193; interview with Jewett, 193; correspondence with Lincoln about the Niagara affair, 195-199; interview with F. P. Blair, Sr., 248; becomes Jefferson Davis's bail, X, 275.

Green, Duff, visit to Lincoln, III, 286.

Green, James S., M. C., Min. to Bogota, U. S. Sen.: Senate discussion, II, 406, 407.

Green, Martin E., Conf. Brig. Gen.: in battle of Corinth, VII, 117; ordered to Grand Gulf, 169; in battle of Port Gibson, 170.

Green, Thomas, Conf. Brig. Gen.: in attack on Brashear City, VII, 321; repulsed at Donaldsonville, 321; in battle of Sabine Cross Roads, VIII, 293; attack on Red River fleet defeated, 296.

Greene, S. D., Commander U. S. N.: directs firing in turret of the Monitor, V, 229; succeeds Worden in command, 231.

Greene, William G., buys store of Radford, I, 110.

Greer, James A., Capt. U. S. N.: officer of the San Jacinto, V, 24.

Gregg, David McM., Bvt. Maj. Gen. U. S. Vols.: cavalry battle at Brandy Station, June 9, 1863, VII, 205, 206; cavalry successes under, 215; in battle of Gettysburg, 268; in Army of Potomac, VIII, 353; in battle of the Wilderness, 363; in battle of Yellow Tavern, 371; in siege of Petersburg, IX, 429, 430; in battle of Hatcher's Run, 433, 434.

Gregg, J. Irvin, Bvt. Maj. Gen. U. S. Vols.: captured in march to Appomattox, X, 189.

Gregg, John, Conf. Brig. Gen.: in engagement at Raymond, VII, 177; in battle of Chickamauga, VIII, 106.

Gregory, Dudley S., proposed for Assistant Treasurer at New York, IX, 93.

Grey, Sir George, M. P., Home Secretary: protest against proposition of mediation to the United States, VI, 67; speech on Lincoln's death, X, 342.

Grider, Henry, M. C.: votes for Wilmot Proviso, I, 269; second interview with Lincoln about compensated emancipation, VI, 111.

Grier, Robert C., Assoc. Justice U. S. Sup. Ct.: opinion in the Dred Scott case, II, 72.

Grierson, B. H., Bvt. Maj. Gen. U. S. A.: cavalry raid in Mississippi, VII, 162–164.

Griffin, Charles, Bvt. Maj. Gen. U. S. A.: in battle of Fredericksburg VI, 206; in Army of Potomac, 353; in battle of the Wilderness, 361; in attack on Petersburg, IX, 411; in battle of Five Forks, X, 172; in march to Appomattox, 194; at grand review in Washington, 332.

Grigsby, Aaron, brother-in-law of Pres. Lincoln, I, 45.

Grimes, James W., Gov. of Iowa, U. S. Sen.: member of Senate Committee of Thirteen, II, 414; moves appointment of Committee on Conduct of the War, V, 150; present at interview between Lincoln, Cabinet, and Republican Senators, VI, 266; favors dismissal of Seward, 266.

Grinnell, Moses H., authorized to organize troops, IV, 138.

Griswold, John A., M. C.: first vote for Thirteenth Amendment, X, 78; second vote for Thirteenth Amendment, 83.

Groesbeck, William S., M. C.: recommends McClellan for command at Cincinnati, IV, 282.

Grose, William, Bvt. Maj. Gen. U. S. Vols.: in battle of Chattanooga, VIII, 141.

Grover, Cuvier, Bvt. Maj. Gen. U. S. A.: sent to occupy Baton Rouge, VII, 313; in Sheridan's army, IX, 182; in battle of Winchester, 301.

Groveton, Va., engagement at, Aug. 29, 1862, VI, 9.

Grow, Galusha A., Speaker of H. R.: elected Speaker of House of Representatives in Thirty-seventh Congress, IV, 370.

Gurley, John A., M. C.: letter to Lincoln, III, 254.

Gurley, Rev. Dr. P. D., present at Lincoln's deathbed, X, 300; address at Lincoln's funeral at Washington, 318.

Guthrie, James, Sec. of Treas. under Pierce, U. S. Sen.: voted for in Charleston Convention, II, 244; member of Peace Convention, III, 230; chairman of leading committee in Peace Convention, 231; recommends Sherman's retention in Kentucky, V, 64, 65; chairman of Platform Committee of Democratic National Convention, 1864, IX, 256, 257; receives votes for Vice-President at Chicago Convention, 258, 259.

Guthrie, James V., Col. U. S. Vols.: establishes Camp Clay, IV, 239.

Gwin, William M., M. C., U. S. Sen.: supports demand for a Congressional Slave Code, II, 175; reported emigration scheme of, VII, 420.

Gwynn, Walter, Conf. Col.: ordered to prepare a plan to reduce Fort Sumter, III, 124.

Habeas corpus, case of John Merryman, IV, 174–177; Lincoln's conditional order to suspend at St. Louis, 212; Merryman case reviewed by Atty. Gen. Bates, VIII, 28; opinion on, by Theophilus Parsons, 29; treatise on, by Joel Parker, 29; pamphlet on, by Horace Binney, 29–31; bill to suspend, introduced by Thaddeus Stevens, 34; Act authorizing President to suspend, passed March 3, 1863, 35; proclamation of President suspending, 37–39; Act suspending, passed by Confederate Congress, 42.

Hahn, Michael, M. C., Gov. of La.: elected to Congress, VI, 353; admitted to a seat, 353; elected governor of Louisiana, VIII, 432–434; appointed military governor of Louisiana, 434.

Haight, Edward, M. C.: signs memorial about Frémont and colored troops, VI, 456.

Hale, John P., U. S. Sen., Min. to Spain: leaves Democratic party, I, 277; Senate discussion, II, 403, 406.

Hall, A. Oakey, New York Dist. Atty.: action about suppression of "World" and "Journal of Commerce," IX, 49, 50.

Hall, A. S., Col. U. S. Vols.: defeats Morgan, VIII, 50.

Hall, Rev. Charles H., reads burial service at Lincoln's funeral at Washington, X, 317.

Hall, Levi, marries great-aunt of Lincoln, I, 24.

Hall, Mrs. Levi, step-sister of Pres. Lincoln, I, 45.

Hall, Norman J., Bvt. Lieut. Col. U. S. A.: commander of schooner employed in the transfer to Fort Sumter, III, 50; sent to Washington by Maj. Anderson, 113.

Hall, Willard P., M. C., Lieut. Gov. of Mo.: supports first Nebraska bill, I, 338; appoints Robert Wilson and J. B. Henderson U. S. Senators, VIII, 469.

Hall, William A., M. C.: second interview with Lincoln about compensated emancipation, VI, 111; opposes bill to aid Missouri emancipation, 396.

Halleck, Henry Wager, Maj. Gen. and Gen. in Chief U. S. A.: assigned to command Department of Missouri, V, 81: complains of Lane's men, 83; biographical sketch, 85, 86; correspondence with Price, 90; orders Curtis to pursue Price, 92, 93; issues Order No. Three, 94; explains Order No. Three, 95; reply to Lincoln about coöperation, 100; letters to Lincoln and Buell about Western campaign, 102, 103; directs Grant to demonstrate against Mayfield and Murray, 104; suggests Tennessee movement to McClellan, 109; orders attack on Fort Henry, 120; views about Tennessee movement, 186, 187; calls on Buell for assistance, 188; reply to McClellan about Tennessee movement, 189; asks for command in the West, 200; orders Curtis not to penetrate further into Arkansas, 290; informs Pope of Union success at Shiloh, 299; interview with Asst. Sec. Scott, 299; orders Pope up the Tennessee River, 300; directs Foote to bombard Fort Pillow, 301; asks Buell to take command on the Cumberland, 306; appeals urgently to him for help, 306; asks McClellan for superior command in the West, 307; asks McClellan, "May I assume command?" 307; receives refusal from McClellan, 308; receives complimentary dispatch from Stanton, 308; asks Stanton for control of Buell's army, 309, 310; receives answer that Lincoln decides against any change, 309; orders Grant to command expedition up the Tennessee, 311; accusations against Grant, 312; orders Grant to remain at Fort Henry, 312; assigns C. F. Smith to command Tennessee expedition, 312; orders Grant to resume his command, 312; asks Buell to come to the Tennessee, 313; reports preparations for the Tennessee expedition, 314; complains to McClellan of his refusal to give him command, 314; assigned to command the three Western Departments, 316; assumes command, March 13, 1862, 317; orders Buell to move by land to the Tennessee, 317; arrives at Shiloh, 337; organizes his army, 337; assigns Grant to duty as second in command, 337; assigns Thomas to command right wing, 337; assigns McClernand to command reserve corps, 337; telegraphs Stanton, "We are now at the enemy's throat," 339; letter to Stanton, "We are operating on too many points," 340; report about prisoners at Corinth, 340; replies to Farragut that he cannot send him troops, 349; replies to Stanton that he cannot aid Farragut at Vicksburg, 350; cessation of military activity, 351; transmits McPherson's report about railroad repairs, 352; telegram protesting against sending troops to the East, 354; made general-in-chief, 355; assumes chief command, July 23, 1862, 455; visits McClellan, 455; instructions to McClellan, 455, 456; orders McClellan's withdrawal from the James, 457-459; appointment to chief command favored by Scott, Stanton, and Pope, VI, 2; orders about battle of second Bull Run, 17-21; telegrams to McClellan about Pope's movements, 20; interview with Lincoln and McClellan, 21; effect of his Order No. Three, 98; instructions to McClellan, 134, 135; transmits Lincoln's instructions of Oct. 6, 1862, to McClellan, 175, 176; answer to McClellan's complaint about supplies, 178; writes McClellan there is a want of legs in his army, 179; transmits Lincoln's instructions of Oct. 21, 1862, to McClellan, 184; directs McClellan to use his own discretion, 184, 185; visit to Burnside, 198; comments on Burnside's movement, 199; sends encouraging letter to Burnside after Fredericksburg, 211; dispatch to Burnside to occupy and press the enemy, 214; asks to be relieved as general-in-chief, 215; withdraws his request, 215; indefinite answer to Burnside, 217; instruction to Schofield to "take care of Missouri," 368;

refuses Schofield independent command in Missouri, 368; letter to Schofield about Missouri, 381, 382; returns letter of Gen. Lee as being "insulting to the United States," 470, 471; approves Grant's campaign in rear of Richmond, VII, 119; promises Grant large reënforcements, 122; correspondence with Grant about campaigns, 122, 123; approves river expedition against Vicksburg, 124, 125; transmits Lincoln's order assigning McClernand to the Vicksburg expedition, 126; authorizes Grant to relieve McClernand, 141; answer to Hooker's questions, 205; misunderstandings with Hooker, 212, 214; refuses to abandon Maryland Heights, 225; urges Meade to pursue and attack Lee, 274; telegraphs Meade, "Do not let the enemy escape," 277; criticism of Gen. Banks, 314; praises Grant, 326; offers Lee equivalents for all Union prisoners in Richmond, 460; letter about promotion, VIII, 48; letter to Rosecrans about using the telegraph, 49; answer to Rosecrans about forward movement, 60, 61; orders junction between Rosecrans and Burnside, 81; warning to Rosecrans, 82; orders Burnside towards Chattanooga, 83; advises Rosecrans to give up Chattanooga, 83; at council of war, 112; orders Burnside to connect with Rosecrans, 164; letter to Schofield, 205; at military conference, 236; urges Red River movement, 286; proposes plan for Red River campaign, 288; asks to be relieved from duties of general-in-chief, 342, 343; advises pursuit of Early, IX, 173; telegram to Grant suggesting reënforcements for Sheridan, 298; controversy with Blair, 338; approves Sherman's course at Atlanta, 467; declines to remove Thomas, X, 24; appointed commander of Armies of the Potomac and James, 254; present at Lincoln's deathbed, 300; commands Military Division of the Pacific, 338.

Hamilton, Andrew J., M. C., Prov. Gov. of Texas: member of House Committee of Thirty-Three, II, 417; persuades Banks to send an expedition to Texas, VII, 313.

Hamilton, D. H., interview with Buchanan, III, 4.

Hamilton, Schuyler, Maj. Gen. U. S. Vols.: claims idea of canal at Island No. 10, V, 296.

Hamlin, Hannibal, U. S. Sen., Vice-Pres. with Lincoln: agrees upon the Wilmot Proviso, I, 268; reminiscence about first Nebraska bill, 350; nominated for Vice-President, II, 277; public services, 277, 278; interview with Lincoln, III, 347; receives votes for Vice-President at Baltimore Convention, IX, 72–74.

Hampton, L. J., goes to Kansas, I, 448.

Hampton, Wade, Conf. Lieut. Gen., U. S. Sen.: in army of Northern Virginia, VIII, 354; defeated at Trevilian Station, IX, 405; retreat to Fayetteville, X, 233; engagement with Kilpatrick, 234.

Hampton Roads Conference between Lincoln and Peace Commissioners, Feb. 3, 1865, X, 118–129; Lincoln's message about, Feb. 10, 1865, 137, 138.

Hancock, Winfield S., Maj. Gen. U. S. A.: in battle of Williamsburg, V, 377; orders for Hermann Haupt, VI, 15; in battle of Fredericksburg, 205; losses in his division, 206; in battle of Chancellorsville, VII, 93, 96; in battle of Gettysburg, 243, 244, 246, 250, 258, 266; wounded at Gettysburg, 269; commands Second Corps, Army of the Potomac, VIII, 353; crosses the Rappahannock, 357, 358; in battle of the Wilderness, 360, 362–364, 366; in battle of Spotsylvania, 374, 376, 377, 379–381, 385; in battle of North Anna, 387, 389; in battle of Cold Harbor, 391, 401; in attack on Petersburg, IX, 410, 411; in siege of Richmond, 427; in siege of Petersburg, 429, 430; in battle of Hatcher's Run, 433–435; made Department commander, X, 338.

Hanks, Dennis, emigrates to Illinois, I, 45.

Hanks, Mrs. Dennis, step-sister of Pres. Lincoln, I, 45.

Hanks, John, emigrates to Illinois, I, 45; goes to Springfield with Lincoln, 70; assists to build a flatboat, 70; flatboat voyage to New Orleans, 72; appearance in the Decatur Convention, II, 283.

Hanks, Lucy, grandmother of Pres. Lincoln, I, 24.

Hanks, Nancy, mother of Pres. Lincoln: marries Thomas Lincoln, June 12, 1806, I, 23. See also LINCOLN, NANCY.

Hansell, ——, wounded by Payne, X, 305.

Hansen, Nicholas, claimant for seat in Illinois legislature, I, 143.

Hardee, William J., Lieut. Col. U. S. A., Conf. Lieut. Gen.: sent to drill and review camp of instruction for Gov. Letcher of Virginia, III, 128; inspects camp of instruction in Virginia, 418; sent to Bowling Green, V, 56; attends council of war at

Bowling Green, 185; retreats to Nashville, 186; commands Confederate center at Pittsburg Landing, 321; attacked by Buell's advance at Perryville, VI, 278; in battle of Murfreesboro, 282; in battle of Chattanooga, VIII, 145, 152; march to Kingston, IX, 15; in battles of Dallas, 18, 19; in battles of Kenesaw, 21; requests suspension of order removing Johnston, 265-267; in battle of Peach Tree Creek, 269; in battles of Atlanta, 270-274, 286-288; placed in command of South Carolina and Florida, 472; defense of Savannah, Dec. 10-20, 1864, 487-492; declines to surrender Savannah, 491, 492; evacuates Savannah, Dec. 20, 21, 1864, 492; evacuates Charleston, X, 231; occupies Cheraw, 232; retreat to Fayetteville, 233; defeated by Slocum, 234.

Hardie, James A., Bvt. Maj. Gen. U. S. A.: carries orders for battle to Franklin at Fredericksburg, VI, 203; carries order appointing Meade to command, VII, 226; at council of war, VIII, 112.

Hardin, John J., M. C., Col. U. S. Vols.: mediator in the Lincoln-Shields duel, I, 207; elected to Congress, 222; commands regiment in Mexican war, 250; withdraws from canvass for nomination to Congress, 255; regiment of, at battle of Buena Vista, II, 26.

Harding, ——, Capt. Ill. militia: stationed at Big Muddy Bridge, IV, 194, 195.

Harding, Aaron, M. C.: second interview with Lincoln about compensated emancipation, VI, 111.

Harding, George, associated with Lincoln in a law case, V, 133, 134.

Harker, Charles G., Brig. Gen. U. S. Vols.: in battle of Murfreesboro, VI, 287, 289; in battle of Chickamauga, VIII, 98; in battle of Chattanooga, 148, 153; assault on Rocky Face, IX, 11; killed at Kenesaw Mountain, 23.

Harlan, J., member of committee to distribute Union arms, IV, 237.

Harlan, James, U. S. Sen., Sec. of Int. under Lincoln and Johnson: member of Peace Convention, III, 230; presents address of Quakers of Iowa to Lincoln, VI, 327.

Harmon, Oscar F., Col. U. S. Vols.: killed at Kenesaw Mountain, IX, 23.

Harnden, Henry, Bvt. Brig. Gen. U. S. A.: in capture of Jefferson Davis, X, 269, 270.

Harney, William S., Bvt. Maj. Gen. U. S. A.: concentrates troops at St. Louis arsenal, III, 135; refuses arms to Gov. Yates, IV, 198; relieved from command in Missouri, 209; restored to command, 215; loyal proclamation, 217, 218; agreement with Price, 219; relieved from command, 222.

Harper's Ferry, Va., John Brown's raid, II, 205-208; U. S. armory burned, IV, 122; capture of, Sept. 15, 1862, VI, 137.

Harriet Lane, The, Union gunboat: captured at Galveston, VII, 313.

Harrington, F. C., Capt. U. S. Vols.: crosses Warwick River with 400 men, V, 369.

Harris, Benjamin G., M. C.: votes against resolutions to support the war, VII, 395.

Harris, Miss Clara W., attends Ford's Theater with Mrs. Lincoln, X, 292.

Harris, Ira, U. S. Sen.: votes for National Bank Act, VI, 244; present at interview between Lincoln, Cabinet, and Republican Senators, 266.

Harris, Isham G., M. C., Gov. of Tenn., U. S. Sen.: answers Lincoln's call for troops, IV, 90; letter to Lincoln, 196; secession action of, 250; convenes legislature, 250; reply to Lincoln's proclamation, 250; convenes legislature a second time, 251; protests against rebel invasion of Kentucky, V, 44; asks reënforcements to hold East Tennessee, 59; dispatch about Union rising, 76; seeks the protection of Maximilian, VII, 420.

Harris, Rev. Matthias, U. S. chaplain: offers prayer at Sumter flag-raising, X, 278.

Harris, Thomas L., M. C.: candidate for Congress, I, 373.

Harris, Thomas M., Bvt. Maj. Gen. U. S. Vols.: member of military commission for trial of Lincoln's assassins, X, 312.

Harris, William L., Secession Comr. of Miss.: address before legislature of Georgia, III, 202.

Harrison, Benjamin, Bvt. Brig. Gen. U. S. Vols., twenty-third Pres. U. S.: in battle of Peach Tree Creek, IX, 269.

Harrison, Burton N., Priv. Sec. to Jefferson Davis: captured with Jefferson Davis, X, 273, 274.

Harrison, George M., statement about Iles's company, I, 94; takes canoe to Pekin, 98.

Harrison, N. B., Capt. U. S. N.: commands the Cayuga in Farragut's fleet, V, 261.

Harrison, William G., elected to Maryland legislature, IV, 165.

Harrison, William Henry, ninth Pres. U. S.: campaign for President, 1840, I, 172-178; elected President, 183.

Harrow, William, Brig. Gen. U. S. Vols.: in battles of Atlanta, IX, 286.

Hart, ——, guides Union troops at Rich Mountain, IV, 334.

Hartford, The, Union cruiser: in battle of Mobile Bay, IX, 231, 233, 234, 236.

Hartranft, John F., Bvt. Maj. Gen. U. S. Vols.: in recapture of Fort Stedman, X, 162, 163.

Hartstene, Henry J., Commander U. S. N., Commander Conf. navy: introduces Fox to Gov. Pickens, III, 389; accompanies Fox to Sumter, 389; report to Beauregard, IV, 43.

Hartsuff, George L., Bvt. Maj. Gen. U. S. A.: wounded at Antietam, VI, 142; in march to East Tennessee, VIII, 162.

Harvey, James E., Min. to Portugal: dispatch to Magrath, IV, 31, 32.

Haskell, Frank A., Col. U. S. Vols.: killed at Cold Harbor, VIII, 405.

Haskell, William T., Col. U. S. Vols., M. C.: colonel in Mexican war, I, 260.

Hatch, Edward, Bvt. Maj. Gen. U. S. A.: in Grierson's cavalry raid, VII, 163; in battle of Nashville, X, 30.

Hatch, John P., Bvt. Maj. Gen. U. S. Vols.: repulsed by Smith, IX, 487.

Hatch, O. M., relates Lincoln's criticism of McClellan, VI, 175.

Hatcher's Run, Va., battle of, Oct. 27, 1864, IX, 433–435.

Hathaway, Lee, Conf. Lieut.: captured with Jefferson Davis, X, 274.

Hatteras, The, Union excursion boat: sunk by the *Alabama*, VI, 56.

Hatteras Inlet, N. C., expedition against, V, 12; capture of forts at, Aug. 29, 1861, 13.

Haupt, Hermann, Brig. Gen. U. S. Vols.: interview with McClellan, VI, 14, 15; orders from Gen. Hancock, 15.

Hawes, Richard, inaugurated Confederate governor at Frankfort, Ky., VI, 277, 278.

Hawkins, George S., M. C.: House discussion, II, 416–418; member of House Committee of Thirty-three, 417; signs secession address, 436; refuses to attend meetings of House Committee of Thirty-three, III, 214.

Hawley, Joseph R., Bvt. Maj. Gen. U. S. Vols., U. S. Sen.: information about Wide Awakes, II, 284; in battle of Olustee, VIII, 284, 285.

Hay, John, Asst. Priv. Sec. to Pres. Lincoln, Bvt. Col. and Asst. Adj. Gen. U. S. Vols.: member of Lincoln's suite, III, 290; mission to Rosecrans about alleged plot of American Knights, VIII, 11–13; obtains leave to join Gillmore's expedition, 282; commissioned major and assistant adjutant general, 282; charged with duties about reconstruction, 283; writes safeconduct for Clay, Thompson, Holcombe, and Sanders, IX, 190; interview with Greeley and Confederate emissaries, 193; present at Lincoln's deathbed, X, 300.

Hay, Milton, account of law practice in Springfield, I, 167–169; anecdote about Lincoln, 171, 172; prominent lawyer of Illinois, 214.

Hayes, Rutherford B., Bvt. Maj. Gen. U. S. Vols., nineteenth Pres. U. S.: recommends McClellan for command at Cincinnati, IV, 282; orders Porter court-martial case reexamined, VI, 13; wounded at South Mountain, 137; in battle of Cedar Creek, IX, 317; anecdote of, X, 286, 287.

Hayne, I. W., S. C. Atty. Gen.: sent to Washington by Gov. Pickens, III, 113; calls on Buchanan, 153; withholds Gov. Pickens's letter, 155; reply to secession Senators, 156; correspondence with Senators sent to the President, 159, 160; refers Holt's reply to Gov. Pickens, 162; resumes his mission, 170; letter to Buchanan, 170, 171; rejoinder to Buchanan, 172.

Hays, Alexander, Bvt. Maj. Gen. U. S. Vols.: in battle of Gettysburg, VII, 266; killed in battle of the Wilderness, VIII, 363.

Hays, Harry T., Conf. Maj. Gen.: surrenders at Rappahannock Station, VIII, 243.

Hays, William, Bvt. Brig. Gen. U. S. A.: in assault on Petersburg, X, 179.

Hayti, lease of Ile A'Vache to Bernard Kock for colonization, VI, 360; action towards the colonists, 364.

Hazel, Caleb, teacher of Pres. Lincoln, I, 27, 34.

Hazen, W. B., Bvt. Maj. Gen. U. S. A.: in battle of Murfreesboro, VI, 287; march on Chattanooga, VIII, 71; in battle of Chickamauga, 88, 89, 99; occupies Brown's Ferry, 124; in battle of Chattanooga, 148; in battles of Atlanta, IX, 286; in March to the Sea, 481; capture of Fort McAllister, Dec. 13, 1864, 488, 489; at grand review in Washington, X, 333.

Hazlitt, Charles E., Lieut. U. S. A.: in battle of Gettysburg, VII, 254; killed at Gettysburg, 255.

Head, Rev. Jesse, marries Thomas Lincoln and Nancy Hanks, June 12, 1806, I, 23.

Hébert, Louis, Conf. Brig. Gen. : in battle of Corinth, VII, 117.

Heckman, C. A., Brig. Gen. U. S. Vols. : made prisoner at Bermuda Hundred, VIII, 398; in siege of Richmond, IX, 431.

Heffren, Horace, testimony about American Knights, VIII, 7.

Heintzelman, Samuel P., Bvt. Maj. Gen. U. S. A. : in battle of Bull Run, IV, 342, 348; attends council of war, V, 167; assigned to command Third Army Corps, Army of Potomac, 169; attends council at Fairfax Court House, 179; marches to the front of Yorktown, 360; thinks he could have isolated Yorktown, 367; arrives at Williamsburg, 376; established across the Chickahominy, 385; assists Keyes's corps, 388; in battle of Malvern Hill, 438; interview with Lincoln at Harrison's Landing, 453; ordered to report to Hooker, VII, 215.

Helm, B. H., Conf. Brig. Gen. : killed at Chickamauga, VIII, 92.

Helper, H. R., author of "The Impending Crisis," II, 214.

Hemphill, John, U. S. Sen. : signs secession address, II, 436; signs Senatorial secession caucus resolutions, III, 181.

Henderson, John B., U. S. Sen. : second interview with Lincoln about compensated emancipation, VI, 112; introduces bill in Senate to aid Missouri emancipation, 396; appointed U. S. Senator to succeed Trusten Polk, VIII, 469; elected U. S. Senator, 470; joint resolution to abolish slavery by Constitutional amendment, X, 75; advocates Thirteenth Amendment, 76.

Henderson, Richard, settles in Kentucky, I, 7.

Henry, Dr. A. G., recommended for postmaster by Lincoln, I, 183.

Henry, Guy V., Bvt. Brig. Gen. U. S. Vols. : commands advance to Baldwin, VIII, 283.

Henry, James B., Priv. Sec. to Pres. Buchanan : statement about Pres. Buchanan's inaugural address, II, 72.

Henry, James D., Gen. Ill. Vols. : defeats Black Hawk, I, 94.

Henry, John, elected to Congress, I, 257.

Henry, Joseph, Sec. Smithsonian Inst. : report on Chiriqui coal, VI, 358, 359.

Herndon, "Jim," sells Wm. F. Berry his share in a store, I, 110.

Herndon, "Row," sells Lincoln his share in a store, I, 110.

Herndon, William H., complains of old men in politics, I, 67, 68; one of the "Long Nine," 128; law partner of Abraham Lincoln, 216.

Herold, David E., in conspiracy to assassinate Lincoln, X, 289; receives Booth's directions to aid his escape, 291, 292; escape from Washington, 307; assisted by Samuel Mudd, 307, 308; assisted by Samuel Cox, 308; rowed across the Potomac by Thomas Jones, 308, 309; assisted by William Jett, 311; goes to Garrett's farm, 311; surrenders to Doherty, 311, 312; tried and hanged, 312, 313.

Herrick, Anson, M. C. : vote for Thirteenth Amendment, X, 83.

Herron, Francis J., Maj. Gen. U. S. Vols. : victory in battle of Prairie Grove, Dec. 7, 1862, VI, 383; in siege of Vicksburg, VII, 289.

Heth, Henry, Conf. Maj. Gen. : takes position near Covington, VI, 275; rejoins Kirby Smith, 275; in battle of Gettysburg. VII, 239, 240, 263; in Army of Northern Virginia, VIII, 354; in battle of Spotsylvania, 376; in siege of Petersburg, IX, 428, 432; in retreat from Petersburg, X, 179.

Hicks, Thomas H., Gov. of Md., U. S. Sen. : urged to convene Maryland legislature, III, 304; sentiments of, IV, 93, 94; reply to Secretary of War, 94; equivocal proclamation, 95; speech in Monument Square, 119; alleged order to burn railroad bridges, 120; denies consent to bridgeburning, 121; telegram to Secretary of War, 123; orders Pikesville arsenal occupied, 123; requests that transit of troops be stopped, 125; answer to Lincoln's letter, 126; returns to Annapolis, 135; suggestions to the President, 138; protests against landing troops at Annapolis, 154; opposes secession intrigues, 162, 163; convenes Maryland legislature, 164; special message, 168, 169; orders election for Members of Congress, 170; proclamation to form Union regiments, 174; declines aid from Gen. Butler, 385.

Higgins, Edward, Conf. Lieut. Col. : reply to Porter's second demand for surrender of Forts Jackson and St. Philip, V, 272; surrenders the forts April 28, 1862, 273.

Higginson, Thomas Wentworth, Col. U. S. Vols. : receives letters from John Brown, II, 196; informed of John Brown's plans,

200; commands 1st South Carolina Volunteers, VI, 445; ordered to cut Charleston and Savannah railroad, VII, 427.

Hill, Ambrose P., Conf. Lieut. Gen.: attacks Union forces at Beaver Dam Creek, V, 425; pursues Union army towards James River, 434; attacks Union army at Glendale, 435; corps of, in battle of Cedar Mountain, VI, 6; marches seventeen miles in seven hours, 141; attacks Union left at Antietam, 141; in battle of Fredericksburg, 203; in battle of Chancellorsville, VII, 103; commands corps of Lee's army, 201; begins march to the North, 210; crosses the Potomac, 217, 218; march towards Gettysburg, 233; in battle of Gettysburg, 239, 244, 249, 255, 261; commands Confederate center at Gettysburg, 249; attacks Warren, VIII, 240; commands left wing of Army of Northern Virginia, 352; marches to attack Grant, 358; in battle of the Wilderness, 360, 362, 363; in battle of North Anna, 387; in battle of Cold Harbor, 391, 401; in siege of Petersburg, IX, 429, 430, 432; killed at Petersburg, X, 178.

Hill, Daniel H., Conf. Lieut. Gen.: attacks Casey's division, V, 388; attacks Union forces at Beaver Dam Creek, 425; comment on battle of Gaines's Mill, 432; advice against attacking McClellan at Malvern Hill, 437; with Lee at Sharpsburg, VI, 137; arranges cartel with Dix for exchange of prisoners, VII, 451; ordered to join Hindman, VIII, 78; in battle of Chickamauga, 89, 91.

Hillhouse, Thomas, proposed for Assistant Treasurer at New York, IX, 93.

Hindman, Thomas C., M. C., Conf. Maj. Gen.: plan of compromise, II, 423; signs secession address, 436; remarks in House of Representatives, III, 147; report about results of Pea Ridge, VI, 372; sent to command in Arkansas, 373; censured by Jefferson Davis, 373; authorizes guerrillas in Missouri, 373; defeated at battle of Prairie Grove, Dec. 7, 1862, 383; ordered to Davis's Cross Roads, VIII, 78; in battle of Chickamauga, 93, 95, 99-101; in battle of Chattanooga, 145.

Hitchcock, E. A., Maj. Gen. U. S. Vols.: ordered to verify Gen. Wadsworth's statement, V, 184; reason for declining command of Army of Potomac, VI, 24; letter about retaliation, VII, 456; report on prisoners of war, 459; offers an exchange of

12,000 prisoners, 460; statement about exchange of prisoners, 461.

Hobson, E. H., Brig. Gen. U. S. Vols.: pursuit of Morgan, VIII, 57.

Hodges, Henry C., Capt. U. S. A.: assists John Tucker, V, 167.

Hoke, Robert F., Conf. Maj. Gen.: in battle of Bermuda Hundred, VIII, 398; joins Lee's army, 399; sent to reenforce Beauregard, IX, 410; in siege of Richmond, 433; marches against Plymouth, X, 39; defense of Wilmington, 68, 69; evacuates Wilmington, 69; in defense of Goldsboro, 70.

Holcombe, James P., Confederate agent in Canada, VIII, 15; offered safe-conduct to Washington, IX, 190; replies he is not accredited from Richmond, 191.

Hollins, George N., Capt. Conf. Navy: commands Confederate gunboats at New Madrid, V, 295; attack on Union gunboats, 301.

Holman, William S., M. C.: plan of compromise, II, 423; comment on Thirteenth Amendment, X, 82.

Holmes, Theophilus H., Conf. Lieut. Gen.: called to Beauregard's support, IV, 342; pursues Union army towards James River, V, 434; commands rebel forces in Arkansas, VI, 380, 381; report of summary executions in Texas, 476; repulsed at Helena, July 4, 1863, VII, 323.

Holt, Hines, peace resolution in Confederate Congress, VII, 365.

Holt, Joseph, P. M. Gen. and Sec. of War under Buchanan, Judge Adv. Gen. U. S. A.: opinion on disunion, II, 362; placed in charge of War Department, III, 74; approves Black's memorandum, 82; made Secretary of War ad interim, nominated, and confirmed, 89; letter approving Anderson's forbearance to return fire on Star of the West, 109; proposes measures to defend Washington, 129; action in behalf of the government, 130; countermands Floyd's order to ship the Pittsburg guns, 130; interview with Buchanan, 130, 131; report on Burnett's resolution, 147-149; asks Buchanan to publish his report, 149; orders for military parade on Feb. 22, 1861, 149; instructions to Anderson, 158; gives President's reply to secession Senators, 160; note about the Fort Pickens truce, 169; letter to Hayne, 171; letter to Anderson, 173; letter transmitting news from Anderson, 376, 377; report on Knights of the Golden Circle, VIII, 2-5; report as judge advocate general about political prisoners, 40; urged for Vice-President at Baltimore Convention, IX, 73; declines Attorney-Generalship, 346, 347; judge advocate and recorder in trial of Lincoln's assassins, X, 312.

Homans, Charles, private 8th Mass. Militia: repairs locomotive, IV, 154.

Hood, John B., Conf. Gen.: commands under Lee on the Peninsula, V, 428; in battle of Gaines's Mill, 429; with Lee at Sharpsburg, VI, 139; march to Culpeper Court House, VII, 205; in battle of Gettysburg, 250, 251, 254; in battle of Chickamauga, VIII, 84, 88, 93, 95, 97, 106; in expedition against Burnside, 129; criticism of Johnston, IX, 9; march to Cassville, 15; in battles of Dallas, 18; in battles of Kenesaw Mountain, 21, 22; requests suspension of order removing Johnston, 265-267; accepts Johnston's plan, 267; battle of Peach Tree Creek, July 20, 1864, 269; siege of Atlanta, July 22 to Sept. 1, 1864, 270-289; suggests plan to Jefferson Davis, 281; evacuates Atlanta, Sept. 1, 1864, 289; correspondence with Sherman, 465-467; interview with Jefferson Davis, 471-473; sends French against Allatoona, 473, 474; marches to Dalton, 475, 476; scheme of counter-invasion, X, 1-4; action at Decatur, 5; march to Tuscumbia, 5; army of, 6, 7; announces intention to move into Tennessee, 8; march to Franklin, Nov. 23-30, 1864, 10-18; battle of Franklin, Nov. 30, 1864, 18-21; campaign against Nashville, 22-29; battle of Nashville, Dec. 15, 16, 1864, 29-34; retreat of, 34; succeeded by Johnston, 35; visits Jefferson Davis, 36; surrenders to Davidson, 37.

Hood, J. R., postmaster at Chattanooga, Tenn.: letter to Lincoln about Etheridge, VII, 389, 390.

Hooker, Joseph, Bvt. Maj. Gen. U. S. A.: position at Williamsburg, V, 377; attacks the enemy, 377; complains that he was not assisted, 377; advice to McClellan, 457, 458; leads attack at Antietam, VI, 139; severely wounded, 140; recommends renewal of the fight, 144; asks permission to cross the Rappahannock, 199; commands Union reserve at Fredericksburg, 202; ordered to attack Marye's Heights, 206; remonstrates against the order, 206; accompanies his troops in the assault, 206; criticisms on Burnside and the government, 213; advice against Burnside's "Mud March," 218; lack of confidence in Burnside, 218; assigned to command Army of Potomac, VII, 87; plan of campaign, 90-92; orders to Stoneman, 92; begins movement against Lee, 93-96; battle of Chancellorsville, May 1-3, 1863, 96-107; note to Sedgwick, 99; warns Slocum and Howard against a flank attack, 99; withdraws his line nearer Chancellorsville, 104; accident to, 104; peremptory order to Sedgwick, 105; alleged intoxication, 107, 108; council of war, May 4, 1863, 108, 109; recrosses the Rappahannock, 109; comment on Chancellorsville, 109; letter to Lincoln asking a reserve of 25,000 infantry, 198, 199; sends the Sixth Corps across the Rappahannock, 203; asks advice on Lee's probable move against Washington, 204; suggests a march on Richmond, 206, 207; begins march to the upper Potomac, 210; complains that he does not enjoy Halleck's confidence, 210, 211; misunderstandings with Halleck, 212-214; asks reenforcements, 223; asks that Maryland Heights be abandoned, 224; asks to be relieved, 225; relieved from command, 226; sent to Rosecrans, VIII, 112; occupies Lookout Valley, 124, 127; in battle of Chattanooga, 139-144, 147, 148, 152, 154, 157; skirmishes at Buzzard's Roost, IX, 11; advance on Cassville, 15; in battles of Dallas, 17, 19; in battles of Kenesaw Mountain, 22; in march to the Chattahoochee, 26; relieved from command of Twentieth Corps, 277, 278; made Department commander, X, 338.

Hooper, Samuel, M. C.: introduces bill for National Bank Act, VI, 241; aids in preparing National Bank Act, 242.

Hopoeithleyohola, Creek chief: organizes loyal Indians, V, 82.

Housatonic, The, Union blockading vessel: engagement with rebel rams at Charleston, VII, 59-61.

House Committee of Thirty-three, appointment of, moved, II, 415; members, 417; propositions submitted to, 422-426; meetings, Dec. 12, 13, 1860, 433, 434; Rust's statement, 433; Dunn's resolution adopted, 433, 434; Southern members absent themselves, III, 214; report by the chairman, 216; minority reports, 217.

Houston, D. C., Bvt. Col. U. S. A.: prepares memorandum for Red River campaign, VIII, 288.

Houston, George S., M. C.: member of House Committee of Thirty-three, II, 417.

Houston, Sam, U. S. Sen., Gov. of Texas: captures Santa Anna, I, 233; opposes first Nebraska bill, 340; opposes secession, III, 193; characterization of Jefferson Davis, 208; opposes secession, IV, 181; ambition to establish a separate nation, 181 ; letter to Calhoun, 181, 182; refuses to convene Texas legislature, 182 ; calls extra session of legislature, 183; message to legislature, 183; protest, 183; refuses to recognize secession ordinance, 186, 187 ; deposed from office of governor, 187; address to the people, 187, 188; declines military help from the government, 189.

Hovey, Alvin P., Brig. Gen. U. S. Vols.: in battle of Port Gibson, VII, 171; march to Edwards's Station, 187; in battle of Champion's Hill, 189-192; in siege of Vicksburg, 289; advance north of Dalton, IX, 11.

How, John, member of Union Safety Committee at St. Louis, IV, 212.

Howard, Jacob M., M. C., U. S. Sen.: votes for National Bank Act, VI, 244 ; present at interview between Lincoln, Cabinet, and Republican Senators, 266; comment on Thirteenth Amendment, 76.

Howard, John R., construction of the "two-thirds rule," II, 243.

Howard, Joseph, Jr., false dispatch about Lincoln, III, 315.

Howard, Mark, nomination of, rejected, IX, 87.

Howard, Oliver O., Bvt. Maj. Gen. U. S. A.: in battle of Chancellorsville, VII, 93, 98-100; present at council of war, 109; in battle of Gettysburg, 242, 244-246, 249, 258; favors attacking Lee at the Potomac, 275-277; in march on Lookout Valley, VIII, 125; engagement in Lookout Valley, 126; in battle of Chattanooga, 134, 140, 146, 154; in Sherman's march to Knoxville, 182; bridges the Tennessee at Davis's Ford, 182; skirmishes at Buzzard's Roost, IX, 11; in battles of Resaca, 13, 14; in march to the Chattahoochee, 26; assigned to command Army of the Tennessee, 277; assigned to command Northern Department, 278; commands Department of the East and Department of the Lakes, 278; in battles of Atlanta, 280, 285-287; in March to the Sea, 477, 481; in march to Columbia, X, 230, 231; in march to Goldsboro, 233, 234; appointed Chief of Freedmen's Bureau, 333.

Howard, Volney E., M. C.: opposes first Nebraska bill, I, 338.

Howard, William A., M. C., U. S. Sen.: member of Investigating Committee, I, 451; member of House Committee of Thirty-three, II, 417 ; offers resolution to appoint Select Committee of Five, III, 141.

Howarth, W. L., U. S. N.: in expedition against the Albemarle, X, 47.

Howell, J. C., recommended for postmaster by Lincoln, I, 183.

Howell, Jefferson D., Conf. midshipman: captured with Jefferson Davis, X, 274.

Howell, Miss Maggie, sister of Mrs. Jefferson Davis: captured with Jefferson Davis, X, 274.

Howe, Albion P., Bvt. Maj. Gen. U. S. A.: in battle of Chancellorsville, VII, 106 ; testimony about Gettysburg, 269 ; succeeds Sigel in command, IX, 161; member of military commission for trial of Lincoln's assassins, X, 312.

Howe, Dr. Samuel G., informed of John Brown's plans, II, 200.

Huey, Pennock, Bvt. Brig. Gen. U. S. Vols.: in battle of Chancellorsville, VII, 102.

Huger, Benjamin, Bvt. Col. U. S. A., Conf. Maj. Gen.: visit to Charleston authorities with Anderson, II, 356; hopeful of settlement of difficulties, 357; assists Hill's attack on Casey's division, V, 388; left to guard south side of Chickahominy, 428; pursues Union army towards James River, 434.

Hughes, John, Archbishop of New York: supports the government and the war, VI, 325; address to New York rioters, July 17, 1863, VII, 24, 25.

Huidekoper, Col., Lincoln's order to permit recruiting at Rock Island prison, V, 145, 146.

Hume, John F., moves that Lincoln's nomination be declared unanimous, IX, 72.

Humphrey, James, M. C.: member of House Committee of Thirty-three, II, 417.

Humphreys, Andrew A., Bvt. Maj. Gen. U. S. A.: selects positions for Union army at Malvern Hill, V, 436, 437; in battle of Fredericksburg, VI, 206-208; in battle of Chancellorsville, VII, 97; in battle of Gettysburg, 250, 251, 255; in Army of Potomac, VIII, 353; in battle of Spotsylvania, 381; in recapture of Fort Stedman, X, 163, 164; in battle of Five Forks, 173; in assault at Petersburg, 177, 179, 181; in march to

Appomattox, 186, 187, 189; at grand review in Washington, 332.

Humphreys, F. C., U. S. military storekeeper at Charleston: issues forty muskets to Foster, II, 443; demands their return, 444.

Hunt, Henry J., Bvt. Maj. Gen. U. S. A.: in battle of Gettysburg, VII, 249, 250, 261; testimony about Gettysburg, 269.

Hunt, Randall, mentioned for the Cabinet, III, 362, 363.

Hunt, Washington, M. C., Gov. of N. Y.: chairman of Constitutional Union Convention, II, 253; resolution in Democratic National Convention, IX, 255.

Hunter, David, Bvt. Maj. Gen. U. S. A.: member of Lincoln's suite, III, 290; arm broken at Buffalo, 309; attends meeting of Lincoln's suite, 314; in battle of Bull Run, IV, 342, 348; requested to assist Frémont, 413; commands division under Frémont, 429; opinion of Frémont, 430; succeeds Frémont, 435, 436; retires to Rolla, 438; assigned to command Department of Kansas, V, 81; order of military emancipation in Georgia, Florida, and South Carolina, VI, 90; condition of his Department, 91; order revoked by the President, 94–96; asks authority to organize negro soldiers, 124; effort to organize a negro regiment, 443; answer to the Wickliffe resolution, 443; proclaimed an outlaw by the rebel government, 471; relieved by Gen. Gillmore, VII, 85; defeats Gen. Jones, IX, 159; advance on Lynchburg, 159; retreats down the Kanawha, 159; joins in pursuit of Early, 175; interview with Grant and Sheridan at Monocacy, 180–182; member of military commission for trial of Lincoln's assassins, X, 312.

Hunter, R. M. T., U. S. Sen., Conf. Sec. of State: voted for in Charleston Convention, II, 244; called by Floyd to influence Buchanan, 396; member of Senate Committee of Thirteen, 414; interview with Seward, III, 401; appointed Peace Commissioner, X, 110; asks permission to go to Washington, 113; interview with Grant, 114–116; interview with Lincoln, 118–129; report to Davis, 129.

Hunter, William, Second Asst. Sec. State: appointed Acting Secretary of State, X, 317.

Hurlbut, Stephen A., Maj. Gen. U. S. Vols.: visits Charleston, III, 390, 391; report to the President, 391, 392; position of division at Pittsburg Landing, V, 324; position at sundown, April 6, 1862, 330; promises to organize negro troops, VI, 459; commands Sixteenth Army Corps, VII, 144; left to guard Memphis and Charleston railroad, 144; organizes Grierson's cavalry raid, 162; in Sherman's movement to Meridian, VIII, 330, 331; letter to Lincoln about Tennessee reconstruction, 440.

Hurst, ——, pension agent: complimented by Lincoln, I, 291.

Huston, W. B., member of committee to distribute Union arms, IV, 237.

Hutchins, John, M. C.: plan of compromise, II, 422.

Hutchins, Wells A., M. C.: vote for Thirteenth Amendment, X, 83.

Ile A'Vache, Hayti, description of, VI, 359, 360; contract to establish a negro colony on, 360; emigrants arrive from Fort Monroe, 363; Bernard Kock as governor, 363; Kock driven from the island, 364; arrival of Special Agent Donnohue, 364; Donnohue's report, 365, 366; relief to the colonists, 365; colonists brought back to the United States, 366.

Iles, Elijah, Capt. Ill. Vols.: commands company in Black Hawk war, I, 93.

Illinois, State of, in 1830, I, 47–69; population of, 50; manners and customs in, 50–63; Sangamon County created, 59; early politics in, 63–68, 101–109; population in 1834, 123; legislative schemes of internal improvement, 133–136; growth of Chicago, 133, 134; an era of speculation, 133–136; railroad system in, proposed, 135; movement in 1822–23 to introduce slavery, 143–146; murder of Lovejoy, 146–148; action of legislature on slavery, 150; failure of internal improvement system, 160; campaign of 1840 in, 172–178; volunteers from, in Mexican war, 250, 255; characteristics of the Eighth Circuit Bar about 1850, 300; free in consequence of Ordinance of 1787, 317; geographical situation of, 365; political condition in 1854, 366; Republican party formed in, II, 23–29; the Decatur Convention, 23; "Know-Nothing" party in, 24, 25; the Bloomington Convention, 27–30; vote of, in 1856, 43; Republican State Convention of 1858, 136–138; Lincoln-Douglas debates, 135–163; election of Nov. 2, 1858, 164, 165; meeting of Republican National Convention at Chicago, May 16, 1860, 255; response to Lincoln's proclamation, IV, 86; departure of troops from Quincy, 87;

412 INDEX

American Knights, etc., in, VIII, 2; plot to liberate prisoners at Camp Douglas, 21; ratifies Thirteenth Amendment, X, 88.

Imboden, John D., Conf. Brig. Gen.: raiding in Maryland, VII, 233; in Shenandoah campaign, IX, 292.

Indiana, State of, state of society in, I, 39–42; free in consequence of Ordinance of 1787, 317; response to Lincoln's proclamation, IV, 86; Caleb B. Smith appointed district judge in, VI, 300; American Knights, etc., in, VIII, 2; obstructive action of legislature, 9, 10; Morgan's raid, 53–55; instructs delegates in favor of Lincoln's renomination, IX, 56; ratifies Thirteenth Amendment, X, 89.

Ingalls, Rufus, Bvt. Maj. Gen. U. S. A.: assists John Tucker, V, 167; statement about McClellan's supplies, VI, 178, 179.

Ingersoll, C. J., M. C.: remarks on the boundary question, I, 265.

Iowa, State of, admitted as a State, I, 324; response to Lincoln's proclamation, IV, 86; ratifies Thirteenth Amendment, X, 89.

Isherwood, Benj. F., Eng. in Chief, U. S. N.: mission to Gosport navy yard, IV, 145, 146.

Island No. 10, Tenn., situation of, V, 294; rebel defenses at, 294; surrender of, April 7, 1862, 299.

Island Queen, The, unarmed steamer: scuttled by John Y. Beall, VIII, 19.

Iverson, Alfred, M. C., U. S. Sen.: signs address commending the Charleston disruption, II, 245, 246; Senate discussion, 400, 401, 408, 409; signs secession address, 436; remarks in Senate, III, 137; signs Senatorial secession caucus resolutions, 181.

Jacks, T. M., elected to Congress, VIII, 418.

Jackson, Miss., battle of, May 14, 1863, VII, 182, 183.

Jackson, Andrew, seventh Pres. U. S.: letter about Texas annexation, I, 226; interview with Gen. Scott about nullification, II, 338.

Jackson, Claiborne F., Gov. of Mo.: answer to Lincoln's call for troops, IV, 90; secession conspiracy of, 206–208; refuses Lincoln's call for troops, 207, 208; convenes Missouri legislature, 208; forms "Camp Jackson" at St. Louis, 209; correspondence with Jefferson Davis, 210; correspondence with Walker, 210, 211; destroys railroad bridge over the Osage River, 219; interview with Lyon, 222; calls out 50,000 Missouri militia, 223; flight from Jefferson

City, 224; commissions rebel officers, 397; convenes rebel legislature at Lexington, 426, 427; convenes rebel legislature at Neosho, V, 88.

Jackson, James, M. C.: signs secession address, II, 436.

Jackson, James S., M. C., Brig. Gen. U. S. Vols.: second interview with Lincoln about compensated emancipation, VI, 111.

Jackson, N. J., Bvt. Maj. Gen. U. S. Vols.: in March to the Sea, IX, 481.

Jackson, Thomas Jonathan ("Stonewall"), Conf. Lieut. Gen.: collects rebel forces at Harper's Ferry, IV, 310, 311; forms second line of battle at Bull Run, 348, 349; biographical notice, V, 393, 394; singularities of character, 394; his religious enthusiasm, 395, 396; self-confidence, 397; promotions, 397; treatment of his slaves, 398; resemblance to John Brown, 398, 399; hatred of his enemies, 399; love of fame, 399, 400; ordered to the Shenandoah Valley, 400; defeated by Shields and Kimball, 400; report of his defeat, 400; begins his second campaign in the Shenandoah Valley, 401; defeats Milroy at McDowell, 401; moves to Harrisonburg, 401; marches to Front Royal, 402; objects of his Shenandoah Valley campaign, 404; retreat up the Valley, 404; his escape, 409; battle of Cross Keys, June 8, 1862, 411; defeats Shields at Port Republic, June 9, 1862, 411; ordered to join Lee, 422; reports at Richmond, June 23, 1862, 423; attacks Porter's right at Gaines's Mill, 429; pursues Union army towards James River, 434; arrives at Malvern Hill, 437; attacked by Banks at Cedar Mountain, Aug. 9, 1862, VI, 6; retires to the Rapidan, 6; flank movement against Pope's line of communications, 7; flank movement against Chantilly, 11; repulsed at Chantilly, Sept. 1, 1862, 11; sent to capture Harper's Ferry, 133; marches to join Lee at Sharpsburg, 137; ordered to turn the Federal right, 144; position at Fredericksburg, 201; sent to attack Hooker's rear in battle of Chancellorsville, VII, 98–100; attacks Hooker, 101, 102; mortally wounded by his own men, 103.

Jackson, Zadock, denounces sack of Lawrence, I, 456.

James, ——, Maj. U. S. Vols., M. C.: major in Mexican war, I, 260.

Jamison, D. F., commissioner to Anderson, III, 110.

Japan, The, or Georgia, The, Conf. cruiser: escapes from England, VIII, 256.

Jaquess, James F., Col. U. S. Vols.: letter to Garfield about peace, IX, 201, 202; report about peace, 204-206; visit to Richmond, 208; interview with Davis and Benjamin, 208-211.

Jefferson, Thomas, third Pres. U. S.: reprobates slave trade, I, 314; drafts Ordinance of 1784 prohibiting slavery, 316; purchase of Louisiana, 319; originates policy of slavery restriction, 359.

Jenkins, Albert G., M. C., Conf. Brig. Gen.: compromise proposition of, II, 424, 425.

Jenkins, Micah, Conf. Brig. Gen.: killed in battle of the Wilderness, VIII, 366.

Jett, William, assists Booth and Herold, X, 311.

Jewett, William Cornell, writes letters to Greeley and others, IX, 215; correspondence with Confederate emissaries, 193, 194.

Johnson, Andrew, seventeenth Pres. U. S.: voted for in Charleston Convention, II, 244; compromise proposition, 425; remains a loyal Senator from Tennessee, IV, 371; offers Crittenden resolution, 379; inquiry addressed to Buell, V, 68; member of Committee on Conduct of the War, 150; appointed military governor of Tennessee, VI, 344; sketches his official functions, 344, 345; deprecates colored recruiting in Tennessee, 464; efforts for East Tennesseans, VIII, 160-162; orders elections: for Congress, 439 — for county officers, 443 — for President, 447; proclaims amendments to Constitution adopted, 449; nominated for Vice-President at Baltimore Convention, IX, 72-74; disapproves Sherman's agreement, X, 250; proclamation of amnesty, Dec. 25, 1868, 275; sworn in as President, 317; at grand review in Washington, 331; proclaims end of rebellion, 338, 339.

Johnson, Bradley T., Conf. Brig. Gen.: sent towards Point Lookout, IX, 162, 163; raid in Maryland, 165.

Johnson, Bushrod R., Conf. Maj. Gen.: captured at Fort Donelson, V, 200; in battle of Chickamauga, VIII, 84; report about Chickamauga, 106.

Johnson, Edward, Conf. Maj. Gen.: in battle of Gettysburg, VII, 246, 258; in Army of Northern Virginia, VIII, 354; captured at Spotsylvania, 380, 382.

Johnson, George W., "Provisional Gov. of Ky.": killed in the ranks at Shiloh, VI, 277.

Johnson, J. M., elected to Congress, VIII, 418.

Johnson, Oliver, anti-slavery editorials of, I, 148.

Johnson, Reverdy, U. S. Sen., Atty. Gen. under Taylor, Min. to Eng.: argument in Dred Scott case, II, 64; member of Peace Convention, III, 230; interview with Lincoln, IV, 164; answers Lincoln's letter, 165; resolutions in Senate about Arguelles case, IX, 46; approves Lincoln's message, 109; advocates and votes for Thirteenth Amendment, X, 76, 77.

Johnson, Robert W., Bvt. Maj. Gen. U. S. A.: signs the Senatorial Secession Caucus resolutions, III, 181; in battle of Murfreesboro, VI, 285; in battle of Chickamauga, VIII, 88, 89, 92, 104; in battle of Chattanooga, 135, 148, 153, 155.

Johnson, Thomas, elected president of council in Kansas Territorial legislature, I, 415.

Johnson, Waldo P., U. S. Sen.: expelled from Congress, VIII, 469.

Johnston, Albert S., Conf. Gen.: assigned to command Department Number Two, V, 44, 45; orders Buckner to Bowling Green, 45; orders Hardee to Bowling Green, 56; attends council of war at Bowling Green, 185; resolves "to fight for Nashville at Donelson," 185; evacuates Nashville, 190; retreats towards Chattanooga, 303; joins Beauregard near Corinth, 321; telegraphs Jefferson Davis his intention to attack Grant at Pittsburg Landing, 321; council of Confederate commanders; rejects Beauregard's advice, 322; attack on Union troops, April 6, 1862, 325; killed at Pittsburg Landing, April 6, 1862, 326.

Johnston, Daniel, first husband of Sarah Bush Lincoln, I, 32.

Johnston, J. D., Commander Conf. navy: commands the Tennessee, IX, 227.

Johnston, John, step-brother of Pres. Lincoln, I, 37; goes to Springfield with Lincoln, 70; assists to build a flatboat, 70; flatboat voyage of, to New Orleans, 72.

Johnston, Joseph E., Q. M. Gen. U. S. A., Conf. Gen., M. C.: interview with Drayton, II, 322; sent to command Harper's Ferry, IV, 317; evacuates Harper's Ferry, 318; ordered to join Beauregard, 346; arrives at Bull Run, 346; adopts Beauregard's plans of battle, 347; report of forces, V, 149, 150, 152; council of war at

Fairfax Court House, 153, 154; prepares to retire to Gordonsville, 164; embarrassed by accumulation of provisions, 165; opinion on McClellan, 175; receives news of McClellan's advance on Yorktown, 176; statement about "quaker guns," 177; desires the *Merrimac* to go to York River, 233; regards Magruder's position as untenable, 367; assumes Confederate command on the Peninsula, 371; statement of forces, 371; orders evacuation of Yorktown, 374, 375; retreats to Williamsburg, 376; posts Longstreet as a rearguard, 376; battle with McClellan's advance, May 5, 1862, 377; continues his retrograde march, 379; crosses the Chickahominy, May 15, 1862, 379; encamps before Richmond, 379; comment on battle of Hanover Court House, 386; orders an attack on Heintzelman and Keyes, 387; accompanies reserves under G. W. Smith, 388; orders Smith to attack Union right flank, 388; wounded, 389; estimate of "Stonewall" Jackson, 396; orders Jackson to the Shenandoah Valley, 400; comment on battle of Gaines's Mill, 432, 433; sent to command rebel armies in the West, VII, 129; conference at Grenada, Miss., with Pemberton and Jefferson Davis, 131; warning to Pemberton, 166; sent with reenforcements to the Mississippi, 178, 179; telegram to Richmond: "I am too late," 180; directs Pemberton to come up in Sherman's rear, 181; dispatches of, intercepted, 183; controversy with Jefferson Davis, 183; censure of Pemberton, 183; orders Pemberton to Clinton, 186; advises Pemberton to evacuate Vicksburg, 194; gathers an army to relieve Vicksburg, 294; directs evacuation of Port Hudson, 295; correspondence with Pemberton about relief of Vicksburg, 295, 296; correspondence with Jefferson Davis about Vicksburg, 296; correspondence with Seddon about Vicksburg, 296-298; movements to relieve Vicksburg, 298, 299; defense of Jackson, Miss., 324, 325; evacuates Jackson, 325; sends Bragg two divisions, VIII, 76; assumes chief command in the West, 326; report on Confederate Western operations, 327-329; strength of army, IX, 5; criticism of Bragg's plan, 8; position of, 9, 10; battles of Resaca, May 13-16, 1864, 13, 14; retires to Adairsville, 14, 15; retires towards Cassville and Kingston, 15; abandons Cassville, 16; battles of Dallas, May 25 to June 4, 1864, 17-19; battles of Kenesaw Mountain, June 9-30, 1864, 19-25; retires across the Chattahoochee, 25-28; relieved from command, 263; transfers his command to Hood, 264; succeeds Hood in command, X, 35; appointed to command Confederate Western armies, 153, 157; supersedes Beauregard, 233; battle of Bentonville, March 19, 1865, 234, 235; retreats from Bentonville, 236, 237; retreat from Smithfield, 242; proposes an armistice to Sherman, 243, 244, 263; interview with Sherman, 245; interview with Sherman and Breckinridge, 246-248; signs Sherman's memorandum agreement, 248; distributes silver among his troops, 251; disregards Davis's instructions, 252; surrenders to Sherman, April 26, 1865, 252, 253; interviews with Davis and Beauregard, 257-263; account of interviews with Davis, 261.

Johnston, R. D., Conf. Brig. Gen.: wounded at Spotsylvania, VIII, 382.

Johnston, Sarah Bush, marries Thomas Lincoln, I, 32; improves the condition of his household, 32; testifies to Abraham's good conduct, 37.

Johnston, William F., receives votes for Vice-President in Philadelphia Convention, II, 35.

Joinville, Prince de, comment on battle of Seven Pines, V, 391; advice about battle of Glendale, 436.

Jones, Dr. Anson, elected President of Texas, I, 237.

Jones, Catesby Ap R., Lieut. U. S. N., Commander Conf. navy: commands the *Merrimac*, V, 228; fight of *Monitor* and *Merrimac*, March 9, 1862, 228-231.

Jones, D. R., Conf. Maj. Gen.: with Lee at Sharpsburg, VI, 139.

Jones, Edward F., Col. 6th Mass. Militia: warned of danger in Baltimore, IV, 110; order to his regiment, 111; orders delayed companies to join him, 114; keeps his men under control, 117.

Jones, George W., U. S. Sen., Min. to New Granada: imprisoned in Fort Lafayette, VIII, 39; brings suit for false imprisonment, 39; suit dismissed by Supreme Court of New York, 39.

Jones, John J., M. C.: House discussion, II, 416; signs secession address, 436.

Jones, John M., Conf. Brig. Gen.: killed in battle of the Wilderness, VIII, 361.

Jones, John R., Conf. Brig. Gen.: with Lee at Sharpsburg, VI, 139.

Jones, Dr. Joseph, report on Andersonville prison, VII, 468–470.

Jones, Lieut. Roger, burns armory at Harper's Ferry, IV, 122.

Jones, Samuel, Conf. Maj. Gen.: captures one of Burnside's outposts, VIII, 171; reply to an order, 397.

Jones, Samuel J., sheriff of Douglas Co., Kas.: arrests Branson, I, 441; Branson rescued from, 441; demands 3,000 men from governor to carry out the laws, 442; attempt to assassinate, 450; orders burning and sack of Lawrence, 455.

Jones, Thomas, rows Booth and Herold across the Potomac, X, 308, 309.

Jones, W. E., Conf. Brig. Gen.: defeated by Hunter, IX, 159; killed in engagement at Piedmont, 403.

Juarez, Benito Pablo, Pres. of Mex. Republic: origin and career of, VI, 30, 31; condition of Mexico, 31; measures against French expedition, 45; demands expulsion of Almonte, 45; reply to Maximilian's invitation, VII, 416; takes refuge in Chihuahua, 419.

Judd, Norman B., Min. to Prussia, M. C.: speech in Illinois legislature against Nebraska bill, I, 366; member of Bloomington Convention, II, 28; delegate to Chicago Convention, 1860, 271; nominates Lincoln, 271; member of Lincoln's suite, III, 290; conference with Felton and Pinkerton, 307; interview with Lincoln, 308; arrangements for Lincoln's night journey, 309; conference with Pinkerton, Franciscus, and Sanford, 310; calls a meeting of Lincoln's suite, 314; describes Lincoln's starting, 315; approves Lincoln's message, IX, 110.

Julian, George W., M. C.: member of Committee on Conduct of the War, V, 150; statement about caucus after Lincoln's death, X, 316.

Jurien de la Gravière, Pierre Roch, French admiral: named to command French part of Mexican expedition, VI, 39.

Kane, George P., chief of police, Baltimore: hastens to scene of riot, IV, 114; holds pursuing rioters in check, 117; dismisses his force, 118; orders and heads party to burn bridges, 120, 121; telegram to Johnson, 122.

Kansas, State of, bill to organize Territory of, I, 139; Lawrence founded by Emigrant Aid Company, 395; town of Atchison founded, 402; Reeder appointed governor, 402; invaded by Missouri voters, Nov. 29, 1854, 404; frauds at election, 406; population as shown by Reeder's census, January and February, 1855, 409; second invasion by Missouri voters, 410; election frauds of March 30, 1855, 410; number of slaves in, in 1855, 422; Lecompton founded and made the capital, 424; meeting and resolutions of Big Springs Convention, 428; Free State Constitutional Convention, 429; frames Topeka Constitution, 429; Charles D. Robinson elected governor under Topeka Constitution, 430; Congressional investigating committee sent to, 431, 432; Pierce's proclamation against Topeka movement, 433; resignation of Gov. Shannon, 435; Woodson's proclamation against Free State legislature, 435; Free State legislature dispersed by Col. Sumner, 436; condition of civil war in the Territory, 451, 452; civil war in, II, 1–20; guerrilla bands dispersed by Col. Sumner, 2; Gen. P. F. Smith supersedes Col. Sumner, 3; Gov. Shannon removed, 3; J. W. Geary appointed governor, 9; third Missouri raid against Lawrence, 14–18; skirmish at Hickory Point, 18; imprisonment of Free State men, 19; cessation of guerrilla war, 20; summary of its results, 20; removal and flight of Gov. Geary, 22; convention of proslavery party, 90; Act for Constitutional Convention, 91; Enabling Acts by Douglas and Toombs, 93, 94; Free State mass-meeting at Topeka, 97; Proslavery Convention at Lecompton, 98; defective census and registry, 99; election of delegates, 100; Lecompton Constitutional Convention, 103, 106–108; October election, 1857, 104; Oxford and McGee frauds, 105; candle-box fraud, 106; Lecompton Constitution, 108, 109; extra session of legislature called, 114; votes on Lecompton Constitution, 115; vote under the English bill, 115; popular vote rejecting the English bill, 133; admitted as a free State, III, 237; Quantrell's massacre at Lawrence, Aug. 21, 1863, VIII, 211, 212; resolution of legislature renominating Lincoln, IX, 55; ratifies Thirteenth Amendment, X, 89.

Kautz, August V., Bvt. Maj. Gen. U. S. A.: commands cavalry under Butler, VIII, 392; in siege of Richmond, IX, 433; member of military commission for trial of Lincoln's assassins, X, 312.

Kearny, Philip, Maj. Gen. U. S. Vols. : killed at Chantilly, Sept. 1, 1862, VI, 11.

Kearsarge, The, Union cruiser: blockades the *Alabama* at Cherbourg, IX, 144 ; sinks the *Alabama*, 146–149.

Keenan, Peter, Maj. U. S. Vols. : in battle of Chancellorsville, VII, 102.

Keitt, Lawrence M., M. C. : interferes in the Sumner assault, II, 51 ; course disapproved by the House, 53.

Kelley, Benjamin F., Bvt. Maj. Gen. U. S. Vols. : organizes Union regiment, IV, 330, 331; attacks and defeats Porterfield, 331; skirmish with McCausland, IX, 178.

Kelley, William D., M. C. : favors Lincoln's renomination, IX, 62.

Kellogg, Francis W., M. C. : approves Lincoln's message, IX, 110.

Kellogg, William, M. C., Min. to Guatemala; member of House Committee of Thirty-three, II, 417; writes to Lincoln for advice, III, 258, 259; visit to Lincoln, 259.

Kenesaw Mountain, Ga. : battles of, June 9–30, 1864, IX, 19–25.

Kennebec, The, Union gunboat: in battle of Mobile Bay, IX, 235.

Kennedy, Dr., mission to the President, VI, 350, 351.

Kennedy, John A., Supt. of police in New York city: sends detectives to Baltimore, III, 312.

Kennedy, Robert C., employed by Thompson to burn New York city, VIII, 23 ; captured and hung, 23.

Kennon, Beverly, Lieut. U. S. N., Capt. Conf. navy : commands Confederate gunboat *Gov. Moore*, V, 263.

Kentucky, State of, exploration by Daniel Boone, I, 6; Harrodsburg founded, 7; settlement at the Falls of the Ohio, 7, 8; emigration to the Falls of the Ohio, 15; Louisville incorporated, 15; answer to Lincoln's proclamation, IV, 90, 230; vote for President in 1860, 232 ; legislature convened in second special session, 234; legislative measures, 234; legislature adjourns *sine die*, 238; election for Congress, 238 ; election for legislature, 239, 240; rebel invasion, V, 43–46; legislature demands withdrawal of Confederate forces, 46; governor vetoes joint resolution, 46; legislature invites Anderson to take command, 46; legislature calls out 40,000 Union volunteers, 47; Anderson removed from command, 52; battle of Mill Springs, Jan. 19, 1862, 116, 117; attack and surrender

of Fort Donelson, Feb. 12–16, 1862, 192–200; Bragg's invasion, VI, 274–279; defeat of Nelson, 274; Buell marches to Louisville, 276; inauguration of a Confederate government at Frankfort, 277; battle of Perryville, Oct. 8, 1862, 278 ; retreat of Bragg from the State, 279; American Knights, etc., in, VIII, 2, 12; Morgan's raid, 53.

Keokuk, chief of Sac and Fox Indians : loyal to the whites, I, 89.

Kershaw, J. B., Conf. Maj. Gen. : in battle of Spotsylvania, VIII, 374 ; in Shenandoah campaign, IX, 293; sent to Early, 312; in battle of Cedar Creek, 316, 317, 322, 325; captured in retreat to Appomattox, X, 187.

Ketchum, Edgar, signs memorial about Frémont and colored troops, VI, 456.

Ketchum, Morris, signs memorial about Frémont and colored troops, VI, 456.

Key, John J., Maj. U. S. Vols. : remark about "the game" of the army, VI, 186; interview with the President, 186, 187; dismissed from military service, 187.

Keyes, Erasmus D., Maj. Gen. U. S. Vols.: ordered to prepare plan to reënforce Fort Pickens, III, 436; submits plan, 437; attends council of war, V, 167; assigned to command Fourth Corps, Army of Potomac, 169; attends council at Fairfax Court House, 179; marches to Lee's Mills, 360; arrives at Williamsburg, 376; establishes himself across the Chickahominy, 385; attacked by D. H. Hill, 388; moves across White Oak Swamp, 433; establishes himself at Malvern Hill, 433; interview with Lincoln at Harrison's Landing, 453; estimate of rebel strength, 456.

Keystone State, The, Union gunboat: attacked at Charleston by rebel ram *Chicora*, VII, 59–61.

Kilgore, David, M. C. : plan of compromise, II, 423.

Kilpatrick, Judson, Bvt. Maj. Gen., U. S. A. Min. to Chili: cavalry successes under, VII, 215 ; in battle of Gettysburg, 268 ; cavalry raid towards Richmond, VIII, 251, 252; destroys railroad at Jonesboro, IX, 281; in March to the Sea, 481; in march to Columbia, X, 230; engagement with Hampton, 234.

Kimball, Nathan, Bvt. Maj. Gen. U. S. Vols. : repulses Stonewall Jackson at Kernstown, V, 400 ; in siege of Vicksburg, VII, 290; in march to Franklin, X, 11, 16.

King, Austin A., Gov. of Mo., M. C.: vote for Thirteenth Amendment, X, 83.

King, John A., M. C., Gov. of N. Y.: present at Lincoln's Cooper Institute speech, II, 217.

King, Preston, M. C., U. S. Sen.: agrees upon Wilmot Proviso, I, 268; leaves the Democratic party, 277; receives votes for Vice-President in Philadelphia Convention, II, 35; Senate discussion, 405, 406; votes against National Bank Act, VI, 244; informs Seward of action of Senate caucus, 264.

King, William R., U. S. Sen., Min. to France, Vice-Pres. with Pierce: death of, I, 397.

Kingsbury, Charles P., Bvt. Brig. Gen. U. S. A.: sent to Harper's Ferry, IV, 96.

Kinney, J. C., information about Wide Awakes, II, 284.

Kinney, Miss, present at Lincoln's deathbed, X, 300.

Kinney, Mrs., present at Lincoln's deathbed, X, 300.

Kinney, William, Lieut. Gov. of Ill.: defeated by Reynolds for governor of Illinois, I, 103.

Kirk, Edward N., Brig. Gen. U. S. Vols.: in battle of Murfreesboro, VI, 286; severely wounded, 286.

Kirkpatrick, ——, volunteer in Lincoln's company in Black Hawk war, I, 89; defeated for the legislature in 1832, 109.

Kirksville, Mo., action at, Aug. 6, 1862, VI, 379.

Knapp, Dr., candidate for Illinois legislature, I, 179.

Knights of the Golden Circle, extensive organization in Texas, IV, 181; order of, VIII, 2-27.

"Know-Nothing," or American, Party, influence on elections in 1854, I, 358; nominates Fillmore and Donelson, II, 24; action in Illinois, 24, 25; Lincoln's views on, 181.

Knox, John J., comptroller of currency: quotations from, VI, 237, 244, 245, 252.

Knoxville, Tenn., siege of, Nov. 16 to Dec. 3, 1863, VIII, 174-181.

Kock, Bernard, description of Ile A'Vache, VI, 359, 360; contract with the President to form negro colony on Ile A'Vache, 360; his scheme of speculation, 361; preparations and expenditures for his project, 362; the President cancels his contract, 362; assignment of his lease, 362; accompanies the colony as governor of Ile A'Vache, 363; driven from the island, 364.

Lackawanna, The, Union cruiser: in battle of Mobile Bay, IX, 235, 236.

Laird, John, M. P.: builder of the Alabama, VI, 53.

Lamb, William, note about the Virginia election of 1860, III, 417.

Lamb, William, Conf. Col.: wounded at Fort Fisher, X, 67.

Lamborn, Josiah, prominent lawyer of Illinois, I, 213.

Lamon, Ward H., marshal D. C.: member of Lincoln's suite, III, 290; selected to accompany Lincoln on his night journey to Washington, 310; attends meeting of Lincoln's suite, 314; visit to Charleston, 390, 391.

Lancaster, John, owner of English yacht Deerhound: carries off crew of the Alabama, IX, 150, 151.

Landrum, J. M., M. C.: signs secession address, II, 436.

Lane, Henry S., M. C., U. S. Sen.: permanent chairman of Philadelphia Convention, II, 32; votes for re-passage of National Bank Act, VI, 245.

Lane, James H., U. S. Sen., Brig. Gen. U. S. Vols.: elected U. S. Senator, I, 430; commands Free State forces in Kansas, 443; goes East to recruit help, 450; organizes "Frontier Guards," IV, 106; receives authority to raise a brigade, V, 83; endeavors to supplant Hunter, 84; asks permission to receive colored recruits, VI, 445; favors Lincoln's renomination, IX, 61, 62.

Lane, John Q., Bvt. Brig. Gen. U. S. Vols.: in march to Franklin, X, 11, 12.

Lane, Joseph, Bvt. Maj. Gen. U. S. A., Gov. of Oreg., U. S. Sen.: voted for, in the Charleston Convention, II, 244; remarks about resistance, 316.

Larrabee, Charles H., M. C.: plan of compromise, II, 423.

Latham, George C., member of Lincoln's suite, III, 290.

Lauman, Jacob G., Bvt. Maj. Gen. U. S. Vols.: in siege of Vicksburg, VII, 289; repulsed at Jackson, 324; relieved from command at Ord's request, 324.

Lawrence, Kas., founded by Emigrant Aid Company, I, 395; Border Ruffian foray against, organized, 442; threatened by Border Ruffian army, 443; Gov. Shannon's compromise with, 447; threatened a second time by guerrillas, 455; Free State Hotel burned, 455; Free State Hotel declared a rebellious fortification, 456; Quantrell's massacre, Aug. 21, 1863, VIII, 211, 212.

Lawton, Alexander R., Conf. Brig. Gen.: strength of brigade after Antietam, VI, 143.

Lawton, G. W., Capt. U. S. Vols.: in capture of Jefferson Davis, X, 270; statement about capture of Davis, 271, 272.

Leadbetter, Danville, Conf. Brig. Gen.: moves his command to East Tennessee, V, 77.

Leake, Shelton F., M. C.: plan of compromise, II, 422.

Leale, Dr., present at Lincoln's death-bed, X, 300.

Leary, Cornelius L. L., M. C.: second interview with Lincoln about compensated emancipation, VI, 111; member of Select Committee on Emancipation, 395.

Leasure, Daniel, Col. U. S. Vols.: in battle of the Wilderness, VIII, 366.

Leavitt, Humphrey H., M. C., Judge U. S. Circuit Ct.: denies motion for habeas corpus for Vallandigham, VII, 336-338.

Lecompte, Samuel D., Chief Justice Kansas Territory, I, 423; doctrine of "constructive treason," 434; speech at Leavenworth meeting, 440; instructions on "constructive treason," 440; issues writ against ex-Governor Reeder, 451.

Lecompton, Kas., founded, I, 424; made capital of the Territory, 424.

Lecompton Constitution, brought to Buchanan by Calhoun, II, 125; transmitted to Congress, 125; rejected by Congress, 130, 131; Crittenden-Montgomery substitute, 131; English bill passed, 133.

Lecompton Constitutional Convention, meeting of, Sept. 7, 1857, II, 103; recess of, 103; reassembles Oct. 19, 1857, 106, 107; Constitution framed by, 108, 109.

Ledlie, James H., Brig. Gen. U. S. Vols.: in assault at Petersburg mine, IX, 421, 422; censured for Petersburg mine affair, 425.

Lee, Albert L., Brig. Gen. U. S. Vols.: in Red River expedition, VIII, 292; in battle of Sabine Cross Roads, 293, 294; in battle of Pleasant Hill, 295.

Lee, Fitzhugh, Conf. Maj. Gen.: in Army of Northern Virginia, VIII, 354; in battle of Spotsylvania, 374; in battle of Cold Harbor, 400; in Shenandoah campaign, IX, 293, 295; wounded at Winchester, 305; defeated at Trevilian Station, 405; in march to Five Forks, X, 168; in retreat to Appomattox, 185, 194.

Lee, G. W. Custis, Conf. Maj. Gen.: captured in retreat to Appomattox, X, 187.

Lee, Robert E., Col. U. S. A., Conf. Gen.: commands marines sent against John Brown, II, 208; personal description, IV, 97; interview with F. P. Blair, Sr., 98; offered command of Union army, 98; contradictory reports of his reply, 98, 99; interview with Gen. Scott, 100; letter to Gen. Scott resigning his commission, 101; takes command of Virginia secession troops, 101; conference with A. H. Stephens, 158, 159; opposes projects to capture Washington, 161; instructs Virginia forces to act on the defensive, 161; letter about securing provisions, 195; opinion of Harper's Ferry, 318; assumes command of Confederate army before Richmond, V, 390; statement of his force, 421; Davis's friendship for, 422; orders Jackson to join him, 422; plan for attacking McClellan's army, 423, 424; commands in person at battle of Gaines's Mill, June 27, 1862, 428; losses at Gaines's Mill, 429; pursues McClellan towards James River, 434; attacks Union army at Malvern Hill, July 1, 1862, 437; withdraws his army to Richmond, July 8, 1862, 440; concentrates large force against Pope's advance, VI, 6; forces of, 6; states strength of Confederate army in battle of Antietam, 131; crosses the Potomac into Maryland, 132; sends detachment to capture Harper's Ferry, 133; captures Harper's Ferry, Sept. 15, 1862, 137; takes position at Sharpsburg, 137; battle of Antietam, Sept. 17, 1862, 139-141; report to Jefferson Davis about stragglers, 143; report of the battle, 144; retreats across the Potomac, 145; arrives at Fredericksburg to oppose Burnside, 199; concentrates his army, 201; battle of Fredericksburg, Dec. 13, 1862, 203-208; dispatch to Richmond that enemy has disappeared, 209; plan to retire to the Annas, 209, 210; charges Hunter and Phelps with inaugurating servile war, 470; recommends negro soldiers for rebel service, 487; battle of Chancellorsville, May 1-3, 1863, VII, 96-107; sends Jackson to attack Hooker's rear, 98; beset with the cry, "On to Washington," 201; reasons for invading Pennsylvania, 201, 203; advance to the Shenandoah Valley, 205-210; withdraws Longstreet to the Shenandoah Valley, 216; crosses the Potomac, 217, 218; asks for reënforcements, 217; learns that Meade is advancing northward, 232, 233; selects Gettysburg to concentrate his army, 236; battle of Gettysburg, July 1–3, 1863, 239–268; arrives at Gettysburg, 246; resolves to renew his attack, 247, 248; orders Longstreet to attack on July 2, 251; orders Longstreet to attack on July 3, 258, 259; proposes to exchange prisoners, 272; retreats from Gettysburg, 273, 274; delayed at the Potomac, 275; crosses the Potomac, 277; retires behind the Rapidan, VIII, 233; offers his resignation, 234; begins flanking movement, 238; returns to the Rappahannock, 241; concentrates behind the Rapidan, 245; activity at Mine Run, 248; strength of Army of Northern Virginia, 352; marches to attack Grant, 358; battle of the Wilderness, May 5, 6, 1864, 360–367; begins march to Spotsylvania, 368; battle of Spotsylvania, May 8–19, 1864, 372–385; battle of North Anna, May 23–27, 1864, 387–390; battle of Cold Harbor, June 1–12, 1864, 391, 400–405; sends Early to Lynchburg, IX, 160; letter to Jefferson Davis, 160; sends Early reënforcements, 311, 312; sends Beauregard reënforcements, 410; commands defenses of Petersburg, 411, 419, 420; siege of Richmond, 427; made Confederate general-in-chief, X, 153; assumes command of all Confederate forces, 155; reports want of rations, 156; proposes a military convention to Grant, 157, 158; conference with Jefferson Davis, 159, 160; directs Gordon to break the Union lines, 160; march to Five Forks, 168–172; battle of Five Forks, April 1, 1865, 172–174; retreat from Petersburg, 175; directs evacuation of Richmond, 180, 181; letter to Davis, 182, 183; evacuates Petersburg, April 2, 1865, 183; retreat to Appomattox, 183–195; asks Grant's terms, 190; proposes to meet Grant, 192; orders of, 193; asks Grant for interview, 194; interview with Grant at Appomattox, 195; surrender to Grant, April 9, 1865, 195, 197; farewell interview with Grant, 197, 198; dispatch, "Richmond must be evacuated," 201.

Lee, Stephen D., Conf. Lieut. Gen.: in battles of Atlanta, IX, 280, 283, 286, 287; demands surrender of Resaca, 475; in army of Hood, X, 7: in march to Franklin, 10, 13; in campaign against Nashville, 23; in battle of Nashville, 33; joins Johnston, 36.

Lee, S. Phillips, Rear Adm. U. S. N.: commands the *Oneida* in Farragut's fleet, V,
261; report of, 263; transmits Stephens's request to Sec. Welles, VII, 373.

Lee, W. H. F., Conf. Maj. Gen.: capture of, VII, 458; in Army of Northern Virginia, VIII, 354.

Lee, William R., Bvt. Brig. Gen. U. S. Vols.: in battle of Ball's Bluff, IV, 456.

Lefferts, Marshall, Col. 7th New York Militia: asks orders to proceed via Annapolis, IV, 134; proceeds by steamer, 135.

Leggett, M. D., Maj. Gen. U. S. Vols.: in battles of Atlanta, IX, 273; in March to the Sea, 481.

Lehman, William E., M. C.: member of Select Committee on Emancipation, VI, 395.

Leigh, Watkins, places Clay's name in nomination, I, 225.

Lellyett, John, interview with Lincoln, IX, 358.

Leopold I, King of the Belgians: letter to Napoleon the Third, urging mediation in America, VI, 81.

Le Roy, W. E., Rear Adm. U. S. N.: commands the *Ossipee* in Mobile Bay, IX, 237.

Letcher, John, M. C., Gov. of Va.: thinks disunion probable, III, 418; message to Virginia legislature, 419, 420; design on Fort Monroe, 421; answer to Lincoln's call for troops, IV, 91; proclaims dissolution of the Union, 92; orders military seizures and movements, 92; efforts to capture Gosport navy yard, 145; informs Jefferson Davis of Virginia's secession, 158; advises resumption of peaceful pursuits, 261; calls out Virginia forces, 310, 330.

Lexington, Mo., siege and surrender of, Sept. 18–20, 1861, IV, 426–429.

Lexington, The, Union gunboat· assists in defense of Milliken's Bend, VII, 293; passage through dam on Red River, VIII, 300.

Libby Prison, mine under, VII, 471.

Liberty, Mo., U. S. arsenal robbed of arms, I, 442; arsenal seized, IV, 211.

Lilley, R. D., Conf. Brig. Gen.: in battle of Waynesboro, IX, 330.

Lincoln, Abraham, sixteenth Pres. U. S.: born Feb. 12, 1809, I, 25; childhood, 25–27; early schooling in Indiana, 33, 34; home studies and youthful habits, 34–38; conditions and influences surrounding, 39–43; flatboat journey to New Orleans, 44; farm work, 46; election incident concerning, 67; letter to Herndon, 1848, 68; goes to Springfield, 70; assists to build a flatboat, 70; incident at Rutledge's mill-dam, 71; patents an invention, 1849, 71,

Lincoln, Abraham — continued.
flatboat voyage to New Orleans, May, 1831, 72; sight of slavery, and feelings thereon, 72-74; letter to Speed, 1855, 72-74; returns to Coles County, Ill., 74; letters to John Johnston, 75-77; returns to New Salem, 1831, 78; acts as clerk at an election, 78; manages a store and mill for Offut, 78; wrestling-match with Jack Armstrong, 80, 81; studies " Kirkham's Grammar," 84; goes to meet and pilot the steamboat *Talisman* up the Sangamon River, 86; volunteers for the Black Hawk war, 89; elected captain, May 27, 1832, 89; mustered out as captain, 93; reënlists as private, June 16, 1832, 96; returns to New Salem, 96-100; humorous speech in Congress on his services in Black Hawk war, 100; announces himself candidate for legislature, March 9, 1832, 101; political opinions of, 102-106; circular of, 106; defeated for legislature, 109; vote of New Salem for, 109; purchases share in a store, 110; buys stock of goods from Greene, 111; obtains license to keep a tavern with Berry, 112; begins reading law books, 113; appointed postmaster of New Salem, 114; appointed deputy surveyor, 115; certificate of survey by, 119; elected to State legislature, 122; service in legislature, 1834-1836, 124-128; becomes candidate for reëlection, 128; circular to voters, June 13, 1836, 129; reëlected in 1836, 131; services in legislature, 1836-1837, 131-138, 140, 150-152; secures removal of the State capital to Springfield, 131-138; votes for internal improvements, 137; protest of, with Dan Stone, against certain resolutions on slavery, 140, 151; friendship with William Butler and Joshua F. Speed, 153; removes to Springfield, 153; becomes law partner of John T. Stuart, 157; reëlected to legislature in 1838 and 1840, 158; receives Whig nomination for Speaker, 160; financial plan of, 161; first meeting with Douglas, 163; protest against the Judicial Reform scheme, 164, 165; his gift of story-telling, 170; sudden appearance at a political meeting, 171; nominated for Presidential elector, 172; political speech at Springfield in 1840, 173-177; letters to Stuart: Nov. 14, 1839, about politics, 178, 179 — Jan. 1, 1840, 179, 180 — Jan. 20, 1840, 180, 181 — March 1, 1840, 181 — Dec. 17, 1840, about appointments, 183 — Jan. 23, 1841, about Congressional election, 184, 185; engaged to Miss Mary Todd, 186; experiences in his love affairs, 186-200; his proposal of marriage to Mary S. Owens, 192; becomes morbid over his engagement with Mary Todd, 186-200; goes to Kentucky with Speed, 194; letters of counsel to Speed, 196-198; married to Mary Todd, Nov. 4, 1842, 200; children of, 200; letter about Shields from the "Lost Townships," 205, 206; challenged by Shields, 206, 207; prescribes terms of the duel, 207; meets Shields opposite Alton, Ill., 208; becomes Merryman's second, 210; letter of explanation to W. G. Anderson, 211; advice on quarrelling, 212; dissolves partnership with Stuart, 213; becomes law partner of Judge Logan, 213; opens a law office for himself, 216; his home in Springfield, 216; work in the legislature, 217; declines to be candidate for governor, 217; temperance address, Feb. 22, 1842, 218; work in politics, 1843-1844, 219, 235; fails to secure nomination to Congress, 222; nominated for Presidential elector, 223; resolutions against " Native Americanism," 235; canvass for Congress, 242-245; minute knowledge of local politics, 244, 245; receives the nomination, 245; elected to Congress, 249; service in Thirtieth Congress, 258, 272, 273; speech on the Mexican war, 261, 262; resolutions on the Mexican war, 270-272; letter to Rev. J. M. Peck, 274; supports Gen. Taylor for President, 275; correspondence with Usher F. Linder, 275, 276; speech in Congress for Gen. Taylor, 279, 280; campaign speeches in New England, 1848, 281; votes for Wilmot Proviso, 285; bill to abolish slavery in District of Columbia, 285-288; declines to become a candidate for renomination to Congress, 290; recommendations for appointments, 291, 292; applies for appointment as Commissioner of the General Land Office, 292, 293; offered governorship of Oregon, 297; resumes law practice at Springfield, Ill., 298; studies the first six books of Euclid, 299; Judge David Davis's opinion of, 301-303; Judge Drummond's opinion of, 303, 304; anecdotes of his cases, 305, 306; his grave and serious temper, 306; method of argument, 307; cordiality and wit, 308; his largest fee, 308; political advancement of, 310-312; partial withdrawal from politics, 372; re-appearance on the stump, 373; speech in Springfield, Ill., at State fair, Oct. 4, 1854, 375-380;

Lincoln, Abraham — *continued.*
candidate for legislature in Sangamon
County, 375; speech at Peoria, Oct. 16,
1854, 380-383; candidate for U. S. Senator
before Illinois legislature in 1855, 383-390;
elected member of legislature from Sangamon County, 384; resigns his seat, 384;
named as member of Republican Central
Committee of Illinois in 1854, 386; letter to
Codding, Nov. 27, 1854, 386, 387; urges his
friends to vote for Trumbull for Senator,
389; letter to Washburne, Feb. 9, 1855, 389;
letter to Robertson, Aug. 15, 1855, 391,
392; attends Decatur Convention, II, 24;
speech at Bloomington Convention, 30;
receives votes for Vice-President in Philadelphia Convention, 35; note to John
Van Dyke, June 27, 1856, 36; campaign
work in 1856, 41; speech at Galena, 41-43;
speech at Chicago, 44, 45; speech in reply
to Douglas on the Dred Scott decision,
June 26, 1857, 85-89; nominated for Senator, 136; "House divided against itself"
speech, 136-138, 143; letter to Wilson, June
1, 1856, about Greeley and Seward, 139-
142; correspondence with Crittenden, 142;
speech at Springfield, Ill., July 17, 1858,
143, 144; begins Senatorial campaign, 145;
challenges Douglas to joint debate, 145;
method of debate, 147; answers to Douglas's questions, 156, 157; questions to
Douglas at Freeport, 157, 158; comments
on Douglas's answers, 161, 162; defeated
for Senator, 165; letter to Judd, Nov. 15,
1858, about his defeat, 167, 168; favors
Trumbull's reëlection, 167; letter to Judd,
Nov. 16, 1858, about campaign expenses,
168; letter to Dr. Henry, Nov. 19, 1858,
about the election, 168, 169; letter to As-
bury, Nov. 19, 1858, "The fight must go
on," 169; receives many invitations to
speak, 177; growing party authority of,
178; correspondence with Colfax, 178-180;
letter to Canisius, May 17, 1859, about
Know-Nothingism, 181; letter to Pierce
and others, April 6, 1859, 182, 183; Ohio
speeches, 185-188; comment on the John
Brown raid, 212, 213; invited to lecture in
New York, 216; Cooper Institute speech,
218-225; speeches in New England, 226;
candidate before Chicago Convention,
1860, 256, 271; letter to Pickett, April 16,
1859, 256; letter to Judd, Dec. 9, 1859, 257;
letter to Frazer, Nov. 1, 1859, 257, 258; letter
to Judd, Feb. 9, 1860, 258, 259; votes for: on
first ballot, 273 — on second ballot, 274 — on

third ballot, 274, 275; nominated for President, 275-277; letter of acceptance, May 23,
1860, 276-281; habits during the Presidential campaign, 286, 287; letter to Edward
Lusk, Oct. 30, 1858, on "Know-Nothings,"
288; letter to A. Jonas, July 21, 1860, on
"Know-Nothings," 288; electoral votes
for, 294; the Presidential count, 294; declared elected President, 294; opinion on
Fugitive Slave law, III, 25; election as
President officially declared, 146; compared and contrasted with Jefferson
Davis, 207-210; approves Constitutional
Amendment, 236; address at Springfield
jubilee, 246; opinions on secession, 247;
correspondence with Gen. Scott, 249-251;
letter to Washburne, Dec. 21, 1860, for Gen.
Scott, 250; letter to Gen. Wool, Jan. 14,
1861, 251; letter to Weed, Dec. 17, 1860,
about governors' meeting, 253; caution to
Greeley, 258; letter to Kellogg, Dec. 11,
1860, about compromise, 259; letter to
Washburne, Dec. 13, 1860, about compromise, 259; letter to Seward, Feb. 1, 1861,
about compromise, 260; interview with
Weed, 261; confidential correspondence
with A. H. Stephens, 271-273; letter to
Speer, Oct. 23, 1860, 276; letter to Prentice,
Oct. 29, 1860, 278; letter to Paschal, Nov.
16, 1860, 279; interview with New England
politician, 279-282; letter to Raymond,
Nov. 28, 1860, 282; letter to Gilmer, Dec. 15,
1860, 284; letter to Duff Green, Dec. 28,
1860, 286; letter to Trumbull, Dec. 28, 1860,
287; letter to Hale, Jan. 11, 1861, 288;
journey from Springfield to Washington,
289-315; members of his suite, 290; farewell address at Springfield, 291; speeches
at Indianapolis, 293-295; speech at Columbus, 295; speech at Steubenville, 296;
speech at Trenton, 297-299; speech at
Philadelphia, 299; speech at Harrisburg,
300; raises flag over Independence Hall,
300, 310; secret night journey from Harrisburg to Washington, 302-315; rumored
plot to assassinate, 303; interview with
Judd and Pinkerton, 308; interview with
F. W. Seward, 311, 313; conference with
members of his suite, 314; arrival in
Washington, 315; consultation with party
leaders, 318; first inaugural address, 319-
344; receives Seward's suggestions for the
inaugural, 321; adopts most of Seward's
suggestions, 322; inauguration of, 324-344;
takes the oath of office, 344; formation of
his Cabinet, 347; interview with Hamlin,

Lincoln, Abraham — *continued.*
347; editorial in Springfield "Journal," 348; letters to Seward, Dec. 8, 1860, tendering him office of Secretary of State, 349; interview with Bates, 351; offers Bates office of Attorney-General, 352; letter to Colfax, March 8, 1861, 353; invites Cameron to Springfield, 355; letter to Cameron, Dec. 31, 1861, tendering him Cabinet appointment, 355, 356; letter to Cameron, Jan. 3, 1861, recalling tender of Cabinet appointment, 356, 357; explanatory letters about the Cameron affair, 356-358; invites Chase to Springfield, 359; conference with Chase, 359; invites Gilmer to Springfield, 362; letter to Seward, Jan. 3, 1861, 362; letter to Seward, Jan. 12, 1861, 364; answer to Judd about Cabinet "slate," 370; letter to Seward, March 4, 1861, asking reconsideration of his withdrawal from the Cabinet, 371; order to maintain all military places, 379; questions to Gen. Scott, 379; first Cabinet meeting, 380; extract from message about Sumter, 382; questions his Cabinet about Sumter, 385; sends Capt. Fox to Sumter, 389; sends Hurlbut to Charleston, 390; invites G. W. Summers to Washington, 423; interview with Baldwin, 423-426; interview with Botts, 423-426; order for the Sumter expedition, 433, 434; interview with Meigs, 435, 436; order to Gen. Scott to reënforce Fort Pickens, 436; signs secret orders, 438; interview with Welles, 440, 441; answer to Seward's memorandum, 448, 449; orders to Lieut. Porter, April 1, 1861, IV, 4; letter to Capt. Mercer, April 2, 1861, 4; interview with Seward and Welles, 5, 6; instructions to Anderson, April 4, 1861, 27, 28; notice to Gov. Pickens, 33, 34; letter to Fox, May 1, 1861, 56; asks Gen. Scott to report military events daily, 64; his equanimity, 70; reply to committee of Virginia Convention, 72-76; proclamation, April 15, 1861, calling out 75,000 militia, and convening Congress, 77; interview with Douglas, 80; proclaims blockade of Southern ports, 89; declares privateering piracy, 89; requests F. P. Blair, Sr., to ascertain Lee's sentiments, 98; described by Bayard Taylor, 108; interview with Baltimore committee, 126; letter, April 20, 1861, in reply to Gov. Hicks and Mayor Brown, 126; interview with Mayor Brown, 127-130; precautionary orders, April 21, 1861, 137, 138; reply to Baltimore committee, 139; letter to Rev-

erdy Johnson, April 24, 1861, 164, 165; letter to Gen. Scott, April 25, 1861, about Maryland legislature, 167, 168; order about habeas corpus, April 27, 1861, 169; interview with committee of Maryland legislature, 171, 172; message about Merryman case, 176, 177; draft of reply to Gov. Harris, May, 1861, 196; reply to Johnson, May 6, 1861, 197; orders transfer of arms to Illinois, 198; directs Lyon to enroll 10,000 volunteers, 212; confidential instructions to Lyon to relieve Harney, 217; approves seizure of war material at Cairo, 232; sends Nelson to Kentucky, 235; commissions Anderson to organize Kentucky troops, 235; letter to Gov. Magoffin, Aug. 24, 1861, 241, 242; call for three years' volunteers, 255; criticism on current events, 258; establishes armory at Rock Island, Ill., 259; corrects Seward's dispatch of May 21, 1861, 270-275; refuses England's conditions to the Declaration of Paris, 279; revokes exequatur of British consul at Charleston, 280; calls council of war, 322, 323; promises to aid western Virginia, 329, 330; authorizes Secretary of War to aid Gov. Peirpoint, 332; receives news of Union success at Bull Run, 352, 353; informed of Union retreat, 353; visits Potomac camps, 357; memorandum on military affairs, 368, 369; message, July 4, 1861, 371-375; instructions to Gen. Scott, July 16, 1861, about fugitive slaves, 391; signs first Confiscation Act, 394; appoints Frémont major general in the U. S. army, 402; assigns him to command Western Department, 402; letter to Hunter, Sept. 9, 1861, 413; letter to Mrs. Frémont, Sept. 12, 1861, 414; criticism on Frémont, 414, 415; letter to Frémont, Sept. 2, 1861, requesting him to modify his proclamation, 418; revokes Frémont's proclamation, 420; letter to Browning, Sept. 22, 1861, 421-423; order to relieve Frémont, 433; letter to Curtis, Oct. 24, 1861, 433; instructions to Hunter, Oct. 24, 1861, 437, 438; comment on Gen. Stone's arrest, 460; interviews with Wade, Chandler, and Trumbull, 467; letter about recruiting at Hatteras, V, 14; instructions about Port Royal expedition, 15, 16; comments on the *Trent* affair, 25, 26; draft of dispatch on the *Trent* affair, 32-34; orders Anderson to assume command in Kentucky, 50; letter to Gov. Morton, Sept. 29, 1861, 54, 55; suggests expedition to East Tennessee, 61, 62; proposes military rail-

Lincoln, Abraham — continued.
road to East Tennessee, 66, 67; inquiry to
Buell, Jan. 4, 1862, 70; letter to Buell, Jan.
6, 1862, about East Tennessee, 71; gives
Lane authority to raise a brigade, 84;
directions about the Lane expedition,
84, 85; authorizes organization of Missouri
State militia, 96; comment on letter from
Halleck, 99; suggestions to Western commanders to coöperate, 100; inquiry about
movement on Bowling Green, 101; directs
coöperation between Halleck and Buell,
103; indorsement on Halleck's letter, Jan.
10, 1862, 103, 104; letter to Halleck and
Buell, Jan. 13, 1862, on Western campaign,
107, 108; letter to McClernand, Nov. 10,
1861, about Belmont, 114, 115; modifies
War Department instruction about employing contrabands, 124; modifies Cameron's report about arming slaves, 126, 127;
nominates Cameron Minister to Russia,
128; defends Cameron in a special message, 130; first meeting with Stanton,
133, 134; relations with Stanton, 139, 140;
relations with his Cabinet, 139; letter to
Stanton, March 1, 1864, about Mrs. Baird,
143; letter to Stanton, March 18, 1864,
about discharge of prisoners of war, 144;
order, Sept. 1, 1864, about prisoners of war
at Rock Island, 145, 146; interview with
Stanton about Rock Island prisoners,
146, 147; letter to Grant, Sept. 22, 1864,
about Rock Island prisoners, 147; suggests
plan of campaign to McClellan, 148, 149;
urges McClellan to prepare for a forward
movement, 151; invites McDowell and
Franklin to a conference, 156; military
council at the White House, Jan. 13, 1862,
157, 158; issues "General War Order No.
One," 160; issues "President's Special War
Order No. One," 160; letter to McClellan,
Feb. 3, 1862, about plan of campaign, 161;
adopts McClellan's plan of movement by
the lower Chesapeake, 166; issues "General War Order No. Two," 169; issues
"General War Order No. Three," 170, 171;
resolves to remove McClellan from chief
command, 178; "President's [Special]
War Order No. Three," 178, 179; approves
plan of council at Fairfax Court House,
March 13, 1862, 181; directs McDowell's
corps to remain in front of Washington,
184; telegram to Halleck, Feb. 16, 1862,
about Fort Donelson, 199; appoints Grant
major general of U. S. volunteers, 200; letter to Bancroft, Nov. 18, 1861, 203; annual

message, Dec. 3, 1861, 204, 205; plan of compensated emancipation for Delaware, 206,
207; special message, March 6, 1862, recommending compensated abolishment,
209, 210; letters advocating compensated
abolishment: to Raymond, March 9,
1862, 210—to McDougall, March 14, 1862,
210, 211; interview, March 10, 1862, with
Border Slave State Representatives,
212-214; signs joint resolution for compensated abolishment, 214; signs Act to
emancipate slaves in District of Columbia,
216; military council at the White House,
221, 222; desires part of McClellan's army
to proceed down the Potomac, 221, 222;
orders Potomac rebel batteries silenced,
222; receives news of the *Merrimac's*
attack, 226; receives news of the *Monitor's*
victory, 231; orders that the *Monitor* be
not unduly exposed, 232; visits Fort Monroe, 234; suggests attack on Sewall's
Point batteries, 234; reconnoiters landing opposite Fort Monroe, 236; visits Norfolk, 237, 238; present at council about
expedition against New Orleans, 254,
255; orders the expedition, 255; decides
against present change of commands in
the West, 309; cautionary dispatch to
Buell, March 10, 1862, 315; War Order
No. Three, March 11, 1862, uniting Western Departments under command of Halleck, 315, 316; letter to Halleck, May 24, 1862,
339, 340; orders Halleck to send 25,000
troops east, 353; telegraphs Halleck, June
30, 1862, to send no troops east if it interferes with Buell's advance on East Tennessee, 353; appoints Halleck general-in-
chief, 355; letter to McClellan, April 9,
1862, answering complaints about Mc-
Dowell's corps, 362-364; asks McClellan,
May 1, 1862, "Is anything to be done?"
374; sends McClellan permission to temporarily suspend the corps organization,
381; letter to McClellan, May 9, 1862,
about corps commanders, 381, 382; informs
McClellan that "the President is not
willing to uncover the capital entirely,"
383; orders McDowell to form a junction
with McClellan, 383; dispatch to McClellan, May 25, 1862, about Jackson's raid and
the detention of McDowell, 402, 403; urges
McClellan to "attack Richmond or give
up the job," 403; directions in regard to
Jackson's raid, 403; orders to McDowell to
move against Jackson, 405, 406; advice and
information to McDowell, 407, 408; orders

Lincoln, Abraham — *continued*.
Frémont to Harrisonburg, 408; orders to abandon pursuit of Jackson, 411; letter to McClellan, June 15, 1862, 416; comment on "Stonewall" Jackson, 417; answers McClellan's dispatch about responsibility, June 26, 1862, 420; telegraphs McClellan, June 28, 1862, "Save your army at all events," 443; orders assistance and reënforcements to McClellan, 444; telegram to McClellan, July 1, 1862, "Maintain your ground if you can," 445; telegram to McClellan, July 2, 1862, about reënforcements, 446; visits McClellan, July 8, 1862, 453; interviews with army officers, 453; questions McClellan about absenteeism, 453, 454; places Halleck in chief command, 455; visits Gen. Scott at West Point, VI, 2; alleged opinion in Porter court-martial case, 13; reply to McClellan's telegram about Pope, 19; interview with McClellan and Halleck, 21; places McClellan in command of defenses of Washington, 21; opinion of McClellan, 23; orders Halleck to form a new army, 28; comment on Hunter's order of emancipation, 94; proclamation revoking Hunter's order, 94–96; admonition to the Southern States, 95, 96; approval of antislavery enactments of Second Session of Thirty-Seventh Congress, 98–102; recommends recognition of Hayti and Liberia, 99; draft of veto message on the Confiscation Act, 102, 103; influence on antislavery movement, 107; second interview with Border State Representatives, 108–111; urges them to accept compensated emancipation, 109–111; letter to Seward, June 28, 1862, "I expect to maintain this contest," etc., 115, 116; letter to governors of loyal States, June 30, 1862, about reënforcements, 116, 117; response to governors issuing call for 300,000 men, 119; private circular to governors, 119; decides to adopt military emancipation, 121; interview with Welles and Seward, 121–123; directs order to be issued about seizing rebel property and employing slaves, 124; averse to arming negroes, 124, 125; reads to his Cabinet first draft of emancipation proclamation, 125; describes comments of members of the Cabinet, 129, 130; postpones issuing first emancipation proclamation, 130; injunction to McClellan to find and hurt the enemy, 132; grotesque simile of, 142; disappointment at Lee's escape from Antietam, 145, 146;

letter to Reverdy Johnson, July 26, 1862, answering conservative complaints in Louisiana, 149, 150; letter to Bullitt, July 28, 1862, answering conservative complaints in Louisiana, 150, 151; letter to Horace Greeley, Aug. 22, 1862, 152, 153; his self-criticism, 154; reply to a Chicago deputation, Sept. 13, 1862, 155, 156; reads preliminary emancipation proclamation to his Cabinet, 158; comment in Cabinet on emancipation proclamation, 163; reply to serenade, 164; statement about Altoona meeting, 164, 165; visits McClellan at Antietam, 174; "McClellan's body-guard," 175; instructions through Halleck to McClellan, Oct. 6, 1862, 175, 176; inquiry about McClellan's horses, 177; reply to McClellan about horses, 179; letter to McClellan, Oct. 13, 1862, of military criticism and advice, 181–184; instructions through Halleck to McClellan, Oct. 21, 1862, urging movement, 184; letter requesting Maj. Key to disprove alleged remarks, 186; interview with Maj. Key and Maj. Turner, 186, 187; record in case of Maj. Key, Sept. 27, 1862, 187; orders dismissal of Maj. Key, 187; intentions towards McClellan, 188; removes McClellan from command, Nov. 5, 1862, 188, 189; consents to Burnside's plan of campaign against Richmond, 198; visits Burnside at Fredericksburg, Nov. 27, 1862, 200; letter to Halleck, Nov. 27, 1862, on Burnside's proposed campaign, 200, 201; dispatch to Army of Potomac, Dec. 22, 1862, 211; telegraphs Burnside, Dec. 30, 1862, not to make a general movement, 213; interview with Gens. Cochrane and Newton, 213; interview with Burnside, 214; letter asking Halleck to approve or disapprove Burnside's plan, Jan. 1, 1863, 215; withdraws the letter, 216; declines to accept Burnside's resignation, 217; gives Burnside leave of absence, 221; assigns Burnside to command Department of the Ohio, 221; signs Act to make paper money legal tender, Feb. 25, 1862, 235; comments on National Bank Act, 243, 244; supports Chase's financial management, 247; estimate of Chase's ability, 262, 263; conference with Republican Senators asking Seward's dismissal, 264, 265; interview with Cabinet and Republican Senate Committee, 265–267; declines to accept resignations of Seward and Chase, 268; comment on Chase's resignation, "Now I can ride,"

Lincoln, Abraham — *continued*.
271; urges relief of East Tennessee, 273; directs Halleck to order Buell to East Tennessee, 280; congratulates Rosecrans on battle of Murfreesboro, 296; asks written opinions of Cabinet on bill to admit West Virginia, 300; opinion on the admission of West Virginia, 309-311; signs Act admitting West Virginia, 311; reply to resolutions of New School Presbyterians, 323; reply to committee of General Conference of the Methodist Episcopal Church, 324; letter to Iowa Quakers, Jan. 5, 1862, 327, 328; letter to Rhode Island Quakers, March 19, 1862, 328; letter to Mrs. Gurney, Sept. 4, 1864, 328, 329; letter to Reed, Feb. 22, 1863, 330; commutes punishment of Norfolk clergyman, 334; letter to Curtis, Jan. 2, 1863, about the churches, 336; letter to Filley, Dec. 22, 1863, about Dr. Mc-Pheeters, 336, 337; letter to Stanton, Feb. 11, 1864, about the Southern churches, 337; orders about a church at Memphis, March 4, 1864, 338; revokes Grant's order expelling Jews, 339; order for observance of the Sabbath, Nov 16, 1862, 340, 341; meditation on Providence, September, 1862, 342; appoints Andrew Johnson military governor of Tennessee, 344; appoints Edward Stanley military governor of North Carolina, 345; appoints G. F. Shepley military governor of Louisiana, 346; appoints John S. Phelps military governor of Arkansas, 346; language of inaugural and special message concerning reconstruction, 347, 348; allusion to reconstruction in letter to Reverdy Johnson, July 26, 1862, 348, 349; allusion to reconstruction in letter to Cuthbert Bullitt, July 28, 1862, 349; letter to Butler and Shepley, Oct. 14, 1862, about reconstruction, 350; same to Grant and Johnson, Oct. 21, 1862, 350; same to Steele and Phelps, Nov. 18, 1862, 350; letters to Shepley, Nov. 21, 1862, about Congressmen from Louisiana, 351, 352; belief in the value of colonization, 354; comment on colonization in the Lincoln-Douglas debates, 355; recommends appropriation of money and acquisition of territory for colonization, 355; asks Prof. Henry for report on Chiriqui coal, 358; signs contract with Bernard Kock for colonization on Ile A'Vache, 360; cancels the contract, 362; sends special agent to investigate the colony at Ile A'Vache, 364; order creating Department of the Mis-

souri, 381; letter to Bates, Nov. 29, 1862, about Missouri State militia, 385, 386; letter to Gamble, and order, 386; order suspending assessments in St. Louis County, 386; letter to Curtis, Jan. 5, 1863, about Missouri difficulties, 387, 388; orders suspension of assessments for damages in Missouri, 390; telegram to Curtis, Jan. 10, 1863, about slaves in Missouri, 396; telegram to B. Gratz Brown, Jan. 7, 1863, about Missouri Senatorial election, 397; answer to Woodruff, April 16, 1863, about Missouri discords, 397, 398; discusses compensated abolishment in annual message of Dec. 1, 1862, 399-401; proposes a Constitutional Amendment, 400; reads draft of final emancipation proclamation to the Cabinet, 405; form of the draft, 414, 415; final revision of the proclamation, 421; signs final emancipation proclamation, 429; letter to Hodges, April 4, 1864, about emancipation proclamation, 430, 431; extract from letter to Conkling, Aug. 26, 1863, 431, 432; extracts from letter to Robinson, Aug. 17, 1863, 432, 433; extract from letter to Schermerhorn, Sept. 12, 1864, 433; remarks in interview with J. T. Mills, 433, 434; letter to Chase, Sept. 2, 1863, 434, 435; question to Gen. Mitchel about opening the Mississippi, 440, 441; answers Butler's inquiry about negro soldiers, 448; letter to Dix, Jan. 14, 1863, about colored troops, 452, 453; letter to Gov. Johnson, March 26, 1863, about colored troops, 453, 454; letter to Banks, March 29, 1863, about colored troops, 454, 455; letter to Hunter, April 1, 1863, about colored troops, 455, 456; letter to Sumner, June 1, 1863, about Frémont and colored troops, 456, 457; urges a vigorous renewal of organizing negro troops, 465; letter to Grant, Aug. 9, 1863, about negro troops, 465; reply to Frederick Douglass about retaliation, 474; order about retaliation, 474, 475; address about Fort Pillow, 478; asks Cabinet opinions on the Fort Pillow massacre, 481; calls for 300,000 volunteers, July 2, 1862, VII, 3; calls for 300,000 nine-months militia, Aug. 4, 1862, 3; approves law for the draft, March 3, 1863, 5; letter to Gov. Seymour, March 23, 1863, 10, 11; letters to Seymour, Aug. 7 and 16, 1863, about the draft, 33, 35, 39; appoints commission on New York enrollment, 41; letter to Stanton, Feb. 27, 1864, on New York enrollment, 42, 43; unpublished opinion on the draft law, 49-57;

Lincoln, Abraham — *continued.*
telegram to Du Pont, April 13, 1863, about
attack on Charleston, 74, 75; instruction
to Hunter and Du Pont, April 14, 1863, 75;
letter of thanks to Hunter, June 30, 1863,
85, 86; letter to Hooker, Jan. 26, 1863,
about dictatorship, 87, 88; memorandum,
April 11, 1863, about Richmond campaign,
90, 91; directs that McClernand command
the Vicksburg expedition, 126; letter to
Hooker, May 7, 1863, asking if he has a
plan of movement, 197, 198; letter to
Hooker, May 14, 1863, against early movement, 199; letter to Hooker, June 5, 1863,
"Would not take any risk of being entan-
gled upon the river like an ox jumped half
over a fence," 204, 205; telegram to
Hooker, June 10, 1863, that Lee's army,
and not Richmond, is his objective, 208;
letter, June 29, 1863, answering Milroy's
complaints, 209; telegram to Hooker, June
14, 1863, about the head and tail of Lee's
army, 210; letter to Hooker, June 16, 1863,
about relations between Hooker and Halleck, 212; issues call for 100,000 militia for
six months, 220; urges pursuit of Lee, 274;
informs Meade of surrender of Vicksburg,
274; appoints Meade brigadier general in
U. S. army, 274; expresses dissatisfaction
at Lee's escape, 277; declines to accept
Meade's resignation, 277; comment on
Lee's escape, 277, 278; unsigned letter to
Meade, July 14, 1863, 279-281; reply, Nov.
22, 1862, to Banks's requisition, 312, 313;
letter of praise to Grant, July 13, 1863,
326, 327; letter to Burnside, May 29, 1863,
about Vallandigham's arrest, 338; commutes Vallandigham's sentence, 339;
orders him sent "beyond our military
lines," 339; letter to Corning and others,
June 12, 1863, about Vallandigham, 343-
349; reply to Ohio committee, June 29,
1863, 352-354; draft of instructions about
Vallandigham, June 20, 1864 (not sent),
359; letter to Schurz, Nov. 24, 1862, about
the elections, 363, 364; letter to Fernando
Wood, Dec. 12, 1862, about amnesty and
negotiation, 368; draft of reply to
Stephens (not sent), 373; draft of reply
to Stephens (sent), 374; letter to Conkling, Aug. 26, 1863, about peace, 380-384;
reply to Chandler's criticism on Weed and
Morgan, 389; warning to Republicans
about Etheridge's alleged plot, 390, 391;
letter to Montgomery Blair, Nov. 2,
1863, about Frank Blair, 392, 393; letter

to Grant, Aug. 9, 1863, about Mexico, 401;
affirms the Monroe doctrine in his second
letter of acceptance, 421; action respecting rebel privateers, 448; authorizes
Grant to reopen the subject of exchange,
463; attitude towards the American
Knights, VIII, 8; remark to Sen. Mc-
Donald, 13; gives respite to John Y.
Beall, 20; refuses to commute Beall's
sentence, 20, 21; modifies Dix's order
about pursuing rebel raiders, 25; order,
Feb. 14, 1862, about political prisoners, 32;
order, Feb. 27, 1863, appointing Dix and
Pierrepont to examine cases of State
prisoners, 32, 33; directs War Department
order of Nov. 22, 1862, discharging prisoners arrested for opposing the draft, etc.,
33, 34; indemnified by Congress for having
suspended writ of habeas corpus, 33-36;
authorized by Congress to suspend writ of
habeas corpus, 33-36; letter to Rosecrans,
March 17, 1863, about rank, 47; letter to
Rosecrans, Feb. 17, 1863, about rebel raids,
50; letter to Rosecrans, Aug. 10, 1863,
about inaction, 64-66; rejoinder to Rosecrans, Aug. 31, 1863, 66, 67; comment on
Chickamauga, 108; instructions to Halleck, Sept. 21, 1863, about Rosecrans, 109;
dispatch to Rosecrans, Sept. 21, 1863, 109,
110; dispatches to Burnside, Sept. 21 and
23, 1863, 110, 111; rides from Soldiers'
Home to War Department at night, 112;
holds council of war, 112; correspondence with Rosecrans, 114-117; letter to
Rosecrans, Sept. 28, 1863, about Hooker
and Slocum, 143; sympathy for Unionists
in East Tennessee, 158, 159; reply to East
Tennesseeans, Aug. 9, 1863, 161, 162; declines to accept Burnside's resignation,
165; draft of telegram to Burnside, Sept.
25, 1863 (not sent), 166; answer to East
Tennesseeans, Oct. 16, 1863, 169; anecdote
illustrating Burnside's situation, 178;
letter to Gov. Johnson, Sept. 18, 1863,
about reconstruction and military affairs,
186, 187; proclamation about Union success in East Tennessee, 187; telegram of
thanks to Grant, Dec. 8, 1863, 187, 188; accepts invitation to Gettysburg dedication,
190; visits Gettysburg, 191; Gettysburg
Address, Nov. 19, 1863, 202; letter to Everett, Nov. 20, 1863, 203; letter to Stanton,
May 11, 1863, about Curtis and Schofield,
204, 205; telegram to Blow, Drake, and
others, May 15, 1863, 205; instructions to
Schofield, May 27, 1863, 205, 206; letter to

Lincoln, Abraham—*continued.*
Schofield, June 22, 1863, about emancipation in Missouri, 208; interview with committee of Missouri radicals, 215-220; written reply to address of Missouri radicals, Oct. 5, 1863, 220-223; instructions to Schofield, Oct. 1, 1863, about Missouri affairs, 225, 226; letter to Gamble, Oct. 19, 1863, about protection to provisional government of Missouri, 227, 228; letter to Halleck, July 29, 1863, about attacking Lee, 233; letter to Halleck, Sept. 15, 1863, advising attack on Lee, 234; letter to Halleck, Sept. 19, 1863, discussing defensive policy, 235, 236; holds military conference, 236; letter to Halleck, Oct. 16, 1863, advising attack on Lee, 242; letter to Gillmore, Jan. 13, 1864, on reconstruction in Florida, 282, 283; letter to William Kellogg, June 29, 1863, about cotton, 307; comment on Chase's course, 316, 317; letter to Chase, Feb 29, 1864, about Pomeroy's circular, 322; appoints Grant lieutenant-general, 335; comment on Halleck, 335; interview with Grant, 340, 341; presents Grant his commission as lieutenant-general, 341; conversation with Grant about his duties, 343; letter to Grant, April 30, 1864, about Virginia campaign, 354, 355; letter to Hurlbut, July 31, 1863, about emancipation and reconstruction in Arkansas, 410, 411; letters to Steele, Jan. 15 and 20, 1864, on Arkansas reconstruction, 412, 413; letter to Murphy, Feb. 6, 1864, about reconstruction in Arkansas, 415, 416; letter to Fishback, Feb. 17, 1864, about reconstruction in Arkansas, 416; letter to Steele, June 29, 1864, about new State government in Arkansas, 418; letter to Louisiana Conservative Committee, June 19, 1863, 420; letter to Banks, Aug. 5, 1863, about Louisiana reconstruction, 421, 422; letter to Banks, Nov. 5, 1863, about Louisiana registration, 423, 424; letter to Flanders, Nov. 9, 1863, about repeal of Louisiana secession ordinance, 424; letter to Cottman, Dec. 15, 1863, about Louisiana reconstruction, 426; letter to Banks, Dec. 24, 1863, making him "master" in Louisiana reconstruction, 427, 428; approves Banks's plan, 430; appoints Hahn military governor of Louisiana, 434; letter to Johnson, Sept. 11, 1863, about Tennessee reconstruction, 441; orders about Tennessee reconstruction, 442; telegram to Maynard, Feb. 13, 1864, 444;

telegram to Warren Jordan, 444; letter to E. H. East, Feb. 27, 1864, about Tennessee reconstruction, 444, 445; proclamation defining the amnesty proclamation, 445, 446; order regulating negro enlistments in Maryland, Missouri, Tennessee, and Delaware, 460; letter to Swann about Maryland elections, 461; letter to Bradford, Nov. 2, 1863, about Schenck's election order in Maryland, 463, 464; letter to Creswell, March 17, 1864, about Maryland emancipation, 465; letter to Hoffman, Oct. 10, 1864, about Maryland Constitution, 467; vote for, in Presidential election, 1864, 468; interview with Schofield, 472; letters to Stanton, Dec. 18 and 21, 1863, about Schofield, 472-474; nominates Schofield major general of U. S. volunteers, 474; transfers Schofield and Rosecrans, 474; letter to Rosecrans, April 4, 1864, about Missouri, 475, 476; instructions to Rosecrans about Missouri election, 480, 481; directions to Missouri office holders, 483; letter to Gov. Fletcher, Feb. 20, 1865, 485; letter, June 3, 1864, in praise of Grant, IX, 50, 51; letter to Washburne, Oct. 26, 1863, about renomination, 58; letters to Schurz, March 13 and 23, 1864, about political canvass, 59, 60; address to Workingmen's Committee, March 21, 1864, 60, 61; nominated for President by Baltimore Convention, 71, 72; declines to interfere about Vice-President and platform, 73; reply to notice of his renomination, 75, 76; letter of acceptance, 77, 78; declines to renominate Howard, 87; note to Chase, May 8, 1863, about Victor Smith, 89, 90; declines to appoint Field Assistant Treasurer at New York, 92, 93; letter to Chase, June 28, 1864, about Field, 93, 94; accepts Chase's resignation, 95; nominates Tod for Secretary of Treasury, 95; nominates Fessenden for Secretary of Treasury, 99; comment on Fessenden's appointment, 100; annual message, Dec. 8, 1863, 104-109; comment on theory of reconstruction, 111; comment on Missouri radicals, 111, 112; letter to Henry Winter Davis, March 18, 1863, 113, 114; interview with Chandler about Reconstruction Act, 120, 121; declines to sign Reconstruction Act, 120-123; proclamation, July 8, 1864, about Reconstruction Act, 123; correspondence with Grant about Early's raid, 166, 167; witnesses skirmish near Washington, 172, 173; issues call for 500,000 men, 176; reply, Aug. 3, 1864, to Grant's dis-

428 INDEX

Lincoln, Abraham — *continued.*
patch, 180; letter to Greeley, July 9, 1864, about peace propositions, 187, 188; letter to Greeley, July 15, 1864, asking him to bring commissioners, 189; letter, July 18, 1864, "To whom it may concern," 192; correspondence with Greeley about publishing the Niagara letters, 195; refuses government authority to Jaquess, 203; letter to Abram Wakeman, July 25, 1864, 213, 214; draft of letter to Robinson, Aug. 17, 1864, 215–217; interview with Raymond and others, 219–221; draft of instructions to Raymond, Aug. 24, 1864, 220, 221; secret memorandum, Aug. 23, 1864, 251; reply to Sherman, July 26, 1864, about Osterhaus, 276; order of thanks on capture of Atlanta, 289, 290; telegram to Grant, Sept. 12, 1864, suggesting movement for Sheridan, 298; dispatch to Grant, Sept. 29, 1864, about Sheridan, 313; telegraphs thanks to Sheridan, 326, 327; comment on the Sumner-Blair controversy, 336; action on the Blair-Halleck controversy, 338, 339; asks Blair's resignation, 340, 341; offers Montgomery Blair Spanish or Austrian mission, 342; offers Bates a District Judgeship, 344, 345; offers Holt Attorney-Generalship, 345, 346; appoints Speed Attorney General, 347, 348; nominates Morgan for Secretary of Treasury, 349; appoints McCulloch Secretary of Treasury, 349; proclamation of thanks for Mobile and Atlanta, Sept. 3, 1864, 351, 352; reply to Rev. Dr. Thompson, 352; remarks to returning regiments, 355, 356; draft of letter, Sept. 12, 1864, to Schermerhorn, 356, 357; interview with Lellyett, 358; letter to Campbell, Oct. 22, 1864, about Tennessee election, 358, 359; speech, Oct. 19, 1864, about election, 360, 361; action in the Scripps-Arnold controversy, 361; letter to Hunt about Conkling, 362; letter to McMichael, Aug. 5, 1864, about Kelley, 362, 363; refuses to suspend the draft, 364, 365; directions to Sherman and Rosecrans about soldiers' vote, 365, 366; receives news of October election, 1864, 369–371; receives news of Presidential election, 1864, 376, 377; reëlected President, Nov. 8, 1864, 377; speech about Presidential election, 380, 381; letter to John Phillips, Nov. 21, 1864, 382; comment on the election in annual message of 1864, 383, 384; comment on Chase, 393, 394; appoints Chase Chief Justice, 394, 395; telegram, June 15,

1864, about movement across James River, 407; telegram to Grant, July 17, 1864, 419; dispatch to Grant, Aug. 17, 1864, 428; letters to Butler, Aug. 9 and Dec. 21, 1864, about Virginia reconstruction, 442–444; letter to Hurlbut, Nov. 14, 1864, about Louisiana reconstruction, 446, 447; letter to Canby, Dec. 12, 1864, about Louisiana reconstruction, 447, 448; letter to Trumbull, Jan. 9, 1865, on Louisiana reconstruction, 453, 454; address on reconstruction, April 11, 1865, 457–463; reply to Sherman about Gov. Brown, 471; letter of thanks to Sherman for Savannah, 494, 495; directs Porter to hold his position off Fort Fisher, X, 65; asks Grant to renew expedition against Fort Fisher, 65; message of Dec. 8, 1863, on emancipation, 73, 74; suggests that Baltimore platform advocate Thirteenth Amendment, 79; message of Dec. 6, 1864, on Thirteenth Amendment, 80; interview with Ashley, 84, 85; address about Thirteenth Amendment, 87, 88; message, Dec. 6, 1864, about peace, 92, 93; gives F. P. Blair, Sr., pass to go South, 94; letter to Blair, Jan. 18, 1865, about peace negotiations, 108; sends Eckert to meet Peace Commissioners, 113; sends Seward to confer with Peace Commissioners, 115; instructions to Seward, Jan. 31, 1865, 115; goes to Fort Monroe, 117; interview with Peace Commissioners in Hampton Roads, Feb. 3, 1865, 118–129; draft of message, Feb. 5, 1865, submitted to Cabinet, 133–135; message, Feb. 10, 1865, about Hampton Roads Conference, 137, 138; message, Feb. 8, 1865, about joint resolution on electoral votes, 140, 141; declared reëlected by joint convention of Congress, 141, 142; reply to notification committee, 142; second inauguration of, March 4, 1865, 143–145; second inaugural address, March 4, 1865, 143–145; letter to Weed, March 15, 1865, about second inaugural, 146; directs Grant not to discuss or confer upon political questions, 158; dispatch to Grant, 188; letter to Grant, Jan. 19, 1865, about his son, 213; visit to Grant's headquarters, 214; interview with Grant, Sherman, and Porter, 215; interview with Grant at Petersburg, 216; visit to Richmond, 216–221; interviews with Campbell, 220–222; memorandum for Campbell, 221; letter to Weitzel, April 6, 1865, about Virginia legislature, 222, 223; dispatch to Grant, April 6, 1865, about Virginia legislature, 223, 224;

dispatch to Weitzel, April 12, 1865, about Virginia legislature, 226–228; remarks at Cabinet meeting, April 14, 1865, 281–285; interview with Colfax, 285; comments on personal threats, 287, 288; attends Ford's Theater, 292; shot by Booth, April 14, 1865, 296; carried across the street, 297; death, April 15, 1865, 301, 302; funeral honors at Washington, 316–318; at Baltimore, Harrisburg, Philadelphia, 320; at New York, Albany, Syracuse, Rochester, Buffalo, Cleveland, 321; at Columbus, Indianapolis, Chicago, Springfield, 322; buried at Oak Ridge, 323; monument at Springfield, 324, 325.

Lincoln, Mrs. Abraham, accompanies the President-elect to Washington, III, 290; invites Gen. and Mrs. Grant to Ford's Theater, X, 292; invites Miss Harris and Maj. Rathbone to Ford's Theater, 292; attends the theater with her husband, 292; present at Lincoln's deathbed, 300, 302.

Lincoln, Abraham, marries Anna Boone, I, 4; serves in Pennsylvania Constitutional Convention, 4.

Lincoln, Abraham, grandfather of the Pres.: emigrates from Virginia to Kentucky, I, 1; son of John Lincoln of Rockingham County, Va., 3; marries Mary Shipley, 5; enters land in Kentucky, 10, 11; list of lands owned by, 11; killed by Indians, 21; widow removes with family to Washington County, Ky., 23.

Lincoln, Abraham, Confederate soldier, I, 4.

Lincoln, David J., of Birdsboro, Berks Co., Pa.: information from, about Lincoln genealogy, I, 4.

Lincoln, Edward Baker, son of the President: born March 10, 1846, I, 200.

Lincoln, Hannaniah, signs surveyor's certificate for Abraham Lincoln's land in Jefferson County, Ky., I, 5.

Lincoln, Isaac, settles on the Holston River in Tennessee, I, 3.

Lincoln, Jacob, Revolutionary soldier, I, 3.

Lincoln, John, son of Mordecai Lincoln of Berks County, Pa., I, 3; goes to Rockingham County, Va., 3.

Lincoln, Josiah, uncle of the President: goes to fort for assistance against Indians, I, 21.

Lincoln, Minor, writes a secession letter to the President, I, 4.

Lincoln, Mordecai, son of Samuel Lincoln, of Hingham, Mass., I, 2.

Lincoln, Mordecai, grandson of Samuel Lincoln, of Hingham, Mass., I, 2; death of, in Berks County, Pa., 3.

Lincoln, Mordecai, preacher: performs marriage ceremony for President Andrew Johnson, I, 3.

Lincoln, Mordecai, uncle of the President: inherits his father's lands in Kentucky, I, 11; defends homestead against Indians, 21; hatred of Indians, 21.

Lincoln, Nancy, personal appearance, I, 24; teaches her husband to write his name, 24; birth of Sarah, or Nancy, 25; birth of Abraham, 25; death, Oct. 5, 1818, 31.

Lincoln, Richard V. B., letter from, about Lincoln genealogy, I, 5.

Lincoln, Robert, captain and commissary of U. S. volunteers, I, 3.

Lincoln, Robert T., son of the Pres., Capt. U. S. Vols., Sec. of War under Garfield and Arthur, Min. to England: erects monument over his grandfather's grave, I, 74; born Aug. 1, 1843, 200, 216; accompanies President-elect to Washington, III, 290; evidence in Porter court-martial case, VI, 13; service on Grant's staff, X, 214; present at Lincoln's deathbed, 300.

Lincoln, Samuel, of Hingham, Mass.: first American ancestor of the President, I, 2.

Lincoln, Sarah or Nancy, sister of the President: born in 1807, I, 25; joins the Baptist Church, 32, 33; marriage to Aaron Grigsby, 45; death, 45.

Lincoln, Thomas, emigrates to Kentucky, I, 3.

Lincoln, Thomas, father of the President: narrowly escapes capture by Indians, I, 21; learns carpenter's trade, 23; personal characteristics, 23; marries Nancy Hanks, June 12, 1806, 23; marriage bond of, 23, 24; home in Elizabethtown, Ky., 25; Sarah or Nancy, daughter of, born, 25; removes to Hardin, now La Rue, County, Ky., 25; Abraham, son of, born, 25; buys farm on Knob Creek, 25; emigrates to Indiana, 28; death of his wife, 31; marries Sarah Bush Johnston, 32; joins the Baptist Church, 32; emigrates to Illinois, 45; death, 1851, 74.

Lincoln, Thomas, son of the President: born April 4, 1853, I, 200; accompanies his father to Washington, III, 290.

Lincoln, William Wallace, son of the President: born Dec. 21, 1850, I, 200; accompanies his father to Washington, III, 290.

Linder, Usher F., correspondence with Lincoln, I, 275, 276.

430 INDEX

Lindsay, W. S., M. P.: interview with Napoleon the Third, VIII, 274.

Lloyd, John M., accessory in plot for Lincoln's abduction, X, 291; gives information of Booth and Herold, 307.

Locke, Vernon, alias Capt. Parker, Conf. Navy: receives the *Chesapeake* from her captors, VIII, 14, 15.

Loewe, William, Prussian Deputy: speech on Lincoln's death, X, 343.

Logan, David, son of Stephen T. Logan: succeeds Lincoln in partnership with his father, I, 215; sergeant in Mexican war, 250.

Logan, John A., Maj. Gen. U. S. Vols.: personal relations to Lincoln, VII, 136; march to Perkins's plantation, 161; in battle of Port Gibson, 171, 172; in engagement at Raymond, 177, 178; in battle of Champion's Hill, 189-192; present at Grant's interview with Pemberton, 303; promoted to command McPherson's corps, VIII, 345; temporarily succeeds McPherson, IX, 271; in battles of Atlanta, 272, 273, 280, 286; sent to relieve Thomas, X, 28; in march to Columbia, 230; at grand review in Washington, 333.

Logan, J. L., Conf. Col.: correspondence with Andrews about negro prisoners of war, VII, 454, 455.

Logan, Stephen T., Judge of Illinois Circuit Ct.: first meeting with Lincoln, I, 108; makes Lincoln his law partner, 213; character as a lawyer, 214; comment on Lincoln's ability, 215; nominated for Congress, 289; defeated for Congress, 290; candidate for legislature in Illinois, 375; announces change of votes from Lincoln to Trumbull, 390; member of Peace Convention, III, 230.

Lomax, L. L., Conf. Maj. Gen.: in battle of Winchester, IX, 300; in battle of Fisher's Hill, 306, 309; defeated by Torbert, 314; stationed at Millford, 327.

Lone Jack, Mo., action at, Aug. 16, 1862, VI, 379.

Long, A. L., Conf. Brig. Gen.: statement about battle of Waynesboro, IX, 330.

Long, Alexander, M. C.: resolution in Democratic National Convention, IX, 255.

Long, Eli, Bvt. Maj. Gen. U. S. A.: in Wilson's raid, X, 239.

Longstreet, James, Conf. Lieut. Gen.: posted as rearguard at Williamsburg, V, 376; repulses Stoneman, 376; assists Hill's attack on Casey's division, 388; attacks Union forces at Beaver Dam Creek, 425; criticism on the results at Beaver Dam, 426, 427; pursues Union army towards James River, 434; attacks Union army at Glendale, 435; ordered to the Rapidan, VI, 6; in battle of second Bull Run, Aug. 30, 1862, 10; with Lee at Sharpsburg, 137; commands Confederate left at Fredericksburg, 201; commands corps in Lee's army, VII, 201; corps of, moves northward, 205; crosses the Potomac, 217, 218; march towards Gettysburg, 233; in battle of Gettysburg, 247, 250, 251, 259, 260, 262, 263, 268; commands Confederate right at Gettysburg, 249; advises Lee to adopt flank movement, 251; ordered by Lee to attack on July 2, 1863, 251; ordered by Lee to attack on July 3, 1863, 258, 259; opinion about Gettysburg, 271; in battle of Chickamauga, VIII, 90, 91, 93, 95, 100, 102, 104, 106, 107; advice to Bragg, 113; engagement in Lookout Valley, 126; expedition against Burnside, 129; detached from Bragg's army and sent against Burnside, 170, 171; asks reënforcements, 171; begins siege of Knoxville, Nov. 16, 1863, 174; forces of, 175; assault on Fort Sanders, Nov. 29, 1863, 179; repulse of, 179, 180; abandons siege of Knoxville, Dec. 3, 1863, 181; winters south of the Holston, 186; sent to the West, 234; commands reserve, Army of Northern Virginia, 352; in battle of the Wilderness, 363-366; wounded, 366; in retreat to Appomattox, X, 188; eulogy of Lincoln, 350.

Loomis, Dwight, M. C.: recommends Goodman for Collector for District of Connecticut, IX, 87.

Loomis, J. M., Col. U. S. Vols.: in battle of Chattanooga, VIII, 146.

Lorencez, Charles Ferdinand de Latrille, Comte de, French General: arrives in Mexico with French reënforcements, VI, 46; defeated before Puebla, 46.

Loring, William W., Conf. Maj. Gen.: forces of, under Pemberton, VII, 164, 165; ordered to Rocky Springs, 171; advice in council of war, 185; in battle of Champion's Hill, 189-192; joins Johnston's army in Mississippi, 294; temporarily succeeds Polk at Pine Mountain, IX, 20; in battles of Kenesaw, 21.

Louisiana, State of, territory purchased from France, I, 319; secession movement in, III, 191; extra session of legislature called, 192; appropriation to arm the State, 192; Convention bill, 192; seizures ordered by governor, 192; meeting of Convention, 192; secession ordinance passed, Jan. 26, 1861, 192; free navigation of Mississippi River recognized, 193; battle of Forts Jackson and St. Philip, April 24, 1862, V, 261-266; Lovell evacuates New Orleans, April 25, 1862, 266; capture of New Orleans by Farragut, April 26, 1862, 268; surrender of Forts Jackson and St. Philip, April 28, 1862, 273; Forts Jackson and St. Philip occupied by Union troops, 275; Butler occupies New Orleans, May 1, 1862, 275; Col. G. F. Shepley appointed military governor, VI, 346; reconstruction alluded to in Lincoln's letter to Reverdy Johnson, 348, 349; reconstruction alluded to in Lincoln's letter to Cuthbert Bullitt, 349; Lincoln's letter to Butler and Shepley about reconstruction, 350; Lincoln's letters to Gov. Shepley about Congressmen from Louisiana, 351, 352; Gov. Shepley orders an election for Congress, 352; B. F. Flanders elected in First District, 353; Michael Hahn elected in Second District, 353; Flanders and Hahn admitted to seats in Congress, 353; siege of Port Hudson, May 25 to July 9, 1863, VII, 317; surrender of Port Hudson, July 9, 1863, 322; battle of Sabine Cross Roads, April 8, 1864, VIII, 292-294; battle of Pleasant Hill, April 9, 1864, 295; Durant appointed attorney general, 419; Gov. Shepley orders registration of voters, 419, 420; orders for registration renewed, 424, 425; conservative programme for election, 425; Banks orders an election for State officers, 431-433; Michael Hahn elected governor, 432-434; Banks orders election for State Convention, 435; State Convention abolishes slavery, 435, 436; Members of Congress elected, 436, 437; legislature elects U. S. Senators, 437; ratifies Thirteenth Amendment, X, 29.

Love, John, member of commission on New York enrollment, VII, 41.

Love, Peter E., M. C.: member of House Committee of Thirty-three, II, 417.

Lovejoy, Elijah P., murder of, in 1837, I, 146-148.

Lovejoy, Owen, M. C.: speeches in Illinois, I, 369; elected to Illinois legislature in 1854, 383; announces Republican State Convention, 385; member of Bloomington Convention, II, 28; favors Lincoln's plan of compensated abolishment, V, 214; prominence as an antislavery leader in Congress, VI, 107; approves Lincoln's message, IX, 109.

Lovell, Mansfield, Conf. Maj. Gen.: evacuates New Orleans, April 25, 1862, V, 266; testimony about insufficiency of provisions at New Orleans, 275; sends troops and guns to Vicksburg, 346; in battle of Corinth, 117.

Lowell, Charles Russell, Jr., Brig. Gen. U. S. Vols.: in Sheridan's army, IX, 182; killed at Cedar Creek, 325.

Lowell, James Russell, Min. to England: eulogy of Lincoln, X, 350.

Lowrie, Walter H., Chief Justice Sup. Ct. of Penn.: decides draft law unconstitutional, VII, 13; defeated for reëlection, 13, 376.

Lubbock, Francis R., Conf. Col.: captured with Jefferson Davis, X, 173.

Lutheran General Synod, resolutions supporting the war and emancipation, VI, 318, 319.

Lyon, Nathaniel, Brig. Gen. U. S. Vols.: at St. Louis arsenal, III, 135; recommends transfer of arms to Illinois, IV, 198; sends arms to Illinois, 199; assigned to command St. Louis arsenal, 208; directed to muster in and arm volunteers, 209; captures Camp Jackson, 213, 214; appointed brigadier general of U. S. volunteers, 217; supersedes Gen. Harney, 222; interview with Gov. Jackson, 222; advance to Jefferson City, 223, 224; orders Springfield, Mo., occupied, 398; moves to Springfield, 399; calls for reënforcements, 407, 408; attacks Confederates at Wilson's Creek, 410; killed at Wilson's Creek, 411.

Lyons, Richard Bickerton Pemell, Baron, afterwards Earl, Brit. Min. at Washington: suggested as mediator, IV, 138; note to Lord Russell, V, 31; instructions concerning Mason and Slidell, 40, 41; letter to British government about war feeling in America, VI, 84, 85; advises against British mediation, 86, 87; his errors of fact or inference, 87, 88; reports the sentiments of New York conservatives, 194, 195.

Lytle, W. H., Brig. Gen. U. S. Vols.: in battle of Chickamauga, VIII, 95.

McAllister, Archibald, M. C.: vote for Thirteenth Amendment, X, 83.

McArthur, John, Bvt. Maj. Gen. U. S. Vols.: in siege of Vicksburg, VII, 289, 292.

McCall, George A., Brig. Gen. U. S. Vols.: ordered to Dranesville, IV, 453; ordered to fall back, 455; attends council of war, V,

167; division sent to reënforce McClellan, 414; commands under Porter on the Peninsula, 428.

McCallum, D. C., Bvt. Maj. Gen. U. S. Vols. : at council of war, VIII, 112; feat of transportation, 113.

McCauley, Charles S., Commodore U. S. N. : commandant at Gosport navy yard, IV, 145; countermands departure of ships, 146; orders ships at Gosport to be scuttled, 147.

McCausland, John, Conf. Brig. Gen. : burns Chambersburg, Pa., July 30, 1864, IX, 176, 177; defeated by Averill at Hancock, 178; skirmish with Kelley, 178; defeated by Averill at Moorefield, 178; in Shenandoah campaign, 296; defeated by Powell, 328.

McClellan, George B., Maj. Gen. and Gen. in Chief U. S. A.: assumes command of Department of Ohio, IV, 200, 201; recommendations for river defense, 201; interviews with Buckner, 202; reports excitement on Kentucky frontier, 231; promises to sustain Kentucky Unionists, 236; recommended for command at Cincinnati, 282; previous services, 283, 284; appointed major general of Ohio militia, 285; assigned to command Department of the Ohio, 285; appointed major general of U. S. Army, 285, 286; proposes plan of campaign, 298-300; promises to aid western Virginia, 329, 330; orders four regiments to Grafton, 330; goes to western Virginia, 334; moves toward Rich Mountain, 334, receives news of Pegram's defeat, 336; occupies Beverly, 336; receives Pegram's surrender, 336; plans for western Virginia, 338, 339; bulletin of victory, 339; ordered to the Shenandoah Valley, 354; called to Washington, 356; orders about slave insurrection, 386; commands Division of the Potomac, 440; reports strength of army, 442; personal characteristics, 443-445; family letters, 445-447; his temper and feeling, 446-448; ideas of his task, 448; adopts Marcy's suggestion, 449; exaggerates strength of the enemy, 449; opinion of the Potomac blockade, 452; orders preliminary to the battle of Ball's Bluff, 453, 454; orders troops to withdraw from Ball's Bluff, 458; directed to arrest Gen. Stone, 460; orders his arrest, 460; letter to Gen. Scott, 461, 462; neglect of Gen. Scott's orders, 464; appointed general-in-chief, 465; treatment of the President, 468, 469; directs East Tennessee movement, V, 66; repeats instructions about East Tennessee, 68; letter to Buell, 69; criticism of Buell's views, 71, 72; advises Halleck to send expedition up Tennessee River, 101; suggests Cumberland River movement to Buell, 103; answers on Lincoln's plan of campaign, 148, 149; inattentive to Committee on Conduct of the War, 151; estimate of rebel forces, October, 1861, 152; illness of, 155; military council at the White House, Jan. 13, 1862, 157, 158; plan of campaign against Richmond by the lower Chesapeake, 159; letter objecting to Lincoln's plan of campaign, and proposing movement by Urbana, 161-163; preparations for a bridge at Harper's Ferry, 168; canal boats found unserviceable, 168; orders an advance, 174; explanation of the march to Manassas, 177; calls council at Fairfax Court House, 179; embarks for Fort Monroe, 182; suggests combined movement up the Tennessee and Cumberland, 188; receives news of Hampton Roads sea fight, 226; present at council about expedition against New Orleans, 254, 255; refuses Halleck superior command in the West, 308; asks Buell when he can advance on Nashville, 309, 310; telegraphs Halleck to direct his efforts on Nashville, 310; advises Halleck to arrest Grant, 312; arrives at Fort Monroe, 358; sends Heintzelman against Yorktown, 359; sends Keyes to the Half Way House, 359; resolves on the siege of Yorktown, 360; complaints to the government, 360; clamor about the retention of McDowell's corps, 361; his force on the Peninsula, 361, 362; letter to Admiral Goldsborough, 364, 365; asks for Franklin's division, 365; reports the incident at Dam No. 1, 370; comments on the authorities at Washington, 370; siege works at Yorktown, 372; letter to Lincoln about Yorktown batteries, 373; asks for Parrott guns, 374; telegraphs, May 4, 1862, "Yorktown is in our possession," 374; forces at evacuation of Yorktown, 375; pursues the enemy from Yorktown, 376; gives his corps commanders no orders, 376; arrives at Williamsburg, 377; telegram from Williamsburg, 378; announces his intention to "resume the original plan," 378; asks for more men, and permission to suspend the corps organization, 380; forms two provisional army corps, 382; joins his

433

army at Cumberland Landing, 382; asks for "all disposable troops," 382; asks that McDowell be placed under his orders in the usual way, 384; establishes permanent depot at White House,385; establishes his army in line on the Chickahominy, 385; sends the corps of Keyes and Heintzelman across the river, 385; telegram to Washington about Johnston, 387; comment on Jackson's raid, 403; says rain will retard his movements, 414; reënforcements received by, 415; strength of his army in June, 1862, 417; intimates intention to fight, 417, 418; report of damage from Stuart's raid, 418, 419; orders Porter to retire from Beaver Dam, 426; indecision at battle of Gaines's Mill, 430, 431; gives orders for movement to James River, 433; army of, at Malvern Hill, 436; withdraws to Harrison's landing, 440; dispatch to Stanton, "You have done your best to sacrifice this army," 441, 442; asks for 50,000 men, 445; asks for 100,000 men, 446; letter to Lincoln on political policy, 447-449; preparation of the Harrison's landing letter, 450, 451; private letters about the government, 452, 453; reply to Lincoln about absentees, 454; interview with Halleck, 455, 456; telegrams asking reënforcements, 457; protests against withdrawal from the James, 458, 459; delays withdrawal from the James, 459, 460; leaves Harrison's Landing, 460; arrives at Alexandria, 460; ordered to send away his sick, VI, 3; directed to move his army to Aquia Creek, 3; reply to Pope's letter, 5; interview with Hermann Haupt, 14, 15; telegrams about second battle of Bull Run, 17, 18; telegram to Lincoln about Pope, 19; telegrams to Halleck about Pope's movements, 20; interview with Lincoln and Halleck, 21; letter to Porter urging support of Pope, 21; new version of his interview with Lincoln and Halleck, 26, 27; telegraphs he will endeavor to outmanœuvre and outfight the enemy, 114; telegraphs Stanton, "You have done your best to sacrifice this army," 115; reports strength of Army of Potomac, 131; asks Halleck for reënforcements, 134; obtains Lee's plans of campaign, 135; telegraphs Lincoln that he has "all the plans of the rebels," 136; battle of South Mountain, Sept. 14, 1862, 136, 137; takes position at Antietam Creek, 138; blames Burnside for slowness, 138; battle of Antietam, Sept. 17,

1862, 139-141; plan of battle, 139; comment on battle of Antietam, 142; decides not to renew the attack, 144; reports victory at Antietam, 145; apprehensive of attack from the enemy, 173, 174; strength of his army, 174; visited by the President, 174; instructed by the President to attack the enemy, 175, 176; report about cavalry, 176; inquiry about hospital tents, 177; complaints about supplies, 177, 178; prepares protest against emancipation proclamation, 180; contemplates retiring from service, 180; order *apropos* of emancipation proclamation, 180, 181; asks whether the President desires him to move at once, 184; asks for detailed instructions, 184; crosses the Potomac with his army, 185; removed from command, Nov. 5, 1862, 188, 189; comments on the order for his removal, 189; review of his military career, 189-193; supports Judge Woodward for governor of Pennsylvania, VII, 376; interview with Weed, IX, 247; interview with F. P. Blair, Sr., 248, 249; nominated for President, 258; letter of acceptance, 260, 261; resigns his commission in the army, 384.

McClelland, R., M. C., Gov. of Mich., Sec. of Int. under Pierce: agrees to Wilmot Proviso, I, 268.

McClernand, John A., M. C., Maj. Gen. U. S. Vols.: votes against Wilmot Proviso, I, 269; motion affecting slavery in California and New Mexico, 284; House discussion, II, 420, 421; plan of compromise, 423; march to Mayfield, V, 105; report of, 106; second in command at Belmont, 114; marches against Fort Henry, 121; occupies Fort Henry, 122; commands division in march against Fort Donelson, 192; right wing of his division driven back by Pillow, 196; left wing repulses Buckner, 196; ordered to attack, 197; position of division at Pittsburg Landing, 323; position at sundown, April 6, 1862, 330; assigned to command reserve corps of Halleck's army, 337; assigned to command Vicksburg expedition, VII, 126; supersedes Sherman at Milliken's Bend, 135; personal relations to Lincoln, 135, 136; plan of recruiting, 136, 137; commands expedition against Arkansas Post, 139; captures Fort Hindman, 140; controversy with Grant, 141-143; commands Thirteenth Army Corps, 144; protests against being superseded by Grant, 146; march to Perkins's plantation, 157; crosses the Mississippi to Bruinsburg, 169; battle of Port Gibson, May 1, 1863, 170, 171; controversy with Grant, 183; march to Edwards's Station, 187; in battle of Champion's Hill, 189–192; battle of the Big Black, May 17, 1863, 192; march on Vicksburg, 195; first assault on Vicksburg, 283; second assault on Vicksburg, 283–288; relieved from command of Thirteenth Army Corps, 288; in siege of Vicksburg, 289; brings reënforcements to Banks at Alexandria, VIII, 297.

McConnell, John L., historian of Western pioneers, I, 189.

McCook, A. McD., Bvt. Maj. Gen. U. S. A.: commands division of Buell's army in battle of Pittsburg Landing, V, 333; appointed by Rosecrans to command right wing of Army of the Cumberland, VI, 281; march on Chattanooga, VIII, 73; ordered towards Alpine, 75; directed to join Thomas, 80; effects junction with Thomas, 81; in battle of Chickamauga, 84, 88, 89, 93, 95, 96, 103; in battle of Chattanooga, 135.

McCook, Daniel, Brig. Gen. U. S. Vols.: in battle of Chickamauga, VIII, 85; killed at Kenesaw Mountain, IX, 22, 23.

McCook, Edward M., Bvt. Maj. Gen. U. S. Vols.: cavalry raid in Georgia, IX, 279; in Wilson's raid, X, 239.

McCormick, Andrew, one of the "Long Nine," I, 128.

McCown, John P., Conf. Maj. Gen.: in battle of Murfreesboro, VI, 282.

McCulloch, Ben, Conf. Brig. Gen.: takes possession of San Antonio, IV, 185; sent to Indian Territory, 409; junction with Pearce and Price, 409; returns to Arkansas, 426; occupies Springfield, Missouri, 439; withdraws his army to Arkansas, V, 88; ordered to join Van Dorn in Arkansas, 290; killed in battle of Pea Ridge, 292.

McCulloch, Hugh, Sec. of Treas. under Lincoln, Johnson, and Arthur: appointed Secretary of Treasury, IX, 349; at Cabinet meeting, April 14, 1865, X, 282; present at Lincoln's deathbed, 300.

McDaniels, ——, chosen to Illinois legislature, I, 385.

McDougall, James A., M. C., U. S. Sen.: defeated for Congress by Hardin, I, 222; resolutions about the French in Mexico, VII, 407.

McDowell, Irvin, Bvt. Maj. Gen. U. S. A.: declines commission of major general, IV, 324; appointed brigadier general, 324; plan of campaign against Manassas, 324; marching orders of, 341; changes his plan of attack, 344; announces his plan of battle, 347; battle of Bull Run, July 21, 1861, 348–351; battle of the morning, 348; battle of the afternoon, 349; defeat of his army, 349; retreat to the Potomac, 350; continued in command in Virginia, 356; invited to a conference with Lincoln, V, 156; recommends movement against rebels, 157; attends council of war, 167; assigned to command First Army Corps, Army of Potomac, 169; attends council at Fairfax Court House, 179; ordered to form junction with Mc-Clellan, 383; ordered to Front Royal, 404; obeys Lincoln's order, 406; sends Shields to Catlett's, 406; commands corps in Army of Virginia, VI, 1; meeting with Porter, 8; receives from Pope joint order to himself and Porter, 8; second battle of Bull Run, Aug. 30, 1862, 9–11; made Department Commander, X, 338.

Mace, Daniel, M. C.: testimony referred to, I, 394.

McFarland, E. J., Sec. to Confederate Commissioners, V, 24; removed from the Trent, 24.

McIlvaine, Bishop Charles P., conducts ceremonies at Lincoln's funeral in Cleveland, X, 322.

McIntosh, James M., Conf. Brig. Gen.: ordered to join Van Dorn in Arkansas, V, 290; killed at battle of Pea Ridge, 292.

McIntosh, John B., Bvt. Maj. Gen. U. S. A.: wounded at Winchester, IX, 304.

McKee, Col., U. S. Vols.: regiment of, at battle of Buena Vista, II, 26.

McKeen, Henry B., Col. U. S. Vols.: killed at Cold Harbor, VIII, 404.

McKensie, Lieut., U. S. Vols.: in defense of Allatoona, IX, 474.

Mackenzie, Ranald S., Bvt. Maj. Gen. U. S. Vols.: in march to Five Forks, X, 172.

McKinstry, Justus, Brig. Gen. U. S. Vols.: commands a division under Frémont, IV, 429.

McLaughlen, Napoleon B., Bvt. Brig. Gen. U. S. A.: made prisoner in Fort Stedman, X, 162.

McLaws, Lafayette, Conf. Maj. Gen.: sent to capture Harper's Ferry, VI, 133; joins Lee at Sharpsburg, 137; in battle of Chancellorsville, VII, 96, 101; division moves to Culpeper Court House, 205; in battle of Gettysburg, 251; in battle of

Chickamauga, VIII, 106; in expedition against Burnside, 129.

McLean, John, Assoc. Justice U. S. Sup. Ct.: dissenting opinion in Dred Scott case, II, 66, 67, 78-80; candidate before Chicago Convention, 1860, 271; votes for: on first ballot, 273 — on second ballot, 274 — on third ballot, 275.

McLean, Wilmer, Lee's surrender in house of, X, 195.

MacMahon, James P., Col. U. S. Vols.: killed at Cold Harbor, VIII, 401, 405.

McMillan, James W., Bvt. Maj. Gen. U. S. Vols.: in battle of Cedar Creek, IX, 325.

McNair, Evander, Conf. Brig. Gen.: joins Johnston's army in Mississippi, VII, 294; in battle of Chickamauga, VIII, 106.

McNeil, John, Bvt. Maj. Gen. U. S. Vols.: executes ten rebel guerrillas, VI, 475; explanation of action, 475.

Macomb, W. H., Commodore U. S. N.: commands Union fleet at Plymouth, X, 46; captures Plymouth, Oct. 30, 1864, 51.

McPheeters, Rev. Dr. Samuel B., arrested for disloyalty, VI, 336.

McPherson, James B., Maj. Gen. U. S. Vols.: report about railroad repairs, V, 352; sent by Grant on reconnaissance towards Holly Springs, VII, 122; commands Seventeenth Army Corps, 144; work on the Lake Providence route, 148; in battle of Port Gibson, 171; drives the enemy through Willow Springs, 172; engagement at Raymond, May 12, 1863, 177, 178; occupies Clinton, 178; battle of Jackson, May 14, 1863, 182; in battle of Champion's Hill, 189-192; march on Vicksburg, 195; first assault on Vicksburg, 283; second assault on Vicksburg, 283-286; in siege of Vicksburg, 289; present at Grant's interview with Pemberton, 303; made brigadier general of U. S. army, 325; in Sherman's movement to Meridian, VIII, 330, 331; succeeds to Sherman's command of Department of the Tennessee, 345; strength of Army of the Tennessee, IX, 4; sent against Resaca, 10; march through Snake Creek Gap, 11, 12; in battles of Dallas, 17-19; in battles of Kenesaw Mountain, 20, 22, 23; in march to the Chattahoochee, 25; in march on Atlanta, 263; in battles of Atlanta, 270; killed at Atlanta, 271.

McQueen, John, M. C.: signs secession address, II, 436; advises with Trescott about withdrawing Gov. Pickens's letter, III, 6.

Maffitt, John N., Commander Conf. navy:

commands Confederate cruiser Florida, IX, 128, 129.

Magoffin, Beriah, Gov. of Ky.: answer to Lincoln's call for troops, IV, 90; message against subjugation, 229, 230; refuses Lincoln's call for troops, 230; convenes legislature in second special session, 234; message declaring the Union broken, 234; letter to Lincoln, 241; vetoes joint resolution of legislature demanding Confederate withdrawal from Kentucky, V, 46.

Magrath, A. G., U. S. Dist. Judge, Conf. Gov. of S. C.: criticism of Buchanan's message, II, 374, 375; commissioner to Anderson, III, 110; speech to military council, 111; transmits Harvey's telegram to Montgomery, IV, 31.

Magruder, John B., Bvt. Lieut. Col. U. S. A., Conf. Maj. Gen.: resignation of, IV, 142; interview with the President, 142; employs slaves to build batteries, 386; force of, on the Peninsula, V, 358; policy of delay, 366; comment on McClellan's inactivity, 366; report of attack at Dam No. 1, 369; left to guard south side of Chickahominy, 428; comment on battle of Gaines's Mill, 432; defeated at Malvern Hill, July 1, 1862, 438; captures Banks's expedition against Galveston, VII, 313; seeks the protection of Maximilian, 420.

Mahone, William, Conf. Maj. Gen., U. S. Sen.: in siege of Richmond, IX, 427; in battle of Hatcher's Run, 434.

Maine, State of, admitted as a State, I, 323; legislature adopts resolutions recommending Lincoln's renomination, IX, 56; ratifies Thirteenth Amendment, X, 89.

Major, J. P., Conf. Brig. Gen.: in attack on Brashear City, VII, 321; repulsed at Donaldsonville, 321.

Major, Minor, employed by Thompson to destroy Union steamboats on the Mississippi, VIII, 22.

Mallory, Col., demands escaped slaves, IV, 387.

Mallory, Robert, M. C.: plan of compromise, II, 423; second interview with Lincoln about compensated emancipation, VI, 111; opposes bill for draft, VII, 5.

Mallory, S. R., U. S. Sen., Conf. Sec. of Navy: visit to Pensacola, III, 167; telegram to Slidell, Hunter, and Bigler, 167; member of caucus committee of secession Senators, 180, 181; signs Senatorial secession caucus resolutions, 181; appointed Confederate Secretary of Navy, 212; present at inter-

views of Davis and Johnston, X, 257-263; account of interviews of Davis and Johnston, 261-263; leaves Davis's party, 267.
Malvern Hill, Va., battle of, July 1, 1862, V, 437-439.
Manhattan, The, Union monitor: in battle of Mobile Bay, IX, 236.
Manigault, Edward, Conf. Col.: ordered to prepare a plan to reduce Fort Sumter, III, 124.
Mann, W. D., elected to Congress, VIII, 437.
Mansfield, J. K. F., Maj. Gen. U. S. Vols.: ordered to seize Arlington Heights, IV, 310; goes to Meade's assistance at Antietam, VI, 140; killed at Antietam, 140.
Marcy, R. B., Bvt. Maj. Gen. U. S. A.: advises McClellan to demand a draft, IV, 448, 449.
Marcy, William L., U. S. Sen., Sec. of War under Polk, Sec. of State under Pierce: votes for, in Baltimore Convention of 1852, I, 332.
Marmaduke, J. S., Conf. Maj. Gen.: captured by Pleasonton, VIII, 479.
Marshall, ——, in Mexican war, I, 262.
Marshall, Col., U. S. Vols.: killed at Cold Harbor, VIII, 405.
Marshall, Charles, Conf. Col.: present at Lee's surrender, X, 195.
Marshall, Charles A., advice about organizing Kentucky troops, IV, 236, 237.
Marshall, Humphrey, Conf. Brig. Gen.: organizes insurrectionary force in Kentucky, IV, 243; flight from Lexington, V, 51.
Marshall, Thornton F., member of committee to distribute Union arms, IV, 237.
Martin, ——, testimony concerning Lecompton Convention, II, 110.
Martin, Col., Conf. emissary in Canada: employed by Thompson to burn New York city, VIII, 22, 23.
Martin, Henri, French historian: eulogy of Lincoln, X, 349.
Martin, John W., Capt. Kickapoo Rangers: guards Gov. Robinson, I, 450.
Marvin, William, Judge of U. S. Dist. Ct.: apprehensions of, IV, 15.
Maryland, State of, meetings of adjourned Charleston Convention at Baltimore, II, 250, 251; meeting of Constitutional Union National Convention at Baltimore, 253; condition of Baltimore in January and February, 1861, III, 304-307; response to Lincoln's proclamation, IV, 94; the Baltimore riot, 111-119; railroad bridges burned, 121; secession plottings in, 162; members of legislature elected, 165; legislature meets at Frederick, 168; Department of Annapolis created, 169; election of members of Congress, 170; transit of troops through Baltimore reëstablished, 172, 173; battle of South Mountain, Sept. 14, 1862, VI, 136; capture of Harper's Ferry, Sept. 15, 1862, 137; battle of Antietam, Sept. 17, 1862, 139; A. W. Bradford elected governor, VIII, 450; resolutions of legislature about emancipation, 454; Union League Convention in Baltimore, 458, 459; State Central Committee Convention in Baltimore, 458, 459; Gen. Schenck's orders about Maryland elections, 462-464; vote on emancipation, 465; Constitutional Convention, 465, 466; slavery abolished by Convention, 466; vote on amended Constitution, 467, 468; Bradford's proclamation declaring Constitution adopted, 468; instructs delegates in favor of Lincoln's renomination, IX, 55; meeting of Republican National Convention at Baltimore, 63-74; battle of Monocacy, July 9, 1864, 165; ratifies Thirteenth Amendment, X, 88.
Mason, James M., U. S. Sen., Conf. Comr. to Europe: supports demand for a Congressional slave code, II, 175; cross-examines John Brown, 209; member of committee to investigate John Brown raid, 210; signs address commending Charleston disruption, 245, 246; letter to Jefferson Davis proposing secession, 300; called by Floyd to influence Buchanan, 396; Senate discussion, 402; work on Fugitive Slave law, III, 26; sent to Baltimore to assist secession, IV, 161; unsuccessful mission to Maryland legislature, 171; Confederate commissioner to England, V, 21; arrives at Havana, 21; removed from the Trent, 23, 24; imprisoned in Fort Warren, 24; delivered to Lord Lyons, 39; negotiates cotton bonds in England, VI, 250; management of Slidell's loan, 251, 252; interview with Lord Palmerston, VIII, 264, 265.
Massachusetts, State of, draft riot in Boston, VII, 26; ratifies Thirteenth Amendment, X, 89.
Massachusetts Emigrant Aid Company, formed in Boston, I, 394; work of, 394, 395; founds town of Lawrence, Kas., 395.
Matheny, Noah W., candidate for county clerk, I, 179.
Mattabesett, The, Union gunboat: fight with the Albemarle, X, 41-43.

Matteson, Joel A., Gov. of Ill. : votes for, for U. S. Senator, I, 388, 389.

Matthews, A. C., Col. U. S. Vols.: finds MS. patent of lands to Abraham Lincoln, the President's grandfather, I, 11.

Matthews, J., burns Booth's letter, X, 293.

Maurin, ——, Conf. Maj.: captured with Jefferson Davis, X, 274.

Maury, Dabney H., Conf. Maj. Gen. : in battle of Corinth, VII, 117 ; commands defenses of Mobile, IX, 239.

Maury, Matthew F., Commander Conf. navy : fits out Confederate cruiser *Georgia*, IX, 137, 138.

Maury, William L., Commander Conf. navy : commands Confederate cruiser *Georgia*, IX, 137, 138.

Maxey, Samuel B., Conf. Brig. Gen., U. S. Sen.: joins Johnston's army in Mississippi, VII, 294.

Maximilian (Ferdinand Maximilian Joseph), Archduke of Austria and Emperor of Mexico : selected as Emperor of Mexico, VII, 398, 399 ; reply to the offer, 399, 400; accepts the crown of Mexico, 411, 412 ; message to Slidell, 412 ; arrival in Mexico, 415 ; invitation to Juarez, 416 ; administration in Mexico, 416-420 ; captured and shot, 423.

May, William L., M. C. : defeats Stuart for Congress, I, 157 ; prominent lawyer of Illinois, 214.

Maynard, Horace, M. C., Min. to Turkey: elected to Congress, V, 59; inquiry to Buell, 68 ; second interview with Lincoln about compensated emancipation, VI, 112 ; efforts for East Tennesseeans, VIII, 160-162; remonstrance against Burnside's leaving East Tennessee, 167 ; signs call for Union Convention at Nashville, 440; complaint to Lincoln, 444.

Mead, Larkin G., designs Lincoln monument at Springfield, X, 325.

Meade, George G., Maj. Gen. U. S. A. : commands Union brigade under McCall, V, 425; succeeds to command of Hooker's corps at Antietam, VI, 140; in battle of Fredericksburg, 203 ; in battle of Chancellorsville, VII, 93, 96, 97 ; present at council of war, 109; appointed to command Army of Potomac, 226; assumes command, 229; asks that Farnsworth, Custer, and Merritt be made brigadier generals, 232; crosses the Pennsylvania line, 234 ; selects line of Pipe Creek for a defensive battle, 235; battle of Gettysburg, July 1-3, 1863, 239-268;

adopts Gettysburg instead of Pipe Creek as the battlefield, 244, 245; telegram to Halleck, 247; controversy about intention to retreat, 248 ; orders Slocum to prepare to attack Ewell, 248; disapproves Sickles's positions, 250; holds council of war, 258 ; attacks the enemy on Culp's Hill, July 3, 1863, 259, 260; telegram to French, 259, 260 ; reports "a handsome repulse of the enemy," 268; declines exchange of prisoners, 272; holds council of war, July 4, 273; moves his army southward, 273, 274; made brigadier general of U. S. army, 274 ; answers to Halleck's urgency, 274, 275 ; follows Lee to the Potomac, 275 ; calls a council of war, 275; favors an attack on Lee, 275 ; asks to be relieved from command, 275 ; informs Halleck of Longstreet's being sent from Lee's army, VIII, 82; crosses the Potomac, 231; letter to Stanton about attacking Lee, 234; moves to Centreville, 239, 240; moves against Lee, 242 ; movement against Mine Run, 247; countermands attack on Mine Run, 249; withdraws from Mine Run, 251; conversation with Grant, 344; in battle of the Wilderness, 360, 362, 363; reconnaissance after the Wilderness, 368; suggested for command of Middle Military Division, IX, 179; in attack on Petersburg, 410-412; in siege of Petersburg, 420, 432; orders about assault at Petersburg mine, 424-426 ; in march to Five Forks, X, 169; in assault on Petersburg, 179 ; in march to Appomattox, 186 ; at grand review in Washington, 331; commands Military Division of the Atlantic, 338.

Meade, R. K., Lieut. U. S. A. : engineer assistant to Capt. Foster, III. 51.

Medill, Joseph, editor of Chicago "Tribune": letter about Lincoln's nomination, VIII, 323.

Meigs, Montgomery C., Bvt. Maj. Gen. and Q. M. Gen. U. S. A. : interview with Lincoln, III, 435, 436 ; ordered to prepare plan to reënforce Fort Pickens, 436; submits plan, 437; sails for Fort Pickens, IV, 6 ; mission at Key West, 14; arrives at Fort Pickens, 16; visit to Frémont, 413; ordered to make preparations to obstruct the Potomac, V, 227; estimate of rebel strength, 456; report about cavalry horses, VI, 176, 177; reply to McClellan about hospital tents, 177 ; urges Burnside to advance, 214, 215; feat of transportation, VIII, 113; organizes quartermaster's employees, IX, 163; present at Lincoln's deathbed, X, 300.

Mejia, Tomas, Mex. Gen.: captured and shot, VII, 423.

Memminger, C. G., Conf. Sec. of Treas.: appointed Confederate Secretary of Treasury, III, 212.

Memphis, Tenn., river battle, June 6, 1862, V, 344; occupied by Union troops, 345.

Memphis, The, Union gunboat: engagement with rebel rams at Charleston, VII, 59-61.

Menzies, John W., M. C.: second interview with Lincoln about compensated emancipation, VI, 111.

Mercedita, The, Union gunboat: disabled by rebel ram Palmetto State at Charleston, VII, 59-61.

Mercer, Samuel, Capt. U. S. N.: report to Secretary of Navy, IV, 5.

Mercier, Henri, French Minister in Washington: sympathy with the South, VI, 83; comment on Greeley's letter, 84; visits Richmond, 84.

Meredith, Solomon, Bvt. Maj. Gen. U. S. Vols.: in battle of Gettysburg, VII, 240.

Merrimac, The, Conf. ironclad: burned and sunk at Gosport, V, 218; raised and ironclad by the rebels, 218; description of, 218, 219; called the Virginia by the rebels, 220; appears in Hampton Roads, March 8, 1862, 222; consorts of, 222, 223; steams for Newport News, 222; rams and sinks the Cumberland, 223, 224; damaged in the encounter, 224; shells and burns the Congress, 225; ceases action for the day, 225; renews her attack, March 9, 1862, 228; fight with the Monitor, 228; commanded by C. Ap R. Jones, 228, 229; retreats from the fight, 231; reappears in Hampton Roads, May 8, 1862, 235; abandoned and burned by the rebels, 237.

Merritt, Wesley, Bvt. Maj. Gen. U. S. A.: made brigadier general of U. S. volunteers, VII, 232; in battle of Yellow Tavern, VIII, 371; in Shenandoah campaign, IX, 294; in battle of Winchester, 303; in battle of Cedar Creek, 324, 325; raid in Loudon County, Va., 328; destroys James River Canal, 331; in march to Five Forks, X, 171; in march to Appomattox, 185, 187; at grand review in Washington, 331.

Merryman, Dr. E. H., becomes a second to Lincoln, I, 206, 207; prints account of the Lincoln-Shields duel, 208; correspondence with Whitesides, 209, 210.

Merryman, John, arrested for rebel recruiting, IV, 174; habeas corpus issued for, 174.

Metacomet, The, Union gunboat, in battle of Mobile Bay, IX, 231, 233, 234.

Methodist Episcopal Church, action supporting the war and emancipation, VI, 324, 325.

Methodist Episcopal Church South, action on secession, VI, 332, 333.

Mexican war, Congress authorizes 50,000 volunteers, I, 250; three regiments raised in Illinois, 250; battles of, mentioned, 242, 250-252, 255, 261-263; Ashmun's amendment on, 259; Taylor's success, 260, 261; Lincoln's speech on, 261, 262; Scott's march and victories, 262, 263; Calhoun's remarks on, 264, 265; treaty of peace signed, 266; extent of territory conquered, 266, 267; Lincoln's resolutions upon, 270.

Mexico, boundary claims of, I, 240; protest against annexation of Texas, 240, 241: war with the United States, 242; condition of, VI, 31; Congress of, suspends payment on national debt, 31; imposes tax on capital, 32; occupation of Vera Cruz by the allies, 42; convention of Soledad, 44; withdrawal of English and Spanish expeditions, 45; defeat of French at Puebla, 46; defeat of Berthier and Forey before Puebla, 47; Blair's project concerning, X, 96-106.

Michigan, State of, free in consequence of Ordinance of 1787, I, 317; admitted as a State, 324; ratifies Thirteenth Amendment, X, 88.

Michigan, The, U. S. steamer on Lake Erie: plot to capture, VIII, 18, 19.

Miles, Dixon S., Col. U. S. A.: commands division at Bull Run, IV, 342; killed at Harper's Ferry, VI, 137.

Miles, Nelson A., Bvt. Maj. Gen. U. S. A.: in march to Five Forks, X, 169; in assault at Petersburg, 177, 179; at grand review in Washington, 332.

Miles, William Porcher, M. C., Conf. Col.: speech to Buchanan, II, 383, 384; House discussion, 416; signs secession address, 436.

Mills, John T., interview with Lincoln about emancipation, VI, 433.

Millson, John S., M. C.: member of House Committee of Thirty-three, II, 417.

Mill Spring, Ky., battle of, Jan. 19, 1862, V, 116, 117.

Milroy, Robert H., Maj. Gen. U. S. Vols.: defeated at McDowell, V, 401; refuses to evacuate Winchester, VII, 208; defeated at Winchester, 209; defeats Bate at Murfreesboro, X, 23.

Milwaukee, The, Union gunboat; sunk by a torpedo at Mobile, IX, 240.

Minnesota, State of, instructs delegates in favor of Lincoln's renomination, IX, 55, 56; ratifies Thirteenth Amendment, X, 89.

Minnesota, The, Union steam frigate: at Fort Monroe, V, 223; starts to encounter the *Merrimac*, 223; runs aground, 223.

Minty, R. H. Q., Bvt. Maj. Gen. U. S. Vols.: march on Chattanooga, VIII, 71.

Miramon, Miguel, Mex. Gen. and diplomatist: captured and shot, VII, 423.

Mississippi, State of, secession movement in, III, 183; military appropriation in, 184; arms purchased by, 184; legislature convened, 184; commissioners appointed by legislature, 185; meeting of convention, 185; secession ordinance passed, Jan. 9, 1861, 185; seizures of Ship Island and Marine Hospital, 185; declaration of causes for secession, 201; Corinth captured by Halleck, May 30, 1862, V, 340, 341; Vicksburg fortified by the rebels, 346; battle of Corinth, Oct. 3, 4, 1862, VII, 116-118; assault on Chickasaw Bluffs, Dec. 28, 29, 1862, 133, 134; bombardment of Grand Gulf, April 29, 1863, 167; battle of Port Gibson, May 1, 1863, 170, 171; Grand Gulf occupied, 172; battle of Raymond, May 12, 1863, 177, 178; battle of Jackson, May 14, 1863, 182, 183; battle of Champion's Hill, May 16, 1863, 189-192; battle of the Big Black, May 17, 1863, 192; Grant's army invests Vicksburg, May 18, 1863, 282; siege of Vicksburg begun, May 22, 1863, 288; surrender of Vicksburg, July 4, 1863, 305.

Missouri, State of, applies for admission as a State, I, 322, 323; admitted as a State, 323; U. S. arsenal at Liberty robbed of arms, 442; answer to Lincoln's proclamation, IV, 90; Presidential election in 1860, 206, 207; secession movement in, 206-226; legislature, 207; State Convention condemns secession, 207; legislature convened, 208; arsenal at Liberty seized, 211; Lyon ordered to enroll 10,000 volunteers, 212; Lyon captures Camp Jackson, 213, 214; Harney reinstated, 215; legislature passes military bill, 219; Lyon supersedes Harney, 222; Gov. Jackson's proclamation, 223; battle of Boonville, 224; State Convention called together, 225; battle of Wilson's Creek, Aug. 10, 1861, 410, 411;

siege and surrender of Lexington, Sept. 18-20, 1861, 426-429; admitted to Confederate States, V, 88; Convention called together, 96; State militia organized, 96; amnesty, 97, 98; battle of Belmont, Nov. 7, 1861, 113, 114; loss at, 114; Curtis's midwinter campaign, 288; Pope captures New Madrid, March 13, 1862, 295; capture of Island No. 10, April 7, 1862, 299; made a separate military district, VI, 368; social and political conditions, 370, 371; Hindman authorizes guerrillas, 373; Gov. Gamble's order creating Enrolled Missouri Militia, 375; registration of rebel sympathizers, 376; general guerrilla rising, 378; action at Kirksville, Aug. 6, 1862, 379; action at Lone Jack, Aug. 16, 1862, 379; Curtis assumes command of Department of Missouri, 382; Lincoln's order suspending assessments in St. Louis County, 386; Lincoln orders suspension of assessments for damages in Missouri, 390; Breckinridge's bill in State Convention for compensated abolishment, 391; bill laid on the table, 391; Convention resolution respecting compensated abolishment, 392; mass convention of emancipationists at Jefferson City, 392, 393; emancipation victory in November election, 1862, 394; Gov. Gamble's message to legislature on emancipation, 394; bills in Congress to aid emancipation in, 394-397; assignment to command and death of Col. Sumner, 398; McNeil executes ten rebel guerrillas, 475, 476; American Knights, etc., in, VIII, 2; Constitutional Convention called to meet, June 15, 1863, 207; Convention refuses to accept Gov. Gamble's resignation, 207; Convention adopts ordinance of prospective emancipation, 209; Convention adjourns *sine die*, 210; Radical Emancipation Convention meets at Jefferson City, 210; resolutions of that Convention, 213, 214; proclamation of Gov. Gamble, 226, 227; death of Gov. Gamble, 470; Henderson and Brown elected U. S. Senators, 470; Rosecrans succeeds Schofield in command, 474, 475; political movements in, 477, 478; Price's invasion, 478-480; Rosecrans's election order, 481, 482; Presidential vote in 1864, 483; Constitutional Convention abolishes slavery, 484; action of Assembly on Lincoln's renomination, IX, 56; ratifies Thirteenth Amendment, X, 89.

Missouri Compromise, remarks upon, by J. R. Giddings, I, 339; remarks upon, by D.

440 INDEX

R. Atchison, 340, 341; Archibald Dixon offers amendment repealing, 344; Atchison's proposition to Douglas concerning, 346; Douglas's reply to Atchison, 346; Pierce agrees to make repeal an administration measure, 349; declared "inoperative and void" in Douglas's bill, 350; repealed by the Kansas-Nebraska Act, 351; repeal of, defended by the South, 357, 358; elections in New Hampshire and Connecticut adverse to repeal of, 362.

Mitchel, Ormsby M., Maj. Gen. U. S. Vols.: designated to command East Tennessee expedition, V, 63; occupies line of Tennessee River between Tuscumbia and Stevenson, 345; reply to Lincoln's question about opening the Mississippi River, VI, 441.

Mitchell, John G., Bvt. Maj. Gen. U. S. Vols.: in battles of Kenesaw Mountain, IX, 22.

Moall, Edward, remains with rearguard in Fort Moultrie, III, 50, 51.

Mobile, Ala., seizure of Forts Morgan and Gaines, III, 186; siege of, IX, 239-242; surrender of, April 11, 1865, 242.

Mobile Bay, Ala., battle of, Aug. 5, 1864, IX, 230-239.

Mocquard, Constant, Priv. Sec. to Napoleon III: notes to Slidell, VIII, 272-274.

Moir, James, Capt. British mail steamer Trent, V, 22.

Monitor, The, Union ironclad: invented by Ericsson, V, 219; plan of, 219, 220; expected at Fort Monroe, 222; ordered to engage Potomac rebel batteries, 222; arrives at Fort Monroe, 227; fight with Merrimac, March 9, 1862, 228-231; construction of pilot house, 230; Worden wounded, 230; Greene succeeds to command, 231; sunk off Cape Hatteras, 238.

Monocacy, Md., battle of, July 9, 1864, IX, 165.

Monongahela, The, Union gunboat: in battle of Mobile Bay, IX, 235, 236.

Monroe doctrine, origin of, VII, 405, 406; reaffirmed in Republican Baltimore Platform of 1864, 421; indorsed by Lincoln in letter of acceptance of 1864, 421.

Monroe, John T., mayor of New Orleans: correspondence with Farragut, V, 267, 268; promises to yield obedience to the conqueror, 268; contumacy of, 269.

Monsarrat, G. H., Conf. Capt.: report on East Tennessee persecutions, V, 79.

Montalembert, Charles Forbes, Comte de, criticism of Lincoln's style, X, 351.

Montauk, The, Union monitor: attacks Fort McAllister, Jan. 27 and Feb. 1, 1863, VII, 61-63; destroys blockade-runner Nashville, 61-64; commanded by Worden, 63.

Montgomery, Ala., meeting of rebel Provisional Congress, III, 196.

Montgomery, L. M., Conf. Col.: present at Pemberton's interview with Grant, VII, 303.

Moody, Capt., captured with Jefferson Davis, X, 274.

Moore, A. B., Gov. of Ala.: reply to Gist about proposed secession, II, 311-313; letter of, III, 185; proclamation of, 185; seizures ordered by, 186; causes banks to suspend payment, 186.

Moore, O. H., Col. U. S. Vols.: repulses Morgan's cavalry, VIII, 53.

Moore, Sydenham E., M. C.: signs secession address, II, 436.

Moore, Thomas O., Gov. of La.: reply to Gist about proposed secession, II, 308-310; calls extra session of legislature, III, 192; orders for seizures, 192; organizes colored rebel troops, VI, 450.

Moravian Synod, resolutions supporting the war and emancipation, VI, 319.

Morell, G. W., Maj. Gen. U. S. Vols.: commands under Porter on the Peninsula, V, 428; in battle of Gaines's Mill, 429.

Morfitt, H. M., elected to Maryland legislature, IV, 165.

Morgan, —, assists Sumner, II, 51.

Morgan, Edwin D., Gov. of N. Y., U. S. Sen.: chairman National Republican Committee, II, 265; calls Chicago Convention to order, 265; authorized to organize troops, IV, 138; conference with Seward about recruiting, VI, 117; supports the government, VII, 9; letter to Lincoln about renomination, IX, 55; address calling Baltimore Convention to order, 65; protests against Field for Assistant Treasurer at New York, 92; declines nomination for Secretary of Treasury, 349.

Morgan, George D., authorized to organize troops, IV, 138.

Morgan, G. W., Brig. Gen. U. S. Vols.: division of, at Chickasaw Bluffs, VII, 134; in attack on Fort Hindman, 140.

Morgan, James D., Bvt. Maj. Gen. U. S. Vols.: in March to the Sea, IX, 481.

Morgan, John H., Conf. Brig. Gen.: imprisoned in retaliation, VII, 457; escapes from prison, 457; defeated by Hall, VIII, 50; driven from Snow Hill by Stanley, 50;

imprisoned in Ohio penitentiary, 52; commands cavalry raid into northern States, 53; skirmish with Col. Moore, 53; burns Lebanon, Ky., 53; crosses into Indiana, 53, 54; raid through Indiana and Ohio, 55–57; capture of, 58; raid into Kentucky, 58; defeated by Burbridge, 58; death, 58.

Morrill, Justin S., M. C., U. S. Sen.: member of House Committee of Thirty-three, II, 417; deprecates making paper money legal tender, VI, 235; votes for National Bank Act, 244; votes for re-passage of the Act, 245.

Morrill, Lot M., Gov. of Me., U. S. Sen.: member of Peace Convention, III, 230.

Morrill Tariff Act, passed, March 2, 1861, III, 243; financial provisions of, 243.

Morris, Achilles, elected to Illinois legislature in 1832, I, 109.

Morris, Buckner S., votes for, for governor of Illinois, II, 43.

Morris, C. M., Lieut. Conf. navy: commands the *Florida*, IX, 129.

Morris, Edward Joy, M. C., Min. to Turkey: plan of compromise, II, 422.

Morris, H. W., Commodore U. S. N.: commands the *Pensacola* in Farragut's fleet, V, 261; ordered to hoist Union flag over the Mint in New Orleans, 268.

Morris, Orlando H., Col. U. S. Vols.: killed at Cold Harbor, VIII, 404.

Morris, Thomas A., Maj. Gen. U. S. Vols.: moves towards Laurel Hill, IV, 334; pursues Garnett, 337.

Morrison, James L. D., Col. U. S. Vols., M. C.: in Mexican war, I, 262; favorably mentioned by Lincoln for appointment, 293.

Morse, Freeman H., M. C., consul at London: member of House Committee of Thirty-three, II, 417.

Morton, O. P., Gov. of Ind., U. S. Sen.: telegram about Ohio River commerce, IV, 200; reports danger from Kentucky, 231; contest with Indiana legislature, VIII, 9, 10.

Moss, Charles E., speech in Cleveland Convention, IX, 34, 35.

Mott, Gershom, Maj. Gen. U. S. Vols.: in battle of the Wilderness, VIII, 362; in battle of Spotsylvania, 377; in battle of Hatcher's Run, IX, 434; in assault on Petersburg, X, 179.

Mott, Thaddeus P., Capt. U. S. Vols.: battery of, attacks Dam No. One, V, 368.

Mouton, Alfred, Conf. Brig. Gen.: in attack on Brashear City, VII, 321; in battle of

Sabine Cross Roads, VIII, 293; killed at Sabine Cross Roads, 295.

Mower, Joseph A., Bvt. Maj. Gen. U. S. A.: in Red River expedition, VIII, 292; in battle of Pleasant Hill, 295; in March to the Sea, IX, 481; in march to Goldsboro', X, 235; assigned to command Twentieth Corps, 241; at grand review in Washington, 333.

Mudd, Samuel, assists Booth and Herold, X, 307, 308; tried and imprisoned, 312, 313.

Mullany, J. R. M., Rear Adm. U. S. N.: wounded in Mobile Bay, IX, 235.

Mulligan, James A., Bvt. Brig. Gen. U. S. Vols.: sent to reënforce Lexington, IV, 427; surrenders to Price, 428; engagement at Leetown, IX, 161.

Mumford, William B., tears down Union flag in New Orleans, V, 268, 269; arrested and tried for treason, 278; convicted and hanged, 278.

Munford, Thomas T., Conf. Brig. Gen.: in retreat to Appomattox, X, 187.

Murfreesboro, Tenn., battle of, Dec. 31, 1862, to Jan. 2, 1863, VI, 285–295; losses at, 294, 295.

Murphy, Isaac, Gov. of Ark.: appointed provisional governor of Arkansas, VIII, 415; elected governor of Arkansas, 417.

Murphy, Robert C., Col. U. S. Vols.: evacuates Iuka, VII, 113; surrenders Holly Springs, Dec. 20, 1862, 127.

Murray, E. H., Bvt. Brig. Gen. U. S. Vols.: in March to the Sea, IX, 481.

Murray, John P., resolution in Confederate Congress about Mexico, VII, 422.

Murray, Robert, U. S. marshal for New York: indicted for arresting Arguelles, IX, 47; indictment quashed, 47.

Naglee, Henry M., Brig. Gen. U. S. Vols.: attends council of war, V, 167.

Nail, J. L., information from, about the Lincoln genealogy, I, 5.

Napoleon III., letter to Gen. Forey about Mexico, VI, 33, 34; conversation with Schele de Vere, 34, 35; proposes to increase French expedition to Mexico, 41; sends reënforcements to Lorencez in Mexico, 46; sends Gen. Forey to Mexico with 35,000 men, 46; admission concerning concession of belligerent rights to the Confederate States, 62; expresses sympathy with the South to Slidell, 76–79; interview with Slidell, Oct. 28, 1862, about American affairs, 80, 82; suggests to

Slidell building Confederate ships in France, 82; withdraws French army from Mexico, VII, 423; comments on the American war, VIII, 266, 267; suggestion to Slidell about Confederate navy, 269; interview with Voruz and Slidell, 270; promises to Arman, 271; sends Slidell confidential dispatch from Adams to Dayton, 272; conversation with Slidell, 272, 273; steps towards recognizing Confederate government, 273, 274; interview with Roebuck and Lindsay, 274; letter to Drouyn de l'Huys, 275; interview with Arman, 279; action concerning the *Rappahannock*, IX, 138-142.

Nashville, Tenn., battle of, Dec. 15, 16, 1864, X, 29-34.

Nashville, The, Conf. blockade-runner: destroyed by Union monitor *Montauk*, VII, 61-64.

Navy of the United States, reduction of, X, 337, 338.

Neale, T. M., employs Lincoln as deputy surveyor, I, 115.

Nebraska, State of, first bill to organize Territory, I, 338; second bill, 343; third bill, 349.

Nebraska Bill, first bill passes House, sent to Senate, referred, and reported back to Douglas, I, 339, discussed in Senate, 340, and laid on table, 341; second bill reported to Senate by Douglas, 343; " Peculiar provision" concerning slavery in second bill, 344; Kansas-Nebraska Act introduced by Douglas, 349; bill further amended, 350; Act passed, 351; petition of 3050 New England clergymen against, 361; speeches in Illinois legislature against: of N. B. Judd, 366 — of B. C. Cook, 366, 367 — of J. M. Palmer, 366, 367.

Negley, James S., Maj. Gen. U. S. Vols.: in battle of Murfreesboro, VI, 288, 292; march on Chattanooga, VIII, 71; advances into McLemore's Cove, 76; withdraws from Bragg's attack, 79; in battle of Chickamauga, 89, 92, 93, 105.

Negro soldiers, in the Revolutionary War, I, 314; Lincoln expresses his intention to use them, VI, 441; Stanton's orders to Saxton concerning, 441; laws authorizing, 441, 442; employment of, announced in final emancipation proclamation, 442; Hunter's effort to organize a regiment, 443; the Wickliffe resolution, and Hunter's answer, 443; Sergeant Trowbridge's company, 444, 445; Col. Higginson's regiment,

445; "First Kansas Colored" organized, 446; Lincoln's answer to Butler, 448; Butler refuses Phelps's project, 448, 449; Phelps's resignation and offensive answer, 449; a rebel colored regiment, 450; Butler's regiment of free negroes, 450, 451; Butler organizes three additional regiments, 451, 452; Lincoln's letters about colored troops, 452-457; rebel proclamation of outlawry against officers of negro regiments, 454; proposal to give Frémont a command of, 456; Gen. Thomas sent west to organize, 459; special bureau for organizing in War Department, 461; Gov. Sprague's application, 462; Gov. Andrew's regiments, 462, 463; War Department orders for recruiting, 463; Lincoln pushes organization of, 465; Act of Congress to enroll negroes for the draft, 467; number of, 468; efficiency in battle, 469; rebel threats against officers organizing, 471-473; Lincoln's order of retaliation, 474, 475; the Fort Pillow massacre, 478-480; Cabinet opinions on Fort Pillow massacre, 481-483; Jefferson Davis on arming negroes for rebel service, 485, 486; his letter to Gov. Smith on same subject, 486, 487; Lee recommends them for rebel service, 487; action of the Confederate Congress, 487; Lincoln's order regulating enlistment of, in Maryland, Missouri, Tennessee, and Delaware, VIII, 460.

Nelson, Homer A., M. C., Col. U. S. Vols.: vote for Thirteenth Amendment, X, 83.

Nelson, Samuel, Assoc. Justice U. S. Sup. Ct.: opinion in Dred Scott case, II, 66; accompanies Justice Campbell to an interview with Seward, III, 406.

Nelson, Thomas A. R., M. C.: member of House Committee of Thirty-three, II, 417.

Nelson, William, Lieut. Comm. U. S. N., Maj. Gen. U. S. Vols.: sent to Kentucky, IV, 235; brings 5000 muskets to arm Union men of Kentucky, 236; establishes "Camp Dick Robinson," 240; forwards arms to East Tennessee, V, 59; ordered to reënforce Grant, 191; occupies Nashville under Grant's orders, 311; leads advance from Duck River to Savannah, 319; arrives at Savannah with advance division of Buell's army, 328; reaches Pittsburg Landing, 333; defeated by Smith, VI, 274; prepares to defend Louisville, 274.

Neosho, The, Union gunboat: passage through the dam on Red River, VIII, 300, 301.

Nesmith, James W., U. S. Sen.: votes for Thirteenth Amendment, X, 77.

Nevada, State of, organized as a Territory, III, 237; ratifies Thirteenth Amendment, X, 89.

Newcastle, Duke of, protest against proposition of mediation to the United States, VI, 67.

Newell, W. A., M. C., Gov. of N. J.: evidence in Porter court-martial case, VI, 12, 13.

New Hampshire, State of, ratifies Thirteenth Amendment, X, 89.

New Jersey, State of, fusion movement in, II, 292; legislature passes anti-war resolutions, VI, 218; Union members of legislature renominate Lincoln, IX, 55; ratifies Thirteenth Amendment, X, 89.

Newman, J. P., Bish. M. E. Church: comment on action of Methodist Episcopal Church, VI, 324, 325.

New Mexico, territory of, acquired, I, 325; Territory of, organized, 328.

New Orleans, La., situation on the Mississippi, V, 254; arrival of Farragut's fleet, 266; surrender of, April 26, 1862, 268; occupied by Butler, May 1, 1862, 275; insufficient supply of provisions, 275; Butler's successful effort to feed the population, 276; martial law established, 276; arrest, trial, and execution of Mumford, 278; Butler's description of disloyalty in the city, 279; the "Woman Order," 281; efficiency of Butler's military government, 284; assessments and charities, 284, 285; the public health maintained, 285; quarantine and yellow fever, 285, 286; rebel contumacy and intrigue, 286, 287.

New School Presbyterians, resolutions supporting the war and emancipation, VI, 322, 323.

Newton, John, Bvt. Maj. Gen. U. S. A.: interview with Lincoln, VI, 213; in battle of Kenesaw Mountain, IX, 22, 23; sent to Chattanooga, 281.

New York, State of, fusion movement in, II, 289, 290; Seymour elected governor, VII, 10; draft proceedings in, 13–18; draft riots in, 17–26; ratifies Thirteenth Amendment, X, 88.

New York "Journal of Commerce" publishes forged proclamation, IX, 48; order for suppression of, 48; arrest and release of editor, 48, 49; publication resumed, 49.

New York "World," publishes forged proclamation, IX, 48; order for suppression

of, 48; arrest and release of editor, 48, 49; publication resumed, 49.

Niagara, The, Union cruiser: captures Confederate cruiser Georgia, IX, 138.

Niblack, William E., M. C.: plan of compromise, II, 423.

Nichols, E. T., Rear Adm. U. S. N.: commands the Winona in Farragut's fleet, V, 261.

Nicolay, John G., Priv. Sec. to Pres. Lincoln: member of Lincoln's suite, III, 290; present at interview between Lincoln and Grant, VIII, 341; inquiry about Lincoln's preference for Vice-President at Baltimore Convention, IX, 72, 73; report on Missouri politics, 369; interview with Ashley, X, 84, 85; at Sumter flag-raising in Charleston, 301.

Noell, John W., M. C.: compromise proposition of, II, 425; second interview with Lincoln about compensated emancipation, VI, 112; introduces bill in House to aid Missouri emancipation, 396.

Norfolk, Va., evacuated by rebels, V, 236; occupied by Union troops, May 10, 1862, 237.

North Anna, Va., battle of, May 23–27, 1864, VIII, 387–390.

North Carolina, State of, answer to Lincoln's proclamation, IV, 90; course of secession movement in, 246–248; seizure of Forts Johnston and Caswell, 246; Convention voted down, 247; military bill passed, 247; Fayetteville arsenal seized, 247; the governor's usurpation, 248; a second Convention called, 248; secession ordinance passed, May 20, 1861, 248; capture of Hatteras, Aug. 29, 1861, V, 12, 13; recruiting in, 14; Roanoke Island fortified by Confederates, 239, 240; Department created for Burnside, 242; Union victory at Roanoke Island, Feb. 8, 1862, 245; capture of Elizabeth City, Feb. 10, 1862, 246; reduction of New Berne, March 14, 1862, 246; capture of Fort Macon and Beaufort, April 26, 1862, 247; Edward Stanley appointed military governor, VI, 345; capture of Fort Fisher, Jan. 15, 1865, X, 67; Schofield occupies Wilmington, Feb. 22, 1865, 69; Schofield occupies Goldsboro', March 21, 1865, 70, 71; ratifies Thirteenth Amendment, 89; Goldsboro' occupied by Sherman, March 23, 1865, 237; Johnston surrenders to Sherman, April 26, 1865, 252, 253.

Norton, Elijah H., M. C.: opposes bill to aid Missouri emancipation, VI, 396.

Nott, Charles C., Judge U. S. Ct. of Claims: present at Lincoln's Cooper Institute speech, II, 217.

Noyes, E. M., Lieut. U. S. Vols.: crosses Warwick River at Dam No. One, V, 368; reports to Gens. Smith and McClellan, 368.

Noyes, William Curtis, signs memorial about Frémont and colored troops, VI, 456.

Nugent, Robert, appointed provost marshal general for New York, VII, 15.

Nye, James W., Gov. of Nev., U. S. Sen.: present at Lincoln's Cooper Institute speech, II, 217.

O'Brien, H. T., Col. of militia: murdered in New York draft riots, VII, 21, 22.

O'Conor, Charles, remarks about slavery, II, 211.

O'Laughlin, Michael, in conspiracy to assassinate Lincoln, X, 289; tried and imprisoned, 312, 313.

O'Rorke, Patrick H., Col. U. S. Vols.: killed at Gettysburg, VII, 255.

Octorara, The, Union gunboat: in battle of Mobile Bay, IX, 231; in siege of Mobile, 240, 242.

Odell, Moses F., M. C.: member of Committee on Conduct of the War, V, 150; first vote for Thirteenth Amendment, X, 78; second vote for Thirteenth Amendment, 83.

Odonnell, Leopold, Duke of Tetuan, Spanish statesman: reply to Great Britain about joint intervention in Mexico, VI, 36.

Offut, Denton, employs Lincoln to take a flatboat to New Orleans, I, 70; buys Cameron's mill, 78.

Oglesby, Richard J., Maj. Gen. U. S. Vols., Gov. of Ill., U. S. Sen.: orator of the day, at Lincoln's funeral at Springfield, X, 325.

Ohio Democratic Convention, 1863, nominates Vallandigham for governor, VII, 350, 351; resolutions about Vallandigham's arrest, 351; appoints committee to present resolutions to Lincoln, 351, 352; resolutions censuring Gov. Tod, 354, 355.

Ohio, State of, free in consequence of Ordinance of 1787, I, 317; response to Lincoln's proclamation, IV, 86; arrest and trial of Vallandigham, VII, 332-334; Vallandigham nominated for governor, 350, 351; John Brough nominated for governor, 355; American Knights in, VIII, 12; Morgan's raid, 56-58; Republican members of

legislature renominate Lincoln, IX, 56; ratifies Thirteenth Amendment, X, 89.

Olin, A. B., M. C., Judge Sup. Ct. of D. C.: remarks on bill for draft, VII, 4.

Oliver, Mordecai, M. C.: member of investigating committee, I, 451.

Olustee, Fla., battle of, Feb. 20, 1864, VIII, 285; losses at, 285.

Oneida, The, Union gunboat: disabled in Mobile Bay, IX, 233, 235.

Opdycke, Emerson, Bvt. Maj. Gen. U. S. Vols.: in march to Franklin, X, 11, 12, 17; in battle of Franklin, 19, 20.

Opdyke, George, authorized to make government purchases, IV, 137.

Ord, Edward O. C., Bvt. Maj. Gen. U. S. A.: sent by Grant to attack Iuka, VII, 113; attacks Van Dorn's retreat, 118; assigned to command Thirteenth Army Corps, 288; present at Grant's interview with Pemberton, 303; in Sherman's campaign against Jackson, 323, 324; requests that Lanman be relieved from command, 324; in assault at Petersburg mine, IX, 423, 424; wounded at Richmond, 431; in assault on Petersburg, X, 177; in march to Appomattox, 187, 194; made Department commander, 338.

Ordinance of 1784, Jefferson's draft of, prohibiting slavery in the Northwest Territory, I, 316; vote of Congress rejecting Jefferson's prohibition, 316.

Ordinance of 1787, adopted by Congress, I, 316; provides for forming not less than three nor more than five States, 317; Ohio, Indiana, Illinois, Michigan, free in consequence of, 317.

Oregon, State of, ratifies Thirteenth Amendment, X, 89.

Oreto (or Florida), The, Conf. cruiser: built in Liverpool, VI, 52; sails to Nassau, 52; enters Mobile Bay under British flag, 52; sails as Confederate cruiser under the name of the Florida, 52.

Orr, James L., M. C., Comr. of S. C., Gov. of S. C., Min. to Russia: arrives in Washington, III, 62; interview with Pres. Buchanan, 70.

Osage, The, Union gunboat: sunk by a torpedo at Mobile, IX, 240.

Ossipee, The, Union gunboat: in battle of Mobile Bay, IX, 235, 237.

Osterhaus, Peter J., Maj. Gen. U. S. Vols.: in battle of Port Gibson, VII, 170, 171; march to Edwards's Station, 187; in battle of Champion's Hill, 191; in siege of

Vicksburg, 292; in battle of Chattanooga, VIII, 139, 140, 152; in battles of Atlanta, IX, 286; in March to the Sea, 481.

Ould, Robert, Conf. Col.: appointed Confederate commissioner of exchange, VII, 451; remarks on negro prisoners of war, 453; refuses to exchange certain prisoners, 458; comment on exchange of prisoners, 459, 460; refuses proposed exchange of 12,000 prisoners, 460; directed to refuse communication with Butler, 460; asks Butler for a conference, 460; intimates readiness to exchange prisoners, 462; proposes mutual forwarding of supplies to prisoners, 462, 463.

Owens, Mary S., Lincoln's attentions to, correspondence with, and proposal of marriage to, I, 192.

Page, R. L., Conf. Brig. Gen.: surrenders Fort Morgan, IX, 238, 239.

Paine, Charles J., Bvt. Maj. Gen. U. S. Vols.: in second Fort Fisher expedition, X, 65.

Palfrey, F. W., Bvt. Brig. Gen. U. S. Vols.: statement about strength of Army of Potomac, VI, 136.

Palfrey, John G., M. C., historian: comment on Calhoun, I, 264; comment on slavery, 266.

Palmer, James S., Rear Adm. U. S. N.: commands the Octorara in siege of Mobile, IX, 242.

Palmer, John M., Maj. Gen. U. S. Vols., Gov. of Ill.: prominent lawyer of Illinois, I, 214; speech in Illinois legislature against Nebraska bill, 366, 367; in battle of Murfreesboro, VI, 283; march on Chattanooga, VIII, 71; in battle of Chickamauga, 92, 104; in march to Lookout Valley, 125; in battle of Chattanooga, 135, 154; skirmishes at Buzzard's Roost, IX, 11; in march to the Chattahoochee, 26; made Department commander, X, 338.

Palmer, Roundell (Lord Selborne), Lord Chancellor of England: opinion on the Alabama, VI, 54.

Palmer, W. J., Bvt. Brig. Gen. U. S. Vols.: defeats W. W. Russell, X, 36.

Palmerston, Henry John Temple, Viscount, Prime Minister of England: note to the Queen, V, 27; censures of Gen. Butler, 282; answered in Gen. Butler's farewell address, 282, 283; rejects Earl Russell's suggestion to propose mediation to the United States, VI, 66; revives the proposition, 66; opinion on the American war, VIII, 261; interview with Mason, 264, 265.

Palmetto State, The, Conf. ram: attempts to break blockade at Charleston, VII, 59–61.

Paris, Comte de (Louis Philippe d'Orléans): comment on Napoleon the Third's offer of mediation in the United States, VI, 70, 71.

Parke, John G., Bvt. Maj. Gen. U. S. A.: commands division under Burnside, V, 242; commands right in attack on Roanoke Island, 244; captures Fort Macon at Beaufort, N. C., 247; in siege of Vicksburg, VII, 290, 292; in Sherman's campaign against Jackson, 324; starts in pursuit of Longstreet, VIII, 185; in Army of Potomac, 353; in attack on Petersburg, IX, 411; in siege of Petersburg, 432; recapture of Fort Stedman, X, 161–164; in assault at Petersburg, 175, 178, 179; at grand review in Washington, 332.

Parker, Capt., alias Vernon Locke, Conf. navy: receives the Chesapeake from her captors, VIII, 14.

Parker, Foxhall A., Commodore U. S. N.: commands breaching battery against Fort Wagner, VII, 433.

Parker, Joel, Chief Justice N. H. Sup. Ct.: treatise on habeas corpus, VIII, 29.

Parker, Rev. Theodore, receives letters from John Brown, II, 196; informed of John Brown's plans, 200; remarks on John Brown's execution, 211.

Parrott, Marcus J., M. C.: elected to Congress, II, 104.

Parsons, M. M., Conf. Brig. Gen.: in battle of Pleasant Hill, VIII, 295.

Parsons, Theophilus, Chief Justice, Mass. Sup. Jud. Ct.: opinion on habeas corpus, VIII, 29.

Patterson, Robert, Maj. Gen. Penn. militia: organizes Pennsylvania troops, IV, 110; directions from Gen. Scott, 129, 130; assigned to command Department of Pennsylvania, 315; letter to Cameron, 316; reports a victory, 316; letter to Townsend, 325; crosses to Martinsburg, 326; letter to Townsend, 326; answers Scott, "Enemy has stolen no march," 345; intention to offer battle, 345; persuaded to change his plan, 345, 346; marches to Charleston, 346; mustered out of service, 356; orders about slave insurrection, 386.

Patton, W. T., Conf. Col.: killed at Winchester, IX, 305.

Paulding, Hiram, Rear Adm. U. S. N.: sent to Gosport with the *Pawnee*, IV, 146; burns Gosport navy yard, 147.

Payne, Henry B., M. C., U. S. Sen.: presents minority report in Charleston Convention, II, 234, 235.

Payne, Lewis, *alias* Lewis Powell. See POWELL, LEWIS.

Peace Convention, origin of, III, 227; States represented in, 229; prominent members of, 230; Constitutional Amendment recommended by committee of, 231; contradictory votes of, 231; conflicting views in, 231; resolutions of, transmitted to Congress, 233; members make a visit of ceremony to Lincoln, 317.

Peach Tree Creek, Ga., battle of, July 20, 1864, IX, 269.

Pearce, N. B., Conf. Brig. Gen.: commands Arkansas troops, IV, 409; junction with McCulloch and Price, 409; returns to Arkansas, 426.

Pea Ridge, Ark., battle of, March 6–8, 1862, V, 291, 292.

Peck, Ebenezer, Judge U. S. Ct. of Claims: organizes the convention system in Illinois, I, 127; member of Bloomington Convention, II, 28.

Pegram, John, Conf. Maj. Gen.: occupies pass at Rich Mountain, IV, 333; defeat of his rearguard, 335; retreats towards Laurel Hill, 336; surrenders to McClellan, 336; in battle of Murfreesboro, VI, 282; in battle of Fisher's Hill, IX, 306; in battle of Cedar Creek, 316, 321, 325.

Peirpoint, Francis H., Gov. of Va.: appointed governor of Virginia, IV, 331; applies for aid to suppress rebellion, 332; removes seat of "restored government of Virginia" to Alexandria, VI, 313; gathers a legislature at Alexandria, IX, 438; controversy with Butler, 439–442.

Pelletan, Eugène, French Deputy: remarks on Lincoln's death, X, 345.

Pelouze, Louis H., Bvt. Brig. Gen. U. S. A.: present at Lincoln's deathbed, X, 300.

Pemberton, John C., Conf. Lieut. Gen.: supersedes Van Dorn in Mississippi, VII, 119; conference with Johnston and Jefferson Davis at Grenada, Miss., 131; forces of, 164, 165; doubts as to Grant's movements, 166; orders reënforcements to Grand Gulf, 166; sends reënforcements to Grand Gulf, 170; arrives at Vicksburg, 171; consults Bowen at Grand Gulf, 172; forces of, 182; dispatches of, intercepted,

183; blame of Johnston, 183; council of war, 185; ordered to Clinton, 186; battle of Champion's Hill, May 16, 1863, 189–192; retreat to Vicksburg, 193; decides to hold Vicksburg, 194, 195; besieged in Vicksburg, May 18 to July 4, 1863, 282–305; correspondence with Johnston about relief of Vicksburg, 295, 296; council of war, 302; proposes to surrender Vicksburg, 302; interview with Grant, 303; accepts Grant's terms of surrender, 304, 305; forces surrendered at Vicksburg, 306–310; defeated by Stoneman, X, 238.

Pendleton, George H., M. C., Min. to Prussia: deprecates making paper money legal tender, VI, 235; resolution in House of Representatives about Vallandigham, VII, 358; nominated for Vice-President by Chicago Democratic Convention, IX, 258, 259; opposes Thirteenth Amendment, X, 83.

Pendleton, William N., Conf. Brig. Gen.: advises Lee to surrender, X, 189, 190.

Penn, D. B., Conf. Col.: defeated at Rappahannock Station, VIII, 243.

Pennington, William, Gov. of N. J., Speaker H. R.: receives vote for Vice-President in Philadelphia Convention, II, 35; elected Speaker, 215.

Pennsylvania, State of, Pittsburgh Republican Convention, II, 30, 31; Philadelphia Convention, 31–37; fusion movement in, 290, 291; meeting of governors at Altoona, Sept. 24, 1862, VI, 164–166; organization to resist the draft, VII, 3; Supreme Court decides draft law unconstitutional, but reverses its decision, 13; battle of Gettysburg, July 1–3, 1863, 239–264; dedication ceremonies at Gettysburg, Nov. 19, 1863, VIII, 191–202; address of legislature to Lincoln, asking his renomination, IX, 53, 54; Chambersburg burned, July 30, 1864, 176, 177; ratifies Thirteenth Amendment, X, 89.

Pennypacker, Galusha, Bvt. Maj. Gen. U. S. A.: wounded in assault on Fort Fisher, X, 66, 67.

Penrose, Charles B., Bvt. Lieut. Col. U. S. A.: in Lincoln's visit to Richmond, X, 218.

Pensacola, Fla., navy yard and forts at, III, 162; navy yard and forts surrendered, Jan. 12, 1861, 163, 164; occupied by rebels, 164.

Perrin, Abner, Conf. Brig. Gen.: killed at Spotsylvania, VIII, 382.

Perry, Aaron F., argument against habeas corpus for Vallandigham, VII, 335.

Perry, Edgar, Col. U. S. Vols.: killed at Cold Harbor, VIII, 405.

Perry, M. S., Gov. of Fla.: reply to Gov. Gist about proposed secession, II, 313, 314.

Perryville, Ky., battle of, Oct. 8, 1862, VI, 278.

Personal liberty bills, complaints of, III, 19; renewed and remodeled, 30; summary of, 30.

Petersburg, Va., operations against, IX, 403-426; importance of securing, 406, 407; attack by Gen. W. F. Smith, 407-410; Union advantages lost, 410; Hancock's attack, 410, 411; Potter's attack, 411; assault of June 18, 1864, 411; Union losses in four days' fighting, 412; investment of, 412; Lee's efforts to divert the besieging force, 419; Pleasants proposes a mine, 420; explosion of the mine, 421; disorder in the crater, 422, 423; attack repulsed, 424; court of inquiry, 425; investigation by Committee on Conduct of the War, 426; evacuation of, April 2, 1865, X, 183.

Pettigrew, James J., Conf. Brig. Gen.: in battle of Gettysburg, VII, 239, 261, 263.

Pettigru, James L., opinion on secession in South Carolina, III, 391, 392.

Pettit, John, M. C., U. S. Sen.: votes against Wilmot Proviso, I, 269; characterization of Declaration of Independence, II, 153.

Pettus, E. W., Conf. Brig. Gen.: statement about Lookout Mountain, VIII, 142.

Pettus, John J., Gov. of Miss.: reply to Gist about proposed secession, II, 310; sentiments of, III, 184; convenes legislature to aid Pemberton, VII, 130.

Phelps, Edward H., Col. U. S. Vols.: in battle of Chattanooga, VIII, 148; killed at Chattanooga, 155.

Phelps, John S., M. C., Mil. Gov. of Ark.: member of House Committee of Thirty-three, II, 417; second interview with Lincoln about compensated emancipation, VI, 111; appointed military governor of Arkansas, 346.

Phelps, J. W., Brig. Gen. U. S. Vols.: suggests enlistment of negro soldiers, VI, 447; makes requisition to organize negro regiments, 448; resignation and offensive reply to Butler, 449; proclaimed an outlaw by the rebel government, 471.

Phelps, S. L., Lieut. Comm. U. S. N.: commands gunboat Eastport in Red River expedition, VIII, 297.

Philadelphia Convention, 1856, Republican National: meeting, June 17, 1856, II, 31: nominations, 32; platform, 36, 37.

Philippi, Va., battle of, June 3, 1861, IV, 331.

Phillips, John, reply to Lincoln's letter, IX, 382.

Phillips, P. J., Conf. Brig. Gen.: defeated by Walcutt, IX, 485.

Phillips, Wendell, remarks on the John Brown raid, II, 211; approves of Cleveland Convention, IX, 32; letter to Cleveland Convention, 37, 38.

Philo Parsons, The, mrch. vessel: seized by John Y. Beall, VIII, 19.

Pickens, Francis W., M. C., Min. to Russia, Gov. of S. C.: interviews with Floyd, II, 317; elected governor and inaugurated, III, 1; letter to Buchanan demanding possession of Fort Sumter, 2, 3; withdraws his letter to Buchanan, 7; interview with Caleb Cushing, 12; inquires about recruits for Fort Sumter, 43; message to Anderson demanding his return to Fort Moultrie, 57; orders seizure of Fort Moultrie and Castle Pinckney, 58; takes possession of Charleston arsenal and other Federal buildings, 59; letter to Anderson justifying firing on the Star of the West, 107; communication to South Carolina legislature, 108; sends commissioners to Anderson to demand possession of Fort Sumter, 110, 111; accepts Anderson's proposal " to refer this matter to Washington," 113; orders for military preparation, 116; authorized by Convention to declare martial law, 117; reply to report of Gen. Simons, 121; indorsement on report of ordnance board, 122; orders engineers to prepare a plan to reduce Fort Sumter, 124; letter to Buchanan demanding possession of Fort Sumter, 154; abates his urgency for an answer, 170; letter to Cobb, 174; interview with Fox, 389; inquiry about expeditions, IV, 3; proposes to assault Fort Sumter, 18, 19; letter to Beauregard, 23: interview with Chew, 35; opens Anderson's mail, 39; reports preparations for defense, 42; telegram about purchasing provisions, 195.

Pickett, Geo. E., Conf. Maj. Gen.: in battle of Gettysburg, VII, 251, 258-260, 262, 263, 266; makes final charge at Gettysburg, July 3, 1863, 263-268; joins Lee's army, VIII, 399; retakes works at Bermuda Hundred, IX, 410; in march to Five Forks, X, 169, 171, 172; in battle of Five Forks, 173.

Pickett, John T., requests answer to the commissioners' formal note, III, 403; interview with Assistant Secretary of State, 405.

Pickett, T. J., letter to Lincoln suggesting him as a candidate for President, II, 256.

Pierce, Franklin, fourteenth Pres. U. S.: nominated for President, I, 332; elected, 337; inaugural address, 341, 342; remarks on Compromise of 1850, 342; interview with Democratic Senators, 349; agrees to make repeal of Missouri Compromise a party measure, 349; amendment written by, 350; appoints A. H. Reeder governor of Kansas Territory, 402; denounces Topeka movement as insurrectionary, 431, 449; proclamation against Topeka movement, 433, 449; defeated in Cincinnati Convention, II, 38; voted for in Charleston Convention, 244; appoints Jefferson Davis Secretary of War, III, 206; put in nomination for President in 1864, IX, 258.

Pierrepont, Edwards, Atty. Gen. under Grant: appointed by Lincoln to examine cases of State prisoners, VIII, 32, 33.

Pike, Albert, Conf. Brig. Gen.: secures adhesion of Indian chiefs to the rebels, V, 82; ordered to join Van Dorn in Arkansas, 290; commands Indian regiments at Pea Ridge, 292, 293; ordered back to Indian Territory, 293.

Pillow, Gideon J., Conf. Maj. Gen.: crosses to New Madrid, IV, 405; ordered to occupy Columbus, V, 43; reënforces Belmont, 113; sent to reënforce Fort Donelson, 185; attacks McClernand's division, 196; attends council of war in Donelson, 198; relinquishes command to Buckner, 198; leaves Fort Donelson, 198.

Pinkerton, Allan, detective work of, February, 1861, III, 304-306; conference with Judd, Franciscus, and Sanford, 310.

Pitcher, Thomas G., Bvt. Brig. Gen. U. S. A.: musters in Grant as colonel of 21st Illinois Volunteers, IV, 293.

Pitts, Charles H., elected to Maryland legislature, IV, 165.

Pittsburg Landing (or Shiloh), skirmish at, V, 317; Sherman's and Hurlbut's divisions at, 317; Grant unites his army at, 320; situation of battlefield, 322; positions of Union division commanders, 323, 324; battle of Sunday, April 6, 1862, 325; death of A. S. Johnston, 326; capture of Prentiss, 327; W. H. L. Wallace mortally wounded, 327; condition of the battle at sundown, April

6, 1862, 330, 331; arrival of Buell with his army, April 6, 1862, 333; battle of April 7, 1862, 334; defeat and retreat of Confederates, 334; Union and Confederate loss, 335.

Pittsburgh Republican Convention, meeting of, Feb. 22, 1856, II, 30, 31.

Pleasant Hill, La., battle of, April 9, 1864, VIII, 295.

Pleasants, Henry, Bvt. Brig. Gen. U. S. Vols.: proposes Petersburg mine, IX, 420, 421; at explosion of the mine, 422.

Pleasonton, Alfred, Bvt. Maj. Gen. U. S. A.: in battle of Chancellorsville, VII, 93-102; cavalry battle at Brandy Station, June 9, 1863, 205, 206; cavalry successes under, 215; recommends Farnsworth, Custer, and Merritt for brigadier generals, 232; testimony about Gettysburg, 269; drives Price from Missouri, VIII, 479.

Plumb, David, speech in Cleveland Convention, IX, 35.

Poindexter, J. A., capture of, VI, 379.

Polignac, C. J., Conf. Maj. Gen.: in battle of Pleasant Hill, VIII, 295; defeated by A. J. Smith, 301.

Polk, James K., eleventh Pres. U. S.: Democratic nominee for President in 1844, I, 227; measures to complete annexation of Texas, 238; orders Gen. Taylor to the Rio Grande, 241; asks appropriation for a treaty, 267; asks appropriation to promote acquisition of territory, 268.

Polk, Leonidas, Conf. Lieut. Gen.: takes command on the Mississippi River, IV, 203; commands at Memphis, 399; plan to invade Missouri, 399, 400; message to Magoffin, V, 43; orders Pillow to Columbus, 43; defends Confederate invasion of Kentucky, 44; reënforces Belmont, 113; commands Confederate left wing at Pittsburg Landing, 321; in battle of Murfreesboro, VI, 282, 291, 292; recommends retreat from Murfreesboro, 293; pastoral letter about secession, 331; ordered to attack Crittenden, VIII, 79; requests reënforcements, 80; in battle of Chickamauga, 84, 90, 91, 93, 101; succeeds Johnston in command in Mississippi, 326; joins Johnston's army, IX, 13; in battles of Resaca, 13; march to Cassville, 15; in battles of Dallas, 18; killed at Pine Mountain, 20.

Polk, Trusten, Gov. of Mo., U. S. Sen.: expelled from Congress, VIII, 469.

Pomeroy, Samuel C., U. S. Sen.: receives votes for Vice-President in Philadelphia

Convention, II, 35; present at interview between Lincoln, Cabinet, and Republican Senators, VI, 266; favors dismissal of Seward, 266; secret circular of, VIII, 318-321.

Pope, John, Bvt. Maj. Gen. U. S. A.: attends meeting of Lincoln's suite, III, 314; offers to assist Grant, IV, 288; commands in northern Missouri, 405; describes bushwhackers, 405; opinion of Frémont, 431; report of victory near Milford, V, 91; assigned to command campaign against Island No. Ten, 294; lands at Commerce, Missouri, 294; invests New Madrid, 295; erects battery at Point Pleasant, 295; New Madrid evacuated, 295; requests Foote to attack Island No. Ten with gunboat fleet, 296; captures Confederate troops, 299; prepares to advance against Memphis, 299; advance to Fort Pillow, 300; ordered up the Tennessee River, 300; arrives at Pittsburg Landing, 301; lands with his army near Shiloh battlefield, 337; assigned to command left wing of Halleck's army, 337; statement concerning prisoners at Corinth, 341; appointed to command Army of Virginia, VI, 1; takes the field, July 29, 1862, 2; doubts the coöperation of McClellan, 3; address to Army of Virginia, 4; cordial letter to McClellan, 5; retreats behind the Rappahannock, 6; orders Fitz John Porter to Bristoe Station, 8; joint order to McDowell and Porter, 8; battle at Groveton, 9; sends Porter peremptory order to go into action, 9; sends Porter peremptory order to report in person on the field, 10; battle of second Bull Run, Aug. 30, 1862, 10, 11; withdraws to intrenchments before Washington, 12; letter asking Grant to examine Porter court-martial case, 12; comment in report on second Bull Run, 16; made Department commander, X, 338.

Porter, Andrew, Brig. Gen. U. S. Vols.: provost marshal at Washington, IV, 441; attends council of war, V, 167.

Porter, Benjamin H., Lieut. U. S. N.: killed at Fort Fisher, X, 66.

Porter, David D., Adm. U. S. N.: selected for Fort Pickens expedition, III, 452; claims command of the *Powhatan*, IV, 4; sails for Fort Pickens, 5, 6; arrival at Fort Pickens, 16; brings information about New Orleans defenses, V, 253; consulted about expedition against New Orleans, 253; suggests a mortar flotilla, 254; present at council about expedition against New Orleans, 254; assigned to organize and command mortar flotilla, 255; bombardment of Forts Jackson and St. Philip, April 18, 1861, 260; demands surrender of the forts, 270; sends six mortar schooners to the rear of Fort Jackson, 272; again demands surrender of Forts Jackson and St. Philip, 272; receives surrender, April 28, 1861, 273; accompanies Farragut to Vicksburg with mortar flotilla, 348; bombards Vicksburg batteries, June 27, 1862, 348; commands flotilla in expedition against Arkansas Post, VII, 139; in attack on Fort Hindman, 140; attempts the Steele's Bayou route, 150-152; passes the Vicksburg batteries, 158-161; bombards Grand Gulf, April 29, 1863, 167; occupies Grand Gulf, 172; attacks Vicksburg batteries, 293; joins Banks's expedition at Alexandria, La., 314, 315; commands gunboats in Red River expedition, VIII, 289; retreat down Red River, 297-301; commands fleet in Fort Fisher expeditions, X, 55; first bombardment of Fort Fisher, 61; directed to hold position off Fort Fisher, 65; second bombardment of Fort Fisher, 65, 66; interview with Lincoln, Grant, and Sherman, 215; Lincoln's visit to Richmond, 216-219.

Porter, Fitz John, Maj. Gen. U. S. Vols.: inspects Charleston forts, II, 345, 346; persuades Patterson not to attack, IV, 346; commands provisional brigades at Washington, 441; attends council of war, V, 167; assigned by McClellan to command provisional army corps, 381; established north of the Chickahominy, 385; battle near Hanover Court House, 385; statement about McClellan's change of base, 419; repulses rebels at Beaver Dam Creek, June 26, 1862, 425; urges McClellan to move on Richmond, 426; strength of command, 428; losses at Gaines's Mill, 429; crosses White Oak Swamp, 433; establishes his corps at Malvern Hill, 433; interview with Lincoln at Harrison's Landing, 433; ordered to Bristoe Station, Centreville, and Gainesville, VI, 8; advance arrives at Dawkins Branch, 8; meeting with McDowell, 8; receives from Pope joint order to himself and McDowell, 8; receives from Pope peremptory order to go into action, 9; receives from Pope peremptory order to report in person on the field, 10; reports to Pope, Aug. 30, 1862,

10; in battle of second Bull Run, Aug. 30, 1862, 10; tried by court martial and cashiered, 12; letters to Burnside, 13, 14; sent with his corps to McClellan, 134.

Porter, J. K., Lieut. Conf. navy : surrenders the *Florida*, IX, 132.

Porter, Joseph C., guerrilla leader in Missouri in 1862, VI, 378; pursuit and dispersion of his band, 379.

Porter, Peter, Col. U. S. Vols.: killed at Cold Harbor, VIII, 405.

Porterfield, G. A., Conf. Col.: retires to Philippi, IV, 330; attacked and routed, 331.

Port Gibson, Miss., battle of, May 1, 1863, VII, 170, 171.

Port Hudson, La., first assault on, May 25, 1863, VII, 317; second assault, June 14, 1863, 317; siege begun May 25, 1863, 317; surrender, July 9, 1863, 322.

Port Royal, S. C., expedition against, V, 14–17; capture of, Nov. 7, 1861, 17–19.

Posey, ——, a settler in Indiana, I, 28, 29.

Post, P. Sidney, Bvt. Brig. Gen. U. S. Vols.: in battle of Murfreesboro, VI, 286; in march to Franklin, X, 11; in battle of Nashville, 30, 32, 33.

Potter, Robert B., Maj. Gen. U. S. Vols.: in battle of Spotsylvania, VIII, 381; in attack on Petersburg, IX, 411; in assault at Petersburg mine, 422, 424, 432; in recapture of Fort Stedman, X, 162.

Powell, Lazarus W., Gov. of Ky., U. S. Sen.: moves to appoint Senate Committee of Thirteen, II, 405; member of that committee, 414; amendment to Crittenden compromise plan, III, 225; Senate resolution about political prisoners, VIII, 39, 40; put in nomination for President, IX, 258.

Powell, Lewis (*alias* Lewis Payne), in conspiracy to assassinate Lincoln, X, 289; receives Booth's directions to murder Seward, 291; gains entrance to Seward's house, X, 303, 304; attacks and wounds Frederick Seward and Robinson, 304; stabs Sec. Seward, 304; stabs Augustus Seward, 305; wounds Hansell, 305; escapes from Seward's house, 305; arrested at Mrs. Surratt's house, 306; tried and hanged, 312, 313.

Powell, W. H., Bvt. Maj. Gen. U. S. Vols.: defeats McCausland, IX, 328.

Powers, Frank, Conf. Col.: report about negro prisoners of war, VII, 455.

Prairie Grove, Ark., battle of, Dec. 7, 1862, VI, 383.

Preble, G. H., Rear Adm. U. S. N.: commands the *Katahdin* in Farragut's fleet, V, 261.

Prentice, George D., editor of "Louisville Journal": letter to Lincoln, III, 277.

Prentiss, Benjamin M., Maj. Gen. U. S. Vols.: departure with his company for Springfield, IV, 87; takes command at Cairo, Ill., 195; asks assistance at Cairo, 406; portion of division at Pittsburg Landing, V, 323; taken prisoner at Pittsburg Landing, 327; repulses Holmes's attack on Helena, July 4, 1863, VII, 323.

Presbyterian General Assembly, resolutions supporting the war and emancipation, VI, 319–321.

Presbyterian General Assembly of the South, formed, Dec. 4, 1861, VI, 331.

Prescott, Royal B., Lieut. U. S. Vols.: enters Richmond, X, 208.

Presidential campaign of 1860: candidates and platforms, II, 279, 280; the "Wide Awakes," 284–286; fusion, 289–292; vote of Maine, 293; the October States, 293; electors chosen, 294; results of fusion, 294; electors cast their votes, 294; the Presidential count, 294; Lincoln declared elected, 294; electoral vote, 294.

Preston, S. W., Lieut. U. S. N.: fires powder-boat at Fort Fisher, X, 61; killed at Fort Fisher, 66.

Preston, William, Conf. Maj. Gen.: leaves Kentucky to join the South, IV, 244; in battle of Chickamauga, VIII, 100, 102, 106.

Preston, William Ballard, member of committee from Virginia Convention, IV, 72.

Pretorius, Emil, fails to attend Cleveland Convention, IX, 34.

Price, Sterling, Conf. Maj. Gen.: appointed major general of Missouri militia, IV, 219; agreement with Harney, 219; collects an army in southwest Missouri, 398; defeats Sigel at Carthage, 398, 399; junction with McCulloch and Pearce, 409; marches on Lexington, 426; besieges Lexington, 427, 428; retreats southward, 429; calls for 50,000 volunteers, V, 88; correspondence with Halleck, 90; retreat from Springfield, 289; opposed to Grant in the West, VII, 112; captures Iuka, 113; joins Van Dorn at Ripley, 113; seeks the protection of Maximilian, 420; invasion of Missouri, VIII, 478–480.

Price, Thomas L., M. C.: second interview with Lincoln about compensated emancipation, VI, 111; opposes bill to aid Missouri emancipation, 396; resolution in Democratic National Convention, IX, 255.

Prim, Don Juan, Marquis de los Castillejos: named to command Spanish part of Mexican expedition, VI, 39; appointed diplomatic commissioner of Spain, 39; executes convention of Soledad with Doblado, 44; sails for Spain from Mexico, 46.

Prisoners of war, Lincoln's letter to Stanton, March 18, 1864, about discharging, V, 144; Lincoln's order about prisoners at Rock Island, 145, 146; his interview with Stanton about them, 146, 147; Lincoln's letter to Grant about Rock Island prisoners, 147; Canby's report on, VII, 445; Lincoln's action about rebel privateers, 448; commission for relief of, 449; cartel for exchange of, 451; Confederate action about negro soldiers, 452–456; Butler appointed commissioner of exchange, 460; Grant's instructions to Butler, 461; treatment of, 463–465; Col. Chandler's report on Andersonville, 465–468; Dr. Jones's report on Andersonville, 468–470; numbers and mortality of, 470; Winder's order to Andersonville guards, 471.

Pritchard, Benjamin D., Bvt. Brig. Gen. U. S. Vols.: in capture of Jefferson Davis, X, 269, 270; statement about conversation with Davis, 272, 273; report of persons captured, 273, 274.

Privateering, invited by Jefferson Davis, IV, 88; Lincoln proclaims it piracy, 89.

Protestant Episcopal Church, Diocese of Pennsylvania, resolutions supporting the war and emancipation, VI, 323, 324.

Protestant Episcopal Church in the South, action on secession, VI, 331, 332.

Provisional Congress of Seceding States, meeting of, at Montgomery, Ala., Feb. 4, 1861, III, 196; elects Howell Cobb chairman, 197; Provisional Constitution adopted, 198; adopts name of Confederate States of America, Feb. 8, 1861, 198; elects President and Vice-President, 198; Permanent Constitution adopted, 198; summary of Acts of, 212.

Public debt, amount of: July 1, 1861, VI, 226; July 1, 1862, 230; July 1, 1863, 230; June 30, 1864, 237; June 30, 1865, 237; maximum amount (Aug. 31, 1865), 237.

Pugh, George E., U. S. Sen.: opposes a Congressional slave code, II, 175; speech in the Charleston Convention, 238; Senate discussion, 404; recommends McClellan for command at Cincinnati, IV, 282; counsel for Vallandigham, VII, 335; applies to Judge Leavitt for writ of habeas corpus for Vallandigham, 335.

Pugh, James L., M. C.: House discussion, II, 416, 417; signs secession address, 436.

Purcell, John B., Archbishop of Cincinnati: supports the government and the war, VI, 325.

Purinton, Lieut., U. S. Vols.: in capture of Jefferson Davis, X, 270.

Putnam, Harvey, M. C.: offers resolution embodying Wilmot Proviso, I, 269.

Putnam, H. S., Col. U. S. Vols.: killed in second assault on Fort Wagner, VII, 429, 431.

Quakers, or Society of Friends, action on the war and emancipation, VI, 326–329.

Quantrell, W. C., Conf. guerrilla: massacre at Lawrence, Kas., Aug. 21, 1863, VIII, 211, 212.

Quincy, Josiah, M. C.: comment on Lincoln's Conkling letter, VII, 385.

Quitman, John A., Bvt. Maj. Gen. U. S. A.: candidate for governor of Mississippi in 1861, III, 206.

Radford, Reuben, sells store to Greene, I, 110.

Radford, William, M. C.: votes for Thirteenth Amendment, X, 83.

Ramseur, Stephen D., Conf. Maj. Gen.: in Army of Northern Virginia, VIII, 354; wounded at Spotsylvania, 382; defeated by Averell, IX, 175; in battle of Winchester, 300, 301, 304; in battle of Fisher's Hill, 306; in battle of Cedar Creek, 316, 321; killed at Cedar Creek, 325.

Ramsey, Alexander, U. S. Sen., Sec. of War under Hayes: votes for re-passage of National Bank Act, VI, 245.

Randall, A. W., Gov. of Wis., Min. to Italy, P. M. Gen. under Johnson: letter to Lincoln, IV, 305.

Randolph, George W., member of committee from Virginia Convention, IV, 72.

Randolph, The, Union gunboat: sunk by a torpedo at Mobile, IX, 240.

Ransom, ——, defeated for delegate to Congress, II, 104.

Ransom, George M., Commodore U. S. N.: commands the Kineo in Farragut's fleet, V, 261.

Ransom, Robert, Jr., Conf. Maj. Gen.: in battle of Bermuda Hundred, VIII, 398.

Ransom, T. E. G., Bvt. Maj. Gen. U. S. Vols.: captures works at Aransas Pass, VIII, 287; in Red River expedition, 292; in battle of Sabine Cross Roads, 293; wounded, 294; in battles of Atlanta, IX, 286.

Rappahannock, The, Conf. cruiser: action of French government about, IX, 138-142.

Rathbone, Henry R., Bvt. Col. U. S. A.: attends Ford's Theater with Mrs. Lincoln and Miss Harris, X, 292; wounded by Booth, 296; directs Lincoln's removal from Ford's Theater, 296.

Raymond, Miss., battle of, May 12, 1863, VII, 177, 178.

Raymond, Henry J., editor of "New-York Times," M. C.: reports feeling in Burnside's army, VI, 212, 213; reports Baltimore platform of 1864, IX, 69-71; speech in Baltimore Convention, 71; letter to Lincoln about peace negotiations, 218, 219.

Raynor, Kenneth, M. C.: suggested for the Cabinet, III, 362.

Read, John Meredith, Justice Sup. Ct. of Pa., Min. to Greece: dissents from decision that draft law is unconstitutional, VII, 13.

Read, Theodore, Bvt. Brig. Gen. U. S. Vols.: killed in march to Appomattox, X, 187, 188.

Reagan, John H., M. C., Conf. P. M. Gen., U. S. Sen.: signs secession address, II, 436; appointed Confederate Postmaster General, III, 212; arrest of, X, 151; present at interviews of Davis and Johnston, 257-263; continues with Davis's party, 267; statement about Pritchard's conversation with Davis, 273; captured with Jefferson Davis, 273.

Reconstruction, changes of authority in localities and States occupied by Union armies, VI, 343, 344; appointment of military governors, 344; Andrew Johnson appointed military governor of Tennessee, 344; he sketches his official functions, 344, 345; Edward Stanley appointed military governor of North Carolina, 345; his commission and instructions, 345; G. F. Shepley appointed military governor of Louisiana, 346; John S. Phelps appointed military governor of Arkansas, 346; language of Lincoln's inaugural concerning, 347; language of special message of July 4, 1861, concerning, 347, 348; Lincoln's allusions to, in letter to Reverdy Johnson, 348, 349; in letter to Cuthbert Bullitt, 349; Lincoln's letters to Butler and Shepley, 350; to Grant and Johnson, 350; to Steele and Phelps, 350; Lincoln's letters to Gov. Shepley about Congressmen from Louisiana, 351, 352; election for Congress in Louisiana, 352, 353; B. F. Flanders and Michael Hahn elected and admitted to seats, 353; Lincoln's letter to Gillmore about, in Florida, VIII, 282, 283; mission of Major Hay, 282, 283; failure in Florida, 283; Lincoln's letters about, in Arkansas, 410-418; State Convention at Little Rock, 414; Arkansas Constitution amended to abolish slavery, 415; provisional government formed in Arkansas, 415; Arkansas adopts new Constitution, 416, 417; Arkansas State government elected and organized, 417; Senators and Congressmen elected from Arkansas, 418; Congress refuses to admit them, 418; Lincoln's letters about, in Louisiana, 420-430; State officers elected in Louisiana, 431-434; Louisiana State Convention elected, 435; Louisiana Convention abolishes slavery, 435, 436; amended Constitution adopted in Louisiana, 436; Senators and Members of Congress elected in Louisiana, 436, 437; Lincoln's letters about, in Tennessee, 441-445; election for county officers in Tennessee, 443-445; Tennessee Convention abolishes slavery, 447, 448; amended Constitution adopted, 448, 449; Tennessee legislature ratifies Thirteenth Amendment, 449; Senators and Members of Congress elected in Tennessee, 449; Lincoln's comment on theory of, IX, 111; Henry Winter Davis's bill, 115-117; Act for, passed by Congress, 120; Lincoln declines to sign Act, 120-123; Lincoln's proclamation about, 123; Peirpoint-Butler controversy, 439-442; Lincoln's letters to Butler about Virginia reconstruction 442-444; Lincoln's letters to Hurlbut and Canby about Louisiana reconstruction, 446, 447; House of Representatives defeats Ashley's bills for, 449-453; Lincoln's letter to Trumbull about Louisiana reconstruction, 453, 454; Trumbull reports joint resolution on Louisiana reconstruction, 454; Lincoln's address on, 457-463; discussed at Hampton Roads Conference, X, 122, 123.

Rector, Henry M., Gov. of Ark.: answer to Lincoln's call for troops, IV, 90.

Redfield, James, Lieut. Col. U. S. Vols.: killed at Allatoona, IX, 474.

Reed, John M., vote for, in Chicago Convention, 1860, II, 273.

Reeder, Andrew H., Gov. of Kas. Ter.: appointed governor of Kansas Territory, I, 402; powers as governor, 403; arrives in Territory, 403; orders election for Territorial Delegate, 404; orders census of inhabitants of Kansas, 409; orders election of legislature for March 30, 1855, 409; regulations for election of March 30, 1855, 409, 410; removes his office to Shawnee Mission, 411; issues certificate of election to members of bogus legislature, 412; convenes legislature at Pawnee, 414; goes to Washington, 414; his political dilemma, 416; legislature asks his removal, 417; removed by the President, 417; nominated for Territorial Delegate by Free State party, 428; receives Free State vote for Delegate, 429, 439; elected U. S. Senator, 430; writ against, issued by Lecompte, 451; resists arrest, 451; flees in disguise, 451; speech at Bloomington, II, 29.

Reformed Presbyterian Church, resolutions supporting the war and emancipation, VI, 322.

Reid, J. W., M. C.: commands in Border Ruffian camp, II, 16.

Reid, Whitelaw, editor of N. Y. "Tribune," Min. to France: statement about Grant at Pittsburg Landing, V, 331.

Reno, Jesse L., Maj. Gen. U. S. Vols.: commands division under Burnside, V, 242; commands left in attack on Roanoke Island, 244; killed at South Mountain, VI, 137.

Republican Party, proposed, I, 159; organized in Illinois, II, 23–30; Pittsburg Convention, 30, 31; Philadelphia Convention, 31; nominates J. C. Frémont for President, 32; nominates William L. Dayton for Vice-President, 35; Philadelphia platform, 36, 37; growing chances of, 255; leaders in, 255, 256; National Convention at Chicago in 1860, 255, 259–277; candidates and platform in 1860, 279; electors chosen by, 294; Baltimore Convention of 1864 adopts resolutions affirming Monroe doctrine, VII, 421; National Convention of 1864 at Baltimore, IX, 65–74; nominates Lincoln and Johnson, 71–74; victory in October States, 1864, 369–371; reëlection of Lincoln, Nov. 8, 1864, 377.

Resaca, Ga., battles of, May 13–16, 1864, IX, 13, 14.

Retaliation, rebel threats of, about negro troops, VI, 471–473; Lincoln's order for, 474, 475; McNeil executes ten rebel guerrillas, 475, 476; Van Dorn authorizes Breckinridge to threaten, 477; Fort Pillow massacre, 478–480; threats of rebel officers, 480; Cabinet action on Fort Pillow massacre, 481–483.

Reynolds, J. J., Bvt. Maj. Gen. U. S. A.: march on Chattanooga, VIII, 71; in battle of Chickamauga, 88, 92, 94, 95, 98, 99, 104; made Department commander, X, 338.

Reynolds, John, Gov. of Ill.: relates pioneer incidents, I, 53–55; call for volunteers to expel the Indians, 87–89; elected governor, 103.

Reynolds, John F., Maj. Gen. U. S. Vols.: commands brigade under McCall, V, 425; makes a reconnaissance at Chancellorsville, VII, 108; arrives at Gettysburg, 238; selects Gettysburg for the battlefield, 239, 240; killed at Gettysburg, 240.

Reynolds, John H., M. C.: member of Select Committee of Five, III, 142.

Rhind, Alexander C., Commodore U. S. N.: commands ironclad Keokuk in attack on Charleston, VII, 69; fires powder-boat at Fort Fisher, X, 61.

Rhode Island ratifies Thirteenth Amendment, X, 88.

Rice, Henry M., U. S. Sen.: member of Senate Committee of Thirteen, II, 414; proposition in that committee, III, 222.

Rice, James C., Brig. Gen. U. S. Vols.: killed at Spotsylvania, VIII, 376.

Richardson, A. D., correspondent of N. Y. "Tribune": cruelly treated as prisoner of war, VII, 458.

Richardson, Israel B., Maj. Gen. U. S. Vols.: mortally wounded at Antietam, VI, 140.

Richardson, William A., M. C., U. S. Sen.: chairman of House Committee on Territories, I, 337; introduces first Nebraska Bill, 338; nominated for Speaker of House of Representatives, 363; nominated by Democrats for governor of Illinois, II, 25; votes for, for governor, 43; criticism on Bull Run, IV, 359; fault-finding speech about Bull Run, 364; opposes bill for draft, VII, 4; opposes commutation clause, 27; presides over peace meeting at Springfield, 378.

Richardson, William P., Maj. Gen. Kas. militia: orders out his division of militia, II, 6.

Richmond, Va., made capital of the Confederate States, IV, 264; effect of the war, X,

148-150; evacuation of, April 2, 1865, 201-206; conflagration in, 205-207; surrender of, 208; occupied by Gen. Weitzel, 208.

Richmond, The, Union cruiser : in·battle of Mobile Bay, IX, 233, 235.

Rich Mountain, Va., battle of, July 11, 1861, IV, 334, 335.

Ricketts, James B., Bvt. Maj. Gen. U. S. A.: in Army of Potomac, VIII, 353; sent to Baltimore, IX, 164; wounded at Monocacy, 165; in battle of Fisher's Hill, 307, 309.

Riney, Zachariah, teacher of Pres. Lincoln, I, 27.

Ripley, E. H., Bvt. Brig. Gen. U. S. Vols.: brigade of, occupies Richmond, X, 209.

Rippit, Mrs., housekeeper in Fort Moultrie : transfer to Fort Sumter, III, 54.

Roanoke, The, Union steam frigate : at Fort Monroe, V, 223; starts to meet the *Merrimac*, 223; runs aground, 223.

Roanoke Island, N. C., situation of, V, 239; fortified by Confederates, 240; Goldsborough attacks the shore batteries, 243; defenses of, 244; attacked by Union army, 244, 245; surrendered by Confederates, Feb. 8, 1862, 245.

Roberts, George W., Col. U. S. Vols. : killed at Murfreesboro, VI, 288, 289.

Robertson, Judge, interview with Scott, IV, 104.

Robertson, John, Peace Commissioner from Virginia to seceding States, III, 165, 228; report of, 229.

Robinson, Charles, elected governor of Kansas under Topeka Constitution, I, 430; arrested at Lexington on requisition of governor of Kansas, 434, 450; indictment against, for "constructive treason," 434; given command of Free State forces, 443; house of, in Lawrence, burned, 455.

Robinson, Charles D., letter to Lincoln about war policy, IX, 214.

Robinson, Christopher, M. C., Min. to Peru: member of House Committee of Thirty-three, II, 417.

Robinson, Sergeant George F., wounded by Payne, X, 304.

Robinson, J. F., member of committee to distribute Union arms, IV, 237.

Robinson, Lucius, Gov. of N. Y.: signs call for Cleveland Convention, IX, 32; letter to Cleveland Convention, 38.

Robinson, M. S., Bvt. Brig. Gen. U. S. Vols.: in battle of Chickamauga, VIII, 104.

Rockwell, A. F., Bvt. Lieut. Col. U. S. A.: present at Lincoln's deathbed, X, 300.

Rodes, Robert E., Conf. Maj. Gen.: in battle of Chancellorsville, VII, 103; losses at Kelly's Ford, VIII, 245; in Army of Northern Virginia, 354; in campaign against Washington, IX, 172; in Shenandoah campaign, 296; in battle of Winchester, 300, 301; killed at Winchester, 301, 304.

Rodgers, George W., Commander U. S. N.: commands Union gunboat *Catskill* in attack on Charleston, VII, 69.

Rodgers, John, Rear Adm. U. S. N.: mission to prepare Western gunboats, IV, 201; describes bombardment of Port Royal, V, 18; sent West to construct gunboats, 118; commands monitor *Weehawken*, VII, 66; leads attack on Charleston, April 7, 1863, 66; captures rebel ram *Atlanta*, 79-81.

Rodman, Isaac P., Brig. Gen. U. S. Vols.: killed at Antietam, VI, 141.

Roe, F. A., Captain U. S. N.: fight with the *Albemarle*, X, 41-43; commands the *Sassacus*, 43.

Roebuck, John Arthur, M. P.: interview with Napoleon the Third, VIII, 274.

Rogers, A. A. C., M. C.: elected to Congress, VIII, 418.

Rollins, James S., M. C.: second interview with Lincoln about compensated emancipation, VI, 111; vote for Thirteenth Amendment, X, 83.

Roman, A. B., Conf. Comr.: arrives in Washington, III, 413.

Root, Joseph M., M. C.: resolutions to make California and New Mexico free Territories, I, 284.

Rosecrans, William S., Bvt. Maj. Gen. U. S. A.: battle of Rich Mountain, July 11, 1861, IV, 335, 336; assigned to command in western Virginia, 356; supersedes Buell in command of the Army of the Cumberland, Oct. 30, 1862, VI, 281; appoints Thomas to command center, McCook right wing, and Crittenden left wing of his army, 281; establishes headquarters at Nashville, 281; marches against Bragg, 282; plan of battle at Murfreesboro, 283, 284; battle of Murfreesboro, Dec. 31, 1862, to Jan. 2, 1863, 285-295; occupies Murfreesboro, 294; order respecting church assemblages, 334, 335; sent by Grant to attack Iuka, VII, 113; attacked by the rebels, 113; defeats Van Dorn's attack on Corinth, 117; pursues Van Dorn, 118; made major general of U. S. volunteers, 118; assigned to command Army of the Cumberland, 118; apprehension about conspiracy of American

Knights, VIII, 10; sends report on American Knights to Lincoln, 11–13; defends his inactivity, 43; fortifies Murfreesboro, 44; idiosyncrasies of, 45; complaints about cavalry, 46; sends Rousseau to Washington, 46; controversies with Halleck, 47; complaints about rank, 47; reply to Halleck's letter about promotion, 48, 49; reply to Halleck about telegraphing, 49; organizes cavalry expedition under Col. Streight, 51; council of war, 59; adopts Garfield's plan, 60; telegram to Halleck about council of war, 60; drives Bragg out of middle Tennessee, 61, 62; letter to Lincoln, 64; answer to Lincoln's letter, 66; questions Halleck about his orders, 67; march on Chattanooga, 67–73; occupies Chattanooga, Sept. 9, 1863, 73; telegraphs Halleck, "Chattanooga is ours," 75; censures Thomas, 79; reply to Halleck, 81; battle of Chickamauga, Sept. 18–20, 1863, 84–107; dispatch about Chickamauga, 108; dispatches to Lincoln, 110, 111; retires to Chattanooga, 113; correspondence with Lincoln, 114–117; relieved from command, 119; denies intention to retreat from Chattanooga, 121; plan of, 121–123; interview with Grant, 122; answer to Lincoln about Potomac troops, 143; transferred to Missouri, 474; order concerning church organizations, 475; election order in Missouri, 481, 482; approves Jaquess's application to go South, IX, 202, 203.

Rosser, Thomas L., Conf. Maj. Gen.: in battle of the Wilderness, VIII, 363; sent to Early, IX, 312; defeated by Torbert, 314; in battle of Cedar Creek, 317; stationed at Stony Creek, 327; raid on Baltimore and Ohio railroad, 328; in battle of Waynesboro, 329, 330; in retreat to Appomattox, X, 187.

Rouher, Eugène, French Minister of State: interview with Slidell, VIII, 270.

Rousseau, Lovell H., Bvt. Maj. Gen. U. S. A.: establishes "Camp Joe Holt," IV, 239; organizes Union brigade of Kentuckians, V, 47; in battle of Murfreesboro, VI, 287, 293; sent to Washington by Rosecrans, VIII, 46; cavalry raid from Decatur, IX, 27; receives votes for Vice-President at Baltimore Convention, 72; defense of Murfreesboro, X, 23.

Rowan, Stephen C., Vice Adm. U. S. N.: destroys rebel fleet in Albemarle Sound, V, 246; captures Elizabeth City, Feb. 10, 1862, 246; in bombardment of Fort Sumter, VII, 437.

Rowett, Richard, Bvt. Brig. Gen. U. S. Vols.: wounded at Allatoona, IX, 474.

Ruffin, Thomas, M. C.: signs secession address, II, 436.

Ruger, T. H., Bvt. Maj. Gen. U. S. Vols.: in march to Franklin, X, 13.

Runyon, Theodore, Brig. Gen. N. J. militia: commands division under McDowell, IV, 342.

Russell, ——, City Judge of New York: action about suppression of the "World" and "Journal of Commerce," IX, 49, 50.

Russell, D. A., Bvt. Maj. Gen. U. S. A.: storms rebel works at Rappahannock Station, VIII, 243; sent to Washington, IX, 164; killed at Winchester, 301.

Russell, Lord John, afterwards Earl, British Minister of Foreign Affairs: reply to Dallas, IV, 268; receives Southern commissioners, 268; disclaims England's intention to aid the rebellion, 277; says he does not expect to see Southern commissioners again, 277; proposes that the Declaration of Paris shall not apply to the rebellion, 278; notes on the Trent affair, V, 29, 30; views on the Trent affair, 39, 40; correspondence about intervention of France, Spain, and England, VI, 35, 36; thinks adhesion of United States ought to be invited, 36; announces English part of Mexican expedition, 39; comment on rumored designs of France and Spain in Mexico, 42; reply to Adams that the Oreto was built for peaceful commerce, 52; interview with Adams about the Oreto, 52; alleged views on the Alabama, 54; replies that British government is "unable to go beyond the law," 57; correspondence with Adams on proposed changes in Foreign Enlistment Act, 57, 58; answer to Adams's presentation of evidence, 58, 59; interview with Adams, March 26, 1863, 59; comments on blockade-running, 60; suggestion to Palmerston to propose mediation to the United States, 66; indorses Palmerston's suggestion to propose mediation to the United States, 66; proposes recognition of Confederate States, 66; dispatch about the Alabama, VIII, 254, 255; dispatch about Confederate cruisers, 256; correspondence with Adams about Confederate rams, 258, 259; remarks on the American war, 260; speech on Lincoln's death, X, 343.

Russell, John H., Capt. U. S. N.: commands the Kennebec in Farragut's fleet, V, 261.

Russell, W. W., Conf. Brig. Gen. : defeated by Palmer, X, 36.

Russia, invited by France to mediate in American affairs, VI, 63 ; refuses to join France in effort to obtain armistice in United States, 65, 66.

Rust, Albert, M. C., Conf. Brig. Gen. : member of House Committee of Thirty-three, II, 417 ; statement to that committee, 433.

Rutledge, Ann, Lincoln's interest in, I, 191, 192.

Sabine Cross Roads, La., battle of, April 8, 1864, VIII, 292-294.

Sabine Pass, Texas, Union defeat at, Sept. 8, 1863, VIII, 287.

St. Albans, Vt., rebel raid on, from Canada, Oct. 19, 1864, VIII, 23-27.

St. Lawrence, The, Union sailing frigate : at Fort Monroe, V, 223 ; starts to encounter the *Merrimac*, 223 ; runs aground, 223.

Salas, Mariano, member of Mexican provisional government, VII, 398.

Saligny, M. de, French diplomatist : assists Forey to organize a provisional government, VII, 397, 398.

Sanborn, F. B., receives letters from John Brown, II, 196.

Sanders, George N., offered safe-conduct to Washington, IX, 190 ; replies he is not accredited from Richmond, 191.

Sanderson, J. P., Col. U. S. A. : permission to visit Washington asked for, VIII, 10, 11 ; report on Order of American Knights, 11-13.

Sandford, C. W., Maj. Gen. N. Y. militia : sent to aid Patterson, IV, 326.

Sandford, John F. A., owner of Dred Scott, II, 63.

Sanford, E. S., acknowledgments to, from Secretary of War, IV, 129.

Sanford, Henry, conference with Judd, Pinkerton, and Franciscus, III, 310.

Sangamon County, Ill., created by the legislature in 1821, I, 59 ; commissioners of, elected, 59 ; county-seat established, 60, 61.

Sangston, Lawrence, elected to Maryland legislature, IV, 165.

Sanitary commissions, work of, VI, 329.

Sanitary fairs, work of, VI, 329, 330.

San Jacinto, The, U. S. war steamer : detains the *Trent*, V, 22-24 ; proceeds to Boston, 24.

Santa Anna, Antonio Lopez de, Pres. of Mexico : captured by Houston, I, 233 ; advance on Saltillo, 255.

Saulsbury, Willard, U. S. Sen. : opposes repeal of commutation clause of Draft Act, VII, 27 ; puts Powell in nomination for President, IX, 258.

Savage's Station, Va., engagement at, June 29, 1862, V, 434.

Savannah, Ga., siege of, Dec. 10-20, 1864, IX, 487-492 ; occupied by Sherman, Dec. 21, 1864, 492.

Savannah, The, Conf. privateer : crew indicted and tried, V, 10, 11 ; exchanged, 11.

Saxton, Rufus, Bvt. Maj. Gen. U. S. Vols. : reports the enemy still at Harper's Ferry, V, 408.

Schaefer, Frederick, Col. U. S. Vols. : killed at Murfreesboro, VI, 288.

Schele de Vere, Prof. Univ. of Va. : conversation with Napoleon the Third, VI, 34, 35.

Schenck, Robert C., Maj. Gen. U. S. Vols. : placed under Hooker's orders, VII, 215 ; order about Maryland election, VIII, 462 ; supplementary order about Maryland election, 464.

Schnierle, ——, Conf. Maj. Gen. : warns Humphreys of danger of a violent demonstration, II, 444 ; interview with Foster, 445 ; directed to carry out certain military details, III, 116 ; illness of, 122.

Schofield, J. M., Bvt. Maj. Gen. and Gen. in Chief U. S. A. : commands Missouri State militia, V, 97 ; member of advisory board to reëxamine Porter court-martial case, VI, 13 ; instructed to "take care of Missouri," 368 ; assigned to command District of Missouri, 368 ; order to hunt down and destroy guerrillas, 374 ; assessments on rebel sympathizers, 374, 375 ; registration of rebel sympathizers, 376 ; provisional regiments from Enrolled Militia, 377 ; report on guerrilla rising of 1862, 378, 379 ; takes the field towards southwest Missouri, 382 ; reports no rebel forces north of Arkansas River, 396 ; inquiry about Missouri Convention, VIII, 207, 208 ; letter to governor of Kansas, 212 ; letter to Lincoln about Missouri affairs, 224 ; reports on Missouri affairs, 229 ; interview with Lincoln, 472 ; nominated major general of U. S. volunteers, 474 ; transferred to Tennessee, 474 ; strength of Army of the Ohio, IX, 4 ; advance north of Dalton, 11 ; advance on Cassville, 15 ; in battles of Dallas, 17-19 ; in battles of Kenesaw Mountain, 20, 25 ; in march on Atlanta, 263 ; in battles of Atlanta, 272-274, 285, 286 ; sent to Thomas, 477 ; in army of Thomas,

X, 7, 8; march to Franklin, Nov. 23-30, 1864, 10-18; battle of Franklin, Nov. 30, 1864, 18-21; in defense of Nashville, 21, 22; in battle of Nashville, 30-33; assigned to command Department of North Carolina, 68; advance on Wilmington, 68, 69; occupies Wilmington, Feb. 22, 1865, 69; occupies Goldsboro, March 21, 1865, 70, 71; made Department commander, 338.

Schurz, Carl, Maj. Gen. U. S. Vols., U. S. Sen., Sec. of Int. under Hayes: in battle of Chancellorsville, VII, 99; in battle of Gettysburg, 242; engagement in Lookout Valley, VIII, 126.

Scott, Dred, condition as a slave, II, 58, 59; declared to be not a citizen, 73; manumitted by his owners, 81. See also DRED SCOTT DECISION.

Scott, Robert E., suggested by Seward for the Cabinet, III, 362; promises Seward an interview, 363; interview with Seward, 365.

Scott, Robert N., Bvt. Lieut. Col. U. S. A.: opinion of Lincoln's military ability, X, 354.

Scott, Thomas A., Asst. Sec. of War: telegram to Halleck, V, 299; interview with Halleck, 299; asks for reënforcements for Halleck, 299; suggestion about continuing the campaign, 300.

Scott, T. Parkin, elected to Maryland legislature, IV, 165.

Scott, Winfield, Bvt. Lieut. Gen. U. S. A.: march and victories in Mexico, I, 262, 263; biographical sketch, II, 337, 338; his nullification experience, 338, 339; "Views" addressed to Buchanan and Floyd, 339-341; reply to Buchanan's criticism, 342; interview with Anderson, 347; orders to Anderson, Nov. 15, 1860, 348; letter to Twiggs by G. W. Lay about instructions to Anderson, 388; goes to Washington to advise the government, 434; message to Buchanan, III, 68; letter to Floyd, 87; letter to Larz Anderson, 88; confidential letter to Buchanan, 88; letter of additional suggestions to Buchanan, 89; notifies commanders of forts to be on the alert, 129; recommendation to reënforce Forts Taylor and Jefferson, 134; orders St. Louis arsenal reënforced, 135; concentrates regular troops at Washington, 139-145; precautionary measures for Lincoln's inauguration, 146, 324; orders military parade for Feb. 22, 1861, 149; instructions to Lieut. Slemmer, 162; criticism of the

joint instructions sent to Pensacola, 170; correspondence with Lincoln, 249, 251; letter to Seward, 311; opinion on reënforcing Sumter, 378; recommends evacuating Sumter, 382; sends Capt. Fox to Sumter, 389; letter to Seward, 393; advises evacuation of Fort Pickens, 394; gives Capt. Fox confidential orders, IV, 28; daily reports to the President, 64-67, 95-97; approves intention to give Lee command of Union army, 98; interview with Lee, 100; example and loyalty, 102-104; reply to Robertson, 104; telegram to Crittenden, 104; interview with Baltimore Committee, 126; directions to Gen. Patterson, 129, 130; report of April 22, 1861, 143, 144; orders to Butler about Maryland legislature, 168; letter to Gen. Twiggs, 180; orders troops withdrawn from Texas, 184; instructs Col. Waite to form intrenched camp, 188; alternative instruction to evacuate Texas, 189; order about provisions on the Ohio, 200; approves McClellan's appointment to command, 285; indorsement on McClellan's plans, 300; general plan of campaign, 301-303; comments on the governors' memorial, 305, 306; letter to Cameron, 308; orders Arlington Heights occupied, 310; discusses campaign against Manassas, 323; orders to Patterson, 325; encouragement to McClellan in western Virginia, 339; orders Gen. Patterson to detain Johnston, 344; warns McDowell of rebel reënforcements, 351; confidence in McDowell's success, 351, 352; discredits reports of defeat, 352, 354; criticisms on the disaster, 358; urges Frémont to proceed west, 402; friendliness to McClellan, 461; asks to be retired, 462, 463; complaints of McClellan, 463; General Order of Sept. 16, 1861, 464; second remonstrance against McClellan, 464; retirement of, 464, 465; approves sending McDowell's corps to McClellan, VI, 2; circular to army, recommending acceptance of paper money, 228; attends Lincoln's funeral at New York, X, 321.

Scripps, John L., answer to Arnold's complaint, IX, 361.

Seaton, William W., editor of "National Intelligencer": approves Lincoln's bill abolishing slavery in District of Columbia, I, 286.

Secession, agitation in 1852, II, 297; movement in 1850, 297; conspiracy in 1856, 299; letter of Gov. Wise to Southern governors, 299; letter of J. M. Mason to Jefferson Davis, 300; letter of Wm. L. Yancey to Slaughter, 301; letter of Gov. Wise to Wm. Sergeant, 302; The 1860 Association, 305; letter of Gov. Gist to Southern governors, 306, 307; replies of Southern governors to Gov. Gist, 307-314; Jackson's instructions to Gen. Scott about nullification, 338; Gen. Scott's mission to Charleston, 338; address of Senators and Representatives, Dec. 14, 1860, 436; ordinance of South Carolina passed Dec. 20, 1860, III, 13; Senatorial caucus of Jan. 5, 1861, 155, 180; Senators' letter to Hayne, 155; Senators send Holt's reply to Hayne, 162; movement of, 175-182, 193; committee of Senatorial caucus appointed, 180; resolutions of Senatorial caucus, 180; date of, in different States, 181; duration of movement in the Cotton States, IV, 245; course of: in Virginia, 246 — in North Carolina, 246-248 — in Arkansas, 248, 249 — in Tennessee, 249-251; first and second periods of, 251, 252; denounced: by Baptist Convention of New York, VI, 315 — by American Baptist Missionary Union, 316 — by American Board of Foreign Missions, 317 — by Congregational Conference of Massachusetts, 317, 318 — by Congregational General Association of New York, New Jersey, and Pennsylvania, 318 — by German Reformed Synod, 318 — by Lutheran General Synod, 318, 319 — by Moravian Synod, 319 — by Presbyterian General Assembly, 319-321 — by United Presbyterian Church General Assembly, 321 — by Reformed Presbyterian Church, 322 — by New School Presbyterians, 322, 323 — by Protestant Episcopal Church, Diocese of Pennsylvania, 323, 324 — by Methodist Episcopal Church, 324, 325 — by Catholic Church, 325; action of the Society of Friends, 326-329; supported by Baptist State Convention of Alabama, 331; action: of Presbyterian General Assembly of the South, 331 — of Protestant Episcopal Church in the South, 331, 332 — of Methodist Episcopal Church, South, 332, 333.

Seddon, James A., M. C., Conf. Sec. of War: remarks about battle of Buena Vista, II, 26; instruction to E. K. Smith to deal "red-handed" with white officers of colored troops, VI, 473; correspondence with Johnston about Vicksburg, VII, 296-298; appointed Confederate commissioner to negotiate an exchange of prisoners, 449;

instructions to Beauregard about captured negro soldiers, 452; instructions to Johnston, VIII, 326, 327; dispatch about Richmond, 396; urges Beauregard to attack, 397; resignation of, X, 153.

Sedgwick, John, Maj. Gen. U. S. Vols.: wounded at Antietam, VI, 140; in battle of Chancellorsville, VII, 106, 107; crosses the Rappahannock with the Sixth Corps, 203; in battle of Gettysburg, 249; crosses the Rappahannock, VIII, 243; in movement at Mine Run, 249, 250; commands Sixth Corps, Army of Potomac, 353; march to the Wilderness, 358; in battle of the Wilderness, 360, 362, 363; in battle of Spotsylvania, 374; killed at Spotsylvania, 375.

Segar, Joseph, M. C.: admitted to seat in House of Representatives, IX, 437.

Selma, Ala., captured by Wilson, April 2, 1865, X, 240.

Selma, The, Conf. gunboat: captured in Mobile Bay, IX, 234.

Semmes, Raphael, Commander U. S. N., Capt. Conf. navy: commands the Alabama, VI, 55; procedure of, 55; sinks the Hatteras, 56; commands the Alabama, IX, 142; accepts challenge of the Kearsarge, 144; escapes on the Deerhound, 150.

Semple, James, U. S. Sen.: defeated for U. S. Senator, 126.

Senate Committee of Thirteen, appointment of, moved, II, 405; members of, 414; Jefferson Davis's excuse, III, 219; propositions submitted to, 220; reports inability to agree, 222.

Seven Pines, Va., battle of, May 31 and June 1, 1862, V, 388-390; withdrawal of Confederates, 390.

Seventh New York Militia, arrival in Philadelphia, IV, 134; arrives before Annapolis, 135; landed at Annapolis, 154; march to Annapolis Junction, 155; arrives in Washington, 156.

Seward, Augustus H., Bvt. Col. U. S. A.: stabbed by Payne, X, 304.

Seward, Clarence A., proposed as colonel for Hatteras Volunteers, V, 14.

Seward, Frederick W., Asst. Sec. of State: visits Lincoln in Philadelphia, III, 311; carries a verbal message to his father, 313; valuable manuscripts from, 321; tenders his resignation, VI, 264; wounded by Payne, X, 304.

Seward, William H., Gov. of N. Y., U. S. Sen., Sec. of State under Lincoln and Johnson: fails to annex St. Thomas, I, 234; remarks in Senate speech, 393; candidate before Chicago Convention, II, 255, 271; political antecedents, 260, 261; "higher law" doctrine, 261; "irrepressible conflict" doctrine, 261; votes for: on first ballot, 273 — on second ballot, 274 — on third ballot, 275; criticism on Buchanan's message, 371; member of Senate Committee of Thirteen, 414; letter about Stanton's relations to Republican leaders, III, 142; propositions in Senate Committee of Thirteen, 222; letter to Lincoln about Senate Committee of Thirteen, 261; letters to Lincoln about crisis at Washington, 264, 265; letter to Lincoln, 311; meets Lincoln at railway station in Washington, 315; letter to Lincoln, 319; suggestions about Lincoln's inaugural, 319-323, 327-343; tendered office of Secretary of State, 349; letter to Lincoln about Secretaryship, 350; accepts office of Secretary of State, 351; advises Lincoln to put a Southerner in his Cabinet, 362; letters to Lincoln: Jan. 4, 1861, 363 — Jan. 27, 1861, 365; withdraws acceptance of place in Cabinet, 370; interview with Lincoln, 371; renews his acceptance of place in Cabinet, 372; appointed Secretary of State, 372; first opinion on Sumter, 386, 387; refuses to see commissioners, 402; memorandum declining official interview with commissioners, 403, 404; interviews with Campbell: March 14 or 15, 1861, 406, 407 — March 21 and 22, 1861, 409, 410 — March 30 and April 1, 1861, 410; memorandum of April 1, 1861, 410; recommends G. W. Summers for Supreme Court, 423; second opinion on Sumter, 430; interview with Lincoln and Meigs, 435, 436; "Some thoughts for the President's consideration," 445-447; interviews with Lincoln and Welles, IV, 5, 6; telegram to Porter, 6; comment on Harvey's telegram, 32; gives Campbell written memorandum, 34; answer to Campbell, 36; reply to Gov. Hicks, 139; dispatch to Dayton, 260; circular to foreign governments, 267, 268; dispatch of May 21, 1861, 269-275; instructs Adams to propose the adhesion of the United States to the Declaration of Paris, 278; brings news of defeat at Bull Run, 353; opinion on closing insurrectionary ports, V, 8; hears Lord Lyons about the Trent affair, 31; receives formal dispatch of British government, 31; letter to Weed, 31; confidential dispatch to Adams, 32; dis-

patch on the Trent affair, 38, 39; suggests to England, France, and Spain a scheme of financial aid to Mexico, VI, 38; reply to invitation to adhere to tripartite convention, 40, 41; circular, March 3, 1862, about affairs in Mexico, 48; repeats declaration of unfriendliness of the Queen's proclamation of neutrality, 51; comment on treaty to oppose African slave trade, 61; dispatch to Dayton about European mediation, 68; dispatch declining mediation proposed by France, 71-76; denies having given authority to make representations to the rebel government, 84; visits New York, 117; conference with governors about recruiting, 117; telegram about number of troops to be called, 118; Lincoln communicates his decision to adopt military emancipation, 121-123; favors employment of negro soldiers, 124; favors delay in publishing first emancipation proclamation, 128, 130; suggestions relative to preliminary emancipation proclamation, 161; personal attitude towards the President, 253; quotation from diplomatic dispatches, 263, 264; resolutions against, by caucus of Republican Senators, 264; tenders his resignation, 264; Lincoln declines to accept his resignation, 268; resumes duty as Secretary of State, 268; opinion on the admission of West Virginia, 300, 301; circular to foreign governments about colonization, 357; stipulations of the circular, 361; suggestions for final emancipation proclamation, 415, 416; opinion on the Fort Pillow massacre, 481; comment on the Democratic party, VII, 387; dispatches to Dayton about Mexico: Sept. 26, 1863, 401, 402 — Oct. 23, 1863, 403, 404 — April 7, 1864, 408, 409; at council of war, VIII, 112; response to serenade at Gettysburg, 191; at military conference, 236; dispatch about the Alabama, 255; comment on the Alexandra case, 257, 258; answer to Senate about Arguelles case, IX, 46, 47; correspondence about the Florida, 133; comment on McClellan's action, 252; speech at Auburn, 353, 354; proclaims Thirteenth Amendment ratified, X, 89; sent to confer with Peace Commissioners, 115; stabbed by Payne, 304.

Seymour, Horatio, Gov. of N.Y.: defeats Wadsworth for governor of New York, VII, 10, 362; reply to Lincoln's letter, April 14, 1863, 11; refuses Stanton's invitation for a consultation, 12; controversy with the government about the draft, 13–17; remarks to rioters, July 13, 1863, 22, 23; proclamations of July 14, 1863, 23; letters to Lincoln against the draft, 32–38; correspondence with Dix about the draft, 36, 37; proclamation about the draft, 37; correspondence with Stanton about the draft, 43, 45; letter about Vallandigham case, 341, 342; defeated for governor of New York in 1863, 377; letter about suppression of the "World" and "Journal of Commerce," IX, 49; chairman Democratic National Convention, 256; speech of, 256; letter informing McClellan of his nomination for President, 259, 260; proclamation about Presidential election, X, 374.

Seymour, Thomas H., M. C., Gov. of Conn., Min. to Russia: put in nomination for President, IX, 258.

Seymour, Truman, Bvt. Maj. Gen. U. S. A.: proceeds with his company to Fort Sumter, III, 53; commands brigade under McCall, V, 425; wounded in second assault on Fort Wagner, VII, 431; commands expedition to Florida, VIII, 283; interview with Gillmore at Baldwin, 283; announces intention to advance to the Suwanee River, 284; battle of Olustee, Feb. 20, 1864, 285; withdraws to Jacksonville, 285; in Wilderness campaign, 285; in battle of the Wilderness, 367; in march to Appomattox, X, 187.

Shackleford, James M., Brig. Gen. U. S. Vols.: captures Morgan, VIII, 58; captures Gen. Frazer, 165.

Shaler, Alexander, Bvt. Maj. Gen. U. S. Vols.: in battle of the Wilderness, VIII, 367.

Shannon, Wilson, Gov. of O., Min. to Mexico, Gov. of Kas. Ter.: appointed governor of Kansas, I, 439; arrival in the Territory, 439; reception speech at Westport, 439; presides at Law and Order meeting at Leavenworth, 440; order to militia to report to Sheriff Jones, 442; compromise with people of Lawrence, 447; orders the Wakarusa forces to disband, 447; sends requisition for Gov. Robinson, 450; refuses to interfere to protect Lawrence, 453; asks for troops to protect Topeka and Lecompton, II, 1; proclamation commanding military organizations to disperse, 2; removal of, 3; flight of, 11.

Sharpe, Jacob, Bvt. Brig. Gen. U. S. Vols.: wounded at Winchester, IX, 304.

Shaw, Francis George, letter to Lincoln about his son, VII, 431.

Shaw, H. M., Conf. Col.: surrender at Roanoke, Feb. 8, 1862, V, 245.

Shaw, John, claimant for seat in Illinois legislature, I, 143.

Shaw, Robert G., Col. U. S. Vols.: in second attack on Fort Wagner, VII, 429–431; killed in the assault, 431.

Shenandoah, The, Conf. cruiser: burns American whalers, IX, 156, 157; surrenders to United States, 157.

Shepherd, Oliver L., Bvt. Brig. Gen. U. S. A.: in battle of Murfreesboro, VI, 289.

Shepley, G. F., Brig. Gen. U. S. Vols., Mil. Gov. of La.: appointed military governor of Louisiana, VI, 346; orders election for Congress, 352; appoints Durant attorney general for Louisiana, VIII, 419; orders registration of voters in Louisiana, 419, 420; renews order of registration, 424, 425; order about Norfolk election, IX, 439, 440.

Sheridan, Philip H., Lieut. Gen., Gen. in Chief, U. S. A.: drives enemy through Perryville, Oct. 8, 1862, VI, 278; in battle of Murfreesboro, 285; in battle of Chickamauga, VIII, 94–97, 100, 105; in battle of Chattanooga, 135, 138, 148, 150, 152, 153, 155; commands cavalry in Army of Potomac, 353; leads advance in Wilderness campaign, 357; defeats Stuart, 368; expedition to join Butler, 370, 371; defeats Stuart at Yellow Tavern, 371; joins Butler, 371; rejoins Grant, 371; in battle of Cold Harbor, 391, 400; sent north on temporary duty, IX, 179; interview with Grant and Hunter at Monocacy, 180–182; assumes command of Middle Military Division, 182; personal description of, 291; Shenandoah campaign, Aug. 10 to Sept. 19, 1864, 291–299; battle of Winchester, Sept. 19, 1864, 299–305; made brigadier general U. S. A., 305; battle of Fisher's Hill, Sept. 22, 1864, 306–310; campaign of Cedar Creek, Oct. 6–18, 1864, 312–315; visits Washington, 314, 315; returns to Winchester, 315; battle of Cedar Creek, Oct. 19, 1864, 316–326; made major general U. S. A. 327; retires to Kernstown, 328; campaign against Virginia Central Railroad, 329–321; battle of Waynesboro, March 2, 1865, 329–331; raid to Trevilian Station, 405, 413; suggestions to Grant, X, 167, 168; advance to Five Forks, 168, 169, 171; battle of Five Forks, April 1, 1865, 172–174; relieves Warren from command, 173; in march to Appomattox, 185–189, 191, 194; commands Military Division of the Gulf, 338.

Sherman, Francis T., Brig. Gen. U. S. Vols.: in battle of Chattanooga, VIII, 148.

Sherman, John, M. C., Sec. of Treas. under Hayes, U. S. Sen.: member of Investigating Committee, I, 451; candidate for Speaker of House of Representatives, II, 214; ballotings for, 214; indorses Helper's book, 214; declaration about slavery, 214; withdraws his name, 215; plan of compromise, 422; introduces National Bank Act in Senate, VI, 243; votes for National Bank Act, 244; votes for re-passage of the Act, 245.

Sherman, Thomas W., Bvt. Maj. Gen. U. S. A.: recruits forces for Port Royal expedition, V, 14; reports extent of victory at Port Royal, 19; address to white inhabitants of Department of the South, VI, 91.

Sherman, W. Tecumseh, Lieut. Gen. and Gen. in Chief, U. S. A.: occupies Muldraugh's Hill, V, 51; succeeds Anderson in Kentucky, 52; military consultation with Cameron, 53, 54; discouragement of, 64; relieved from command, 64; river raid to Eastport, 316; returns to Pittsburg Landing, 316; position of his division, 323; position at sundown, April 6, 1862, 330; opinion of McClellan's correspondence, 453; arranges plan of operations with Grant, VII, 123; appointed by Grant to command Vicksburg expedition, 125; arrives at Milliken's Bend, 129; lands his expedition at Walnut Hills, 129; assault on Chickasaw Bluffs, Dec. 29, 1863, 133; returns to Milliken's Bend, 135; superseded by McClernand, 135; in attack on Fort Hindman, 140; commands Fifteenth Army Corps, 144; attempts the Steele's Bayou route, 150–152; letter to Grant, suggesting plan of campaign, 155; occupies Clinton, 178; battle of Jackson, May 14, 1863, 182, 183; ordered to Bolton's Station, 187; occupies Haines's Bluff, 195; first assault on Vicksburg, 283; second assault on Vicksburg, 283–286; in siege of Vicksburg, 289; campaign against Jackson, Miss., 323–325; made brigadier general of U. S. army, 325; praises Grant, 326; arrives at Memphis, VIII, 131, 132; march to Chattanooga, 132; in battle of Chattanooga, 134, 138–140, 144–147, 149, 154, 157; ordered to Knoxville, 154; sent to relieve Burnside, 181; enters Knoxville with

Granger's corps, 183; returns to Chattanooga, 186; visit to Banks, 289; movement to Meridian, 330, 331; returns to Vicksburg, 331, 332; reply to Grant's letter of thanks, 337–339; commands Military Division of the Mississippi, 346; plan of campaign, IX, 1–4; armies of, 4; begins campaign to the Chattahoochee, May 5, 1864, 4; operations against Johnston, 11; battles of Resaca, May 13–16, 1864, 13, 14; battles of Dallas, May 25 to June 4, 1864, 17–19; battles of Kenesaw Mountain, June 9–30, 1864, 19–25; advance to the Chattahoochee, 25–28; marches on Atlanta, 263; comment on Hood, 268; siege of Atlanta, July 22 to Sept. 1, 1864, 270–289; comment on McPherson, 275; dispatch about Osterhaus, 276; selects Howard to command Army of Tennessee, 277; approves Stoneman's raid, 279; instructions about destroying railroads, 285; occupies Atlanta, 289; opposes suspension of the draft, 364, 365; returns to Atlanta, 464; removes inhabitants from the city, 465; correspondence with Hood, 465–467; correspondence with Grant, 468, 469; sends messages to Gov. Brown, 469–471; communicates to Lincoln negotiations with Gov. Brown and A. H. Stephens, 471; sends Corse to defend Allatoona, 474; prepares for March to the Sea, 476–479; letter to Halleck about southward march, 476, 477; orders to Thomas, 477; sends Schofield to Thomas, 477; correspondence with Grant, 478, 479; army of, 481; orders for the march, 484; begins March to the Sea, Nov. 16, 1864, 484; occupies Milledgeville, Nov. 23, 1864, 486; arrives at Savannah, Dec. 10, 1864, 487; orders to assault Fort McAllister, 488; capture of Fort McAllister, Dec. 13, 1864, 488, 489; interview with Dahlgren, 489; summons Hardee to surrender Savannah, 491; occupies Savannah, Dec. 21, 1864, 492; letter to Lincoln, 493; orders to Thomas, X, 6; interview with Lincoln, Grant, and Porter, 215; returns to North Carolina, 216; march to Columbia, 229–232; occupies Columbia, Feb. 17, 1865, 232; march to Goldsboro, 232–237; occupies Goldsboro, March 23, 1865, 237; assigns Mower to command Twentieth Corps, 241; march to Raleigh, 242, 243; interview with Johnston, 244–246; interview with Johnston and Breckinridge, 246–248; memorandum of agreement with Johnston, 246–248; letter to Johnston, 248, 249; notifies Johnston of disapproval of agreement, 251; receives Johnston's surrender, April 26, 1865, 252, 253; letter to Grant, 253; controversy with Stanton and Halleck, 254; eulogy of Lincoln at Springfield, 325; at grand review in Washington, 332, 333; commands Military Division of the Mississippi, 338; eulogy of Lincoln, 350, 353.

Shields, James, U. S. Sen., Brig. Gen. U. S. Vols.: Illinois State Auditor, I, 203; letters about, from the "Lost Townships," 204, 205; his eccentricities, 204, 205; challenges Lincoln to a duel, 206, 207; meets Lincoln opposite Alton, Ill., 208; challenges William Butler, 209; subsequent political and military career, 210, 211, 251; appointed brigadier general of Illinois volunteers in Mexican war, 251; wounded at Cerro Gordo, 255; candidate for reëlection to U. S. Senate, 376; supported by the Democrats, 387; dropped by the Democrats, 388; ordered to reënforce McDowell, V, 392; wounded at Kernstown, 400; sent to Catlett's Station, 406; his grumbling and boasting, 407; pursuit of Jackson, 410; defeated at Port Republic, June 9, 1862, 411.

Shiloh, Tenn. (see PITTSBURG LANDING), battle of, April 6, 7, 1862, V, 317–335.

Shipley, Mary, marries Abraham Lincoln, grandfather of the President, I, 5.

Sickles, Daniel E., M. C., Bvt. Maj. Gen. U. S. A., Min. to Spain: House discussion, II, 418, 419; offers resolution to celebrate February 22, III, 149; interview with Buchanan, 151; in battle of Chancellorsville, VII, 93, 102; present at council of war, 109; in battle of Gettysburg, 245, 249–251; wounded at Gettysburg, 251; testimony about Gettysburg, 269; made Department commander, X, 338.

Sigel, Franz, Maj. Gen. U. S. Vols.: advance to Carthage, Mo., IV, 398; routed at Wilson's Creek, 410; commands division under Frémont, 429; succeeds to command of Frémont's corps in Army of Virginia, VI, 1; ordered to Culpeper Court House, 5; retreats to Maryland Heights, IX, 161; removed from command, 161.

Sill, J. W., Brig. Gen. U. S. Vols.: in battle of Murfreesboro, VI, 288; killed at Murfreesboro, 288.

Simms, James P., Conf. Brig. Gen.: opinion about Gettysburg, VII, 271.

Simons, James, Conf. Brig. Gen.: report to Gov. Pickens on military situation, 118;

ordered to assume command of State forces at Charleston, 122.

Simpson, M., Bish. Meth. Ch.: offers prayer at Lincoln's funeral at Washington, X, 317, 318; oration at Lincoln's funeral at Springfield, 323.

Singleton, Otho R., M. C.: House discussion, II, 416; signs secession address, 436.

Sixth Massachusetts Militia, departure for Washington, IV, 110; arrival in Baltimore, 112; insulted and attacked, 113–119; casualties in Baltimore riot, 118; arrival in Washington, 123.

Slavery, opinions for and against, I, 143–152; action of Illinois legislature, 150; discussed in the Thirtieth Congress, 263–266; Palfrey's comment on, 266; McClernand's motion in House of Representatives, 284; Thompson's amendment, 284; Lincoln's bill to abolish in District of Columbia, 285–288; estimated value of slaves in 1861, 313; origin of, in United States, 313; institution of, in United States, 313–329; Ordinance of 1784, 316; prohibited in Northwest Territory by Ordinance of 1787, 316, 317; Constitutional provisions respecting fugitive slaves, 318; relative strength of North and South in Congress when Constitution was formed, 318; abolished in all Eastern and Middle States except Delaware, 319; increase in number of slaves before slave trade ceased, 321; remarks of Sherrard Clemens on value of slaves, 321; relative increase of free and slave States, 322; Missouri Compromise, 323; compromise measures of 1850, 328; Senate caucus agreement on, 344; Dixon's amendment to the Nebraska bill, 344; Douglas's amendments, 349, 350; Kansas-Nebraska Act passed, 351; Thomas Jefferson originates policy of restriction, 359; growth of, in Missouri, 398; provisions in bogus laws of Kansas, 419–421; John Brown's plan and attempt against, II, 193–209; Fugitive Slave law of 1793, III, 20; decision in Prigg vs. Pennsylvania, 21; Fugitive Slave law of 1850, 26, 27; fugitive slaves: escape of, 1850 and 1860, 31 — Cameron's instructions to Butler about, IV, 389, 390 — Lincoln's instructions to Gen. Scott about, 391 — Cameron's rules about, 394 — Gen. Wool's regulations about employing, 396; Lincoln modifies War Department instruction about employing contrabands, V, 124; Cameron's report about arming slaves, 125, 126; Lincoln modifies Cameron's report, 126, 127; Lincoln's letter to Bancroft, 203; treaty between United States and Great Britain to suppress African slave trade, VI, 60, 61; industrial and educational organization of abandoned slaves in Department of the South, 93; law forbidding the army to return fugitive slaves, 98; virtual amendment of Fugitive Slave law, 98; Act for recognition of Hayti and Liberia, 99; Act for suppression of African slave trade, 99; trial and execution of Gordon, the slave trader, 99; prohibition of slavery in the Territories, 99, 100; abolished in West Virginia, 313; denounced: by Baptist Convention of New York, 315 — by American Baptist Missionary Union, 316 — by American Board of Foreign Missions, 317 — by Congregational General Association of New York, New Jersey, and Pennsylvania, 318 — by Lutheran General Synod, 318, 319 — by Moravian Synod, 319 — by Presbyterian General Assembly, 319-321 — by United Presbyterian Church General Assembly, 321 — by Reformed Presbyterian Church, 322 — by New School Presbyterians, 322, 323 — by Protestant Episcopal Church, Diocese of Pennsylvania, 323, 324; action on, of Society of Friends, 326-329; abolished: by Arkansas, VIII, 415 — by Louisiana, 435, 436 — by Tennessee, 447, 448 — by Maryland, 466 — by Missouri, 484 — in Virginia, IX, 438, 439; Thirteenth Amendment: Trumbull reports it, X, 75 — adopted by the Senate, 77 — rejected by the House, 77, 78 — adopted by the House, 85, 86 — ratified, 88, 89.

Slave trade, Gott's resolution to prohibit in District of Columbia, I, 286; provisions of the Constitution concerning, 318; abolished in District of Columbia, 328; treaty between United States and Great Britain to suppress, VI, 60; Act for suppression of, 99; trial and execution of Gordon, 99.

Slemmer, Adam J., Bvt. Brig. Gen. U. S. A.: commands Fort Barrancas, Pensacola, III, 162; transfers his command to Fort Pickens, 163.

Slidell, John, Min. to Mexico, U. S. Sen., Conf. Comr. to Europe: signs address commending Charleston disruption, II, 245, 246; signs secession address, 436; member of caucus committee of secession Senators, III, 180, 181; signs Senatorial se-

cession caucus resolutions, 181; Confederate Commissioner to France, V, 21; arrives at Havana, 21; removed from the Trent, 23, 24; imprisoned in Fort Warren, 24; delivered to Lord Lyons, 39; submits propositions from rebel government to Napoleon the Third, VI, 76-79; interview with Napoleon, Oct. 28, 1862, about American affairs, 80, 81; promises Napoleon help in Mexico and the West Indies, 82; scheme of cotton loan, 251; dispatches to Benjamin about Maximilian, VII, 413-415; relations with Napoleon, VIII, 267-269, conversation with Thouvenel, 269; relations with Drouyn de l'Huys, 269, 270; interview with Rouher, 270; interview with Napoleon and Voruz, 270; conversation with Napoleon, 272, 273; letter to Napoleon, 275, 276; interview with Drouyn de l'Huys, 276, 277; letters to Benjamin about Confederate ships in France, 278, 280; correspondence about the Rappahannock, IX, 139-142; interview with Drouyn de l'Huys, 153-155.

Slocum, Henry W., Maj. Gen. U. S. Vols.: division of, sent to Porter, V, 428; in battle of Chancellorsville, VII, 93, 96; in battle of Gettysburg, 245, 246, 248, 249; in battles of Atlanta, IX, 288; in March to the Sea, 481; in siege of Savannah, 490; in march to Columbia, X, 230; defeats Hardee, 234; battle of Bentonville, March 19, 1865, 234, 235; at grand review in Washington, 333.

Small, Col. William F., commands brigade of Pennsylvania militia, IV, 111.

Smith, ——, Canadian judge: discharges the rearrested St. Albans raiders, VIII, 26.

Smith, Andrew J., Bvt. Maj. Gen. U. S. A.: sent to break Shreveport railroad, VII, 129; joins Sherman at Walnut Hills, 129; in battle of Port Gibson, 171; march to Edwards's Station, 188; in battle of Champion's Hill, 191; present at Grant's interview with Pemberton, 303; in Banks's Red River expedition, VIII, 289, 292; captures Fort de Russy, March 13, 1864, 289; in battle of Pleasant Hill, 295; defeats rebels under Polignac and Wharton, 301; sent against Price, 479; in siege of Mobile, IX, 240; in army of Thomas, X, 7, 8; in defense of Nashville, 22; in battle of Nashville, 30-32.

Smith, A. N., Commodore U. S. N.: commands the Wissahickon in Farragut's fleet, V, 261.

Smith, Caleb B., M. C., Sec. of Int. under Lincoln, Judge U. S. Dist. Ct. : recommended for Secretary of Interior, III, 352; appointed Secretary of Interior, 372; first opinion on Sumter, 387, 388; second opinion on Sumter, 431, 432 ; signs remonstrance against McClellan's continuance in command, VI, 21; retires from Lincoln's Cabinet, 300; appointed U. S. District Judge for Indiana, 300, 418.

Smith, Charles, elected U. S. Senator, VIII, 437.

Smith, Charles F., Maj. Gen. U. S. Vols.: thinks Washington safe, IV, 95; march to Calloway, V, 105, 106; report of reconnaissance to Fort Henry, 119; invests Fort Henry, 121; commands division in march against Fort Donelson, 192; storms intrenchments at Donelson, 197; ordered to command Tennessee River expedition, 312; superseded by Grant, 312.

Smith, Chauncey, member of Commission on New York Enrollment, VII, 41.

Smith, E. Kirby, Conf. Gen.: sent by Bragg into eastern Kentucky, VI, 274; defeats Union force under Nelson, 274; occupies Lexington, 275; rejoins Bragg at Frankfort, 275; attempts to inaugurate a Confederate government at Frankfort, 277; in battle of Murfreesboro, 282; sends Walker to attack Milliken's Bend, VII, 293; instructions about captured negro soldiers, 454; report of battle of Pleasant Hill, VIII, 295; surrenders to Canby, X, 328, 329.

Smith, George W., Bvt. Brig. Gen. U. S. Vols. : in battles of Atlanta, IX, 273.

Smith, Gerrit, M. C.: present at John Brown's council, II, 196; supports John Brown, 199; becomes Jefferson Davis's bail, X, 275.

Smith, Giles A., Maj. Gen. U. S. Vols. : in March to the Sea, IX, 481.

Smith, Green Clay, Bvt. Maj. Gen. U. S. Vols., M. C., Gov. of Montana: resolutions supporting the war, VII, 395.

Smith, Gustavus W., Conf. Maj. Gen.: council of war at Fairfax Court House, V, 153, 154; forces in reserve accompanied by Gen. Johnston, 388; attacks Union right flank, 388; repulsed by Sumner, 389; succeeds to Confederate command after Johnston's wound, 389; in defense of Savannah, IX, 487.

Smith, John E., Bvt. Maj. Gen. U. S. A.: in battle of Chattanooga, VIII, 139, 146; in March to the Sea, IX, 481.

Smith, Martin L., Conf. Maj. Gen. : advises capitulation of Vicksburg, VII, 302.

Smith, Melancton, Rear Adm. U. S. N.: commands the *Mississippi* in Farragut's fleet, V, 261; captures rebel ram *Manassas*, 265; battle with the *Albemarle*, X, 41–43.

Smith, Morgan L., Brig. Gen. U. S. Vols.: in battle of Chattanooga, VIII, 139, 146.

Smith, Persifor F., Bvt. Maj. Gen. U. S. A.: supersedes Col. Sumner in Kansas, II, 3; reënforcements ordered to, 5; orders against Border Ruffians, 6; report of, 7, 8; consultation with Gov. Geary, 11.

Smith, Prescott, feat of transportation, VIII, 113.

Smith, T. Kilby, Bvt. Maj. Gen. U. S. Vols.: in Red River expedition, VIII, 292.

Smith, T. W., Judge, Ill. Sup. Ct. : action on the "alien" question, I, 164.

Smith, Victor, Collector at Puget's Sound : complaints against, IX, 89.

Smith, William, M. C. : plan of compromise, II, 422.

Smith, William F., Bvt. Maj. Gen. U. S. A.: attends council of war, V, 167; ordered to reconnoiter Dam No. One, 368; ordered to hold his position at Dam No. One, 368; withdraws his forces from across Warwick River, 369; position at Williamsburg, 377 ; states that McClellan prepared a protest against the emancipation proclamation, VI, 180; advises McClellan against publishing it, 180; prepares plan at Chattanooga, VIII, 122, 123; occupies Brown's Ferry, 124; reports against attack on Missionary Ridge, 130; in battle of Chattanooga, 139, 151; in battle of Cold Harbor, 391, 400, 401, 404; commands Eighteenth Corps, under Butler, 392, 393; in battle of Bermuda Hundred, 398; joins Army of Potomac, 399; advance on Petersburg, IX, 407–409; opinion of Lincoln's military ability, X, 353, 354.

Smith, W. Sooy, Brig. Gen. U. S. Vols. : in siege of Vicksburg, VII, 290; defeated by Forrest, VIII, 331.

Snyder, G. W., Bvt. Maj. U. S. A. : engineer assistant to Capt. Foster, III, 51; report to Anderson, IV, 25, 26; hoists flag of Sumter on a jury mast, 59.

Society of Friends (or Quakers), action on the war and emancipation, VI, 326–329.

Soley, J. R., Prof., U. S. N., Asst. Sec. of Navy : describes the *Monitor's* fighting, V, 229, 230.

Sons of Liberty, Order of, VIII, 2-27.

South Carolina, State of, meeting of Democratic National Convention, 1860, at Charleston, II, 243; legislature convened by Gov. Gist, 328, 329; legislature chooses Presidential electors, 331, 332; military appropriation, 333; Convention bill passed, 333, 334; secession mass-meeting in Charleston, 334, 335; Federal forts at Charleston, 343; delegates to Secession Convention elected, III, 1; convention organizes at Columbia and adjourns to Charleston, 1; legislature adjourns to Charleston, 1; F. W. Pickens elected and inaugurated governor, 1; ordinance of secession adopted, Dec. 20, 1860, 13; Convention adopts Declaration of Causes, 15; Convention adopts Address to Slaveholding States, 15; Anderson transfers his command to Fort Sumter, 50-54; rebels occupy Fort Moultrie and Castle Pinckney, 60, 61; commissioners from Secession Conventon reach Washington, 62; commissioners inform Buchanan of Anderson's movement, 64; interview of commissioners with Buchanan, 70; commissioners receive the President's reply, 83; commissioners send rejoinder to Pres. Buchanan, 83-86; Star of the West fired on, 100, 103; Convention authorizes Gov. Pickens to declare martial law, 117; siege of Fort Sumter begun, 126; bombardment of Sumter, IV, 50-59; capitulation and evacuation of Sumter, 60, 61; capture of Port Royal, Nov. 7, 1861, V, 16-19; attack on defenses of Charleston, April 7, 1863, VII, 65-71; rebels evacuate Fort Wagner, Sept. 7, 1863, 437; bombardment of Charleston, Aug. 23, 1863, 439-441; ratifies Thirteenth Amendment, X, 89; capture of Charleston, Feb. 18, 1865, 231; Columbia occupied, Feb. 17, 1865, 232.

Southfield, The, Union gunboat: sunk by the Albemarle, X, 39, 41.

South Mountain, Md., battle of, Sept. 14, 1862, VI, 136.

Spain, alleged causes of intervention in Mexico, VI, 33; signs tripartite convention, 38; Spanish fleet sails for Vera Cruz, 41; withdraws from Mexican expedition, 45; regards with disfavor treaty for suppressing African slave trade, 61; asks extradition of Arguelles, IX, 46.

Spangler, Edward, tried and imprisoned, X, 312, 313.

Sparrow, Thomas, married great-aunt of Pres. Lincoln, I, 24.

Sparrow family, the, mentioned, I, 29, 31.

Spaulding, Elbridge G., M. C.: deprecates making paper money legal tender, VI, 235; aids in preparing National Bank Act, 242.

Spear, S. P., Bvt. Brig. Gen. U. S. Vols.: captures Gen. W. H. F. Lee, VII, 221.

Speed, James, Atty. Gen. under Lincoln: member of Committee to Distribute Union Arms, IV, 237; appointed Attorney General, IX, 347, 348; present at Lincoln's deathbed, X, 300.

Speed, Joshua F., friendship with Lincoln, I, 153, 194; engaged to be married, 195; his morbid anxiety, 195; represents Kentucky Unionists, IV, 235, 236; advice about organizing Kentucky troops, 236, 237; member of Committee to Distribute Union Arms, 237.

Speed, Mrs. Lucy, mother of Joshua F. Speed: presents Bible to Lincoln, I, 195.

Spotswood, Alexander, Gov. of Va.: urges the building of frontier forts, I, 12.

Spotsylvania, Va., battle of, May 8-19, 1864, VIII, 372-385.

Sprague, J. W., Bvt. Maj. Gen. U. S. Vols.: in battles of Atlanta, IX, 270.

Sprague, William, Gov. of R. I., U. S. Sen.: sailing of, IV, 160; visits Halleck, V, 356; asks permission to raise a colored regiment, VI, 462.

Springfield, Ill., made county seat of Sangamon County, I, 60, 61; State capital located at, 131, 138; condition of society at, in 1837, 153-156; law practice at, in early days, 167-169; members of the Bar at, about 1840, 213; Lincoln's debate with Douglas at, 375; Lincoln's farewell address at, III, 291; Democratic peace meeting at, VII, 378; Union mass meeting at, 380; Lincoln's funeral at, X, 323-325.

Stafford, F. E. P., Conf. Col.: killed at Franklin, X, 20.

Stafford, Leroy A., Conf. Brig. Gen.: killed in battle of the Wilderness, VIII, 362.

Stallworth, J. A., M. C.: signs secession address, II, 436.

Stanley, David S., Bvt. Maj. Gen. U. S. A.: drives Morgan from Snow Hill, VIII, 50; in army of Thomas, X, 7, 8; in march to Franklin, 10, 11; in battle of Franklin, 19, 20.

Stanley, Edward, M. C., Mil. Gov. of N. C.: appointed military governor of North

Carolina, VI, 345; commission and instructions of, 345.

Stannard, George J., Bvt. Maj. Gen. U. S. Vols.: in battle of Gettysburg, VII, 266; in siege of Richmond, IX, 431, 432.

Stansbury, Edward A., signs memorial about Frémont and colored troops, VI, 456.

Stanton, Edwin M., Atty. Gen. under Buchanan, Sec. of War under Lincoln and Johnson, Assoc. Justice U. S. Sup. Ct.: advice on Buchanan's message, II, 365; appointed Attorney General, III, 66, 139; describes Floyd's last appearance in the Cabinet, 73, 74; announces his intention to resign, 80; copies Black's memorandum, 82; urges Holt to accept post of Secretary of War, 89; confidential relations with Republican leaders, 140; believed to have written the Howard resolution, 142; answer to Tyler about the *Brooklyn*, 166; statement about the joint instructions sent to Pensacola, 169; criticism of Lincoln, IV, 362; appointed Secretary of War, V, 129; biographical sketch, 130, 131; relations with the Buchanan administration, 131; criticized by J. S. Black, 131, 132; relations with prominent Republicans, 132; interviews with Sumner, 133; first meeting with Lincoln, 133, 134; letters criticizing Lincoln, 134, 135; personal characteristics, 136; letters to Buchanan and Dyer, 137, 138; relations to Pres. Lincoln, 139, 140; reply to Lincoln about discharge of prisoners of war, 144; interview with Lincoln about Rock Island prisoners, 146, 147; incites McClellan to activity, 159; orders preparations to obstruct the Potomac, 227; visits Fort Monroe, 234; reconnoiters landing opposite Fort Monroe, 236; sends complimentary dispatch to Halleck, 308; asks Halleck to designate limits of his desired command, 315; telegraphs Halleck, " I have no instructions to give you," 337; orders Ellet to construct a ram fleet, 343 ; orders Halleck to send 25,000 troops east, 353; comment on McClellan, 366; congratulations to McClellan upon incident at Dam No. One, 370; signs remonstrance against McClellan's continuance in command, VI, 21; telegram to Seward about call for troops, 117, 118; telegram to Seward about advancing bounty, 118; order about seizing rebel property and employing slaves, 124; favors employment of negro soldiers, 124; memorandum about first emancipation proclamation, 128; favors immediate announcement of first emancipation proclamation, 128; comment on preliminary emancipation proclamation, 162; sends encouraging letter to Burnside after Fredericksburg, 211; opinion on admission of West Virginia, 303, 304; order about churches, 333, 334; order modifying the preceding, 337, 338; instructions to military governor of North Carolina, 345; transmits Lincoln's answer about negro troops to Butler, 448; sends Gen. Thomas west to organize colored troops, 459 ; establishes special bureau to organize colored troops, 461; order establishing recruiting stations for colored troops in border slave States, 463; reports on negro soldiers, 468; opinion on the Fort Pillow massacre, 481, 482; invites Gov. Seymour to a consultation, VII, 12; correspondence with Seymour about the draft, 43, 44; telegram giving Grant "full and absolute authority," 143; comment on the Democratic party, 387; order about rebel prisoners, 459; action relative to Indiana conspiracy, VIII, 9, 10; order discharging prisoners arrested for opposing the draft, etc., 34; transmits to Senate Holt's report about prisoners, 40; sends for the President, 112; at council of war, 112; meets Grant at Indianapolis, 119; telegram about Chattanooga, 121; at military conference, 236; present at interview between Lincoln and Grant, 341; orders suppression of New York " World " and " Journal of Commerce," IX, 48; precaution for Lincoln's safety, 169; sends Butler to New York to preserve order at Presidential election, 374; recommends Chase for Chief Justice, 391; letter to Grant about Thomas, X, 24; visit to Sherman, 229; prints disapproval of Sherman's agreement, 250; at Cabinet meeting, April 14, 1865, 283, 284; present at Lincoln's deathbed, 300; statement about organization of armies, 335, 336.

Stanton, Elizabeth Cady, signs call for Cleveland Convention, IX, 31.

Stanton, Frederick P., M. C., Sec. of Kas. Ter.: appointed Secretary of Kansas Territory, II, 95; proclamation about attempted frauds, 105, 106; becomes acting governor, 113; convenes extra session of the legislature, 114; removal of, 116; speeches against Lecompton Constitution, 130.

Stanton, Lewis H., son of E. M. Stanton: thanks for valuable MSS., V, 137.

Star, Order of the, VIII, 2–27.

Starkweather, John C., Brig. Gen. U. S. Vols.: in battle of Murfreesboro, VI, 291.

Star of the West, The, merchant vessel: sails with troops and supplies to relieve Fort Sumter, III, 96; enters Charleston harbor, 99, 103, 104; fired into by Morris Island battery, 100, 103; retreats from Charleston harbor, 101.

Stearns, George L., receives letters from John Brown, II, 196; informed of John Brown's plans, 200.

Steedman, James B., Maj. Gen. U. S. Vols.: in battle of Chickamauga, VIII, 101, 104; in defense of Nashville, X, 22; in battle of Nashville, 29, 31; made Department commander, 338.

Steele, Frederick, Bvt. Maj. Gen. U. S. A.: division of, at Chickasaw Bluffs, VII, 134; raid to Greenville, 157; march to Little Rock, VIII, 411; orders an election in Arkansas, 415–417; in siege of Mobile, IX, 240, 241; defeats Clanton's cavalry, 240; storms Fort Blakely at Mobile, 241; made Department commander, X, 338.

Steele, John B., M. C.: vote for Thirteenth Amendment, X, 83.

Steinwehr, A. von, Brig. Gen. U. S. Vols.: in battle of Gettysburg, VII, 242; engagement in Lookout Valley, VIII, 126.

Stephens, Alexander H., M. C., Conf. Vice-Pres.: criticizes South Carolina Declaration of Causes, III, 17; comment on Personal Liberty bills, 19; views on slavery, 189; elected Confederate Vice-President, 198; takes official oath, 199; "Cornerstone" speech, 202; Union speech at Milledgeville, Nov. 14, 1860, III, 266; views on slavery, 268; views on disunion, 269, 274; confidential correspondence with Lincoln, 271–273; plenipotentiary to Virginia, IV, 158; conference with Lee, 158, 159; concludes league of Confederate States with Virginia, 159; proposes a mission to Washington, VII, 370, 371; conference with Davis and Confederate Cabinet about peace mission to Washington, 371, 372; authorized by Davis to proceed to Washington, 372; asks permission of Admiral Lee to visit Washington, 372; declines conference with Sherman, IX, 471; appointed Peace Commissioner, X, 110; asks permission to go to Washington, 113; interview with Grant, 114–116; interview

with Lincoln, 118–129; report to Davis, 129; retires to Georgia, 199.

Steuart, George H., Conf. Brig. Gen.: captured at Spotsylvania, VIII, 380, 382.

Steuart, George H., Pres. of Christian Commission: consults with Mr. Lincoln, VI, 330.

Steever, Charles, Asst. Eng. U. S. N.: in expedition against the Albemarle, X, 47.

Stevens, ——, Conf. Major: ordered to erect a battery on Morris Island, III, 116.

Stevens, A. H., Maj. U. S. Vols.: enters Richmond, X, 208; raises guidons over Richmond State House, 208, 209.

Stevens, Isaac I., Maj. Gen. U. S. Vols.: killed at Chantilly, Sept. 1, 1862, VI, 11.

Stevens, Thaddeus, M. C.: speech on Confiscation Act, IV, 382; prominence as an antislavery leader in Congress, VI, 107; votes for re-passage of National Bank Act, 245; introduces bill authorizing the President to suspend habeas corpus, VIII, 34.

Stevenson, Carter L., Conf. Maj. Gen.: forces of, under Pemberton, VII, 164; ordered to Grand Gulf, 166; sent to reënforce Port Gibson, 170; advice in council of war, 185; in battle of Champion's Hill, 189–192; in battle of Chattanooga, VIII, 140, 145; joins Johnston, X, 36.

Stevenson, John W., M. C., U. S. Sen.: plan of compromise, II, 423.

Stewart, Alexander P., Conf. Maj. Gen.: in battle of Chickamauga, VIII, 91, 93; in battle of Chattanooga, 145.

Stewart, Ambrose P., Conf. Lieut. Gen.: succeeds to Polk's command, IX, 20; requests suspension of order removing Johnston, 265–267; in battle of Peach Tree Creek, 269; in battles of Atlanta, 280, 283; in army of Hood, X, 7; in march to Franklin, 12; in battle of Franklin, 18; in campaign against Nashville, 23; joins Johnston, 36.

Stewart, James A., M. C.: plan of compromise, II, 422.

Stewart, John A., offered appointment of Assistant Treasurer at New York, IX, 91, 92.

Stidger, ——, detective among the American Knights, VIII, 5.

Stillman, ——, Maj. Ill. Vols.: commands battalion in Black Hawk war, I, 91; defeated by Black Hawk, 91.

Stockton, John P., Min. to Rome, U. S. Sen.: puts McClellan in nomination for President, IX, 258.

Stokes, James H., superintends transfer of arms, IV, 199.

Stone, Charles P., Brig. Gen. U. S. Vols.: organizes militia of District of Columbia, III, 137; report, Feb. 5, 1861, 138; report, Feb. 21, 1861, 311; employs detectives, 312; preparations for Lincoln's first inauguration, 324; sent to coöperate with Patterson, IV, 315; joins Patterson, 316; reconnaissance towards Leesburg, 454; battle of Ball's Bluff, Oct. 21, 1861, 455–457; suspicions against, 459, 460; arrest of, 460.

Stone, Dan, member of Ill. legislature: one of the "Long Nine," I, 128; speech in canvass of 1836, 130; protest with Lincoln against resolutions on slavery, 140, 151.

Stone, Dr. Robert K., called to attend Pres. Lincoln, X, 297; present at Lincoln's deathbed, 300.

Stoneman, George, Bvt. Maj. Gen. U. S. A.: chief of cavalry at Washington, IV, 441; repulsed at Williamsburg by Longstreet, V, 376; sent on cavalry raid by Hooker, VII, 92; result of his expedition, 111; in battles of Resaca, IX, 13; cavalry raid in Georgia, 279; position near Lynchburg, X, 192; raid through Tennessee and Virginia, 237, 238; captures Salisbury, 238; made Department commander, 338.

Stonewall, The, Conf. ram: surrendered to the Spanish government, IX, 135–137; sold to the Emperor of Japan, 137.

Storrs, Rev. Richard S., D. D.: reads selection of psalms at Sumter flag-raising, X, 278.

Stotesbury, William, Asst. Eng. U. S. N.: in expedition against the Albemarle, X, 47.

Stoughton, William L., Bvt. Maj. Gen. U. S. Vols.: in battle of Chattanooga, VIII, 148.

Stout, Lansing, M. C.: member of House Committee of Thirty-three, II, 417.

Strahl, O. F., Conf. Brig. Gen.: killed at Franklin, X, 20.

Stratton, John L. N., M. C.: member of House Committee of Thirty-three, II, 417.

Streight, A. D., Bvt. Brig. Gen. U. S. Vols.: placed in close confinement by the rebels, VII, 457; commands cavalry expedition into Georgia and Alabama, VIII, 50; forms junction with Gen. Dodge, 50; defeats rebels at Tuscumbia, 51; surrenders to Forrest, 52; escapes from prison, 52.

Stringfellow, J. H., editor of "Squatter Sovereign": protest against Pawnee mission, I, 413; elected Speaker of House in Kansas Territorial legislature, 416; comment on the governor, 417.

Stringham, Silas H., Rear Adm. U. S. N.: opinion on relief of Sumter, III, 381; commands fleet of Hatteras expedition, V, 12; report on the Hatteras victory, 13.

Strong, George C., Maj. Gen. U. S. Vols.: assaults Fort Wagner, July 11, 1863, VII, 427; in second assault on Fort Wagner, July 18, 1863, 429–431; killed in the assault, 431.

Strong, Schuyler, prominent lawyer of Illinois, I, 213.

Strong, William, M. C., Justice Sup. Ct. of Penn., Assoc. Justice U. S. Sup. Ct.: dissents from decision that draft law is unconstitutional, VII, 13.

Stuart, —, puts T. H. Seymour in nomination for President, IX, 258.

Stuart, Alexander H. H., M. C., Sec. of Int. under Fillmore: member of committee from Virginia Convention, IV, 72.

Stuart, Charles E., M. C., U. S. Sen.: votes against Lecompton Constitution, II, 130; opposes a Congressional slave code, 175; construction of the "two-thirds" rule, 243.

Stuart, David, Brig. Gen. U. S. Vols.: position of brigade at Pittsburg Landing, V, 323; gallant resistance against Confederate assaults, 327.

Stuart, J. E. B., Conf. Maj. Gen.: raid around McClellan's army, V, 418; ordered to the Rapidan, VI, 6; second cavalry raid around McClellan's army, 176; position at Fredericksburg, 201; in battle of Chancellorsville, VII, 98; succeeds Jackson in command of his corps, 104; retires to Ashby's Gap, 216; rides around Hooker's army, 217; raiding in Pennsylvania, 233; in battle of Gettysburg, 268; commands cavalry in Army of Northern Virginia, VIII, 354; defeated by Sheridan, 368; killed at Yellow Tavern, 371.

Stuart, John T., Maj. Ill. Vols., M. C.: serves in Black Hawk war, I, 93; reënlists as a private, 93; candidate for legislature in 1832, 109; elected, 109; lends Lincoln law books, 112; advises Lincoln to become a candidate for the legislature, 121; elected to legislature in 1834, 122; forms law partnership with Lincoln, 156; defeated for Congress in 1836, 157; elected to Congress in 1838, 157; rencontre with Douglas, 182; dissolves partnership with Lincoln, 213; reëlected to Congress, 217.

Studebaker, P. E., marks grave of Nancy Hanks Lincoln, I, 31.

Sturgis, Samuel D., Bvt. Maj. Gen. U. S. A.: succeeds Lyon in command at Wilson's Creek, IV, 411; in battle of Fredericksburg, VI, 206.

Sullivan, Jeremiah C., Brig. Gen. U. S. Vols.: assists in Kimball's repulse of Jackson, V, 400.

Summers, George W., M. C.: member of Peace Convention, III, 230; recommended by Seward for the Supreme Court, 423; invited to Washington, 423.

Sumner, Charles, U. S. Sen.: characterization of Baker, I, 221; amendment to first Nebraska bill, 344, 345; address against Nebraska bill, 360; receives votes for Vice-President in Philadelphia Convention, II, 35; his character, 47, 48; Senate speech of, May 19, 20, 1856, 48, 49; criticism of Sen. Butler, 48, 49; assaulted by Preston S. Brooks, 50, 51; his serious malady, 55; reëlected to the Senate, 56; reappearance in the Senate, 56; vote for, in Chicago Convention, 1860, on first ballot, 273; relates interview with Stanton, V, 133; favors Lincoln's plan of compensated abolishment, 214; prominence as an antislavery leader in Congress, VI, 107; remarks on legal tender, 233; votes for National Bank Act, 244; present at interview between Lincoln, Cabinet, and Republican Senators, 266; favors dismissal of Seward, 266; comment on Lincoln's Conkling letter, VII, 385; approves Lincoln's message, IX, 109; amendment to Reconstruction Act, 120; opposed to Lincoln, 367; recommends Chase for Chief Justice, 391; opposes recognition of Louisiana, 455; joint resolution to abolish slavery by Constitutional amendment, X, 75, 76; present at Lincoln's deathbed, 300.

Sumner, Edwin V., Bvt. Maj. Gen. U. S. A.: disperses Free State legislature in Kansas, I, 436; declines to interfere in Wakarusa war, 446; only permitted to act at the call of governor or marshal, 454; disperses guerrilla bands in Kansas, II, 2; superseded by Gen. P. F. Smith, 3; member of Lincoln's suite, III, 290; attends meeting of Lincoln's suite, 314; attends council of war, V, 167; assigned to command Second Corps, Army of Potomac, 169; attends council at Fairfax Court House, 179; arrives at Williamsburg, 376;

establishes himself on north side of Chickahominy, 385; marches with two divisions to the bridges, 389; crosses the Chickahominy and repulses Smith's attack, 389; defeats Magruder at Allen's Farm and Savage's Station, 428; interview with Lincoln at Harrison's Landing, 453; comment on second battle of Bull Run, VI, 16; corps engaged at Antietam, 140; asks permission to cross the Rappahannock, 199; commands Union right at Fredericksburg, 202; in battle of Fredericksburg, 205, 206; ordered to assault with the Ninth Corps on Dec. 14, 1862, 208; remonstrates with Burnside, 209; admits there is "too much croaking in the army," 212; lack of confidence in Burnside, 218; relieved from command in Army of Potomac, 221; death of, at Syracuse, N. Y., March 21, 1863, 222, 398; assigned to command Department of Missouri, 398.

Sumter, The, Confederate privateer, V, 8, 9.

Supreme Court of the United States, Dred Scott case in, II, 63–80; arguments of the Court, case, 63–65; members of the Court, 64; Justice Nelson instructed to prepare the opinion, 65; opinion of Justice Nelson, 66; suggestions of members, 72; decision announced, 72; opinions of all the Justices, 72, 73; opinion of the Court by Chief Justice Taney, 73–76; dissenting opinion by Justice Curtis, 77–79; dissenting opinion by Justice McLean, 78–80; decision in case of Prigg vs. Commonwealth of Pennsylvania, III, 23; decision declaring Fugitive Slave law of 1850 constitutional, 31.

Surratt, John H., in conspiracy to assassinate Lincoln, X, 289, 291, 292; escape to Europe, 313; arrested in Egypt, 313; trial of, in Washington, 313.

Surratt, Mrs. Mary E., in conspiracy to assassinate Lincoln, X, 289, 291, 293; statement about Payne, 306; tried and hanged, 312, 313.

Swan, Francis H., Paymaster U. S. N.: in expedition against the Albemarle, X, 46, 48.

Swaney, ——, teacher of Pres. Lincoln, I, 34.

Swasey, Charles H., Lieut. U. S. N.: report of, V, 263, 264.

Sweeney, Thomas W., Brig. Gen. U. S. Vols.: occupies Springfield, Mo., IV, 398; in battles of Resaca, IX, 14.

Sweet, Benjamin J., Bvt. Brig. Gen. U. S. Vols.: commands Camp Douglas at Chicago, VIII, 21; captures leaders of plot to liberate rebel prisoners, 21, 22.

Swett, Leonard, member of Bloomington Convention, II, 28; urges Holt for Vice-President at Baltimore Convention, IX, 73.

Swift, ——, Gen. Ill. militia : ordered to Cairo, Ill., IV, 194.

Swinton, William, comment on McClellan's Antietam campaign, VI, 136.

Sykes, George, Bvt. Maj. Gen. U. S. A.: commands under Porter on the Peninsula, V, 428; in battle of second Bull Run, VI, 11; in battle of Fredericksburg, 206; in battle of Chancellorsville, VII, 93, 96.

Taft, Dr., present at Lincoln's deathbed, X, 300.

Talbot, Theodore, Maj. U. S. A.: statement about Anderson's condition, III, 158; obtains interview for Mr. Chew with Gov. Pickens, IV, 35.

Taliaferro, James G., loyalty of, III, 193.

Taliaferro, R. W., elected to Congress, VIII, 437.

Taney, Roger B., Atty. Gen. under Jackson, Chief Justice U. S. Sup. Ct.: opinion in Dred Scott case, II, 73-76; says Declaration of Independence does not include negroes, 153; administers oath of office to Lincoln, III, 344; issues writ of habeas corpus for Merryman, IV, 174; issues attachment for Gen. Cadwalader, 175; opinion in Merryman case, 175; sends his opinion to the President, 175; death of, IX, 385, 386.

Tappan, Mason W., M. C.: member of House Committee of Thirty-three, II, 417.

Tatnall, Josiah, Capt. U. S. N., Capt. Conf. navy: refuses to send the *Merrimac* to York River, V, 233.

Taylor, Bayard, Min. to Russia: description of Washington, IV, 107, 108; description of Lincoln, 108.

Taylor, E. D., elected to Illinois legislature in 1832, I, 109; discussion at Illinois State fair, 375.

Taylor, Miles, M. C.: member of House Committee of Thirty-three, II, 317.

Taylor, Richard, Conf. Lieut. Gen.: commands rebel forces in Louisiana, VII, 314; captures Brashear City, 321; sends Green and Major against Donaldsonville, 321; battle of Sabine Cross Roads, April 8, 1864, VIII, 292-294; battle of Pleasant Hill,

April 9, 1864, 295; statement about Grant's plans, 343; in command at Mobile, IX, 239; capitulation of, 242; retreats to Demopolis, X, 240; surrenders to Canby, 327, 328.

Taylor, W. H., Conf. Col.: in battle of the Wilderness, VIII, 364.

Taylor, Zachary, Maj. Gen. U. S. A., Twelfth Pres. U. S.: sent to Corpus Christi, I, 241; ordered to the Rio Grande, 241; victories of, 242; success in Mexican war, 260, 261; supported by Lincoln for President, 275; nominated for President, 276; elected 282.

Tebbs, W. H., leaves letter for publication in the Washington "Union," II, 111.

Tecumseh, The, Union ironclad: in battle of Mobile Bay, IX, 230; sunk by a torpedo, 232.

Ten Eyck, John C., U. S. Sen.: votes for National Bank Act, VI, 244.

Tennessee, State of, response to Lincoln's proclamation, IV, 90, 250; course of secession movement in, 249-251; Convention voted down, 250; military league with Confederate States, 251; vote on separation in East Tennessee, V, 58; Maynard and Clements elected to Congress, 59; Union rising in East Tennessee, 74-76; persecutions in East Tennessee, 76-80; capture of Fort Henry, Feb. 6, 1862, 121, 122; Union forces occupy Nashville, Feb. 25, 1862, 311; battle of Pittsburg Landing (or Shiloh), April 6, 7, 1862, 317-335; evacuation of Forts Randolph and Pillow, 340; river battle at Memphis, June 6, 1862, 344; Memphis occupied by Union troops, 345; battle of Murfreesboro, Dec. 31, 1862, to Jan. 2, 1863, VI, 285-295; Andrew Johnson appointed military governor, 344; Lincoln's letter to Grant and Johnson, Oct. 21, 1862, about reconstruction, 350; capture of Fort Pillow, April 12, 1864, 479, 480; massacre of colored troops at Fort Pillow, 479; Rosecrans occupies Chattanooga, VIII, 73; battle of Chickamauga, Sept. 18-20, 1863, 84-107; battle of Chattanooga, Nov. 23-25, 1863, 134-157; Longstreet's siege of Knoxville, Nov. 16 to Dec. 3, 1863, 174-181; Gov. Johnson orders election for Congress, 439; Union Convention at Nashville, July 1, 1863, 440; Johnson orders election for county officers, 443, 445; Union Convention at Knoxville, April, 1864, 446; Union Convention at Nashville, Sept. 5, 1864, 446; Johnson orders election for

President, 447; Constitutional Convention abolishes slavery, 447, 448; popular vote on amended Constitution, 448, 449; W. G. Brownlow elected governor, 449; legislature ratifies Thirteenth Amendment, 449; Senators and Members of Congress elected, 449; battle of Franklin, Nov. 30, 1864, X, 18-21; battle of Nashville, Dec. 15, 16, 1864, 29-34; Thirteenth Amendment ratified, 89.

Tennessee, The, Conf. ram: fitted out at Mobile, IX, 227-230; in battle of Mobile Bay, 234-237.

Terry, Alfred H., Bvt. Maj. Gen. U. S. A.: member of advisory board to reëxamine Porter court-martial case, VI, 13; makes demonstration against James Island, VII, 427; commands second Fort Fisher expedition, X, 65; capture of Fort Fisher, Jan. 15, 1865, 67; advance on Wilmington, 68, 69; in advance on Goldsboro, 70, 71; made Department commander, 338.

Texas, annexation of, opposition to, defeats Van Buren, I, 225; urged on Pres. Tyler, 225; Andrew Jackson's letter in favor of, 225, 226; Calhoun's views, 227; Clay's views, 228-230; opposed by John Quincy Adams, 230, 231; effect on Presidential election, 231; popular sentiment in favor of, 232, 233; Tyler's measures to secure, 237; condition of the Republic, 237; joint resolution for, passed, 237, 238; Polk's measures to complete, 238; Convention in Texas, 238; objections of antislavery men, 238, 239; protest of Mexican government against, 240, 241.

Texas, State of, annexation of, I, 225-234; Dr. Anson Jones elected President, 237; admitted as a State, 1845, 238, 325; western boundary of, 239; joint resolution authorizing acquisition, annexation, and admission as a State, 324; four additional States to be formed out of, 325; indemnity, 328; illegal secession convention in, III, 193: secession ordinance passed, Feb. 1, 1861, 193; election to ratify secession ordinance, 193; the army in, IV, 179; Gov. Houston's attitude, 181, 182; revolutionary State Convention, 182, 183; extra session of legislature called, 183; legislature approves Convention, 183; ordinance of secession passed, Feb. 1, 1861, 183; delegates to Confederate Congress appointed, 183; Ben McCulloch takes possession of San Antonio, 185; vote to ratify secession ordinance, 186; Provisional Confederate

Constitution ratified, 186; Gov. Houston deposed, 187; Lieut. Gov. Clark made governor, 187; Union defeat at Sabine Pass, Sept. 8, 1863, VIII, 287; Banks's expedition to the Rio Grande, 287, 288; ratifies Thirteenth Amendment, X, 89.

Thatcher, Henry K., Rear Adm. U. S. N.: commands naval forces before Mobile, IX, 239; receives Farrand's surrender, X, 328.

Thayer, Eli, M. C.: trustee of Massachusetts Emigrant Aid Society, I, 394; plan of compromise, II, 422.

Thiers, Louis Adolphe, French statesman and historian: Constitutional maxim of, III, 78.

Thirteenth Amendment, reported by Trumbull, X, 75; adopted by Senate, 77; rejected by the House, 77, 78; Lincoln's message about, 80; called up in House for reconsideration, 81; adopted by House, 85, 86; Lincoln's address on, 87, 88; ratification of, 88, 89; discussed at Hampton Roads Conference, 125, 126.

Thoburn, Joseph, Col. U. S. Vols.: in battle of Winchester, IX, 303; killed at Cedar Creek, 317.

Thomas, Francis, M. C., Gov. of Md., Min. to Peru: second interview with Lincoln about compensated emancipation, VI, 111; House resolution about Maryland emancipation, VIII, 456, 457.

Thomas, George H., Maj. Gen. U. S. A.: persuades Patterson not to attack, IV, 346; sent to Camp Dick Robinson, V, 49; orders a regiment to Lexington, 51; recommends movement on East Tennessee, 62, 63; asks to be relieved, 63; repeats his request to march to East Tennessee, 63; commands in eastern Kentucky, 115; ordered to dislodge Zollicoffer, 116; battle of Mill Springs, Jan. 19, 1862, 116, 117; supersedes Grant in command of right wing of Halleck's army, 337; assigned to supersede Buell, VI, 276; protests against Buell's being relieved from command, 277; order relieving Buell withdrawn, 277; appointed by Buell second in command, 277; appointed by Rosecrans to command center of Army of the Cumberland, 281; defends Rosecrans's inactivity, VIII, 43; march on Chattanooga, 71; ordered towards Lafayette, 75; in battle of Chickamauga, 84, 85, 88-90, 92-94, 97-99, 101-105, 107; supersedes Rosecrans in command of Army of the Cumberland, 119; answer to Grant, 120; confirms Rosecrans's statement about Chattanooga, 122; obtains revocation of order to attack Missionary Ridge, 129, 130; in battle of Chattanooga, 134, 135, 139, 144, 147, 148, 150, 154, 157; strength of Army of the Cumberland, IX, 4; advance on Kingston, 15; in battles of Dallas, 17, 19; in battles of Kenesaw Mountain, 20, 22-24; in march to the Chattahoochee, 26; in march on Atlanta, 263; in battle of Peach Tree Creek, 269; in battles of Atlanta, 285-287, 289; orders from Sherman, 477; commands Departments of the Ohio and Tennessee, X, 6; army of, 7, 8; battle of Franklin, Nov. 30, 1864, 18-21; defense of Nashville, 21-29; reply to Grant's criticisms, 25; battle of Nashville, Dec. 15, 16, 1864, 29, 34; pursuit of Hood, 34-36; commands Military Division of the Tennessee, 338.

Thomas, Jesse B., U. S. Sen.: elected to U. S. Senate, I, 143; prominent lawyer of Illinois, 213.

Thomas, J. Hanson, elected to Maryland legislature, IV, 165.

Thomas, Lorenzo, Bvt. Maj. Gen. U. S. A.: ordered to verify Gen. Wadsworth's statement, V, 184; reports the President's requirement not complied with, 184; sent West to organize negro troops, VI, 459; reports of his mission, 459-461.

Thomas, Philip F., M. C., Gov. of Md., Sec. of Treas. under Buchanan: appointed Secretary of Treasury, III, 66, 240; resignation of, 132, 241; advertises $5,000,000 Treasury notes, 240.

Thomasson, William P., M. C.: votes for Wilmot Proviso, I, 269.

Thompson, C. R., Bvt. Brig. Gen. U. S. A.: in battle of Nashville, X, 32, 33.

Thompson, Jacob, M. C., Sec. of Int. under Buchanan: instructions to Martin, II, 109; interviews with Floyd, 317; interviews with Clingman, 325, 326; opinion on disunion, 362, 363; advocates evacuation of Fort Sumter, III, 73; sends notice of relief expedition to Charleston, 99; notifies Gov. Pickens of permanent postponement of the Sumter expedition, 122; commissioner of Mississippi to North Carolina, 129; resignation of, 132; Confederate agent in Canada, VIII, 16; organizes conspiracies in United States, 16-27; employs Major to burn steamboats on the Mississippi, 22; employs Col. Martin to burn New York city, 22, 23; employs Kennedy to burn New York city, 23; offered safe-conduct to Washington, IX, 190; replies he is not accredited from Richmond, 191.

Thompson, Jeff. M., Conf. Brig. Gen.: organizes a secession camp at St. Joseph, IV, 211.

Thompson, Richard W., M. C., Sec. of Navy under Hayes: amendment affecting slavery in California and New Mexico, I, 284.

Thompson, Samuel, Col. Ill. Vols.: commands regiment in Black Hawk war, I, 90.

Thompson, Waddy, M. C., Min. to Mexico: negotiations with Texas, I, 240.

Thomson, J. Edgar, Pres. Penn. R. R.: suggests new route to Washington, IV, 129.

Thoreau, Henry D., remarks on John Brown's execution, II, 211.

Thouvenel, Edouard Antoine, French Min. of Foreign Affairs: resignation of, VIII, 268; conversation with Slidell, 269.

Tidball, John C., Bvt. Maj. Gen. U. S. Vols.: in recapture of Fort Stedman, X, 163.

Tilghman, Lloyd, Conf. Brig. Gen.: surrenders Fort Henry, Feb. 6, 1862, V, 121; sent to Grindstone Ford, VII, 171; killed at Champion's Hill, 191.

Titus, H. T., Col. Kas. militia: arrives in Kansas, I, 448; interview with Walker, II, 21.

Tod, David, Min. to Brazil, Gov. of Ohio: censured by Ohio Democratic Convention, VII, 354, 355; calls out militia to meet Morgan's raid, VIII, 56; letter about Lincoln's nomination, 323, 324; declines nomination for Secretary of Treasury, IX, 95-99.

Todd, John, great-uncle of Mrs. Abraham Lincoln: appointed lieutenant of county of Illinois by Patrick Henry, I, 186; death of, 186.

Todd, John B. S., Bvt. Brig. Gen. U. S. Vols.: present at Lincoln's deathbed, X, 300.

Todd, Lockwood, member of Lincoln's suite, III, 290.

Todd, Mary, lineage and relatives of, I, 186; engaged to Abraham Lincoln, 186; married to Abraham Lincoln, 200.

Todd, Robert S., father of Mrs. Abraham Lincoln, I, 186.

Tompkins, C. H., Bvt. Brig. Gen. U. S. Vols.: member of military commission for trial of Lincoln's assassins, X, 312.

Toombs, Robert, U. S. Sen., Conf. Sec. of State, Conf. Brig. Gen.: introduces enabling bill for Kansas, II, 93; signs address commending the Charleston disruption, 245, 246; member of Senate Committee of Thirteen, 414; signs Senatorial secession caucus resolutions, III, 181; appointed Confederate Secretary of State, 212; propositions in Senate Committee of Thirteen, 220; speech at Milledgeville to promote secession, 266; instructions to ˌ Commissioners, Feb. 27, 1861, 396; instructions of March 11, 1861, 401; instructions of March 14, 1861, 401; instructions of March 20, 1861, 403; instructions of April 2, 1861, 413.

Topeka Constitution, framed by Free State Constitutional Convention at Topeka, I, 429; submitted to popular vote, 429; presented to Congress as a petition, 429, 430; advocated by Republicans in Congress, 430; reported against in Senate by Douglas, 431; House of Representatives passes bill to admit Kansas under, 431; provisional legislature under, dispersed by Col. Sumner, 436; never legalized, 436, 437.

Topp, Robertson, letter about persecution in East Tennessee, V, 60.

Torbert, Alfred T. A., Bvt. Maj. Gen. U. S. A.: commands cavalry rearguard in Wilderness campaign, VIII, 357; in battle of Spotsylvania, 385; in Sheridan's army, IX, 182; in Shenandoah campaign, 295; in battle of Winchester, 303; in campaign of Fisher's Hill, 309, 310; defeats Rosser and Lomax, 314; raid on Virginia Central Railroad, 328, 329.

Totten, Joseph G., Bvt. Maj. Gen. U. S. A.: opinion on evacuation of Fort Sumter, III, 380.

Toucey, Isaac, Atty. Gen. under Polk, U. S. Sen., Sec. of Navy under Buchanan: voted for in the Charleston Convention, II, 244; opinion on disunion, 362; approves Buchanan's draft of reply to South Carolina commissioners, III, 75; informs Buchanan of threatened resignation of Black and Stanton, 80; instructions to Capt. Armstrong, 163; orders ships of war to Pensacola, 164.

Tourtellotte, J. E., Bvt. Brig. Gen. U. S. Vols.: wounded at Allatoona, IX, 474.

Townsend, E. D., Bvt. Maj. Gen. U. S. A.: reads original dispatch at Sumter flag-raising, X, 279; represents Secretary of War at Lincoln's funeral, 320.

Townsend, Frederick, Bvt. Brig. Gen. U. S.

A.: appointed Provost Marshal General for New York, VII, 15.

Townsend, George Alfred, account of Booth's escape, X, 308.

Tracy, E. D., Conf. Brig. Gen.: in battle of Port Gibson, VII, 170, 171.

Transylvania Presbytery, action of, VI, 332.

Trapier, J. H., Conf. Brig. Gen.: ordered to prepare a plan to reduce Fort Sumter, III, 124.

Travis, Wm. Barrett, defense of the Alamo, I, 233.

Treadwell, ——, goes to Kansas, I, 448.

Treasury notes, issue of $10,000,000 authorized, III, 240; $5,000,000 advertised by Secretary Thomas, 240; offers for, 240; authorized by Morrill Tariff Act, 243.

Treat, Samuel H., U. S. Dist. Judge: prominent lawyer of Illinois, I, 213.

Trenholm, George A., Conf. Sec. of Treas.: goes to Greensboro, X, 257.

Trent, The, British mail steamer: detained by the San Jacinto, V, 22–24; permitted to proceed, 24.

Trent Brothers, purchase Berry & Lincoln's store, I, 112.

Trescott, W. H., Asst. Sec. of State under Buchanan: interviews with Floyd, II, 317; letters: to Rhett, 317–319 — to Drayton, 322, 323 — to Gov. Gist, 378, 379; interview with Buchanan, 379; agent of South Carolina, III, 4; advises with South Carolina Congressmen, 6; interview with Buchanan, 7; letter to Gov. Pickens, 7–9.

Trimble, Isaac R., Conf. Maj. Gen.: in battle of Gettysburg, VII, 261, 263; opinion about Gettysburg, 271.

Trowbridge, C. T., Lieut. Col. U. S. Vols.: maintains a company of negro soldiers, VI, 444, 445.

Trumbull, Lyman, M. C., U. S. Sen.: discussion at Illinois State fair, I, 375; votes for, for U. S. Senator, 388; elected U. S. Senator, 390; member of Bloomington Convention, II, 28; letters to Lincoln, III, 252, 254; attends meeting at Seward's house, 253; amendment to Confiscation Act, IV, 380, 381; interview with Lincoln, 467; interview with McClellan, 467; votes for re-passage of National Bank Act, VI, 245; present at interview between Lincoln, Cabinet, and Republican Senators, 266; favors dismissal of Seward, 266; Senate resolution about political prisoners, VIII, 31; reports joint resolution on Louisiana reconstruction, IX, 454; advocates recognition of Louisiana, 455; reports Thirteenth Amendment, X, 75; speech on Thirteenth Amendment, 76.

Tucker, John, Asst. Sec. of War: charged with transportation of Army of Potomac, V, 167; report of army transportation, 182.

Turchin, J. B., Brig. Gen. U. S. Vols.: in battle of Chickamauga, VIII, 104; in battle of Chattanooga, 148.

Turner, John W., Bvt. Maj. Gen. U. S. A.: in assault at Petersburg mine, IX, 423; in assault on Petersburg, X, 179, 180.

Turner, Levi C., Maj. U. S. Vols.: interview with the President, VI, 186, 187.

Turner, Thomas, Rear Adm. U. S. N.: commands Union frigate *New Ironsides* in attack on Charleston, VII, 67.

Tuttle, James M., Brig. Gen. U. S. Vols.: in siege of Vicksburg, VII, 292.

Twiggs, David E., Bvt. Maj. Gen. U. S. A., Conf. Maj. Gen.: in command of Department of Texas, IV, 179; asks instructions of Gen. Scott, 180; correspondence with Gen. Scott, 180; asks to be relieved, 181; relieved from command, 184; surrenders military posts and government property in Texas, 185; agrees to withdraw the army by sea, 185; dismissed from U. S. army, 191; terms to U. S. prisoners of war, VII, 447.

Tyler, Daniel, Brig. Gen. U. S. Vols.: commands division under McDowell, IV, 342; brings on battle of Blackburn's Ford, July 18, 1861, 343; in battle of Bull Run, 348.

Tyler, Erastus B., Bvt. Maj. Gen. U. S. Vols.: assists Kimball in repulse of Jackson, V, 400.

Tyler, John, tenth Pres. U. S.: measures to secure annexation of Texas, I, 237; signs Act to admit Iowa and Florida, 324; signs joint resolution admitting Texas, 324, 325; protests against military parade on Feb. 22, 1861, III, 150; appointed commissioner to Washington by Virginia legislature, 165, 228; interview with Buchanan, 165; interview with Black and Stanton, 166; note to Buchanan, 166; called to preside over Peace Convention, 231.

Tyler, Robert O., Bvt. Maj. Gen. U. S. A.: wounded at Cold Harbor, VIII, 404.

Ullman, Daniel, Bvt. Maj. Gen. U. S. Vols.: volunteers to organize negro troops, VI, 454, 455.

Underwood, John C., Judge U. S. Dist. Ct.: certificate of division in the Jefferson Davis case, X, 275.

Underwood, J. W. H., M. C.: signs secession address, II, 436.

United Presbyterian Church, General Assembly, resolutions supporting emancipation, VI, 321.

Upsher, Abel P., Sec. of Navy and Sec. of State under Tyler: negotiations with Texas, I, 240.

Upton, Emory, Bvt. Maj. Gen. U. S. A.: storms rebel works at Rappahannock Station, VIII, 243; in battle of Spotsylvania, 377; in battle of Winchester, IX, 301; wounded at Winchester, 304; in Wilson's raid, X, 239.

Uraga, José Lopez, Gen., Mex. army: made general-in-chief of Mexican army, VII, 400; goes over to Maximilian, 419.

Usher, John P., Sec. of Int. under Lincoln: appointed Secretary of Interior to succeed Caleb B. Smith, VI, 419; opinion on Fort Pillow massacre, 482; resignation of, IX, 349, 350; statement about Lincoln's emancipation message, X, 136; present at Lincoln's deathbed, 300.

Utah, Territory of, organized, I, 328.

Vallandigham, Clement L., M. C.: cross-examines John Brown, II, 209; House discussion, 419, 420; compromise proposition, 426; comment on Burnside's Order No. Thirty-eight, VII, 329, 330; attacks on the government war policy, 329, 330; speech at Mt. Vernon, O., 330, 331; arrested and imprisoned, 332; tried by military commission, 333, 334; sentenced to close confinement during the war, 334; sentence commuted by Lincoln, 339; sent within the Confederate lines, 339; nominated for governor of Ohio, 354; goes to Richmond, 355; escapes to Bermuda, 355, 356; arrives in Canada, 356; address to the people of Ohio, 356; defeated by 101,000 majority, 357, 377; returns to United States, June 1864, 359; political speeches, 360; takes part in Chicago Convention, 360; House resolutions for peace, 365; statement of numbers of American Knights, etc., VIII, 2; on Platform Committee of Democratic National Convention, IX, 255; writes peace resolution of Democratic Platform of 1864, 257; comment on Democratic Platform, 261, 262.

Van Bergen, ——, sues Lincoln for debt, I, 117.

Van Buren, Martin, eighth Pres. U. S.: defeated for Presidential nomination in 1844, I, 227; receives Free-soil nomination for President, 277; popular vote for, 282.

Vance, R. B., Conf. Brig. Gen.: moves his command to East Tennessee, V, 77.

Vance, Zebulon B., M. C., Conf. Gov. of N. C., U. S. Sen.: flight from Raleigh, X, 243.

Van Cleve, H. P., Bvt. Maj. Gen. U. S. Vols.: in battle of Murfreesboro, VI, 287, 289, 292; in battle of Chickamauga, VIII, 88, 95.

Vanderbilt, Cornelius, becomes Jefferson Davis's bail, X, 275.

Vanderbilt, The, merchant steamer: chartered and prepared to run down the *Merrimac*, V, 227.

Van Derveer, Ferdinand, Brig. Gen. U. S. Vols.: in battle of Chickamauga, VIII, 94; in battle of Chattanooga, 148.

Van Dorn, Earl, Conf. Maj. Gen.: mission to induce U. S. troops to rebel, IV, 190; ordered to capture U. S. troops and stores, 190; captures remnants of U. S. troops, 191; captures Union troops in Texas, 262; sent to command the trans-Mississippi district of Department No. Two, V, 290; orders McCulloch, McIntosh, and Pike to join him in Arkansas, 290; proposes a haversack campaign against St. Louis, 290, 291; writes to Johnston that he will give battle at Cross Hollow, 291; battle of Pea Ridge, March 6–8, 1862, 291, 292; moves towards Pocahontas, 293; authorizes Breckinridge to threaten retaliation, VI, 477; opposed to Grant in the West, VII, 112; attacks Rosecrans at Corinth, Oct. 3, 1863, 116; battle of Corinth, Oct. 3, 4, 1863, 116, 117; repulsed at Corinth, 117; retreat of, 118; superseded by Pemberton, 119; captures Holly Springs, Dec. 20, 1862, 127; death of, 179; defeats Coburn, VIII, 50.

Venable, Charles S., Conf. Col.: in battle of the Wilderness, VIII, 364.

Vermont, State of, response to Lincoln's proclamation, IV, 86: rebel raid from Canada on St. Albans, Oct. 19, 1864, VIII, 23–27; ratifies Thirteenth Amendment, X, 89.

Vicksburg, Miss., fortified by rebels, V, 346; passed and repassed by Farragut's fleet, 347–350; situation of, VII, 121, 282; first assault on, May 19, 1863, 282, 283; second assault on, May 22, 1863, 283–286; siege of, May 22 to July 4, 1863, 288–305; privations of inhabitants, 300, 301; surrender of, July 4, 1863, 305; occupied by Grant, 305–307.

Victoria, Queen of Great Britain and Ireland: proclamation of neutrality, IV, 268; note to Lord John Russell, V, 28.

Vidaurri, Santiago, Mex. Gen.: deserts from Monterey, VII, 419.

Vincent, Strong, Col. U. S. Vols.: in battle of Gettysburg, VII, 254; killed at Gettysburg, 255.

Vincent, Thomas M., Bvt. Brig. Gen. U. S. A.: present at Lincoln's deathbed, X, 300.

Vinton, S. F., M. C.: recommends McClellan for command at Cincinnati, IV, 282.

Virginia, State of, legislature incorporates Louisville, Ky., I, 15; endows Transylvania University, 15, 16; John Brown's raid, II, 205–208; legislature appoints John Tyler commissioner to Washington, III, 165, 228; legislature appoints John Robertson commissioner to seceding States, 165, 228; resolutions of legislature suggesting Peace Convention, 227; effect of John Brown's raid, 416; preparations for arming, 416; declines the South Carolina proposition for a conference, 417; vote at Presidential election of 1860, 417; military organization, 418; extra session of legislature, 419; legislative resolution against coercion, 421; State Convention elected, 421; meeting of Convention, 422; Committee of Convention visits the President, IV, 72; response to Lincoln's proclamation, 91; ordinance of secession passed, April 17, 1861, 91, 92; armory at Harper's Ferry burned, 122; burning of Gosport Navy Yard, 147; military league with Confederate States, 158–162; Richmond made the rebel capital, 264; Gov. Letcher calls out State forces, 310, 330; popular movement in western Virginia against secession, 329; provisional State government formed, 331, 332; Peirpoint appointed governor, 331; he applies for aid to suppress rebellion, 332; battle of Rich Mountain, July 11, 1861, 334, 335; engagement at Blackburn's Ford, July 18, 1861, 343; battle of Bull Run, July 21, 1861, 348–351; battle of Ball's Bluff, Oct. 21, 1861, 455–457; Norfolk occupied by Union troops, May 10, 1862, V, 237; McClellan's Richmond campaign begun, 358; capture of Yorktown, May 3, 1862, 374, 375; battle of Williamsburg, May 5, 1862, 377; battle of Seven Pines, May 31 and June 1, 1862, 388–390; engagement at Beaver Dam, June 26, 1862, 425; battle of Gaines's Mill, June 27, 1862, 428–430; engagement at Savage's Station, June 29, 1862, 434; engagement at Glendale, June 30, 1862, 435; battle of Malvern Hill, July 1, 1862, 437–439; engagement at Cedar Mountain, Aug. 9, 1862, VI, 6; engagement at Groveton, Aug. 29, 1862, 9; battle of second Bull Run, Aug. 30, 1862, 10; engagement at Chantilly, Sept. 1, 1862, 11; battle of Fredericksburg, Dec. 13, 1862, 203–208; consent of Wheeling legislature to division of the State, 298; (as to organization of West Virginia, see WEST VIRGINIA); the Peirpoint government removes to Alexandria, 313; battle of Chancellorsville, May 1–3, 1863, VII, 96–107; cavalry battle at Brandy Station, June 9, 1863, 205, 206; battle of the Wilderness, May 5, 6, 1864, VIII, 360, 367; battle of Spotsylvania, May 8–19, 1864, 372–385; battle of North Anna, May 23–27, 1864, 387–390; battle of Cold Harbor, June 1–12, 1864, 391, 400–405; battle of Bermuda Hundred, May 16, 1864, 397–399; battle of Winchester. Sept. 19, 1864, IX, 299–305; battle of Fisher's Hill, Sept. 22, 1864, 306–310; battle of Cedar Creek, Oct. 19, 1864, 316–326; battle of Waynesboro, March 2, 1865, 329–331; battle of Hatcher's Run, Oct. 27, 1864, 433, 434; elects State Convention, 438; abolishes slavery, 438, 439; ordinance to establish restored government, 439; legislature ratifies Thirteenth Amendment, 439, X, 89; battle of Five Forks, April 1, 1865, 172–174; evacuation of Petersburg, April 2, 1865, 183; Lee's surrender at Appomattox, April 9, 1865, 195–197; evacuation of Richmond, April 2, 1865, 201–207; Richmond occupied by Gen. Weitzel, 208.

Vogdes, Israel B., Bvt. Brig. Gen. U. S. A.: sent with artillery company to reënforce Fort Pickens, III, 164, 165; ordered to land his company at Fort Pickens, 394; asks facilities for landing, IV, 7; lands, 12, 13; constructs batteries on Folly Island, VII, 426.

Voruz, ——, French Deputy: interview with Napoleon the Third and Slidell, VIII, 270.

Waddell, J. I., Lieut. Conf. Navy: commands Confederate cruiser Shenandoah,

IX, 155; burns American whaling-vessels, 156, 157.

Wade, Benjamin, F., U. S. Sen.: votes for, in Chicago Convention, 1860, on first ballot, I, 273; Senate speech for the Union, 412–414; member of Senate Committee of Thirteen, 414; interview with Pres. Lincoln, IV, 467; interview with McClellan, 467; member of Committee on Conduct of the War, V, 150; urges active army operations, 150; votes for National Bank Act, VI, 244; advocates Reconstruction Act, IX, 119; signs Wade-Davis manifesto, 124–127; opposes recognition of Louisiana, 455; comment on Lincoln's death, X, 316.

Wadsworth, James S., Bvt. Maj. Gen. U. S. Vols.: assigned to command defenses of Washington, V, 169; reports only 19,000 men under his command, 184; reports the President's requirement not complied with, 184; defeated by Seymour for governor of New York, VII, 10, 362; in battle of Gettysburg, 239, 240, 244, 249; testimony about Gettysburg, 269; favors attacking Lee at the Potomac, 275–277; in battle of the Wilderness, VIII, 361, 363, 364; killed in battle of the Wilderness, 366.

Wagner, George D., Brig. Gen. U. S. Vols.: in battle of Chattanooga, VIII, 148, 149, 153; in battle of Kenesaw Mountain, IX, 23; in march to Franklin, X, 11, 17; in battle of Franklin, 18.

Wainwright, Jonathan M., Commander U. S. N.: commands the Harriet Lane, VII, 313; killed at Galveston, 313.

Wainwright, Richard, Commander U. S. N.: commands the Hartford in Farragut's fleet, V, 261.

Waite, Carlos A., Bvt. Brig. Gen. U. S. A.: assigned to command Department of Texas, IV, 184; arrives in San Antonio 185; complies with agreement entered into by Twiggs, 185; capture of, 191.

Walcutt, C. C., Bvt. Maj. Gen. U. S. Vols.: defeats Phillips, IX, 485.

Walke, Henry, Rear Adm. U. S. N.: runs gunboat Carondelet past Island No. Ten, V, 298.

Walker, Cyrus, prominent lawyer of Illinois, I, 213.

Walker, Duncan S., Bvt. Brig. Gen. U. S. Vols.: valuable manuscripts from, II, 112.

Walker, James A.: Conf. Brig. Gen.: wounded at Spotsylvania, VIII, 382.

Walker, J. G., Conf. Maj. Gen.: sent to capture Harper's Ferry, VI, 133; sent to attack Milliken's Bend, VII, 293; in battle of Sabine Cross Roads, VIII, 293.

Walker, Leroy P., Conf. Sec. of War and Brig. Gen.: appointed Confederate Secretary of War, III, 212; letter to Pickens, 397; dispatches about Fort Pickens, IV, 9–11, 13; telegrams to Beauregard, 19, 20; instructions to Beauregard, 29, 30, 38; order to reduce Sumter, 45, 46; sends agent West to purchase provisions, 195; directs withdrawal of Confederate troops from Kentucky, V, 44.

Walker, Moses B., Bvt. Brig. Gen. U. S. Vols.: in battle of Murfreesboro, VI, 291.

Walker, Robert J., U. S. Sen., Sec. of Treas. under Polk, Gov. of Kas.: appointed governor of Kansas, II, 93; conditions of acceptance, 93; promises a submission of the Constitution to popular vote, 93, 97, 101; his inaugural address, 95; arrival in Kansas, 96; speech at Topeka, 97; letter to Pres. Buchanan, 102; rejects the Oxford and McGee fraudulent returns, 105; proclamation about the attempted frauds, 105, 106; goes to Washington on leave of absence, 112; resignation of, 117; opposition to Lecompton Constitution, 130.

Walker, Samuel, Bvt. Brig. Gen. U. S. Vols.: interview with Titus, II, 21.

Walker, W. H. T., Conf. Maj. Gen.: in engagement at Raymond, VII, 177; ordered towards Lee and Gordon's Mills, VIII, 79; in battle of Chickamauga, 84, 88, 91; in battle of Chattanooga, 145.

Wallace, Lew, Maj. Gen. U. S. Vols.: division ordered to attack at Fort Donelson, V, 197; position of division at Crump's Landing, 324; ordered to battlefield of Pittsburg Landing, 329; arrival and position of, 334; commands at Baltimore, IX, 163; battle of Monocacy, July 9, 1864, 165; member of military commission for trial of Lincoln's assassins, X, 312.

Wallace, W. H. L., Brig. Gen. U. S. Vols.: commands Smith's division at Pittsburg Landing, V, 324; position of division, 324; mortally wounded at Pittsburg Landing, 327.

Wallace, Dr. W. S., member of Lincoln's suite, III, 290.

Wallis, S. Teackle, elected to Maryland legislature, IV, 165.

Walthall, E. C., Conf. Maj. Gen.: in retreat of Hood, X, 35.

Ward, James H., Capt. U. S. N.: project to relieve Fort Sumter, III, 172; interview with Gen. Scott about relief of Sumter, 383.

Ward, W. T., Bvt. Maj. Gen. U. S. Vols.: in March to the Sea, IX, 481.

Warfield, Henry M., elected to Maryland legislature, IV, 165.

Warren, Gouverneur K., Bvt. Maj. Gen. U. S. A.: in battle of Chancellorsville, VII, 97; opinion of Hooker, 110, 111; in battle of Gettysburg, 248, 254, 261; wounded at Gettysburg, 269; testimony about Gettysburg, 271; sent to Culpeper, VIII, 237, 238; repulses A. P. Hill's attack, 240; movement at Mine Run, 248–250; opinion on lost opportunities, 252, 253; commands Fifth Corps Army of Potomac, 353; crosses the Rappahannock, 357, 358; in battle of the Wilderness, 360, 361, 363; reaches Spotsylvania, 368, 369; in battle of Spotsylvania, 374, 376, 381, 383, 385; in battle of North Anna, 387, 389; in battle of Cold Harbor, 391, 404; in movement across James River, IX, 407; in siege of Petersburg, 412; in march to Five Forks, X, 169, 171; in battle of Five Forks, 172, 173; relieved from command, 173, 174; at grand review in Washington, 332.

Washburn, Cadwalader C., M. C., Maj. Gen. U. S. Vols.: member of House Committee of Thirty-three, II, 417; in siege of Vicksburg, VII, 290, 292; commands advance on Matagorda Bay, VIII, 287.

Washburn, Francis, Bvt. Brig. Gen. U. S. Vols.: killed in march to Appomattox, X, 187, 188.

Washburne, Elihu B., M. C., Min. to France: interview with Gen. Scott, III, 250; letter to Lincoln, 250; meets Lincoln at railway station in Washington, 315; recommends Grant, IV, 293; candidate for Speaker of House of Representatives, VII, 391; nominates Colfax for Speaker, 393, 394; introduces bill to revive grade of lieutenant general, VIII, 334; statement about Schofield, 471; letter expressing doubt about Lincoln's reëlection, IX, 372.

Watson, Benjamin, Lieut. Col. 6th Mass. Militia: in Baltimore riot, IV, 113.

Watson, P. H., Asst. Sec. of War: at council of war, VIII, 112.

Wayne, James M., Assoc. Justice U. S. Sup. Ct.: moves to reconsider Dred Scott decision, II, 67; opinion in Dred Scott case, 72.

Waynesboro', Va., battle of, March 2, 1865, IX, 329–331.

Wead, Fred F., Col. U. S. Vols.: killed at Cold Harbor, VIII, 405.

Webb, Alexander S., Bvt. Maj. Gen. U. S. A.: statement of strength of Johnston's army, V, 176, 177; comment on landing of Franklin's division, 365, 366; says Warwick line could have been broken, 367; says a fair opportunity to break the Warwick line was missed, 369; comment on McClellan's report, 384; in battle of Gettysburg, VII, 261, 266; wounded at Gettysburg, 269: testimony about Gettysburg, 269; assists in repulsing Hill, VIII, 240; wounded at Spotsylvania, 382.

Webb, The, Conf. ram: burned on the Mississippi River, IX, 242, 243.

Webster, Charles R., Ould refuses to exchange him, VII, 458.

Webster, Daniel, U. S. Sen., Sec. of State under W. H. Harrison, Tyler, and Fillmore: amendment to Fugitive Slave law, III, 25.

Webster, Edwin H., M. C.: second interview with Lincoln about compensated emancipation, VI, 111.

Webster, J. D., Bvt. Maj. Gen. U. S. Vols.: posts a reserve battery at Pittsburg Landing, V, 328.

Weed, Stephen H., Brig. Gen. U. S. Vols.: killed at Gettysburg, VII, 255.

Weed, Thurlow, editor of Albany "Evening Journal": invites Lincoln to speak at Albany, II, 177; letter to Lincoln, III, 252; visit to Lincoln at Springfield, 261; statement about Lincoln and Seymour, VII, 12, 13; interview with McClellan, IX, 247; letter to Seward about politics, 250; letter about opposition to Lincoln, 366.

Weehawken, The, Union monitor: captures the Atlanta, VII, 79–81; sinking of, 81, 82.

Weitzel, Godfrey, Bvt. Maj. Gen. U. S. A.: in siege of Richmond, IX, 434; assigned to command first Fort Fisher expedition, X, 55; reconnoiters Fort Fisher, 61, 62; occupies Richmond, April 3, 1865, 208; present at interviews of Lincoln and Campbell, 220–222; statement about interview between Lincoln and Campbell, 222; interview with Campbell, 224–226.

Welles, Edgar T., valuable manuscripts from, VI, 123.

Welles, Gideon, Sec. of Navy under Lincoln: opinion about the Lincoln genealogy, I, 5; selected for the Cabinet, III, 367; appointed Secretary of Navy, 372; first opinion on Sumter, 387; second opinion on Sumter, 430, 431; interview with Lincoln, 440, 441; orders for Fort Sumter expedition, IV, 4; interview with Lincoln and Seward, 5, 6; instructions to Capt. Adams, 9; order to prepare Western gunboats, 201; opinion on closing insurrectionary ports, V, 7; approves course of Capt. Wilkes, 25; present at council about expedition against New Orleans, 254, 255; statement about Farragut's confidence and enthusiasm, 257; signs remonstrance against McClellan's continuance in command, VI, 22; describes Lincoln's reading of emancipation proclamation, 160; comment on emancipation proclamation, 163; present at interview between Lincoln, Cabinet, and Republican Senators, 266; opinion on admission of West Virginia, 304–306; comments on Lincoln's draft of final emancipation proclamation, 405; proposes amendments to draft, 415, 416; opinion on the Fort Pillow massacre, 482; letter of thanks to Du Pont, VII, 86; statement about Grant's plans, VIII, 343; memorandum about Lincoln's emancipation message, X, 136; at Cabinet meeting, April 14, 1865, 282, 284; present at Lincoln's deathbed, 300; statement about reduction of navy, 337, 338.

Welles, T. M., elected to Congress, VIII, 437.

Wessells, Henry W., Bvt. Brig. Gen. U. S. A.: commands at Plymouth, N. C., X, 39.

Weston, ——, guerrilla leader in Kansas, I, 453.

West Virginia, State of, popular movement against secession, IV, 329; consultation at Wheeling, 329; Union Convention at Wheeling, 331; provisional State government formed, 331, 332; Peirpoint appointed governor, 331; legislature elects U. S. Senators, 332; ordinance to create State of Kanawha, 332; recapitulation of formation of the new State, VI, 297, 298; popular vote for the new State, October, 1861, 298; Constitutional Convention at Wheeling, 298; name of West Virginia adopted, 298; popular vote on the Constitution, 298; consent of legislature of the "restored government of Virginia" to the erection of the new State of West Virginia, 298; report of Senate Committee on Territories on the division of the State, 299; conditions of the Senate bill, 299; Senate bill passed, July 14, 1862, 299; passage of the bill by House of Representatives, Dec. 10, 1862, 299; Cabinet consideration of the bill, 300; opinions: by Seward, 300, 301 — by Chase, 301-303 — by Stanton, 303, 304 — by Welles, 304-306 — by Blair, 306-308 — by Bates, 308, 309 — by Lincoln, 309-311; Lincoln approves the Act, 311; Constitutional Convention reassembled, 312; conditions of Congress adopted, 312; Lincoln's proclamation of admission, 312; inauguration of new State government, 312; legislative Acts concerning slavery, 312, 313; abolition of slavery in, 313; ratifies Thirteenth Amendment, X, 88, 89.

Wever, Clark R., Bvt. Brig. Gen. U. S. Vols.: defense of Resaca, IX, 475, 476.

Whaley, Kellian V., M. C.: member of Select Committee on Emancipation, VI, 395.

Wharton, Gabriel C., Conf. Brig. Gen.: in battle of Fisher's Hill, IX, 306; in battle of Cedar Creek, 316, 320, 321, 325; winter quarters at Staunton, 329; in battle of Waynesboro, 329, 330.

Wharton, John A., Conf. Maj. Gen.: in battle of Murfreesboro, VI, 282; defeated by A. J. Smith, VIII, 301.

Wheaton, Frank, Bvt. Maj. Gen. U. S. A.: in march to Appomattox, X, 187.

Wheeler, Ezra, M. C.: first vote for Thirteenth Amendment, X, 78; second vote for Thirteenth Amendment, 83.

Wheeler, Joseph, Conf. Lieut. Gen.: in battle of Murfreesboro, VI, 282, 293; repulsed at Fort Donelson, VIII, 50; defeats Coburn, 50; in expedition against Burnside, 129; in battles of Resaca, IX, 13; in battles of Atlanta, 270; raid in Sherman's rear, 281-283.

Whipple, Amiel W., Bvt. Maj. Gen. U. S. A.: in battle of Chancellorsville, VII, 101.

White, Albert S., M. C., U. S. Sen., Judge of Dist. Ct. of Ind.: chairman of Select Committee on Emancipation, VI, 395; reports bill to aid emancipation in Delaware, Maryland, Virginia, Kentucky, Tennessee, and Missouri, 395.

White, E. B., Conf. Col.: ordered to prepare a plan to reduce Fort Sumter, III, 124.

White, Harry, Bvt. Brig. Gen. U. S. Vols.: exchange of, refused, VII, 458.

White, Hugh L., U. S. Sen.: Presidential candidate, I, 125.

Whiteley, William G., M. C.: member of House Committee of Thirty-three, II, 417.

Whitesides, John D., bears a challenge from Shields to Lincoln, I, 206, 207; publishes account of the Lincoln-Shields duel, 208; correspondence with Merryman, 209, 210.

Whitesides, Samuel, Gen. Ill. Vols.: commands volunteer expedition in Black Hawk war, I, 90; march of, to Dixon, 91; march to Stillman's Run, 91; reënlists as a private, 93.

Whitfield, J. W., Delegate from Kas. Ter.: voted for, for Delegate in 1854, I, 406; elected to Congress, 408; elected Delegate by Pro-Slavery party, 1855, 428, 429, 438; driven out of Kansas, II, 2; leaves letters for publication in the Washington "Union," 111.

Whiting, W. H. C., Conf. Maj. Gen.: commands under Lee on the Peninsula, V, 428; at battle of Bermuda Hundred, VIII, 398, 399; wounded at Fort Fisher, 67.

Whitney, Eli, inventor of the cotton gin, I, 320, 321; fame of, neglected, 322.

Whitney, E. W., letter about his father, I, 322.

Wickham, W. C., Conf. Brig. Gen.: in campaign of Fisher's Hill, IX, 306, 309, 310.

Wickliffe, Charles A., M. C., P. M. Gen. under Tyler: member of committee to distribute Union arms, IV, 237; second interview with Lincoln about compensated emancipation, VI, 111; opposes bill for draft, VII, 5; puts Pierce in nomination for President, IX, 258.

Wide Awakes, origin and campaign work of, II, 284-286.

Wigfall, Louis T., U. S. Sen., Conf. Brig. Gen.: Senate discussion, II, 401, 402, 410; signs secession address, 436; signs the Senatorial secession caucus resolutions, III, 181; retains his seat in Senate, 195; visits Fort Sumter, IV, 59, 60; establishes rebel recruiting office in Baltimore, 93.

Wilcox, Cadmus M., Conf. Maj. Gen.: in battle of Gettysburg, VII, 261, 263, 267; in siege of Richmond, IX, 427; in siege of Petersburg, 432; defense of Petersburg, X, 178.

Wilder, John T., Bvt. Brig. Gen. U. S. Vols.: march on Chattanooga, VIII, 71.

Wilderness, Va., battle of, May 5, 6, 1864, VIII, 360-367.

Wilkes, ——, goes to Kansas, I, 448.

Wilkes, Charles, Rear Adm. U. S. N. : commands U. S. war steamer, *San Jacinto*, V, 22; overhauls the *Trent*, 22; commended by Secretary of Navy, 25; receives thanks of House of Representatives, 25.

Willcox, O. B.. Bvt. Maj. Gen. U. S. A. : in Army of Potomac, VIII, 353; in attack on Petersburg, IX, 411; in assault at Petersburg mine, 422; censured for Petersburg mine affair, 425; in recapture of Fort Stedman, X, 162.

Willey, Waitman T., U. S. Sen. : second interview with Lincoln about compensated emancipation, VI, 112.

Williams, Archibald, U. S. Dist. Judge: member of Bloomington Convention, II, 28; letter to Lincoln, III, 256.

Williams, A. S., Bvt. Maj. Gen. U. S. A. : succeeds to command of Mansfield's corps at Antietam, VI, 140; in March to the Sea, IX, 481; in march to Columbia, X, 230.

Williams, John E., signs memorial about Frémont and colored troops, VI, 456.

Williams, Richard, Commander, R. N. : mail agent of the *Trent*, V, 23.

Williams, Thomas, Brig. Gen. U. S. Vols. : commanding land forces, accompanies Farragut to Vicksburg, V, 348; defeats attack on Baton Rouge, VII, 122; killed at Baton Rouge, 122; began Vicksburg Canal, 146.

Williamsburg, Va., battle at, May 5, 1862, V, 377.

Williamson, Alexander, present at Lincoln's deathbed, X, 300.

Willich, August, Bvt. Maj. Gen. U. S. Vols.: in battle of Murfreesboro, VI, 286; taken prisoner, 286; in battle of Chickamauga, VIII, 104; in battle of Chattanooga, 148.

Wills, David, Special Agent of Gov. Curtin: invites Lincoln to Gettysburg dedication ceremonies, VIII, 190.

Wilmington, N. C., occupied by Schofield, Feb. 22, 1865, X, 69.

Wilmot, David, M. C., U. S. Sen. : offers Wilmot Proviso, I, 268; leaves Democratic party, 277; receives votes for Vice-President at Philadelphia Convention, II, 35; temporary chairman Chicago Convention, 1860, 266; member of Peace Convention, III, 230; writes to Gen. Scott, IV, 129; votes for National Bank Act, VI, 244.

Wilmot Proviso, adopted by House of Representatives, I, 268; votes upon, 269.

Wilson, Henry, U. S. Sen., Vice-Pres. with Grant: receives votes for Vice-President in Philadelphia Convention, II, 35; denounces Brooks's assault, 54; challenged by Brooks, 54; votes for National Bank Act, VI, 244; defends bill for draft, VII, 4; comment on Lincoln's Conkling letter, 385; approves Lincoln's message, IX, 109; comment on Blair, 339.

Wilson, James F., Gov. of Iowa, M. C. : member of Select Committee on Emancipation, VI, 395; joint resolution to abolish slavery by Constitutional amendment, X, 78.

Wilson, James H., Bvt. Maj. Gen. U. S. A. : work on the Yazoo Pass route, VII, 149; bridges the Tennessee at Morgantown, VIII, 182; in Army of Potomac, 363; in battle of the Wilderness, 363; in battle of Yellow Tavern, 371; in battle of Cold Harbor, 391; in Sheridan's army, IX, 182; in battle of Winchester, 300, 303; in movement across James River, 406, 407; raid on the Weldon Railroad, 413, 418; in army of Thomas, X, 8; in march to Franklin, 11; in defense of Nashville, 22; in battle of Nashville, 30, 33; raid through Alabama, 237, 238; defeats Forrest, 239, 240; captures Selma, April 2, 1865, 240; sends parties in pursuit of Davis, 269; capture of Jefferson Davis, May 10, 1865, 270-274; paroles rebel prisoners, 329; opinion of Lincoln's military ability, 354.

Wilson, R. L., one of the "Long Nine," I, 128.

Wilson, Robert, U. S. Sen. : second interview with Lincoln about compensated emancipation, VI, 111; appointed U. S. Senator, VIII, 469.

Wilson, Thomas F., U. S. consul at Bahia: protest against the *Florida*, IX, 130, 131; dismissal of, 133.

Wilson's Creek, Mo., battle of, Aug. 10, 1861, IV, 410, 411.

Winans, Ross, elected to Maryland legislature, IV, 165.

Winchester, Va., battle of, Sept. 19, 1864, IX, 299, 305.

Winder, John H., Conf. Brig. Gen. : censured by Col. Chandler, VII, 467, 468; promotion of, 468; order to guards at Andersonville prison, 471.

Windom, William, M. C., U. S. Sen., Sec. of Treas. under Garfield and B. Harrison :

member of House Committee of Thirty-three, II, 417; votes for re-passage of National Bank Act, VI, 245.

Winnebago, The, Union monitor: in battle of Mobile Bay, XI, 235.

Winslow, John A., Rear Adm. U. S. N.: commands the *Kearsarge*, IX, 143; blockades the *Alabama*, 144; sinks the *Alabama*, 146-149, 152, 153; letter about battle of the *Alabama* and *Kearsarge*, 152.

Winslow, Warren, M. C.: member of House Committee of Thirty-three, II, 417.

Winters, Hannah, niece of Daniel Boone: marries Abraham Lincoln, I, 5.

Winthrop, Robert C., Speaker H. R., U. S. Sen.: chosen Speaker of House of Representatives, I, 259; comment on provision of Fugitive Slave Law, III, 25, 26.

Winthrop, Theodore, Maj. U. S. Vols.: killed at Big Bethel, IV, 320.

Wisconsin, State of, admitted as a State, I, 325; instructs delegates in favor of Lincoln's renomination, IX, 56; ratifies Thirteenth Amendment, X, 89.

Wise, Henry A., Min. to Brazil, Gov. of Va., Conf. Brig. Gen.: cross-examines John Brown, II, 209; letter to governors proposing consultation, 299; letter to William Sergeant exposing secession intrigues, 302; preparations for secession, III, 416; remarks in Virginia Convention, 417; sent to the Kanawha Valley, IV, 332; summarizes effect of Union victory at Roanoke Island, V, 245, 246.

Withers, Jones M., Conf. Maj. Gen.: in battle of Murfreesboro, VI, 293.

Witzig, J., member of Union Safety Committee at St. Louis, IV, 212.

Wood, Fernando, M. C.: advice to Lincoln about Vallandigham, VII, 359, 360; letters to Lincoln about peace, 366; letters to Seward explaining his speech, 367; letter to Lincoln about amnesty, 367; rejoinder to Lincoln's reply, 368, 369; House resolution to appoint peace commissioners, 394, 395.

Wood, Gustavus A., Col. U. S. Vols.: in battle of Chattanooga, VIII, 153.

Wood, R. C., Bvt. Brig. Gen. U. S. A.: made Department commander, X, 338.

Wood, Thomas J., Bvt. Maj. Gen. U. S. A.: march on Chattanooga, VIII, 71; in battle of Chickamauga, 94, 95, 98-100, 103, 104; in battle of Chattanooga, 135, 138, 146, 148, 152, 155; in march to Franklin, X, 16; in defense of Nashville, 22; in battle of Nashville, 30-32; in pursuit of Hood, 34; made Department commander, 338.

Wood, W. B., Conf. Col.: moves his command to East Tennessee, V, 77.

Wood, W. S., member of Lincoln's suite, III, 290.

Woodbury, Daniel P., Bvt. Maj. Gen. U. S. A.: advice against Burnside's "Mud March," VI, 218.

Woodman, John, U. S. N.: in expedition against the *Albemarle*, X, 47, 51.

Woodruff, William E., Col. U. S. Vols.: establishes "Camp Clay," IV, 239; in battle of Murfreesboro, VI, 286.

Woods, C. R., Bvt. Maj. Gen. U. S. A.: in battle of Chattanooga, VIII, 142: in March to the Sea, IX, 481.

Woodson, Daniel, Sec. Kas. Ter.: becomes acting governor of Kansas Territory, I, 417; proclamation forbidding provisional Free State legislature to assemble, 435; becomes acting governor, II, 3; proclaims the Territory in insurrection, 6; sent to the Border Ruffian camp, 14; promotion of, 95.

Woodward, George W., M. C., Judge Sup. Ct. of Penn.: decides draft law unconstitutional, VII, 13; defeated for governor of Pennsylvania, 13, 375, 376.

Wool, John E., Maj. Gen. U. S. A.: correspondence with Lincoln, III, 251, 252; regulates pay and rations of contrabands, IV, 396; advises holding the Hatteras forts, V, 13; commands march to Norfolk, 236; telegram about McClellan's despondent tone, 378; transferred to Baltimore, 413; ordered to report to Hooker, VII, 215; notifies Confederate government of the mission of Commissioners Fish and Ames, 449; meeting with Cobb to arrange exchange of prisoners, 449, 450; letter to Benjamin about Confederate privateers, 450.

Woolsey, Dr. Theodore D.: remarks on civil war, VII, 446.

Worden, John L., Rear Adm. U. S. N.: sent to Pensacola, IV, 9; arrival, 11; visits the fleet, 12; arrested and imprisoned, 13; commands the *Monitor*, V, 228; fight of *Monitor* and *Merrimac*, March 9, 1862, 228-231; wounded, 230; directs Greene to take command, 231; commands monitor *Montauk*, VII, 63; attacks Fort McAllister, 63; in attack on Charleston, 67.

Wright, Horatio G., Bvt. Maj. Gen. U. S. A.:

commands troops in expedition to occupy coast of Florida, V, 251; in Army of Potomac, VIII, 353; in battle of the Wilderness, 363, 367; succeeds Sedgwick in command of Sixth Corps, 375; in battle of Spotsylvania, 375, 378, 381-383; wounded, 382; in battle of Cold Harbor, 391, 400, 401; sent to Washington, IX, 164; lands two divisions at Washington, 171; begins pursuit of Early, 173, 174; in Sheridan's army, 182; in battle of Winchester, 300, 303; in battle of Fisher's Hill, 307, 309; in campaign of Cedar Creek, 314, 315, 317, 320-325; in movement across James River, 407; in siege of Petersburg, 412; in recapture of Fort Stedman, X, 163, 164; in assault at Petersburg, 175, 177-181; made Department commander, 338.

Wyke, Sir Charles Lennox, British Min. to Mexico: correspondence with Mexican foreign office, VI, 32; ceases diplomatic relations with Mexico, 32; sails for England from Mexico, 45.

Yancey, William L., M. C., Conf. Comr. to Europe: characteristics of, II, 236; speech in Charleston Convention, 237; leads secession from Charleston Convention, 240; his prophecy, 242; speech in Seceders' Convention, 244; inconsistencies of, 249; present at Baltimore, 251; letter to Slaughter, proposing revolution, 301; prints explanatory statement, 303; speech in Alabama Convention, III, 187.

Yates, Richard, M. C., Gov. of Ill., U. S.
Sen.: candidate for Congress, I, 373; member of Bloomington Convention, II, 28; orders Gen. Swift to Cairo, IV, 194; orders Prentiss to seize arms and munitions, 195, 196; applies to Gen. Harney for arms, 198; asks Grant to assist the adjutant general, 287; sends him to muster in new regiments, 288; appoints him colonel of 21st Illinois Volunteers, 292; apprehension about conspiracy of American Knights, VIII, 10.

Yeaman, George H., M. C., Min. to Denmark: resolution in House of Representatives censuring emancipation proclamation, VI, 171; vote for Thirteenth Amendment, X, 83.

Yorktown, Va., siege of, April 5 to May 3, 1862, V, 368-374; evacuation of, May 3, 1862, 374, 375.

York, Zebulon, Conf. Brig. Gen.: wounded at Winchester, IX, 305.

Yulee, David L., U. S. Sen.: letter to Finegan, III, 180; signs the Senatorial secession caucus resolutions, 181.

Zamacona, Manuel Maria de, Mex. diplomatist: correspondence with Sir Charles Wyke, VI, 32.

Zollicoffer, Felix K., M. C., Conf. Brig. Gen.: invades eastern Kentucky, V, 45, 46; commands in East Tennessee, 60; guards Cumberland Gap, 116; attacks Thomas, 116; killed at Mill Springs, 117.

Zook, Samuel K., Bvt. Maj. Gen. U. S. Vols.: killed at Gettysburg, VII, 255.

COSIMO

COSIMO is a specialty publisher of books and publications that inspire, inform, and engage readers. Our mission is to offer unique books to niche audiences around the world.

COSIMO BOOKS publishes books and publications for innovative authors, nonprofit organizations, and businesses. **COSIMO BOOKS** specializes in bringing books back into print, publishing new books quickly and effectively, and making these publications available to readers around the world.

COSIMO CLASSICS offers a collection of distinctive titles by the great authors and thinkers throughout the ages. At **COSIMO CLASSICS** timeless works find new life as affordable books, covering a variety of subjects including: Business, Economics, History, Personal Development, Philosophy, Religion & Spirituality, and much more!

COSIMO REPORTS publishes public reports that affect your world, from global trends to the economy, and from health to geopolitics.

FOR MORE INFORMATION CONTACT US AT
INFO@COSIMOBOOKS.COM

※ if you are a book lover interested in our current catalog of books

※ if you represent a bookstore, book club, or anyone else interested in special discounts for bulk purchases

※ if you are an author who wants to get published

※ if you represent an organization or business seeking to publish books and other publications for your members, donors, or customers.

**COSIMO BOOKS ARE ALWAYS
AVAILABLE AT ONLINE BOOKSTORES**

VISIT COSIMOBOOKS.COM
BE INSPIRED, BE INFORMED

CPSIA information can be obtained at www.ICGtesting.com
Printed in the USA
BVOW02s0251040815

411548BV00002B/525/P